PROPORTIONALITY IN INVESTOR–STATE ARBITRATION

Proportionality in Investor–State Arbitration

GEBHARD BÜCHELER

OXFORD
UNIVERSITY PRESS

Great Clarendon Street, Oxford, OX2 6DP,
United Kingdom

Oxford University Press is a department of the University of Oxford.
It furthers the University's objective of excellence in research, scholarship,
and education by publishing worldwide. Oxford is a registered trade mark of
Oxford University Press in the UK and in certain other countries

Published in the United States of America by Oxford University Press
198 Madison Avenue, New York, NY 10016, United States of America

British Library Cataloguing in Publication Data
Data available

Library of Congress Control Number: Data Available

ISBN 978–0–19–872433–9

Printed and bound by
CPI Group (UK) Ltd, Croydon, CR0 4YY

To my parents, wife, and children

Foreword

Let me begin with a disclosure: I am the *Doktorvater* of the thesis which the author submitted at the University of Munich, for which he obtained the highest academic honors and which is now to be presented to the public in this beautiful book. Speaking of the public: the book arrives at the right moment. Never before in its history has investor–State arbitration "enjoyed" a degree of attention comparable to the situation at present. I put "enjoyed" in quotation marks on purpose because I would go as far as saying that what we are currently observing (or many of us are participating in) is no less than a battle for the survival of the system of investor–State arbitration as we know it. After a few decades during which this system developed rather quietly – as a specialty of a few academics in international economic law and a small group of practitioners mainly with a civil/commercial law background – before it started to grow exponentially, it had not caught public attention until very recently, when some Western industrialized countries suddenly found out that BITs were actually capable of displaying the reciprocity that the capital-exporting nations had hitherto regarded as a formality due to the sovereignty of the investments' host States. Such experiences of 'backfiring' BITs are now coinciding with an extremely fierce public debate triggered by the negotiation of so-called 'mega-regionals', that is, free-trade agreements covering a significant part of world GDP such as the envisaged Transatlantic Trade and Investment Partnership (TTIP) between the European Union and the United States, which are (or were) supposed to also provide for investor–State dispute settlement machineries along ICSID or UNCITRAL lines. Unfortunately, this debate has developed strong traits of a 'dialogue des sourds'. While investor–State arbitration is praised as a great advancement in the international rule of law, and sometimes even given a human rights flair, by some, what is probably the majority of voices is now perceiving it as a threat to the regulatory freedom of States, as a system of parallel justice, of undeserved privilege, for the rich and powerful devoid of any democratic legitimacy, ultimately transferring the risks combined with expensive foreign ventures to the taxpayers of the host countries. In this situation, any serious attempt at 'objectifying' the discussion is welcome; and Gebhard Bücheler's book is an important contribution to this endeavor indeed.

In the last instance, the future of investor–State arbitration will depend on whether the relevant stakeholders – foremost States (both their legal elites and their civil societies) and foreign investors – consider their sometimes conflicting interests well-served by this system in the long run. Bücheler's book analyses one of the most promising tools to reconcile conflicting interests: the principle of proportionality. The doctrinal basis employed by the author for the application of proportionality is the notion of general principles emanating from domestic legal systems, a source of international law strangely underutilized in international dispute resolution. As somebody who in his judicial and arbitral practice of international law is frequently encountering the preponderance of the Common Law, I cannot suppress taking pride in mentioning that we owe the development and refinement of the concept of proportionality to Civil Law, particularly German post-World War II doctrine. Returning to Bücheler's work, by harnessing and delimiting the concept of systemic integration, his book makes a convincing argument as to when arbitrators should – and when they should not – have recourse to proportionality in investment disputes. Four norms, or sets thereof, that regularly play a key role in investor–State arbitration are analysed in particular depth: treaty provisions on expropriation, the standard of fair and equitable treatment, Article XI of the US-Argentina BIT (representing the most-often litigated non-precluded-measures clause in investment disputes) and the customary international law defence of necessity. Based on the methodology developed in Chapters 3 and 4, Chapters 5 through 8 of the book thus analyse the potential role of proportionality in the context of these norms.

Bücheler's analysis comprises a number of valuable contributions to unresolved issues in international (investment) law, for example to the question of both potential and boundaries of systemic integration and to the influence States can have on the interpretation of investment treaties short of renegotiating them. Moreover, the author's treatment of proportionality is not limited to an analysis of the use that arbitrators can make of the principle under existing treaties. It also contains interesting comments on what States can do to recalibrate the balance between investment protection and other interests if they wish do so, for example when it comes to the conclusion of the next generation of investment treaties or a refinement of the customary international law defence of necessity.

Bücheler's book represents a most welcome voice in the present discourse. It not only contributes to academic clarification of its topic, but is also a guide to the practical application of the proportionality principle. I therefore commend *Proportionality in Investor–State Arbitration* to scholars, counsel and arbitrators as well as to domestic decision-makers, in particular to treaty negotiators.

The Hague/Munich
Bruno Simma

Acknowledgements

It is a pleasure to record my gratitude to a number of people whose guidance, inspiration, and companionship was crucial in writing and finishing this book. First of all, I would like to thank Judge Bruno Simma, the supervisor of my doctoral thesis on which this book is based. The German term for doctoral supervisor, *Doktorvater*, invokes connotations of a bond similar to the one between father and son, and Bruno Simma was a *Doktorvater* in the best possible sense. He fostered intellectual curiosity and provided invaluable advice whenever sought, all accompanied by an abundance of personal warmth and generosity. I also thank Professor Rudolf Streinz, who reviewed my thesis for the law faculty of the University of Munich in a timely fashion and provided valuable comments that have benefitted this book, in particular its Chapter 3.

I am much indebted to the late Professor Horst G. Krenzler for enriching debates in the early phases of my doctoral research and his benign mentorship over many years. I am very sad that he did not see the completion of this book, and I hope it has come some way in meeting his expectations.

Furthermore, I would like to express my profound gratitude to Judge Andreas L. Paulus, who as my first teacher of international law instilled a passion for this area of law in me that I am confident will last a lifetime, as will hopefully our friendship. I have learned more about the theory and practice of international law from him than from any textbook.

I also wish to thank some past and present members of two institutions that provided me with an ideal environment to live my enthusiasm for international law in general and investor–State arbitration in particular. First, at Columbia Law School, Professor Pieter Bekker greatly enhanced my understanding of investor–State arbitration and Professor Michael W. Doyle introduced me to the law and politics of what he summarizes as 'global constitutionalism'. With José Burmeister, Adam Douglas, Gonzalo Navarro, and Dr Niklas Maydell, I had and continue to have fruitful discussions about many of the issues discussed in this book.

Second, at the Institute of International Law at the University of Munich, I enjoyed an immensely friendly and collegiate atmosphere during various stages of my career, most recently when reviewing the proofs of this book. I am grateful for the hospitality and support of Professor Christian Walter and Professor Georg Nolte, current and former chair of international law at the University of Munich, respectively. I also wish to thank Professor Bardo Fassbender, Professor Hans-Peter Folz, Professor Daniel-Erasmus Khan, and Professor Thilo Rensmann, who as interim heads of the institute helped me in numerous ways. Finally, I had the privilege to debate issues relevant to this book with many colleagues and scholars at the institute, of which I want to mention in particular Dr Helmut Aust,

Fredrik von Bothmer, Professor Thomas Burri, Dr Thomas Meerpohl, Paulus Suh, Pascal Schonard and Dr Markus Zöckler.

One of the reasons why the writing of this book took a long time is that I had started to practice international arbitration with Freshfields Bruckhaus Deringer LLP in Paris before finishing it. I am very grateful to my colleagues at Freshfields for intellectually enriching and professionally rewarding years. Particular thanks go to Dr Georgios Petrochilos for his mentorship and to Francisco Abriani, Jonathan Jacob Gass, Dr Ben Juratowitch, Robert Kirkness, Ben Love, Dr Sam Luttrell, and Dr Kate Parlett for many stimulating discussions on arbitration and international law. Dr Sam Luttrell read through more than half of an early draft of this book, and I thank him for his valuable comments.

I have since returned to Munich and joined the dispute resolution firm Wach+Meckes LLP. I am very grateful to my colleagues, in particular to Dr Karl J. T. Wach, for finding the time and space to finish this book. It is to state the obvious that the opinions expressed in it are solely mine and reflect neither the views of my current or former firm nor those of their clients.

At Oxford University Press, my gratitude goes especially to Emma Endean for ably supporting the publication process along the way.

Finally, and most importantly, I owe the greatest debt to my family. My parents, Veronika and Gebhard A. Bücheler, relentlessly encouraged me to pursue my interests and supported me in any way they could. I am immeasurably grateful to my wife, Dr Emese Bücheler, for her patience throughout the years and summer vacations of research and writing. I dedicate this book to our family, blessed with Maja and her little sister Emilia, born one week before these lines were written.

Contents

Table of Cases

Table of Cases

WTO DISPUTE SETTLEMENT BODY

EUROPEAN COURT OF HUMAN RIGHTS (ECHR)

EUROPEAN COURT OF JUSTICE (ECJ)

OTHER INTERNATIONAL COURTS AND TRIBUNALS

DOMESTIC COURTS

Canada

Germany

List of Abbreviations

ASEAN	Association of Southeast Asian Nations
ASEAN–ANZ FTA	Agreement establishing the ASEAN–Australia–New Zealand Free Trade Area
ASR	Articles on Responsibility of States for Internationally Wrongful Acts
BVerfG	*Bundesverfassungsgericht* (German Constitutional Court)
BVerfGE	*Entscheidungen des Bundesverfassungsgerichts* (Decisions of the German Constitutional Court)
BIT	bilateral investment treaty
CETA	Comprehensive Economic and Trade Agreement between the EU and Canada
CFI	Court of First Instance (now called General Court of the European Union)
EC	European Communities
ECHR	European Convention for the Protection of Human Rights and Fundamental Freedoms
ECJ	European Court of Justice
ECOSOC	United Nations Economic and Social Council
ECR	Reports of the Court of Justice of the European Communities
ECT	Energy Charter Treaty
ECtHR	European Court of Human Rights
EU	European Union
FCN Treaty	Treaty of Friendship, Commerce, and Navigation
FET	fair and equitable treatment
FTA	Free Trade Agreement
GA	General Assembly of the United Nations
GATS	General Agreement on Trade in Services
GATT	General Agreement on Tariffs and Trade
GG	*Grundgesetz* (German Basic Law)
ICCPR	International Covenant on Civil and Political Rights
ICESCR	International Covenant on Economic, Social and Cultural Rights
ICJ	International Court of Justice
ICSID	International Centre for the Settlement of Investment Disputes
IIA	international investment agreement
ILA	International Law Association
ILC	International Law Commission
ILM	International Legal Materials
KORUS FTA	United States–Korea Free Trade Agreement
NAFTA	North American Free Trade Agreement
NAFTA FTC	NAFTA Free Trade Commission
NGO	non-governmental organization
NPM clause	non-precluded measures clause
OECD	Organisation for Economic Co-operation and Development
PCA	Permanent Court of Arbitration

PCIJ	Permanent Court of International Justice
PPI	Producer Price Index
SC	Security Council of the United Nations
SCR	Canadian Supreme Court Reports
TTIP	Transatlantic Trade and Investment Partnership
UDHR	Universal Declaration of Human Rights
UK	United Kingdom of Great Britain and Northern Ireland
UNCITRAL	United Nations Commission on International Trade Law
UNCLOS	United Nations Convention on the Law of the Sea
UNCTAD	United Nations Conference on Trade and Development
UNTS	United Nations Treaty Series
US	United States of America
VCLT	Vienna Convention on the Law of Treaties
WWI	World War I
WWII	World War II
WTO	World Trade Organization

1

Introduction

International investment agreements (IIAs) seek to ensure that States treat foreign nationals and corporations fairly and equitably, do not discriminate against them, and do not deprive them of their property without paying compensation. A State's failure to live up to these or similar standards can give rise to neutral third-party adjudication through arbitral tribunals, which may result in enforceable awards in favour of foreign investors. Based on a dense web of more than 3000 IIAs, investor–State arbitration is one of the most tangible elements in the judicialization of international relations after World War II. In recent years, however, this system has drawn increasing criticism. The reasons for and intensity of this criticism are not uniform, but one recurring theme is that tribunals would strike an unfair balance between the rights of investors and host States, leaving insufficient room for States to regulate in the public interest.[1] These concerns are particularly strong where arbitrators adjudicate claims arising from State measures adopted to protect the environment or human health, to cope with financial crises, or to provide the population with basic utilities.

Virtually every legal order has to deal with collisions between different rights and interests. A tool applied by many domestic and some international courts to resolve such conflicts is the principle of proportionality. Used at times to reconcile conflicting private rights, the most important function of this principle is to provide for an appropriate balance between individual rights and the public interest. While there are subtle differences among the practices of various courts,

---

[1] Regarding the increasing scepticism of certain States toward investor–State arbitration, *see* UNCTAD, 'World Investment Report 2012, Towards a New Generation of Investment Policies' (2012), at 86–8. For a particularly fierce NGO criticism, *see* Corporate Europe Observatory & Transnational Institute, *Profiting from Injustice* (2012). Summaries and overviews of scholarly concerns offer, *e.g.,* Waibel, Michael et al., 'The Backlash against Investment Arbitration: Perceptions and Reality', *in The Backlash against Investment Arbitration* (Michael Waibel, et al., eds, 2010) xxxvii–li, at xxxviii–xliv; José E. Alvarez & Kathryn Khamsi, 'The Argentine Crisis and Foreign Investors: A Glimpse into the Heart of the Investment Regime', *in Yearbook on International Investment Law & Policy 2008–2009* (Karl P. Sauvant, ed, 2009) 379–478, at 462–3; Stephan W. Schill, 'International Investment Law and Comparative Public Law—an Introduction', *in International Investment Law and Comparative Public Law* (Stephan W. Schill, ed, 2010) 3–35, at 4–7; Charles Brower & Sadie Blanchard, 'What's in a Meme? The Truth about Investor–State Arbitration: Why It Need Not, and Must Not, Be Repossessed by States', *Columbia Journal of Transnational Law* 52 (2014) 689–779, at 692–700; and Gus Van Harten, et al., *Public Statement on the International Investment Regime* (31 August 2010) *available at* <http://www.osgoode.yorku.ca/public-statement-international-investment-regime-31-august-2010/>.

adjudicators generally consider three elements in determining the proportionality of a certain State measure. First, the relevant measure must be a *suitable* means to achieve a *legitimate* goal. Second, the chosen measure must be the *least restrictive* means to attain the relevant goal. This part of the analysis requires that there exists no other equally effective means of achieving the relevant objective that would infringe the individual right to a lesser extent. Third, the measure adopted must be proportionate in the narrow sense (*proportionality stricto sensu*), which involves a weighing and balancing of the different interests at stake.

Several scholars think that investor–State tribunals should make (more) use of the principle of proportionality to provide for a fair balance between investor rights and the public interest. The norms and concepts for which proportionality ought to play a role, however, vary significantly among authors.[2] While some tribunals have already made use of proportionality or similar concepts, the relevant jurisprudence is far from being consistent, and tribunals have so far not adequately explained why proportionality does (or does not) matter. This book offers an analytical framework to decide whether and in what legal settings tribunals should resort to the principle of proportionality. It also identifies limits to judicial balancing, and discusses other means for States to recalibrate the balance between private property rights and the public interest if they wish to do so. The structure of the book is as follows.

Chapter 2 introduces the current system of investor–State arbitration in historical perspective. It also contains an introduction to a series of cases that have fuelled the debate on the legitimacy of investor–State arbitration: the arbitral jurisprudence arising from the 2001–3 Argentine financial crisis. This jurisprudence is particularly instructive for how tribunals handle conflicts between investor rights

---

[2] Benedict Kingsbury & Stephan W. Schill, 'Investor–State Arbitration as Governance: Fair and Equitable Treatment, Proportionality and the Emerging Global Administrative Law', *in 50 Years of the New York Convention—ICCA International Arbitration Conference* (Albert Jan van den Berg, ed, 2009) 5–68, at 31–2; Benedict Kingsbury & Stephan W. Schill, 'Public Law Concepts to Balance Investors' Rights with State Regulatory Actions in the Public Interest—the Concept of Proportionality', *in International Investment Law and Comparative Public Law* (Stephan W. Schill, ed, 2010) 75–104, at 88–103; Alec Stone Sweet & Florian Grisel, 'Transnational Investment Arbitration: From Delegation to Constitutionalization?', *in Human Rights in International Investment Law and Arbitration* (Pierre-Marie Dupuy, Ernst-Ulrich Petersmann, and Francesco Francioni, eds, 2009) 118–36, at 131–2; Annika Wythes, 'Investor–State Arbitrations: Can the "Fair and Equitable Treatment" Clause Consider Human Rights Obligations?', *Leiden Journal of International Law* 23 (2010) 241–56, at 254–5; Jasper Krommendijk & John Morijn, '"Proportional" by What Measure(s)? Balancing Investor Interests and Human Rights by Way of Applying the Proportionality Principle in Investor–State Arbitration', *in Human Rights in International Investment Law and Arbitration* (Pierre-Marie Dupuy, et al. eds, 2009) 422–51, at 449–50; Anne van Aaken, 'Defragmentation of Public International Law through Interpretation: A Methodological Proposal', *Indiana Journal of Global Legal Studies* 16 (2009) 483–512, at 506–12; Caroline Henckels, 'Indirect Expropriation and the Right to Regulate: Revisiting Proportionality Analysis and the Standard of Review in Investor–State Arbitration', *Journal of International Economic Law* 15 (2012) 223–55, at 228–9; August Reinisch, 'Necessity in International Investment Arbitration—an Unnecessary Split of Opinions in Recent ICSID Cases? Comments on *CMS v. Argentina* and *LG&E v. Argentina*', *Journal of World Investment & Trade* 8 (2007) 191–214, at 201; Andrea K Bjorklund, 'Emergency Exceptions: State of Necessity and Force Majeure', *in The Oxford Handbook of International Investment Law* (Peter Muchlinski, et al. eds, 2008) 459–522, at 485.

and the public interest in the context of certain treaty provisions and other concepts that frequently lie at the core of investor–State arbitrations. The jurisprudence in the Argentine cases will frame the debate throughout the book.

Chapter 3 turns to the principle of proportionality and examines why it should be relevant to investor–State arbitration at all. Relying on general principles within the meaning of Article 38(1)(c) ICJ Statute as legal foundation for proportionality in investor–State arbitration, Chapter 3 includes a comparative study of proportionality in various domestic jurisdictions. This analysis helps to identify three factors arbitral tribunals should consider before engaging in a proportionality analysis: (1) the threat of unwarranted judicial lawmaking; (2) the rule of law; and (3) the availability of a value system that guides the weighing and balancing involved in a proportionality analysis. Regarding the last factor, domestic constitutions usually provide the relevant value systems for proportionality on the domestic level. International law does not offer a unitary value system equivalent to domestic constitutions. Still, several elements in international law may provide guidance in a proportionality analysis. Sometimes, adjudicators will find a value system in the treaty provision giving rise to a proportionality analysis itself or at least in its context. But even in the absence of such assistance, the international community has produced significant 'value glue'[3] that may guide a proportionality analysis. Chapter 4 discusses the relevant legal instruments and the vehicle that can—under certain conditions—import them into investor–State arbitration: the concept of systemic integration enshrined in Article 31(3)(c) VCLT.

The subsequent chapters build on the analytical framework developed in Chapters 3 and 4 and assess the role, potential, and limits of proportionality in specific legal settings in investor–State arbitration. Chapter 5 examines whether and under what circumstances IIA provisions on expropriation involve a proportionality analysis. *Tecmed* is usually considered to be the leading case for excluding general regulatory measures in the public interest—as long as they are proportionate—from the scope of IIA provisions on expropriation. We will see that the methodology adopted by the *Tecmed* tribunal—reference to ECtHR jurisprudence—is insufficient reason to resort to proportionality analysis under each and every IIA provision on expropriation. Still, Chapter 5 identifies several avenues that may justify a proportionality analysis under expropriation provisions.

Chapter 6 makes a case for the application of the principle of proportionality in the context of arguably the most important treaty protection in the current system of investor–State arbitration: the standard of fair and equitable treatment (FET). While applying this standard will always remain a highly case-specific exercise, proportionality analysis adds analytical rigour and transparency to the reasoning of arbitral tribunals. Chapter 6 also contains some remarks of caution regarding possible ramifications of the 2012 *Occidental v Ecuador* decision, with $1.77 billion probably the largest award in ICSID history. Some

---

[3] Andreas L. Paulus, 'Commentary to Andreas Fischer-Lescano & Gunther Teubner: The Legitimacy of International Law and the Role of the State', *Michigan Journal of International Law* 25 (2004) 1047–58, at 1050.

might understand this decision to stand for the proposition that a State's exercise of its contractual rights automatically triggers a proportionality analysis under the FET standard. Chapter 6 explains why this is not the case.

Chapter 7 addresses one of the most effective means for States to ensure they are not liable to foreign investors when they adopt (proportionate) measures in furtherance of governmental goals in the public interest: non-precluded measures (NPM) clauses. An increasing number of IIAs contain such exception clauses for the protection of specific values such as international peace and security, labour standards, and the stability of financial systems.[4] One of these clauses is Article XI of the US–Argentina BIT, which played a key role in several of the Argentine cases. It reads as follows:

This Treaty shall not preclude the application by either Party of measures necessary for the maintenance of public order, the fulfillment of its obligations with respect to the maintenance or restoration of international peace or security, or the protection of its own essential security interests.

Chapter 7 analyses the most important interpretative issues that arose in the context of Article XI, in particular whether the term 'necessary' in this provision triggers a proportionality analysis. Answering this question is of little value without knowing whether it is for tribunals to decide that a certain measure was 'necessary' or whether Article XI is a 'self-judging' clause subject to very limited judicial review. In a similar vein, establishing the proper understanding of the term 'necessary' does not make much of a difference if States do not escape liability even if the requirements of Article XI are met. Chapter 7 deals with these issues. While each NPM clause has to be interpreted individually and Chapter 7 contains a case study of Article XI of the US–Argentina BIT only, many of the considerations in that chapter are relevant to other NPM clauses as well.

Chapter 8 examines the legal concept that arguably drew most scholarly attention in the context of the Argentine cases: the customary international law defence of necessity. Argentina argued that it experienced a state of necessity during its 2001–3 financial crisis. While all tribunals acknowledged that such a defence exists under customary international law and was accurately codified by the ILC in Article 25 ASR,[5] none of the tribunals found that Argentina could rely on it to justify its emergency measures. Nevertheless, some authors think that the doctrine of necessity should be harnessed—and modified—to readjust the 'balance'

---

[4] *See e.g.,* UNCTAD, Bilateral Investment Treaties 1959–1991, at 80–99, and the values and interests listed in Articles 10 and 11 of the 2004 Canadian Model BIT (*available at* <http://ita.law.uvic.ca/documents/Canadian2004-FIPA-model-en.pdf>).

[5] This provision reads as follows:
   1. Necessity may not be invoked by a State as a ground for precluding the wrongfulness of an act not in conformity with an international obligation of that State unless the act:
      (a) is the only way for the State to safeguard an essential interest against a grave and imminent peril; and
      (b) does not seriously impair an essential interest of the State or States towards which the obligation exists, or of the international community as a whole.

between investor rights and the public interest in investor–State arbitration.[6] We will see that an annulment decision in one of the Argentine cases, *Enron*, lends support to such efforts. To assess the current and potential role of necessity in investor–State arbitration, Chapter 8 first analyses why the necessity defence as currently codified is of little use for States in investor–State arbitration. We will see that the necessity defence may—in principle—justify internationally wrongful acts not only vis-à-vis States but also in relation to foreign investors, despite a judgment of the German Constitutional Court that casts doubt on this proposition. Chapter 8 identifies the 'only way' and 'non-contribution' requirements in Article 25 as reasons for why Argentina could not successfully rely on the necessity defence to justify the measures taken during its 2001–3 crisis. Based on this finding, Chapter 8 evaluates whether arbitrators should expand the scope of necessity by applying a proportionality analysis to assess whether regulatory measures in the public interest are justified. Chapter 8 also asks what will actually happen when a tribunal finds—through a proportionality analysis or otherwise—that the elements of Article 25 are met: will the State invoking necessity have to compensate those who suffered from the exercise of this defence, and if yes, to what degree?

Chapter 9 summarizes the main findings of this book and contains some concluding remarks.

2. In any case, necessity may not be invoked by a State as a ground for precluding wrongfulness if:
   (a) the international obligation in question excludes the possibility of invoking necessity; or
   (b) the State has contributed to the situation of necessity.

[6] Avidan Kent & Alexandra R. Harrington, 'The Plea of Necessity under Customary International Law: A Critical Review in Light of the Argentine Cases', *in Evolution in Investment Treaty Law and Arbitration* (Chester Brown & Kate Miles eds, 2011) 246–70, at 270.

2

Investor–State Arbitration and
the Argentine Cases: an Overview

Under the current system of international investment arbitration, foreign investors can bring claims against sovereign States before international tribunals without the State's specific consent to arbitrate the relevant dispute. Instead, the State's
consent is typically included in a bilateral or multilateral treaty, and extends to
a potentially unlimited number of claims arising from events that occur after
the conclusion of the respective treaty. The awards obtained by investors in these
proceedings can be enforced against the respondent State through its domestic
courts or the courts of other States with only very limited judicial review, if any,
by domestic courts. To the reader who is familiar with the principles of investor–
State arbitration, these sentences contain nothing new. From a broader perspective, however, they reflect some of the most dynamic developments and profound
changes in international law since WWII. The result of this development is a
system of international dispute resolution with individuals and other non-State
actors as the main beneficiaries of a mix of substantive treaty protections, procedural mechanisms, and robust enforcement mechanisms without historical
precedent.[1] While the current system of investor–State arbitration is evidence of
significant progress in the international rule of law, the system is increasingly
under attack. The reasons for and intensity of this criticism are not uniform, but
generally critics doubt the legitimacy of the current system for one or more of the
following reasons—whether perceived or real: a pro-investor bias of arbitrators;
a lack of transparency in arbitral proceedings; the fact that IIAs contain legal
obligations for States only; the lack of an appellate system that could provide for
consistency in arbitral jurisprudence; the notion that it is for domestic actors and/
or democratic institutions to decide on the handling of foreign investors and not
for international tribunals; and a narrowing of the regulatory leeway of States to
pursue the public interest without incurring international liability.[2]

Jurisprudence frequently adduced in the debate on the legitimacy of investor–
State arbitration are the cases arising from the 2001–3 Argentine financial

---

[1] For a comparison between the current system of investor–State arbitration and the dispute
resolution mechanism of the 1794 Jay Treaty, *see infra* notes 33–7 and accompanying text.
[2] *See* the references provided in Chapter 1, note 1.

crisis.[3] As at 2014, Argentina was the respondent in at least 54 pending or concluded investor–State arbitrations.[4] Many of these proceedings were brought in connection with Argentina's 2001–3 financial crisis. The amount of damages awarded to claimants for measures Argentina deemed necessary to handle its crisis is substantial.[5] Furthermore, some tribunals reached diverging decisions on identical legal issues. While these factors are reason enough for a detailed analysis of the Argentine cases, the relevant jurisprudence is instructive as to how tribunals tend to deal with conflicting interests when interpreting and applying IIAs. This is particularly true for the concept of indirect expropriation, the FET standard, Article XI of the US–Argentina BIT, and the customary international law defence of necessity. Thus, the Argentine cases provide an illustrative starting point to assess the (current and potential) role of proportionality in providing for a fair balance between conflicting interests in investor–State arbitration. While the individual chapters in this book deal with the relevant jurisprudence in depth, sections IV and V of this chapter provide an overview of the factual background and the main findings of the tribunals. Before we turn to the Argentine cases, sections I–III outline important characteristics of the current system of investor–State arbitration and some developments that formed this system.

I. The protection of foreign investment in the past

The history of the protection of foreign investment can be traced back to the middle ages and even Roman law.[6] National legislation, customary international law, and bilateral and multinational treaties, regulating either substantive or procedural aspects or both, all played an important role in the evolution of international investment law. This section focuses on developments at the international level and starts in the late eighteenth century, when instruments reminiscent of the

---

[3] *See, e.g.,* Stephan W. Schill, 'Deference in Investment Treaty Arbitration: Re-conceptualizing the Standard of Review', *Journal of International Dispute Settlement* 3 (2012) 577–607, at 577; William W. Burke-White & Andreas von Staden, 'Private Litigation in a Public Law Sphere: the Standard of Review in Investor–State Arbitrations', *Yale Journal of International Law* 35 (2010) 283–346, at 299; Barnali Choudhury, 'Recapturing Public Power: Is Investment Arbitration's Engagement of the Public Interest Contributing to the Democratic Deficit?', *Vanderbilt Journal of Transnational Law* 41 (2008) 775–831, at 805–7. *See also* Alvarez & Khamsi, 'The Argentine Crisis', at 382–7 and 460–78; Kingsbury & Schill, 'Public Law Concepts', at 75–6.

[4] In April 2014, UNCTAD counted 53 cases against Argentina as at the end of 2013 (UNCTAD, Recent Developments in Investor–State Dispute Settlement (ISDS), IIA Issues Note, No. 1 (2014), at 8). At least one additional case was filed against Argentina in 2014 (*Casinos Austria International GmbH and Casinos Austria Aktiengesellschaft v. Argentine Republic*, ICSID Case No. ARB/14/32).

[5] *E.g.,* *CMS*, $133 million; *Enron*, $106 million; *Sempra*, $128 million; *BG Group*, $185 million; *National Grid*, $54 million; *LG&E*, $57 million (all without interest and costs).

[6] *See, e.g.,* Peter Fischer, 'Transnational Enterprises' *in Encyclopedia of Public International Law*, Vol. IV (Rudolf Bernhardt ed., 1985) 921–6, at 922–3 and Tillmann R. Braun, 'Investitionsschutz durch internationale Schiedsgerichte', *TranState Working Papers* 89 (2009) 1–23, at 20–2.

current legal framework of foreign investment started to evolve.[7] At that time, the US began to conclude an array of treaties addressing both security issues and commercial matters. These treaties came to be known as 'Treaties of Friendship, Commerce and Navigation' (FCN).[8] Probably the first agreement of this sort was the 'Treaty of Amity and Commerce' between the US and France, signed in 1778.[9] While this treaty dealt primarily with trade and navigation matters, later FCN treaties increasingly included investment protections. With foreign investment addressed under the more general provisions on the protection of aliens, Article 13 of a treaty between the US and Venezuela of 1836, for example, stated that:

Both the contracting parties, promise, and engage formally, to give their special protection to the persons and property of the citizens of each other, of all occupations, who may be in the territories subject to the jurisdiction of the one or the other, transient or dwelling therein, leaving open and free to them the Tribunals of Justice for their judicial recourse on the same terms which are usual and customary with the natives or citizens of the country in which they may be.[10]

In addition to such treaty stipulations, customary international law offered a certain degree of protection to aliens and their property. The precise content of these rules of customary international law was controversial. According to one widespread view, foreigners could not expect better treatment than nationals. This view was most prominently promoted by the Argentine jurist Carlos Calvo in the nineteenth century, and came to be known as the 'Calvo doctrine' or the 'principle of national treatment'.[11] The Calvo doctrine is usually juxtaposed with the concept of an 'international minimum standard'. Lord Palmerston vividly described this standard in a speech to the House of Commons in 1850. With regard to the conflict between Greece and the United Kingdom in the *Don Pacifico Affair*, Lord Palmerston observed that:

We shall be told, perhaps, as we have already been told, that if the people of the country are liable to have heavy stones placed upon their breasts, and police officers to dance upon them; if they are liable to have their heads tied to their knees, and to be left for hours in that state; or to be swung like a pendulum, and to be bastinadoed as they swing, foreigners

---

[7] There are many ways to summarize and portray the history of international investment law. For approaches less focused on the perspective of traditionally capital-exporting States than the brief account provided here (and most of the sources on which it relies), *see, e.g.*, Kate Miles, *The Origins of International Investment Law—Empire, Environment and the Safeguarding of Capital* (2013), at 19–121; M. Sornarajah, *The International Law on Foreign Investment* (2010), at 19–46.

[8] Kenneth J. Vandevelde, 'A Brief History of International Investment Agreements', *UC Davis Journal of International Law & Policy* 12 (2005) 157–94, at 158 n.7.

[9] *Available at* <http://avalon.law.yale.edu/18th_century/fr1788-1.asp>.

[10] Treaty of Peace, Friendship, Navigation and Commerce between the United States and Venezuela of 18 May 1836, <http://avalon.law.yale.edu/19th_century/venez_001.asp>.

[11] For an in-depth discussion of this doctrine, *see, e.g.*, Kurt Lipstein, 'The Place of the Calvo Clause in International Law', *British Yearbook of International Law* 22 (1945) 130–45 and Alwyn V. Freeman, 'Recent Aspects of the Calvo Doctrine and the Challenge to International Law', *American Journal of International Law* 40 (1946) 121–47.

have no right to be better treated than the natives, and have no business to complain if the same things are practised upon them. We may be told this, but that is not my opinion, nor do I believe it is the opinion of any reasonable man.[12]

In the 1920s, the US and Mexico set up a general claims commission, which would shed further light on the international minimum standard of treatment. The purpose of the underlying treaty was to settle claims by individuals,[13] but it was still the US and Mexico, respectively, who brought the claims before the commission on behalf of their nationals. The *Neer* case involved an alleged failure of Mexican authorities to punish the murderers of an American citizen, and when investor–State tribunals today comment on the content of the international minimum standard they usually refer to *Neer*, where the commission held that:

(first) the propriety of governmental acts should be put to the test of international standards, and (second) that the treatment of an alien, in order to constitute an international delinquency, should amount to an outrage, to bad faith, to willful neglect of duty, or to an insufficiency of governmental action so far short of international standards that every reasonable and impartial man would readily recognize its insufficiency.[14]

Another case decided by the commission, *Hopkins*, contains important remarks on the relationship between the international minimum standard and a State's treatment of its own citizens. The commission found that:

[i]t not infrequently happens that under the rules of international law applied to controversies of an international aspect a nation is required to accord to aliens broader and more liberal treatment than it accords to its own citizens under its municipal laws.[15]

While the commission recognized that the international minimum standard might lead to differences in treatment, rights, and remedies between nationals and foreigners, it found that this would not give rise to serious concerns:

The citizens of a nation may enjoy many rights which are withheld from aliens, and, conversely, under international law aliens may enjoy rights and remedies which the nation does not accord to its own citizens.[16]

The international minimum standard of treatment received widespread support through both State practice and scholarly writings in the early twentieth century.[17] Still, the conflict between the 'international minimum standard' and

---

[12] *Cited in* Elihu Root, 'The Basis of Protection of Citizens Residing Abroad', *American Journal of International Law* 4 (1910) 517–28, at 523.

[13] Preamble of the General Claims Convention between the United States of America and the United Mexican States of 8 September 1923, *US Treaty Series*, No. 678, *reprinted in* 18 *AJIL* (1924) *Supplement: Official Documents*, 147–51, at 147.

[14] *United States (Neer) v. Mexico*, General Claims Commission—United States and Mexico, Decision, 15 October 1926, 21 *American Journal of International Law* (1927) 555–7, at 556.

[15] *United States (Hopkins) v. Mexico*, General Claims Commission—United States and Mexico, Decision, 31 March 1926, IV Reports of International Arbitral Awards (1926) 41–7, at 47.

[16] Id., at 47.

[17] For a list of references, *see* Ian Brownlie, *Principles of Public International Law* (2008), at 525 n 30.

the 'standard of national treatment' continued to exist. Particularly illustrative in this regard is the Convention on Rights and Duties of States adopted by the Seventh International Conference of American States in 1933. While the US on other occasions actively promoted the international minimum standard, it ratified this convention, which embraced the standard of national treatment in Article 9:

Nationals and foreigners are under the same protection of the law and the national authorities and the foreigners may not claim rights other or more extensive than those of the nationals.[18]

Five years after its signing, Mexico relied on this convention in a correspondence with the US in which Mexico denied the illegality of the expropriation committed against US citizens, arguing that the relevant measures affected both Mexicans and foreigners alike.[19] In a note of 22 August 1938, Secretary of State Hull acknowledged 'the right of all sovereign nations to expropriate private property'. But no government should be allowed to do so 'without provision for prompt, adequate, and effective' compensation.[20] This formulation eventually came to be known as the *Hull* formula, which was to have significant impact on the content of future IIAs.[21]

In the mid-twentieth century, however, the Hull formula could not resolve the ongoing controversy about the proper standard of protection for foreign investors. This is borne out by the failure of the Havana Charter, signed on 23 March 1948 by 54 countries to create the International Trade Organization (ITO).[22] The charter contained substantive and procedural rules regarding trade matters and the protection of foreign investment. The project was abandoned in 1948 after it had become clear that an insufficient number of countries would ratify the charter. One of the reasons for the failure of the charter was the opposition of many developing countries to the incorporation of the international minimum standard of treatment.[23] Another multilateral attempt in the 1960s failed on similar grounds. In 1967, the OECD introduced a 'Draft Convention on the Protection of Foreign Property'.[24] The draft convention drew much criticism, inter alia because it came from a forum of mainly capital-exporting countries but sought universal application.[25]

While multilateral efforts were not successful, States enhanced the protection of foreign investment through bilateral treaties, often in the form of FCN

---

[18] Convention on Rights and Duties of States adopted by the Seventh International Conference of American States, 26 December 1933, 165 LNTS 19.

[19] Green Haywood Hackworth, *Digest of International Law*, Vol. III (1942) 655–65, at 659.

[20] Id., 658.   [21] *See infra* notes 60–1 and accompanying text.

[22] United Nations Conference on Trade and Employment, Havana Charter for an International Trade Organization, *available at* <http://www.worldtradelaw.net/misc/havana.pdf>.

[23] Christopher F. Dugan, et al., *Investor–State Arbitration* (2008), at 48. Exporting countries and business groups were dissatisfied with the resulting compromise as well, and the Charter was not even presented to the US Congress for ratification (*see* Gus Van Harten, *Investment Treaty Arbitration and Public Law* (2007), at 20).

[24] 7 ILM (1968) 117–43.

[25] *See, e.g.*, Rudolf Dolzer & Christoph Schreuer, *Principles of International Investment Law* (2008), at 19.

treaties.[26] The first treaty that dealt exclusively with the protection of foreign investment was the Germany–Pakistan BIT concluded in 1959. Germany was particularly sensitive to issues of foreign investment because of the loss of both public and private property abroad as a consequence of its defeat in WWII.[27] The 1960s saw the signing of further BITs, especially by European countries.[28] These treaties contained far-reaching substantive provisions for the protection of foreign investment. While not all of the early BITs contained investor–State dispute resolution clauses, such clauses became increasingly prevalent over time. The overview of the concept of diplomatic protection in the next subsection will show that it is difficult to overestimate the importance of this development.

II. Diplomatic protection and the traditional role of the individual in international dispute resolution

One of the main characteristics of international law prior to WWII was the limited access of individuals to international courts and tribunals. Of course, there were notable exceptions. Individuals could for example instigate proceedings against States before the Central American Court of Justice. Between 1907 and 1918, the Court heard five cases. However, the respondent State had to consent to each individual case, and none of the cases was decided in favour of the individual.[29] The Hague Convention XII of 1907 established the International Prize Court, to which individuals were supposed to have access. But this convention never came into force and hence the Court never heard a single case.[30] Another example are the mixed arbitral tribunals created by the peace treaties after WWI, which could render awards directly payable to individual claimants.[31]

There were a significant number of other arbitral tribunals and commissions that decided cases concerning the treatment of aliens prior to WWII.[32] The proceedings before most of these adjudicatory bodies, however, were controlled by States, and are, as we will see below, instances of diplomatic protection. This is arguably also true for the commission established by Article 6 of the famous 1794 Jay Treaty.[33] The US and Great Britain concluded this treaty to ameliorate

---

[26] *See, e.g.*, Vandevelde, 'A Brief History of International Investment Agreements', at 162–4.

[27] Dolzer & Schreuer, *Investment Law*, at 18.

[28] Switzerland alone signed 19 such treaties in this decade. The Netherlands and France each concluded four bilateral investment treaties during this time (UNCTAD, Bilateral Investment Treaties 1959–1991 (1992), Annex, at 20, 28, 33).

[29] *See* W. Paul Gormley, *The Procedural Status of the Individual before International and Supranational Tribunals* (1966), at 32–3.

[30] D. H. N. Johnson, 'Prize Law', *in Encyclopedia of Public International Law*, Vol. III (Rudolf Bernhardt ed., 1997) 1122–8, at 1123.

[31] *See, e.g.*, Kate Parlett, *The Individual in the International Legal System—Continuity and Change in International Law* (2011), at 72–3.

[32] For an overview of the different tribunals, *see* id., at 124–75.

[33] Jay Treaty of Amity, Commerce, and Navigation between the United States and Great Britain of 1794 (*available at* <http://avalon.law.yale.edu/18th_century/jay.asp>).

their relationship, which had suffered from the aftermath of the American War of Independence (1775–1783). In addition, Great Britain's entry into war with France in 1793 exposed American vessels to significant peril.[34] The commission established under Article 6 of the Jay Treaty dealt with legislation of several US states that made it impossible for British nationals to collect debts from American debtors. Article 6 provided for 'full and adequate compensation' from the US for losses suffered from state legislation to the extent that British nationals could not recover their debts by the 'ordinary course of judicial proceedings'. Furthermore, the provision stipulated that an award of the commission should be 'final and conclusive both as to the Justice of the Claim, and to the amount of the Sum to be paid to the Creditor or Claimant.'[35] The subject matter of Article 6 (confiscated debts) and its procedure (claims brought by individuals and final awards for monetary compensation) displays remarkable similarities with the current legal framework of the protection of foreign investment.

Barton Legum put Article 6 of the Jay Treaty on the same footing as Chapter 11 of NAFTA regarding the consequences for State sovereignty.[36] It is important to bear in mind, however, that Article 6 covered only certain types of controversies related to historical events that had occured prior to the conclusion of the Jay Treaty. Chapter 11 of NAFTA, in contrast, covers a possibly unlimited number of *future* disputes, and foreign investors securing a NAFTA award can rely on an effective enforcement mechanism. The position of British nationals under the Jay Treaty was not strong enough to be independent of the diplomatic realm. This became particularly clear in the dissolution of the commission. Between 1797 and 1799, the commission reached a set of important decisions on some fundamental questions. Before the commission could apply the agreed principles to the merits of a single case, the US and Great Britain abolished the Article 6 commission and agreed to settle all claims for a total sum of £600,000. This sum was later distributed proportionately to the individual claimants by a domestic commission.[37]

Hence, the main mechanism to enforce the substantive rules on the treatment of aliens and their property prior to WWII was diplomatic protection. In general terms, diplomatic protection is the protection given by a State to individuals against a violation of international law by another State.[38] The ILC sought to codify the customary rules on diplomatic protection in its 2006 draft articles.[39] Article 1 describes the means of diplomatic protection broadly as ranging from

---

[34] For the historical background of the Jay Treaty, *see* Hans-Jürgen Schlochauer, 'Jay Treaty' *in Encyclopedia of Public International Law*, Vol. III (Rudolf Bernhardt ed., 1997) 4–7, at 4–5 and John Basset Moore, *International Adjudications* (1931), at 10–14.

[35] Reprinted in Moore, *International Adjudications*, at 5–7.

[36] Barton Legum, 'Investment Disputes and NAFTA Chapter 11, Remarks', *ASIL Proceedings* 95 (2001) 202–5, at 203.

[37] *See* Moore, *International Adjudications*, at 359–74.

[38] Wilhelm Karl Geck, 'Diplomatic Protection', *in Encyclopedia of Public International Law*, Vol. I (Rudolf Bernhardt ed., 1992) 1045–67, at 1046.

[39] ILC, Articles on Diplomatic Protection with Commentaries (2006). The UN General Assembly 'welcomed' the adoption of the draft articles and 'commended' the articles to the attention of the governments: Res. 62/67 of 6 December 2007.

'diplomatic action' to 'other means of peaceful settlement'. The latter includes the most important means for the purposes of the protection of foreign investment: arbitral and judicial proceedings.[40]

The position of the individuals and other non-State actors in the realm of diplomatic protection is very weak, for a number of reasons. First, a State exercises diplomatic protection in its own right.[41] This notion rests on the fiction that an injury to a foreign national is an injury to the home State itself. The Permanent Court of International Justice (PCIJ) found in the *Mavrommatis Palestine Concessions* case that:

[b]y taking up the case of one of its subjects and by resorting to diplomatic action or international judicial proceedings on its behalf, a State is in reality asserting its own right—its right to ensure, in the person of its subjects, respect for the rules of international law.[42]

According to this traditional approach, it is in the sole decision of the home State when and how to exercise diplomatic protection. The decision of the ICJ in *Barcelona Traction* illustrates the irrelevance of the interests of the individual:

[A] State may exercise diplomatic protection by whatever means and to whatever extent it thinks fit, for it is its own right that the State is asserting. Should the natural or legal person on whose behalf it is acting consider that their rights are not adequately protected, they have no remedy in international law [...] The State must be viewed as the sole judge to decide whether its protection will be granted, to what extent it is granted, and when it will cease. It retains in this respect a discretionary power the exercise of which may be determined by considerations of a political or other nature, unrelated to the particular case.[43]

This statement makes abundantly clear that States are under no duty to exercise diplomatic protection.[44] Even today, there is very limited support for the notion that a State might under certain circumstances be obliged to grant diplomatic protection. In his 2000 report to the ILC, Special Rapporteur John Dugard suggested that States should have an obligation to exercise diplomatic protection in instances of grave breaches of *jus cogens* norms.[45] This narrowly tailored duty was further mitigated by several exceptions, such as the invocation of overriding interests of the State or its people.[46] Still, the ILC could not agree on Dugard's suggestion. Rather, the commission adopted Article 2, which simply states that:

[a] State has *the right* to exercise diplomatic protection in accordance with the present draft articles. (Emphasis added)

---

[40] Id., Article 1, para. 8.   [41] Id., Article 1, para. 3.

[42] *Mavrommatis Palestine Concessions* (Greece v. United Kingdom), Judgment, 30 August 1924, PCIJ Reports, Series A, No. 2 (1924) 6–37, at 12.

[43] *Case concerning the Barcelona Traction Light and Power Company Limited* (Belgium v. Spain), Judgment, 5 February 1970, ICJ Reports (1970) 3, at 44.

[44] For attempts to establish an obligation to exercise diplomatic protection as a matter of domestic law, *see* John R. Dugard, First Report on Diplomatic Protection at the 52nd Session of the International Law Commission, A/CN.4/506 (2000), Article 4, paras. 80–87.

[45] Id., Article 4, at 27.   [46] Id., Article 4(2)(a).

According to the ILC, this provision does not constitute a decision against the more progressive view that States exercise diplomatic protection not only in their own right, but also in that of their nationals.[47] The emphasis on the *right* to exercise diplomatic protection, however, reflects the still predominant view that States are under no duty to exercise diplomatic protection.[48] The ILC merely 'recommends' in Article 19 that States 'should' take into account the interests of their nationals.[49] Another disadvantageous feature of diplomatic protection for individuals is the 'local remedies rule'. According to this rule, foreign investors must first exhaust all domestic legal remedies of the host State before their home States may exercise diplomatic protection. The ICJ called the rule 'a well-established rule of customary international law' resting on the *ratio* 'that the State where the violation occurred should have an opportunity to redress it by its own means, within the framework of its own domestic legal system'.[50] Consequently, the ILC included the 'local remedies rule' in its draft articles (as Article 14).

Moreover, a State can abandon its efforts at all times. This is the consequence of the notion that a State is asserting its own right when granting diplomatic protection. In the context of arbitral proceedings, for example, States may agree on a settlement whenever they deem fit. And finally, even a successful exercise of diplomatic protection does not necessarily have beneficial effects for the individual. It is at the discretion of the home State whether its nationals participate in any benefits resulting from a successful exercise of diplomatic protection. In this vein, Article 19(c) ILC draft articles merely recommends that the home State transfer any compensation obtained for the injury (minus a 'reasonable' deduction) to its nationals.[51]

III. The modern system of the protection of foreign investment

The current system of investor–State arbitration operates largely independently of diplomatic protection and its inherent limitations. One element in this system is the ICSID convention, which entered into force in 1966. The ICSID convention does not contain substantive standards for the protection of foreign investment. Rather, the convention constitutes a very effective procedural instrument due to a combination of various progressive elements and its interplay with dispute resolution clauses in IIAs. For example, the convention abandoned the long-standing 'local remedies rule', even though States can agree to the contrary according to Article 26. One of the most important features of the ICSID convention is the direct enforceability of an arbitral award within the territory of all parties to the convention (Article 54). Domestic courts cannot review ICSID awards on the

---

[47] ILC, *Commentaries on Diplomatic Protection*, Article 2, para. 1 and Article 1, para. 5.
[48] Id., Article 2, para. 2.   [49] Id., Article 19, paras. 1–8.
[50] *Interhandel Case* (Switzerland v. United States), Judgment, 21 March 1959, ICJ Reports 1959, 6, at 27.
[51] ILC, *Commentaries on Diplomatic Protection*, Article 19.

merits. It is only during the execution of the award that domestic law comes to play a significant role: Article 55 clarifies that the convention does not interfere with the law of State immunity that is in place in the State where execution is sought.[52]

Under Article 25 ICSID convention, foreign companies and individuals can directly bring arbitral proceedings against host States. As Article 25(1) requires the host State to consent to the submission of a dispute to ICSID, the convention is in line with traditional concepts of sovereignty under public international law. However, foreign investors benefit from the general consent of host States to the jurisdiction of an arbitral tribunal in IIAs. As explained in section II, private actors were involved in international dispute resolution even before the current system of investor–State arbitration had emerged. However, consent to arbitration in these treaties was *retroactive*, i.e. the events giving rise to the relevant claims had occurred before the contracting States decided to refer the dispute to arbitration. Therefore, States had a very concrete notion of what would be at stake before they took the decision to arbitrate.[53] The consent to arbitration in IIAs, on the contrary, is *prospective*, and relates to disputes that arise after the relevant treaty has entered into force. Through the ratification of IIAs with arbitration clauses, States expose themselves to a theoretically unlimited number of arbitral proceedings.[54]

Dispute resolution clauses in early BITs had been limited to inter-State proceedings.[55] In the 1970s, the incorporation of investor–State arbitration clauses into investment treaties started to spread slowly but steadily.[56] Many States, however, turned against a robust protection of foreign investment. On 1 May 1974, the UN General Assembly adopted the 'Declaration on the Establishment of a New International Economic Order'.[57] The resolution stipulates under section 4(c)

---

[52] Christoph Schreuer, et al., *The ICISD Convention—a Commentary* (2009), Article 55, para. 13.

[53] *See* Van Harten, *Investment Treaty Arbitration and Public Law*, at 100.

[54] Of course, this is not only true for arbitration clauses that refer disputes to ICSID, but also for those that (in addition or exclusively) provide for dispute resolution under the auspices of other administering bodies, such as the International Chamber of Commerce (ICC), or for ad hoc arbitration, often under the UNCITRAL rules. For the differences between retrospective and prospective consent, *see also* Andrea Marco Steingruber, *Consent in International Arbitration* (2012), paras. 11.91–7.

[55] *See, e.g.,* Article 11 of the Germany–Pakistan BIT of 25 November 1959, which referred 'disputes as to the interpretation or application' of the treaty '(a) to the International Court of Justice if both Parties so agree or (b) if they do not so agree to an arbitration tribunal upon the request of either Party'.

[56] *See, e.g.,* Article 9 of the Netherlands–Yugoslavia BIT of 16 February 1976, which states that 'the investor shall be entitled to submit the dispute, at his choice, for settlement to: (a) the International Centre for the Settlement of Investment Disputes…; (b) the International Centre for the Settlement of Investment Disputes, under the Rules Governing the Additional Facility for the Administration of Conciliation, Arbitration and Fact-Finding Proceeding (Additional Facility Rules)…; (c) a sole arbitrator or an international ad hoc tribunal under the Arbitration Rules of the United Nations Commission on International Trade Law (UNCITRAL); (d) the Court of Arbitration of the International Chamber of Commerce (ICC)'.

[57] A/Res/3202 (S-VI), UN Doc A/9559. The Resolution was adopted without a vote; *see* 13 ILM (1974) 715–66, at 715. For a summary of the constitutive parts of the 'New International Economic Order' in general, *see* Bruno Simma & Alfred Verdross, 'Universelles Völkerrecht' (1984), para. 506.

that the new order should be founded on the '[f]ull permanent sovereignty of every State over its natural resources and all economic activities'.[58] Furthermore, the resolution considered the 'right to nationalization or transfer of ownership to its nationals' as a suitable means to achieve this objective. An obligation to pay compensation was not mentioned. In light of the uncertainty regarding the substantive rules for the protection of foreign investment, the UK and the US decided to launch their respective BIT programmes in the second half of the 1970s.[59] One of the main targets of the US BIT programme was to promote the Hull formula,[60] and the fair market value, as the applicable standard of compensation for expropriation.[61]

During the 1970s and 1980s, the total number of BITs continued to grow. While only two BITs were signed in the 1950s, the number of worldwide BITs rose to 83 until 1969 and 176 until 1979. By the end of 1989, States had concluded 377 BITs.[62] While this is a considerable number, it pales in comparison to the more than 2600 BITs signed since the end of the Cold War.[63] From a substantive viewpoint, these treaties display a remarkable degree of consistency. They typically include guarantees of fair and equitable treatment (FET), most-favoured-nation (MFN) treatment, compensation for expropriation, and the right to transfer revenues out of the host state. Moreover, violations of these provisions regularly lead to enforceable arbitral awards in favour of foreign investors, which are not (in the case of ICSID) or only to a very limited extent (under the New York Convention)[64] subject to review by domestic courts.

Commentators have offered both practical and ideological explanations for the stark increase in the total number of BITs in the 1990s. The most often cited factors are the sovereign debt crisis in the 1980s,[65] the collapse of communism,[66] and the widespread support for the so-called 'Washington Consensus'.[67] Latin

---

[58] This formulation relates back to the General Assembly Resolution on Permanent Sovereignty over Natural Resources of 14 December 1962, GA Res 1803, UN Doc A/5217.

[59] Vandevelde, 'A Brief History of International Investment Agreements', at 169.

[60] On the Hull formula, *see* note 20 and accompanying text.

[61] Vandevelde, 'A Brief History of International Investment Agreements', at 171.

[62] UNCTAD, Bilateral Investment Treaties 1959–1991, at 3.

[63] As at 28 January 2015, the total number of worldwide BITs was 2924, and the number of other IIAs was 345 (<http://investmentpolicyhub.unctad.org/IIA>).

[64] Convention on the Recognition and Enforcement of Foreign Arbitral Awards of 10 June 1958 ('New York Convention'), 330 UNTS 38.

[65] UNCTAD, International Investment Rule-Making: Stocktaking, Challenges and the Way Forward, UNCTAD Series on International Investment Polices for Development (2008), at 14; Vandevelde, 'A Brief History of International Investment Agreements', at 177–8.

[66] Dolzer & Schreuer, 'Investment Law', at 15.

[67] For the genesis of this term *see* John Williamson, 'From Reform Agenda to Damaged Brand Name—a Short History of the Washington Consensus and Suggestions for What to do Next', *Finance & Development* 40 (2003) 10–13. Williamson, who coined the term 'Washington Consensus', reports that he initially chose this term to describe ten policy reforms that he thought were necessary to cope with the debt crisis in Latin America (at p 10). In 1989, these proposals reflected the policies pursued by the following Washington-based institutions: the IMF, the World Bank, the Inter-American Development Bank, the US Treasury, and probably also the US Federal Reserve (at 11). In the following years, however, commentators began to use this term to describe neoliberal agendas or policies of the Washington-based institutions that only partly matched the

American countries in particular concluded a large number of BITs in the early 1990s.[68] This positive attitude towards foreign investment on the international level is reflected in the 1992 World Bank Guidelines on the Treatment of Foreign Direct Investment. The preamble of these guidelines states:

that a greater flow of foreign direct investment brings substantial benefits to bear on the world economy and on the economies of developing countries in particular, in terms of improving the long term efficiency of the host country through greater competition, transfer of capital, technology and managerial skills and enhancement of market access and in terms of the expansion of international trade.[69]

In addition to BITs concluded between developed and developing countries, the 1990s witnessed the beginning of a trend towards treaties between developing countries.[70] The most important multilateral treaties for the protection of foreign investment were also concluded in the 1990s. In 1994, the NAFTA entered into force between Canada, Mexico, and the US.[71] The treaty guarantees, inter alia, 'fair and equitable treatment' and 'full protection and security' (Article 1105(1)) for investments and provides for the possibility of investor–State arbitration. A multilateral treaty with a broader territorial scope is the Energy Charter Treaty of 1994 (ECT).[72] According to its Article 2, the ECT 'establishes a legal framework in order to promote long-term cooperation in the energy field' among its more than 40 signatories from Europe, Asia, Japan, and Australia.[73] The treaty deals with a variety of issues such as trade, transit, and investment, but it exclusively focuses on the energy sector, and its substantive rules on investment protection (Articles 10–17) are very similar to those in BITs. The ECT offers four options for investors to instigate arbitral proceedings: the ICSID convention, the Additional Facility Rules of ICSID, the UNCITRAL Arbitration Rules, and the Arbitration Institute of the Stockholm Chamber of Commerce (Article 26(4)).

While investors started to make significant use of arbitration clauses in IIAs in the 1990s, this development greatly accelerated in this millennium. Prior to the year 2000, the total number of all publicly known treaty-based investor–State arbitrations was below 50. By the end of 2010, the total number of known cases was 390,[74] and at

---

original meaning of the term (at 11). Williamson's original concept included trade liberalization and privatization but also emphasized the need of supervision and regulation (at 10).

[68] The BITs that became the basis of the proceedings against Argentina discussed in this book were concluded in the 1990s, except for the Italy–Argentina BIT, which was signed on 10 September 1989. (*See* UNCTAD, Bilateral Investment Treaties 1959–1991, Annex, at 15.)

[69] World Bank Guidelines on the Treatment of Foreign Direct Investment, ILM 31 (1992) 1379–84.

[70] By the end of 2007, 27% of all BITs had been concluded between developing countries. (*See* UNCTAD, World Investment Report 2008, Transnational Challenge and the Infrastructure Challenge (2008), at 15–16.)

[71] NAFTA regulates the free movement of goods, services, people, and investment. Chapter 11 deals specifically with issues of foreign investment. For the text of Chapter 11, *see* 32 ILM (1993) 605–803, at 639–49.

[72] For the text of the ECT and related documents, *see* 34 ILM (1995) 373–454.

[73] Russia has signed but not ratified the ECT.

[74] UNCTAD, World Investment Report 2011, Non-Equity Modes of International Production and Development (2011), at 101.

the end of 2013, this number stood at 568.[75] With 56 cases, the year 2013 alone saw more newly instigated investor–State arbitrations than the entire twentieth century.[76] The importance of ICSID in the current system is borne out by the fact that more than 60% of all publicly known cases were brought under the ICSID convention or the ICSID additional facility rules.[77] Interestingly, States have more often won than lost investment disputes.[78] Still, as mentioned above, States, NGOs, and scholars increasingly voice concerns about the current system of investor–State arbitration for public interest reasons.[79] An important role in this debate is played by the jurisprudence arising from the 2001–3 financial crisis in the State sued before arbitral tribunals more often than any other: Argentina.[80]

IV. The 2001–3 Argentine financial crisis

This section provides a short introduction to the historical and economic background of the arbitral jurisprudence related to the 2001–3 Argentine financial crisis. Most of the relevant claimants invested in Argentina's public utilities sector, and the dismantling of the regulatory regime in this sector played a key role in the tribunals' findings on liability. Therefore, subsection 1 briefly outlines the main features of the relevant regulatory framework when the crisis started. Subsection 2 addresses the developments and events before and during the Argentine financial crisis, and subsection 3 outlines Argentina's emergency measures.

1. The privatization of public utilities in the late 1980s

In the 1980s, Argentina went through various economic and financial crises, during which the country experienced, inter alia, four currency devaluations of over 90%.[81] As a result, Argentina passed a state reform law in 1989 acknowledged that Argentina's state-run public services were in a state of emergency and called for their privatization.[82] In the gas sector, a 1992 law (the 'Gas Law') and various consecutive decrees regulated the privatization of the gas industry,

---

[75] UNCTAD, World Investment Report 2014, Investing in the SDGs: an Action Plan, at 124.

[76] *See* the data provided in id., at 124.

[77] UNCTAD, Recent Developments in Investor–State Dispute Settlement (ISDS), IIA Issues Note, No. 1, at 9.

[78] *See, e.g*, UNCTAD, World Investment Report 2014, Investing in the SDGs: an Action Plan, at 125; UNCTAD, Latest Developments in Investor–State Dispute Settlement, IIA Issue Note No. 1 (2011), at 2.

[79] *See* Chapter 1, note 1 and accompanying text.

[80] See *supra* notes 3 and 4 and accompanying text

[81] Law No. 23.696 of 17 August 1989. (*Suez, Sociedad General de Aguas de Barcelona SA, and Vivendi Universal SA v. Argentine Republic*, ICSID Case No. ARB/03/19, para. 28, and *AWG Group v. Argentine Republic*, UNCITRAL Arbitration, Decision on Liability, 30 July 2010, para. 28).

[82] *LG&E Energy Corp v. Argentine Republic*, ICSID Case No. ARB/02/1, Decision on Liability, 3 October 2006, para. 35; *Suez-Vivendi* and *AWG Group*, Decision on Liability, paras. 28–9.

and reorganized the transport and distribution of gas.[83] Similar legislation was passed in the same year for the electricity sector and the water sector.[84] By way of example, I will briefly outline the relevant regulatory framework in the gas sector.[85]

As part of its privatization programme, Argentina dismantled the State-owned gas transportation and distribution monopoly, Gas del Estado. At the beginning of this process, the company was divided into two transportation and eight distribution business units according to different geographic regions. These business units were then transferred to ten newly created companies, including TNG, Centro, GasBan, and Cuyana. Consecutively, the Argentine State transferred licences to the ten companies so that they could operate within the new system.[86] The actual privatization part of the reform involved establishing Argentine investment companies, which served as vehicles for those shares of the ten companies that were destined for the private sector. Through a bidding process, foreign and domestic investors could acquire shares in the investment companies.[87] To attract foreign investors to this process, Argentina targeted them with marketing material and presentations on the new regulatory framework.[88]

An important role in this regulatory framework was played the public agency *Ente Nacional Regulador del Gas* (ENARGAS), established through the Gas Law. The agency was responsible for supervising the gas industry and setting the maximum tariff that each transport and distribution company was allowed to charge. The tariffs were to be reviewed and adjusted every five years. ENARGAS had to set the tariffs at levels that were sufficient to (a) cover operating costs, taxes, and depreciation, (b) allow a reasonable rate of return on invested capital, and (c) guarantee continuous supply by providing sufficient means for maintenance and expansion.[89] To achieve these goals, the government adopted legislation that granted several benefits to the investors. First, investors were allowed to calculate tariffs in US dollars and only had to express them in Argentine peso at the time of the billing. Second, the investors had a right to a tariff review based on the US Producer Price Index (PPI adjustment) every six months. Third, investors could demand a revision of the tariffs every five years to ensure that they were at a sufficient level to provide a reasonable rate of return. Finally, Argentina guaranteed that the licences could not be modified against the will of the licensees. If the government were to change the tariff system, investors would be entitled

---

[83] *See, e.g., CMS Gas Transmission Company v. Argentine Republic*, ICSID Case No. Arb/01/08, Decision of the ad hoc Committee on the Application for Annulment of the Argentine Republic, para. 31; *Suez-Vivendi* and *AWG Group*, Decision on Liability, para. 30.

[84] Law No. 24,065. For the content of this law, *see, e.g., National Grid plc v. Argentina*, UNCITRAL Arbitration, Award, 3 November 2008, paras. 52–5.

[85] On the regulatory framework for the privatization of the water distribution and sewage system, *see, e.g., Suez-Vivendi* and *AWG Group*, Decision on Liability, paras. 72–88.

[86] Decrees Nos 2454/92, 2460/92, 2453/92. (*See, e.g., LG&E*, Decision on Liability, paras. 44, 47.)

[87] Id., paras. 45, 48.   [88] Id., paras. 48–9.

[89] Andres Gomez-Lobo & Vivien Foster, The 1996–97 'Gas Price Review in Argentina', *in Natural Gas: Private Sector Participation and Market Development* (Suzanne Smith ed., 1999) 78–87, at 78–9.

to compensation.[90] Apart from this sector-specific framework, a 1991 law established a fixed exchange rate of 1:1 between the US dollar and the Argentine peso to counter the previous period of hyperinflation (the 'Convertibility Law').[91]

2. The 2001–3 crisis and its precursors

The measures mentioned in the previous subsection contributed to a significant increase of foreign investment in Argentina. In the gas sector, the legal framework provided a stable tariff system until the end of the 1990s.[92] In 1998, however, the economic situation started to deteriorate. According to the IMF, three factors played a particularly important role in the emergence of the crisis: adverse developments abroad, a flawed fiscal policy, and the fixed exchange rate system, which formerly provided stability but turned out to be disadvantageous under new circumstances.[93] Regarding adverse developments abroad, the IMF mentioned the following points: the Russian default in August 1998, the fall in oil and other commodity prices, and the decrease in demand from Argentina's major trading partner Brazil due to a massive devaluation of the Brazilian real against the US dollar.[94] Moreover, the IMF criticized Argentina for accumulating further public debt even though the economy was already shrinking in the second half of 1998.[95] In 2000, the situation further deteriorated with the continued appreciation of the US dollar. According to the IMF, such a situation would normally require the depreciation of the real exchange rate.[96] The convertibility regime, however, deprived Argentina of this possibility.

The so-called bank run on 28 November 2001 has come to be considered the starting point of the major crisis. Within three days, more than 60% of total private sector deposits were withdrawn from Argentine banks.[97] The government's response included a strict cap on bank withdrawals. An executive order of 1 December 2001, which became known as the *Corralito*, prohibited the withdrawal of more than 250 dollars per week from private bank accounts and the transfer of currency abroad.[98] These measures led to massive riots, causing President de La Rua to resign on 20 December 2001. Between 20 December and 30 December of that year, three different presidents were appointed by Congress. The following economic indicators affirm the view that the crisis was 'among the most severe of recent currency crises':[99] GDP fell by 4.5% in 2001 and by 11% in 2002, resulting

---

[90] Decree No. 1738/92 of 28 September 1992 and Decree No. 2255/92 (*Reglas Básicas de la Licencia*— Basic Rules of the License). *See also LG&E*, Decision on Liability, paras. 41–2; *BG Group plc v. Argentina*, UNCITRAL Arbitration, Final Award, 24 September 2007, para. 305.

[91] Law No. 23, 928. *See* IMF, *Evaluation Report, The IMF and Argentina 1991-2001* (Washington 2004), at 1; *Continental Casualty Company v. Argentine Republic*, ICSID Case No. ARB/03/9, Award, 5 September 2008, para. 105.

[92] *LG&E*, Decision on Liability, paras. 52–3.   [93] IMF, *Evaluation Report*, at 14.

[94] Id., at 12, 13.   [95] Id., at 13.   [96] Id.

[97] IMF, *Lessons from the Crisis in Argentina* (Washington, 2003), para. 61.

[98] *LG&E*, Decision on Liability, para. 63; IMF, Lessons from the Crisis in Argentina, para. 61.

[99] IMF, *Evaluation Report*, at 8.

in an overall shrinking of the Argentine economy by 20% from 1998 to 2002. The unemployment rate exceeded 20% in 2002. The inflation rate was 10% in April 2002 alone and averaged 40% for the year as a whole.[100] While presidents during the crisis were appointed by the Argentine congress, the first popular presidential election since the beginning of the crisis took place on 26 April 2003. On 25 May 2003, new president Néstor Kirchner took office, and the economic and financial situation in Argentina started to stabilize.[101]

3. Argentina's measures in response to the crisis

As explained in subsection 1, the regulatory framework had granted gas transportation and distribution companies a semi-annual right to a tariff review based on the US PPI.[102] When the tariffs were due to be adjusted in January 2000, Argentina's deflationary period met with an inflationary period in the US. Under these circumstances, adjustment as envisioned by the Gas Law would have resulted in a large increase in utility rates for consumers.[103] The Argentine government, therefore, sought an agreement with licensees to suspend the semi-annual tariff adjustment. The gas companies finally agreed to a postponement of the tariff adjustment in January 2000. The agreement stipulated that the costs of the postponement would be recovered from 1 July 2000 to 30 April 2001, and that resulting income losses would be indemnified.[104]

When the situation did not improve over the following six months, the government managed to convince the companies to agree to a second postponement for two years. The decree establishing this postponement envisaged a stabilization fund to recover the postponed amounts.[105] Furthermore, the decree reaffirmed the government's commitments regarding the semi-annual PPI adjustment. After a national ombudsman had filed a lawsuit against the decree and a provisional order enjoined its application, the regulatory authority declared at the end of 2001 that no PPI adjustment would be approved.[106]

After Argentina had announced suspension of all payments on its external debt on 24 December 2001, it proclaimed a public emergency 'with respect to social, economic, administrative, financial and exchange matters' in a 6 January 2002 law (the Emergency Law).[107] This law abolished the peg of the peso to the US dollar, which had been established by the Convertibility Law of 1991, and empowered the executive to set up a system for the determination of the peso exchange

---

[100] IMF, Lessons from the Crisis in Argentina, paras. 62, 66.

[101] *See, e.g., LG&E*, Decision on Liability, para. 70.

[102] *See supra* note 90 and accompanying text, and id., paras. 41–2.

[103] Id., paras. 55–6.

[104] *CMS Gas Transmission Company v. Argentine Republic*, ICSID Case No. ARB/01/8, Award, 12 May 2005, para. 60.

[105] Decree No. 669/00 of 17 July 2000, effective as of 4 August 2000.

[106] *LG&E*, Decision on Liability, paras. 601.

[107] Law No. 25561 of 6 January 2012 (*see Continental*, Award, paras. 140–1; *Impregilo SpA v. Argentine Republic*, ICSID Case No. ARB/07/17, Award, 21 June 2011, para. 202).

rate.[108] On 9 January 2002, the executive set the exchange rate at 1.4 pesos per dollar for all public sector and some trade-related transactions and left all other transactions to prevailing market rates.[109] This dual system was abandoned only one month later, when the fixed exchange rate was abolished in favour of market rates.[110] The peso depreciated immediately to 1.8 peso per dollar when the market opened on 11 February 2002.[111]

Apart from leading to changes in the applicable exchange rate, the Emergency Law also abolished the right of licensees of public utilities to a tariff review based on the US PPI.[112] Moreover, the Emergency Law converted the calculation of tariffs for public services from dollars into pesos, at a rate of 1:1.[113] Furthermore, in February 2002, an executive act converted all dollar-denominated obligations between private persons (and debt owed to financial institutions) into pesos, again at a rate of 1:1.[114] Dollar deposits with banks were converted at a rate of 1.40 peso for each US dollar.[115] In March 2002, government debt denominated in US dollars was also converted into pesos at a rate of 1.40 peso for each US dollar.[116] This measure affected in particular the US dollar denominated treasury bills and government loans held by some of the claimants in the arbitral proceedings against Argentina.[117]

V. The jurisprudence arising from the Argentine financial crisis

The measures adopted by Argentina during its 2001–3 financial crisis have given rise to several arbitral awards and decisions on liability.[118] Most of these decisions

---

[108] Gabriel Goméz Giglio, 'Emergency Law and Financial Entities in Argentina', *Journal of International Banking Law and Regulation* 10 (2003) 397–405, at 400; IMF, *Evaluation Report*, at 14; *CMS*, Award, para. 65.

[109] Executive order 71/2002 (*see* Goméz Giglio, 'Emergency Law', at 400; *Continental*, Award, para. 142).

[110] Executive order 260/2002 of 11 February 2002 (*see* Goméz Giglio, 'Emergency Law', at 400; *Continental Casualty Company v. Argentine Republic*, ICSID Case No. ARB/03/9, Decision on the Application for Partial Annulment of Continental Casualty Company and the Application for Partial Annulment of the Argentine Republic, 16 September 2011, para. 142).

[111] *Continental*, Award, para. 142. The peso reached its lowest value of almost 4 pesos to one dollar on 25 June 2002 (*see* id., para. 142).

[112] *CMS Gas Transmission Company v. Argentine Republic*, ICSID Case No. ARB/01/08, Decision of the ad hoc Committee on the Application for Annulment of the Argentine Republic, 25 September 2007, para. 36; *LG&E*, Decision on Liability, para. 65; *Suez-Vivendi* and *AWG Group*, Decision on Liability, para. 44.

[113] *LG&E*, Decision on Liability, para. 65; *Enron Corporation and Ponderosa Assets, L.P. v. Argentine Republic*, ICSID Case No. ARB/01/3, Award, 22 May 2007, para. 72; *Impregilo*, Award, para. 258.

[114] Executive order 214/2002 of 3 February 2002 (*see Continental*, Award, para. 144; Goméz Giglio, 'Emergency Law', at 401).

[115] Id.   [116] Executive order 471/2002 of 8 March 2002 (*Continental*, Award, para. 145).

[117] Id., para. 145.

[118] *CMS*, Award, *LG&E Energy Corp. v. Argentine Republic*, ICSID Case No. ARB/02/1, Award, 25 July 2007; *Enron*, Award, *Sempra Energy International v. Argentine Republic*, ICSID Case No. ARB/02/16, Award, 28 September 2007; *BG Group*, Final Award, *Metalpar SA and Buen Aire SA v. Argentine Republic*, ICSID Case No. ARB/03/5, Award, 6 June 2008; *Continental*,

were brought before annulment committees, and some of these committees have already rendered their decisions.[119] Some other investment disputes brought by foreign investors against Argentina since 2001 are, for various reasons, of less relevance for our purposes: The tribunal in *Wintershall* upheld Argentina's preliminary objection to jurisdiction and therefore did not proceed to the merits of the case.[120] The decision was based on Article 10(2) and (3) of the Argentina–Germany BIT, which provides for an eighteen-month waiting period during which the claimant must resort to domestic remedies. In *TSA Spectrum*, the tribunal 'pierced the corporate veil' and identified an Argentine citizen as the ultimate owner of the claimant. Consequently, the tribunal denied jurisdiction on the basis of Article 25(2)(b) ICSID Convention.[121] In *Siemens* and *Azurix,* the tribunals had to decide on the lawfulness of measures taken prior to the beginning of the economic crisis in the autumn of 2001.[122]

The various decisions by arbitral tribunals dealing with the 2001–3 Argentine crisis differ in important respects. There are, however, also considerable similarities between the different rulings. While all tribunals but that for *Metalpar* found that Argentina was in breach of at least one of its obligations under the applicable

Award, *National Grid plc v. Argentina*, UNCITRAL Arbitration, Award, 3 November 2008; *Suez-Vivendi* and *AWG Group*, Decision on Liability; *Suez, Sociedad General de Aguas de Barcelona SA, and InterAgua Servicios Integrales del Agua SA v. Argentine Republic*, ICSID Case No. ARB/03/17, Decision on Liability, 30 July 2010 (note that *Suez–Vivendi, AWG Group*, and *Suez–InterAgua* were heard and decided by the same tribunal; the arbitral tribunal rendered one decision on liability for *Suez–Vivendi* and *AWG Group* and issued another, largely identical, decision for *Suez–InterAgua*); *Impregilo*, Award (collectively referred to in this book as 'the Argentine cases'). There are at least four additional decisions by arbitral tribunals concerning the 2001–3 Argentine financial crisis: *Total SA v. Argentine Republic*, ICSID Case No. ARB/04/1, Decision on Liability, 27 December 2010; *El Paso Energy International Company v. Argentine Republic*, ICSID Case No. ARB/03/15, Award, 31 October 2011; *EDF International SA, SAUR International SA and León Participaciones Argentinas SA v. Argentine Republic*, ICSID Case No. ARB/03/23, Award, 11 June 2012; and *SAUR International SA v. Republic of Argentina*, ICSID Case No. ARB/04/4, Award, 22 May 2014. While these decisions have partly made their way into the public domain though different channels, the parties did not agree to their publication by ICSID (see Article 48(5) ICSID Convention), and they will not be discussed in this book.

[119] *CMS*, Decision of the Annulment Committee; *Continental*, Decision of the Annulment Committee; *Sempra Energy International v. Argentine Republic*, ICSID Case No. ARB/02/16, Decision on the Argentine Republic's Application for Annulment of the Award, 29 June 2010; *Enron Creditors Recovery Corp v. Argentine Republic*, ICSID Case No. ARB/01/3, Decision on the Application for Annulment of the Argentine Republic, 30 July 2010 (in chronological order).

[120] *Wintershall Aktiengesellschaft v. Argentine Republic*, ICSID Case No. ARB/04/14, Award, 8 December 2008, paras. 108–97.

[121] *TSA Spectrum de Argentina, SA v. Argentine Republic*, ICSID Case No. ARB/05/5, Award, 19 December 2008, paras. 133–62.

[122] See *Azurix Corp v. Argentine Republic*, ICSID Case No. ARB/01/12, Award, 14 July 2006, para. 57. (An annulment committee dismissed Argentina's application for annulment, *Azurix Corp v. Argentine Republic*, ICSID Case No. ARB/01/12, Decision of the ad hoc Committee on the Application for Annulment of the Argentine Republic, 1 September 2009.) The *Siemens* case involved the termination of a concession in the public utilities sector (electricity). The contract was terminated on 18 May 2001 by a decree under the terms of a law enacted in 2000 (*Siemens AG v. Argentine Republic*, ICSID Case No. ARB/02/8, Award, 6 February 2007, para. 97) The parties agreed to settle the case before a constituted annulment committee rendered a decision.

BIT, none of the tribunals considered Argentina's measures to be expropriatory. Furthermore, the *Metalpar* tribunal did not rule differently because of an antithetical understanding or interpretation of the applicable law. Rather, the underlying reason for the diverging holding of the tribunal was the particular situation of the claimant and a different regulatory framework in the claimant's industry. The cases *CMS, LG&E, Enron, Sempra*, and *BG Group* involved claimants from the gas sector. The decisions in *Suez–Vivendi, AWG Group, Suez–InterAgua*, and *Impregilo* concerned the water and sewage services. The claimant in *National Grid* had also invested into Argentina's public utilities (electricity), privatized in the 1990s. *Continental* invested in the sector of workers' accident insurance, which had been privatized in 1996.[123] The investor in *Metalpar*, in contrast, was from a sector unaffected by the privatization programme of the 1990s—automotives.[124] Consequently, the claimant did not suffer from the regulatory measures that were taken in the formerly state-owned industry sectors during the 2001–3 crisis.[125]

The jurisprudence of the tribunals was much less consistent regarding the extent to which Argentina incurred international responsibility because of its noncompliance with BIT provisions. The tribunals in *CMS, LG&E, Enron, Sempra*, and *Continental* had to decide on the basis of the Argentina–US BIT. This is of particular importance since the Argentina–US BIT contains a non-precluded measures (NPM) clause in Article XI:

This Treaty shall not preclude the application by either Party of measures necessary for the maintenance of public order, the fulfillment of its obligations with respect to the maintenance or restoration of international peace or security, or the protection of its own essential security interests.

The BITs underlying the claims in *BG Group, Metalpar, National Grid, Suez-Vivendi, AWG Group, Suez-InterAgua*, and *Impregilo* do not contain a treaty emergency exception similar to Article XI of the Argentina–US BIT.[126] Argentina was ordered to pay compensation in all of these cases except for the *Metalpar* case, where the tribunal found that Argentina's measures did not interfere with any treaty protections.[127] The other tribunals deciding on the basis of a BIT different from the Argentina–US BIT found that Argentina failed to meet the strict requirements of the customary international law defence of necessity. It was common ground among the tribunals that Article 25 ILC Articles on State Responsibility (ASR) constitutes an accurate codification of the necessity defence.[128] This provision reads as follows:

---

[123] *Continental*, Award, para. 104.

[124] For an overview of the privatization programme, *see supra* subsection IV.1.

[125] For the content of these measures, *see supra* subsection IV.3.

[126] The *Metalpar* case involved the BIT between Chile and Argentina. The investors in *GB Group* and *National Grid* both relied on the Argentina–UK BIT.

[127] *See supra* notes 124–5 and accompanying text.

[128] *See, e.g., BG Group*, Final Award, para. 255; *National Grid plc v. Argentina*, UNCITRAL Arbitration, Award, 3 November 2008, para. 256.

1. Necessity may not be invoked by a State as a ground for precluding the wrongfulness of an act not in conformity with an international obligation of that State unless the act:
   (a) is the only way for the State to safeguard an essential interest against a grave and imminent peril; and
   (b) does not seriously impair an essential interest of the State or States towards which the obligation exists, or of the international community as a whole.
2. In any case, necessity may not be invoked by a State as a ground for precluding wrongfulness if:
   (a) the international obligation in question excludes the possibility of invoking necessity; or
   (b) the State has contributed to the situation of necessity.

All tribunals deciding on the basis of a BIT other than the Argentina–US BIT ruled that Argentina could not rely on Article 25 ASR: they found that the relevant State measures did not constitute the 'only way' to cope with the crisis as required by Article 25(1)(a) and/or held that Argentina 'contributed to the situation of necessity' within the meaning of Article 25(2)(b).[129] The jurisprudence of the tribunals deciding on the basis of the Argentina–US BIT is more complex. The *CMS, Enron,* and *Sempra* tribunals ruled largely in favour of the claimants. These tribunals followed the same approach in one decisive aspect: they all relied on necessity under customary international law in order to interpret Article XI of the Argentina–US BIT. Since the tribunals inter alia found that Argentina contributed to the emergence of the economic crisis and that its measures had not been the 'only way' to cope with the crisis, they rejected Argentina's arguments based on both Article XI of the Argentina–US BIT and Article 25 ASR.

The *LG&E* and *Continental* tribunals ruled to a considerable extent in favour of Argentina. The factual circumstances in *LG&E* hardly differed from those in the other cases involving investors in the gas sector. Nevertheless, the *LG&E* tribunal drew different conclusions from these circumstances for Argentina's necessity defence. Most notably, the tribunal held that Argentina's emergency measures had been the 'only way' to overcome the economic crisis.[130] After the awards in *CMS, LG&E, Enron,* and *Sempra* had been rendered, the *CMS* annulment committee criticized that the *CMS* tribunal did not properly distinguish between Article XI of the Argentina–US BIT and the customary international law defence of necessity. The committee stressed that Article XI needs to be interpreted independently, and not merely by reference to customary international law.[131] The *Continental* tribunal followed the guidelines of the *CMS* annulment committee by distinguishing between the two provisions. Moreover, the tribunal introduced a WTO-inspired 'least restrictive means' test to Article XI. The 'least restrictive

---

[129] *National Grid plc v. Argentina*, UNCITRAL Arbitration, Award, 3 November 2008, paras. 259–260; *Suez-Vivendi* and *AWG Group*, Decision on Liability, paras. 260 ('only way') and 263 ('contribution'); *Impregilo*, Award, paras. 356–359 ('contribution').

[130] For this (*obiter dicta*) finding on Article 25, *see* Chapter 8, notes 119–21 and accompanying text. For the tribunal's analysis of Article XI, *see* Chapter 7, notes 16–24 and accompanying text.

[131] For the reasoning of the *CMS* tribunal and the corresponding criticism by the annulment committee, *see* Chapter 7, notes 6–15 and accompanying text.

means' test constitutes a significantly lower threshold than the 'only way' requirement. In this regard, the tribunal found that there was no less infringing, equally
effective way to deal with the financial crisis than the approach taken by the
Argentine government. Consequently, the tribunal ruled largely in favour of
Argentina.[132]

The tribunals in *Enron* and *Sempra* adopted essentially the same approach
regarding the relationship between Article XI of the Argentina–US BIT and
Article 25 ASR as the *CMS* tribunal. In 2010, the annulment committees in
Enron and *Sempra* went one step further than the annulment committee in *CMS*.
They did not only criticize the reasoning of the respective tribunal concerning
the customary international law defence of necessity and/or Article XI of the
Argentina–US BIT, but they annulled the awards. Interestingly, the reasons on
which the two annulment committees based their decisions differ significantly.
The *Sempra* annulment committee followed essentially the same approach as the
CMS annulment committee and criticized that the tribunal conflated Article XI
of the treaty and Article 25 ASR.[133] Contrary to the *CMS* annulment committee,
however, it decided that the tribunal's approach amounted to an outright failure
to apply the applicable law.[134] In the view of the *Sempra* annulment committee,
this failure provided a sufficient basis for the finding that the tribunal 'manifestly
exceeded its powers' within the meaning of Article 52(1)(b) ICSID Convention.[135]

Only one month later, the *Enron* annulment committee rendered its decision
on Argentina's application for annulment of the *Enron* award. While the committee took note of the *CMS* annulment committee's harsh criticism of the conflation of Article XI of the BIT and Article 25 ASR, it held that it was for the
arbitral tribunal to decide on the relationship between these two provisions.[136]
However, the committee took issue with the way the *Enron* tribunal applied
Article 25. It found that the tribunal did not apply certain elements of this provision *at all* and therefore annulled the award on the basis of Article 52(1)(b) ICSID
Convention.[137] In particular, the committee criticized that the *Enron* tribunal
failed to clarify both the meaning of the 'only way' requirement of Article 25(1)(a)
and the legal elements of Article 25(2)(b) ('necessity may not be invoked...if the

---

[132] The tribunal awarded 2.8 million US dollars to the claimant. The claimant had demanded
damages in the amount of 'not less' than 31 million US dollars for violations of contract obligations
and 'not less' than 38 million for expropriation (*Continental*, Award, para. 22). The recovery is rather
small compared to the sums that had been awarded in the other cases mentioned in this chapter
(*CMS*, 133 million; *Enron*, 106 million; *Sempra*, 128 million; *BG Group*, 185 million; *National Grid*,
54 million. Even the *LG&E* award—which is often considered a success for Argentina—contains
an order to pay 57 million US dollars in damages).

[133] *Sempra Energy International v. Argentine Republic*, ICSID Case No. ARB/02/16, Decision on
the Argentine Republic's Application for Annulment of the Award, 29 June 2010, paras. 186–204.

[134] Id., paras. 205–10.   [135] Id., paras. 211–19.

[136] *Enron Creditors Recovery Corp v. Argentine Republic*, ICSID Case No. ARB/01/3, Decision on
the Application for Annulment of the Argentine Republic, 30 July 2010, para. 405.

[137] Id., paras. 374, 377, 393. Furthermore, the *Enron* annulment committee found that 'the
award has failed to state the reasons on which it is based' within the meaning of Article 52(1)(e)
ICSID Convention (paras. 378, 384).

State has contributed to the situation of necessity').[138] Unlike its peers in *Sempra* and *Enron*, the *Continental* annulment committee did not annul the relevant award, which was rendered largely in favour of Argentina. In its 2011 decision, the *Continental* committee found no error meeting the high threshold for annulment under the ICSID Convention, without rejecting or embracing the views taken by the *Continental* tribunal on Article XI of the US–Argentina BIT.[139]

The reasoning of the Argentina tribunals will be analysed in depth in other chapters of this book. The short overview in this section revealed that Argentina did not avoid liability for its emergency measures as a matter of the customary international law defence of necessity. When it came to Article XI of the Argentina–US BIT, the tribunals were divided, and the outcome of the different cases hinged on how the tribunals interpreted the relationship between Article XI and customary international law. The *CMS, Enron*, and *Sempra* tribunals relied on the 'only way' requirement from Article 25 in the context of Article XI, and found that Argentina's measures to combat the crisis were not covered by this treaty provision. The *LG&E* and *Continental* tribunals granted Argentina greater leeway to regulate in the public interest under Article XI without being liable to foreign investors, and dismissed significant parts of the relevant claims. Chapters 5 and 6 will reveal that Article XI of the US–Argentina BIT and Article 25 ASR were not the only normative contexts in which the tribunals had to resolve conflicts between the interests of foreign investors and the public. Rather, such conflicts played a key role in the tribunals' analyses of the FET standard and were relevant (albeit not decisive) in their jurisprudence on BIT provisions on expropriation. Much of the remainder of this book will analyse in which of the normative settings just mentioned—expropriation, FET, Article XI, and Article 25 ASR—proportionality may help to resolve conflicts between investor rights and the public interest.

---

[138] Id., paras. 371–6, 392–3.
[139] *Continental*, Decision of the Annulment Committee, paras. 110–43.

3

Proportionality as a General Principle of Law

Conflicts between different rights and interests arise in virtually every legal order. The principle of proportionality is a tool to resolve such conflicts. Today, a large number of domestic courts make use of this principle, in particular when individual rights collide with the public interest. The principle of proportionality has also made its way into international law. Proportionality analysis is an integral part of the jurisprudence of the ECtHR and the ECJ. The WTO adjudicatory bodies follow a very similar approach when weighing and balancing the relevant interests at stake. Proportionality is also part of other areas of international law, for example of the rules governing self-defence and countermeasures.

A considerable number of scholars suggest that international investment tribunals should apply the principle of proportionality when determining whether a State is liable under an IIA. The norms and concepts in international investment law for which proportionality should play a role vary significantly from author to author.[1] The most prominent examples are IIA provisions on expropriation and

---

[1] Kingsbury & Schill, 'Investor–State Arbitration as Governance: Fair and Equitable Treatment, Proportionality and the Emerging Global Administrative Law', at 31–32 (indirect expropriation and FET); Kingsbury & Schill, 'Public Law Concepts to Balance Investors' Rights with State Regulatory Actions in the Public Interest—the Concept of Proportionality', at 88–103 (indirect expropriation, FET, and NPM clauses); Stone Sweet & Grisel, 'Transnational Investment Arbitration: From Delegation to Constitutionalization?', at 131–2 (indirect expropriation, FET, Article XI of the Argentina–US BIT); Whythes, 'Investor–State Arbitrations: Can the 'Fair and Equitable Treatment' Clause Consider Human Rights Obligations?' at 254–5 (FET); Krommendijk & Morijn, '"Proportional' by What Measure(s)? Balancing Investor Interests and Human Rights by Way of Applying the Proportionality Principle in Investor–State Arbitration', at 449–50 (indirect expropriation); Alvarez & Khamsi, 'The Argentine Crisis and Foreign Investors: a Glimpse into the Heart of the Investment Regime', at 447–9 (balancing in the context of indirect expropriation, FET, national treatment, jurisdictional objections, most favoured nations treatment, umbrella clauses, and damages, but not Article XI of the Argentina–US BIT); José E. Alvarez & Tegan Brink, 'Revisiting the Necessity Defense: Continental Casualty v. Argentina', *in Yearbook on International Investment Law & Policy* 2010–2011 (Karl P. Sauvant ed., 2012) 319–74, at 357–8 (balancing in all substantive guarantees contained in BITs); Roland Kläger, 'Fair and Equitable Treatment' in *International Investment Law* (2011), at 235–56 (FET); van Aaken, 'Defragmentation of Public International Law Through Interpretation: a Methodological Proposal', at 506–12 (indirect expropriation and FET); Henckels, 'Indirect Expropriation and the Right to Regulate: Revisiting Proportionality Analysis and the Standard of Review in Investor–State Arbitration', at 228–9 (indirect expropriation); Reinisch, 'Necessity', at 201 (Article 25 ASR); Bjorklund, 'Emergency Exceptions: State of Necessity and Force Majeure', at 485 (Article 25 ASR); and Andreas Kulick, *Global Public Interest in International Investment Law* (2012), at 209–13 (compensation and damages).

FET, NPM clauses, and the customary international law defence of necessity. Chapters 5, 6, 7, and 8 examine these four normative settings in depth. This chapter analyses why proportionality should matter in investor–State arbitration at all. Answering this question is not only necessary to demonstrate that proportionality can be part of the applicable law in investor–State arbitration; it also provides valuable insights to decide whether and when arbitrators should use proportionality to interpret, apply, and—as some might argue—overwrite treaty provisions.

Aharon Barak, the former president of the Israeli Supreme Court, rightly notes that '[a]ny legal system wishing to adopt proportionality...must provide a legal foundation for such an adoption'.[2] The legal foundation for the application of the principle of proportionality in investor–State arbitration suggested in this book is Article 38(1)(c) ICJ Statute, which refers to 'general principles of law'. While this provision addresses the law the ICJ shall apply, the sources of international law mentioned in Article 38(1) matter beyond the ICJ context.[3] It reads as follows:

The Court, whose function is to decide in accordance with international law such disputes as are submitted to it, shall apply:

a. international conventions, whether general or particular, establishing rules expressly recognized by the contesting states;
b. international custom, as evidence of a general practice accepted as law;
c. *the general principles of law* recognized by civilized nations... (emphasis added)

Determining the law applicable to an investor–State arbitration is not always a straightforward task. In some investor–State arbitrations, international law is irrelevant to the substance of the dispute. This can be the case when the host State has given its consent to arbitration in a private contract governed by *domestic law*. The tribunal might then have to apply the principle of proportionality as part of the relevant domestic legal system. No meaningful generalization is possible as to whether and to what extent proportionality comes into play in such situations: much depends on the relevant domestic law, the specific contractual relationship, and the rights and interests at stake in the particular dispute.

We are interested in situations in which an arbitral tribunal should apply the principle of proportionality as a matter of *international law*. For disputes arbitrated under the ICSID Convention, Article 42 describes the law applicable to the substance of a dispute as follows:

[t]he Tribunal shall decide a dispute in accordance with such rules of law as may be agreed by the parties. In the absence of such agreement, the Tribunal shall apply the law of the Contracting State party to the dispute (including its rules on the conflict of laws) and such *rules of international law as may be applicable*. (Emphasis added)

---

[2] Aharon Barak, *Proportionality* (2012), at 211.
[3] Allain Pellet, 'Article 38', *in The Statute of the International Court of Justice* (Andreas Zimmermann, et al. eds., 2012) 731–870, paras. 49–54. *See also* note 5 and accompanying text.

According to the second sentence of Article 42(1), 'rules of international law' may govern the dispute if the parties did *not agree* on the applicable law.[4] The drafters of the ICSID Convention clarified that the term 'international law' should have the same meaning as it does in the context of Article 38(1)(c) ICJ Statute.[5] The rules of international law mentioned in Article 38(1)(c) may also become relevant when the parties *did agree* on the applicable law. Most investor–State tribunals owe their jurisdiction to an investment treaty. Many of these treaties specify that the arbitral tribunal shall apply the treaty provisions and applicable rules of 'international law'.[6] Tribunals have no difficulties in finding that such treaty stipulations constitute choice of law clauses for the purposes of the first sentence of Article 42(1) ICSID.[7] Some tribunals have even held that instituting proceedings based on BITs *without* a choice of law clause complete an implicit agreement on the choice of 'international law'.[8]

This short account of Article 42(1) ICSID illustrates why general principles within the meaning of Article 38(1)(c) ICJ Statute may be relevant in an ICSID arbitration. Of course, general principles of law matter in treaty arbitrations outside the ICSID context as well. Article 26(6) ECT, for example, provides that '[a] tribunal...shall decide the issues in dispute in accordance with this Treaty and applicable rules and principles of international law'—regardless of whether the investor opted for ICSID or a different forum. Other IIAs contain similar provisions.[9] Even in the absence of such provisions, arbitral tribunals should and

---

[4] For the intricate relationship between domestic and international law in the context of the second sentence of Article 42(1), *see* Schreuer, et al., *The ICISD Convention—a Commentary*, Article 42, paras. 204–44.

[5] The First Draft of the ICSID Convention contained an explicit clarification of this point in the text of the Convention (ICSID, *History of the Convention*, Volume I (1970) at 192). The relevant sentence was finally transferred from the Convention to the Report of the Executive Directors (ICSID, *Report of the Executive Directors* (1965), para. 40). The chairman of the Legal Committee clarified that this transfer was not meant to change the meaning of Article 42(1) (ICSID, *History of the Convention*, Volume II, Part 2 (1968), at 984, para. 19). It is important to note that the term *'rules'* in the English version of Article 42(1) ICSID does not exlcude *'general principles'* from the scope of the applicable international law. The First Draft of Article 42(1)—former Article 45(1)—referred to *'règles* de droit...international' and *'reglas* de derecho...internacional' in the authentic French and Spanish versions of the Convention respectively (ICSID, *History of the Convention*, Volume I, at 192–3 (emphasis added). The final Spanish version of Article 42(1), however, reads *'normas* de derecho internacional', and the French version refers to 'les *principes* de droit international' (emphasis added). For the interchangeable use of the terms 'rules' and 'principles' by international tribunals, *see, e.g., Case Concerning Delimitation of the Maritime Boundary in the Gulf of Maine Area* (Canada v. United States of America), Judgment, 12 October 1984, ICJ Reports 1984, 246–346, at 288–99, para. 79; *Compañia del Desarrollo de Santa Elena SA v. Republic of Costa Rica*, ICSID Case No. ARB/96/1, Final Award, 12 February 2000, para. 64; *Suez-Vivendi* and *AWG Group*, Decision on Liability, para. 185.

[6] *See, e.g.,* Article 26(6) ECT, Article 1131(1) NAFTA and Article 30(1) of the US Model BIT (*available at* <http://italaw.com/sites/default/files/archive/ita1028.pdf>). Some IIAs add the domestic law of the contracting State that is a party to the dispute to this list (*see, e.g.,* Article 10(7) of the Argentina–Netherlands BIT, *available at* <investmentpolicyhub.unctad.org/Download/TreatyFile/107>).

[7] *See* Schreuer, et al., *The ICISD Convention—a Commentary*, Article 42, paras. 80–8.

[8] For the divided jurisprudence on this point, *see* id., Article 42, paras. 89–95.

[9] *See supra* note 6 and accompanying text.

do apply general international law (consisting of custom and general principles) simply because IIAs do not constitute 'self-contained' regimes operating in a legal vacuum—a point that will be discussed in more depth in Chapter 4.[10]

If we accept the proposition that general international law matters in treaty-based arbitrations, the applicability of proportionality hinges on two questions. First, is proportionality a general principle of law within the meaning of Article 38(1)(c) ICJ Statute? Second, when and how should arbitrators use this principle to interpret, apply, or overwrite treaty stipulations? This chapter analyses the first question, i.e. whether proportionality constitutes a general principle—an issue on which scholars disagree.[11] To tackle this issue, it is first necessary to sketch out what legal norms may constitute general principles within the meaning of Article 38(1)(c) ICJ Statute. There is some debate on this question, structured around the following four categories:

1. principles and rules emanating from domestic legal systems;
2. principles grounded in the very nature of the international community or in other words 'general principles of international law';[12]
3. principles applicable to all legal systems and principles of legal logic;[13] and

---

[10] *See* Chapter 4, notes 50–77 and accompanying text.

[11] Scholars that consider proportionality to constitute a general principle include the following: Alec Stone Sweet & Giacinto della Cananea, 'Proportionality, General Principles of Law, and Investor–State Arbitration: a Response to José Alvarez', *NYU Journal of International Law and Politics* 46 (2014) 911–54, at 937–8; Robert Kolb, 'Principles as Sources of International Law (With Special Reference to Good Faith)', *Netherlands International Law Review* 53 (2006) 1–36, at 8, 25; Ernst-Ulrich Petersmann, 'International Rule of Law and Constitutional Justice in International Investment Law and Arbitration', *Indiana Journal of Global Legal Studies* 16 (2009) 513–33, at 531; Georg Nolte, 'Thin or Thick? The Principle of Proportionality and International Humanitarian Law', *Law & Ethics of Human Rights* 4 (2010) 244–55, at 254; Jost Delbrück, 'Proportionality', *in Encyclopedia of Public International Law,* Vol. III (Rudolf Bernhardt ed., 1997) 1140–44 at 1144; van Aaken, 'Defragmentation of Public International Law Through Interpretation: a Methodological Proposal' at 502. Scholars who deny that proportionality constitutes a general principle of law include Michael Krugmann (Michael Krugmann, Der Grundsatz der Verhältnismäßigkeit im Völkerrecht (2004), at 124) and José E. Alvarez, 'Beware Boundary Crossings', New York University Public Law & Legeal Theory Research Paper Series, Working Paper No. 14-51 (September 2014) *available at* <http://papers.ssrn.com/sol3/papers.cfm?abstract_id=2498182> at 12–13, 28, 37, and 57. Rosalyn Higgins finds it 'doubtful' that proportionality is 'a general principle of law' (Rosalyn Higgins, *Problems & Process: International Law and How We Use It* (1995), at 236). Orakhelashvili leaves the question unanswered—despite his overview of the significant role of proportionality in the law of the sea, the ECHR, WTO law, international humanitarian law, and the law of the use of force (Alexander Orakhelashvili, *The Interpretation of Acts and Rules in Public International Law* (2008), at 266–70). Meron seems to be undecided as well when he states (with respect to the protection of civilians in armed conflict) that 'the core of the principle [of proportionality] is customary and *perhaps* also a general principle of law.' (Theodor Meron, *Human Rights and Humanitarian Norms as Customary Law* (1989), at 65 n.178, emphasis added).

[12] Typical examples in this context are basic rules such as non-intervention, self-defence, the sovereign immunity of States, and territorial integrity (Hermann Mosler, 'General Principles of Law', *in Encyclopedia of Public International Law,* Vol. II (Rudolf Bernhardt ed., 1995) 511–27, at 513, 522–4; Olufemi Elias & Chin Lim, '"General Principles of Law", "Soft" Law and the Identification of International Law', *Netherlands Yearbook of International Law* 28 (1997) 3–49, at 28).

[13] Some scholars state that certain principles are so fundamental to every legal order that they are valid at both the domestic and the international level. Typical examples are the principle of *pacta sunt servanda*, the *lex specialis derogat legi generali* rule, and the *lex posterior derogat legi priori* rule (Mosler, 'General Principles of Law', at 513–14; Elias & Lim, '"General Principles"' at 31–5; Stefan

4. a group Elias and Lim refer to as 'inchoate custom', i.e. legal expressions within the international community that do not meet the requirements of custom.[14]

There is no consensus on whether the second ('general principles of international law') and third ('principles applicable to all legal systems and principles of legal logic') categories fall indeed under Article 38(1)(c) ICJ Statute or whether they simply reflect customary international or treaty law.[15] Regarding the fourth category ('inchoate custom'), there are serious doubts whether the relevant legal expressions give rise to binding rules of international law at all.

Scholars and practitioners agree, however, that the first category of norms ('principles and rules emanating from domestic legal systems') may give rise to rules of international law under certain conditions.[16] We focus on this category here. Identifying such general principles involves a two-step process. The first step is a comparative study of national legal systems.[17] Once it has been shown that a particular principle is sufficiently established at the domestic level, it is necessary to demonstrate in a second step that the relevant principle is transposable to the international level.[18] To be noted at the outset, Article 38(1)(c) does not require recognition by *all* domestic legal orders; an analysis of a fair number of representative legal systems is sufficient.[19] In 1944, H. C. Gutteridge offered the following guidelines for identifying general principles of law:

Kadelbach & Thomas Kleinlein, 'Überstaatliches Verfassungsrecht. Zur Konstitutionalisierung im Völkerrecht', *Archiv des Völkerrechts* 44 (2006) 235–66, at 255–6).

[14] Elias & Lim, '"General Principles"', at 35.

[15] *See, e.g.*, id., at 29, 35; Simma & Verdross, *Universelles Völkerrecht*, para. 605 (with respect to general principles of international law). Pellet restricts the scope of Article 38(1)(c) to principles emanating from domestic law (Pellet, 'Article 38', paras. 259–60).

[16] Pellet, 'Article 38', paras. 261–3. Before the end of the Cold War, communist scholars, in particular, were sceptical about the prospect of identifying common principles in light of the fundamental differences between 'capitalist' and 'socialist' legal systems (*see* Simma & Verdross, *Universelles Völkerrecht*, para. 603).

[17] The phrase 'recognized by civilized nations' does not constrain the scope of Article 38(1)(c). Even the drafters of the corresponding article in the PCIJ Statute in the 1920s seem to have considered all nations to be civilized (Pellet, 'Article 38', para. 261, referring to the Procès-verbaux of the Proceedings of the the the Advisory Committee of Jurists of 1920). It is, therefore, more appropriate to speak of the general principles of law 'common to the major legal systems of the world' (Louis Henkin, *International Law: Politics and Values* (1995), at 39–40, who harshly criticized the 'arrogantly Eurocentric' formulation in Article 38(1)(c) ICJ Statute).

[18] Brownlie, *Public International Law*, at 16–17; Tarcisio Gazzini, 'General Principles of Law in the Field of Foreign Investment', *Journal of World Investment & Trade* 10 (2009) 103–19, at 107: Pellet, 'Article 38', para. 269; Giorgio Gaja, 'General Principles of Law', *in The Max Planck Encyclopedia of Public International Law* Volume IV (Rüdiger Wolfrum ed., 2012) 370–8, para. 7.

[19] Pellet, for example, stresses that 'probably all contemporary municipal laws borrow part of their rules ... [from] civil (or continental) law and common law' and that it is 'enough to ascertain that such principles are present in any (or some) of the laws belonging to these various systems' (Pellet, 'Article 38', para. 263 and n.755). In a similar vein, Georg Schwarzenberger, *A Manual of International Law* (1967) 34; Michael Bogdan, 'General Principles of Law and the Lacunae in the Law of Nations', *Nordic Journal of International Law* 46 (1977) 37–53, at 46; Kadelbach & Kleinlein, 'Überstaatliches Verfassungsrecht', at 257. The ICJ tends to circumvent the comparative law exercise by referring to 'general conception[s] of law', 'general and well recognized principles', 'principles governing the judicial process', or similar concepts, without attributing these rules to one of the sources of international law listed in Article 38(1) (*See* Pellet, 'Article 38', para. 265). For an enumeration of ICJ cases in which individual judges embraced the comparative task to identify a

If any real meaning is to be given to the [word] 'general'... the correct test would seem to be that an international judge before taking over a principle from *private law* must satisfy himself that it *is recognized in substance* by all the *main systems of law* and that in applying it he will not be doing violence to the fundamental concepts of any of those systems.[20]

Gutteridge naturally focused on 'private law' systems when he wrote his seminal essay in 1944—a time in which States were more or less the sole actors in international law.[21] Indeed, the relationship between equal and independent private actors might offer the most appropriate analogies for the relationships between sovereign States. But with the increasing role of non-State actors in international law, comparative law analysis in other areas of law becomes more and more important. Issues involved in human rights cases or investor–State arbitrations often resemble situations for which domestic legal systems have developed solutions in their administrative or constitutional law jurisprudence. There is no reason why international tribunals should not draw on this experience.[22] In the end, the migration of decision-making powers from the domestic to the international level and the greater involvement of non-State actors in international law could give rise to a development that some had expected to set in many decades ago: a more significant role of general principles of law in international dispute resolution.[23]

This chapter analyses whether proportionality should be one of these principles. It is structured as follows: Section I examines the role of the principle of proportionality in various domestic legal systems, in particular in Germany, Canada, South Africa, Israel, and the United States. While the courts in the first four States regularly apply the principle of proportionality, the US Supreme Court considers proportionality irrelevant for its fundamental rights jurisprudence. We will see that this does not necessarily mean that proportionality falls short of constituting a general principle of law. Still, the reasoning of the US Supreme Court helps to identify some factors that speak against resorting to proportionality analysis in certain normative settings on both the domestic and the international level. Section II categorizes these factors and discusses three main concerns regarding proportionality that arbitrators ought to assess before applying proportionality in a particular normative setting: (1) unwarranted judicial lawmaking; (2) the rule

---

general principle of law, *see* id., para. 264 n.757. Particularly illustrative is Bruno Simma's approach to base a rule of joint and several liability in international law on Article 38(1)(c) (*see Case concerning Oil Platforms* (Iran v. United States of America), Judgment, 6 November 2003, ICJ Reports 2003, 161 (Simma, J, partly dissenting) 352–7).

[20] H. C. Gutteridge, 'Comparative Law and the Law of Nations', *British Yearbook of International Law* 21 (1944) 1–10, at 5 (emphases added).

[21] For notable exceptions to this rule (and their limitations), *see* Chapter 2, notes 29–51 and accompanying text.

[22] *See also* Gazzini, 'General Principles of Law in the Field of Foreign Investment', at 139; Kingsbury & Schill, 'Investor–State Arbitration as Governance', at 15–16, 27–8; Schill, 'International Investment Law and Comparative Public Law', at 23–35. Under certain circumstances, one may even consider the use of criminal law concepts (*see, e.g.,* Anne Peters, 'Humanity as the A and Ω of Sovereignty', *European Journal of International Law* 20 (2009) 513–544, at 536).

[23] *See, e.g.,* Rudolf B. Schlesinger, 'Research on the General Principles of Law Recognized by Civilized Nations', *American Journal of International Law* 51 (1957) 734–53, at 734.

of law; and (3) the risk of arbitrary outcomes due to the lack of a relevant value system. Section III examines the role of proportionality in several subsystems of international law. This analysis shows that—as a matter of principle—proportionality is transposable to the international level. Furthermore, it sheds light on the typical situations in which international courts and tribunals resort to proportionality, and how these bodies deal with specific issues that arise when applying proportionality. Section IV concludes.

I. The principle of proportionality in domestic legal systems

This section focuses on the first step of identifying a general principle of law within the meaning of Article 38(1)(c) ICJ Statute: a comparative study of national legal systems. Scholars trace early versions of proportionality back to Babylonian times and Hammurabi,[24] classical Greek and Roman law,[25] the Magna Carta,[26] and the Middle Ages.[27] We are interested in the practice of contemporary courts and tribunals to use proportionality as a means to resolve conflicts between the rights of individuals and the public interest. Several authors consider German public law to be the very cradle of this practice, from which the principle of proportionality spread into various domestic and international legal regimes.[28] Georg Nolte doubts that the widespread use of proportionality analysis by different courts and tribunals around the world results from such a success story of another 'German export product'.[29] Rather, Nolte considers the prevalence of proportionality to be the result of human rights instruments such as the Universal Declaration of Human Rights[30] (UDHR) and the International Covenant on Civil and Political Rights[31] (ICCPR).[32] For the purposes of determining whether proportionality constitutes a general principle within the meaning of Article 38(1)(c) ICJ Statute, its exact roots are of little importance. The

---

[24] Eric Engle, 'The General Principle of Proportionality and Aristotle', *Ius Gentium* 23 (2013) 265–75, at 265; Jonas Christoffersen, *Fair Balance: Proportionality, Subsidiarity and Primarity in the European Convention on Human Rights* (2009), 33–4.

[25] Erich Vranes, 'Der Verhältnismäßigkeitsgrundsatz', *Archiv des Völkerrechts* 47 (2009) 1–35, at 10; Barak, *Proportionality*, at 176, n.8 & 9 (both with further references).

[26] Engle, 'The General Principle of Proportionality and Aristotle', at 270–1; Barak, *Proportionality*, at 176, n.10 (with further references).

[27] Barak, *Proportionality*, at 176, n.12 (with further references).

[28] Klaus Stern, 'Zur Entstehung und Ableitung des Übermaßverbots', *in Wege und Verfahren des Verfassungslebens: Festschrift für Peter Lerche zum 65. Geburtstag* (Peter Badura & Rupert Scholz eds., 1993) 165–75, at 168; Dieter Grimm, 'Proportionality in Canadian and German Constitutional Jurisprudence', *University of Toronto Law Journal* 57 (2007) 383–97, at 384–5; Alec Stone Sweet & Jude Mathews, 'Proportionality Balancing and Global Constitutionalism', *Columbia Journal of Transnational Law* 47 (2008) 73–165, at 98–103; Barak, *Proportionality*, at 178–83.

[29] Nolte, 'Thin or Thick?', at 246.

[30] Universal Declaration of Human Rights, G.A. Res. 217A (III), UN Doc A/810 (December 10, 1948).

[31] International Covenant on Civil and Political Rights, 16 Dec 1996, 999 UNTS 171.

[32] Nolte, 'Thin or Thick?', at 246–7.

principle of proportionality is well established in Germany, and the practice of its courts constitutes a convenient starting point in analysing the role of proportionality in various legal systems.

1. The principle of proportionality in German law

The overview of proportionality in German law in this subsection falls into three parts. Subsection (a) reviews some pre-World War I case law from German administrative courts in the nineteenth century. While not strictly necessary for the identification of a general principle, this short historical account sheds light on the development of the three-step proportionality test applied by the German Constitutional Court (*Bundesverfassungsgericht*). Subsection (b) will discuss the jurisprudence of this court. Virtually all publications on proportionality arrive eventually at the work of the German jurist Robert Alexy.[33] One may wonder whether proportionality would play the same key role in scholarship and jurisprudence around the world as it does today if Alexy had not written on the subject. Alexy's theory is closely related to the jurisprudence of the German Constitutional Court, and will be discussed in subsection (c).

a) Proportionality in German administrative law before World War I

The Prussian General Law of 1794 codified various areas of law. Its section 10 II 17 regulated the State's police powers, and stated in material part that:

[t]he office of the police is to take the necessary measures for the maintenance of public peace, security, and order...[34]

After the establishment of the first administrative law courts in Germany in the 1860s and '70s, this provision gave rise to a number of rulings that contained—in

---

[33] *See, e.g.,* Mads Andenas & Stefan Zleptnig, 'Proportionality: WTO Law in Comparative Perspective', *Texas International Law Journal* 42 (2007) 372–427, at 376–9; Jacco Bomhoff, 'Balancing, the Global and the Local: Judicial Balancing as a Problematic Topic in Comparative (Constitutional) Law', *Hastings International and Comparative Law Review* 31 (2008) 555–86, at 574–5; Niels Petersen, 'Customary Law Without Custom? Rules, Principles, and the Role of State Practice in International Norm Creation', *American University International Law Review* 23 (2008) 275–310, at 286–91; Stone Sweet & Mathews, 'Proportionality Balancing' at 94–97; van Aaken, 'Defragmentation of Public International Law', at 502–4; Thomas Kleinlein, 'Judicial Lawmaking by Judicial Restraint? The Potential of Balancing in International Economic Law', *German Law Journal* 12 (2011) 1141–74, at 1149–50; 1168–9; Barak, *Proportionality*, at 235–7; Klaus Stern, *Das Staatsrecht der Bundesrepublik Deutschland–Band III/2–Allgemeine Lehren der Grundrechte* (1994), at 818.

[34] Translation provided by Stone Sweet & Mathews, 'Proportionality Balancing', at 101. The text in the original German version reads as follows: 'Die nöthigen Anstalten zur Erhaltung der öffentlichen Ruhe, Sicherheit, und Ordnung, und zur Abwendung der dem Publico, oder einzelnen Mitgliedern desselben, bevorstehenden Gefahr zu treffen, ist das Amt der Polizey.' (*available at* <http://www.smixx.de/ra/Links_F-R/PrALR/PrALR_II_17.pdf>).

today's terminology—the 'least restrictive means' test. According to this test, a government measure may not interfere with individual rights to a greater extent than is necessary to achieve the stated public goal. In 1886, the Prussian Higher Administrative Court (*Preußisches Oberverwaltungsgericht*) had to decide on the lawfulness of a police order that obliged a landowner to remove a number of posts from his property. The landowner had erected these posts in order to keep people from entering his territory. As the posts were hard to see at night, the police had them removed to prevent accidents. The Prussian Higher Administrative Court held that in order to attain this goal, it would have been sufficient to light the posts. Consequently, the Court considered the order to remove the post to be unlawful as it was not 'necessary' within the meaning of paragraph 10 II 17 of the Prussian General Law of 1794.[35]

In 1907, the Prussian Higher Administrative Court rendered another decision that contained an analysis reminiscent of the principle of proportionality. In this case, the administration ordered the owner of a machine factory to empty a pond for cleaning by the local authorities. The pond was crucial for the operation of the factory, and the police issued the order only 20 hours before it expected the claimant to empty the pond. The claimant refused to follow the order since it was impossible to make arrangements to prevent economic damage to his factory under such short notice. The Court reiterated the principle enshrined in paragraph 10 II 17 of the 1794 Prussian General Law, according to which the State administration may adopt measures that are 'necessary' for the fulfillment of a public purpose (here, the protection of human health).[36] However, the Court found that an order to empty the pond within such a short period of time would have been 'necessary' only in case of an imminent peril, which was not present on the facts.

Furthermore, the Court held that the administration would have had to balance the public interest against the economic interests of the claimant before issuing its order.[37] This consideration is reminiscent of what is known today as 'proportionality balancing' or 'proportionality in the strict sense'. In this vein, the Court held that the administration must take account of the economic interests of the individual to the greatest extent possible under the particular circumstances of the case.[38] The Court pointed out that the authorities had neither involved the claimant in ongoing deliberations about the cleaning of the pond nor contacted him before issuing the order.[39] Hence, the Court held that the order was unlawful.

---

[35] Preußisches Oberverwaltungsgericht [PrOVG] [Prussian Higher Administrative Court] July 3, 1886, 13 Entscheidungen des Preußischen Oberverwaltungsgerichts [PrOVGE] 426–8, at 427. The research of Alec Stone Sweet and Jude Mathews drew my attention to this and the following case (Stone Sweet & Mathews, 'Proportionality Balancing', at 101, n.70).

[36] PrOVG May 27, 1907, 51 Entscheidungen des Preußischen Oberverwaltungsgerichts [PrOVGE] 284–9, at 287.

[37] Id., at 288–99.   [38] Id, at 299.   [39] Id.

b) Proportionality in German constitutional law

Following the entry into force of the German Basic Law (*Grundgesetz*) in 1949, the principle of proportionality migrated from the administrative to the constitutional level. Proportionality is today a core element of the jurisprudence of the German Constitutional Court. Its establishment on the constitutional level, however, was not as smooth as its present deep entrenchment in the Court's jurisprudence may suggest. Rather, it was the scholarship of Rupprecht von Krauss[40] and Peter Lerche[41] that paved the way for the Court to test all State measures that interfere with individual rights against the requirements of this principle.[42] The interplay between academia and the German Constitutional Court resulted in a proportionality test that strictly differentiates between three different analytical steps.[43] First, the Court examines whether the State measure in question is suitable to achieve a legitimate end (*Geeignetheit*).[44] It is rare that a State measure does not pass this first step of the analysis.[45] Second, the Court scrutinizes whether the chosen means was necessary to attain the particular goal (*Erforderlichkeit*).[46] A State measure will only pass this step if it was the least restrictive means available. In other words, a State measure is not proportionate if a less infringing means could have achieved the same result as effectively (hence, this step of the analysis can also be called the least restrictive means test). If a State measure passes this second prong, the analysis will continue to its third level. If it does not, the State measure is automatically considered disproportionate without any balancing or weighing of the different interests.

The third stage of the analysis is called proportionality in the narrow sense (*Verhältnismäßigkeit im engeren Sinne* or *Zumutbarkeit*) or proportionality *stricto sensu*.[47] It is only at this stage that actual balancing of the competing interests takes place. This 'proportionality balancing' involves weighing the infringement of the individual freedom against the benefits of the relevant State measure. Factors which play a decisive role in this balancing process include: the importance of the governmental goal and the individual right in question (both in the abstract as well as in the particular circumstances of the case); the degree to which the State measure interferes with the individual right; and the severity of the consequences that would have occurred without the infringing act. In the *Pharmacy*

---

[40] Rupprecht von Krauss, *Der Grundsatz der Verhältnismäßigkeit in seiner Bedeutung für die Notwendigkeit des Mittels im Verwaltungsrecht* (1955).

[41] Peter Lerche, *Übermaß und Verfassungrecht* (1961).

[42] *See* Stone Sweet & Mathews, 'Proportionality Balancing', at 105–112; Stern, 'Zur Entstehung', 173–175; Grimm, 'Proportionality in Canadian and German Constitutional Jurisprudence', 385–7.

[43] Strictly speaking, proportionality involves a four-step analysis since the first prong comprises two different questions. First, is the goal pursued by the legislator or the executive a legitimate one? Second, is the State measure a suitable means to attain this goal? Hence, Aharon Barak rightly counts 'four components' of proportionality (Barak, *Proportionality*, at 131). I will stick to the established terminology and divide the proportionality analysis into three parts.

[44] Michael Sachs, 'Artikel 20', *in Grundgesetz* (Michael Sachs ed., 2011) 787–849, paras. 150–1.

[45] Id., para. 150.   [46] Id., para. 152.

[47] Id., para. 154; Barak, *Proportionality*, at 340.

case of 1958, the German Constitutional Court described proportionality balancing in the context of the freedom of occupation (Article 12 of the German Basic Law) as follows:

The [purpose of] the constitutional right should be to protect the freedom of the individual [while the purpose of] the regulation should be to ensure sufficient protection of societal interests. The individual's claim to freedom will have a stronger effect... the more his right to free choice of a profession is put into question; the protection of the public will become more urgent, the greater the disadvantages that arise from the free practicing of professions. When one seeks to maximize both... demands in the most effective way, then the solution can only lie in a careful balancing [*Abwägung*] of the significance of the two opposed and perhaps conflicting interests.[48]

Since the 1960s, every infringement of a constitutionally guaranteed individual right or freedom has had to pass the three-pronged proportionality test in order to be constitutional. The consistency of this practice is remarkable. After all, the various constitutional rights and freedoms of the German Basic Law are phrased in very different terms. While some of these rights and freedoms contain specific limitations, others do not. And even among the conditionally guaranteed rights, the wording of the different limitation clauses varies greatly. Articles 2(1), 2(2), and 12(1) of the German Basic Law provide a good example of this variation.[49]

Article 2 [Personal Freedoms]

(1) Every person shall have the right to free development of his personality insofar as he does not violate the rights of others or offend against the constitutional order or the moral law.
(2) Every person shall have the right to life and physical integrity. Freedom of the person shall be inviolable. These rights may be interfered with only pursuant to a law.

Article 12 [Occupational Freedom]

(1) All Germans shall have the right freely to choose their occupation or profession, their place of work and their place of training. The practice of an occupation or profession may be regulated by or pursuant to a law.

The application of the principle of proportionality is arguably even more surprising in the case of individual rights and freedoms that are guaranteed without reservations. For example, Article 4 of the German Basic Law (Freedom of faith and conscience) states that:

(1) Freedom of faith and of conscience, and freedom to profess a religious or philosophical creed, shall be inviolable.
(2) The undisturbed practice of religion shall be guaranteed.

---

[48] BVerfGE 7, 377, 404–5. In contrast to later decisions, the Constitutional Court did not provide an English translation for its decision in the *Pharmacy* case. I slightly modified the translation provided by Stone Sweet & Mathews, 'Proportionality Balancing', at 108.

[49] *See also* the jurisprudence of the German Constitutional Court on Article 14 of the Basic Law, Chapter 5, notes 51–6 and accompanying text.

[...] Similarly, Article 5(3) of the German Basic Law guarantees the freedom of arts and science by broadly stipulating that:

[a]rts and sciences, research and teaching shall be free. The freedom of teaching shall not release any person from allegiance to the constitution.

Despite the lack of any constraints on the freedom of faith and conscience and freedom of arts and science in the text of the Basic Law, the German Constitutional Court decided that these freedoms are not guaranteed without limitations. This does not mean that the legislator can interfere with these freedoms for any legitimate purpose as long as such measures meet the proportionality test. Rather, limitations on unconditionally guaranteed rights must be rooted in the value system of the constitution itself. In 1971, The German Constitutional Court expressed this idea very clearly in the *Mephisto* case, where it had to resolve a conflict between artistic freedom (Article 5 (3)) and human dignity (Article 1(1)):

[T]he right of artistic liberty is not unlimited.... But the unconditional nature of [this] basic right means that limits on artistic freedom can only be determined by the Constitution itself. Since freedom of arts does not grant the legislature the authority to restrict this right, this freedom may not be curtailed either by the general legal system or [by] an indefinite clause that permits [limitations on artistic expression] if values necessary for the existence of the national community are endangered. [Courts] must resolve a conflict involving artistic freedom by interpreting the Constitution according to the value order established in the Basic Law and the unity of its fundamental system of values.[50]

And similarly, in the *Religious Oath* case of 1972, the German Constitutional Court stated with respect to religious freedom that:

[t]he Constitution grants the right of religious freedom unreservedly.... Its limits may be drawn only by the Constitution itself; that is according to the directives of the constitutional value order and the unity of this fundamental value system.[51]

In other words, the State may even interfere with unconditional fundamental rights of the German Basic Law for the protection of the fundamental rights of others or other constitutional values. The decisive tool in resolving such conflicts is the principle of proportionality. Its application is intended to ensure that each of the two conflicting values is taken into account to the greatest extent possible. Konrad Hesse coined the term 'practical concordance' (*praktische Konkordanz*) for this balancing process:

The principle of the Constitution's unity requires the *optimization* of [*values* in conflict]: Both legal values need to be limited so that each can attain its optimal effect. In each concrete case, therefore, the limitations must satisfy the principle of proportionality;

---

[50] BVerfGE 30, 173, 193 (translation in Donald P. Kommers, *The Constitutional Jurisprudence of the Federal Republic of Germany* (1997), at 428).
[51] BVerfGE 33, 23, 29 (translation in id., at 454).

that is, they may not go any further than necessary to produce a concordance of both legal values.[52]

c) *Robert Alexy on principles and proportionality*

The notion of *praktische Konkordanz* described in the last paragraph is closely related to Robert Alexy's theory on rules and principles and the role proportionality plays within this theoretical framework.[53] Key to Alexy's theory is the difference between 'rules' and 'principles'. His understanding of these terms is unrelated to their use in international law, where legal instruments and adjudicators often do not draw a clear line between the two concepts.[54] Rather, Alexy's understanding of rules and principles builds on the work of Ronald Dworkin, who explained the difference between the two concepts as follows:

The difference between legal principles and legal rules is a logical distinction. Both sets of standards point to particular decisions about legal obligation in particular circumstances, but they differ in the character of the direction they give. Rules are applicable in an all-or-nothing fashion. If the facts a rule stipulates are given, then either the rule is valid, in which case the answer it supplies must be accepted, or if is not, in which case it contributes nothing to the decision.[55]

Dworkin provides a very illustrative example for such a rule: in baseball, a batter is out if he has three strikes. There is no room for the referee to decide that a batter who has had three strikes is not out.[56] Robert Alexy builds on Dworkin's differentiation,[57] but focuses on the feature of principles as 'optimization requirements'. This means that principles need to be realized to the greatest extent possible under the particular legal and factual circumstances.[58]

The differences between rules and principles become most apparent in collision scenarios. If *two rules collide*, there are only two possible solutions: either an exception clause in one of the two rules solves the conflict, or a conflict rule renders one of the two rules inapplicable.[59] The *lex posterior derogat legi priori* and *lex specialis derogat legi generali* rules constitute prominent examples of such conflict rules.[60] A *collision of two principles* is not resolved by exception clauses or collision rules but by balancing the competing interests at stake.[61] Conflicts between two

---

[52] Konrad Hesse, *Grundzüge des Verfassungsrechts der Bundesrepublik Deutschland* (1999), para. 72 (translation in Kommers, *The Constitutional Jurisprudence*, at 46, emphases added). *See also* Hesse, *Grundzüge des Verfassungsrechts*, paras. 317–20. The German Constitutional Court referred to the concept of 'practical concordance' in BVerfGE 77, 240, 255 and BVerfGE 83, 130, 143–6.

[53] For the similarities between 'practical concordance' and Robert Alexy's theory on rights and principles, *see* Robert Alexy, *Theorie der Grundrechte* (1986), at 152.

[54] *See infra* note 5.   [55] Ronald Dworkin, *Taking Rights Seriously* (1977), at 24.

[56] Id., at 24–5. There seem to be narrowly defined exceptions to this rule, which are beyond the scope of this book and the author's understanding of the game (*see* id. for further information).

[57] *See* Alexy, *Theorie der Grundrechte*, at 77 n.27.

[58] Robert Alexy, 'Constitutional Rights, Balancing, and Rationality', *Ratio Juris* 16 (2003) 131–140, at 135.

[59] Alexy, *Theorie der Grundrechte*, at 77.   [60] Id., at 78.

[61] Alexy, 'Constitutional Rights', at 133; Alexy, *Theorie der Grundrechte*, at 78–9.

principles are never decided in the abstract. This means that one principle is not inapplicable only because it collides with another principle. At most, one principle has to yield to the other under the particular circumstances of the case at hand.[62] The three steps of the proportionality analysis shall ensure that the detriment to the yielding principle is no greater than factually and legally necessary for the purposes of the prevailing principle.[63] The third possible scenario under this model is the *collision between a rule and a principle*. In this case, the rule prevails because of the legislative or constitutional preferences articulated in its wording.[64] Something different may only be true if the rule itself refers to a principle.[65]

To understand the functions that Alexy attaches to principles in a legal system, the *Lüth* decision of the German Constitutional Court is of central importance.[66] In this case, Lüth complained against a state court decision prohibiting his calls to boycott the movies of a former Nazi film director. The state court found that Lüth's statement interfered with the business of the film director in violation of section 826 of the German Civil Code.[67] The German Constitutional Court held that the state court failed to properly take into account Lüth's constitutional right to free speech (Article 5(1) of the German Basic Law) in determining whether he acted 'contrary to public policy' as required by section 826.[68] Consequently, the German Constitutional Court reversed the decision of the state court. The most important passage in this decision reads as follows:

[T]he Basic Law is not a value-neutral document....Its section on basic rights establishes an *objective order of values*...This value system, which centers upon dignity of the human personality developing freely within the social community, must be looked upon as a fundamental constitutional decision affecting all spheres of law....Every provision of private law must be compatible with this system of values, and every such provision must be interpreted in its spirit.[69]

Alexy interprets this notion of an 'objective order of values' as an acknowledgment that the fundamental rights enshrined in the German Basic Law do not only constitute 'rules' but also 'principles'.[70] Regarding the effect of the basic rights on other spheres of law, the German Constitutional Court spoke of a 'radiating effect',[71] which in Alexy's view renders constitutional rights 'ubiquitous'.[72]

---

[62] Alexy, *Theorie der Grundrechte*, at 79, 85–6.
[63] Alexy, 'Constitutional Rights', at 135–6.
[64] *See* Petersen, 'Customary Law Without Custom?', at 291.
[65] Section 826 reads as follows: 'A person who, in a manner contrary to public policy, intentionally inflicts damage on another person is liable to the other person to make compensation for the damage.' (<http://www.gesetze-im-internet.de/englisch_bgb/englisch_bgb.html#BGBengl_000P826>).
[66] BVerfGE 7, 198 (1958). For an English translation of parts of the judgment, *see* Norman Dorsen, et al., *Comparative Constitutionalism: Cases and Materials* (2003) 824–9.
[67] Section 826 reads as follows: 'A person who, in a manner contrary to public policy, intentionally inflicts damage on another person is liable to the other person to make compensation for the damage.' (<http://www.gesetze-im-internet.de/englisch_bgb/englisch_bgb.html#BGBengl_000P826>).
[68] Dorsen, et al., *Comparative Constitutionalism*, at 828–9.
[69] BVerfGE 7, 198, 205; id., at 825 (emphasis added).
[70] Alexy, 'Constitutional Rights', at 133.   [71] BVerfGE 7, 198, 207.
[72] Alexy, 'Constitutional Rights', at 133.

2. The establishment of the principle of proportionality in various constitutional orders

Today, the principle of proportionality is not only part of German law but of many domestic legal orders. Aharon Barak provides a concise overview of the establishment of proportionality as a legal concept within and outside Europe. Western European jurisdictions that employ proportionality analysis include the following: Austria, Portugal, Ireland, Spain, Belgium, the Netherlands, Switzerland, Greece, Italy, and France.[73] Barak also lists several Central and Eastern European countries that apply the principle of proportionality in their public law jurisprudence, in particular Hungary, Poland, Lithuania, Slovenia, and the Czech Republic.[74] Furthermore, proportionality plays an important role in certain Asian and South American jurisdictions, for example in Hong Kong, India, South Korea, Argentina, Chile, Columbia, Mexico, and Peru.[75] In the UK, courts have to a certain extent abandoned the more deferential 'Wednesbury unreasonableness' standard in favour of the principle of proportionality (albeit reluctantly and in response to some pressure from the ECtHR).[76] Furthermore, proportionality has become an integral part of the constitutional jurisprudence of Canada, New Zealand, South Africa, and Israel.[77]

Outlining the relevant jurisprudence on proportionality of all jurisdictions mentioned in the last paragraph is beyond the scope of this book. I will focus on Canada, South Africa, and Israel.[78] While one could choose different jurisdictions for good reason, three considerations are responsible for the choice made here. First, since the previous subsection described the practice of the German Constitutional Court and section III will address the relevance of proportionality in EU law and the ECHR, this subsection focuses on proportionality outside

---

[73] Barak, *Proportionality*, at 182, 189. The European Union and the ECtHR are important catalysts for spreading the proportionality test in domestic jurisdictions. Angelika Nußberger, for example, reports that until recently French courts had used the strict proportionality test only for administrative acts related to EU law or the ECHR. This changed in 2011, when the *Conseil d'Etat* established a German-style proportionality test for all administrative acts, and abandoned a more deferential practice that had provided the executive with greater leeway (Angelika Nußberger, 'Das Verhältnismäßigkeitsprinzip als Strukturprinzip richterlichen Entscheidens in Europa', *Neue Zeitschrift für Verwaltungsrecht* (NVwZ) Supplement 32 (2013) 36–44, at 38, 40). For the role of EU law and the ECHR in establishing proportionality within domestic legal systems in Europe, *see also* Barak, *Proportionality*, at 181–6.

[74] Barak, *Proportionality*, at 182, 198–9. For an additional analysis of proportionality in Central and Eastern Europe, *see* Wojciech Sadurski, *Rights Before Courts: a Study of Constitutional Courts in Postcommunist States of Central and Eastern Europe* (2005), at 266–82.

[75] Barak, *Proportionality*, at 182, 199–202. For proportionality in Ecuadorian law, *see Occidental Petroleum Corporation and Occidental Exploration and Production Company v. The Republic of Ecuador*, ICSID Case No. ARB/06/11, Award, 5 October 2012, paras. 396–401.

[76] *See* Stone Sweet & Mathews, 'Proportionality Balancing', at 148–52. For proportionality balancing by the Irish High Court, *see* id., at 123. For the differences between the reasonableness test and other standards of review, *see* Chapter 3, note 232.

[77] Barak, *Proportionality*, at 182, 188–98.

[78] For an in-depth analysis of proportionality in these jurisdictions, *see* Stone Sweet & Mathews, 'Proportionality Balancing', at 113–38.

the European Union. Second, the analysis of proportionality in one common law jurisdiction (Canada) and two mixed jurisdictions (South Africa and Israel) ought to work against possible misconceptions that proportionality is a civil law concept incompatible with other legal traditions. Third, the application of the principle of proportionality by the Israeli Supreme Court is particularly illustrative and impressive. The Court applies this principle to decide conflicts between individual rights and security concerns in a highly volatile geopolitical and social environment.[79] It is difficult to imagine a more sensitive and vital issue, and the practice of the Court illustrates that no area of life or law is per se too important or 'political' to be left to the proportionality analysis of a judicial body.

a) *The jurisprudence of the Canadian Supreme Court*

In 1982, the Canadian Charter of Rights and Freedoms entered into force. A few years later, in 1986, the Canadian Supreme Court elaborated on the principle of proportionality in *R v. Oakes*.[80] In this case, the Supreme Court had to decide on the constitutionality of a criminal law provision that required a person found in the possession of drugs to prove that he or she did not also intend to traffic the drugs. If the person could not meet this burden of proof, he or she would be convicted of both crimes, i.e. of possessing *and* trafficking drugs. The Court found that such a rebuttable presumption violated the presumption of innocence protected by section 11 of the Canadian Charter of Rights and Freedoms.[81] After the Court had established the violation of the constitutional right, it examined whether the provision could still be upheld under the general limitation clause in section 1 of the Charter.[82] Section 1 provides that:

[t]he *Canadian Charter of Rights and Freedoms* guarantees the rights and freedoms set out in it subject only to such reasonable limits prescribed by law as can be demonstrably justified in a free and democratic society.

The Supreme Court clarified that section 1 'states explicitly the exclusive justificatory criteria' against which limitations on the rights and freedoms of the Charter are to be measured.[83] In order to decide whether a measure is justified under

---

[79] For an overview of cases of the Israeli Supreme Court on targeted killings, torture, detention, the wall/separation fence, etc, *see* Eileen Kaufman, 'Deference or Abdiction: a Comparison of the Supreme Courts of Israel and the United States in Cases Involving Real or Perceived Threats to National Security', *Washington University Global Studies Law Review* 12 (2013) 95–159, at 117–152.

[80] *R. v. Oakes* [1986] 1 S.C.R. 103 (Can.).

[81] Id., para. 61. Section 11 reads in relevant part as follows: 'Any person charged with an offence has the right...to be presumed innocent until proven guilty according to law in a fair and public hearing by an independent and impartial tribunal.'

[82] Note the terminological differences between the German Constitutional Court and the Canadian Supreme Court: the German Constitutional Court would speak of a 'violation' of a fundamental right (*Grundrechtsverletzung*) only after it had established that the relevant act was not justified. While the Canadian Supreme Court identified a 'violation' of section 11(d) before turning to its possible justification, the German Constitutional Court would use the term 'infringement' (*Grundrechtsbeeinträchtigung*) in such situations.

[83] *R v. Oakes*, [1986] 1 S.C.R. 103 (Can.), para. 63.

section 1, the Court established a two-step test. First, it needs to be established that the objective of the measure in question must be 'of sufficient importance to warrant overriding a constitutionally protected right or freedom'.[84] Second, the Court considered the requirement that the measures be 'reasonable' and 'demonstrably justified in a free and democratic society' to entail a proportionality test.[85] The Court's description of this proportionality test is worth quoting in full:

> Although the nature of the proportionality test will vary depending on the circumstances, in each case courts will be required to balance the interests of society with those of individuals and groups. There are, in my view, three important components of a proportionality test. First, the measures adopted must be carefully designed to achieve the objective in question. They must not be arbitrary, unfair or based on irrational considerations. In short, they must be rationally connected to the objective. Second, the means, even if rationally connected to the objective in this first sense, should impair 'as little as possible' the right or freedom in question. . . . Third, there must be a proportionality between the effects of the measures which are responsible for limiting the *Charter* right or freedom, and the objective which has been identified as of 'sufficient importance'.[86]

The similarities between the Canadian and the German proportionality test are obvious: both contain a three-step approach that differentiates between suitability, necessity, and proportionality in the strict sense. The Court put particular emphasis on the third prong of the analysis, i.e. the actual balancing process. The Court's reasoning reads in material part as follows:

> With respect to the third component, it is clear that the general effect of any measure impugned under s. 1 will be the infringement of a right or freedom guaranteed by the *Charter*; this is the reason why resort to s. 1 is necessary. The inquiry into effects must, however, go further. A wide range of rights and freedoms are guaranteed by the *Charter*, and an almost infinite number of factual situations may arise in respect of these. Some limits on rights and freedoms protected by the *Charter* will be more serious than others in terms of the nature of the right or freedom violated, the extent of the violation, and the degree to which the measures which impose the limit trench upon the integral principles of a free and democratic society. Even if an objective is of sufficient importance, and the first two elements of the proportionality test are satisfied, it is still possible that, because of the severity of the deleterious effects of a measure on individuals or groups, the measure will not be justified by the purposes it is intended to serve. The more severe the deleterious effects of a measure, the more important the objective must be if the measure is to be reasonable and demonstrably justified in a free and democratic society.[87]

As we will see later, the balancing part outlined in this passage has proved to be its most controversial aspect of proportionality, especially in the US. Nevertheless, a number of common law jurisdictions, including New Zealand and (parts of) Australia, have followed Canada's example and adopted proportionality balancing

---

[84] Id., para. 69.   [85] Id., para. 70.   [86] Id. (internal quotations omitted).
[87] Id., para. 71 (emphasis in the original).

in their constitutional jurisprudence, often explicitly on the basis of *R v. Oakes*.[88] The following subsection provides an overview of proportionality in South Africa.

b) *The jurisprudence of the Constitutional Court of South Africa*

In 1995, the Constitutional Court of South Africa had to decide on the constitutionality of the death penalty in *S v. Makwanyane* under the Interim Constitution of 1993.[89] The Court found that the death penalty was unconstitutional since it violated the prohibition of cruel, inhuman, or degrading punishment under section 11(2)[90] without being justified by section 33. Section 33 contained a general limitation clause, which provided that:

the rights entrenched in this Chapter may be limited by law of general application, provided that such limitation:
(a) shall be permissible only to the extent that it is:
  (i) reasonable, and
  (ii) justifiable in an open and democratic society based on freedom and equality; and
(b) shall not negate the essential content of the right in question, and provided further that any limitation to…a right entrenched in Section 15, 16, 17, 18, 23 or 24, in so far as such right relates to free and fair political activity, shall, in addition to being reasonable as required in Paragraph (a)(i), also be necessary.[91]

The president of the Court interpreted the key elements of this provision, that is that the limitation be 'reasonable' and 'necessary' and 'justifiable in an open and democratic society', to entail a proportionality analysis. He found that:

[t]he limitation of constitutional rights for a purpose that is reasonable and necessary in a democratic society involves the weighing up of competing values, and ultimately an assessment based on proportionality. This is implicit in the provisions of *section* 33(1).[92]

The different factors of this analysis are highly reminiscent of the German and the Canadian approaches. The South African proportionality analysis, however, does not follow the three-step analysis of the German Constitutional Court or Canadian Supreme Court. Rather, it addresses the different elements of the proportionality test on the same level of the analysis without putting them into a particular sequence. Therefore, one could speak of a 'horizontal' proportionality test as opposed to the 'vertical' approach of the German Constitutional Court and the Canadian Supreme Court.[93] The following statement of the President

---

[88] *See* Moshe Cohen-Eliya & Iddo Porat, 'The Hidden Foreign Law Debate in Heller: the Proportionality Approach in American Constitutional Law', *San Diego Law Review* 46 (2009) 367–413, 381.

[89] *S v. Makwanyane & Another* 1995 (3) SA 391 (CC) (S Afr).

[90] Section 11(2) of the Interim Constitution read as follows: 'No person shall be subject to torture of any kind, whether physical, mental or emotional, nor shall any person be subject to cruel, inhuman or degrading treatment or punishment.'

[91] *Available at* <http://www.servat.unibe.ch/icl/sf10000_.html>.

[92] *S v. Makwanyane & Another* 1995 (3) SA 391 (CC) (S Afr), para. 104.

[93] Christoffersen, *Fair Balance*, at 72–3.

of the Constitutional Court in the *Makwanyane* case illustrates this 'horizontal' approach:

[The] requirement of proportionality...calls for the balancing of different interests. In the balancing process, the relevant considerations will include the nature of the right that is limited, and its importance to an open and democratic society based on freedom and equality; the purpose for which the right is limited and the importance of that purpose to such a society; the extent of the limitation, its efficacy, and particularly where the limitation has to be necessary, whether the desired ends could reasonably be achieved through other means less damaging to the right in question. In the process regard must be had to the provisions of *section* 33(1), and the underlying values of the Constitution.[94]

In 1996, the (final) Constitution of South Africa entered into force. Its general limitation clause reflects in almost identical terms the passage on proportionality balancing in the *Makwanyane* case. Section 36 provides that:

1. The rights in the Bill of Rights may be limited only in terms of law of general application to the extent that the limitation is reasonable and justifiable in an open and democratic society based on human dignity, equality and freedom, taking into account all relevant factors, including
   a. the nature of the right;
   b. the importance of the purpose of the limitation;
   c. the nature and extent of the limitation;
   d. the relation between the limitation and its purpose; and
   e. less restrictive means to achieve the purpose.
2. Except as provided in subsection (1) or in any other provision of the Constitution, no law may limit any right entrenched in the Bill of Rights.

Today, proportionality balancing is deeply entrenched in the jurisprudence of South Africa's Constitutional Court. According to one estimate, the Constitutional Court engages in proportionality balancing in roughly 75% of its cases.[95]

c) The jurisprudence of the Israeli Supreme Court

Proportionality plays a key role in the jurisprudence of the Israeli Supreme Court. In *Mizrahi v. Migdal Cooperative Village*, the Israeli Supreme Court decided for the first time that it has the power to strike down a law passed by the Knesset if this law violates a Basic Law.[96] To be noted at the outset, Israel does not have a constitution in the sense of a single written document but several Basic Laws enacted by the Knesset under the same procedure as ordinary legislation. Furthermore, the Basic Law at issue in *Mizrahi*—Basic Law: Human Dignity and Freedom—does not specify how it relates to laws passed or amended by the

---

[94] *S v. Makwanyane & Another* 1995 (3) SA 391 (CC) (S Afr), para. 104.
[95] Stone Sweet & Mathews, 'Proportionality Balancing', at 130.
[96] CA 6821/93 *Bank Mizrahi v. Migdal Cooperative Village* [1995] IsrSC 49(4) 221, *translated in* [1995] IsrLR 1 (citations refer to the English translation), at 3.

Knesset after its adoption.[97] In the absence of such a 'supremacy clause', it was argued that the principle of *lex posterior* applies and that Knesset may enact legislation contrary to the Basic Laws. The majority of the Supreme Court, however, concurred with the President of the Court, Aharon Barak, who found that the Basic Laws possess constitutional status superior to ordinary legislation.[98] After an analysis of judicial review in other constitutional orders, Barak concluded that the Israeli Supreme Court has the power to declare laws unconstitutional and void if they contradict the Basic Laws.[99]

The specific issue that the Israeli Supreme Court had to decide in *Mizrahi* was the constitutionality of a law that entitled a governmental body to restructure and cancel unpaid private debts. The Court had little difficulty finding that such a regulation infringed section 3 of Basic Law: Human Dignity and Freedom which stipulates that '[t]here shall be no violation of the property of a person'.[100] For our purposes, however, the most interesting part of the judgment is the way in which the Court interpreted the limitation clause in section 8 of the same Basic Law. Section 8 reads as follows:

There shall be no violation of rights under this Basic Law except by a law befitting the values of the State of Israel, enacted for a proper purpose, and to an extent no greater than is required.

Barak found that the phrase 'to an extent no greater than is required' gives rise to a review of the infringing law along the lines of the principle of proportionality.[101] He supported this finding with references to other constitutional systems. On this basis, he held that:

the principle of proportionality does not reflect a unique social history or particular constitutional position. Rather, it is a general analytical position according to which we may examine a law infringing constitutional human rights.[102]

Regarding the different elements of this proportionality test, Barak referred to the *Oakes* test of the Canadian Supreme Court and the *Pharmacy* case of the German Constitutional Court. Barak called the three steps in the proportionality analysis of these courts (a) 'fitness test (*geeignet*)', (b) 'test of minimal harm', and (c) 'proportionality in the strict sense'.[103] Furthermore, Barak commented on some of the more controversial issues in the context of the principle of proportionality. One of the most delicate tasks in applying the proportionality test is to determine whether a less infringing means would have been available. Critics of the principle of proportionality argue that it is for the legislator to weigh the advantages and disadvantages of different policy options. Courts are ill-equipped to determine whether a less infringing but equally effective means would have been available. If they still decide to embark on such an analysis, they unduly

---

[97] In section 10 the Basic Law on Human Dignity and Freedom merely clarifies that it does not affect the validity of a law in force *prior* to the commencement of the Basic Law.

[98] *Bank Mizrahi v. Migdal Cooperative Village*, at 210, 232, 256.   [99] Id., at 218–32.

[100] Id., at 249–50.   [101] Id., at 242–3.   [102] Id., at 243.   [103] Id., 243–4.

interfere with the competencies of the legislator. In addressing these concerns, Barak made clear that the Court should not shy away from evaluating intricate social facts in order to determine whether a less infringing means would have been available. He stated that:

[i]n addressing the question of whether a piece of legislation violates a protected human right to an extent no greater than is required, it is sometimes necessary to examine alternative means. Thus, just as the proportionality test requires that the Court examine the various alternatives that present themselves to the administrative authority, so the Court must examine the various alternatives that were available to the legislature. This is not a task that is beyond the Court's ability.[104]

Barak conceded that 'in marginal cases, the legislature must be given reasonable latitude in its legislative options', but he unequivocally demanded that '[t]he court must be convinced that, among the available legislative options, the legislature chose that which least infringed the constitutional right'.[105] In the case at hand, Barak found that the law in question was necessary and proportionate to handle the severe financial crisis in the agricultural sector. Barak held that voluntary settlement of the debts would not have been a viable alternative since such an attempt had already failed in the past. Furthermore, Barak noted that other legislative alternatives mentioned by the parties had not been supported with sufficient evidence.[106]

Another illustrative example is the judgment of the Israeli Supreme Court in *Beit Sourik*.[107] In this case, the Court had to decide whether the erection of a separation fence[108] in the so-called 'belligerent territories' to prevent terrorists from entering Israel was in compliance with international law and Israeli administrative law. It is important to note that the Court applied the principle of proportionality even in the absence of a particular limitation clause. The Court stated that:

balancing between security and liberty . . . is a general problem in the law . . . [whose] solution is universal. . . . [and] found deep in the general principles of law . . . One of those foundational principles which balance between the legitimate objective and the means of achieving it is the principle of proportionality.[109]

---

[104] Id., at 247.   [105] Id., at 249.   [106] Id., at 255.

[107] HCJ 2056/04 *Beit Sourik Village Council v. The Government of Israel* [2004] *available at* <http://elyon1.court.gov.il/files_eng/04/560/020/A28/04020560.a28.pdf>.

[108] Some parts of this security installation are more reminiscent of a 'wall' than of a 'fence', and there is significant political controversy about the right terminology. Here, I will adhere to the term used by the Israeli Supreme Court.

[109] HCJ 2056/04 *Beit Sourik Village Council v. The Government of Israel* [2004], at 21. One of the international law sources that Barak cited as being relevant for this dispute contained a textual marker for a proportionality analysis. Article 27 of the Fourth Geneva Convention provides that '[p]rotected persons are entitled, in all circumstances, to respect for their persons, their honour, their family rights, their religious convictions and practices, and their manners and customs . . . However, the Parties to the conflict may take such measures of control and security in regard to protected persons as may be *necessary* as a result of the war.' (Emphasis added).

In addition, the Court categorized proportionality as a 'general principle of international law'.[110] Regarding the domestic sphere, the Court held that proportionality is 'today one of the basic values of the Israeli administrative law... [that] applies to every act of the Israeli administrative authorities'.[111] The Court then applied the three-step proportionality test, of which the separation fence passed the first two steps.[112] The Court found, however, that considerable parts of the fence were disproportionate in the strict sense. Particularly noteworthy in the Court's analysis is the relationship between the second and the third steps of the proportionality test. With respect to the second step of the analysis, the Court asked whether an alternate route causing less injury to inhabitants would have fulfilled the security objective to the same extent as the route chosen by the military leadership. The Council on Peace and Security, an NGO who joined the proceedings as *amicus curiae,* argued that an alternative route would have been less infringing and at the same time provided the same or even a greater degree of security.[113] After careful consideration of the arguments, the Court acknowledged that both parties had presented credible arguments as to the necessity of the particular route of the fence. Finally, the burden of proof became the crucial factor in the decision of whether the chosen route of the fence was the least restrictive means to satisfy Israel's security needs.[114] Before embarking on its proportionality analysis, the Court dedicated several pages to some general remarks on the scope of its judicial review.[115] One of the key elements in this passage was a reference to an earlier decision of the Court:

In such a dispute regarding military-professional questions, in which the Court has no well founded knowledge of its own, the witness of respondents, who speaks for those actually responsible for the preservation of security in the administered territories and within the Green Line, shall benefit from the assumption that his professional reasons are sincere reasons. Very convincing evidence is necessary in order to negate this assumption.[116]

Since the Court was not convinced that the route suggested by the Council on Peace was indeed preferable or at least equally effective from a security perspective, the Court decided that the fence met the second prong of the proportionality analysis.[117] It is not clear whether the Court placed the burden of proof on the petitioner *ab initio* or whether the Court considered the burden of proof to have shifted at some point. The wording of the passage quoted above ('assumption') might suggest that the Court considered the petitioner to bear that burden of proof from the very beginning. It is clear from the Court's summary of the arguments provided by the parties, however, that it was initially the respondent who argued at length that it had adopted several measures to ensure that the disadvantages for the inhabitants were no greater than necessary to protect Israel's security interests.[118] The alternative route for the fence was suggested by the Council for

---

[110] Id., at 21.   [111] Id., at 23.   [112] Id., at 33.   [113] Id., at 11, 31–2.
[114] Id., at 32–3.   [115] Id., at 26–9.
[116] Id., at 28, the Court citing HCJ 258/79 *Amira v. Defense Minister*, 92.
[117] Id., at 29, 33.   [118] Id., at 8–9, especially para. 13.

Peace and Security only at a later stage of the proceedings.[119] This indicates that the Court expected the respondent to make at least a credible case as to the least restrictive character of its adopted measures before it was willing to grant the 'benefit of the doubt' in the face of contrary evidence.

The most remarkable part of the judgment in the *Beit Sourik* case is the fact that the Court considered certain parts of the fence to be disproportionate in the narrow sense. The Court explained that this step of the analysis is meant to ensure 'a reasonable balance between communal needs and the damage done to the individual' and it must be 'made against the background of the general normative structure of the legal system, which recognizes human rights and the necessity of ensuring the provision of the needs and welfare of local inhabitants'.[120] It is precisely at this point of the analysis that the alternate route suggested by the Council for Peace and Security assumed crucial importance. As mentioned above, the Court was not convinced at the second stage of the proportionality test that the alternate route would have yielded the same level of security. At the third stage of the analysis, the Court considered any potential security gains from the chosen route to be too marginal to justify the significant additional suffering that this route entailed for the inhabitants as compared to the alternate route.[121] In other words, the Court compared the consequences of the decision taken by the military leadership to the hypothetical situation that would have existed if it had chosen the alternate route. In juxtaposing these different scenarios, the Court took into account that the State did not offer substitute land to the inhabitants, even though the Court had proposed such a solution during the course of the proceedings.[122]

3. The principle of proportionality, balancing, and similar concepts in US constitutional law

In contrast to the domestic jurisdictions discussed above, the principle of proportionality is not well established in the jurisprudence of US courts. Some scholars even claim that the US is the only jurisdiction in the Western world that rejects the principle of proportionality.[123] Indeed, the three-step proportionality test has never been applied in a majority opinion of the US Supreme Court.[124] That said, there are several concepts in US constitutional law that perform a similar function. These concepts seek to resolve conflicts between the federal government and State governments or between fundamental rights of individuals and the public interest. They are sometimes highly reminiscent of the principle of proportionality, or at least of some of its elements.[125] In this subsection, I will provide an

---

[119] Id., at 11.   [120] Id., at 34.   [121] Id., at 35.   [122] Id., at 34.

[123] Cohen-Eliya & Porat, 'The Hidden Foreign Law Debate', at 381 (with further references, n.111).

[124] For references to proportionality in individual opinions of Justice Breyer, *see infra* notes 173-198 and accompanying text.

[125] *See also* Bernhard Schlink, 'Proportionality in Constitutional Law: Why Everywhere but Here?', *Duke Journal of Comparative and International Law* 22 (2012) 291–302, who observed that

overview of some of these concepts and address the efforts by Justice Breyer to establish the principle of proportionality in the jurisprudence of the US Supreme Court. Before turning to these issues, I will outline why the debate on proportionality balancing in the US deserves particular attention.

a) The relevance of the debate on proportionality balancing in the US

The critical attitude toward the principle of proportionality in the US is of importance for this book for two reasons. First, the extent to which this principle, some of its elements, or very similar concepts are accepted in the US is relevant to the question of whether the principle of proportionality constitutes a general principle of law. As shown above, the first step in identifying a general principle within the meaning of Article 38(1)(c) ICJ Statute is a comparative analysis of the 'major legal systems of the world'. It is particularly important that the application of the legal concept in question is not 'doing violence to the fundamental concepts of any of those systems.'[126] One might argue that the application of the principle of proportionality in a considerable number of common law jurisdictions such as Canada and New Zealand is sufficient. Such a view could find further support in the notion that the reasons for the scepticism towards proportionality balancing in the US are very specific to that country's history.

Stephen Gardbaum, for example, insists that the few differences that exist between fundamental rights jurisprudence in the US and other modern constitutional systems stem from greater age and the absence of express limitation clauses.[127] In a similar vein, Cohen-Eliya and Porat submit that the US attitude toward balancing is dominated by a unique 'suspicion based conception of the State' motivated by the idea of 'individual autonomy and self-rule'.[128] Because of a particular fundamental distrust of government, US Americans put overwhelming emphasis on a clear separation of its different branches. Consequently, the role of the judiciary needs to be clearly distinguished from the role of the legislature and the executive as political decision-makers.[129] Moreover, some argue that the overwhelming emphasis on the 'original intent' of the 'Founding Fathers' is unique to US constitutionalism and less prominent in other domestic jurisdictions.[130] Regardless of the merits of these arguments, it is submitted that a resort to the principle of proportionality in international investment law is greatly facilitated if its application does not contradict constitutional tenets of an important actor in this area of law.

---

the 'U.S. Supreme Court, shy about using the term [principle of proportionality] . . . follows the rule in substance again and again' (at 302).

[126] Gutteridge, 'Comparative Law and the Law of Nations', at 5 (*see supra* note 20).

[127] Stephen Gardbaum, 'The Myth and the Reality of American Constitutional Exceptionalism', *Michigan Law Review* 107 (2008) 391–466, at 431.

[128] Cohen-Eliya & Porat, 'The Hidden Foreign Law Debate', at 396.   [129] Id., at 396.

[130] Bardo Fassbender, *The United Nations Charter as the Constitution of the International Community* (2009), at 132–3 with further references (n.569).

The second reason is that US scepticism toward the principle of proportionality is of particular importance because scholars who argue against its application at the international level often resort to arguments that originated in the US constitutional context. It is not the purpose of this book to contribute to the debate between 'balancers' and 'absolutists' in the US constitutional context.[131] Instead, this subsection 3 outlines the legal settings in US constitutional law that give rise to this debate and the competing arguments. It thus lays the basis for the analysis in section II, which identifies several factors that speak against applying a proportionality analysis in certain situations.

b) The dormant commerce clause

Article I, section 8 of the US Constitution empowers congress '[t]o regulate Commerce...among the several States'. There is no provision in the US Constitution, however, that bars states from passing legislation that has an effect on interstate commerce. In other words, the Constitution does not clarify to what extent state legislation may interfere with inter-State commerce in the absence of a federal law. This lacuna in the text of the US Constitution has been filled with a doctrine called the 'dormant commerce clause'.[132] The rationale of this doctrine is to prevent 'economic protectionism' in the form of state laws 'designed to benefit in-state economic interests by burdening out-of-state competitors'.[133] The Supreme Court acknowledges that this aspiration may sometimes conflict with the local autonomy of individual states, which the Constitution seeks to protect.[134]

Therefore, the US Supreme Court differentiates in its 'dormant commerce clause' jurisprudence between discriminatory and non-discriminatory laws: a State law that *discriminates* against interstate commerce—'either on its face or in practical effect'—is only constitutional if the law 'serves a legitimate local purpose' that 'could not be served as well by available nondiscriminatory means'.[135]

---

[131] For the extensive literature in this field, *see* Cohen-Eliya & Porat, 'The Hidden Foreign Law Debate', at 379 n.47. For a particularly fierce debate on balancing with respect to the First Amendment protection of free speech, *see* Richard A. Posner, 'Pragmatism versus Purposivism in First Amendment Analysis', *Stanford Law Review* 54 (2002) 737–52, on one side, and Jed Rubenfeld, 'A Reply to Posner', *Stanford Law Journal* 54 (2002) 753–67, on the other.

[132] On the 'dormant commerce clause' in general, *see* John R. Vile, *A Companion to the United States Constitution and its Amendments* (2006), at 44; Laurence H. Tribe, *American Constitutional Law—Volume One* (2000), at 1029–43; Louis Henkin, 'Infallibility under Law: Constitutional Balancing', *Columbia Law Review* 78 (1978) 1022–49, at 1037–41.

[133] *New Energy Co. of Indiana v. Limbach*, 486 US 269 (1988) at 273.

[134] *Department of Revenue of Kentucky v. George W. Davis*, 553 US 328 (2008) at 338.

[135] *Maine v. Taylor*, 477 US 131 (1986) at 138. An even more explicit and arguably stricter formulation of the same rule can be found in *C & A Carbone, Inc. v. Town of Clarkstown*, 511 US 383 (1994): 'Discrimination against interstate commerce in favour of local business or investment is *per se* invalid, save in a narrow class of cases in which the municipality can demonstrate, under rigorous scrutiny, that it has no other means to advance a legitimate local interest' (Id., at 392).

The doctrine for *non-discriminatory* laws, on the other hand, was famously summarized in Pike:

> Where the statute regulates even-handedly to effectuate a legitimate local public interest, and its effects on interstate commerce are only incidental, it will be upheld unless the burden imposed on such commerce is clearly excessive in relation to the putative local benefits.[136]

These formulations illustrate that some elements of the 'dormant commerce clause' doctrine are very similar to the different steps of the proportionality analysis. The requirements that a law discriminating against inter-State commerce (1) serve a 'legitimate local purpose' which (2) cannot be 'achieved by a nondiscriminatory means' are reminiscent of the first two prongs of the proportionality analysis (*suitability* and *least restrictive means*). The *Pike* test for non-discriminatory measures corresponds to the first prong of the proportionality analysis ('to effectuate a legitimate local public interest') and the balancing process on the third stage of the analysis ('clearly excessive in relation to the...benefit').[137]

c) *The equal protection clause and its different levels of scrutiny*

The different levels of scrutiny for the equal protection clause is another area of US constitutional law that displays certain similarities with the three elements of the principle of proportionality.[138] The US Supreme Court distinguishes between three degrees of judicial deference to legislative and administrative decision-making. Proceeding from the most deferential to the least deferential standard, these different levels of scrutiny are: (i) the rational basis test, (ii) intermediate scrutiny, and (iii) strict scrutiny. The rational basis test applies to economic regulations that do not contain any suspect classifications but whose differentiations are still challenged on 'equal protection' grounds. Such a law passes the rational basis test if it is *rationally related* to a *legitimate* government purpose.[139] The party challenging the constitutionality of the law has the burden to show that there is no conceivable basis on which the differentiation could be based.[140] It is also irrelevant whether the legislator has actually based its differentiation on such legitimate considerations or whether it was motivated by different reasons and the legitimate purpose is merely conceivable.[141]

---

[136] *Pike v. Bruce Church Inc*, 397 US 137 (1970) at 142.

[137] For balancing in the context of the 'dormant commerce clause' in general, *see* Henkin, 'Infallibility under Law', at 1040–1.

[138] The equal protection clause of the Fourteenth Amendment provides that '[no State shall] deny to any person within its jurisdiction the equal protection of the laws.' However, 'equal protection' issues may also arise from the 'due process' clause in the Fifth Amendment. For further textual sources of 'equal protection' (e.g. the Thirteenth and Fifteenth Amendments in race-related differentiations), *see* Laurence H. Tribe, *American Constitutional Law* (1988), at 1437.

[139] *Federal Communications Commission v. Beach Communications*, 508 US 307 (1993) at 313–14; *Schweiker v. Wilson*, 450 US 221 (1981) at 242.

[140] *Federal Communications Commission v. Beach Communications*, 508 US 307 (1993), at 315; *Lehnhausen v. Lake Shore Auto Parts Co*, 410 US 356 (1973) at 364.

[141] *Federal Communications Commission v. Beach Communications*, 508 US 307 (1993) at 315; *Nordlinger v. Hahn*, 505 US 1 (1993) at 15.

A law that differentiates on the basis of gender triggers 'intermediate scrutiny'. Under this test, a law is only in line with the equal protection clause if the classification is *'substantially related* to an *important* governmental objective'.[142] Contrary to the rational basis test, the government bears the burden of proof.[143] Moreover, the governmental objective put forward as justification must have been the actual reason for the classification. In other words, in contrast to the rational basis test, it is not sufficient for the government to articulate a sufficiently important reason 'post hoc' in the course of legal proceedings.[144]

'Strict scrutiny' shares some of the characteristics of 'intermediate scrutiny': the government bears the burden of proof and the relevant governmental goal must have actually existed at the time of the legislative action. Strict scrutiny applies, for example, to classifications based on race or national origin[145] and to all infringements of 'fundamental rights'.[146] Laws subject to strict scrutiny are only constitutional if they are *'narrowly tailored* to achieve a *compelling* government interest'.[147] In analysing whether a particular law meets this level of scrutiny, the Supreme Court has repeatedly resorted to a least restrictive means test.[148] Hence, 'strict scrutiny' contains the same considerations that constitute the first two prongs of a proportionality analysis (suitability and least restrictive means).[149]

d) Balancing and the First Amendment to the US Constitution

One of the most controversial issues of US constitutional law is whether and to what extent the rights enshrined in the First Amendment can be restricted for public policy reasons. The First Amendment to the US Constitution reads as follows:

---

[142] *Heckler v. Mathews*, 465 US 728 (1984), at 744; *Mississippi University for Women v. Hogan*, 458 US 718 (1982), at 724; *Wengler v. Druggists Mutual Ins. Co.*, 446 US 142 (1980) at 150 (emphasis added).

[143] *Heckler v. Mathews*, 465 US 728 (1984) at 745; *Wengler v. Druggists Mutual Ins. Co.*, 446 US 142 (1980) at 150.

[144] *United States v. Virginia*, 518 US 515 (1996), at 533; *Weinberger v. Wiesenfeld*, 420 US 636 (1975) at 643.

[145] *Adarand Constructors Inc v. Peña*, 515 US 200 (1995) at 220; *Grutter v. Bollinger*, 539 US 206 (2003) at 326.

[146] For a criticism of the vagueness of the term 'fundamental rights', *see United States v. Virginia*, 518 US 515 (1996) (dissenting opinion of Scalia, J) at 567–8. However, it is uncontroversial that the right to vote, the freedom to associate (*Illinois State Bd of Elections v. Socialist Workers Party*, 440 US 173 at 184), the freedom of speech, and the freedom of religion qualify as fundamental rights.

[147] *Parents Involved in Community Schools v. Seattle School Dist No 1*, 551 US 701 (2007) at 720 (quotations omitted) (emphasis added). *See also Adarand Constructors Inc v. Peña*, 515 US 200 (1995) at 227 and *Grutter v. Bollinger*, 539 US 206 (2003) at 326.

[148] *Illinois State Bd of Elections v. Socialist Workers Party*, 440 US 173, at 186; *Bernal v. Fainter*, 467 US 216 (1984) at 219–20; *Randall v. Sorrell*, 548 US 230 (2006) at 283.

[149] Cohen-Eliya & Porat, 'The Hidden Foreign Law Debate' go even one step further and claim that the third stage of the proportionality analysis is 'implicitly present' in the least restrictive means requirement (at 386).

Congress shall make no law respecting an establishment of religion, or prohibiting the free exercise thereof; or abridging the freedom of speech, or of the press; or the right of the people peaceably to assemble, and to petition the Government for a redress of grievances.

This provision does not contain a limitation clause. However, the Supreme Court decided that certain expressions fall outside the protection of the First Amendment, and it did so on the basis of a balancing approach. The 'weighing' of free speech against the public interest in these cases is similar to the third prong of the proportionality analysis. In its 1942 *Chaplinsky* decision, the Supreme Court had to determine the constitutionality of a criminal statute prohibiting the utterance of any 'offensive' or 'derisive' word to another person in public. The Court broadly stated that 'obscene', 'profane', or 'insulting'

utterances are no essential part of any exposition of ideas, and are of such slight social value as a step to truth that any benefit that may be derived from them is clearly outweighed by social interest in order and morality.[150]

In *Miller v. California*, a case involving adult pornography decided in 1973, the Supreme Court refined the *Chaplinsky* standard in regard of obscenity. In light of the 'inherent danger of undertaking to regulate any form of expression',[151] the Court held that only such sexually oriented works fall categorically outside the scope of the First Amendment that:

taken as a whole, appeal to the prurient interest in sex, which portray sexual conduct in a patently offensive way, and which, taken as a whole, do not have serious literary, artistic, political, or scientific value.[152]

The Supreme Court explained (in its later *Ferber* decision) that this standard was the result of a balancing process, or, in the words of the Court, 'an accommodation between the State's interests in protecting the "sensibilities of unwilling recipients" from exposure to pornographic material and the dangers of censorship inherent in unabashedly content-based laws'.[153]

In 1978, five years after *Miller*, the Supreme Court had to decide in *Pacifica* on the constitutionality of restrictions on sexually offensive radio speech that was not offensive enough to reach the *Miller* obscenity threshold. The Court held that such speech 'is not entitled to absolute constitutional protection under all circumstances'. Rather, the constitutional protection of offensive speech would depend on its context.[154] The Court outlined two factors that would both justify a lower protection of broadcast speech in general and support the constitutionality of the particular action of the Federal Communication Commission. First, the Court focused on the exposure of all citizens to the broadcasting media in the 'privacy' of their home. The Court held that 'the individual's right to be left alone plainly *outweighs* the First Amendment

---

[150] *Chaplinsky v. New Hampshire*, 315 US 568 (1942) at 571–2.
[151] *Miller v. California*, 413 US 15 (1973) at 23.   [152] Id., at 24.
[153] *New York v. Paula Ira Ferber*, 458 US 747 (1982), at 756.
[154] *Federal Communications Commission v. Pacifica Foundation*, 439 US 883 (1978) at 747–8.

Rights of an intruder'.[155] The second factor mentioned by the Court contains a similar process of weighing and balancing the conflicting interests at stake. In light of the ready accessibility of broadcasting for children, the Court recalled and summarized its findings in *Ginsburg v. New York*, according to which:

the government's interest in the 'well-being of its youth' and in supporting 'parents' claim to authority in their own household' justified the regulation of otherwise protected expression.[156]

In its 1982 *Ferber* decision, the US Supreme Court adopted a similar balancing approach in the context of child pornography:

it is not rare that a content-based classification of speech has been accepted because it may be appropriately generalized that within the confines of the given classification, the evil to be restricted so overwhelmingly outweighs the expressive interests, if any, at stake, that no process of case-by-case adjudication is required.[157]

Furthermore, the Supreme Court found that child pornography

bears so heavily and pervasively on the welfare of children engaged in its production [that] we think the balance of competing interests is clearly struck and that it is permissible to consider these materials as without the protection of the First Amendment.[158]

In *Reno*, the Supreme Court had to decide a case with a similar subject matter to *Pacifica*: the protection of minors from harmful content—this time not on the radio but on the internet. In its 1997 decision, the Supreme Court relied on a least restrictive means test in deciding the case. The Court found that the provision in question suppressed a significant amount of speech that adults have a First Amendment right to receive and to exchange. Such a burden on adult speech was unconstitutional 'if less restrictive alternatives would be at least as effective in achieving the legitimate purpose' of preventing minors from accessing harmful speech on the internet.[159] The Court noted that there would be a 'heavy burden on the Government to explain why a less restrictive provision would not be as effective'.[160] In light of the possible alternatives that had been discussed before the Court (for example 'tagging' incoming material to make paternal control possible), the Court held that the provision was not 'narrowly tailored', and hence unconstitutional.[161]

In *Stevens*, decided in 2010, the government sought to exclude an additional category of speech from the protection of the First Amendment: the depiction of animal cruelty. The government argued that the exclusion of a certain category from the protection of the First Amendment depends on a 'balancing of the value of the speech against its societal costs'.[162] Even though the majority

---

[155] Id. at 748 (emphasis added).
[156] Id. at 749 (citing *Ginsberg v. New York*, 390 US 629 at 640 and 639).
[157] *New York v. Paula Ira Ferber*, 458 US 747 (1982) at 763–4.   [158] Id. at 764.
[159] *Reno v. American Civil Liberties Union*, 521 US 844 (1997) 874.   [160] Id. at 879.
[161] Id., at 879.   [162] *United States v. Stevens*, 2010 WL 1540082 (US), at 6.

opinion conceded that the government's view finds some support in decisions such as *Chaplinsky* and *Ferber*,[163] it did not resort to a balancing test in its decision. The Court stated that:

The First Amendment's guarantee of free speech does not extend only to categories of speech that survive an ad hoc balancing of relative social costs and benefits. The First Amendment itself reflects a judgment by the American people that the benefits of its restrictions on the Government outweigh the costs. Our Constitution forecloses any attempt to revise that judgment simply on the basis that some speech is not worth it. The Constitution is not a document 'prescribing limits, and declaring that those limits may be passed at pleasure.'[164]

Still, even the majority opinion in *Stevens* recognized that there are some categories of speech that are historically not protected by the First Amendment ('fraud', 'speech integral to criminal conduct', etc)[165]—but the depiction of animal cruelty was found not to be one of them.

The 2012 US Supreme Court decision *Xavier Alvarez* dealt with the Stolen Valor Act, a law that had made it a crime to falsely claim receipt of certain military decorations and medals.[166] The Court renewed its scepticism towards free-floating balancing articulated in *Stevens* and recalled:

this Court has rejected as 'startling and dangerous' a 'free-floating test for First Amendment coverage... [based on] an ad hoc balancing of relative social costs and benefits.' [...] Instead, content-based restrictions on speech have been permitted, as a general matter, only when confined to the few 'historic and traditional categories [of expression] long familiar to the bar'.[167]

The Court held that there is no *historic* category that would deny statements First Amendment protection only because they are 'false'.[168] Furthermore, the

---

[163] Id. at 7. Finally, however, the Court rejected the government's arguments based on *Ferber* and *Chaplinsky*. It held that:

Our decisions in *Ferber* and other cases cannot be taken as establishing a freewheeling authority to declare new categories of speech outside the scope of the First Amendment. Maybe there are some categories of speech that have been historically unprotected, but have not yet been specifically identified or discussed as such in our case law. But if so, there is no evidence that 'depictions of animal cruelty' is among them. We need not foreclose the future recognition of such additional categories to reject the Government's highly manipulatable balancing test as a means of identifying them.

(id., at 7)

The Court also pointed out that the subject matter of *Ferber*, child pornography, was 'intrinsically related' to child abuse as an illegal activity (id., at 7).

[164] Id. at 6 (the quotation in the last sentence refers to *Marbury v. Madison*, 5 US 137 (1803)).

[165] *See United States v. Stevens*, 2010 WL 1540082 (US) at 5. For further examples of categories of speech unprotected by the First Amendment, *see* Federal Communications *Commission v. Pacifica Foundation*, 439 US 883 (1978) at 745 ('words used to create a clear and present danger', 'speech calculated to provoke a fight').

[166] *United States v. Xavier Alvarez*, 132 S.Ct. 2537 (2012), at 2543.   [167] Id., at 2544.

[168] For false statements to fall outside the scope of protected free speech, additional elements have to be present, i.e. defamation, fraud, or some other legally cognizable harm associated with a false statement (id., at 2545).

government did not demonstrate that 'false statements' should constitute a *new* unprotected category based on 'a long (if heretofore unrecognized) tradition'.[169] The Court then applied the 'most exacting scrutiny' to the Stolen Valor Act,[170] which the act failed for two independent reasons. First, the Court found that there was no 'direct causal link between the restriction imposed and the injury to be prevented'. Quoting an *amicus curiae*, the Court opined 'there is nothing that charlatans such as Xavier Alvarez can do to stain [the Medal winners'] honor.'[171] Second, the Court held that criminalizing false statements was not the 'least restrictive means among available, effective alternatives' to protect the military awards system: a governmental database listing the true medal holders could expose false statements as well.[172] This second consideration ('least restrictive means among available, effective alternatives') is identical to the second step of a proportionality analysis (least-restrictive means test). In addition, it is difficult not to see the strong similarities between the first consideration ('lack of causal link') and the first step of a proportionality analysis (suitability).

e) *The struggle of Justice Breyer for an explicit endorsement of the principle of proportionality by the US Supreme Court*

The first decision of the Supreme Court dealing in depth with the Second Amendment of the US Constitution concisely illustrates the debate on balancing and proportionality in US constitutional law.[173] In *Heller*, the Court had to decide on the constitutionality of a District of Columbia law restricting the holding and use of handguns, inter alia by requiring that lawfully owned handguns be kept locked or otherwise inoperable at home. The Supreme Court started with an in-depth analysis of the drafting history of the Second Amendment.[174] The Court found that the Second Amendment contains a right to possess and use handguns even outside service in a militia.[175] In a second step, the Court stated that this right is 'not unlimited', and that it is 'not a right to keep and carry any weapon whatsoever in any manner whatsoever and for whatever purpose'.[176] Still, the Supreme Court held that restrictions to the right to bear arms are only permissible if they are historically established. In this vein, the Court recognized 'such longstanding' Second Amendment restrictions as forbidding felons to possess

---

[169] Id., at 2547 (internal references omitted).

[170] Id., at 2548 (internal references omitted). Before the Court applied 'most exacting scrutiny' to the Stolen Valor Act, it held that a general ban on false speech is unconstitutional, and concluded that '[t]he previous discussion suffices to show that the Act conflicts with free speech principles' (id., at 2548). This indicates that the Court's analysis on whether the Stolen Valor Act satisfies 'most exacting scrutiny' was *obiter dictum*.

[171] Id., at 2549 (internal references omitted).   [172] Id., at 2551.

[173] *Columbia v. Heller*, 128 S.Ct. 2783 (2008). The Court noted that this case constitutes its first detailed analysis of the Second Amendment (*see* id., at 2821).

[174] The Second Amendment of the US Constitution reads as follows: 'A well regulated Militia being necessary to the security of a free State, the right of the people to keep and bear Arms, shall not be infringed.'

[175] *Columbia v. Heller*, 128 S.Ct. 2783 (2008) at 2788–816.   [176] Id. at 2816.

firearms, banning firearms from schools and government buildings, or qualifying the commercial sale of guns.[177] Since the law in question did not fall under any of those 'historical justifications for the exceptions',[178] the majority opinion declared the law unconstitutional.

Justice Breyer preferred a different methodology. He stated that in Second Amendment cases, there will typically be a conflict between the individual right and the 'governmental public safety concerns'. Breyer submitted that these conflicts—as well as other instances of 'competing constitutionally protected interests'—could be resolved by proportionality balancing.[179] Breyer's notion of proportionality is highly similar to the approaches of other domestic courts. Breyer suggested that the Court:

generally asks whether the statute burdens a protected interest in a way or to an extent that is out of proportion to the statute's salutary effects upon other important governmental interests.... Any answer would take account both of the statute's effects upon the competing interests and the existence of any clearly superior less restrictive alternative. Contrary to the majority's unsupported suggestion that this sort of 'proportionality' approach is unprecedented, the Court has applied it in various constitutional contexts, including election-law cases, speech cases, and due process cases.[180]

For the case at hand, Breyer first established that the law contributed to the governmental purpose, that is saving lives.[181] (This analysis is equivalent to the *suitability* prong of the three-step proportionality analysis.) After that, Breyer inquired into the extent to which the law in question burdened the interests protected by the Second Amendment.[182] Breyer then established that there were no equally effective, less restrictive means (which is equivalent to the second prong of the proportionality test).[183] In a final step (which is arguably identical to proportionality in the strict sense), Breyer asked whether the law 'disproportionately burden[s] Amendment-protected interests'.[184] Since he answered this last question in the negative, he considered the law to be constitutional.[185]

The majority of the Court explicitly dismissed Breyer's proportionality analysis, or what Justice Scalia called a 'freestanding "interest-balancing" approach'.[186] The following passage, in which Justice Scalia argues against Breyer's approach, epitomizes the reasons why proportionality analysis is so controversial in US constitutional law.

The very enumeration of the right takes out of the hands of government—even the Third Branch of Government—the power to decide on a case-by-case basis whether the right is *really worth* insisting upon. A constitutional guarantee subject to future judges' assessments of its usefulness is no constitutional guarantee at all. Constitutional rights are enshrined with the scope they were understood to have when the people adopted them, whether or not future legislatures or (yes) even future judges think that scope too broad.

---

[177] Id., at 2816–17.   [178] Id., at 2821.   [179] Id. (Breyer, J, dissenting) at 2582.
[180] Id. at 2852 (internal references omitted).   [181] Id. at 2854–61.
[182] Id. at 2861–4.   [183] Id. at 2864–5.   [184] Id. at 2865.
[185] Id. at 2865–8.   [186] Id. at 2821.

We would not apply an 'interest-balancing' approach to the prohibition of a peaceful neo-Nazi march through Skokie. The First Amendment contains the freedom-of-speech guarantee that the people ratified... The Second Amendment is no different. Like the First, it is the very product of an interest-balancing by the people—which Justice BREYER would now conduct for them anew.[187]

In 2009, Breyer followed a line of argument very similar to the one he adopted in *Heller* in his partly concurring and partly dissenting opinion in *Ysursa*. The subject matter of this case was a state law that barred public employees from opting for a payroll deduction for political activities. Contrary to the majority opinion of the Court, Breyer found that this regulation restricted the free speech of unions. Breyer considered intermediate scrutiny to be the appropriate level of judicial review in this case,[188] and he identified proportionality as the relevant test. In this vein, he examined 'whether the statute imposes a burden upon speech that is disproportionate in light of the other interests the government seeks to achieve'.[189] In contrast to his dissenting opinion in *Heller*, Breyer cited not only US jurisprudence in support of his view but also judgments of foreign constitutional courts (Canada, South Africa, and Israel) and the ECtHR.[190] Factors that Breyer considered relevant for such a proportionality analysis were the 'seriousness of the speech-related harm the provision will likely cause, the importance of the provision's countervailing objectives, the extent to which the statute will tend to achieve those objectives, and whether there are other less restrictive ways of doing so'.[191] Interestingly, Breyer clarified that he would not necessarily use the principle of proportionality for cases involving 'strict scrutiny',[192] which implies that Breyer considers 'strict scrutiny' to be a stricter standard of review than proportionality analysis.

In *Alvarez*, the 2012 free-speech decision discussed above,[193] Breyer agreed with the plurality that the Stolen Valor Act violates the First Amendment. However, Breyer rejected the plurality's 'strict categorical analysis', which distinguished between categories of free speech that were protected under the First Amendment and those that were not.[194] The decisive criterion for Breyer was the 'fit between statutory ends and means': a statute violates the First Amendment if its 'speech related harm is out of proportion to its justification'.[195] Breyer considered both 'proportionality review' and 'intermediate scrutiny' to be appropriate labels for such an analysis.[196] Part of this analysis is the question 'whether it is possible substantially to achieve the Government's objective in less burdensome ways'.[197] For the Stolen Valor Act, Breyer answered this question in the affirmative, identifying a publicly available database as an adequate protection for the integrity of the

---

[187] Id. at 2821 (emphasis in the original) (internal references omitted).
[188] *Ysursa v. Pocatello Education Association*, 129 S.Ct. 1093 (2009) (concurring and dissenting opinion of Breyer, J), at 1102–3.
[189] Id., at 1103.   [190] Id., at 1103.   [191] Id., at 1103.   [192] Id., at 1103.
[193] Chapter 3, notes 22-28 and accompanying text.
[194] *United States v. Xavier Alvarez*, 132 S.Ct. 2537 (2012) (concurring opinion Breyer, J, at 2551).
[195] Id., at 2551.   [196] Id., at 2551–2.   [197] Id., at 2555.

military award system.[198] Hence, Breyer found the Stolen Valor Act to be unconstitutional through an inquiry identical to the second prong of a proportionality review, the least restrictive means test.

4. Summary of the comparative analysis

A great number of constitutional systems apply the principle of proportionality. Of these systems, we have examined the constitutional orders in Germany, Canada, South Africa, and Israel in some depth to illustrate how proportionality works in practice. The comparative analysis did not reveal that domestic legal systems apply a free-floating proportionality test whenever individual rights collide with the public interest. Rather, the normative setting of the relevant provision is key. If a fundamental right is subject to a general or specific limitation clause, proportionality resolves conflicts between the relevant rights and interests at stake. Canadian, South African, and Israeli jurisprudence are fine examples for proportionality analysis triggered by limitation clauses. If the fundamental right at issue is on its face guaranteed unconditionally, restricting it by way of a proportionality analysis is a much more complicated matter. Some say that German law is the cradle of modern proportionality analysis, and there is arguably no judicial body in the world that is more willing to apply proportionality than the German Constitutional Court. Nevertheless, even this court restricts unconditionally guaranteed rights through proportionality only for the sake of *constitutionally* protected rights or interests. Interests that enjoy no constitutional protection—whether private or public—cannot trump unconditionally guaranteed rights.

The US Supreme Court—or at least the majority of its justices—rejects proportionality as a legal concept relevant to its fundamental rights jurisprudence. This may be partly due to the lack of general or specific limitation clauses in the relevant amendments to the US Constitution. Still, the Court engages in the weighing and balancing of different rights and interests in a variety of different normative settings, for example in the context of the dormant commerce clause. Furthermore, the Supreme Court has employed in several instances a balancing test to decide whether some categories of speech fall outside the scope of the First Amendment. Moreover, the Supreme Court resorts to certain components of proportionality such as the least restrictive means test on several occasions. This is particularly true for 'strict scrutiny' in the Court's equal protection clause jurisprudence and 'most exacting scrutiny', recently employed by the Court in First Amendment cases.

In sum, the jurisprudence of the US Supreme Court is no reason to deny proportionality the status of a general principle of law within the meaning of Article 38(1)(c) ICJ Statute. At the same time, the practice of other courts examined in this section does not suggest that it is appropriate to resort to proportionality

---

[198] Id., at 2556.

whenever a conflict arises between two rights or interests. Two conclusions follow from this account. First, proportionality is sufficiently prevalent on the domestic level to pass the first step of identifying a general principle of law—a comparative analysis of domestic legal systems. Second, this alone tells us very little about when adjudicators should apply proportionality at the international level. All depends on the relevant normative setting. Taking into account insights from the comparative analysis in this section, the next section introduces three factors adjudicators should consider before they engage in a proportionality analysis.

II. The 'dark sides' of proportionality

As demonstrated in the previous section, domestic courts apply the principle of proportionality or very similar concepts in a variety of different settings. Proportionality balancing is more problematic in some of these than it is in others. Notably, it is not only the US Supreme Court or US scholars that are sceptical about proportionality balancing or who subject proportionality balancing to certain limitations. Even the most ardent supporters of proportionality recognize that fundamental rights jurisprudence cannot be reduced to a pure exercise of weighing and balancing. Robert Alexy, for example, stresses that the wording of constitutional provisions needs to be taken seriously and both guides and restricts the balancing process.[199] Furthermore, the practice of domestic courts reveals that the concrete legal settings greatly prejudice the balancing process. Limitation clauses that enumerate certain public policy goals for the sake of which an individual right or freedom may be restricted are a good example. Such limitation clauses exist both on the domestic and the international level.[200] In these scenarios, all

---

[199] Alexy, *Theorie der Grundrechte*, at 121.
[200] *See, e.g.,* Articles 8(2), 9(2), 10(2), and 11(2) of the ECHR, which read as follows (emphases added):

Article 8 —Right to respect for private and family life

...There shall be no interference by a public authority with the exercise of this right except such as is in accordance with the law and is *necessary* in a democratic society in the interests of national security, public safety or the economic well-being of the country, for the prevention of disorder or crime, for the protection of health or morals, or for the protection of the rights and freedoms of others.

Article 9—Freedom of thought, conscience and religion

...Freedom to manifest one's religion or beliefs shall be subject only to such limitations as are prescribed by law and are *necessary* in a democratic society in the interests of public safety, for the protection of public order, health or morals, or for the protection of the rights and freedoms of others.

Article 10—Freedom of expression

...The exercise of these freedoms, since it carries with it duties and responsibilities, may be subject to such formalities, conditions, or penalties as are prescribed by law and are *necessary* in a democratic society, in the interests of national security, territorial integrity or public safety, for the prevention of disorder or crime, for the protection of health or morals, for the protection of the reputation or rights of others, for preventing the

three steps of the proportionality analysis are circumscribed by the concrete list of public interests. It is not sufficient that the State measure in question is suitable to achieve a public goal, that there is no less restrictive means available, and that the measure is proportionate in the strict sense. Rather, it is necessary that the State measure in question satisfies these requirements with respect to a public purpose enumerated in the relevant limitation clause.

These and other insights from the comparative analysis in section I and further material covered in this section can be translated into three caveats when it comes to the application of the principle of proportionality: (1) the risk of unwarranted judicial lawmaking; (2) rule-of-law concerns; and (3) the risk of arbitrary outcomes due to uncertainty as to what interests and factors matter in a proportionality analysis and what weight they carry. Much of the criticisms voiced against proportionality by courts and scholars relate to one of these—partly overlapping—categories, and they will be addressed in turn.

1. Judicial lawmaking

The first caveat—the risk of judicial lawmaking—addresses the relationship of adjudicatory bodies to other decision-makers. In the domestic context, this issue essentially boils down to a separation-of-powers argument: it is for the legislator or the people to reach decisions on fundamental issues, and not for courts. Rather, courts should apply the legal texts that enshrine such decisions. In *Heller,* Justice Scalia, writing for the majority of the US Supreme Court, criticized Justice Breyer's balancing approach as follows:

The First Amendment contains the freedom-of-speech guarantee that the people ratified ... The Second Amendment is no different. Like the First, it is the very product of an interest-balancing by the people—which Justice BREYER would now conduct for them anew.[201]

This line of argument is not limited to constitutional provisions. Judicial balancing is also perceived as a threat to parliamentary decision-making. Louis Henkin, for example, warned that:

In some contexts, [ad hoc balancing] sets the court to doing, and doing finally, not what 'is emphatically the province of the judicial department'—'to say what the law is'—but what

---

disclosure of information received in confidence, or for maintaining the authority and impartiality of the judiciary.

Article 11—Freedom of assembly and association

...No restrictions shall be placed on the exercise of these rights other than such as are prescribed by law and are *necessary* in a democratic society in the interests of national security or public safety, for the prevention of disorder or crime, for the protection of health or morals or for the protection of the rights and freedoms of others. This article shall not prevent the imposition of lawful restrictions on the exercise of these rights by members of the armed forces, of the police or of the administration of the State.

[201] *See supra* note 187 and accompanying text.

would seem emphatically to be the province or competence of the political branches—the weighing of competing societal interests and values. It makes the courts appellate administrators of every police regulation.[202]

The separation-of-powers model underlying this argument cannot be transferred lock, stock, and barrel to international law. Still, the basic idea applies here as well: it is for the States as the primary law-makers in international law to prioritize among conflicting rights and interests, and not for arbitrators or judges. In this vein, it is sometimes argued that the text of human rights instruments such as the ECHR constitutes the result of a balancing process. Consequently, judicial balancing in this context would raise serious questions of legitimacy.[203] Similar considerations are put forward in the field of international economic law. Jürgen Kurtz, for example, argues against proportionality balancing in investor–State arbitration because parliamentarians would be better equipped to reach 'value laden and empirical judgments' than courts or other adjudicatory bodies.[204] Donald H. Regan advances a similar sovereignty-based argument against proportionality balancing in the context of Article XX GATT. Regan argues that such an approach would be contrary to a basic tenet of WTO law, according to which it is for domestic actors to weigh domestic benefits of a State measure against adverse effects on trade.[205] While generally sympathetic to proportionality analysis in investor–State arbitration, Benedict Kingsbury and Stephan Schill acknowledge that proportionality risks 'legitimating judicial lawmaking'.[206]

It is important to bear in mind that not all authors use the term judicial lawmaking in the same way. Stone Sweet and della Cananea, for example, adopt a rather wide notion of judicial lawmaking. They consider the interpretation of undefined treaty terms and the finding of solutions to procedural issues deliberately left to courts to be examples of judicial lawmaking.[207] Under this wide notion of judicial lawmaking, one could say that we are concerned here only with unwarranted judicial lawmaking. Unwarranted judicial lawmaking is particularly likely to occur when balancing undermines or overwrites legislative decisions taken in the legal instrument responsible for the very jurisdiction of the relevant judicial body.

---

[202] Henkin, 'Infallibility under Law', at 1048 (internal quotation refers to *Marbury v. Madison*, 5 US 137 (1803), at 177). In a similar vein, Stone Sweet and Mathews question whether parliamentary sovereignty will 'survive anywhere' as the principle of proportionality spreads into an ever greater number of domestic legal orders (Stone Sweet & Mathews, 'Proportionality Balancing', at 161). For the at least indirect democratic legitimacy of judges, *see* Schlink, 'Proportionality in Constitutional Law', at 300.

[203] Stavros Tsakyrakis, 'Proportionality: an Assault on Human Rights?', *International Journal of Constitutional Law* 7 (2008) 468–93, at 472.

[204] Jürgen Kurtz, 'Adjudging the Exceptional at International Investment Law: Security, Public Order and Financial Crisis', *International and Comparative Law Quarterly* 59 (2010) 325–71, at 367.

[205] Donald H. Regan, 'The Meaning of "Necessary" in GATT Article XX and GATS Article XIV: the Myth of Cost–Benefit Balancing', *World Trade Review* 6 (2007) 347–69, at 350.

[206] Kingsbury & Schill, 'Public Law Concepts', at 103.

[207] Stone Sweet & della Cananea, 'Proportionality, General Principles of Law', at 942; 948–9.

2. Threat to the rule of law

The second major concern regarding the principle of proportionality is closely related to these warnings against judicial lawmaking. Some arguments against proportionality may be summarized under the notion that it poses a threat to the rule of law. This proposition might be particularly surprising in light of the fact that some scholars consider proportionality to be the very epitomization of the rule of law.[208] There is a lot of discussion on what the term 'rule of law' actually means and what it requires. The extent of this debate is well beyond the scope of this book, but there seems to be consensus on some factors that the rule of law definitely involves. These factors have been summarized as follows:

[L]aw must be set forth in advance (be prospective), be made public, be general, be clear, be stable and certain, and be applied to everyone according to its terms. In the absence of these characteristics, the rule of law cannot be satisfied.[209]

Some of the features of judicial balancing appear to run counter to this characterization of the rule of law. Judicial balancing is generally retrospective, i.e. adjudicators weigh and balance the different factors after the relevant actors have had to make a decision. Also, the outcome of the balancing process might vary from case to case and—probably even worse—from adjudicator to adjudicator. Furthermore, in some instances proportionality balancing restricts individual rights even though the right holders could not foresee such restrictions from the text guaranteeing the right in question. This is, for example, true for restrictions of free speech guaranteed by the text of the First Amendment to the US Constitution unconditionally. In this context, the following statement by Jeremy Waldron on the rule of law comes to mind:

According to most conceptions of the rule of law, individual citizens are entitled to laws that are neither murky nor uncertain but are instead publicly and clearly stated in a text that is not buried in doctrine.[210]

It bears emphasis that reasons why individual interests should yield to an allegedly greater public good are always readily available, both in liberal democracies and in totalitarian regimes. Modern constitutional systems guarantee individual rights regardless of whether public interest agents—that is the members of the different branches of government (including the judiciary)—consider them worth protecting or not. Louis Henkin pointed out that

[ad hoc balancing] tends to balance away rights that were intended to stand even in the face of public need.[211]

---

[208] *See, e.g.,* David M. Beatty, *The Ultimate Rule of Law* (2004).
[209] Brian Z. Tamanaha, 'A Concise Guide to the Rule of Law', *in Relocating the Rule of Law* (Gianluigi Palombella & Neil Walker eds., 2009) 3–15, at 3.
[210] Jeremy Waldron, 'The Rule of International Law', *Harvard Journal of Law & Public Policy* 30 (2006) 15–30, at 17.
[211] Henkin, 'Infallibility under Law', at 1048.

Balancing is sometimes also criticized for being a comfortable alternative to rigorous textual analysis, which might involve greater care and effort.[212] For the international context, such an approach would be at odds with the rules of treaty interpretation, according to which the text of a treaty is the starting point of the analysis.[213] Martti Koskenniemi identified undifferentiated calls for 'equitable solutions or "balancing" whenever conflicts arise' as a threat to the rule of law.[214] He argued with respect to equitable solutions in disputes involving State sovereignty that:

> recourse to the kind of justice involved in such appreciation can only mean, from the perspective of the Rule of Law, capitulation to arbitrariness or undermining the principle of the subjectivity of value, required in the pursuit of a Rule of Law.[215]

3. Arbitrariness and the lack of a unitary value system

The arbitrariness that Martti Koskenniemi mentions in the preceding passage brings us to the third major concern with respect to proportionality balancing: doubts as to what factors enter the balancing process and what weight ought to be attached to them.[216] This consideration is particularly relevant on the international level, where the alleged lack of a common value system constitutes one of the main arguments put forward against proportionality.[217] On the domestic level, proportionality analysis usually occurs against a strong constitutional background. In this vein, Burke-White and von Staden state that proportionality analysis 'may be an ideal mechanism for judicial balancing', but only '[w]ithin a constitutional framework'.[218] In Chapter 4, I will identify some features of the international legal order that could provide a normative framework for proportionality balancing. These features, as well as their inherent limitations, offer valuable clues as to the applicability of the principle of proportionality in investor–State arbitration. Before entering this debate, however, an analysis of the general transposability of proportionality as a general principle emanating from domestic legal systems to the international level is in order.

---

[212] Jeffrey A. Brauch, 'The Margin of Appreciation and the Jurisprudence of the European Court of Human Rights: Threat to the Rule of Law', *Columbia Journal of European Law* 11 (2005) 113–50, at 149–50; Cohen-Eliya & Porat, 'The Hidden Foreign Law Debate', at 398.

[213] *See* Chapter 4, notes 43–4 and accompanying text.

[214] Martti Koskenniemi, *The Politics of International Law*, European Journal of International Law 1 (1990) 4–32, at 20.

[215] Id., at 16.   [216] Henkin, 'Infallibility under Law', at 470.

[217] Vranes, 'Der Verhältnismäßigkeitsgrundsatz', at 21–2.

[218] William W. Burke-White & Andreas von Staden, 'The Need for Public Law Standards of Review in Investor–State Arbitrations', *in International Investment Law and Comparative Law* (Stephan W. Schill ed., 2010) 689–720, at 717.

III. Transposability of proportionality to the international level

As explained above, identifying a general principle within the meaning of Article 38(1)(c) ICJ Statute involves a two-step process: a comparative analysis of domestic legal systems and an inquiry into whether the principle thus identified is transposable to the international level.[219] We have seen in section I that proportionality is sufficiently prevalent at the domestic level to constitute a general principle. This analysis did not reveal, however, that domestic legal systems apply a free-floating proportionality test whenever individual rights collide with the public interest. Rather, context matters. While limitation clauses frequently trigger a proportionality analysis, restricting fundamental rights guaranteed on their face unconditionally is more complex and controversial. Section II identified three factors that may in certain legal settings weigh against a proportionality analysis: the risk of unwarranted judicial lawmaking; the rule of law; and the risk of arbitrary outcomes as a result of uncertainty as to what rights and interests enter the proportionality analysis. With these principles in mind, we now turn to transposability of proportionality to the international level. In *Barcelona Traction*, Justice Fitzmaurice aptly summarized the rationale of analysing the transposability of a given concept to the international level:

> [C]onditions in the international field are sometimes very different from what they are in the domestic, and . . . rules which this latter's conditions fully justify may be less capable of vindication if strictly applied when transposed onto the international level. Neglect of this precaution may result in an opposite distortion—namely that qualifications or mitigations of the rule, provided for on the internal plane, may fail to be adequately reflected on the international—leading to a resulting situation of paradox, anomaly and injustice.[220]

Regarding the transposability of proportionality to the international level, we do not have to start from scratch. Proportionality is already part of certain areas of international law, in most cases as the result of specific treaty provisions. The mere fact that proportionality is applied in international regimes tells us little about what role proportionality should play in investor–State arbitration. Nevertheless, it indicates that proportionality is, in principle, transposable to the international level—regardless of the relevance of proportionality in specific legal settings in investor–State arbitration (discussed in Chapters 5–8). Against this background, subsection 1 provides an overview of proportionality in certain areas of international law, in particular in the law of the European Union, the ECtHR, and international trade law. The legal settings in which the relevant adjudicatory bodies apply proportionality provide certain clues as to the potential role of this principle in investor–State arbitration. Subsection 2 considers whether a particular

---

[219] *See supra* notes 17–8 and accompanying text.
[220] *Case concerning the Barcelona Traction Light and Power Company Limited* (Belgium v. Spain), Judgment, 5 February 1970, ICJ Reports (1970) 3 (Fitzmaurice, J, concurring) 64, at 66–7.

categorization of proportionality in domestic law—whether as 'meta-constitutional rule', 'methodological tool', or otherwise—has any bearing on its transposability. Final subsection 3 shows that there is ample room for general principles in international dispute resolution—even if the relevant issues turn on specific treaty provisions.

1. Proportionality in several subsystems of international law

Proportionality is part of a significant number of subsystems of international law. It is an integral part of the jurisprudence of the ECJ and the ECtHR. The WTO adjudicatory bodies follow a very similar approach when weighing and balancing the relevant interests at stake. Subsections (a)–(c) will outline the relevant jurisprudence in these three regimes. Subsection (d) briefly comments on the relevance of proportionality in a few additional, select subsystems of international law.

a) *Proportionality and the law of the European Union*

The principle of proportionality is deeply ingrained in the law of the EU, and the ECJ refers to proportionality as a 'general principle'.[221] Some authors even call proportionality a 'constitutional principle' of the EU.[222] The following statement of the ECJ in *Fedesa* illustrates that the proportionality analysis of the ECJ follows the three-step approach introduced in the domestic context:

The Court has consistently held that the principle of proportionality is one of the general principles of Community law. By virtue of that principle, the lawfulness of the prohibition of an economic activity is subject to the condition that the prohibitory measures are appropriate and necessary in order to achieve the objectives legitimately pursued by the legislation in question; when there is a choice between several appropriate measures, recourse must be had to the least onerous, and the disadvantages caused must not be disproportionate to the aims pursued.[223]

The EU Treaty mentions the principle of proportionality on several occasions. Most of these refer to the exercise of EU competencies and regulate the relationship between the EU and its member States.[224] Furthermore, proportionality is crucial when member States or EU organs take regulatory actions that interfere with individual freedoms. Regarding the free movement of goods, Article 36 of the Treaty on the Functioning of the European Union provides that:

---

[221] Case C-331/88, *R v. Minister of Agriculture, Fisheries and Food ex parte Fedesa*, 1990 ECR I-4023, para. 13. For a concise historial overview of the establishment of proportionality in the jurisprudence of the ECJ, *see* Stone Sweet & della Cananea, 'Proportionality, General Principles of Law', at 919–20.

[222] Sionaidh Douglas-Scott, *Constitutional Law of the European Union* (2002), 184.

[223] Case C-331/88, *R v. Minister of Agriculture, Fisheries and Food ex parte Fedesa*, 1990 ECR I-4023, para. 13.

[224] *See, e.g.*, Articles 5(1) and (4), 12(b), and 69 of the EU Treaty. In addition, Protocol No. 2 ('On the Application of the Principles of Subsidiarity and Proportionality') elaborates on proportionality.

[t]he provisions of Articles 34 and 35 shall not preclude prohibitions or restrictions on imports, exports or goods in transit justified on grounds of public morality, public policy or public security; the protection of health and life of humans, animals or plants; the protection of national treasures possessing artistic, historic or archaeological value; or the protection of industrial and commercial property.[225]

In determining whether a measure of a EU member State that restricts the free movement of goods is 'justified' because it advances one of the policy objectives listed in Article 36, the ECJ resorts to the principle of proportionality. Obstacles to the free movement of goods survive judicial scrutiny only if they are proportionate to the goal of the State measure.[226] In *Cassis de Dijon*, the ECJ decided that member States may under certain circumstances interfere with the free movement of goods even if the relevant governmental measure does not serve one of the interests enumerated in Article 36. For such measures to be compatible with EU law, the relevant member State must act out of 'imperative requirements in the general interest',[227] and the State measure in question must be proportionate.[228]

   Proportionality is also part of the fundamental rights jurisprudence of the ECJ. In the absence of a (binding) written catalogue of fundamental rights on the EU level prior to the Lisbon Treaty, the ECJ had held that fundamental rights form 'an integral part of the general principles' of EC law. For the content of these rights, the Court resorted to the 'constitutional traditions common to the member states'.[229] With the entering into force of the Treaty of Lisbon on 1 December 2009, the Charter of Fundamental Rights of the European Union became a binding source of EU primary law.[230] Typically, fundamental rights on the EU level protect individuals against acts of EU organs. But there are also situations in which fundamental rights on the EU level may impose restrictions on the actions of member States, for example when it is for member States to implement EU legislation or executive acts. To be in compliance with EU law, these restrictions have to pass the proportionality test.[231] The principle of proportionality is explicitly mentioned in the general limitation clause of Article 52(1) of the Charter of Fundamental Rights:

Any limitation on the exercise of the rights and freedoms recognised by this Charter must be provided for by law and respect the essence of those rights and freedoms. Subject to the principle of proportionality, limitations may be made only if they are necessary and genuinely meet objectives of general interest recognised by the Union or the need to protect the rights and freedoms of others.

---

[225] The text of Article 36 is largely identical to Article 30 of the former EC Treaty.

[226] *See, e.g.,* Case C-24/00, *Commission v. France*, 2004 ECR I-1277, para. 69.

[227] Case 120/78, *Rewe-Zentral AG v. Bundesmonopolverwaltung für Branntwein*, 1979 ECR 649.

[228] Case C-463/01, *Commission v. Germany*, 2004 ECR I-11706, para. 78 for a State measure aimed at the protection of the environment.

[229] Case 11/70, *Internationale Handelsgesellschaft v. Einfuhr- und Vorratsstelle Getreide*, 1970 ECR 1125, para. 4.

[230] *See* Article 6(1) of the EU Treaty. Before Lisbon, the ECJ also referred to the Charter, but it only did so in order to identify general principles.

[231] *See, e.g.,* Case C-292/97, *Kjell Karlsson and Others*, 2000 ECR I-2737, para. 45.

b) Proportionality in the jurisprudence of the WTO adjudicatory bodies

Another instance in international law where the principle of proportionality (or at least some of its elements) plays a crucial rule is the general exceptions clause in Article XX GATT. The so-called *Chapeau* and the first five exceptions of Article XX read as follows:

Subject to the requirement that such measures are not applied in a manner which would constitute a means of arbitrary or unjustifiable discrimination between countries where the same conditions prevail, or a disguised restriction on international trade, nothing in this Agreement shall be construed to prevent the adoption or enforcement by any contracting party of measures:

(a) *necessary* to protect public morals;

(b) *necessary* to protect human, animal or plant life or health;

(c) *relating* to the importations or exportations of gold or silver;

(d) *necessary* to secure compliance with laws or regulations which are not inconsistent with the provisions of this Agreement, including those relating to customs enforcement, the enforcement of monopolies operated under paragraph 4 of Article II and Article XVII, the protection of patents, trade marks and copyrights, and the prevention of deceptive practices;

(e) *relating to* the products of prison labour...

[...]

(g) *relating to* the conservation of exhaustible natural resources if such measures are made effective in conjunction with restrictions on domestic production or consumption... (emphasis added)

In interpreting this provision, WTO adjudicatory bodies are reluctant to mention the principle of proportionality explicitly. Still, the analysis of the Appellate Body and the WTO panels as to whether a certain measure is 'necessary' in the sense of subparagraph (a), (b), or (d) is remarkably similar to the proportionality test.[232] While the WTO adjudicatory bodies usually do not meticulously follow the three-step proportionality test, their reasoning often covers all of its

---

[232] Trachtman offers a concise summary of concepts that are related or very similar to the principle of proportionality. This overview is relevant beyond the WTO context, which is the focus of Trachtman's analysis. The *simple means–end rationality test* considers whether the adopted measure 'is indeed a rational means to the purported end' (Joel P. Trachtman, 'Trade and...Problems, Cost–Benefit Analysis and Subsidiarity', *European Journal of International Law* 9 (1998) 32–85, at 35). This test corresponds to the '*Wednesbury* reasonableness' test developed in UK case law. The ECtHR has repeatedly decided that such a deferential 'rational basis' standard does not satisfy the standards of the ECHR for fundamental rights review (*see* Stone Sweet & Mathews, 'Proportionality Balancing', at 148–51). The *least restrictive alternative test* asks whether the same goal could have been achieved with a less trade-restrictive means (Trachtman, 'Trade and...Problems', at 35). The purpose of *proportionality stricto sensu* is to ascertain whether the costs are excessive in relation to the benefits. In Trachtman's view, *proportionality stricto sensu* may be regarded as 'cost–benefit analysis with a margin of appreciation, as it does not require that costs be less than the benefits'. Trachtman recognizes that this test may include the assessment of the costs and benefits of alternative measures (id.). *Balancing tests* seek to ascertain whether—balancing all relevant factors—the trade impeding measure is 'acceptable'. Trachtman refers to this test as an 'imprecise cost–benefit analysis' (id., at 36). With the latter concept, Trachtman means a measuring of the regulatory benefits of a certain measure against its overall costs, both trade-related and non-trade-related (id.).

elements.[233] In *Korea Beef,* the Appellate Body first analysed the ordinary meaning of the term 'necessary' in Article XX(d). It found that '"necessary" is not limited to that which is "indispensable" or "of absolute necessity"'. Rather, the term
would lie on a 'continuum' ranging from 'making a contribution to' to 'indispensable'.[234] The Appellate Body added that 'necessary' is 'located significantly
closer to the pole of "indispensable" than to the opposite pole of simply "making
a contribution to."'[235] For measures that are not 'indispensable', the Appellate
Body set out a balancing test which is highly reminiscent of the third step of the
proportionality test: the question whether such measures are 'necessary'

involves in every case a process of weighing and balancing a series of factors which prominently include the contribution made by the compliance measure to the enforcement of
the law or regulation at issue, the importance of the common interests or values protected
by that law or regulation, and the accompanying impact of the law or regulation on
imports or exports.[236]

Part of the Appellate Body's analysis is whether an equally effective but less
infringing means would have been available to achieve the governmental goal.
Typically, the Appellate Body incorporates this least-restrictive means test (which
is equivalent to the second step of a proportionality analysis) into its process of
weighing and balancing. In *Korea Beef,* the Appellate Body stated that:

the weighing and balancing process we have outlined is comprehended in the determination of whether a WTO-consistent alternative measure which the Member concerned
could 'reasonably be expected to employ' is available, or whether a less WTO-inconsistent
measure is 'reasonably available'.[237]

The WTO adjudicatory bodies have confirmed the *Korea Beef* approach in several cases.[238] Particularly noteworthy is the report of the Appellate Body in

---

[233] *But see* the comments below on the more recent *Brazil Tyres* report where the Appellate Body
adhered to the three-step approach (*infra* notes 241–50 and accompanying text).

[234] *Korea—Measures Affecting Imports of Fresh, Chilled and Frozen Beef,* AB-2000-8, Report of
the Appellate Body, WT/DS169/AB/R, WT/DS169/AB/R, 11 December 2000, para. 161.

[235] Id., para. 161. The Appellate Body juxtaposed the meaning of 'necessary' in Article XX(d)
with the more lenient nexus requirement ('relating to') of Article XX(e) and (g). It noted that it was
sufficient for this more lenient standard if there was a '"substantial relationship"', *i.e.,* a close and
genuine relationship of ends and means'. In other words, it is enough if the measure is 'reasonably
related' to the stated goal. (Id., n.104).

[236] Id., para. 164.　　[237] Id., para. 166.

[238] *See, e.g., European Communities—Measures Affecting Asbestos and Asbestos-Containing
Products,* AB-2000-11, Report of the Appellate Body, WT/DS135/AB/R, 12 March 2000, paras.
171–2 and also *United States—Measures Affecting the Cross-Border Supply of Gambling and Betting
Services,* AB-2005-1, Report of the Appellate Body, WT/DS285/AB/R, 7 April 2005, paras. 305–8
where the Appellate Body transferred the 'necessity test' from *Korea Beef* to Article XIV(a) GATS.
The text of this provision is the following: 'Subject to the requirement that such measures are not
applied in a manner which would constitute a means of arbitrary or unjustifiable discrimination
between countries where like conditions prevail, or a disguised restriction on trade in services, nothing in this Agreement shall be construed to prevent the adoption or enforcement by any Member
of measures: (a) *necessary* to protect public morals or to maintain public order' (emphasis added).

Brazil Tyres.[239] In this decision, the Appellate Body at various occasions referred to the 'weighing and balancing' approach in *Korea Beef, US Gambling*, and *EC Asbestos*.[240] The issue was whether a Brazilian import ban on (new) treaded tyres was 'necessary' for the protection of human health and the environment (Article XX(b) GATT). The Appellate Body's analysis mirrors the three-step proportionality test—even though it did not mention the term 'proportionality'. The Appellate Body entitled the first step of its analysis 'Contribution of the Import Ban to the Achievement of Its Objective',[241] and noted that it was for the member State to choose a particular objective and level of protection in furtherance of the values mentioned in Article XX(b).[242] The Appellate Body held that the measure chosen by Brazil 'materially contributed' to the achievement of its goal to reduce the health and environmental risks stemming from the accumulation of waste tyres.[243]

The Appellate Body then proceeded to the second step of its analysis. It approvingly quoted a passage from *US Gambling*, according to which the proposed alternative measure must not only be less trade restrictive but also offer the same level of protection for the State interests at stake.[244] The Appellate Body found that the landfilling, stockpiling, and incineration of waste tyres suggested by the European Communities as alternative measures would not have reached the same level of protection as the import ban because these measures entailed separate environmental and health risks.[245] In a similar vein, the Appellate Body did not consider recycling to be a 'reasonably available alternative' because of its high costs. The import ban therefore passed the least restrictive means test.[246]

In a third step, the Appellate Body reviewed the European Communities' allegation that the Panel had not engaged in an adequate 'weighing and balancing' of the relevant factors as required by Article XX.[247] The Appellate Body stressed that the Panel had considered the protection of human life and health from the threat of dengue fever and malaria (caused by the accumulation of waste tyres) to be 'both vital and important in the highest degree'.[248] It further noted that the Panel described the protection of the environment to be an 'important' value.[249] In sum, the Appellate Body found that the Panel correctly interpreted and applied the necessity requirement in Article XX since its approach involved:

first, the examination of the contribution of the Import Ban to the achievement of its objective against its trade restrictiveness in the light of the interests at stake, and,

---

[239] 'Brazil—Measures Affecting Imports of Retreaded Tyres', AB-2007-4, Report of the Appellate Body, WT/DS332/AB/R, 3 December 2007.
[240] Id., paras. 140–3, 178.   [241] Id., paras. 134–55.   [242] Id., para. 140.
[243] Id., paras. 152, 155.
[244] Id., para. 156 citing *United States—Measures Affecting the Cross-Border Supply of Gambling and Betting Services*, AB-2005-1, Report of the Appellate Body, WT/DS285/AB/R, 7 April 2005, para 308.
[245] *Brazi— Measures Affecting Imports of Retreaded Tyres*, AB-2007-4, Report of the Appellate Body, WT/DS332/AB/R, 3 December 2007, paras. 162–5, 173–5.
[246] Id., para. 166, 175.   [247] Id., paras. 176–82.   [248] Id., para. 179.   [249] Id.

secondly, the comparison of the possible alternatives, including associated risks, with the Import Ban.[250]

In *China—Publications and Audiovisual Products*,[251] the Appellate Body had to decide on the public morals exception in Article XX(a) GATT. Its analysis as to whether China's measures were 'necessary to protect public morals' is reminiscent of the proportionality test. The State measure at issue most relevant for our purposes was a State plan regulating the total number and structure of companies importing publications. The Appellate Body found that the Panel erred when it found that China satisfied its burden of proof regarding the 'material contribution' of this measure to the protection of public morals.[252] Furthermore, the Appellate Body analysed whether China could have employed a less restrictive means to protect its public morals.[253] The Appellate Body recalled that the theoretical existence of an alternative means is not sufficient. Rather, the alternative measure must be 'reasonably available', which is not the case if it imposes an 'undue burden' on the State. Such an undue burden may stem from 'prohibitive costs or substantial technical difficulties'.[254] The Appellate Body described the relevant burden of proof as follows:

This burden does not imply that the responding party must take the initiative to demonstrate that there are no reasonably available alternatives that would achieve its objectives. When, however, the complaining party identifies an alternative measure that, in its view, the responding party should have taken, the responding party will be required to demonstrate why its challenged measure nevertheless remains 'necessary' in the light of that alternative or, in other words, why the proposed alternative is not a genuine alternative or is not 'reasonably available'. If a responding party demonstrates that the alternative is not 'reasonably available', in the light of the interests or values being pursued and the party's desired level of protection, it follows that the challenged measure must be 'necessary'.[255]

The US had suggested that China could have protected its public morals as effectively by putting content review under the sole responsibility of the Chinese government.[256] The Appellate Body found that China did not provide sufficient evidence to establish that the alternative means suggested by the US would impose

---

[250] Id., para. 182.
[251] *China—Measures Affecting Trading Rights and Distribution Services for Certain Publications and Audiovisual Entertainment Products*, AB-2009-3, Report of the Appellate Body, WT/DS363/AB/R, 21 December 2009.
[252] Id., paras. 297–299.   [253] Id., paras. 312–335.
[254] Id., para. 318 referring to *United States—Measures Affecting the Cross-Border Supply of Gambling and Betting Services*, AB-2005-1, Report of the Appellate Body, WT/DS285/AB/R, 7 April 2005, para. 308.
[255] *China—Measures Affecting Trading Rights and Distribution Services for Certain Publications and Audiovisual Entertainment Products*, AB-2009-3, Report of the Appellate Body, WT/DS363/AB/R, 21 December 2009, para. 319 referring to *United States—Measures Affecting the Cross-Border Supply of Gambling and Betting Services*, AB-2005-1, Report of the Appellate Body, WT/DS285/AB/R, 7 April 2005, paras. 309–11.
[256] *China—Measures Affecting Trading Rights and Distribution Services for Certain Publications and Audiovisual Entertainment Products*, AB-2009-3, Report of the Appellate Body, WT/DS363/AB/R, 21 December 2009, para. 312.

an undue financial, administrative, or technical burden on China.[257] Anticipating possible concerns regarding state sovereignty, the Appellate Body clarified that its approach did not unduly restrict China's regulatory freedom. The Appellate Body stated that its finding

> does not mean that having the Chinese Government assume sole responsibility for conducting content review is the *only* alternative available to China, nor that China *must* adopt such a scheme. It does mean that China has not successfully justified under Article XX(a) of the GATT 1994 the provisions and requirements found to be inconsistent with China's trading rights commitments under its Accession Protocol and Working Party Report. It follows, therefore, that China is under an obligation to bring those measures into conformity with its obligations under the covered agreements, including its trading rights commitments. Like all WTO Members, China retains the prerogative to select its preferred method of implementing the rulings and recommendations of the DSB for measures found to be inconsistent with its obligations under the covered agreements.[258]

c) Proportionality in the jurisprudence of the ECtHR

The principle of proportionality is well established in the jurisprudence of the ECtHR. This becomes particularly clear in the context of interferences with the right to respect for private and family life (Article 8 ECHR); the freedom of thought, conscience and religion (Article 9); the freedom of expression (Article 10); and the freedom of assembly and association (Article 11). The second paragraphs of these provisions contain limitation clauses that all follow the same pattern. They stipulate that the right or freedom in question may be restricted only if the relevant measures 'are prescribed by law and are *necessary* [emphasis added] in a democratic society in the interests of...or for the protection of'[259] certain enumerated public purposes, e.g. 'public safety' or 'national security'.[260]

In *Handyside*, the ECtHR decided that the expression 'necessary'—despite not being synonymous with 'indispensable'—does not provide the same degree of flexibility for national decision makers as the adjectives 'admissible', 'ordinary', 'useful', or 'reasonable' used in other ECHR provisions.[261] The ECtHR stated that any interference with the right to freedom of expression (Article 10 ECHR) 'must be proportionate to the legitimate aim pursued'.[262] Still, the Court did not enter into an in-depth proportionality analysis. Rather, it relied on the 'national margin of appreciation' doctrine to exclude a violation of Article 10.[263] In the following decades, the ECtHR refined its jurisprudence on limitation clauses. Stone Sweet and Mathews state that the Court uses the three-step 'German-style'

---

[257] Id., paras. 327–34.   [258] Id., para. 335 (emphasis in the original).
[259] The only paragraph which deviates slightly from this formulation is Article 8(2), which asks whether the measure is 'in accordance with the law and is necessary in a democratic society'.
[260] For full texts of the limitation clauses, *see supra* note 200.
[261] *Handyside v. United Kingdom*, ECtHR, A 24, Judgment, 7 December 1976, para. 48.
[262] Id., para. 49.
[263] Id., para. 57. For further comments on this doctrine, *see* Chapter 7, subsection IV.2.

proportionality analysis in its more recent jurisprudence.[264] Jonas Christoffersen, in contrast, argues that the ECtHR rejects the least restrictive means test as a separate step of the analysis.[265]

Regardless of such doctrinal subtleties, it is uncontroversial that the ECtHR opted against a mere 'rational basis' or 'reasonableness' test (such as the UK *Wednesbury* standard) as the appropriate level of review for interferences with fundamental rights.[266] Instead, the Court repeatedly held that a State measure must be 'proportionate' to the aim pursued.[267] The judgment of the ECtHR in the *Stankov* case contains a particularly illustrative explanation of the applicable level of scrutiny for State measures interfering with the freedom of assembly (Article 11). The Court held that:

[t]he expression 'necessary in a democratic society' implies that the interference corresponds to a 'pressing social need' and, in particular, that it is proportionate to the legitimate aim pursued. The Contracting States have a certain margin of appreciation in assessing whether such a need exists, but it goes hand in hand with European supervision, embracing both the legislation and the decisions applying it, even those given by an independent court.... When the Court carries out its scrutiny, its task is not to substitute its own view for that of the relevant authorities...This does not mean that it has to confine itself to ascertaining whether the respondent State exercised its discretion reasonably, carefully and in good faith; [the Court] must...determine, after having established that [the respondent State] pursued a 'legitimate aim', whether it was proportionate to that aim and whether the reasons adduced by the national authorities to justify it are 'relevant and sufficient'.[268]

The ECtHR does not explicitly break down its analysis into the three steps of the proportionality test.[269] In most cases, the ECtHR decides the issue of whether a State measure was 'necessary in a democratic society' after a balancing process equivalent to the third stage of the three-step proportionality analysis.[270] Often,

---

[264] *See, e.g.,* Stone Sweet & Mathews, 'Proportionality Balancing', at 148; Dirk Ehlers, 'Die Europäische Menschenrechtskonvention: Allgemeine Lehren der EMRK', *in Europäische Grundrechte und Grundfreiheiten* (Dirk Ehlers ed., 2009) 25–80, para. 65.

[265] Christoffersen, *Fair Balance*, at 135.

[266] For a historical survey on the Court's rejection of the *Wednesbury* standard, *see* Stone Sweet & Mathews, 'Proportionality Balancing', at 148–52. For the differences between proportionality and the *Wednesbury* standard, *see* Richard Clayton & Hugh Tomlinson, *The Law of Human Rights* Vol. I (2008), paras 6.92–6.93.

[267] *Dudgeon v. United Kingdom*, ECtHR, A 45, Judgment (Merits), 22 October 1981, para. 53; *Leyla Şahin v. Turkey*, ECtHR, Application no. 44774/98, Judgment, 10 November 2005, para. 117. *Tuomela and Others v. Finland*, ECtHR, Application no. 24711/04, Judgment, 6 April 2010, para. 44; *AD & OD v. United Kingdom*, ECtHR, Application no. 28680/06, Judgment, 16 March 2010, para. 91.

[268] *Stankov and the United Macedonian Organisation Ilinden v. Bulgaria*, ECtHR, Applications nos. 29221/95 and 29225/95, Judgment, 2 October 2001, para. 87.

[269] The ECtHR tends to examine the question of whether a State measure was 'necessary in a democratic society' in two steps: it first examines whether there was a 'pressing social need' for the measure in question, and then analyses whether the interference was 'proportionate to the legitimate aim pursued' (*see, e.g., Open Door and Dublin Well Woman v. Ireland*, ECtHR, A 332, Judgment (Merits and Just Satisfaction), 20 November 1995, para. 70).

[270] Ehlers, 'Die Europäische Menschenrechtskonvention', para. 65.

the Court does not address the question of whether a less infringing means would have been available.[271] In various cases, however, the ECtHR has included the question of whether the State had chosen the least restrictive means in its analysis. In the *Barthold* case, for example, the ECtHR found that a Court injunction based on professional rules limiting advertising and publicity for veterinarians 'went further than the requirements of the legitimate aim pursued', and hence violated the veterinarian's freedom of expression (Article 10 ECHR).[272] In the *Campbell* case, the ECtHR had to decide whether the reading of potentially every letter from a prisoner to his lawyer or vice versa violates the right to respect for private and family life (Article 8 ECHR). The Court recognized that a certain measure of control over prisoners' correspondence was necessary for the prevention of 'disorder or crime' as a legitimate aim under Article 8(2).[273] The Court held, however, that it would have been sufficient to allow for the reading of a letter only if certain facts give rise to a 'reasonable cause' to believe that its content jeopardizes prison security or the safety of others.[274]

The case *Informationsverein Lentia and Others v. Austria* provides a particularly clear example of the relevance of the least restrictive means test in the jurisprudence of the ECtHR. The Court did not deny that the monopoly for the State-owned Austrian broadcasting corporation was capable of contributing to the legitimate aim of guaranteeing high-quality and balanced programming.[275] But the Court held that there existed 'equivalent less restrictive' means to achieve this goal. The Court listed the possibility of issuing licences that are conditioned on a variety of contents and the participation of private actors in the broadcasting corporation as possible alternatives.[276] Finally, the Court found the public monopoly to be 'disproportionate' and in violation of Article 10 ECHR.[277]

In *Ahmed and Others v. United Kingdom*, the Court put the question of whether 'the aim of the legislature in enacting the Regulations was pursued with minimum impairment of the applicants' rights under Article 10'[278] at the centre of its proportionality analysis. It stressed that the relevant regulation limiting the political comments of government officers covered a smaller number of officers than an expert report suggested that it should. The Court further noted that the regulation did not intend to suppress all political comments but only some of a

---

[271] Christoph Grabenwarter & Thilo Marauhn, 'Grundrechtseingriff und –schranken', *in EMRK/GG—Konkordanzkommentar* (Rainer Grote & Thilo Marauhn eds., 2006) 332–77, para. 44.

[272] *Barthold v. Germany*, ECtHR, A 90, Judgment (Merits), 25 March 1985, para. 58. The Court discussed this issue in the context of whether the injunction achieved 'a fair balance between the two interests' at stake (id.).

[273] *Campbell v. United Kingdom*, ECtHR, A 233, Judgment (Merits and Just Satisfaction), 25 March 1992, paras. 39–41, 45.

[274] Id., para. 48.

[275] *Informationsverein Lentia and Others v. Austria*, ECtHR, A 276, Judgment (Merits and Just Satisfaction), 24 November 1993, paras. 33, 36.

[276] Id., para. 39.   [277] Id., para. 43.

[278] *Ahmed and Others v. the United Kingdom*, ECtHR, Reports 1998-VI, Judgment (Merits and Just Satisfaction), 2 September 1998, para. 63.

partisan nature, and that it did not limit the right of the applicants to join a political party or to generally engage in political activities.[279] Hence, the Court found
the regulation in question to be a proportionate interference with the applicants'
freedom of expression.[280]

In *AD & OD v. United Kingdom*, the British authorities placed the second
applicant, the first applicant's son, with foster parents due to allegations of child
abuse. The placement with foster parents was ordered after a 12-week stay of the
two applicants in a family resource center where the authorities failed to make a
proper risk assessment. Under the specific circumstances of the case, the Court
found that it 'was not persuaded that less intrusive measures' than placing the
child with foster parents had not been available. The Court mentioned the possibility of placing the whole family in an assessment center or sending the child
to relatives as less-infringing available alternatives.[281] Consequently, the Court
found the relevant State measure to be disproportionate and in violation of the
applicants' right to respect for their family life (Article 8 ECHR).[282]

Another area in which the ECtHR makes extensive use of the principle of
proportionality is the right to property protected under Article 1 of the First
Additional Protocol to the ECHR. The relevant jurisprudence will be discussed
at length in the context of its transferability to the question of whether a certain
State measure constitutes an indirect expropriation under IIAs.[283] It suffices at
this point to anticipate some elements of this later analysis: The ECtHR scrutinizes interferences with Article 1 of the First Additional Protocol along the lines
of the principle of proportionality. This is true regardless of whether the measure
in question constitutes an expropriation within the meaning of the second sentence of Article 1(1),[284] a measure affecting the 'use of property' in the sense of
Article 1(2),[285] or a general interference with the peaceful enjoyment of property
under the first sentence of Article 1(1).[286]

In sum, the principle of proportionality is deeply embedded in the jurisprudence of the ECtHR. Contrary to the German Constitutional Court or the ECJ,
the ECtHR does not find it necessary to establish the absence of a less infringing means before entering into the balancing process. The proportionality analysis of the ECtHR is, therefore, closer to the 'horizontal approach'[287] of the
Constitutional Court of South Africa than it is to the strict three-step approach
of the German Constitutional Court. Still, the question whether a less restrictive
means would have been available in a particular situation is an important factor
in the proportionality analysis of the ECtHR.

---

[279] Id., para. 63.   [280] Id., para. 65.
[281] *See AD & OD v. United Kingdom*, ECtHR, Application no. 28680/06, Judgment, 16 March
2010, para. 89.
[282] Id., paras. 91–2.   [283] *See* Chapter 5, section IV.   [284] *See infra* at 146–8.
[285] *See infra* at 148–50.   [286] *See infra* at 150–1.   [287] *See supra* note 93.

d) The principle of proportionality in other areas of international law

The principle of proportionality is also well established in certain areas of international law beyond the EU, WTO, and ECHR context. In the realm of humanitarian international law, for example, Article 51(5)(b) of the First Additional Protocol to the Geneva Convention states that an attack is indiscriminate and hence prohibited if it:

> may be expected to cause incidental loss of civilian life, injury to civilians, damage to civilian objects, or a combination thereof, which would be excessive in relation to the concrete and direct military advantage anticipated.

Most scholars consider this provision for the protection of civilians during armed conflicts to constitute a rule of customary international law.[288] While Article 51(5)(b) does not explicitly refer to the principle of proportionality, it requires the balancing of the military advantage expected from an attack against the probable level of civilian casualties.[289] This practice resembles the third step of the proportionality analysis introduced above.[290]

In the realm of *ius ad bellum*, the principle of proportionality limits a State's right of self-defence under Article 51 of the UN Charter.[291] Article 51 of the UN Charter does not explicitly mention such a limitation. However, Article 51 refers to the 'inherent right' of self-defence, and the ICJ held in the *Nicaragua* case that it is 'a rule well established in customary international law' that self-defence 'warrant[s] only measures which are proportional to the armed attack and necessary to respond to it'.[292]

Another area of law in which the ICJ referred to proportionality is the law of the sea. In the *Continental Shelf* case, the ICJ found that maritime delimitation according to equitable principles involves a

> reasonable degree of proportionality... between the extent of the continental shelf areas appertaining to the coastal State and the length of its Coast measured in the general direction of the coastline, account being taken for this purpose of the effects, actual or prospective, of any other continental shelf delimitations between adjacent States in the same region.[293]

---

[288] *See, e.g.*, Judith Gail Gardam, *Necessity, Proportionality and the Use of Force by States* (2004), at 15.

[289] Id., at 3.

[290] The terms 'superfluous injury' or 'unnecessary suffering' in the realm of international humanitarian law for the protection of combatants (*see* id., at 15), on the other hand, are more reminiscent of the second stage of the proportionality analysis, i.e. the least restrictive means test.

[291] Albrecht Randelzhofer, 'Article 51', *in The Charter of the United Nations—a Commentary* (Bruno Simma, et al. eds., 2002) 788–806, para. 42. For a discussion of the content of the principle of proportionality in this respect, *see* Gardam, *Necessity*, at 155–87.

[292] *Case concerning Military and Paramilitary Activities in and against Nicaragua* (Nicaragua v. United States of America), Judgment, Merits, 27 June 1986, ICJ Reports 1986, 4, para. 176.

[293] *North Sea Continental Shelf* (Germany v. Denmark; Germany v. Netherlands), Judgment, 20 February 1969, ICJ Reports 1969, 3, para. 101.

Furthermore, proportionality is relevant for the question of whether counter-measures are admissible.[294] Article 51 of the ASR is entitled 'Proportionality' and states that:

[c]ountermeasures must be commensurate with the injury suffered, taking into account the gravity of the internationally wrongful act and the rights in question.

The ILC explained that the proportionality analysis under Article 51 ASR does not only include a 'quantitative' assessment of the injury 'but also "qualitative" factors such as the importance of the interest protected by the rule infringed and the seriousness of the breach'.[295] Article 49(1) ASR clarifies that the only permissible purpose of countermeasures is to induce the other State to comply with its international obligation. Article 49(2) limits the duration of countermeasures to the period of non-compliance of the other State with its international obligation.[296] The ILC stated that a measure that was required to induce the responsible State to comply with its obligation (Article 49) may still be found to be disproportionate under Article 51.[297] This differentiation suggests that the function of Article 49 is comparable to the first two steps of the three-step proportionality analysis introduced above (*suitability* and *least restrictive means test*), while Article 51 is reminiscent of the process of weighing and balancing characteristic for the third step of this analysis (*proportionality in the strict sense*).

2. Proportionality as a 'principle'

To be part of international law as a matter of Article 38(1)(c) ICJ Statute, proportionality needs to be a 'general *principle* of law'. There is significant academic discussion on the proper categorization of proportionality. Some consider proportionality to be a 'meta-constitutional *rule*'.[298] Others regard proportionality as a tool of 'neutral, rational decision-making',[299] which follows from the very

---

[294] For an in-depth analysis, *see* Elena Katselli Proukaki, *The Problem of Enforcement in International Law—Coutermeasures, the Non-Injured State and the Idea of International Community* (2010), at 260–79.

[295] ILC, 'Articles on Responsibility of States for Internationally Wrongful Acts with Commentaries', *Yearbook of the International Law Commission*, Vol. II, 20–143 (2001), Article 51, para. 6.

[296] Article 49 reads as follows:

Object and limits of countermeasures
1. An injured State may only take countermeasures against a State which is responsible for an internationally wrongful act in order to induce that State to comply with its obligations under part two.
2. Countermeasures are limited to the non-performance for the time being of international obligations of the State taking the measures towards the responsible State.
3. Countermeasures shall, as far as possible, be taken in such a way as to permit the resumption of performance of the obligations in question.

[297] ILC, *Commentaries on State Responsibility*, Article 51, para. 7.

[298] Stone Sweet & Mathews, 'Proportionality Balancing', at 95 (emphasis added).

[299] Bomhoff, 'Balancing, the Global and the Local', at 574.

characterization of principles as optimization requirements.[300] Aharon Barak calls proportionality a 'legal construction' and a 'methodological tool'.[301] While some seem to consider proportionality to be a *'principle'*,[302] Barak states that '[p]roportionality is not an inherent part of the idea of a principle', '[i]t is external to it'.[303] All of these different views build on or relate to the rules/principles dichotomy developed by Dworkin and Alexy.[304]

Given the complexity of this debate, it is fortunate that we do not have to take sides here. Barak is right when he states that '[a]ny legal system wishing to adopt proportionality...must provide a legal foundation for such an adoption'.[305] In the domestic context, Barak identified four 'legal sources' from which proportionality may be derived as a 'constitutional concept': the very notion of 'democracy', the 'rule of law', the 'conflict between legal principles', and 'constitutional interpretation'. Each of these four sources may be a valid foundation for proportionality at the domestic level under certain circumstances.[306] In the absence of a specific treaty provision (or an applicable rule of custom), the 'legal foundation' for proportionality in international law is Article 38(1)(c) ICJ Statute. For proportionality to be a general principle within the meaning of this provision, it is necessary that proportionality is sufficiently prevalent in domestic legal systems and that it is transposable to the international level. The way in which proportionality has become a 'constitutional concept' of domestic legal systems and why and in what form it is part of them does not matter for the purposes of Article 38(1)(c) ICJ Statute.[307]

3. Why general principles if there is a treaty?

Some might ask why general principles such as proportionality should have any role to play in the context of investor–State arbitrations that deal with alleged breaches of specific treaty provision. To recall, Article 38(1) ICJ Statute lists three sources of international law, starting with treaties, then turning to custom, and concluding with general principles. Some factors suggest a certain hierarchy

---

[300] Alexy, *Theorie der Grundrechte*, at 100.   [301] Barak, *Proportionality*, at 131.

[302] *See, arguably,* Andenas & Zleptnig, 'Proportionality: WTO Law', at 378.

[303] Barak, *Proportionality*, at 241.   [304] *See supra* notes 54–72 and accompanying text.

[305] *Supra* note 2 and accompanying text.

[306] Barak, *Proportionality*, at 240 (and 213–39).

[307] Pellet states that only 'unwritten legal norms of wide-ranging character' fall under Article 38(1)(c) of the ICJ Staute (Pellet, 'Article 38', para. 254). While proportionality seems to fit these criteria, there is no reason to exclude specific and written rules from the scope of Article 38(1)(c). In this vein, Judge Simma analysed both common law jurisprudence and written domestic rules such as section 831 of the German Civil Code to identify 'joint and several liability' as a general principle of law (*Case concerning Oil Platforms* (Iran v. United States of America), Judgment, 6 November 2003, ICJ Reports 2003, 161 (Simma, J, partly dissenting), at 354–7). For a compilation of instances in which ICSID tribunals have referred to general principles such as 'prohibition of corruption', 'unjust enrichment', and 'the duty to mitigate damages'—which are written in some jurisdictions and unwritten in others—*see* Schreuer, et al., *The ICISD Convention—a Commentary*, Article 42, para. 180).

among these sources, with international treaties at the top and general principles at the bottom. These considerations include the order in which the three sources are listed in Article 38(1), the allegedly non-consensual character of general principles,[308] and the view that general principles of law would (merely) be meant to prevent a *non-liquet*.[309] The orthodox and better view, however, is that none of the three source listed in Article 38(1) enjoys preeminence over the others. Rather, the structure of Article 38(1) reflects a certain 'order of consideration' based on the *lex specialis* principle.[310] Except for the narrow notion of *jus cogens* norms, no rule or principle in international law—whether it is derived from treaty, custom, or a general principle—is non-derogable. It is, therefore, only logical to assume that a treaty in a particular area of international law supersedes certain rules of customary international law or general principles in the same field. Moreover, there is no reason to deviate from custom if State practice accompanied by *opinio juris* demonstrates that States want to regulate certain issues on the international level differently from similar issues in the domestic realm.

Two functions of general principle that are of particular relevance for our purposes follow from this account. First, if a treaty or customary rule does not regulate an issue that is crucial for deciding a case, general principles may fill the lacunae. In *Barcelona Traction*, for example, the ICJ held with respect to the relationship between corporations and their shareholders that:

[i]f the Court were to decide the case in disregard of relevant institutions of municipal law it would, without justification, invite serious legal difficulties. It would lose touch with reality, for there are no corresponding institutions of international law to which the Court could resort...It is to rules generally accepted by municipal legal systems which recognize the limited company...and not to the municipal law of a particular State, that international law refers.[311]

Second, general principles provide guidance for the meaning of treaty stipulations that are textually open to different interpretations.[312] Of particular relevance in this context is Article 31(3)(c) VCLT, which states that 'any relevant rules of international law applicable in the relations between the parties' should be 'taken into account' in the interpretation of a treaty. General principles within the meaning of Article 38(1)(c) ICJ Statute can also qualify as such 'relevant rules of international law'.[313] As we will see below, it is exactly through the interpretation of

---

[308] For a discussion of this issue, *see, e.g.,* Elias & Lim, '"General Principles of Law"', at 27–8.

[309] *See* Mosler, 'General Principles of Law', at 516.

[310] Brownlie, *Public International Law*, at 5; Pellet, 'Article 38', para. 277; Mosler, 'General Principles of Law', at 518; Simma & Verdross, *Universelles Völkerrecht*, paras. 607–8; Alfred Verdross, *Die Quellen des universellen Völkerrechts* (1973), at 129–30.

[311] *Case concerning the Barcelona Traction Light and Power Company Limited* (Belgium v. Spain), Judgment, 5 February 1970, ICJ Reports (1970) 3, at 37, para. 50.

[312] Simma & Verdross, *Universelles Völkerrecht*, para. 610; Kolb, 'Principles as Sources of International Law', at 32–3.

[313] *See* Chapter 4, notes 87–8.

specific treaty provisions according to Article 31 VCLT that proportionality may assume a key role in investor–State arbitration.

IV. Conclusion

Proportionality is part of many constitutional systems, both in the common law and in the civil law worlds. Of the domestic jurisdictions analysed in this chapter, Germany, Canada, South Africa, and Israel are particularly committed to the principle of proportionality. Nevertheless, even the courts in these jurisdictions do not apply a proportionality test whenever individual rights collide with the public interest. Rather, the relevant courts follow a more nuanced approach. If a fundamental right is subject to a general or specific limitation clause, proportionality resolves conflicts between the relevant rights and interests at stake. If the text of the constitution guarantees a fundamental right unconditionally, restricting it by way of a proportionality analysis is more complicated. The German Constitutional Court limits such rights only for the sake of rights or interests protected by the constitution. Public interest considerations not anchored in the constitution cannot trump rights that the text of the constitution guarantees unconditionally. The unity of the value order provided by the constitution plays a particularly important role in this context.

Contrary to its peers, the US Supreme Court considers proportionality irrelevant for fundamental rights jurisprudence. The lack of general or specific limitation clauses in the relevant provisions of the US Constitution may be one reason for this practice. Still, the Court weighs and balances rights and interests in several normative settings, and its jurisprudence regularly reflects certain components of proportionality. In this vein, the analysis in section I demonstrated that the jurisprudence of the US Supreme Court does not bar proportionality from being a general principle within the meaning of Article 38(1)(c) ICJ Statute. Moreover, the jurisprudence of several international courts and tribunals analysed in this chapter illustrated that proportionality is—in principle—transposable to the international level. We have also seen that legal concepts such a proportionality may qualify as general principles under Article 38(1)(c) ICJ Statute regardless of whether they constitute rules, principles, or something different on the domestic level. Furthermore, a brief inquiry into the relationship between general principles and other sources of international law has illustrated that general principles may play a meaningful role in the process of treaty interpretation.

That said, categorizing proportionality as a general principle of law does not tell us when arbitrators or other international adjudicatory bodies should apply proportionality to resolve conflicts between different rights and interests. This chapter has identified three factors arbitrators should bear in mind before engaging in a proportionality analysis: (1) the danger of unwarranted judicial lawmaking; (2) the rule of law; and (3) the availability of a value system that guides the proportionality analysis and prevents arbitrary outcomes. Regarding the last point, constitutions usually provide the relevant value systems on the domestic level. International law does not offer a unitary value system equivalent to domestic constitutions. Still, several elements in international law may provide guidance in a proportionality analysis, and the next chapter discusses a gateway that may bring them into the realm of investor–State arbitration: the concept of systemic integration.

4

Proportionality and the Concept
of Systemic Integration

As demonstrated in the preceding chapter, proportionality analysis on the domestic level usually occurs within a strong constitutional framework or an objective order of values.[1] The German Constitutional Court stressed in *Mephisto* that it must resolve conflicts between fundamental rights 'according to the value order established in the Basic Law and the unity of its fundamental system of values'.[2] This constitutional value order is of overwhelming importance for interferences with those rights or freedoms that are guaranteed unconditionally by the text of the Constitution. The German Constitutional Court held in the *Religious Oath* case that limits to the right of religious freedom:

> ...may be drawn only by the Constitution itself; that is according to the directives of the constitutional value order and the unity of this fundamental value system.[3]

As explained above, for a domestic legal concept to be applicable in international law as a matter of Article 38(1)(c) ICJ Statute it needs to be transposable to the international level.[4] In this vein, the transfer of a constitutional law concept requires an analysis of whether conditions on the international level are sufficiently similar to those in the domestic sphere.[5] Regarding proportionality, the lack of a unitary value system at the international level is one of the main arguments against the application of this principle in international law.[6]

To be noted at the outset, the lack of an overarching value system is of minor concern if the relevant international law provision identifies the factors and interests that are to be considered in the proportionality analysis. Article 51(5)(b) of

---

[1] *See, e.g.,* Chapter 3, notes 50–2 & 69–72 and accompanying text. In this vein, Barak emphasizes the importance of the 'entire *value structure* of the particular legal system' for proportionality balancing (Barak, *Proportionality*, at 349, emphasis added). Burke-White and von Staden warn that proportionality analysis 'may be an ideal mechanism for judicial balancing', but only '[w]ithin a constitutional framework' (Burke-White & von Staden, 'The Need for Public Law Standards of Review', at 717).

[2] *See* Chapter 3, note 50.   [3] *See* Chapter 3, note 51.

[4] *See* Chapter 3, note 18 and accompanying text.

[5] *See* Chapter 3, note 220 and accompanying text.

[6] *See* Chapter 3, note 217 and accompanying text.

the First Additional Protocol to the Geneva Convention, for example, provides that an attack is indiscriminate and hence prohibited if it:

may be expected to cause incidental loss of civilian life, injury to civilians, damage to civilian objects, or a combination thereof, which would be excessive in relation to the concrete and direct military advantage anticipated.[7]

Applying this rule will often involve a complex factual analysis, but it is clear what values and interests are to be weighed against each other: civilian life, physical integrity, and property on the one hand, against military advantage on the other. Limitation clauses in the ECHR are similarly prescriptive about the values and interests that enter the analysis, and the ECtHR has no difficulty in resorting to a proportionality analysis.[8] Article 8, for example, provides that there shall be no interference

[with the] right to respect for private and family life…except such as is in accordance with the law and is necessary in a democratic society in the interests of national security, public safety or the economic well-being of the country, for the prevention of disorder or crime, for the protection of health or morals, or for the protection of the rights and freedoms of others.[9]

In the WTO context, adjudicatory bodies balance different interests and values in the context of Article XX GATT,[10] and the text of this provision lists the relevant values for whose sake States may impose certain restrictions on free trade.

In international investment law, the picture is less clear. Scholars have suggested that proportionality should play a role in the context of a variety of different IIA provisions.[11] The relevant provisions do not explicitly call for a proportionality analysis. Moreover, in some of these legal settings, the text of the relevant provision does not provide any guidance as to what factors and interests ought to be weighed against each other. Here, one may legitimately ask whether international law is sufficiently 'constitutionalized' to warrant the application of proportionality as a legal principle emanating from constitutional law. The debate on the 'constitutionalization of international law' has both an *institutional* and a *substantive* dimension. Regarding the institutional level, Bardo Fassbender identified the UN Charter as the constitution of the international community.[12] Other authors have analysed certain subsystems of international law through the constitutional prism. Ernst-Ulrich Petersmann argued for a constitutional perception of the WTO.[13]

---

[7] On this provision, *see* Chapter 3, notes 288–90 and accompanying text.
[8] *See* Chapter 3, notes 260–86 and accompanying text.   [9] Chapter 3, note 260.
[10] *See* Chapter 3, notes 232–50 and accompanying text.   [11] *See* Chapter 3, note 1.
[12] Bardo Fassbender, 'The United Nations Charter as the Constitution of the International Community', at 77–115; 170–1; Fassbender, 'Rediscovering a Forgotten Constitution—Notes on the Place of the UN Charter in the International Legal Order', *in Ruling the World? Constitutionalism, International Law, and Global Governance* (Jeffrey L. Dunoff & Joel P. Trachtman eds., 2009) 133–47, at 134, 147.
[13] Ernst-Ulrich Petersmann, 'Human Rights, Constitutionalism and the World Trade Organization: Challenges for World Trade Organization Jurisprudence and Civil Society', *Leiden Journal of International Law* 19 (2006) 633–67, at 643–6.

In a similar vein, Peter Behrens observed a constitutionalization of international investment protection.[14] One can even add more facets to the constitutionalization debate by focusing on the interaction between constitutional orders on the national, regional, and global levels.[15] Another perspective to the debate is gained by focusing on constitutional constraints for international organizations.[16]

For the purposes of assessing the role of proportionality in investor–State arbitration, the *substantive* dimension of the constitutionalization debate provides certain insights. Proportionality involves the weighing of rights and interests, which requires a certain *substantive* value system—provided either by the applicable legal instrument or the relevant legal system as a whole. In this context, the principle of systemic integration as reflected in Article 31(3)(c) VCLT becomes relevant. Some authors have explicitly referred to Article 31(3)(c) as a 'constitutional norm' of the international legal order.[17] Others might wonder why a provision on treaty interpretation should deserve such a status. This chapter will demonstrate that it is precisely its integration into the law of treaties which makes Article 31(3)(c) such a valuable tool, and which at the same time delineates the limits of its constitutional potential. To this end, section I provides an overview of the rules of treaty interpretation in international law and some jurisprudence related to the concept of systemic integration. Section II will clarify the relationship between Article 31(3)(c) and other means of treaty interpretation. Section III turns to the content and scope of the concept of systemic integration. It seeks to shed light on the role Article 31(3)(c) may play in investor–State arbitration and how this provision may justify and guide the application of the principle of proportionality. Section IV concludes this chapter.

I. Article 31 VCLT and systemic integration: a short overview

The ILC described systemic integration reflected in Article 31(3)(c) VCLT as the interpretation of treaty provisions 'by reference to their normative environment

---

[14] Peter Behrens, 'Towards the Constitutionalization of International Investment Protection', *Archiv des Völkerrechts* 45 (2007) 153–97.

[15] *See, e.g.,* Mattias Kumm, 'The Cosmopolitan Turn in Constitutionalism', *in Ruling the World?* (Dunoff & Trachtman eds., 2009) 258–324, at 272–310 and Christian Walter, 'Constitutionalizing (Inter)national Governance—Possibilities for and Limits to the Development of an International Constitutional Law', *German Yearbook of International Law* 44 (2001) 170–201. Walter explicitly rejects the notion of '*a* constitution' (Id., at 173) (emphasis in the original).

[16] Andrew Clapham, *Human Rights Obligations of Non-State Actors* (2006), at 109–194; Anne Peters, 'Membership in the Global Constitutional Community', *in The Constitutionalization of International Law* (Jan Klabbers, et al. eds., 2009) 153–262 at 210–19; *see also* the remarks in Stephen Gardbaum, 'Human Rights and International Constitutionalism', *in Ruling the World? Constitutionalism, International Law, and Global Governance* (Dunoff & Trachtman eds., 2009) 233–57, at 242–3.

[17] Campbell McLachlan, 'The Principle of Systemic Integration and Article 31(3)(c) of the Vienna Convention', *International and Comparative Law Quarterly* 54 (2005) 279–320, at 280; van Aaken, 'Defragmentation of Public International Law', at 497.

("system")'.[18] This section provides a quick introduction to the concept of systemic integration, and outlines some relevant case law. The text of Article 31 VCLT is key—not only for the concept of systemic integration but for many interpretative issues discussed in this book. It is worth quoting in full:

Article 31

General rule of interpretation

1. A treaty shall be interpreted in good faith in accordance with the ordinary meaning to be given to the terms of the treaty in their context and in the light of its object and purpose.
2. The context for the purpose of the interpretation of a treaty shall comprise, in addition to the text, including its preamble and annexes:
   (a) any agreement relating to the treaty which was made between all the parties in connection with the conclusion of the treaty;
   (b) any instrument which was made by one or more parties in connection with the conclusion of the treaty and accepted by the other parties as an instrument related to the treaty.
3. There shall be taken into account, together with the context:
   (a) any subsequent agreement between the parties regarding the interpretation of the treaty or the application of its provisions;
   (b) any subsequent practice in the application of the treaty which establishes the agreement of the parties regarding its interpretation;
   (c) any relevant rules of international law applicable in the relations between the parties.
4. A special meaning shall be given to a term if it is established that the parties so intended.

Article 31 is not only relevant for the interpretation of treaties between States that are parties to the VCLT. Rather, the ICJ has repeatedly held that Articles 31 and 32 VCLT reflect customary international law.[19] This is not to say that the ICJ has embraced the text of these articles as an accurate statement of the rules of treaty interpretation right from the start. Richard Gardiner aptly described the practice of the ICJ regarding the 1969 VCLT rules as developing from 'initial silence' in the 1970s, over 'ensuing hesitations' in the 1980s, to 'express endorsement'.[20] Against this background, it is not surprising that it took the Court until 2003 to explicitly refer to Article 31(3)(c).[21]

---

[18] ILC, *Fragmentation of International Law: Difficulties Arising from the Diversification and Expansion of International Law* (2006)., para. 413.

[19] *See e.g.,* LaGrand (Germany v. United States of America), Judgment, 27 June 2001, ICJ Reports 2001, 466, para. 99 and the references in Mark E. Villiger, *Commentary on the 1969 Vienna Convention on the Law of Treaties* (2009), Article 31, para. 37 n.121.

[20] Richard K. Gardiner, *Treaty Interpretation* (2008), at 13–17.

[21] This does not mean that the Court has not referred more generally to external rules in treaty interpretation or employed a 'presumption of compliance with international law' prior to 2003. For an analysis of the relevant jurisprudence of the PCIJ and the ICJ, *see* Bruno Simma & Theodore Kill, 'Harmonizing Investment Protection and International Human Rights: First Steps Towards a Methodology', *in International Investment Law for the 21st Century—Essays in Honour of Christoph Schreuer* (Christina Binder, et al. eds., 2009) 678–707, at 683–9. Simma and Kill conclude that this earlier practice of the Court was more reminiscent of Article 32 VCLT, i.e. the Court merely

In that year, the ICJ decided the *Oil Platforms* case. One of the issues was whether the destruction of Iranian oil platforms by the United States violated the 1955 FCN treaty between the two States or whether it was justified by its Article XX(1)(d). This provision reads as follows:

The present Treaty shall not preclude the application of measures... (d) necessary to fulfill the obligations of a High Contracting Party for the maintenance or restoration of international peace and security, or necessary to protect its essential security interests.[22]

The ICJ held that the relevant acts would not be justified under this provision if they did not meet the requirements of self-defence under international law, and the Court relied on Article 31(3)(c) VCLT for this proposition.[23] The Court reasoned that it:

cannot accept that Article XX, paragraph 1 (d), of the 1955 Treaty was intended to operate wholly independently of the relevant rules of international law on the use of force, so as to be capable of being successfully invoked, even in the limited context of a claim for breach of the Treaty, in relation to an unlawful use of force. The application of the relevant rules of international law relating to this question thus forms an integral part of the task of interpretation entrusted to the Court...[24]

The second instance in which the ICJ explicitly held that Article 31(3)(c) VCLT 'is to be regarded as a codification of customary international law' is its judgment in *Certain Questions of Mutual Assistance in Criminal Matters* of 2008.[25] In this case, the Court referred to Article 31(3)(c) when it had to decide on Djibouti's argument that the Convention on Mutual Assistance in Criminal Matters between France and Djibouti of 27 September 1986 had to be interpreted in light of the spirit of friendship and general obligation of co-operation provided for by the Treaty of Friendship and Co-operation between the two States of 27 June 1977.[26] The Court found that the 1977 treaty does indeed 'have a certain bearing on the interpretation and application' of the 1986 convention.[27] Still, the Court reasoned that the relevance of the 1977 treaty cannot go so far as to prevent France from relying on a derogation clause in the 1986 convention. Article 3 of the 1986 convention contains an obligation to execute international letters rogatory in accordance with the legislation of the requested State. Article 2 of the 1986 Convention provides an exception to this obligation:

employed external rules or a presumption of compliance with international law in order to affirm a finding established by other interpretative means (id., at 689 n.62).

[22] *Case concerning Oil Platforms* (Iran v. United States of America), Judgment, 6 November 2003, ICJ Reports 2003, 161, para. 32 (emphasis added).

[23] Id., para. 41. The Court accepted the customary international law character of Article 31(3)(c) VCLT by stating that 'under the general rules of treaty interpretation, as reflected in the 1969 Vienna Convention on the Law of Treaties, interpretation must take into account "any relevant rules of international law applicable in the relations between the parties" (Article 31, para. 3 *(c))*'.

[24] Id., para. 41.

[25] *Certain Questions of Mutual Assistance in Criminal Matters* (Djibouti v. France), Judgment, 4 June 2008, ICJ Reports 2008, 177.

[26] Id., para. 106.   [27] Id., para. 114.

[j]udicial assistance may be refused:

[...]

(c) If the requested State considers that execution of the request is likely to impair its sovereignty, security, public policy or other essential interests.[28]

In light of this stipulation, the Court set a clear limit to the concept of systemic integration by stating that:

[a]n interpretation of the 1986 Convention duly taking into account the spirit of friendship and co-operation stipulated in the 1977 Treaty cannot possibly stand in the way of a party to that Convention relying on a clause contained in it which allows for nonperformance of a conventional obligation under certain circumstances.[29]

In the *Pulp Mills* case, the ICJ again referred to Article 31(3)(c) VCLT. The Court found that the interpretation of treaties that predate the entry into force of the VCLT needs to take into account 'any relevant rules of international law applicable in the relations between the parties' since Article 31(3)(c) reflects customary international law.[30]

Interestingly, the practice of international investment tribunals regarding the VCLT followed a similar pattern as the practice of the ICJ, described above as starting with 'initial silence' and developing via 'ensuing hesitations' to 'express endorsement'.[31] At the beginning of the great surge in the number of investor–State arbitrations (in the late 1990s and the beginning of twenty-first century), arbitral tribunals were still very hesitant to expressly refer to the VCLT in the interpretation of IIAs.[32] This changed between 2003 and 2006, when approximately every second decision mentioned Articles 31–3 VCLT.[33] A look at more recent decisions suggests that investment tribunals today recognize the methodology set out in the VCLT as the 'state of the art approach' for the interpretation of IIAs.

In *National Grid,* for example, the tribunal assumed that it had to interpret the UK–Argentina BIT 'in accordance with Article 31 of the Vienna Convention on the Law of Treaties'.[34] The same is true for the *Continental* tribunal, which

---

[28] Convention on Mutual Assistance in Criminal Matters between France and Djibouti, 27 September 1986, 1695 UNTS 297, at 304.

[29] *Certain Questions of Mutual Assistance in Criminal Matters* (Djibouti v. France), Judgment, 4 June 2008, ICJ Reports 2008, 177, para. 114.

[30] *Pulp Mills on the River Uruguay* (Argentina v. Uruguay), Judgment, 20 April 2010, ICJ Reports 2010, 14, para. 65.

[31] *See supra* note 19 and accompanying text.

[32] According to a survey by Kristian Fauchald only 21% of all decisions between 1999 and 2002 referred to Articles 31–33 of the VCLT (Ole Kristian Fauchald, 'The Legal Reasoning of ICSID Tribunals—an Empirical Analysis', *European Journal of International Law* 19 (2008) 301–64, at 314 n.60.)

[33] Fauchald counted 47%, id., at 314 n.60.

[34] *National Grid plc v. Argentina,* UNCITRAL Arbitration, Award, 3 November 2008, para. 167. Similarly, the *Saba Fakes* tribunal interpreted Article 25(2)(a) of the ICSID Convention '[p]ursuant to the generally accepted rules of treaty interpretation, as codified in Article 31 of the Vienna Convention on the Law of Treaties' (*Saba Fakes v. Republic of Turkey*, ICSID Case No. ARB/07/20, Award, 14 July 2010, para. 76). The *Austrian Airlines* tribunal plainly stated that 'Articles 31 and 32 of the VCLT will guide its interpretation' (*Austrian Airlines v. Slovak Republic*, UNCITRAL Arbitration, Final Award and Dissenting Opinion, 20 October 2009,

explicitly referred to Article 31 VCLT in its interpretation of Article XI of the Argentina–US BIT.[35] Some other tribunals have even reproduced the complete text of Articles 31 and 32 before they interpreted the respective IIA provisions.[36] In *Romak v. Uzbekistan*, the tribunal had to interpret the BIT between Uzbekistan and Switzerland of 16 April 1993. Since Uzbekistan had acceded to the VCLT only in 1995, the tribunal could not apply the VCLT as treaty law.[37] Still, the tribunal based its analysis on the wording of Articles 31 and 32 VCLT since '[t]he Vienna Convention, and in particular its provisions on the interpretation of treaties, has been accepted by the ICJ and by the international community as a codification of customary international law'.[38] Tribunals are less explicit about the legal status of the concept of systemic integration as enshrined in Article 31(3)(c) VCLT than they are regarding the general applicability of Articles 31 and 32.[39] However, arbitral tribunals have never excluded the applicability of paragraph (3)(c), and the concept of systemic integration has been mentioned in arbitral jurisprudence, albeit without detailed analysis.[40] The following sections will demonstrate that Article 31(3)(c) can and should play a more important role in investor–State arbitration than it did so far. Before turning to the content and scope of this provision in section III, a few words on the relationship between Article 31(3)(c) and other means of treaty interpretation are in order.

---

para. 95). The tribunal in the *Suez* water cases was also 'guided by the interpretation rules set forth in Articles 31 and 32 of the VCLT' (*Suez-Vivendi* and *AWG Group*, Decision on Liability, para. 129; *Suez-InterAgua*, Decision on Liability, para. 118).

[35] *Continental*, Award, para. 164.

[36] *Romak SA v. The Republic of Uzbekistan*, PCA Case No. AA280, UNCITRAL Arbitration, Award, 26 November 2009, para. 172; *Chevron Corporation and Texaco Petroleum Company v. The Republic of Ecuador*, UNCITRAL Arbitration, Partial Award on the Merits, 30 March 2010, para. 119.

[37] *See also* Article 4 of the VCLT: 'Without prejudice to the application of any rules set forth in the present Convention to which treaties would be subject under international law independently of the Convention, the Convention applies only to treaties which are concluded by States after the entry into force of the present Convention with regard to such States.'

[38] *Romak SA v. The Republic of Uzbekistan*, PCA Case No. AA280, UNCITRAL Arbitration, Award, 26 November 2009, para. 169. In a similar vein, the *Enron* annulment committee found that it had to interpret the Argentina–US BIT and the ICSID Convention according to the 'customary international law rules of treaty interpretation as codified in the 1969 Vienna Convention on the Law of Treaties' (*Enron Creditors Recovery Corp v. Argentine Republic*, ICSID Case No. ARB/01/3, Decision on the Application for Annulment of the Argentine Republic, 30 July 2010, para. 114(c)).

[39] For an overview of the explicit invocation of Article 31(3)(c) VCLT by other international courts and tribunals, in particular the Iran–US Claims Tribunal, the ECtHR, and the WTO Appellate Body, *see* ILC, *Fragmentation of International Law*, paras. 434–50.

[40] *Merrill & Ring Forestry LP v. Canada*, UNCITRAL Arbitration, ICSID Administered Case (NAFTA), Award, 31 March 2010, para. 84, in particular n.47. The tribunal finally did not rely on Article 31(3)(c) for reasons unrelated to the concept of systemic integration as such (id., paras. 85–7).

II. The relationship between Article 31(3)(c) VCLT and other means of treaty interpretation

The heading of Article 31—'General rule of interpretation'—indicates the central importance of Article 31 in the process of treaty interpretation.[41] Moreover, the use of the singular form *'rule'* illustrates that Article 31 provides a unitary system of treaty interpretation, which involves all of the different means mentioned in this provision.[42] There is no hierarchy among these means: ordinary meaning (paragraph 1), context, object, and purpose (paragraphs 1 and 2), and the different means of interpretation mentioned in paragraph 3 are of equal value.

This is not to say that the particular order of the different means of interpretation in Article 31 is irrelevant. Rather, it reflects a certain logic and order of consideration.[43] Consequently, the starting point for the interpretation of every treaty must be the ordinary meaning of its terms. Furthermore, the context and the purpose of a treaty should be considered before the analysis turns to the means of interpretation listed in paragraph 3.[44] This does not mean, however, that the means of interpretation listed in paragraph 3 are in any way inferior to those listed in the preceding paragraphs. In a similar vein, they are not to be ignored only because an isolated interpretation along the lines of the first two paragraphs of Article 31 yields a seemingly satisfactory result. The ILC stressed that the means of interpretation listed in the third paragraph 'are a mandatory part of the interpretation process'.[45] The drafting history confirms the natural reading of Article

---

[41] Article 32 of the VCLT stipulates that supplementary means of interpretation, i.e. means of interpretation not mentioned in Article 31—such as the preparatory work of the treaty and the circumstances of its conclusion—may only be referred to in order to 'determine' the meaning of a treaty under certain narrowly defined circumstances. It is always possible of course to 'confirm' the result of a treaty interpretation along the lines of Article 31 VCLT by supplementary means of interpretation within the meaning of Article 32 of the VCLT.

[42] Villiger, *Vienna Convention on the Law of Treaties*, Article 31, paras. 29–31; Gardiner, *Treaty Interpretation* at 142; ILC, Draft Articles on the Law of Treaties with Commentaries, Yearbook of the International Law Commission Vol. II, 187–274 (1966), Articles 27–28, paras. 8–9. The ILC—whose draft of Article 27 on the Law of Treaties adopted in 1966 was largely identical to the final version of Article 31—explained that it chose the singular form in order to 'emphasize that the process of interpretation is a unity and that the provisions of the article form a single, closely integrated rule' (id., para. 8).

[43] ILC, *Commentaries on the Law of Treaties*, Articles 27–28, para. 9; Villiger, *Vienna Convention on the Law of Treaties*, Article 31, para. 30.

[44] ILC, *Commentaries on the Law of Treaties*, Articles 27–28, para. 9. *But see* Villiger, *Vienna Convention on the Law of Treaties*, Article 31, para. 30 who argues that only the ordinary meaning of the term enjoys some priority in the order of consideration, while the other means of interpretation are to be taken into account simultaneously.

[45] ILC, *Fragmentation of International Law*, para. 425. The drafting history of Article 31(3) of the VCLT confirms this view (ILC, *Commentaries on the Law of Treaties*, Articles 27–28, para. 9: 'these three elements are all of an obligatory character'). Along the same line, the WTO panel in *EC–Biotech* found 'that Article 31(3)(c) mandates a treaty interpreter to take into account other rules of international law…; it does not merely give a treaty interpreter the option of doing so.' (*European Communities—Measures Affecting the Approval and Marketing of Biotech Products*, WT/DS291/R, WT/DS292/R, WT/DS293/R, Reports of the Panel, 29 September 2006, para. 7.69). At first glance, this view appears to be at odds with the following statement of the ICJ in its advisory

31(3)(c) as a non-inferior means of treaty interpretation. In an early version of Article 27 of the ILC draft Articles on the Law of Treaties, the ILC had integrated the clause that would finally become Article 31(3)(c) VCLT into the first paragraph.[46] The reason for the transfer of the clause to paragraph 3 was editorial: the ILC wanted to address the 'intrinsic' means of interpretation in the first two paragraphs and assemble the 'extrinsic' means in a separate paragraph.[47]

III. The content and scope of Article 31(3)(c) VCLT

As mentioned, the ILC described the principle of systemic integration as the interpretation of treaty provisions 'by reference to their normative environment'.[48] This statement provides a rough idea about the content and scope of the concept of systemic integration. The debate on 'self-contained regimes' in international law sheds further light on this concept. While the term 'self-contained regimes' is not always used consistently, the ILC understands it to describe such treaty regimes that exclude the application of general international law.[49] The concept of systemic integration is not limited to the notion that treaties are to be interpreted

---

opinion on the *Competence of the General Assembly for the Admission of a State to the United Nations*: 'The Court considers it necessary to say that the first duty of a tribunal which is called upon to interpret and apply the provisions of a treaty, is to endeavour to give effect to them in their natural and ordinary meaning in the context in which they occur. If the relevant words in their natural and ordinary meaning make sense in their context, that is an end of the matter' (*Competence of the General Assembly for the Admission of a State to the United Nations*, Advisory Opinion, 3 March 1950, ICJ Reports 1950, 4, at 8). A closer look at the advisory opinion of the ICJ, however, diminishes this apparent contradiction. The ICJ resorted to the wording of Article 4(2) of the UN Charter (which stipulates that membership to the United Nations presupposes a '*recommendation* of the Security Council') in order to defeat an argument based on *travaux préparatoires*. Despite the unequivocal stipulation in Article 4(2) of the UN Charter, it had been submitted that the preparatory works of the San Francisco Conference suggest that *any* finding of the Security Council on the admission of a State (even a negative one) would suffice for the purposes of Article 4(2) UN Charter (id., at 9). Consequently, the 1950 opinion of the Court is in line with the relationship between Article 31 and the supplementary means of interpretation of Article 32. In fact, the ILC even explicitly referred to this opinion in its commentaries as an affirmation for the general structure of Article 31 ILC, *Commentaries on the Law of Treaties*, Articles 27–28, para. 12). Hence, the advisory opinion of the ICJ on the *Competence of the General Assembly for the Admission of a State to the United Nations* cannot be construed as an 'anticipatory assault' on Article 31(3) adopted two decades later.

[46] According to this earlier formulation of paragraph 1, the ordinary meaning of a term had to be determined 'in the light of the general rules of international law in force at the time of its conclusion' (*see* ILC, *Commentaries on the Law of Treaties*, para. 16). In the 1966 draft Articles, the Commission omitted the temporal element, slightly changed the formulation, and moved it to the third paragraph.

[47] Id., para. 16. For the distinction between 'intrinsic' and 'extrinsic' means of interpretation, *see* id., para. 9. Of course, an agreement or an instrument made 'in connection with the conclusion of the treaty' within the meaning of Article 31(2)(a) or (b) VCLT is also 'extrinsic' to the text of the treaty to be interpreted. Because of the temporal and factual relationship between such an agreement or instrument and the treaty itself, however, its attribution to the 'context' of the treaty in Article 31(2) VCLT appears to be appropriate.

[48] *See supra* note 18 and accompanying text.

[49] *See* ILC, *Fragmentation of International Law*, para. 172. For an overview of the different understandings of the term 'self-contained regime', *see* id., paras. 123–9.

against the background of general international law and that they are embedded in an overarching system of international law. But if IIAs constitute self-contained regimes, this is the end of the matter: there is no room for Article 31(3)(c) as external rules have no say in self-contained regimes. Before turning to the different elements of Article 31(3)(c), the next subsection therefore analyses whether the notion of self-contained regimes is relevant to investor–State arbitration.

1. The notion of 'self-contained regimes' and its (ir)relevance for investor–State arbitration

Arbitral tribunals and scholars have referred to the notion of self-contained regimes in international investment arbitration in two different contexts: first, in the interpretation of substantive provisions in IIAs and second, in the characterization of the procedural mechanism set out in the ICSID Convention. I will address these two points in turn.

a) International investment agreements as self-contained regimes?

Kristian Fauchald observed in 2008 that 'ICSID tribunals in general follow an approach that includes important elements of a "self-contained regime"'.[50] Fauchald analysed ICSID decisions rendered between 1998 and 2006, and found that ICSID tribunals made only very limited reference to Article 38 ICJ Statute and the rules of treaty interpretation as set out in the VCLT.[51] These provisions are of central importance to the international legal order, and neglect for them can under certain circumstances indeed be indicative for the development of a self-contained regime. On the other hand, Fauchald provided data according to which tribunals referred extensively to the case law of other courts and tribunals,[52] and put particular emphasis on ICJ decisions.[53] From these and similar factors, Fauchald concluded that ICSID tribunals generally do not 'contribute to a "fragmentation" of international law or international tribunals' and that they are 'far from establishing a "self-contained regime"'.[54] This means that Fauchald identified two contradictory strains in the legal reasoning of ICSID tribunals: while he observed certain factors that are characteristic for self-contained regimes, other elements pointed to another direction.

This ambiguity warrants some further remarks on a possible nexus between investor–State arbitration and the notion of self-contained regimes. Recent jurisprudence of investment tribunals suggests that some factors Fauchald held to be indicative for the creation of 'self-contained regimes' in international investment law have changed or are less severe than suggested.[55] First, arbitral tribunals make frequent reference

---

[50] Fauchald, 'The Legal Reasoning of ICSID Tribunals—an Empirical Analysis', at 314.
[51] Id., at 314.   [52] Id., at 333–42.   [53] Id., at 341–3.   [54] Id., at 343.
[55] Most authors share the view that IIAs do not constitute self-contained regimes, *see, e.g.,* Campbell McLachlan, et al., *International Investment Arbitration—Substantive Principles* (2007), para. 1.38; Alvarez & Khamsi, *The Argentine Crisis,* at 428.

to the rules of treaty interpretation as set out in the VCLT today.[56] Second, the fact that arbitral tribunals refer less frequently to Article 38 ICJ Statute can hardly give rise to serious concerns about the detachment of investor–State arbitration from general international law. It is to state the obvious that virtually every decision of an investment tribunal involves a treaty within the meaning of Article 38(1)(a) of the ICJ Statute.[57] Maybe not so obvious is the fact that it is hard for an investor to win a treaty-based arbitration without reliance on customary international law. IIAs set out certain standards that States need to comply with; they typically do not stipulate what happens when they fall short of these standards. A State owes compensation for the breach of a treaty provision either because the relevant treaty says so—which is typically not the case—or as a matter of customary international law. As far as issues of compensation are concerned, there is little doubt that the principles formulated by the PCIJ in *Factory at Chorzów* are applicable in investor–State arbitration.[58] The PCIJ stated that:

The essential principle contained in the actual notion of an illegal act—a principle which seems to be established by international practice and in particular by the decisions of arbitral tribunals—is that reparation must, as far as possible, wipe-out all the consequences of the illegal act and re-establish the situation which would, in all probability, have existed if that act had not been committed. Restitution in kind, or, if this is not possible, payment of a sum corresponding to the value which a restitution in kind would bear; the award, if need be, of damages for loss sustained which would not be covered by restitution in kind or payment in place of it—such are the principles which should serve to determine the amount of compensation due for an act contrary to international law.[59]

In its decision, the PCIJ distinguished between reparation for an 'illegal act' and 'fair compensation' as prerequisite to lawful expropriation under the relevant treaty (the Geneva Convention).[60] It stressed that 'reparation is in this case the consequence not of the application of Articles 6 to 22 of the Geneva Convention, but of acts contrary to those articles.'[61] The PCIJ was thus in a situation similar

---

[56] *See supra* notes 31–40 and accompanying text.

[57] Something different might under certain circumstances be true for a contract-based arbitration not brought before an ICSID tribunal.

[58] Sergey Ripinsky & Kevin Williams, *Damages in International Investment Law* (2008), at p 31 (with further references); Irmgard Marboe, *Calculation of Compensation and Damages in International Investment Law* (2009), paras. 7.04–7.06. Reisman and Sloane observe that '*Chorzów* Factory remains, notwithstanding the passage of more than 70 years, the seminal international decision about compensation under international law' (W. Michael Reisman & Robert D. Sloane, 'Indirect Expropriation and its Valuation in the BIT Generation', *British Yearbook of International Law* 74 (2003) 115–50, at 135).

[59] *The Factory at Chorzów, Merits* (Germany v. Poland), Judgment, 13 September 1928, PCIJ Reports, Series A, No. 17 (1928) 4–65, at 47.

[60] Convention concerning Upper Silesia concluded at Geneva on 13 May 1922 between Germany and Poland (referred to as 'Geneva Convention' by the PCIJ). For a concise summary of the provisions on expropriation in this treaty (Articles 6 to 22), *see The Factory at Chorzów, Jurisdiction* (Germany v. Poland), Judgment, 26 July 1927, PCIJ Reports, Series A, No. 9–10 (1927) 4–34, at 12–13.

[61] *Factory at Chorzów, Merits*, at 46.

to that of an investment tribunal finding on the consequences of an expropriation that did not comply with the relevant IIA provisions. It is therefore not surprising that many investment tribunals have relied on the *Chorzów* principles in determining compensation for treaty breaches.[62]

The *Chorzów* principles are today codified in Part Two of the ASR, of which the rules on compensation (Article 36)[63] are key to investor–State arbitration and frequently relied on by tribunals.[64] Other rules of customary international law reflected in the ASR that investment tribunals regularly resort to are those on attribution and circumstances precluding wrongfulness. As at 2007, 40% of all references to the ASR by international courts and tribunals came from arbitral tribunals constituted under the ICSID Convention or the ICSID Additional Facility Rules. If one adds other proceedings with a primarily economic subject matter—many of them investor–State arbitrations—this figure goes up to well over 70%.[65] In light of the large number of investment claims decided in recent years, it is safe to assume that these percentages have continued to increase after the UN compilation was concluded in 2007.

This short account of the role of customary international law in investor–State arbitration suffices to demonstrate that it is all but impossible for arbitrators to decide treaty-based arbitrations without resort to rules of international law extrinsic to the relevant treaty. Arbitrators also refer to 'general principles' in their decisions, albeit less often than to customary international law.[66] It is true that many

---

[62] *See, e.g., S.D. Myers, Inc v. Canada*, UNCITRAL Arbitration (NAFTA), First Partial Award, 13 November 2000, paras. 305–11; *CMS*, Award, para. 400; *BG Group*, Final Award, paras. 419–29; and the references provided in *supra* note 58.

[63] Article 36 of the ASR reads as follows:

1. The State responsible for an internationally wrongful act is under an obligation to compensate for the damage caused thereby, insofar as such damage is not made good by restitution.
2. The compensation shall cover any financially assessable damage including loss of profits insofar as it is established.

[64] Some authors argue that not all forms of reparation reflected in Part Two of the ASR are applicable in investor–State arbitration, in particular when it comes to restitution and satisfaction (Zachary Douglas, 'Other Specific Regimes of Responsibility: Investment Treaty Arbitration and ICSID', *in The Law of International Responsibility* (James Crawford, et al. eds., 2010) 815–42, at 820, 829). Others state that the ILC focused on inter-State relationships for historical reasons, and that all provisions of Part Two of the ASR are applicable in investment disputes (Ripinsky & Williams, *Damages in International Investment Law*, at 28–32). This issue is irrelevant for questions of compensation, which lie at the core of investor–State arbitration. For a discussion of the power of tribunals to order non-pecuniary remedies, *see, e.g.,* Christoph Schreuer, 'Non-Pecuniary Remedies in ICSID Arbitration', *Arbitration International* 20 (2004) 325–32, at 325–6, 329; Wälde & Sabahi, 'Compensation, Damages, and Valuation', at 1115–16.

[65] UN, *Responsibility of States for Internationally Wrongful Acts: Compilation of Decisions of International Courts, Tribunals and Other Bodies*, Report of the Secretary General of 1 February 2007, A/62/62 (2007), Annex I, 86–97.

[66] Fauchald, 'The Legal Reasoning of ICSID Tribunals', at 315–26. For compilations of arbitral awards that resorted to general principles such as 'good faith', 'estoppel', 'unjust enrichment', or the 'duty to mitigate damages', *see* Schreuer, et al., *The ICISD Convention—a Commentary*, Article 42, para. 180 and Campbell McLachlan, 'Investment Treaties and General International Law', *International and Comparative Law Quarterly* 57 (2008) 361–401, at 326. The *Merrill* tribunal identified the prohibition of arbitrariness and discrimination as general principles of law. Even

of the relevant tribunals do not explicitly mention Article of the 38(1)(c) in this context,[67] but the same could be said about the ICJ, which is usually not accused of contributing to the fragmentation of international law.[68] Hence, general international law is vital for the jurisprudence of investor–State tribunals, which strongly militates against the existence or emergence of a self-contained regime.

Regarding the question whether *individual* IIAs constitute self-contained regimes, it is worth analysing in what way international investment tribunals refer to the decisions of their peers, particularly when interpreting different IIAs. To state the obvious, there is no *stare decisis* rule in international investment arbitration. Consequently arbitral tribunals are not bound to adopt the solutions other tribunals have developed—even if the underlying circumstances are similar or identical.[69] Still, a continuum bounded by the irrelevance of prior decisions at one end, and the *stare decisis* rule at the other, leaves ample room for the consideration of the jurisprudence of other tribunals. One might say that investment tribunals treat other decisions as 'persuasive authorities' or 'inspirational sources'. Some authors describe this practice with terms that suggest an even greater degree of adherence. Andrea Bjorklund, for example, invoked an analogy from the French civil law tradition by introducing the notion of '*jurisprudence constante*' to investor–State arbitration.[70] Domenico Di Pietro detected a 'de facto doctrine of precedent' in light of the extensive reliance of ICSID tribunals on the case law of other tribunals.[71]

Tribunals sometimes explicitly comment on the relevance of decisions by other tribunals to their decisions. I will shortly introduce two seemingly different theoretical approaches that lead to a remarkably consistent practice. The *Romak* tribunal attached little importance to prior decisision when it stated:

With respect to arbitral awards, this Arbitral Tribunal considers that it is not bound to follow or to cite previous arbitral decisions as authority for its reasoning or conclusions. Even

---

more progressively, the tribunal found that the '[a]vailability of a secure legal environment has a close connection…to such principles[,] and transparency, while more recent, appears to be fast approaching that standard.' (*Merrill & Ring Forestry LP v. Canada*, UNCITRAL Arbitration, ICSID Administered Case (NAFTA), Award, 31 March 2010, at 187).

[67] While many arbitral tribunals refer to 'general principles' without further elaboration of the term, the *Inceysa v. El Salvador* tribunal, for example, explicitly mentioned Article 38(1)(c) of the ICJ Statue in its analysis (*Inceysa Vallisoletana, SL v. Republic of El Salvador*, ICSID Case No. ARB/03/26, Award, 2 August 2006, para. 225).

[68] For the practice of the ICJ regarding Article 38(1)(c) ICJ Statute, *see* Chapter 3, note 19.

[69] *See, e.g., Bayindir Insaat Turizm Ticaret Ve Sanayi AS v. Islamic Republic of Pakistan*, ICSID Case No ARB/03/29, Decision on Jurisdiction, 14 November 2005, para. 76; *AES Corporation v. The Argentine Republic*, ICSID Case No. ARB/02/17, Decision on Jurisdiction, 26 April 2005, para. 30. *See also* Article 53 of the ICSID Convention which states that '[t]he award shall be binding *on the parties*' (emphasis added). This provision is generally understood to explicitly exclude the doctrine of '*stare decisis*' from the ambit of the ICSID Convention (Schreuer, et al., *The ICISD Convention*, Article 53, paras. 16–17).

[70] Andrea K. Bjorklund, 'Investment Treaty Arbitral Decisions as *Jurisprudence Constante*', in *International Economic Law—the State and Future of the Discipline* (Colin B. Picker, et al. eds., 2008) 265–80, at 272.

[71] Domenico Di Pietro, 'The Use of Precedents in ICSID Arbitration: Regularity or Certainty?', *International Arbitration Law Review* 10 (2007) 92–103, at 96.

presuming that relevant principles could be distilled from prior arbitral awards (which has proven difficult with respect of many of the decisions cited by the Parties in these proceedings), they cannot be deemed to constitute the expression of a general consensus of the international community, and much less a formal source of international law. Arbitral awards remain mere sources of inspiration, comfort or reference to arbitrators.[72]

In deciding the issue of whether the rights underlying the claim qualify as an 'investment' under the relevant BIT, the tribunal meticulously followed the methodology set out in Articles 31 and 32 VCLT.[73] After this analysis, however, the tribunal filled several pages with references to other arbitral decisions before it reached its conclusion.[74]

In *Austrian Airlines*, the tribunal seemed to attach greater importance to previous decisions than the *Romak* tribunal. It held that:

> The Tribunal considers that it is not bound by previous decisions. At the same time, it is of the opinion that it must pay due consideration to earlier decisions of international tribunals. It believes that subject to compelling contrary grounds, it has a duty to adopt solutions established in a series of consistent cases.[75]

In deciding the legal issues of the case, however, the *Austrian Airlines* tribunal did not simply adopt solutions developed by other tribunals. Instead, it followed the methodology set out in Articles 31 and 32 VCLT.[76] Consequently, the approaches of the *Romak* and the *Austrian Airlines* tribunals toward previous decisions did not greatly differ from a practical viewpoint. Both put significant weight on previous decisions, but only when and to the extent that the VCLT allows for such practice in the process of treaty interpretation.

In sum, the interactions among arbitral tribunals that apply and interpret different treaties confirm the point that IIAs do not constitute self-contained regimes. Arbitral tribunals seem to be increasingly aware that investor–State arbitration does not take place in a legal vacuum and that IIAs are deeply embedded in the larger systems of general international law. In this vein, more recent jurisprudence confirms what the *Asian Agricultural Products* tribunal held as early as 1997:

> [T]he Bilateral Investment Treaty is not a self-contained closed legal system limited to provide for substantive material rules of direct applicability, but it has to be envisaged

---

[72] *Romak SA v. The Republic of Uzbekistan*, PCA Case No. AA280, UNCITRAL Arbitration, Award, 26 November 2009, para. 170.

[73] *See, in particular*, id., paras. 175–85.

[74] Id., paras. 197–205. The tribunal summarized its approach in para. 206. It stressed that the 'ordinary meaning of the term "'investment"'…entail[s] expenditure or contribution, as well as the purpose of obtaining an economic benefit the existence and extent of which is, by definition, uncertain'. Despite its generally more critical stance towards the relevance of previous decisions (*see supra* note 72), the *Romak* tribunal clarified that '[t]his is not to say that the Arbitral Tribunal will simply ignore awards rendered by distinguished arbitrators. The Arbitral Tribunal may and will examine them, not for the purposes of extracting from them rules of law, but as a means to provide context to the Parties' allegations and arguments, and as to explain succinctly the Arbitral Tribunal's own reasoning' (id., para. 171).

[75] *Austrian Airlines v. Slovak Republic*, UNCITRAL Arbitration, Final Award and Dissenting Opinion, 20 October 2009, para. 84.

[76] *See, e.g.*, id., paras. 95, 121, 135.

within a wider juridical context in which rules from other sources are integrated through implied incorporation methods, or by direct reference to certain supplementary rules, whether of international character or of domestic nature.[77]

b) The ICSID Convention as a self-contained regime?

While the previous subsection focused on IIAs as legal instruments setting out substantive standards of investment protection, it remains to be analysed whether the ICSID Convention constitutes a 'self-contained' regime. Some scholars refer to the 'self-contained nature'[78] of the ICSID Convention or its 'self-contained process'.[79] Some features of the ICSID Convention support this terminology. For example, Article 26 stipulates that the parties to a dispute under the Convention cannot seek relief before another international or domestic judicial body after both parties have consented to ICSID arbitration. Furthermore, Article 26 contains the principle of 'non-interference' according to which domestic courts have no role to play in the arbitral proceedings.[80] In a similar vein, Article 27 excludes the possibility of diplomatic protection. Finally, Article 53 establishes the finality and binding force of an ICSID award without the possibility of further review by domestic courts.

This does not mean that the ICSID Convention is completely isolated from general international law, nor are domestic rules and processes entirely irrelevant. After all, the provision of the ICSID Convention are to be interpreted according to the (customary) rules on treaty interpretation as reflected in Articles 31–33 VCLT. For the enforcement of an arbitral award, the claimant is reliant on domestic institutions, even though not necessarily on those of its host or home State (Article 54). Moreover, the ICSID Convention has no bearing on the rules on State immunity from execution in force at the place where enforcement is sought (Article 55). Another illustrative example for the embeddedness of the ICSID Convention in the international legal order is Article 64. This provision establishes the compulsory jurisdiction of the ICJ for disputes between States concerning the interpretation or application of the ICSID Convention.

Therefore, it is submitted that the use of the term 'self-contained' in the context of the ICSID Convention triggers the wrong connotations, at least if one understands the term to describe such treaty regimes that exclude the application of general international law.[81] Moreover, it does not seem to add much to the special features of the ICSID Convention mentioned above—despite the fact that the

---

[77] *Asian Agricultural Products Ltd v. Sri Lanka*, ICSID Case No. ARB/87/3, Award, 27 June 1990, ICSID Reports 4 (1997) 250–95, para. 21.

[78] Schreuer, et al., *The ICISD Convention*, Article 26, para. 1, Article 54, para. 10.

[79] McLachlan, et al., *International Investment Arbitration*, para. 1.05.

[80] Schreuer, et al., *The ICISD Convention*, Article 26, paras. 2–3.

[81] *See supra* note 49 and accompanying text.

combination of these features makes the ICSID Convention a unique instrument in international law.[82]

2. The different elements of Article 31(3)(c) VCLT

The dismissal of the notion of self-contained regimes in international investment law was the first step in determining the possible scope and content of the principle of systemic integration in this area of law: rules of international law external to an IIA are not per se irrelevant to its interpretation. This subsection focuses on the different elements of Article 31(3)(c) VCLT and will reveal that the very structure of investor–State arbitration lends itself to systemic integration to a greater degree than many other areas of international law. The primary reason for this observation is the largely bilateral framework of IIAs. There are a considerable number of unresolved issues regarding the different elements of Article 31(3)(c). The primary purpose of this subsection, however, is to show that Article 31(3)(c) may play a meaningful role in investor–State arbitration on the basis of rather well-established principles. Additional comments seek to contribute to the discussion on some of the more controversial aspects of Article 31(3)(c). The different elements of Article 31(3)(c) can be easily identified by considering the various terms of the phrase 'any relevant rules of international law applicable in the relations between the parties.' I will analyse each of them in turn.

a) 'Rules of international law'

(1) All sources of international law matter
Scholars usually consider the phrase 'rules of international law' in Article 31(3)(c) VCLT to refer to all sources of international law as reflected in Article 38(1) ICJ Statute.[83] The practice of international courts and tribunals confirms this account. Adjudicators have resorted to external treaties, customary international law, and general principles to interpret a treaty under the heading of Article 31(3)(c). In *Pulp Mills*, the ICJ pointed to the possibility of taking account of 'rules of general international law' and '[rules] contained in multilateral conventions to which the two States are parties'.[84] In *Mutual Assistance*, the ICJ considered a bilateral treaty on friendship and cooperation between France and Djibouti of 1977 in the interpretation of a 1986 Convention on mutual assistance in criminal matters on

---

[82] Georg Nolte reaches a similar conclusion and considers the ICSID Convention to be a 'special regime in a wider sense' but not a 'self-contained regime' (Georg Nolte, 'Reports for the ILC Study Group On Treaties over Time: Report 2—Jurisprudence Under Special Regimes Relating to Subsequent Agreements and Subsequent Practice', *in Treaties and Subsequent Practice* (Georg Nolte ed., 2013) 210–306, at 233).

[83] Simma & Kill, 'Harmonizing Investment Protection and International Human Rights', at 695; Villiger, *Vienna Convention on the Law of Treaties*, Article 31, para. 25; ILC, *Fragmentation of International Law*, paras. 462–70.

[84] *Pulp Mills on the River Uruguay* (Argentina v. Uruguay), Judgment, 20 April 2010, ICJ Reports 2010, 14, para. 66.

the basis of Article 31(3)(c).[85] In addition, in *Oil Platforms*, the ICJ resorted to customary international law and the UN Charter for the interpretation of a bilateral treaty between the US and Iran.[86]

Moreover, international adjudicatory bodies have referred to general principles of law in the context of Article 31(3)(c). In *EC–Biotech Products*, a WTO panel found that

if the precautionary principle is a general principle of international law, it could be considered a 'rule of international law' within the meaning of Article 31(3)(c).[87]

The ECtHR was even more explicit about the relevance of general principles in the interpretation process. In *Golder v. United Kingdom*, it held that:

Article 31 para. 3 (c) of the Vienna Convention indicates that account is to be taken, together with the context, of 'any relevant rules of international law applicable in the relations between the parties'. Among those rules are general principles of law and especially 'general principles of law recognized by civilized nations' (Article 38 para. 1 (c) of the Statute of the International Court of Justice).[88]

(2) Proportionality as a 'rule'

Scholars sometimes emphasize that only '*rules*' of international law fall under the scope of Article 31(3)(c) VCLT.[89] Does this mean it is impossible for treaty interpreters to resort to the '*principle* of proportionality' as a matter of Article 31(3)(c)? The short answer is no, it does not. We have seen above that the academic debate on how to categorize proportionality within Alexy's rules/principles dichotomy is irrelevant in the context of Article 38(1)(c) ICJ Statute. Whether called 'meta-constitutional *rule*', tool of 'neutral, rational-decision making', or '*principle*', for the purposes of Article 38(1)(c) ICJ Statute it only matters that proportionality is a legal concept sufficiently established in domestic law and transposable to the international level.[90] To the extent that we have answered these questions in the affirmative, proportionality is a 'general *principle*' within the meaning of Article 38(1)(c) ICJ Statute. This comports with our findings in

---

[85] *Certain Questions of Mutual Assistance in Criminal Matters* (Djibouti v. France), Judgment, 4 June 2008, ICJ Reports 2008, 177, para. 113.

[86] *Case concerning Oil Platforms* (Iran v. United States of America), Judgment, 6 November 2003, ICJ Reports 2003, 161, paras. 41–42.

[87] *European Communities—Measures Affecting the Approval and Marketing of Biotech Products*, WT/DS291/R, WT/DS292/R, WT/DS293/R, Reports of the Panel, 29 September 2006, para. 7.67. The panel reiterated further down in its analysis that 'the relevant rules of international law to be taken into account include general principles of law' (id., para. 7.76). However, the panel was eventually not convinced that the precautionary principle had already achieved the status of a general principle (id., paras. 7.88–7.89).

[88] *Golder v. The United Kingdom*, ECtHR, Application no. 4451/70, Judgment, 21 February 1975, para. 35.

[89] Simma & Kill, 'Harmonizing Investment Protection and International Human Rights', at 702; Orakhelashvili, *The Interpretation of Acts and Rules in Public International Law*, at 366 (emphasis added).

[90] *See* Chapter 3, notes 298–307 and accompanying text.

the previous subsection, where we have seen that courts and tribunals have no difficulty in applying general *principles* as '*rules* of international law'.[91]

When scholars emphasize that only 'rules' of international law are relevant under Article 31(3)(c), they usually do not seek to exclude legal concepts established as legal principles from the scope of this provision. Rather, they want to clarify that Article 31(3)(c) is concerned with *law* external to the treaty to be interpreted and not with mere notions of equity or policy considerations. Hence, Orakhelashvili juxtaposes the term 'rules of international law' with 'principles of uncertain or doubtful legal status, so-called evolving legal standards, policy factors or more generally related notions'.[92] In a similar vein, Hersch Lauterpacht explained that legal concepts emanating from domestic law are crucial to international arbitration, using the terms 'rules' and 'principles' rather interchangeably:

> The arbitrator called upon to decide in accordance with justice [as opposed to equity] has here recourse to rules of law, more especially to such rules of private law as seem to him most comprehensive and of universal application. We have seen before that 'principles of universal jurisprudence' so frequently resorted to by international publicists prove ultimately to be identical with general principles of law. The same applies, with even greater force, to those 'principles of justice' and 'generally recognized rules of law' which, in the overwhelming majority of cases, are referred to in an arbitration convention, and without resort to which no regular judicial settlement of international disputes is possible...[93]

More than eight decades later, the leading commentary on the ICSID Convention confirmed that 'general principles of law' play a 'prominent role in arbitrations between States and foreign nationals'.[94] There is no reason why proportionality should not be one of them and be applied in investor–State arbitrations through Article 31(3)(c) VCLT, subject to the guidelines provided in much of the remainder of this book. But establishing proportionality as a rule of international law that might assist in the interpretation of a treaty tells us nothing about the rights and interests that are relevant if it comes to a proportionality analysis. The following subsection seeks to shed some light on this issue.

(3) The value glue of the international community

As previously mentioned, proportionality analysis requires a certain value system. If the relevant treaty does not provide such a value system, external norms may under certain circumstances offer guidance. This subsection discusses some of these rules and concepts, all of which share two important characteristics. First, the relevant legal instruments go beyond the mere 'legalization' and 'judicialization' of the international legal system. As Andreas Paulus put it, the terms 'legalization' and 'judicialization' tend to describe 'legal regulation of international

---

[91] *See* Chapter 3, notes 87–8 and accompanying text.
[92] Orakhelashvili, *The Interpretation of Acts and Rules*, at 366.
[93] Hersch Lauterpacht, *Private Law Sources and Analogies of International Law* (1927), at 67.
[94] Schreuer, et al., *The ICISD Convention*, Article 42, para. 178 (with specific examples listed in para. 180).

relations as isolated islands of stability in a sea of international anarchy'.[95] These islands are worth protecting, so to speak, but the concepts discussed in this subsection aspire to be part of an overarching system of international law. Second, it is necessary to distinguish the legal concepts and instruments discussed in this subsection from the discourse about international ethics.[96] International law might provide a certain basis for this discourse, which will in turn hopefully yield further rules of international law in the future. This subsection, however, discusses some of the 'value glue'[97] that the international community has already brought about.

(i) The value system of the Charter of the United Nations

The UN Charter—whether constitution, special treaty, or ordinary treaty[98]—as the only international treaty with universal membership offers a natural starting point in the quest for a value system in international law. Article 1(3) of the UN Charter states that it is one of the purposes of the UN:

[t]o achieve international co-operation in…promoting and encouraging respect for human rights and for fundamental freedoms for all without distinction as to race, sex, language or religion.

The protection of human rights is further mentioned in Articles 13(1) 55(c), 56, 62(2), 68, and 76(c) of the UN Charter. The most notable provisions in this context are Articles 55(c) and 56, especially when read together. Article 55(c) stipulates that 'the United Nations shall promote…universal respect for, and observance of, human rights and fundamental freedoms for all without distinction as to race, sex, language, or religion'. Article 56 adds two important elements to this provision. It directly addresses the member States and its formulation implies a greater degree of commitment ('to pledge') than Article 55:

All Members pledge themselves to take joint and separate action…for the achievement of the purposes set forth in Article 55.

Significantly, the organs of the United Nations and most authors interpret Article 55(c) and 56 to constitute not only vague policy goals of the United Nations but

[95] Paulus, *The International Legal System as a Constitution*, at 82.
[96] *See* Stefan Kadelbach, 'Ethik des Völkerrechts unter Bedingungen der Globalisierung', *Heidelberg Journal of International Law* 64 (2004) 1–20, at 19.
[97] Paulus, 'Commentary to Andreas Fischer-Lescano & Gunther Teubner', at 1050.
[98] Bardo Fassbender argues that the UN Charter constitutes a constitution—not only of the United Nations as an international organization but also of the 'international community in a broader sense' (Fassbender, 'Rediscovering a Forgotten Constitution', at 138–41). Michael W. Doyle juxtaposes the UN Charter with domestic constitutions such as the US Constitution at one end of the spectrum with 'standard contract-like treat[ies]' on the opposite end (Michael W. Doyle, 'The UN Charter—a Global Constitution?', *in Ruling the World?* (Jeffrey L. Dunoff & Joel P. Trachtman eds., 2009) 113–32, at 113–14). Doyle finds that the UN Charter fundamentally differs from both. Hence, Doyle holds that the UN Charter constitutes 'a treaty but a special treaty' (id., at 114), which provides for more supranational elements than its members are willing to acknowledge (id., at 131–132).

legal obligations of its member States.[99] These legal obligations are obviously of a very general character. However, the precision of a legal norm has little to do with its binding character.[100] Furthermore, some think that the UDHR—adopted by the UN General Assembly in 1948—constitutes an authoritative interpretation of the Charter,[101] which would provide greater precision to Article 55(c) and 56. The merits of this view are beyond the scope of this book, and the relevance of human rights considerations in the context of Article 31(3)(c) VCLT do not necessarily depend on its validity, as the next subsection demonstrates.

(ii) Human rights in treaties, custom, and general principles
The binding character of two other important human rights instruments is far less controversial than that of the UDHR. In 1966, the General Assembly of the United Nations adopted the ICCPR[102] and the ICESCR.[103] Both Covenants were opened for signature in 1966 and entered into force in 1976. As at January 2015, the ICCPR had 168 State parties and 163 States have acceded to or ratified the ICESCR. Together with a number of other legal norms—foremost from the area of international humanitarian law—the human rights obligations mentioned in this subsection are said to form the basis of an 'international value system'.[104] Analysing the relationship between this value system and the rest of the international legal order, Thilo Rensmann identified a 'radiating effect' (*Ausstrahlungswirkung*) of the former.[105]

Apart from treaty law, human rights can also find their way into the process of treaty interpretation via Article 31(3)(c) VCLT if they constitute general principles. In his dissenting opinion in *South West Africa,* Judge Tanaka linked the protection of human rights to both natural law and general principles within the meaning of Article 38(1)(c) ICJ Statute:

Who can believe, as a reasonable man, that the existence of human rights depends upon the internal or international legislative measures, etc, of the State and that accordingly

---

[99] *See* Brownlie, *Public International Law*, at 556 and Eibe Riedel & Jan-Michael Arend, 'Article 55(c)', *in The Charter of the United Nations* (Bruno Simma, et al. eds., 2012) 1566–602, para. 15 with further references.

[100] Abbott and Snidal, for example, distinguish so-called 'hard law' from 'soft law' by the help of three indicators, which may be present in a particular norm to varying extents. The 'binding' character of a norm and its 'precision' are two different indicators. The third indicator is 'delegation', i.e. the question whether and to what degree disputes arising in the context of the relevant norm are referred to third-party adjudication (Kenneth W. Abbott & Duncan Snidal, 'Hard and Soft Law in International Governance', *International Organizations* 54 (2000) 421–56, at 421).

[101] *See* Riedel & Arend, 'Article 55(c)', para. 30 (with further references); *South West Africa Cases* (Ethiopia v. South Africa; Liberia v. South Africa), Second Phase, Judgment, 18 July 2003, ICJ Reports 1966, 6 (Tanaka, J, dissenting) at 293.

[102] Chapter 3, note 31.

[103] International Covenant on Economic, Social and Cultural Rights, 16 Dec. 1966, 993 UNTS 3.

[104] Erika de Wet, 'The Emergence of International and Regional Value Systems as a Manifestation of the Emerging International Constitutional Order', *Leiden Journal of International Law* 19 (2006) 611–32 at 614–16; Erika de Wet, 'The International Constitutional Order', *International and Comparative Law Quarterly* 55 (2006) 51–76 at 54–8.

[105] Thilo Rensmann, *Wertordnung und Verfassung* (2007), at 385.

they can be validly abolished or modified by the will of the State? If a law exists independently of the will of the State and, accordingly, cannot be abolished or modified even by its constitution, because it is deeply rooted in the conscience of mankind and of any reasonable man, it may be called 'natural law' in contrast to 'positive law' ... As an interpretation of Article 38, paragraph 1 (c), we consider that the concept of human rights and of their protection is included in the general principles mentioned in that Article.[106]

Hence, Judge Tanaka considered the existence and the protection of human rights to be independent of the will or consent of States as the primary law-makers in international law.

Bruno Simma and Philip Alston, in contrast, advocate a notion of human rights as general principles that is embedded in a consensus-based conception of international law. Simma and Alston build on the majority opinion in *South West Africa*, which dismissed the natural law approach of Judge Tanaka as follows:

[I]n order that [an] interest may take on a specifically legal character, [it] must be or become something more than a moral or humanitarian ideal. In order to generate legal rights or obligations, it must be given juridicial expression and be clothed in legal form.[107]

The crux of Simma's and Alston's argument is that such 'expression[s] in legal form' may not only occur through the conclusion of treaties or State practice that satisfies the requirements of customary international law.[108] Rather, 'more direct and spontaneous' State consensus as expressed, for example, in resolutions of the UN General Assembly could be evidence of general principles of law.[109]

More recently, this line of argument has been advanced within the debate on the constitutionalization of international law. Stefan Kadelbach and Thomas Kleinlein argue that some 'constitutional principles' such as universal respect for human rights, the environment, and the rule of law can be established as general principles of law within the meaning of Article 38(1)(c) ICJ Statute.[110] For the necessary manifestation of State consensus, these authors refer not only to resolutions of the UN General Assembly, but also to the preambles of multilateral treaties and the judgments of national and international courts.[111]

Qualifying human rights as general principles could be particularly important for so-called 'third-generation rights' such as the protection of the environment

---

[106] *South West Africa Cases* (Ethiopia v. South Africa; Liberia v. South Africa), Second Phase, Judgment, 18 July 2003, ICJ Reports 1966, 6 (Tanaka, J, dissenting), at 298.

[107] *South West Africa Cases* (Ethiopia v. South Africa; Liberia v. South Africa), Second Phase, Judgment, 18 July 2003, ICJ Reports 1966, 6, at 34, para. 51.

[108] Bruno Simma & Philip Alston, 'The Sources of Human Rights Law: Custom, Jus Cogens, and General Principles', *Australian Year Book of International Law* 12 (1988–9) 82–107, at 105 (referring to the passage in *South West Africa* quoted in *supra* note 107).

[109] Id., at 105.

[110] Stefan Kadelbach & Thomas Kleinlein, 'International Law—a Constitution for Mankind? An Attempt at a Re-appraisal with an Analysis of Constitutional Principles', *German Yearbook of International Law* 50 (2007) 303–47, at 342.

[111] Id., at 340. In a similar vein, Petersen, 'Customary Law Without Custom?', at 285, 292.

and the common heritage of mankind.[112] Unlike 'first-generation rights' (comprising mainly the liberal rights of the ICCPR) and 'second-generation rights' (denoting the economic, social, and cultural rights of the ICESCR), third-generation rights are not set out in a human rights treaty. Furthermore, it is controversial whether some of the third-generation rights constitute customary international law.[113] The following consideration supports the notion of human rights as general principles: in the past, resort to domestic legal orders was the most promising way to ascertain the existence of a general principle of law, so focusing on domestic law in the text of Article 38(1)(c) ICJ Statute made sense. Today, there exist a significant number of international organizations and more informal transnational fora where States may and do express their legal views.[114]

There are, however, also considerable arguments that speak against the notion that legal concepts that are neither part of an applicable treaty nor of custom nor of the major domestic legal systems should constitute general principles under Article 38(1)(c) ICJ Statute. Acts of States within international organizations (such as voting for or protesting against resolutions of the UN General Assembly) may constitute State practice as an element of customary international law.[115] If this State practice is not extensive and uniform enough to establish custom, one may wonder how it is possible to conclude from the same facts that States accept and recognize a general principle of law.[116] Conversely, if one does not want to accept a lesser standard of consistency of State practice for the creation of general principles than for custom, the only reason why certain legal expressions may give rise to general principles but not to custom appears to be the *opinio juris* element of custom. It might then be more appropriate to focus on a sensible approach towards the *opinio juris* element. An ILA committee on the formation of customary international law, for example, contended that it is not always necessary to positively establish the subjective *opinio juris* element of custom in addition to the objective element of State practice. Instead, the committee suggested that the presence of *opinio juris* may be sufficient to establish custom, while the proof of its absence hinders a customary international law rule from coming into existence.[117]

In any event, whether as custom or general principles, there are some indications that spontaneous legal expressions may give rise to rules of international law. In October 2001, the US and some other nations attacked Afghanistan in the aftermath of 9/11. In case of an attack by private actors, military action against the host State is justified by the right of self-defence only if the attack is attributable

---

[112] For an overview of these 'third-generation rights', *see* Riedel & Arend, 'Article 55(c)', para. 14 and Brownlie, *Public International Law*, at 567–8.

[113] Brownlie, *Public International Law*, at 567.

[114] *See* Simma & Alston, 'The Sources of Human Rights Law', at 102.

[115] ILA, Statement of Principles Applicable to the Formation of General Customary International Law (2000), at 60–1.

[116] Elias & Lim, '"General Principles of Law"', at 36.

[117] ILA, Statement of Principles Applicable to the Formation of General Customary International Law, at 31.

to the host State.[118] It is submitted that none of the rules of attribution seriously discussed within the international community prior to 9/11 would have allowed for military action against Afghanistan.[119] For example, the government (that is the Taliban) did not exercise 'effective control' over al-Qaeda and consequently did not satisfy the criteria set out by the ICJ in *Nicaragua*.[120]

Nevertheless, in its Resolution 1368 of 12 September 2001, the Security Council recognized 'the inherent right of individual or collective self-defense' when condemning the terrorist attacks.[121] After the beginning of military action in Afghanistan, the US reported to the UN Security Council that it acted 'in accordance with the inherent right of individual and collective self-defense'.[122] A similar letter was submitted by the UK one day later.[123] On 8 October 2001, only one day after the US letter and on the same day as the UK letter, a press statement by the president of the UN Security Council read that '[t]he members of the Council were appreciative of the presentation made by the United States and the United Kingdom'.[124] For the relevant standard of attribution, the UN Security Council apparently deemed it sufficient that the Taliban regime provided a 'safe haven' to Al-Qaeda.[125] It is open to debate whether the phrase 'safe haven' accurately describes the pertinent legal test for the attribution of terrorist acts. But the legal expressions of some members of the international community and the silence of others in September/October 2001 seem to have had an effect on the rules on attribution in international law.[126]

(iii) Hierarchical structures in international law
While the international legal order largely lacks a hierarchical framework, there are two notable exceptions: the concept of *jus cogens* and Article 103 of the UN Charter. Regardless of whether one chooses to ascribe constitutional character to

---

[118] Albrecht Randelzhofer & Georg Nolte, 'Article 51', *in The Charter of the United Nations* (Bruno Simma, et al. eds., 2012) 1397–428, para. 37.

[119] For an overview of the different approaches and criteria, *see* id, paras. 30–4.

[120] *Case concerning Military and Paramilitary Activities in and against Nicaragua* (Nicaragua v. United States of America), Judgment, Merits, 27 June 1986, ICJ Reports 1986, 4, at 64–5, para. 115.

[121] SC Res. 1368, Introduction, UN Doc S/RES/1368 (September 12, 2001).

[122] Letter from the Permanent Representative of the US to the United Nations addressed to the President of the Security Council, UN Doc S/2001/946 (October 7, 2001).

[123] Letter from the Permanent Representative of the United Kingdom of Great Britain and Northern Ireland to the United Nations addressed to the President of the Security Council, UN Doc S/2001/947 (October 8, 2001).

[124] Press Release, AFG/152, SC/7176 available at <http://www.un.org/News/Press/docs/2001/afg152.doc.htm>.

[125] *See* SC Res 1373, para. 2(c), UN Doc S/RES/1373 (September 28, 2001).

[126] *See* Torsten Stein & Christian von Buttlar, *Völkerrecht* (2012), at 307–8, para. 846. Formulations for the attribution of terrorist acts have become more sophisticated since 2001. Randelzhofer and Nolte, for example, suggest that terrorist acts are attributable (inter alia) if the relevant State 'was unwilling to take steps which can reasonably be expected of it to prevent these acts after having received substantial information', or if the State 'demonstrably gives shelter to terrorists after they have committed an act of terrorism within another State in a situation in which the attack can still be regarded as ongoing' (Randelzhofer & Nolte, 'Article 51', para. 38).

these concepts, they bring a certain degree of coherence and hierarchy to the international legal system and work against its fragmentation. Rules of international law from which it is impossible to derogate through treaties constitute *jus cogens* or peremptory norms of general international law. While this concept had been disputed in the past, it is today firmly established in both judicial opinion and doctrine.[127] The VCLT expressly mentions peremptory norms in its Article 53, which declares a treaty to be void if it conflicts with a *jus cogens* norm.[128] The list of norms that are—in the words of Article 53—'accepted and recognized by the international community of States' as *jus cogens* may vary over time. While there is even today some controversy about the exact composition of this list,[129] the peremptory character of some norms is rather uncontroversial: the prohibition of aggression and genocide; the principle of racial non-discrimination; the rules on crimes against humanity; and the prohibition of torture, trade in slaves, and piracy are usually considered to constitute *jus cogens*.[130] One might wonder how such norms of *jus cogens*—a rather 'loose, objective standard of a purely negative character'[131]—could ever be relevant in investor–State arbitration. Still, the concept of *jus cogens* has already played a certain role in some investor–State arbitrations. The *Methanex* tribunal, for example, referred to *jus cogens* and put it in context with constitutional ideas. It held that:

as a matter of international constitutional law a tribunal has an independent duty to apply imperative principles of law or jus cogens and not to give effect to parties' choices of law that are inconsistent with such principles.[132]

---

[127] For the concept of jus cogens in general, *see, e.g.,* Alexander Orakhelashvili, *Peremptory Norms in International Law* (2006) and Andreas L. Paulus, 'Jus Cogens in a Time of Hegemony and Fragmentation—an Attempt at a Re-appraisal', *Nordic Journal of International Law* 74 (2005) 297–334.

[128] Article 53 VCLT, which is entitled 'Treaties conflicting with a peremptory norm of general international law ("*jus cogens*")', reads as follows:

A treaty is void if, at the time of its conclusion, it conflicts with a peremptory norm of general international law. For the purposes of the present Convention, a peremptory norm of general international law is a norm accepted and recognized by the international community of States as a whole as a norm from which no derogation is permitted and which can be modified only by a subsequent norm of general international law having the same character.

[129] *Compare e.g.* the extensive compilation by Orakhelashvili, *Peremptory Norms*, at 50–65 with the more restrictive approach of Paulus, *Jus Cogens in a Time of Hegemony and Fragmentation—an Attempt at a Re-appraisal*, at 306.

[130] Brownlie, *Public International Law*, at 510–11 with further references. *See also* the list in ILC, *Commentaries on State Responsibility*, Article 26, para. 5, which additionally includes the right to self-determination.

[131] Andreas L. Paulus, 'The International Legal System as a Constitution', *in Ruling the World?* (Dunoff & Trachtman eds., 2009) 69–109, at 88.

[132] *Methanex v. United States,* Final Award, 3 August 2005, 44 ILM (2005) 1345, Part IV, Chapter C, para. 24. The tribunal found that an interpretative note of the NAFTA Free Trade Commission (FTC) on the minimum standard of treatment in Article 1105 NAFTA of 31 July 2001 (*available at* <http://www.sice.oas.org/tpd/nafta/Commission/CH11understanding_e.asp>) did not violate *jus cogens*.

An investment treaty arbitration in which *jus cogens* arguments were of potentially significant relevance was *Piero Foresti, Laura de Carli and others v. Republic of South Africa*.[133] In 2007, European mining investors instigated arbitral proceedings against South Africa because of the regulatory changes in its mining sector. The relevant legislation was based on Article 25(8) of the Constitution of South Africa, which seeks to 'redress the results of past racial discrimination' in the context of access to land and other natural resources. The investors argued that the new regulatory regime rendered their investment less valuable and amounted to an expropriation of their mining rights. An *amicus curiae*, the International Commisssion of Jurists,[134] referred in its petition for participation to the concept of *jus cogens*. It recalled an ILC statement according to which the 'prohibition against racial discrimination has been "clearly accepted and recognized" as a peremptory norm of international law (*jus cogens*) by the international community as a whole'.[135] The tribunal never commented on the relevance of *jus cogens* as the proceedings came to an end with a default award.[136]

But it is still worthwhile to consider how the *jus cogens* argument might have played out in *Piero Foresti*. In his separate opinion in *Oil Platforms*, Judge Simma held that if the rules to be taken into account according to Article 31(3)(c) VCLT are peremptory norms of international law

then the principle of interpretation just mentioned turns into a legally insurmountable limit to permissible treaty interpretation.[137]

Could this mean that the substantive standards for investment protection in BITs have to yield automatically as soon as *jus cogens* is involved? Is it sufficient for a State to claim that it is regulating for the sake of a *jus cogens* norm in order to defeat all claims based on an IIA?

It is important to bear in mind that Judge Simma's remarks in *Oil Platforms* related to the use of force and its prohibition in Article 2(4) of the UN Charter. Scenarios that might give rise to *jus cogens* arguments in investor–State arbitration, in contrast, will typically involve a duty of the host State to take action as opposed to a duty to refrain from certain conduct. This was also the case in *Piero Foresti*, where the prohibition of racial discrimination as *jus cogens* became relevant in the context of the duty under certain human rights treaties not only to refrain from

---

[133] ICSID Case No. ARB(AF)/07/1.

[134] *See* Luke E. Peterson, 'NGOs Permitted to Intervene in South Africa Mining Case and— for Second Time at ICSID—Tribunal Orders Would-be Petitioners to be Given Access to Case Documents', *International Arbitration Reporter* 2 No. 16 (2009).

[135] *Piero Foresti, Laura de Carli and others v. Republic of South Africa*, ICSID Case No. ARB(AF)/07/1, Petition for participation as non-disputing party pursuant to Article 41(3) of the ICISD Arbitration (Additional Factility) Rules, Petitioner: International Commission of Jurists, 19 August 2009, para. 25, referring to ILC, *Commentaries on State Responsibility*, Article 26, para. 5.

[136] *Piero Foresti, Laura de Carli and others v. Republic of South Africa*, ICSID Case No. ARB(AF)/07/1, Award, 4 August 2010. The tribunal decided that the claimants have to contribute to the costs incurred by the respondent and dismissed all claims of the claimants (id., para. 133).

[137] *Case concerning Oil Platforms* (Iran v. United States of America), Judgment, 6 November 2003, ICJ Reports 2003, 161 (Simma, J, partly dissenting), para. 9.

racial discrimination but also to take positive steps.[138] Positive duties typically offer several means of compliance. While an inquiry into whether a State violates a *jus cogens* norm through its active conduct is rather straightforward, a State will often have a variety of different means at its disposal to comply with a duty to act. In this vein, the ILC found that a conflict between a treaty obligation 'apparently lawful on its face and innocent in purpose' (i.e. for our purposes a BIT provision) and a peremptory norm of international law should not be resolved by invalidating the treaty, but by the 'processes of interpretation and application'.[139] Depending on the particular IIA obligation in question (on which more in Chapters 5 and 6), proportionality analysis is arguably the most appropriate way to deal with such *jus cogens* issues. Questions to be clarified in such a case include whether the State could have achieved its goal as effectively through less infringing means and whether the advancement of the interest protected by *jus cogens* was indeed the regulatory goal.

Similar considerations apply to Article 103 of the UN Charter, one of the few universal conflict rules in international law.[140] This provision grants superiority to the UN Charter and specifies that:

[i]n the event of a conflict between the obligations of the Members of the United Nations under the present Charter and their obligations under any other international agreement, their obligations under the present Charter shall prevail.

Some argue that Article 103 of the UN Charter constitutes a 'constitutional provision'.[141] For the purposes of Article 31(3)(c) VCLT, the constitutional character of Article 103 UN Charter is not crucial; it suffices that the UN Charter is a treaty and Article 103 a 'rule of international law'.

One possible scenario in which Article 103 could play a role in investor–State arbitration is in the context of binding UN Security Council resolutions imposing, say, economic sanctions that have a negative effect on foreign investors.[142]

---

[138] *Piero Foresti, Laura de Carli and others v. Republic of South Africa*, ICSID Case No. ARB(AF)/07/1, Petition for participation as non-disputing party pursuant to Article 41(3) of the ICISD Arbitration (Additional Factility) Rules, Petitioner: International Commission of Jurists, 19 August 2009, para. 24.

[139] ILC, *Commentaries on State Responsibility*, Article 26, para. 3.

[140] The VCLT recognizes the hierarchical superiority of obligations under the UN Charter in Article 30(1) ('Subject to Article 103 of the Charter of the United Nations'), *see* Villiger, *Vienna Convention on the Law of Treaties*, Article 30, para. 10. Other conflct rules are Article 53 VCLT (*jus cogens*) and the *lex specialis* and *lex posterior* principles. The latter two play an important role for intra-regime conflicts or the relationship between general international law and specialized regimes. They rarely, if ever, resolve inter-regime conflicts such as conflicts between WTO law and environmental law (*see* Jasper Finke, *Die Parallelität internationaler Streitbeilegungsmechanismen: Untersuchung der aus der Stärkung der internationalen Gerichtsbarkeit resultierenden Konflikte* (2003), at 210–16).

[141] See the references in Andreas Paulus & Johann Ruben Leiß, 'Article 103', in *The Charter of the United Nations* (Simma, et al. eds., 2012) 2110–37, para. 81, n.175. For a discussion on this issue with a negative conclusion, *see* Kadelbach & Kleinlein, *Überstaatliches Verfassungsrecht*, at 249–51.

[142] Article 103 does not only cover the Charter itself, but also obligations 'under the Charter', which include binding UN Security Council resolutions (*see, e.g.,* Paulus & Leiß, 'Article 103', para. 38; ILC, *Fragmentation of International Law*, para. 331). On the controversial issue of whether

In most cases, States will have several ways at their disposal to comply with the relevant UN Security Council resolution and to minimize adverse effects on foreign-owned assets.[143] If the host State does not make use of these options, there is no reason to release it from its IIA obligations, even if it adopts the relevant measures in compliance with the Security Council resolution. A certain tension between two international obligations does not entitle a State to readily dismiss one of them as non-existent or void. In the words of Paulus and Leiß, Article 103 'is only residual in nature',[144] and all interpretative means have to be exhausted before setting aside an international obligation. Proportionality is a valuable tool to assist arbitrators in determining whether a State complied with two separate obligations to the greatest extent possible under the particular circumstances of the case.

Article 103 of the UN Charter might also become relevant in a human rights context. As noted above, Articles 55(c) and 56 of the UN Charter are widely considered to establish legal obligations for UN member States to promote and respect human rights.[145] One human right that both governments and *amicus curiae* put forward in a number of investor–State arbitrations is the right to water.[146] The argument in these cases goes that the host State in question had to take the regulatory measures interfering with the rights of private investors in the water sector in order to comply with its human rights obligations.[147] The right to water is explicitly mentioned in a number of legal instruments, including the UN Convention on the Rights of the Child[148] and the UN Convention on the Elimination of All Forms of Discrimination against Women.[149] Moreover,

---

Article 103 also applies to non-binding decisions by UN organs, *see* Paulus & Leiß, 'Article 103', paras. 42–3.

[143] In *Kadi*, the ECJ had to decide a case in which the relevant SC resolution arguably left States no latitude in its implementation. The Court of First Instance (CFI) had held that it did not have jurisdiction to review the EU regulation implementing the binding UN resolution since this would run counter to the primacy of the UN Charter enshrined in Article 103 (Case T-315/01, *Kadi v. Council and Commission*, 2005 E.C.R. II-3649, at 3655). The ECJ, in contrast, decided the case without even mentioning Article 103 in the decisive passages of the judgment. Instead, the Court relied on the 'rule of law' (C-402/05 P and C-415/05 P, *Kadi and Al Barakaat International Foundation v. Council and Commission*, Judgment of the Grand Chamber of 3 September 2008, para. 281) within the European Union and the 'constitutional principle' of the EC Treaty according to which all legislative and executive acts of the European Union need to comply with fundamental rights (id., para. 285). Andrea Gattini rightly described this approach of the ECJ as 'EC inward constitutionalism' (Andrea Gattini, 'Case Law: Joined Cases C-402 & 415/05 P', *Common Market Law Review* 46 (2009) 213–39, at 224).

[144] Paulus & Leiß, 'Article 103', para. 21.   [145] *See supra* note 99.

[146] *See, e.g. Suez, Sociedad General de Aguas de Barcelona SA, and Vivendi Universal SA v. Argentine Republic*, ICSID Case No. ARB/03/19, Amicus Curiae Submission by the Center for International Environmental Law (CIEL) et al., 4 April 2007. For an extensive list of further cases in this respect, *see* Luke E. Peterson, *Human Rights and Bilateral Investment Treaties* (2009) at 26 n.59 and Jorge E. Vinuales, 'Access to Water in Foreign Investment Disputes', *Georgetown International Environmental Law Review* 21 (2009) 733–58, at 733 n.1.

[147] Peterson, *Human Rights and Bilateral Investment Treaties*, at 26–31.

[148] Convention on the Rights of the Child, Article 24(2)(c), 20 November 1989, 1577 UNTS 3.

[149] Convention on the Elimination of All Forms of Discrimination against Women, Article 14(2)(h), 18 December 1979, 1249 UNTS 13. For a list of further international documents explicitly or implicitly referring to the human right to water, *see* UN Economic and Social Council,

the right to water is considered to implicitly form part of a number of other human rights norms, particularly the right to an adequate standard of living and the right to health enshrined in the ICSECR (Articles 11(1) and 12).[150] Other norms of the two UN Covenants and the UDHR are also invoked in this context, foremost the right to life and human dignity.[151] In 2010, the UN General Assembly explicitly 'recognize[d] the right to safe and clean drinking water and sanitation as a human right'.[152]

The UN Committee on Economic, Social and Cultural Rights commented in greater detail on the content of the right to water. It held that States have a positive duty to ensure that its population has access to water at an affordable price.[153] As mentioned above, some consider the Universal Declaration of Human Rights and other human rights instruments to concretize the obligations of UN member States under Articles 55(c) and 56 of the UN Charter.[154] It is beyond the scope of this book to comment on the persuasiveness of this notion, or on the existence of a positive duty to ensure access to water. But if one accepts and combines these two propositions for the sake of argument, some might find that if a State's IIA obligations conflict with its duty to ensure access to water, the latter prevails according to Article 103 of the UN Charter.[155] It is to be noted, however, that positive duties of States under human rights instruments can be fulfilled through a variety of different means. It will be for the State to adopt measures that give effect to both human rights and rights protected in the relevant IIA to the greatest extent possible. Again, proportionality provides a useful analytical framework, which includes the question whether the State could have resorted to equally effective but less infringing means to comply with its human rights obligations.

b) Which 'parties'?

We now turn to the relevant 'parties' in the context of Article 31(3)(c) VCLT. To recall, this provision requires a certain rule to be 'applicable in the relations

---

Committee on Economic, Social and Cultural Rights, *General Comment No. 15*, UN Doc E/C.12/2002/11 (20 January 2003), para. 4 n.5.

[150] International Covenant on Economic, Social and Cultural Rights, 16 December 1966, 993 UNTS 3. *See* id., paras. 3, 9.

[151] Id., para. 3. *See also* Article 25(1) of the Universal Declaration of Human Rights. Vinuales, 'Access to Water in Foreign Investment Disputes', at 737 n.12, invokes the right to life in Articles 1(2) and 6 (1) of the ICCPR.

[152] GA Res 64/292, UN Doc A/Res/64/292 (August 3, 2010), para. 1.

[153] Notably, the Committee on Economic, Social and Cultural Rights appears to consider some positive duties in relation to the right to water to belong to *jus cogens*. The Committee opines that some 'core obligations' are 'non-derogable' (UN Economic and Social Council, UN Doc E/C.12/2002/11, para. 40), e.g. the obligation to 'ensure access to the minimum essential amount of water, that is sufficient and safe for personal and domestic uses to prevent disease' (id., para. 37(a)) and the obligation to 'adopt relatively low-cost targeted water programmes to protect vulnerable and marginalized groups' (id., para. 37(h)).

[154] *See supra* note 121 and accompanying text.

[155] For the consequences of norm collisions under Article 103 of the UN Charter, *see* Paulus & Leiß, 'Article 103', paras. 75–80.

between the parties.' Two different strands of inter-State relations are relevant here. For the first, if there is a dispute that involves the interpretation of a treaty, the disputing parties will often be parties to the relevant treaty. In investor–State arbitration, this is different: the foreign investor as one of the disputing parties relies on the treaty membership of its home State. The second relevant strand concerns the rules of international law to be taken into account in the interpreta-tion process. As long as these rules are universal and constitute customary inter-national law or general principles of law within the meaning of Article 38(1)(c) ICJ Statute, no further inquiry regarding the relevant 'parties' is necessary. The situation is more complicated if the relevant rules of international law stem from a treaty without universal membership. Here, the question arises whether all con-tracting States of the treaty being interpreted have to be parties to the treaty that is to assist in the interpretation process.

In *EC–Biotech Products*, the EC argued that the panel had to take into account the *Convention of Biological Diversity* and the *Biosafety Protocol*.[156] The panel rejected this view because not all WTO members were parties to these two mul-tilateral treaties.[157] The main concern of the panel seemed to be that the EC approach would lead to the odd result that some WTO member States would have different obligations under the same WTO provisions as others.[158] Furthermore, the panel expressed some sovereignty-based concerns when it held that the EC approach would entail

as a consequence that the interpretation of a treaty to which that State is a party is affected by other rules of international law which that State has decided not to accept.[159]

Several considerations speak against the restrictive approach adopted in *EC–Biotech Products*. Requiring that all WTO members must have ratified a treaty for the latter to play a role in the interpretation of WTO provisions greatly diminishes the relevance of Article 31(3)(c) in the WTO context. The ILC rightly noted that this approach has the 'ironic effect that the more the membership of a multilateral treaty such as the WTO covered agreements expanded, the more those treaties would be cut off from the rest of international law'. Such a development would be 'contrary to the legislative ethos behind most of multilateral treaty making'.[160] Therefore, the ILC suggested that it should be sufficient that the State parties to a dispute relating to a multilateral treaty are also parties to the treaty assisting in the interpretation of the multilateral treaty.[161]

For the purposes of investor–State arbitration, it is largely irrelevant whether one follows the approach of the WTO panel in *EC–Biotech Products*, the

---

[156] 'European Communities—Measures Affecting the Approval and Marketing of Biotech Products', WT/DS291/R, WT/DS292/R, WT/DS293/R, Reports of the Panel, 29 September 2006, paras. 7.53–7.55.
[157] Id., paras. 7.70, 7.73–7.75.   [158] Id., para. 7.70.   [159] Id., para. 7.71.
[160] ILC, *Fragmentation of International Law*, para. 471.   [161] Id., para. 472.

suggestion of the ILC, or alternative suggestions.[162] For disputes under BITs, all approaches introduced in this subsection lead to the same result: for the purposes of Article 31(3)(c) VCLT it is sufficient that the two parties to the BIT to be interpreted are also parties to the treaty that the arbitrators ought to take into account in the interpretation process. In investor–State arbitrations under Chapter XI of NAFTA, the situation is only slightly more complicated. Even under the more restrictive approach of the WTO panel in *EC–Biotech Products*, it is sufficient that the three NAFTA States are parties to the other treaty—a threshold which is much easier to meet than that in the WTO context.

Admittedly, investor–State arbitrations under the ECT will often require an adoption of the ILC approach in order to interpret ECT provisions in light of other treaties. The number of investor–State arbitrations under the ECT, however, is lower than the number of proceedings based on BITs. Furthermore, the number of member states of the ECT is still moderate when compared to the WTO. Moreover, it is important to keep in mind that the debate about the meaning of the term 'parties' in Article 31(3)(c) only matters when the relevant 'rule of international law' is a treaty provision. Rules of customary international law or general principles within the meaning of Article 38(1)(c) ICJ Statute are universal standards that do not give rise to the controversy introduced in this subsection.

c) Which rules are 'applicable'?

The requirement that the rule of international law needs to be 'applicable' in the relations between the parties raises both temporal and normative issues, which I will now address, in that order.

(1) Temporal issues

Article 31(3)(c) does not specify whether the external norm must have been in force at the time of the conclusion of the relevant treaty or at the time of its interpretation. An early draft of what would become Article 31(3)(c) clarified that the time of the conclusion of the relevant treaty was the decisive point in time.[163] When the ILC adopted the final version of its Draft Articles on the Law of Treaties in 1966, however, it could not agree on this issue. Hence, the ILC dropped the temporal element from the draft article's final version.[164] Today, many commentators focus on the time of the interpretation of the treaty, and thus give effect to the evolution of international law.[165]

---

[162] For a differentiation between 'synallagmatic' and 'interdependent' multilateral treaties, *see* Simma & Kill, 'Harmonizing Investment Protection and International Human Rights', at 699 (with further references).

[163] *See supra* note 46.

[164] ILC, *Commentaries on the Law of Treaties*, Articles 27–8, para. 16.

[165] *See, e.g.,* Simma & Kill, 'Harmonizing Investment Protection and International Human Rights', at 696, and Finke, *Die Parallelität internationaler Streitbeilegungsmechanismen*, at 184–5 (with further references, inter alia, to judicial decision dealing with the intertemporal rule in

In its report on the fragmentation of international law, the ILC tried to strike a balance between these two approaches. The ILC noted that the starting point for determining the relevant point in time is a matter of interpreting the treaty itself. Consequently, interpreters should pay special attention to treaty language that is 'not static but evolutionary'. Furthermore, the object and purpose of a treaty could give rise to the assumption that the parties have 'committed themselves to a programme of progressive development'.[166] The ILC argued that the use of 'very general terms' in a treaty would militate in favour of resort to the rules of international law in force at the date of interpretation.[167] Article XX GATT, for example, which permits measures 'necessary' to protect the environment, human health, or other public interests, should be interpreted in light of the evolving standards in the relevant areas of international law.[168]

It is important to bear in mind that international investment arbitration involves non-State actors. If States conclude a treaty that has the potential to influence the interpretation of a legal instrument that predates this treaty, they do this at their own will, and at the reciprocal risk of adverse effects in future inter-State disputes. Foreign investors, in contrast, have no direct influence on treaty-making activities. If the time of the interpretation of the relevant IIA matters for determining which rules are 'applicable', then a treaty concluded after the investor made its investment might negatively influence the protections of this IIA. IIAs, however, intend to provide foreign investors with some certainty at the time they make their investment as to the treatment of their assets in the host State.[169] This purpose would suffer if States could influence the interpretation of IIAs at will by concluding treaties after the foreign-owned assets are in place. The same considerations apply to subsequent agreements on the interpretation of IIA provisions, and will be discussed below.[170]

(2) Normative issues

So far, adjudicatory bodies and most commentators have assumed that only such rules are 'applicable' within the meaning of Article 31(3)(c) that are *binding* on all the parties to the dispute (or even on all the parties of the treaty to be interpreted, depending on the interpretation of the term 'parties' discussed in

---

general, but not explicitly with respect to Article 31(3)(c) VCLT). *See also* Campbell McLachlan, 'The Evolution of Treaty Obligation in International Law', *in Treaties and Subsequent Practice* (Georg Nolte ed., 2013) 69–81, at 73–76; Bruno Simma, 'Miscellaneous Thoughts on Subsequent Agreements and Practice', at 48. For an overview of evolutionary interpretation by international courts and tribunals in the context of Article 31(3)(a) and (b) VCLT, *see* Georg Nolte, 'Reports for the ILC Study Group On Treaties over Time: Report 1—Jurisprudence of the International Court of Justice and Arbitral Tribunals of ad hoc Jurisdiction Relating to Subsequent Agreements and Subsequent Practice' *see id.* 169–209, at 184–8, 207; Nolte, 'Reports for the ILC Study Group On Treaties over Time: Report 2', at 303.

[166] ILC, *Fragmentation of International Law*, para. 478(a).   [167] Id., para. 478(b).
[168] Id. On the jurisprudence of the WTO adjudicatory bodies with respect to Article XX GATT, *see* Chapter 3, notes 232–58 and accompanying text.
[169] *See* Chapter 5, notes 172–88 and accompanying text.   [170] *See* Chapter 5, subsection V.4.

the previous subsection).[171] In the realm of investor–State arbitration, however, this view can lead to contradictory and unsatisfactory consequences. The following example (borrowed from Simma/Kill and slightly modified)[172] illustrates this claim: Argentina, China, France, and Spain have ratified the ICESCR, but the US has not. We assume that foreign investors from China, France, Spain, and the US instigate arbitral proceedings against Argentina based on the respective BIT between their home State and Argentina. As the ICESCR is not binding for the US, it could play a role only in the arbitral proceedings brought by the Chinese, French, and Spanish investors, but not in the arbitration between the US investor and Argentina. Such practice could lead to divergent interpretations of BIT provisions with virtually identical wording. Human rights treaties can be relevant in the interpretation of IIAs in several respects, both to the advantage and disadvantage of host States.[173] In scenarios in which human rights considerations support the position of the host State, the traditional approach would make States that do not ratify human rights treaties more attractive places of incorporation.[174]

There are several ways to prevent or mitigate such an outcome. First, the problem just described can only arise when the external rule stems from a multilateral treaty without universal membership. To the extent that human rights constitute general principles of law within the meaning of Article 38(1)(c) ICJ Statute, they are binding for all States. We have discussed the arguments for and against the notion of human rights as general principles of law above,[175] and they are no less valid here. Second, the wording of Article 31(3)(c) does not require the relevant external rule to be 'binding' or 'in force', as Simma and Kill point out.[176] Rather, the provision uses a term that is more flexible: 'applicable'. Hence, Simma and Kill argue that it is sufficient if the external rule is '*implicitly* accepted or tolerated' by the relevant States.[177] Finke follows a similar approach and argues that the external rules may stem from non-binding 'soft law'.[178]

Others might argue that this broad reading of the term 'applicable' in Article 31(3)(c) deviates from the interpretation of the same term in other provisions. Article 42 ICSID Convention, for example, obliges arbitral tribunals to decide disputes 'in accordance with…such rules of international law as may be *applicable*'

---

[171] The WTO panel in *EC–Biotech Products* did not even discuss this issue, but rather used the terms 'applicable' and 'binding' interchangeably (*European Communities—Measures Affecting the Approval and Marketing of Biotech Products*, WT/DS291/R, WT/DS292/R, WT/DS293/R, Reports of the Panel, 29 September 2006, para. 7.71). Villiger plainly states that '[t]he term 'applicable' leaves no room for doubt: *non*-binding rules cannot be relied upon.' (Villiger, *Vienna Convention on the Law of Treaties*, Article 31, para. 25, emphasis in the original).

[172] Simma & Kill, 'Harmonizing Investment Protection and International Human Rights', at 700.

[173] *See, e.g.,* Chapter 6, notes 154–6 and accompanying text.

[174] *See also* Simma & Kill, 'Harmonizing Investment Protection and International Human Rights', at 700.

[175] *See supra* notes 106–26 and accompanying text.

[176] Simma & Kill, 'Harmonizing Investment Protection and International Human Rights', at 697.

[177] Id., at 698 (emphasis in the original).

[178] Finke, *Die Parallelität internationaler Streitbeilegungsmechanismen*, at 191.

[emphasis added]. Article 1131(1) NAFTA provides that tribunals 'shall decide the issues in dispute in accordance with this Agreement and *applicable* rules of international law' [emphasis added]. As discussed above, these provisions refer to the sources of international law as reflected in Article 38(1) ICJ Statute, which give rise to binding legal obligations.[179] That said, the following consideration might alleviate concerns about an undue influence of non-binding rules of international law on the interpretation process. Article 31(3)(c) does not say anything about the weight of external rules in the interpretation of a treaty. This weight should vary with the normative force of the external rule. In other words, a *jus cogens* norm will play a greater role in the interpretation of a treaty than an external non-peremptory rule of international law derived from custom, treaty, or general principles.[180] The latter, in turn, will have a stronger influence on the interpretation of a treaty than non-binding legal expressions. Furthermore, it will be difficult for a non-binding norm to have a decisive influence on the interpretation process when the wording and the context of the relevant provision indicate a different direction.

The third notion that might help to avoid unsatisfactory outcomes due to the lack of a binding effect of the relevant rule on all IIA contracting States is the concept of obligations *erga omnes*.[181] In *Barcelona Traction*, the ICJ distinguished the obligations of a State 'vis-à-vis another State' from those 'towards the international community as a whole' which are '[i]n view of the importance of the rights involved...obligations *erga omnes*'.[182] The *Nuclear Tests* case provides a first idea about the potential relevance of obligations *erga omnes* in the context of Article 31(3)(c). In this case, the Court had to decide on the legal effects of a declaration by the French government to abstain from further atmospheric nuclear tests after the conclusion of a series of tests in 1974. The Court found that:

[t]he unilateral statements of the French authorities were made outside the Court, publicly and *erga omnes*,...to have legal effect, there was no need for these statements to be addressed to a particular State, nor was acceptance by any other State required...The objects of these statements are clear and they were addressed to the international community as a whole, and the Court holds that they constitute an undertaking possessing legal effect.[183]

This passage reveals nothing about the *substantive* content of obligations *erga omnes*.[184] However, it is precisely the *formal* notion of obligations toward the international community as a whole that is of interest here. The phrase 'rules of

---

[179] *See* Chapter 3, notes 4–9 and accompanying text.

[180] For the relevance of *jus cogens* norms in treaty interpretation, *see supra* pp. 106–9.

[181] *See also* Simma & Kill, 'Harmonizing Investment Protection and International Human Rights', at 701.

[182] *Case concerning the Barcelona Traction Light and Power Company Limited* (Belgium v. Spain), Judgment, 5 February 1970, ICJ Reports (1970) 3, para. 33.

[183] *Nuclear Tests* (Australia v. France), Judgment, 20 December 1974, ICJ Reports 1974, 253, paras. 50–1.

[184] For comments on the norms that give rise to obligations *erga omnes*, *see* Chapter 8, note 106 and accompanying text.

international law' in Article 31(3)(c) is usually understood as a reference to the sources of international law.[185] Article 38(1)(c) ICJ Statute lists international treaties, customary international law, and general principles of law as sources of international law. This enumeration, however, is not exhaustive—at least not if one considers all instruments that give rise to legal rights and obligations to constitute sources of international law.[186] The ICJ clarified in the *Nuclear Tests* case that legal obligations can arise from unilateral acts of States, at least from those that do not constitute 'purely political commitments'.[187]

If the term 'rules' refers indeed to 'sources' of international law, then unilateral acts that give rise to international obligations may fall under the scope of Article 31(3)(c). While the relevant external 'rule' needs to involve both parties ('applicable *in the relations between the parties*' [emphasis added]), it does not necessarily have to give rise to reciprocal obligations. Multilateral human rights treaties or treaties for the protection of the environment, for example, do create reciprocal obligations (only) among the contracting States. Beyond that, however, they give legal effect to community interests for the benefit of all. In the *Nuclear Tests* case, the ICJ found that a declaration announcing the cessation of nuclear tests constituted a statement made *erga omnes*. It is worth considering whether the ratification of a multilateral treaty for the protection of human rights (or the environment) can also be a legally relevant expression addressed to the international community as a whole.

If the answer is 'yes', then a multilateral treaty for the protection of human rights or the environment could fall under Article 31(3)(c) even if it was ratified only by the State that relies on this external norm in the interpretation process. In order to accept this proposition, it is not necessary to agree that certain obligations in international law are *owed* to all other States, which are entitled to demand *fulfilment* independent of a treaty.[188] Rather, a positive answer to the above question starts from the truism that multilateral treaties for the protection of human rights or the environment fall under Article 38(1)(a) of the ICJ Statute. Hence, they are 'rules of international law' within the meaning of Article 31(3)(c). Furthermore, such treaties create binding legal obligations, and, therefore, fulfil the requirements of the term 'applicable' even under its most restrictive interpretation. Article 31(3)(c) further requires the involvement of both parties in the legal relationship established by the particular rule in question. In this regard, it ought to suffice that the multilateral treaty entails binding obligations for one of the relevant parties. These obligations do not only rest on a *quid pro quo* bargain, but also serve the interests of the international community as a whole. The other party is sufficiently involved in the legal relationships established by such multilateral treaties as a member of this international community.[189]

---

[185] *See supra* note 83 and accompanying text.   [186] Pellet, 'Article 38', para. 90.

[187] Id., para. 95. For an overview of the relevant case law of the ICJ, *see* id., paras. 96–8.

[188] For such an understanding of 'true obligation[s] *erga omnes*', *see* Simma & Kill, 'Harmonizing Investment Protection and International Human Rights', at 701.

[189] Note that the notion of obligations *erga omnes partes* is not a very promising avenue in this context. Such obligations are usually considered to serve the interests of all of the parties to a certain

This approach also yields reasonable outcomes. It does not detach the meaning of the terms 'rules' and 'applicable' from the notion of binding legal obligations. At the same time, it takes account of the fact that Article 31(3)(c) does not explicitly require the rule in question to be binding on *all* the parties to the dispute. Furthermore, this approach does not exclude a multilateral treaty protecting the interests of the international community from the scope of Article 31(3)(c) only because the other contracting State failed to ratify it. Of course, only the State that actually ratified the multilateral treaty should be able to rely on this external norm in the interpretation process. A State that chose not to join a multilateral treaty for the protection of a community interest will not be able to invoke this instrument when it comes to its obligations under the relevant IIA. All this might entail a small incentive for States to ratify multilateral treaties serving the interests of the international community as a whole.

d) Which rules are 'relevant'?

The wording of Article 31(3)(c) VCLT does not only require the 'rule of international law' in question to be 'applicable in the relations between the parties' but also to be 'relevant'. At a first glance, this term merely seems to reflect the truism that a treaty interpreter does not have to go through the whole body of international law to interpret a treaty but merely has to look at rules that are 'relevant' in the particular context.[190] Still, several issues deserve attention here. Richard Gardiner suggests that the term 'relevant' might trigger temporal considerations.[191] This appears to be difficult to reconcile with the decision of the ILC not to include temporal elements in the wording of Article 31(3)(c).[192] Another issue is whether the term 'relevant' requires a unity of 'subject-matter' between the treaty to be interpreted and the external rule. Such a view would reduce the relevance of Article 31(3)(c) to a minimum. Moreover, Article 30 VCLT regulates the relationship between treaties on the same subject matter.[193]

---

regime. This subsection, however, discusses scenarios in which one of the relevant parties within the meaning of Article 31(3)(c) is *not* a party to the treaty regime in question. (For the differences between the notions of obligations *erga omnes partes* and obligations *erga omnes, see* Orakhelashvili, *Peremptory Norms,* at 268.)

[190] In this regard, the term 'relevant' mitigates potentially overreaching consequences of the characterization of Article 31(3)(c) VCLT as a 'mandatory part of the interpretation process' (*see supra* note 502).

[191] Gardiner, *Treaty Interpretation,* at 260.

[192] *See supra* notes 163–5 and accompanying text.

[193] Article 30 of the VCLT (entitled 'Application of successive treaties relating to the same subject-matter') reads as follows:

1. Subject to article 103 of the Charter of the United Nations, the rights and obligations of States parties to successive treaties relating to the same subject-matter shall be determined in accordance with the following paragraphs.
2. When a treaty specifies that it is subject to, or that it is not to be considered as incompatible with, an earlier or later treaty, the provisions of that other treaty prevail.
3. When all the parties to the earlier treaty are parties also to the later treaty but the earlier treaty is not terminated or suspended in operation under article 59, the earlier

It does not seem to be a good idea to undermine the elaborate mechanism set out in this provision by leaving parts of the relationship between treaties on the same subject matter to be governed by Article 31(3)(c).[194]

It appears more reasonable to require that the external rule needs to relate in some way to the same subject matter as the treaty *term* or *provision* (as opposed to the treaty as such).[195] This approach ensures that Article 31(3)(c) has some independent meaning, and it is compatible with ICJ jurisprudence. In *Oil Platforms*, the ICJ interpreted a provision of the US–Iran FCN Treaty dealing with issues of international peace and the security interests of the State parties in the light of the law on the use of force.[196] In another case, the ICJ recognized that a general treaty on friendship and cooperation could have a 'bearing on the interpretation and application' of a treaty on assistance in criminal matters.[197]

It would be contradictory to impose a rigid meaning on the inherently flexible term 'relevant'. The relevance of external rules in treaty interpretation should depend on the particular circumstances of each individual case. If the wording of a treaty term is self-explanatory and unambiguous, the role of external rules in the interpretation process will be minor. Similarly, if the context strongly supports a particular interpretation of the treaty term that is compatible with its ordinary meaning, it will be difficult for external rules to steer the interpretation process in a different direction. Conversely, it matters how specific the external rule regulates

---

treaty applies only to the extent that its provisions are compatible with those of the later treaty.
4. When the parties to the later treaty do not include all the parties to the earlier one:
   (a) as between States parties to both treaties the same rule applies as in paragraph 3;
   (b) as between a State party to both treaties and a State party to only one of the treaties, the treaty to which both States are parties governs their mutual rights and obligations.
5. Paragraph 4 is without prejudice to article 41, or to any question of the termination or suspension of the operation of a treaty under article 60 or to any question of responsibility which may arise for a State from the conclusion or application of a treaty the provisions of which are incompatible with its obligations towards another State under another treaty.

[194] *See* Simma & Kill, 'Harmonizing Investment Protection and International Human Rights', at 693. One author who seems to come close to requiring a unity of subject matter is Henn-Jüri Uibopuu. Even this author, however, only requires the rules to be taken into account to be 'directly applicable to the subject-matter of the *case*' (Henn-Jüri Uibopuu, 'Interpretation of Treaties in the Light of International Law: Art. 31, para. 3(c) of the Vienna Convention on the Law of Treaties', *Yearbook of the Association of Attenders and Alumni of The Hague Academy of International Law* 40 (1970) 1–42, at 4, emphasis added).

[195] *See, e.g.* Villiger, *Vienna Convention on the Law of Treaties*, Article 31, para. 25 (referring to the relevant treaty *term*).

[196] *Supra* notes 22–4. *But see* the separate opinion of Judges Higgins (*Case concerning Oil Platforms* (Iran v. United States of America), Judgment, 6 November 2003, ICJ Reports 2003, 161 (Higgins, J, concurring). Judge Higgins found that the ICJ would have had to provide further explanation when it 'incorporat[ed] the entire substance of international law on a topic not mentioned in [Article XX(1)(d) of the FCN Treaty]' (id., para. 46).

[197] *Certain Questions of Mutual Assistance in Criminal Matters* (Djibouti v. France), Judgment, 4 June 2008, ICJ Reports 2008, 177, para. 114. *See also supra* notes 25–9 and accompanying text.

a certain issue.[198] The influence of a very general rule on the interpretation of a complex and detailed provision providing for a variety of different eventualities will be weak. As Campbell McLachlan rightly observed, external rules are particularly relevant for the interpretation process when the treaty provision is unclear and a more developed area of international law is capable of resolving this ambiguity.[199] The same is true when a treaty uses a term that has an established meaning in other areas of international law.[200] Finally, Article 31(3)(c) should play a crucial role where the treaty terms are, as McLachlan put it, 'by their nature open-textured', and the progressive development of international law may illuminate the meaning of these terms.[201]

IV. Conclusion

To recall, one of the key arguments against the application of proportionality at the international level is the arbitrariness of the balancing process due to the lack of a universal value system. On the domestic level, constitutional systems typically provide value orders that militate against the arbitrariness of the balancing process. There may exist only limited indications of a *universal* value order in international law. It is important to bear in mind, however, that a value system as necessary background of proportionality balancing can also be established by the relevant treaty itself, without a need to resort to external norms. Moreover, international law does not consist of a mere web of unconnected subsystems that operate entirely independently of each other. As demonstrated in this chapter, international investment law is deeply embedded in general international law, and IIAs are far from establishing self-contained regimes.

Article 31(3)(c) VCLT may play a significant role in identifying value systems on a *bilateral* or *multilateral* level. This is true even if one adopts the more restrictive of the various approaches proposed in the context of Article 31(3)(c). It is uncontroversial that the rules of international law to be taken into account in the interpretation process may stem from treaties, customary international law, and general principles of law. The controversy about the relevant 'parties' within the meaning of Article 31(3)(c) is largely irrelevant for investment treaty arbitration on the basis of BITs. In contrast to WTO disputes, a possible requirement that all parties to the treaty that is to be interpreted be also parties to the treaty relied on in the interpretation process constitutes no hurdle in bilateral relationships.

---

[198] In other words, this factor describes the 'degree of abstraction' of the external rule (Simma & Kill, 'Harmonizing Investment Protection and International Human Rights', at 696).

[199] McLachlan, 'The Principle of Systemic Integration and Article 31(3)(c) of the Vienna Convention', at 312, para. 6(a).

[200] Id., para. 6(b).

[201] Id., para. 6(c). In a similar vein, Simma and Kill argue that the principle of systemic integration is particularly relevant in the interpretation of 'generic terms' (Simma & Kill, 'Harmonizing Investment Protection and International Human Rights', at 703–4).

Furthermore, multilateral human rights treaties have reached such widespread membership that they may be resorted to as (binding) external rules in a great number of investor–State arbitrations. Moreover, concepts that are part of customary international law or constitute general principles of law are always 'applicable in the relations between the parties'. In sum, Article 31(3)(c) allows treaty interpreters to resort to external rules that reflect multilateral or bilateral agreement on certain values and policy choices.

That said, Article 31(3)(c) is not a universal conflict rule, nor is it a magic wand that creates universal values or hierarchical structures in international law which States have been unable or unwilling to establish so far. Rather, it is one of several means of treaty interpretation. The principle of systemic integration is not hierarchically inferior to other means of interpretation. Still, treaty interpreters should carefully consider the ordinary meaning of the treaty terms, their context, and the object and purpose of the treaty before they turn to external rules. Furthermore, there is a clear line between the interpretation of a treaty and its modification.[202] Article 31(3)(c) can only be relied on for the purposes of the former. Consequently, where States have made certain choices in BITs, it is not for arbitrators to overturn these decisions. Such an approach would be contrary not only to traditional notions of State sovereignty but also to the international rule of law. In addition, it would be virtually impossible for States to make informed and meaningful changes to their IIAs in the face of changing policy preferences.

Ultimately, the relevance of proportionality in investor–State arbitration, and the rights and interests that enter the balancing process, have to be determined separately for each legal setting. Chapters 3 and 4 have provided the relevant guidelines for this analysis. The following chapters analyse whether proportionality should play a role in IIA provisions on expropriation and FET, NPM clauses, and the customary international law defence of necessity.

---

[202] Simma & Kill, 'Harmonizing Investment Protection and International Human Rights', at 692–4.

5

Proportionality and Expropriation

Many commentators suggest that arbitral tribunals should apply the principle of proportionality (or similar methods of balancing) to determine whether an expropriation has occurred.[1] The relevant practice of arbitral tribunals is far from being uniform. Based on the methodology developed in Chapters 3 and 4, this chapter examines whether and under what circumstances IIA provisions on expropriations warrant a proportionality analysis. Except in cases in which host States deprive investors of their title to property, it is more difficult for investors to succeed on an expropriation claim than on an FET claim. The Argentine cases examined in this book are a case in point: while all tribunals but the *Metalpar* tribunal held that Argentina had violated the FET standard, no tribunal found that an expropriation had occurred.[2] This consistency is remarkable, in particular because the tribunals did not employ a uniform standard regarding expropriation and they disagreed on other issues that would determine the outcome of the cases.[3] Despite the prominent role of the FET standard in the Argentine cases and other contemporary jurisprudence, a clear understanding of what constitutes an expropriation is essential, for several reasons. First, while the FET standard is part of many or most BITs it is not part of all BITs. Second, there is a considerable number of BITs that guarantee FET but provide for investor–State arbitration only for disputes related to expropriation.[4] Third, unlike in the Argentine cases,

---

[1] *See, e.g.,* Kingsbury & Schill, 'Investor–State Arbitration as Governance', at 31–2; Kingsbury & Schill, 'Public Law Concepts to Balance Investors' Rights with State Regulatory Actions in the Public Interest', at 88–103; Stone Sweet & Grisel, 'Transnational Investment Arbitration', at 131–2; Jasper Krommendijk & John Morijn, 'Proportional' by What Measure(s)?'id. 422–51, at 449–50; Alvarez & Khamsi, 'The Argentine Crisis', at 447–9; Alvarez & Brink, 'Revisiting the Necessity Defence', at 357–8; van Aaken, 'Defragmentation of Public International Law', at 506–12; Henckels, 'Indirect Expropriation and the Right to Regulate', at 228–9; Chapter 3, note 1.

[2] *See* Chapter 2, notes 118–23 and accompanying text.

[3] *See* Chapter 2, notes 126–48 & *infra* notes 5–46 and accompanying texts.

[4] *See, e.g., Emmis International Holding, BV, Emmis Radio Operating, BV, and MEM Magyar Electronic Media Kereskedelmi és Szolgáltató Kft v. Hungary*, ICSID Case No. ARB/12/2, Award, 16 April 2014, where the relevant Hungary–Switzerland and Hungary–Netherland BITs limited investor–State arbitration to expropration (paras. 134–45). The tribunal dimissed all claims for lack of jurisdiction as it was not convinced that the dispute concerned issues of expropriation (id., paras. 145, 265). Russian BITs from the Soviet era often contain even more narrow dispute-resolution clauses, restricting investor–State arbitration to issues regarding *compensation* for expropriation, which does not necessarily include the question whether an expropriation has occured in the first place (Sergey Ripinsky, 'Commentary on the Russian Model BIT', *in Commentaries on Selected Model Investment Treaties* (Chester Brown ed., 2013) 593–621, at 614–15).

State action during other financial crises—whether past or future—might justify expropriation claims.[5] Moreover, States interfere with foreign-owned assets not only in times of crisis but also in periods of macroeconomic stability, which further highlights the need for a clear understanding of expropriation provisions. Finally, we will see that analysing the role of proportionality in IIA provisions on expropriation offers valuable insights regarding the relevance of proportionality in other normative settings in investor–State arbitration.

This chapter proceeds as follows. Section I explains the differences between direct and indirect expropriations. It also provides a brief overview of the jurisprudence resulting from the Argentine crisis on direct expropriation. Section II introduces the different approaches of determining an indirect expropriation and their use by the tribunals in the Argentine cases. Section III discusses some policy rationales for determining the existence of an indirect expropriation by applying the principle of proportionality. Section IV examines the legal reasoning in *Tecmed*, which is often adduced as the 'leading case' when it comes to the relevance of proportionality in the context of indirect expropriation. We will see that the methodology adopted by the *Tecmed* tribunal is insufficient reason to resort to proportionality analysis in interpreting each and every IIA provision on expropriation. Still, the different means of treaty interpretation reflected in Article 31 VCLT may justify the application of the principle of proportionality under certain circumstances, as section V illustrates.

I. Direct versus indirect expropriations

Customary international law and most BITs differentiate between direct and indirect expropriations. This dichotomy is also featured in the BITs that the tribunals dealing with the Argentine financial crisis had to analyse. Article IV(1) of the Argentina–US BIT, for example, states that:

[i]nvestments should not be expropriated or nationalized either directly or indirectly through measures tantamount to expropriation or nationalization ('expropriation')…

Similarly, Article 5(1) of the Argentina–UK BIT stipulates that:

[i]nvestments of investors of either Contracting Party shall not be nationalized, expropriated or subjected to measures having effect equivalent to nationalization or expropriation (hereinafter referred to as 'expropriation')…

---

[5] *See, e.g.,* Anne Van Aaken & Jürgen Kurtz, 'Prudence or Discrimination? Emergency Measures, the Global Financial Crisis and International Economic Law', *Journal of International Economic Law* 12 (2009) 859–94; Stefan Hobe & Jörn Griebel, 'New Protectionism—How Binding are International Economic Legal Obligations During a Global Economic Crisis?', *Goettingen Journal of International Law* 2 (2010) 423–35, at 425–8.

Most other BITs contain identical or similar stipulations. Before entering the discussion on *indirect* expropriations in international investment law, I will briefly comment on *direct* expropriations.

In *National Grid,* an investor in Argentina's electricity sector claimed that it suffered losses from a direct expropriation. The claimant was part of a consortium ('Citilec') that was the majority shareholder in 'Transener', the company that had operated Argentina's high-voltage electricity system since 1993.[6] Argentina's emergency measures had an adverse effect on Transener's income situation under the relevant concession and contracts. The claimant argued that its economic interest in Transener's assets would sustain a claim for direct expropriation.[7] The negative finding of the tribunal on this claim reflects the high threshold most tribunals attach to direct expropriations:

No formal right of property has been transferred to the State...Deprivation of title to property is inherent in a direct expropriation and none has been adduced or proven in these proceedings. On the contrary, the claimant retained title to its shares and sold them. The Measures may or may not have destroyed its investment but have not transferred ownership of it.[8]

In *Suez–Vivendi, AWG Group,* and *Suez–InterAgua,* the arbitrators also focused on the loss of ownership and title in determining whether there had been a direct expropriation. In these cases, the claimants argued that they had been directly expropriated by the termination of a concession for water distribution and waste water treatment services in Buenos Aires and some surrounding municipalities. The claimants stressed that their case differed from the situation in the cases involving investors in the Argentine gas sector since investors such as *CMS* retained ownership and control of their investment. In the water sector, however, the termination of the concession would have resulted in the claimants' loss of their investments and a corresponding gain for Argentina (in the form of an improved water and sewage system).[9] The arbitrators first clarified that neither the claimants nor a company of which they were shareholders had any property rights in the physical assets of the water and sewage system.[10] In a second step, the arbitrators recognized that contractual rights may be subject to expropriation. The arbitrators noted, however, that the particular contractual rights in question

---

[6] *National Grid plc v. Argentina*, UNCITRAL Arbitration, Award, 3 November 2008, paras. 52, 56–8.

[7] Id., paras. 59–61, 140.

[8] Id., para. 145. For similar characterizations of direct expropriations, *see* Dolzer & Schreuer, 'Investment Law', at 92; McLachlan, 'Investment Treaties and General International Law', paras. 8.69–8.70. The *LG&E* tribunal described direct expropriation even more drastically as the 'forcible appropriation by the State of the tangible or intangible property of individuals by means of administrative or legislative action' (*LG&E*, Decision on Liability, para. 187).

[9] *Suez–Vivendi* and *AWG Group*, Decision on Liability, para. 147; *Suez–InterAgua*, Decision on Liability, para. 136.

[10] *Suez–Vivendi* and *AWG Group*, Decision on Liability, para. 148; *Suez–InterAgua*, Decision on Liability, para. 137.

were not absolute, but subject to various conditions and to a right to terminate.[11] In the eyes of the arbitrators, it was exactly this right to terminate that Argentina made use of when 'confronted with the overwhelming need and public duty to assure the continued provision of water and waste water services to millions of people'.[12] In this regard, the tribunal distinguished the cases involving investors in the Argentine water sector from cases in which tribunals have identified direct expropriations in measures affecting contracts between foreign investors and third parties. As for contracts between foreign investors and host States, what matters would be whether the State acted in exercise of its sovereign powers (*acta iure imperii*) or as a party to the contract (*acta iure gestionis*). Only actions that qualify as *acta iure imperii* would be capable of giving rise to a breach of IIA provisions on expropriation. *Acta iure gestionis*, on the other hand, could only result in contract claims, which are normally not covered by IIAs. In the matters at hand, the arbitrators found that the termination of the concession contract by Argentina did not constitute an exercise of public authority. The arbitrators held that the behaviour of the Argentine government in the particular contractual setting of its relations with the claimants was comparable to the behaviour of a private contracting party.[13] Consequently, the tribunal rejected the claim of a direct expropriation.[14]

This short account of cases involving investors in the Argentine water sector illustrates that public policy considerations may become relevant when determining the existence of a direct expropriation. While interference with contractual rights can give rise to direct expropriation claims, threats to the public interest may trigger a contractual termination clause and defeat such a claim. Nevertheless, public policy considerations typically play a far greater role in the realm of indirect expropriation, to which we turn now.

II. The different approaches towards the identification of an indirect expropriation

In recent years, a considerable corpus of jurisprudence has developed in relation to indirect expropriation. One of the major points of controversy has been the question of how to identify the very existence of an indirect expropriation.

---

[11] *Suez–Vivendi* and *AWG Group*, Decision on Liability, paras. 148, 151; *Suez–InterAgua*, Decision on Liability, paras. 138, 141.

[12] *Suez–Vivendi* and *AWG Group*, Decision on Liability, para. 149; *Suez–InterAgua*, Decision on Liability, para. 138.

[13] *Suez–Vivendi* and *AWG Group*, Decision on Liability, paras. 152–6; *Suez–InterAgua*, Decision on Liability, paras. 141–5.

[14] Note that the tribunal in the *Siemens* case reached a different conclusion for the termination of a concession contract by the government in the electricity sector. However, this contract was not terminated on the basis of a contractual right to terminate. Rather, it was ended by a governmental decree based on a legislative act (*Siemens AG v. Argentine Republic*, ICSID Case No. ARB/02/8, Award, 6 February 2007, para. 97). Consequently, the tribunal found that Argentina's measures constituted an exercise of its public authority (id., para. 271). On this case, *see also* Chapter 2, note 122.

Some tribunals have focused solely on the effects ('sole effects doctrine') of the State measure on the investment, while others have taken into account the social and political context ('police powers doctrine' and 'mitigated police powers doctrine') of the relevant measure. The following subsections introduce the different approaches towards determining whether an indirect expropriation has occurred, and take the jurisprudence on the Argentine financial crisis as a starting point.

1. Sole effects doctrine

Interpreting Article IV(1) of the Argentina–US BIT, the *CMS* tribunal found that the decisive factor in determining the existence of an indirect expropriation was whether the 'enjoyment of the property has been effectively neutralized'[15]. In analysing whether this standard had been met, the tribunal relied both on *Metalclad* and *Pope & Talbot*.[16] The tribunal in the *Metalclad* case laid down the following characterization of indirect expropriation.

[E]xpropriation under NAFTA includes not only open, deliberate and acknowledged takings of property... but also covert or incidental interference with the use of property which has the *effect* of depriving the owner, in whole or in part, of the use or reasonably-to-be-expected economic benefit of property even if not necessarily to the obvious benefit of the host State.[17]

Hence, the *Metalclad* tribunal focused on the 'effects' of the particular measures in order to decide whether an indirect expropriation had occurred. Accordingly, the tribunal deemed the motivation for the interference with private property rights to be irrelevant. In other words, a State's intention to regulate in the public interest would be immaterial at this early stage of the analysis. Scholars have labeled this approach the 'sole effects' doctrine.[18] Considering the effect on the investment to be the decisive criterion entails the question to what degree a State measure needs to interfere with the investment to amount to an indirect expropriation.

In answering this question, many tribunals refer to the *Pope & Talbot* case, in which the tribunal found that:

the test is whether that interference is sufficiently restrictive to support a conclusion that the property has been 'taken' from the owner.[19]

---

[15] *CMS*, Award, para. 262. The *CMS* tribunal adopted this wording from the *Lauder* case in which the tribunal found that the State's measure 'effectively neutralized the enjoyment of the property' (*Lauder v. Czech Republic*, UNCITRAL Arbitration, Award, 3 September 2001, 9 ICSID Reports (2006) 66–112, para. 200).

[16] *CMS*, Award, paras. 262–3.

[17] *Metalclad Corporation v. United Mexican States*, ICSID Case No ARB(AF)/97/1, Award, 30 August 2000, 5 ICSID Reports (2002) 212–35, para. 103.

[18] *See, e.g.,* Ursula Kriebaum, *Eigentumsschutz im Völkerrecht* (2008), at 334; Thilo Rensmann, 'Völkerrechtlicher Enteignungsschutz', *in Rechtsfragen internationaler Investitionen: Tagungsband zum 13. Münsteraner Außenwirtschaftsrechtstag 2008* (Dirk Ehlers, et al. eds., 2009) 25–54, at 45.

[19] *Pope Talbot v. Canada,* NAFTA Arbitration, Interim Award, 26 June 2000, at 102.

The *Pope & Talbot* tribunal further elaborated that this threshold is reached if the State measure constituted a 'substantial deprivation'.[20] Both the *CMS* and the *Enron* tribunals followed the *Pope & Talbot* tribunal in applying the 'substantial deprivation' test.[21] The *Enron* tribunal rephrased the decisive passages of the *Pope & Talbot* case to arrive at the following characterization of a 'substantial deprivation'.

Substantial deprivation results in that light from depriving the investor of the control of the investment, managing the day-to-day operations of the company, arrest and detention of company officials or employees, supervision of the work of officials, interfering in the administration, impeding the distribution of dividends, interfering in the appointment of officials and managers, or depriving the company of its property or control in total or in part.[22]

Not surprisingly, neither the *CMS* nor the *Enron* tribunal found that Argentina's measures met this high threshold criteria. The *CMS* tribunal stated that

the investor is in control of the investment; the Government does not manage the day-to-day operations of the company; and the investor has full ownership and control of the investment.[23]

The tribunal in *National Grid* took a similar approach. It first provided a survey of some case law and scholarly opinion with respect to indirect expropriation.[24] Finally, however, the tribunal focused solely on the effects of the State measure on the investment of the claimant.[25] The tribunal found that Argentina did not indirectly expropriate the investment, since

the Claimant continued to own its shares and could exercise its rights as a shareholder and disposed of its investment by its own decision. The value of its investment was diminished but not to the extent that it could be considered worthless.[26]

2. Police powers doctrine

Most tribunals that do not exclusively rely on the 'effect' on a claimant's investment take the 'purpose' of a State measure into account. Those tribunals, however,

---

[20] Id., at 102. The *Metalclad* tribunal applied a very similar standard by holding that the measure must 'depriv[e] ... the owner, in whole or in part, of the use of ... property' (*Metalclad*, Award, para. 103). For further formulations employed by arbitral tribunals to describe the necessary degree of interference with the investment, *see* Kriebaum, *Eigentumsschutz im Völkerrecht*, at 313–15.

[21] *CMS*, Award, para. 263; *Enron*, Award, para. 245.   [22] *Enron*, Award, para. 245.

[23] *CMS*, Award, para. 263.

[24] *National Grid plc v. Argentina*, UNCITRAL Arbitration, Award, 3 November 2008, paras. 144–53.

[25] Id., paras. 154–5. The *National Grid* tribunal also quoted a passage from *LG&E* in which the latter tribunal assessed the impact of the State measure on the investment of the claimant (id., para. 155 (referring to *LG&E*, Decision on Liability, para. 200)). For further comments on the decision of the *LG&E* tribunal, *see infra* notes 38–41 and accompanying text.

[26] *National Grid plc v. Argentina*, UNCITRAL Arbitration, Award, 3 November 2008, para. 154.

display significant variation with respect to the importance they attach to the purpose of the measure in question. The tribunals that follow the so-called 'police powers doctrine' focus exclusively on the purpose and goal of the particular State measure.[27] The term 'police powers' triggers varying connotations in different legal cultures; in the context of indirect expropriation it stems from a principle of US constitutional law.[28] The entry in *Black's Law Dictionary* under 'police power' offers a concise explanation of this doctrine:

The inherent and plenary power of a sovereign to make all laws necessary and proper to preserve the public security, order, health, morality, and justice. It is a fundamental power essential to government, and it cannot be surrendered by the legislature or irrevocably transferred away from government.[29]

Tribunals adopting this doctrine find that general regulatory measures in the public interest cannot per se give rise to a claim for expropriation. The *Methanex* tribunal, for example, held that

as a matter of general international law, a non-discriminatory regulation for a public purpose, which is enacted in accordance with due process and, which affects, inter alios, a foreign investor or investment is not deemed expropriatory and compensable unless specific commitments had been given by the regulating government.[30]

The tribunal in the *Saluka* case employed similar reasoning, stating that:

It is now established in international law that States are not liable to pay compensation to a foreign investor when, in the normal exercise of their regulatory powers, they adopt in a non-discriminatory manner *bona fide* regulations that are aimed at the general welfare.[31]

In *Saluka*, the tribunal decided that an expropriation did not take place even though it acknowledged that '[t]here can be no doubt…that Saluka has been deprived of its investment in IPB as a result of the imposition of the forced administration'.[32]

Such a strict application of the 'police powers' doctrine is open to criticism on several levels. First, most BITs require that an expropriation be for a 'public purpose' in order to be lawful. This requirement becomes superfluous if a State measure that is for a 'public purpose' does not even qualify as an expropriation.[33]

---

[27] *See* Dolzer & Schreuer, 'Investment Law', at 109; Rensmann, 'Völkerrechtlicher Enteignungsschutz', at 45–6.

[28] For further remarks on the 'police powers doctrine' in the US constitutional context, *see infra* note 33.

[29] Bryan A. Garner, *Black's Law Dictionary*, Pocket Edition (2006), at 544.

[30] *Methanex v. United States,* Final Award, 3 August 2005, 44 ILM (2005) 1345, Part IV, Chapter D, para, 7.

[31] *Saluka Investments BV v. Czech Republic*, UNCITRAL Arbitration, Partial Award, 17 March 2006, para. 255.

[32] Id., paras. 267, 276.

[33] The limited role of the police powers doctrine in contemporary US constitutional law points in the same direction. Justice Kennedy wrote in a dissenting opinion (*Department of Revenue of Kentucky v. George W. Davis*, 553 US 328 (2008) (Kennedy, J, dissenting)) that the 'phrase "police power" [has been] long abandoned as a mere tautology' (id., at 365) and that '[t]he police power concept is simply a shorthand way of saying that a State is empowered to enact laws in the absence

Therefore, the context of the term 'expropriation' (which is relevant according to Article 31(1) and (2) VCLT) militates against an outright exclusion of State measures from the scope of the term 'expropriation' merely because they were adopted in the public interest and in a non-discriminatory manner. Second, most deprivations of private property through State measures will be (at least to some extent) for a 'public purpose': the 'police powers doctrine' consequently reduces investor protection to a minimum.[34] Third, even a finding of a compensable expropriation does not negate a State's sovereign right to regulate in the public interest. There is no doubt that the financial consequences of an award ordering a host State to pay compensation to a foreign investor may be harsh. Still, the fact that an arbitral award imposes a financial obligation on a host State does not in itself restrict the sovereignty of this State. It is probably on account of these shortcomings of the 'police powers doctrine' that none of the tribunals dealing with the Argentine financial crisis relied on this doctrine in its strict form.

3. Mitigated police powers doctrine

The third approach to determining whether an indirect expropriation has occurred takes into account both the effect of a State measure on the investment and the public purpose for which it was adopted. It could, therefore, be labelled 'mitigated police powers' doctrine.[35] The core element of this doctrine is a process of balancing the public interest and the property rights of the foreign investor. While the label 'mitigated police powers doctrine' accurately describes the relevant substantive analysis, it is rather misleading as to the origins of this approach. The 'police powers doctrine' has its roots in US constitutional law, but the introduction of the element of proportionality to the expropriation analysis was inspired by the jurisprudence of the ECtHR. In 2003, the *Tecmed* tribunal explicitly referred to the jurisprudence of the ECtHR in its interpretation of a BIT provision on expropriation.[36] Since then, several tribunals have followed the *Tecmed* approach and have received significant scholarly applause for this practice.[37] The following passage from the *LG&E* decision on liability is particularly illustrative of the

---

of constitutional constraints' (id, at 366). Even though this passage stems from a dissenting opinion, the very characterization of the 'police powers doctrine' was not the cause of disagreement between the majority opinion and Justice Kennedy (id, at 341 n.9). Transferred to the realm of international investment law, the 'constraints' referred to by Kennedy correspond to the requirement that an expropriation be for a public purpose, non-discriminatory, and accompanied by adequate compensation.

[34] Rensmann, 'Völkerrechtlicher Enteignungsschutz', at 46.

[35] *See also* Kriebaum, *Eigentumsschutz im Völkerrecht*, at 347 ('gemäßigte 'Police-powers'-Doktrin').

[36] *Técnicas Medioambientales Tecmed, SA v. United Mexican States*, ICSID Case No. ARB(AF)/00/2, Award, 29 May 2003, paras. 122–3. For the factual background of this case and the reasoning of the tribunal, *see infra* notes 90–1 & 96–10 and accompanying text.

[37] *See, e.g.,* Rensmann, 'Völkerrechtlicher Enteignungsschutz', at 46–51; Behrens, 'Towards the Constitutionalization of International Investment Protection', at 165–6; Kingsbury & Schill, Investor–State Arbitration as Governance, at 40–8; Krommendijk & Morijn, '"Proportional" by What Measure(s)?', at 445–6.

introduction of proportionality balancing to the process of identifying an indirect expropriation:

With respect to the power of the State to adopt its policies, it can generally be said that the State has the right to adopt measures having a social or general welfare purpose. In such a case, the measure must be accepted without any imposition of liability, except in cases where the State's action is obviously disproportionate to the need being addressed. The proportionality to be used when making use of this right was recognized in *Tecmed*, which observed that 'whether such actions or measures are proportional to the public interest presumably protected thereby and the protection legally granted to investments, taking into account that the significance of such impact, has a key role upon deciding the proportionality.'[38]

The *LG&E* tribunal listed a variety of factors that ought to play a role in this balancing process: inter alia the severity of the economic impact on the investor and the duration of the measure on one hand,[39] and the 'social or general welfare purpose' of the measure on the other.[40] In the application of these principles, however, the *LG&E* tribunal focused exclusively on the impact of the challenged measures on the investment. The tribunal referred to the *Pope & Talbot* case—usually cited as authority for the sole effects doctrine—and found that Argentina's measures did not amount to an expropriation. In particular, the tribunal reasoned that the claimants did not lose control over their shares and that the negative effect on them was not permanent.[41]

Several comments of the arbitral tribunal in the *Continental* case suggest that it was, like the *LG&E* tribunal, sympathetic to the *Tecmed* approach. The tribunal differentiated between indirect expropriations and non-compensable limitations on the use of property in the public interest. Regarding non-compensable limitations, the tribunal specified that:

typical government regulations of property entailing mostly inevitable limitations imposed in order to ensure the rights of others or of the general public (being ultimately beneficial also to the property affected)...do not require indemnification, provided however that they do not affect property in an intolerable, discriminatory, or disproportionate manner.[42]

Despite these general comments on the characteristics of indirect expropriations, the *Continental* tribunal ultimately relied exclusively on the 'effects' of the State measures on the claimant's investment. It found that expropriations would require a 'certain level of sacrifice of private property', which was not met by the '[m]inor losses' the claimant had suffered from delays in the payment of interest and the issuance of certain bonds.[43] It is remarkable that, in principle, both the *LG&E* and

[38] *LG&E*, Decision on Liability, para. 195 (quoting *Tecmed*, Award, para. 122).
[39] *LG&E*, Decision on Liability, paras. 190–4.   [40] Id., paras. 195–6.
[41] Id., paras. 198–200.   [42] *Continental*, Award, para. 276.
[43] Id., para. 284. Notably, the tribunal found it unnecessary to comment on the expropriatory character of other (arguably more severe) measures since the tribunal considered those measures to be in breach of the fair and equitable treatment standard (id., at 285).

Continental tribunals endorsed the ECtHR-inspired proportionality approach of the *Tecmed* tribunal, either explicitly (*LG&E*) or implicitly (*Continental*). When it came down to adjudicating the case at hand, however, both tribunals refrained from entering into a fully fledged proportionality analysis. Instead, the tribunals focused solely on the limited effects of the State measures on the claimants' investments. It is interesting to note how the *Metalpar* tribunal perceived the reasoning of the *LG&E* tribunal. The *Metalpar* tribunal explicitly stated that it shared the understanding of the *LG&E* tribunal on indirect expropriation.[44] Its reference to the *LG&E* decision, however, was limited to the passage in which the *LG&E* tribunal clarified that the impact on the claimant's investment needs to amount to a substantial deprivation in order to constitute an indirect expropriation.[45] Consequently, in its analysis of the case at hand, the *Metalpar* tribunal discussed merely the impact of the State measure on the particular investment along the lines of the 'sole effects doctrine'. It finally dismissed the claim for indirect expropriation without commenting on the regulatory goal of the State measure in question.[46]

In *Glamis v. United States of America*, a NAFTA case unrelated to the Argentine financial crisis, the arbitral tribunal followed an approach similar to those taken in *LG&E* and *Continental*. The tribunal adopted a two-step test that brings more clarity to the reasoning of the tribunals in *LG&E* and *Continental*. The *Glamis* tribunal specified that the purpose and character of a governmental action would only become relevant if the State measure exceeded a certain threshold with respect to the severity of the effect on the investment.[47] The tribunal set this threshold rather high, requiring that 'the Claimant was radically deprived of the economical use and enjoyment of its investments, as if the rights thereto...had ceased to exist'.[48] The infringing acts fell short of this first prong of the indirect expropriation test, given that the claimant's mining right was 'never rendered substantially without value'.[49] Consequently, the tribunal did not comment on the second prong, i.e. the weighing of the severity of the interference with the property right and the governmental purpose.

In conclusion, arbitral tribunals appear to be reluctant to embark on proportionality balancing even if they explicitly endorse the *Tecmed* approach. The analysis in this book will reveal that this is hardly surprising: compared to other legal settings in investor–State arbitration, the case for proportionality balancing in

---

[44] *Metalpar SA and Buen Aire SA v. Argentine Republic*, ICSID Case No. ARB/03/5, Award, 6 June 2008, paras. 172–3.

[45] Id., para. 172 (quoting *LG&E*, Decision on Liability, para. 191).

[46] *Metalpar SA and Buen Aire SA v. Argentine Republic*, ICSID Case No. ARB/03/5, Award, 6 June 2008, paras. 173–4.

[47] *Glamis Gold, Ltd. v. United States of America*, UNCITRAL Arbitration (NAFTA), Award, 8 June 2009, para. 356.

[48] Id., para. 357, citing a formulation in *Tecmed*, Award, para. 115.

[49] *Glamis Gold, Ltd. v. United States of America*, UNCITRAL Arbitration (NAFTA), Award, 8 June 2009, paras. 14, 536.

examining the existence of indirect expropriations is rather weak, at least under traditional BIT provisions on expropriation.

III. Policy rationales for proportionality balancing in the context of indirect expropriations

As the wording of standard IIA provisions on expropriation does not call for a proportionality analysis, one might wonder why some tribunals and scholars seek to build this element into the analysis. The reasons for this ambition reside in the overall structure of typical IIAs. The balance that the wording of these treaties strikes between private property rights and the public interest differs from that in other legal regimes. Regarding the question of whether a State measure triggers a claim for compensation under an IIA provision on expropriation, the public interest typically plays out as follows. Once a State measure is considered to be expropriatory and not for a public purpose, it is unlawful. If the expropriation was for a public purpose—and it will rarely (if ever) be for a different purpose—the State has to compensate the foreign investor. Typically, the State will owe compensation in the amount of the full market value of the asset.[50] The provisions on private property rights in domestic legal orders or the ECHR, in contrast, grant a much greater leeway for legislators to regulate in the public interest. By way of example, the next subsection sketches out the balance between private property rights and the public interest in the German Basic Law and the ECHR.

1. The balance between private property rights and the public interest in the provisions on expropriation in the German Basic Law and the ECHR

Article 14 of the German Basic Law and Article 1 of the First Additional Protocol to the ECHR (and the corresponding jurisprudence of the German Constitutional Court and the ECtHR) furnish fine examples for the balance between private property rights and the public interest outside of international investment law. Article 14 of the German Basic Law reads as follows:

(1) Property and the right of inheritance shall be guaranteed. Their content and limits shall be defined by the laws.
(2) Property entails obligations. Its use shall also serve the public good.
(3) Expropriation shall only be permissible for the public good. It may only be ordered by or pursuant to a law that determines the nature and extent of compensation. Such compensation shall be determined by establishing an equitable balance between the public

---

[50] *See* Chapter 2, note 61 & Chapter 8, note 255 and accompanying texts.

interest and the interests of those affected. In case of dispute concerning the amount of compensation, recourse may be had to the ordinary courts.[51]

The first two sentences of Article 14(3) above address the requirements under which expropriations are permissible. These requirements do not materially differ from provisions on expropriation in IIAs: expropriations have to be for the public good and need to be accompanied by compensation. The third sentence of Article 14(3), however, reveals the first stark difference between the treatment of expropriations under German constitutional law and international investment law. The amount of compensation under Article 14(3) does not need to offer 'full compensation' for the material loss, but has to reflect merely an 'equitable balance between the public interest and the interests of those affected'. The German Constitutional Court explicitly held that this balancing process of the legislator may result in an amount of compensation that lies below the 'market value' of the property right.[52]

The second distinguishing characteristic of 'expropriations' under German constitutional law is not immediately apparent from the wording of Article 14. According to the jurisprudence of the German Constitutional Court, 'expropriations' in the sense of Article 14(3) are only such legislative or administrative acts that are aimed at the deprivation of concrete, subjective property rights.[53] Regulatory measures of a general character—even if they greatly interfere with private property rights—do not qualify as expropriations and have to be measured against the requirements of the first two paragraphs of Article 14.[54] In other words, regulatory measures that may qualify as 'indirect expropriations' under IIAs typically do not constitute 'expropriations' under Article 14 of the German Basic Law. Such regulatory acts of general applicability are lawful as long as they meet the requirements of the principle of proportionality.[55] The wording of Article 14(2) reflects the considerable weight of the public interest in this balancing process. The question of whether the interference with the private property right in question was accompanied by a certain amount of compensation is only one factor in this balancing process (albeit sometimes a decisive one).[56]

The ECHR regulates property rights in its First Additional Protocol, Article 1 of which reads as follows:

(1) Every natural or legal person is entitled to the peaceful enjoyment of his possessions. No one shall be deprived of his possessions except in the public interest and subject to the conditions provided for by law and by the general principles of international law.

---

[51] Official translation provided by the German Bundestag, *available at* <https://www.btg-bestellservice.de/pdf/80201000.pdf>.

[52] BVerfGE 24, 367, 421.

[53] BVerfGE 70, 191, 199–200. *See also* Markus Perkams, 'The Concept of Indirect Expropriation in Comparative Public Law—Searching for Light in the Dark', *in International Investment Law and Comparative Public Law* (Stephan W. Schill ed., 2010) 107–50, at 134.

[54] BVerfGE 58, 137, 144; BVerfGE 72, 66, 76.

[55] BVerfGE 75, 78, 87; VerfGE 92, 262, 273.

[56] BVerfGE 58, 137, 149; BVerfGE 100, 226, 245; BVerfGE 83, 201, 212; BVerfGE 79, 174, 192.

(2) The preceding provisions shall not, however, in any way impair the right of a State to enforce such laws as it deems necessary to control the use of property in accordance with the general interest or to secure the payment of taxes or other contributions or penalties.

Section IV analyses this provision in depth when assessing the approach of the *Tecmed* tribunal. For the purposes of this subsection, it suffices to introduce some salient points on the right to property in the ECHR context. Article 1 seeks to strike a 'fair balance' between the public interest and individual property rights. In this vein, the ECtHR held in *Mellacher* that:

an interference must achieve a 'fair balance' between the demands of the general interest of the community and the requirements of the protection of the individual's fundamental rights. The search for this balance is reflected in the structure of Article 1 (P1-1) as a whole, and therefore also in the second paragraph thereof. There must be a reasonable relationship of proportionality between the means employed and the aim pursued.[57]

The second sentence of Article 1(1) deals with expropriations,[58] and its wording does not require the payment of compensation. Still, the 'fair balance' inherent in Article 1 requires that expropriations be accompanied by compensation, albeit only in principle and not necessarily in the amount of the full market value.[59] Moreover, for an expropriation to be lawful under the ECtHR, it needs to meet a proportionality test. The ECtHR stated in *James* that:

Not only must a measure depriving a person of his property pursue, on the facts as well as in principle, a legitimate aim 'in the public interest', but there must also be a reasonable relationship of proportionality between the means employed and the aim sought to be realised.[60]

This brief account illustrates that the regimes for the protection of private property under the German Basic Law and the ECHR do not subject a State measure to a proportionality analysis when deciding on its expropriatory character. They do, however, provide for the balancing of the different interests at stake at later stages of the analysis, which may bar claims for compensation in the amount of the full market value. IIAs lack such a 'gate-keeping' element: once an expropriation has occurred that was not accompanied by full compensation, the host State has violated its treaty obligations. Some tribunals apparently seek to compensate this perceived shortcoming by inserting an element of proportionality into the question of whether a certain State measure constitutes an expropriation at all.

---

[57] *Mellacher v. Austria*, ECtHR, A 169, Judgment, 19 December 1989, para. 48 (internal references omitted).

[58] The second sentence of Article 1(1) ('deprivation of property') covers both formal (or direct) expropriations as well as de facto (or indirect) expropriations (Karen Kaiser, 'Art. 1 ZP I', *in EMRK—Konvention zum Schutz der Menschenrechte und Grundfreiheiten—Kommentar* (Ulrich Karpenstein & Franz Mayer eds., 2012) 359–76, paras. 29–30).

[59] Id., paras. 39–41.

[60] *James v. United Kingdom*, ECtHR, A 98, Judgment, 21 February 1986, para. 50.

2. Possible reasons for a different balance in international investment law

As demonstrated in the last subsection, expropriation provisions in IIAs often contain a different balance between property rights and the public interest than do domestic constitutions or the ECHR. A glance at the historical roots of the current system of international investment protection provides some possible reasons for this practice. Typical BIT provisions on expropriation reflect a settlement of one of the most persistent conflicts in customary international law related to the treatment of aliens. The proponents of the so-called Calvo doctrine, or of the standard of national treatment, argued that aliens had to accept the policy choices of host States without compensation as long as they receive the same treatment as nationals.[61] The current system of international investment protection has not adopted this approach. Rather, modern investment treaties grant foreign investors a certain minimum level of protection that is not subject to the current policy preferences of host States. One of the key factors in this respect is the incorporation of the Hull formula into IIAs, i.e. the obligation to compensate aliens for expropriations (regardless of the underlying policy reasons of the State's decision to expropriate).

Some might argue that in modern States, where policy choices are often the outcome of democratic processes, it is no longer necessary to provide protection to aliens that goes beyond the Calvo doctrine or the standard of national treatment. This is largely a political question, to which this book does not aspire to give an answer. Nevertheless, it is important to note one structural element: foreign investors typically do not take part in the democratic processes resulting in domestic decisions, at least if one considers the right to vote an intrinsic element of such participation.[62] The ECtHR expressed a similar idea in *James* when it found that 'non-nationals are more vulnerable to domestic legislation' and that 'there may well be legitimate reason for requiring nationals to bear a greater burden in the public interest than non-nationals'.[63]

Another possible reason why IIAs typically strike a different balance between private property rights and the public interest than other legal regimes is the shift in risk and bargaining power once an investment is in place. The *Fedax* tribunal stated that an investment involves 'a certain duration, a certain regularity of profit and return, assumption of risk, a substantial commitment and a significance for the host State development'.[64] There is no consensus on whether these five factors define the term 'investment'[65] or merely describe the features that are typical

---

[61] *See* Chapter 2, note 11.

[62] For comments on the democratic legitimacy in international investment arbitration, *see* Chapter 7, notes 135–45 and accompanying text.

[63] *James v. United Kingdom*, ECtHR, A 98, Judgment, 21 February 1986, para. 63. *See also infra* note 120 and accompanying text.

[64] *Fedax NV v. Republic of Venezuela*, ICSID Case No. ARB/96/3, Decision on Objections to Jurisdiction, 11 July 1997, ICSID Reports 5 (2002) 186–99, para. 43.

[65] Leaning into this direction: UNCTAD, Investor–State Dispute Settlement and Impact on Foreign Investment Rulemaking (2007), at 23.

for investments.[66] Regardless of this doctrinal controversy, the statement of the *Fedax* tribunal illustrates the typical differences between an investment and, for example, a mere trade situation. The main difference is the long-term commitment inherent in a decision to invest abroad, which includes an important shift of risk and bargaining power over time. While an investor might have significant leeway in negotiating with the host State before the transfer of assets, once the investment is in place, it is often difficult for the investor to withdraw from the project (without incurring significant losses).[67] IIAs cater for this—perceived or real—vulnerability of foreign investors. While IIAs do not shield investors from ordinary risks that come with doing business, they seek to mitigate risks running from adverse governmental action once the investment is in place.

3. Recent efforts to readjust the balance between private property rights and the public interest in international investment law

Recent developments have led States to reconsider the balance between the public interest and private investor rights in international investment law. Increasingly, developed countries find themselves at the receiving end of investor–State arbitration. NAFTA and the ever denser web of BITs have sparked a steadily growing number of investment arbitrations against States that in the past had been preoccupied with protecting outward investment flows. In addition, values and interests that are sometimes considered to collide with the interests of foreign investors, such as environmental concerns and labour rights, have come to play a greater role at both the national and the international level. As a result, some States seek to readjust the balance between the public interest and property rights in IIAs to ensure that they can realize their policy preferences without being liable to investors. The 2004 and 2012 Model BITs of the US, the 2004 Model BIT of Canada, and the (abandoned) 2007 Model BIT of Norway reflect this objective. The wording of the provisions on expropriation in the current Model BITs of Canada and the US do not differ from standard IIA provisions on expropriation. But both States have attached annexes to their Model BITs setting out their understandings of the term 'indirect expropriations'. Some of the elements in those annexes open the door to proportionality balancing. Paragraph 4(a) of Annex B of the US Model BIT states—in terms that are reminiscent of the holding of the *Tecmed* tribunal—that:

[t]he determination of whether an action or series of actions by a Party, in a specific fact situation, constitutes an indirect expropriation, requires a case-by-case, fact-based inquiry that considers, among other factors:

---

[66] Schreuer, et al., *The ICISD Convention*, Article 25, para. 153. The *Fedax* tribunal itself acknowledges that it derived its factors from Schreuer's analysis (*Fedax,* Decision on Objections to Jurisdiction, para. 43 n.63). This supports the view that a certain transaction or asset does not automatically fall outside the scope of the term 'investment' simply because one of the five factors listed by the *Fedax* tribunal does not apply.

[67] *See also* Dolzer & Schreuer, 'Investment Law', at 3–4.

(i)   the economic impact of the government action, although the fact that an action or series of actions by a Party has an adverse effect on the economic value of an investment, standing alone, does not establish that an indirect expropriation has occurred;

(ii) the extent to which the government action interferes with distinct, reasonable investment-backed expectations; and

(iii) the character of the government action.[68]

The emphasis on the 'character' of the government action in the last sentence of this passage dismisses the 'sole effects doctrine'. Paragraph 4(b) of Annex B of the US Model BIT confirms this point, and considerably prejudices the balancing process in favour of the public interest. This provision stipulates that

[e]xcept in rare circumstances, non-discriminatory regulatory actions by a Party that are designed and applied to protect legitimate public welfare objectives, such as public health, safety, and the environment, do not constitute indirect expropriations.[69]

Annex B.13(1) of the Canadian Model BIT contains the same provisions as Annex B(4) of the US Model BIT (with some minor stylistic differences).[70]

The 2004 US and Canadian Model BITs have had significant influence on the treaty practice of various States. Both the US and Canada have concluded BITs with other States that largely reflect the provisions on indirect expropriation of their respective Model BITs. For example, the US–Uruguay BIT (entered into force on 1 November 2006) contains a standard BIT provision on expropriation (Article 6) and adds (in Annex B(4)) the same clarification on indirect expropriation as the US Model BIT.[71] The US–Rwanda BIT, signed on 19 February 2008, also follows this pattern.[72] The wording of the US Model BIT is also mirrored in

---

[68] US Model BIT of 2004 (*available at* <http://ita.law.uvic.ca/documents/USmodelbitnov04.pdf>) and US Model BIT of 2012 (*available at* <http://italaw.com/sites/default/files/archive/ita1028.pdf>). The 2012 version of the US Model BIT is in large part identical to the 2004 version. This is also true for Annex B, which remained unchanged.

[69] Id.

[70] Annex B.13.(1)(b) and (c) of the Canadian Model BIT (*available at* <http://ita.law.uvic.ca/documents/Canadian2004-FIPA-model-en.pdf>) reads as follows:

  (b) The determination of whether a measure or series of measures of a Party constitute an indirect expropriation requires a case-by-case, fact-based inquiry that considers, among other factors:

    (i)   the economic impact of the measure or series of measures, although the sole fact that a measure or series of measures of a Party has an adverse effect on the economic value of an investment does not establish that an indirect expropriation has occurred;

    (ii) the extent to which the measure or series of measures interfere with distinct, reasonable investment-backed expectations; and

    (iii) the character of the measure or series of measures.

  (c) Except in rare circumstances, such as when a measure or series of measures are so severe in the light of their purpose that they cannot be reasonably viewed as having been adopted and applied in good faith, non-discriminatory measures of a Party that are designed and applied to protect legitimate public welfare objectives, such as health, safety and the environment, do not constitute indirect expropriation.

[71] The US–Uruguay BIT is *available at* <http://investmentpolicyhub.unctad.org/Download/TreatyFile/2380>.

[72] *See* Article 6 and Annex B(4)(a) and (b) of the US–Rwanda BIT, *available at* <http://investmentpolicyhub.unctad.org/Download/TreatyFile/2241>.

Annex 11-B of the Free Trade Agreement between the US and Australia[73] and Annex 10-D of the Free Trade Agreement between the US and Chile.[74] Canada and Latvia signed a BIT on 5 May 2009,[75] and Annex B(2) and (3) of this treaty adopts verbatim the language of Annex B.13(1)(b) and (c) of the Canadian Model BIT.[76] The same is true of Annex A(b) and (c) of the BIT between Canada and the Czech Republic, signed on 6 May 2009.[77]

In June 2007, the US and South Korea signed the US–Korea Free Trade Agreement (KORUS FTA), and a renegotiated agreement was signed in December 2010. Article 11.6 of the agreement contains a standard IIA provision on expropriation, which is to be interpreted in accordance with Annex 11-B. This annex to the KORUS FTA has the same structure and in parts identical wording as Annex B(4)(a) and (b) of the US Model BIT.[78] Paragraphs (a)(iii) and (b) of Annex 11-B to the KORUS FTA are worth quoting in full since they contain some additional factors and refer to proportionality more explicitly than the US Model BIT:

(a) The determination of whether an action or a series of actions by a Party, in a specific fact situation, constitutes an indirect expropriation, requires a case-by-case, fact-based inquiry that considers all relevant factors relating to the investment, including:

  ...

  (iii) the character of the government action, including its objectives and context. Relevant considerations could include whether the government action imposes a special sacrifice on the particular investor or investment that exceeds what the investor or investment should be expected to endure for the public interest.

(b) Except in rare circumstances, such as, for example, when an action or a series of actions is extremely severe or *disproportionate* in light of its purpose or effect, non-discriminatory regulatory actions by a Party that are designed and applied to protect legitimate public welfare objectives, such as public health, safety, the environment, and real estate price stabilization (through, for example, measures to improve the housing conditions for low-income households), do not constitute indirect expropriations.[79]

Other countries have followed a similar approach to the US and Canada. On 1 January 2010, the Agreement establishing the ASEAN–Australia–New Zealand Free Trade Area (the ASEAN–ANZ FTA) entered into force for Australia, Brunei, Malaysia, Myanmar, New Zealand, Singapore, the Philippines, and Vietnam. Since then, the agreement has also become binding for Thailand, Cambodia, Laos, and Indonesia.[80] It includes a chapter on investment (Chapter 11) with a typical IIA provision on expropriation (Article 9) and an 'Annex on Expropriation and Compensation', which

---

[73] US–Australia FTA, entered into force 1 January 2005, *available at* <https://ustr.gov/sites/default/files/uploads/agreements/fta/australia/asset_upload_file148_5168.pdf>.

[74] US–Chile FTA, entered into force 1 January 2004, *available at* <https://ustr.gov/sites/default/files/uploads/agreements/fta/chile/asset_upload_file232_3988.pdf>.

[75] *Available at* <http://investmentpolicyhub.unctad.org/Download/TreatyFile/618>.

[76] *See supra* note 70.

[77] *Available at* <http://investmentpolicyhub.unctad.org/Download/TreatyFile/606>.

[78] *See supra* notes 68–9.

[79] Annex 11-B(3) KORUS (*available at* <https://ustr.gov/trade-agreements/free-trade-agreements/korus-fta/final-text>) (emphasis added).

[80] *See, e.g.,* <http://www.customs.gov.au/site/page6076.asp>.

clarifies the meaning of the term expropriation. This Annex is very similar to those of the Canadian and US Model BITs, and reads in material part as follows:

3. The determination of whether an action or series of related actions by a Party, in a specific fact situation, constitutes an expropriation of the type referred to in Paragraph 2(b) requires a case-by-case, fact-based inquiry that considers, among other factors:
   (a) the economic impact of the government action, although the fact that an action or series of related actions by a Party has an adverse effect on the economic value of an investment, standing alone, does not establish that such an expropriation has occurred;
   (b) whether the government action breaches the government's prior binding written commitment to the investor whether by contract, licence or other legal document; and
   (c) the character of the government action, including its objective and whether the action is disproportionate to the public purpose.

4. Non-discriminatory regulatory actions by a Party that are designed and applied to achieve legitimate public welfare objectives, such as the protection of public health, safety, and the environment do not constitute expropriation of the type referred to in Paragraph 2(b).[81]

The Model International Agreement on Investment for Sustainable Development by the International Institute for Sustainable Development (IISD)—an independent non-profit and non-governmental organization—is even more regulator-friendly than the IIAs mentioned in this subsection. For the purposes of indirect expropriations, Article 8(I) of the IISD model agreement automatically grants precedence to the regulatory interests of States, without subjecting this primacy to any balancing process:

Consistent with the right of states to regulate and the customary international law principles on police powers, *bona fide*, non-discriminatory regulatory measures taken by a Party that are designed and applied to protect or enhance legitimate public welfare objectives, such as public health, safety and the environment, do not constitute an indirect expropriation under this Article.[82]

The 2007 Norwegian Model BIT had taken a different path in order to expand the role of the public interest in provisions on expropriation. To be noted at the outset, the Norwegian government abandoned its Model BIT in 2009, and has not adopted a new draft since then.[83] Still, it is worth analysing the provision on

---

[81] *Available at* <http://www.asean.fta.govt.nz/assets/Agreement-Establishing-the-ASEAN-Australia-New-Zealand-Free-Trade-Area.pdf>.

[82] Article 8(I) of the IISD Model International Agreement on Investment for Sustainable Development, *available at* <http://ita.law.uvic.ca/documents/investment_model_int_agreement.pdf>.

[83] *Investment Treaty News*, 'Norway shelves its draft model bilateral investment treaty', 8 June 2009, *available at* <http://www.iisd.org/itn/2009/06/08/norway-shelves-its-proposed-model-bilateral-investment-treaty/>. For further comments on the 2007 Norwegian Model BIT, *see* Rumu Sarkar, 'A "Re-Visioned" Foreign Direct Investment Approach From an Emerging Country

expropriation in the 2007 Norwegian Model BIT as it markedly differed from what is common in BITs. Article 6 read as follows:

1. A Party shall not expropriate or nationalise an investment of an investor of the other Party except in the public interest and subject to the conditions provided for by law and by the general principles of international law.
2. The preceding provision shall not, however, in any way impair the right of a Party to enforce such laws as it deems necessary to control the use of property in accordance with the general interest or to secure the payment of taxes or other contributions or penalties.[84]

The similarity between the Norwegian stipulation and Article 1 of the First Additional Protocol to the ECHR is no coincidence. Indeed, the Norwegian government stressed in its comments to the Model BIT that it wanted to adapt the protection of foreign investment to the standards on the protection of private property under the ECHR.[85] Hence, the Norwegian Model BIT was not concerned with defining the term 'indirect expropriation'. Rather, it sought to import the entire structure of Article 1 of the First Additional Protocol (and arguably also the jurisprudence of the ECtHR). Moreover, the Norwegian government found that the obligation common to most BITs to compensate in the amount of the 'fair market value' goes further than the obligation to compensate under the jurisprudence of the ECtHR and Norwegian law.[86] Therefore, the Norwegian government suggested a more flexible standard for compensating expropriatory acts along the lines of the ECtHR jurisprudence on Article 1 of the First Additional Protocol.

The European Union is a relatively new actor in the realm of international investment law. By including investment provisions in the Comprehensive Economic and Trade Agreement (CETA) with Canada, the EU made use of its compentencies in the area of foreign direct investment acquired through the Lisbon treaty. The CETA language on indirect expropriation agreed between the European Commission and Canada mirrors in large part that of the Canadian Model BIT. In particular, the relevant provision states that 'except in the rare circumstance where the impact of the measure or series of measures is so severe in light of its purpose that it appears manifestly excessive, non-discriminatory measures of a Party that are designed and applied to protect legitimate public welfare objectives, such as health, safety and the environment, do not constitute indirect expropriations'.[87]

Perspective: Moving From A Vicious Circle to a Virtuous Circle', *ILSA Journal of International and Comparative Law* 17 (2010–11) 379–392, at 387.

[84] Article 6 Norwegian Model BIT, *available at* <http://www.italaw.com/sites/default/files/archive/ita1031.pdf>.

[85] Commentary on the Norwegian Model BIT, *available at* <http://www.italaw.com/sites/default/files/archive/ita1029.pdf>, at 22.

[86] Id., at 23.

[87] Annex X.11 of the consolidated CETA text published on 26 September 2014. While CETA is not in force yet, its text as it stood at the end of the negotiations between the European Commisssion and Canada is *available at* <http://trade.ec.europa.eu/doclib/docs/2014/september/tradoc_152806.pdf>.

If concluded, the currently negotiated Transatlantic Trade and Investment Partnership (TTIP) between the EU and the US, covering more than 40% of global GDP,[88] is likely to contain similar language: in November 2013, the European Commission outlined its general position towards substantive and procedural issues in investor–State arbitration. Regarding indirect expropriation, the European Commission's position appears to have much in common with the 2012 and 2004 US Model BITs. Under the heading 'Rebalancing the system', the European Commission announced that

> future EU agreements will provide a detailed set of provisions giving guidance to arbitrators on how to decide whether or not a government measure constitutes indirect expropriation. In particular, when the state is protecting the public interest in a non-discriminatory way, the right of the state to regulate should prevail over the economic impact of those measures on the investor.[89]

In sum, the Model BITs, BITs, and FTAs cited in this subsection reflect the growing aspiration of States (and the European Union) to provide greater weight to the public interest in determining the existence of an indirect expropriation. A related but different issue is the question of how these Model BITs may influence the interpretation of BITs concluded before the adoption of the relevant Model BIT. Yet another question is how such Model BITs may influence the understanding of indirect expropriations under customary international law and, through this, the interpretation of the term 'expropriation' in the BITs of third States by way of Article 31(3)(c) VCLT. Before we turn to these issues in section V, the next section analyses whether the jurisprudence of the ECtHR supports the application of proportionality in standard IIA provisions on expropriation.

IV. Harmonizing two areas of international law or comparing apples and oranges? A critical analysis of the *Tecmed* approach

The *Tecmed* tribunal had to decide whether the refusal of a Mexican State entity to renew an annual licence for the claimant's subsidiary to run a landfill of hazardous industrial waste constituted an indirect expropriation under the Mexico–Spain BIT.[90] While the tribunal ultimately found that an indirect expropriation had occured, it held that regulatory actions that further a public interest in a proportionate way are not expropriatory.[91] To support this proposition, the *Tecmed* tribunal drew on the jurisprudence of the ECtHR, and viewed through the prism of the fragmentation debate, the *Tecmed* approach appears to be a laudable development.

---

[88] *See, e.g.,* UNCTAD, World Investment Report 2014, Investing in the SDGs: an Action Plan, at 119.

[89] European Commission, Fact sheet—Investment Protection and Investor-to-State Dispute Settlement in EU agreements (26 November 2013), p. 2 (*available at* <http://trade.ec.europa.eu/doclib/docs/2013/november/tradoc_151916.pdf>).

[90] *Tecmed*, Award, paras. 35–45.   [91] *Tecmed*, Award, paras. 122, 151.

This section analyses in three steps whether the proposition and the reasoning of the *Tecmed* tribunal was justified: subsection 1 provides a brief overview on the debate about the fragmentation of international law; subsection 2 considers the reasoning of the *Tecmed* tribunal in greater detail; and Finally subsection 3 analyses the extent to which the jurisprudence of the ECtHR on Article 1 of the First Additional Protocol to the ECHR supports the approach of the *Tecmed* tribunal.

1. The *Tecmed* approach and the fragmentation of international law

The number of international courts and tribunals has grown dramatically since the end of World War II. This development reflects the remarkable degree of legalization that certain areas of international relations have experienced during the same period, especially with respect to international trade, the environment, human rights, international criminal law, and international investment protection. In most cases, these areas have developed independently of one another and generated their own procedural and substantive characteristics. While this process of proliferation and decentralization has been perceived as evidence of a deepening and fostering of international relations, it has also been identified as a threat to the unity of international law. It is sometimes argued that specialized legal regimes such as human rights law, trade law, or international investment law have developed outside of an overarching legal system. The significance of general international law in these areas of law would consequently be minimal or non-existent.[92] Moreover, some claim that the different subsystems not only lack an overarching system, but ignore each other's legal precepts. In the worst possible scenario, adjudicatory bodies of different regimes reach contradictory conclusions.

The term 'fragmentation' of international law expresses these concerns, and connotes an intense academic debate which has inter alia resulted in an ILC report.[93] Contradictory international obligations (which can force States to breach one international obligation as part of complying with another), diverging judicial decisions on similar questions of law, and inconsistent substantive standards within different legal subsystems are perceived to be the main perils of fragmentation. As mentioned above, the ILC has rightly identified Article 31(3)(c) VCLT (and its principle of 'systemic integration') as one of the most promising tools for mitigating or overcoming these problems.[94] The *Tecmed* tribunal

---

[92] *See* Gunther Teubner & Andreas Fischer-Lescano, 'Regime-Collisions: the Vain Search for Unity in the Fragmentation of Global Law', *Michigan Journal of International Law* 25 (2004) 999–1046, at 1007–9 and 1017–45.

[93] ILC, *Fragmentation of International Law.* For the relationship between the fragmentation of international law and its constitutionalization, *see* Paulus, 'The International Legal System', at 821–87; Jeffrey L. Dunoff & Joel P. Trachtman, 'A Functional Approach to Global Constitutionalism', *in Ruling the World?* (Dunoff & Trachtman eds., 2009) 3–35, at 6–9 and 30–2.

[94] ILC, *Fragmentation of International Law*, paras. 479–80.

considered the jurisprudence of another international judicial body (ECtHR) on a different international treaty (ECHR) concerning a separate, specialized sub-system (international human rights) in its interpretation of the term 'expropriation' in the Spain–Mexico BIT—and it received considerable applause for this approach.[95] But do provisions on expropriation in BITs and in the ECHR indeed share sufficient structural similarities to warrant the transfer of ECtHR jurisprudence to the realm of investor–State arbitration? The following two subsections attempt to answer this question.

2. The reasoning of the *Tecmed* tribunal regarding indirect expropriation

As mentioned, in *Tecmed*, Mexican authorities refused to renew an operating licence for a waste landfill. In order to decide whether this measure constituted an indirect expropriation, the tribunal first focused on its impact on the investment.[96] From its observation that the 'economic or commercial value...was irremediably destroyed', the tribunal drew the somewhat ambiguous conclusion that '[a]s far as the effects...are concerned, the decision can be treated as an expropriation under Article 5(1) of the Agreement'.[97] In a second step, the tribunal examined whether the State measure, 'due to its characteristics and considering not only its effects, is an expropriatory decision'.[98] Interestingly, the tribunal dismissed the 'police powers doctrine', based on the wording of the treaty's (standard) provision on expropriation:

[a]fter reading Article 5(1) of the Agreement and interpreting its terms according to the ordinary meaning to be given to them (Article 31(1) of the Vienna Convention), we find no principle stating that regulatory administrative actions are per se excluded from the scope of the Agreement, even if they are beneficial to society as a whole—such as environmental protection.[99]

---

[95] *See, e.g.,* van Aaken, 'Defragmentation of Public International Law', at 507; Kingsbury & Schill, 'Investor–State Arbitration as Governance', at 31–7; Rensmann, 'Völkerrechtlicher Enteignungsschutz', at 46–51; Ernst-Ulrich Petersmann, Human Rights, International Economic Law and "Constitutional Justice"', *European Journal of International Law* 19 (2008) 769–98, at 795; Steven R. Ratner, 'Regulatory Takings in Institutional Context: Beyond the Fear of Fragmented International Law', American *Journal of International Law* 102 (2008) 475–528, at 527; Vinuales, 'Access to Water in Foreign Investment Disputes', at 753, 758.

[96] *Tecmed*, Award, para. 115.   [97] Id., 117.   [98] Id., para. 118.

[99] Id., para. 121. Article 5(1) of the Mexico–Spain BIT contains a standard formulation on the requirements under which an expropriation is lawful: 'Ninguna Parte Contratante expropiará o nacionalizará una inversión, directa o indirectamente a través de medidas equivalentes a expropiación o nacionalización ("expropiación"), salvo que sea:

    (a) por causa de utilidad pública;
    (b) sobre bases no discriminatorias;
    (c) conforme al principio de legalidad; y
    (d) mediante el pago de una indemnización conforme al párrafo 2 siguiente.'

The tribunal was less clear in its reasoning when it introduced the principle of proportionality to its analysis. In this regard, it did not inquire into the wording of Article 5(1) of the Mexico–Argentina BIT or provide any other rationale for its approach. Instead, the tribunal flatly stipulated that:

the Arbitral Tribunal will consider, in order to determine if [regulatory actions] are to be characterized as expropriatory, whether such actions or measures are proportional to the public interest presumably protected thereby and to the protection legally granted to investments...[100]

This statement was followed by several references to the jurisprudence of the ECtHR without any comment on its relevance to the case at hand.[101]

Like most other provisions on expropriation in BITs, Article 5(1) of the Mexico–Spain BIT does not elaborate on the term 'expropriation'.[102] Rather, it specifies the requirements under which an expropriation will not breach the BIT. An expropriatory act does not violate the Mexico–Spain BIT if it serves a public purpose, is non-discriminatory, and is carried out against the payment of compensation.[103] In other words, if a State measure is considered to be 'expropriatory', the treaty language requires it to be adopted for a 'public purpose' in order to be in compliance with the BIT. The proportionality analysis of the *Tecmed* tribunal, however, prescribes a balancing of the public purpose pursued against the protection of the investment when deciding on the very existence of an expropriation. Against this background, it is surprising that the requirement that the expropriation be for a 'public purpose' should suddenly reappear as a criterion for determining the lawfulness of the same expropriation.

The apodictic reasoning of the *Tecmed* tribunal may be explained by its ultimate finding. The tribunal concluded from the facts of the case that there existed no present or imminent risk to the environment or human health. Furthermore, rather than being motivated by sincere environmental concerns, the State measure was found to be merely the outcome of political pressure and manoeuvring.[104] Consequently, the proportionality analysis of the tribunal did not change its preliminary assessment reached by analysing the effects of the investment. The tribunal held that the State measures constituted an expropriation for the purposes of Article 5(1) of the Mexico–Spain BIT.[105]

3. The *Tecmed* approach and the underlying jurisprudence of the ECtHR

As noted above, the *Tecmed* approach to identifying the existence of an indirect expropriation is becoming increasingly popular among arbitral tribunals. This subsection analyses to what extent the jurisprudence of the ECtHR, on which

---

[100] Id., para. 122.   [101] Id., para. 122 nn. 140, 141, and 143.
[102] *See supra* note 99.   [103] Id.
[104] *Tecmed*, Award, especially paras. 145–9.   [105] Id., para. 151.

the tribunal relied, actually supports the tribunal's reasoning. This question is relevant not only to those cases in which Article 1 of the First Additional Protocol to the ECHR might be adduced for the interpretation of the term 'expropriation' by virtue of Article 31(3)(c) VCLT. Rather, an investment tribunal might also resort to the jurisprudence of the ECtHR as an inspirational source (or as a source of persuasive authority), even if none of the parties to the underlying investment treaty has ratified the ECHR. In any event, the importation of the ECtHR proportionality test in the context of the right to property into IIA provisions on expropriation requires a certain degree of structural similarity between the two legal settings. To recall, the relevant provision of the First Additional Protocol, its Article 1, reads as follows:

(1) Every natural or legal person is entitled to the peaceful enjoyment of his possessions. No one shall be deprived of his possessions except in the public interest and subject to the conditions provided for by law and by the general principles of international law.
(2) The preceding provisions shall not, however, in any way impair the right of a State to enforce such laws as it deems necessary to control the use of property in accordance with the general interest or to secure the payment of taxes or other contributions or penalties.

The ECtHR has repeatedly held that Article 1 of the First Additional Protocol contains 'three distinct rules', corresponding to the three sentences of this provision. The first sentence of the first paragraph guarantees the peaceful enjoyment of property in a very general manner. The second rule (paragraph 1, second sentence) subjects the deprivation of possessions, or in other words expropriations,[106] to certain conditions. The second paragraph of Article 1 contains the third rule, and recognizes that States may control the use of property. [107] The second and the third rules regulate special instances of the interference with the right to the peaceful enjoyment of property. Consequently, the ECtHR first resorts to these rules (that is, Article 1(1) second sentence and Article 1(2)) when evaluating the lawfulness of an interference with a property right. If it finds that the interference falls under neither of these two rules (which is the case, for example, for measures that precede expropriations),[108] the Court bases its analysis on Article 1(1) first sentence and its underlying 'fair balance' requirement.[109] The following

---

[106] The ECtHR applies the second sentence of the first paragraph of Article 1 to both 'formal expropriations' and 'de facto expropriations', or, in other words, direct and indirect expropriations (*Sporrong and Lönnroth v. Sweden*, ECtHR, A 52, Judgment (Merits), 23 September 1982, para. 63; *Erkner and Hofauer v. Austria*, ECtHR, A 117, Judgment (Merits), 23 April 1987, para. 74; *Poiss v. Austria*, ECtHR, A 117, Judgment (Merits), 23 April 1987, para. 64.)

[107] *Sporrong and Lönnroth v. Sweden*, ECtHR, A 52, Judgment (Merits), 23 September 1982, para. 61; *James v. United Kingdom*, ECtHR, A 98, Judgment, 21 February 1986, para. 37; *Mellacher v. Austria*, ECtHR, A 169, Judgment, 19 December 1989, para. 42; *Anheuser-Busch v. Portugal*, ECtHR, Application no. 73049/01, Judgment (Grand Chamber), 11 January 2007, para. 62.

[108] Hans-Joachim Cremer, 'Eigentumsschutz', *in EMRK/GG—Konkordanzkommentar* (Grote & Marauhn eds., 2006) 1222–345, para. 136.

[109] *Sporrong and Lönnroth v. Sweden*, ECtHR, A 52, Judgment (Merits), 23 September 1982, para. 69.

subsection (a) will first address the jurisprudence of the ECtHR on expropriations before subsection (b) turns to other interferences with private property rights.

a) Jurisprudence of the ECtHR on the lawfulness of expropriations

For the purposes of interpreting the term 'expropriation' in IIAs, the most informative source in the realm of the ECHR is the jurisprudence of the ECtHR on Article 1(1) second sentence of the First Additional Protocol, which governs expropriations. In *James v. United Kingdom*, the applicants complained against the consequences of an act that granted long-term tenants the right to purchase the landlord's interest against his or her will.[110] The Court plainly stated that the applicants were 'deprived of their possessions' by operation of the contested legislation.[111] It was only after the ECtHR had found on the existence of an expropriation that it weighed the public interest against the interests of the applicants to determine whether this expropriation met the requirements of Article 1(1) second sentence. In this vein, the ECtHR included its proportionality analysis in a chapter entitled 'The "public interest" test and the remaining requirements of the deprivation rule'.[112] Against this background, it is surprising that the *Tecmed* tribunal cited *James* as authority for the inclusion of proportionality in determining whether there was an expropriation in the first place.[113]

The very purpose of the balancing test in the jurisprudence of the ECtHR speaks against the transfer of this test into standard BIT provisions on expropriation. In *James,* the ECtHR noted that the State enjoys some 'margin of appreciation' when deciding which measures lie 'in the public interest' and which do not. This means that the Court still reviews the State measure, but that it 'will respect the legislature's judgment as to what is "in the public interest" unless that judgment be manifestly without reasonable foundation'.[114] Consistent with this doctrinal framework, the Court found that the State's aim of 'eliminating social injustices' was a 'legitimate' one.[115] The Court's decisive and often quoted statement on proportionality came after this clarification. It reads as follows:

Not only must a measure depriving a person of his property pursue, on the facts as well as in principle, a legitimate aim 'in the public interest', but there must also be a reasonable relationship of proportionality between the means employed and the aim sought to be realised.[116]

This means that the principle of proportionality might still negate the lawfulness of a State measure even if it is otherwise in compliance with the requirements of Article 1(1) second sentence. Transferring this line of thought to IIA provisions on expropriation would have consequences completely different from those assumed by the *Tecmed* tribunal. IIAs typically require that an expropriation be for a public

---

[110] *James v. United Kingdom*, ECtHR, A 98, Judgment, 21 February 1986, paras. 10–11.
[111] Id., para. 38.   [112] Id., after para. 45.   [113] *See Tecmed*, Award, para. 122.
[114] *James v. United Kingdom*, ECtHR, A 98, Judgment, 21 February 1986, paras. 46.
[115] Id., paras. 47–9.   [116] Id., para. 50.

purpose, non-discriminatory, and against the payment of compensation (in the amount of the fair market value of the investment). Subjecting the lawfulness of an expropriatory act to the additional requirement that it be proportionate would, in fact, restrict the regulatory freedom of host States to a greater degree than the strict wording of standard BIT provisions: even if a substantial deprivation of property was for a public purpose, not 'discriminatory', and accompanied by 'adequate compensation', it could still be unlawful if it does not meet the proportionality test.

Instead, the *Tecmed* tribunal integrated the proportionality test into the process of identifying an indirect expropriation—an approach not taken by the ECtHR. This twist causes the proportionality test to have exactly the opposite effect as it does under the ECtHR approach in *James*: even if a deprivation of property is discriminatory and not accompanied by compensation, it does not trigger a claim under an IIA provision on expropriation as long as the State measure is proportionate. While *James* proportionality provides an extra shield for non-State actors, the *Tecmed* approach will typically diminish treaty protections.

It is also important to bear in mind that the ECtHR derived the 'fair balance' requirement that gives rise to a proportionality analysis from the very structure of Article 1.[117] It is difficult to transpose this context-specific rationale to standard BIT provisions on expropriation, the structure and wording of which are very different to those of Article 1. Furthermore, the ECtHR considers the payment of compensation to be an important factor in judging the compliance of a State measure with Article 1(1) second sentence. Even though the text of Article 1 does not expressly refer to the issue of compensation, the Court confirmed that Article 1

in general impliedly require[s] the payment of compensation as a necessary condition for the taking of property of anyone within the jurisdiction of a Contracting State.[118]

This statement stands in stark contrast to the potential role of proportionality in determining the existence of an indirect expropriation under standard IIA provisions. According to the current structure of expropriation clauses in most IIAs, the parties to an investment dispute are basically faced with an 'all-or-nothing' scenario. If the tribunal finds that the State measure amounts to an expropriation, the host State will have to fully compensate the investor according to the *Chorzów* principles.[119] If proportionality leads to the result that the State measure in question did *not* constitute an indirect expropriation, then the amount of compensation under the relevant BIT provision will automatically be zero. Under the jurisprudence of the ECtHR, however, the question of whether the private actor

[117] Id., para. 50, *Sporrong and Lönnroth v. Sweden*, ECtHR, A 52, Judgment (Merits), 23 September 1982, para. 69.

[118] *James v. United Kingdom*, ECtHR, A 98, Judgment, 21 February 1986, para 54. For a very similar formulation, *see Pressos Compania Naviera v. Belgium*, ECtHR, A 332, Judgment (Merits and Just Satisfaction), 20 November 1995, para. 38.

[119] *See* Chapter 8, notes 256–8 and accompanying text.

was compensated for the taking constitutes a crucial factor in deciding on the proportionality of the expropriation.

Another key factor in the proportionality analysis of the ECtHR is the question of whether the private actor is a national or a non-national of the expropriating State. For cases in which States deprive non-nationals of their property, the Court identified several considerations that speak in favour of a duty to compensate. The Court found that

non-nationals are more vulnerable to domestic legislation; unlike nationals, they will gen-erally have played no part in the election or designation of its authors nor have been con-sulted on its adoption. Secondly, although a taking of property must always be effected in the public interest, different considerations may apply to nationals and non-nationals and there may well be legitimate reason for requiring nationals to bear a greater burden in the public interest than non-nationals.[120]

Consistent with this holding of the ECtHR, the drafters of Article 1 appar-ently assumed that depriving non-nationals of their property would require the payment of compensation.[121] Foreign investors are by definition exactly that—non-nationals. As noted above, determining the existence of an indirect expropriation under an IIA by a proportionality analysis could reduce the amount of compensation owed for the deprivation of property to zero. Such a result is dif-ficult to reconcile with the drafting history of Article 1 as described by the ECtHR and the weak position of non-nationals in the democratic decision-making pro-cesses of host States.

In conclusion, there are considerable structural differences between stand-ard BIT provisions on expropriation and the way the ECHR and the ECtHR deal with issues of expropriation. These differences weigh against resorting to an ECtHR-inspired proportionality test in determining indirect expropriations in investor–State arbitrations. But the *Tecmed* tribunal did not only rely on ECtHR decisions on expropriation.[122] We turn now to the relevant jurisprudence on other interferences with the right to property.

b) Jurisprudence of the ECtHR on interferences with the right to property other than expropriatory acts

To recall, Article 1 of the First Additional Protocol to the ECHR contains three distinct rules.[123] The ECtHR does not always deem it necessary to allocate a certain State measure to one of the three rules.[124] This practice can partly be

---

[120] *James v. United Kingdom*, ECtHR, A 98, Judgment, 21 February 1986, para. 63.
[121] Id., para. 64; *see also Lithgow v. United Kingdom*, ECtHR, A 102, Judgment, 8 July 1986, para. 117.
[122] *See Tecmed*, Award, para. 122 nn.140–1.
[123] *See supra* notes 106–9 and accompanying text.
[124] *See, e.g.,* the examples listed in Arjen van Rijn, 'Right to the Peaceful Enjoyment of One's Possessions (Article 1 of Protocol No. 1)', *in Theory and Practice of the European Convention on Human Rights* (Pieter van Dijk et al. eds., 2006) 863–93, at 874–5.

explained by the central importance of the right to 'peaceful enjoyment of property' (set out in the first rule of Article 1) to the interpretation of the entire provision. The Court held repeatedly that

the rules are not 'distinct' in the sense of being unconnected: the second and third rules are concerned with particular instances of interference with the right to peaceful enjoyment of property. They must therefore be construed in the light of the general principle laid down in the first rule.[125]

In *Mellacher v. Austria*, for example, the ECtHR had to decide on whether the compulsory reduction of negotiated rent based on the 1981 Rent Act was in compliance with Article 1 of the First Additional Protocol.[126] The Court found that there was no formal or de facto expropriation of the landlords' property and instead measured the compulsory rent reduction against the requirements of Article 1(2). According to the wording of Article 1(2), a State may enforce all laws 'that it deems necessary to control the use of property in accordance with the general interest'. In line with this wording of Article 1(2), the Court generally grants States

a wide margin of appreciation both with regard to the existence of a problem of public concern warranting measures of control and as to the choice of the detailed rules for the implementation of such measures.[127]

Examining the goal of the State measure, the Court in *Mellacher* limited its review to whether the judgment of the domestic legislator was 'manifestly without reasonable foundation.'[128] Once the Court had answered this question in the negative, it did not automatically consider the State's measure to be in compliance with Article 1. Rather, the Court inquired as to the proportionality of the interference. It derived this element from the relevance of the general principle in the first sentence of Article 1(1) for the interpretation of Article 1(2):

... an interference must achieve a 'fair balance' between the demands of the general interest of the community and the requirements of the protection of the individual's fundamental rights. The search for this balance is reflected in the structure of Article 1 (P1-1) as a whole, and therefore also in the second paragraph thereof. There must be a reasonable relationship of proportionality between the means employed and the aim pursued.[129]

The *Mellacher* case illustrates the function of proportionality in the context of the second paragraph. The State enjoys a 'wide margin of appreciation' in deciding

[125] *Mellacher v. Austria*, ECtHR, A 169, Judgment, 19 December 1989, para. 42; *see also* the almost identical formulations in *James v. United Kingdom*, ECtHR, A 98, Judgment, 21 February 1986, para. 37; *Lithgow v. United Kingdom*, ECtHR, A 102, Judgment, 8 July 1986, para. 106; *Bäck v. Finland*, ECtHR, Application no. 37598/97, Judgment, 20 July 2004, para. 52; *Anheuser-Busch v. Portugal*, ECtHR, Application no. 73049/01, Judgment (Grand Chamber), 11 January 2007, para. 62; *Pressos Compania Naviera v. Belgium*, ECtHR, A 332, Judgment (Merits and Just Satisfaction), 20 November 1995, para. 33.
[126] *Mellacher v. Austria*, ECtHR, A 169, Judgment, 19 December 1989, paras. 11–4.
[127] Id., para. 45.   [128] Id., paras. 45–8.
[129] Id., para. 48 (internal references omitted).

which measures lie in the public interest. If the burden on the applicant is disproportionate to this aim, however, the ECtHR will still find this State measure to be
contrary to Article 1. Hence, in the ECHR setting, the principle of proportionality has a corrective function and protects private actors. If the Court finds the
State measure to be proportionate, the Court's determination that the State acted
within its margin of appreciation and in accordance with the ECHR stands. If
the Court finds the State measure to be disproportionate, the measure violates the
private property rights of the claimant.

In contrast, the application of the principle of proportionality in determining the existence of an expropriation would have the effect that a substantial
deprivation might not qualify as an expropriatory act. As already explained
in the previous subsection, this means that proportionality would work to the
disadvantage of private actors. In some situations, there might be good reasons for
cross-fertilization and transporting legal principles from one specialized regime
to another. If the relevant legal principle has diametrically opposed effects in two
regimes, however, it is difficult to make a case for such cross-fertilization.

The jurisprudence of the ECtHR on the first sentence of Article 1(1) does not
offer more compelling reasons for the determination of the very existence of an
indirect expropriation through proportionality balancing than Article 1(2). The
Court bases its analysis on the first sentence of Article 1(1) only if it finds neither
the second sentence of Article 1(1) nor Article 1(2) to be applicable.[130] But the
wording of the first sentence of Article 1 does not contain any criteria under which
an interference with property rights might be permissible. It merely states that
'[e]very natural or legal person is entitled to the peaceful enjoyment of his possessions'. This does not mean that a State measure is automatically unlawful only
because it does not fall under the two other, more specific categories of Article 1.[131]
In this vein, the Court stated that it

must determine whether a fair balance was struck between the demands of the general
interests of the community and the requirements of the protection of the individual's
fundamental rights.[132]

Once again, the Court justified its approach by relying on the general structure of
Article 1 and the ECHR. Indeed, any other result would be utterly absurd. There
is no reason why a mere interference with a property right should be subject to
more severe restrictions than the outright deprivation of the same right. Contrary
to the first sentence of Article 1(1), standard IIA provisions on expropriation very
clearly spell out the criteria (non-discrimination, due process, compensation)
under which an expropriation is lawful.

---

[130] *See, e.g., Matos e Silva v. Portugal*, ECtHR, Reports 1996-IV, Judgment (Merits and Just
Satisfaction), 16 September 1996, para. 85; *Sporrong and Lönnroth v. Sweden*, ECtHR, A 52,
Judgment (Merits), 23 September 1982, paras. 61–6.
[131] *Sporrong and Lönnroth v. Sweden*, ECtHR, A 52, Judgment (Merits), 23 September 1982,
para. 69.
[132] Id., para. 69.

In sum, the jurisprudence of the ECtHR and the underlying text of Article 1 are structurally very different from the legal setting in which the term 'expropriation' must be interpreted in investor–State arbitrations. Therefore, the jurisprudence of the ECtHR does not provide convincing reasons to determine the existence of an indirect expropriation under standard BIT provisions on expropriation by way of a proportionality analysis.

V. Identifying indirect expropriation in accordance with Article 31 VCLT

The criticism of the *Tecmed* approach in section IV did not seek to exclude for good proportionality from the process of determining the existence of an indirect expropriation. Rather, the analysis aimed to demonstrate that reference to the jurisprudence of the ECtHR on the right to property is insufficient reason to apply proportionality in investor–State arbitration. This section considers other avenues for both arbitral tribunals and States to integrate proportionality in the process of identifying an indirect expropriation. The different means of treaty interpretation as set out in Article 31 VCLT provide the relevant analytical framework, and the following subsections follow the structure of this provision. Subsection 1 embarks from the ordinary meaning and the context of standard IIA provisions on expropriation. Before subsection 3 turns to the object and purpose of investment treaties, subsection 2 examines selected IIAs that provide explicit guidance for arbitrators on how to identify an indirect expropriation. Subsection 4 then analyses to what extent recent State practice supports the application of proportionality in determining the existence of an indirect expropriation—and what States can do to establish or foster such an approach, short of renegotiating IIAs. Subsection 5 examines whether and under what circumstances the concept of systemic integration may warrant a proportionality analysis.

1. The ordinary meaning and context of the treaty term

The starting point for the interpretation of every treaty provision is the ordinary meaning of its terms.[133] Dictionaries are an important tool in this regard.[134] *Black's Law Dictionary* defines the term 'expropriation' as '[a] governmental taking or modification of an individual's property rights'.[135] Obviously, this definition does not include an element of proportionality balancing. Rather, it suggests

---

[133] *See* Chapter 4, notes 43–4 and accompanying text.
[134] *See* Gardiner, *Treaty Interpretation*, at 166–9.
[135] Garner, *Black's Law Dictionary*, Pocket Edition, at 271. Gardiner notes that the ordinary meaning of a term is not solely determined by how a layperson understands this term. Rather, it would be appropriate to take into account the understanding of a 'person reasonably informed in that subject' (Gardiner, *Treaty Interpretation*, at 174). Hence, a standard legal dictionary appears to be a valid resource for identifying the ordinary meaning of the term 'expropriation'.

that it is the 'effect' of the State measure on the property right which informs the natural understanding of the term 'expropriation'. The *Oxford* dictionaries equate the verb 'to expropriate' with the phrases 'to dispossess someone of property' or 'to take property from the owner for public use or benefit.'[136] To recall, according to the 'police powers doctrine' general regulatory measures in the public interest cannot per se constitute indirect expropriations.[137] The definition provided by the *Oxford* dictionaries, in contrast, suggests that the public purpose pursued by a measure is a constitutive element of an expropriation.

This quick glance at selected dictionary definitions of the term 'expropriation' weighs against the notion that a State measure automatically fails to qualify as an expropriatory act under an IIA when it serves the public interest in a 'proportionate' way. In fact, the 'ordinary meaning' of the term 'expropriation' provides only very limited guidance for the interpretation of standard IIA provisions on expropriation. Proceeding in the order of consideration set out in Article 31 VCLT, the next interpretative means to be taken into account is the 'context' of the term expropriation (or the words 'shall not be expropriated', depending on the wording of the relevant IIA).[138] As outlined above, the provisions on expropriation in IIAs usually include detailed requirements for an expropriation to be in compliance with the relevant IIA. One of these requirements is that the expropriation be for a 'public purpose'. This requirement makes no sense if the prior step of determining the existence of an indirect expropriation already involves the weighing of the very same 'public purpose' against the investor's interests.[139]

In sum, neither the wording nor the context of standard BIT provisions on expropriation support the view that the deprivation of property falls short of constituting an expropriation as long as it serves a public purpose in a proportionate way. While not decisive for the purposes of treaty interpretation, it is interesting to note that Alexy's theory on rules and principles confirms this account. According to Alexy, a collision between a rule and a principle should be resolved in favour of the rule, because the rule reflects an explicit legislative choice.[140] The following example from the international realm illustrates this point: the prohibition of the use of force in Article 2(4) of the UN Charter constitutes a rule and not a principle.[141] Most authors agree that the only exceptions to this rule are the right to self-defence in Article 51 and resolutions by the UN Security Council under Chapter VII authorizing the use of force (and possibly the rescue of nationals abroad).[142] Conflicting principles (such as human rights considerations triggering military interventions)[143] cannot trump the prohibition on the use of force—neither through proportionality nor otherwise. Against this background,

---

[136] *Available at* <http://oxforddictionaries.com/view/entry/m_en_gb0281880#m_en_gb0281880.005>.

[137] *See supra* notes 30–3 and accompanying text.   [138] *See* Chapter 4, notes 43–4.

[139] *See supra* note 34 and accompanying text.

[140] *See* Chapter 3, note 64 and accompanying text.

[141] *See, e.g.,* Petersen, 'Customary Law Without Custom?', at 289–90.

[142] *See, e.g.,* Randelzhofer & Dörr, 'Article 2(4)', paras. 44–63.

[143] *See, e.g.,* id., para. 54.

it does not take a lot of creativity to characterize standard IIA provisions on expropriation as rules: expropriations are only lawful if they are accompanied by compensation, adopted for a public purpose, and performed on a non-discriminatory basis. Or, in other words, even if an expropriation is for a public purpose and non-discriminatory, it triggers a claim for compensation—regardless of whether the deprivation of property was proportionate or not.

2. Special case: clarification of the notion of 'indirect expropriation' in an IIA

As explained in section III.3, States increasingly define the concept of 'indirect expropriation' in annexes to BITs.[144] The methodology set out in these annexes amounts to a codification of the 'mitigated police powers' doctrine—at least in essence. Significantly, stipulations that follow the example of Annex B(4)(a),(b) of the US Model BIT[145] and Annex B.13(1)(b),(c)[146] of the Canadian Model BIT frame the balancing process in favour of the public purpose ('except in rare circumstances, non-discriminatory regulatory actions...do not constitute indirect expropriations'). Furthermore, these annexes often list factors that ought to play a crucial role in the analysis, that is 'the economic impact of the government action'; 'the extent to which the government interferes with distinct, reasonable investment-backed expectations'; and 'the character of the government action'.[147] We have seen that the Korean–US and ASEAN–ANZ FTAs contain textual elements that more or less explicitly mandate a proportionality analysis.[148] The analysis that follows will reveal that even in the context of provisions on indirect expropriation that strictly follow the wording of the 2004 US Model BIT, there is little reason not to resort to the principle of proportionality. On the contrary, in these legal settings, proportionality is arguably the most appropriate analytical tool available to arbitral tribunals when determining the existence of an indirect expropriation.

---

[144] *See supra* pp. 160–3. One may wonder whether those annexes (a) clarify the 'ordinary meaning' of the term (Article 31(1) VCLT), (b) form part of its context (Article 31(1) and (2) VCLT), or (c) prove that the parties intended to give a 'special meaning' (Article 34(4) VCLT) to the term 'expropriation'. For all practical purposes, however, this question seems to be irrelevant: All means of interpretation listed in Article 31 of the VLCT are of the same hierarchical value (*see* Chapter 4, notes 41–7 and accompanying text). The ILC stated in 1966 that 'the ordinary meaning of a term is not to be determined in the abstract but in the context of the treaty and in the light of its object and purpose' (ILC, *Commentaries on the Law of Treaties*, Articles 27–8, para. 12). Some members of the ILC doubted that Article 31(4) was necessary at all since a 'special meaning' would follow from the particular 'context'. The primary reason why the ILC still included Article 31(4) in its draft articles was to stress that is was for the party relying on Article 31(4) to prove that the parties had indeed intended such a 'special meaning' (id. Article 27, para. 17; *see also* Gardiner, *Treaty Interpretation*, at 292)—a burden of proof evidently met if the special meaning is explained in an annex.

[145] *See supra* notes 68–9.   [146] *See supra* note 70.

[147] *See supra* notes 68 and 70. But note that these provisions also clarify that the three factors explicitly mentioned are not exhaustive ('among other factors').

[148] *See supra* notes 79–81 and accompanying text.

The annexes in the BITs between Canada and the Czech Republic, Canada and Latvia, the US and Rwanda, and the US and Uruguay, and in similar treaties, clarify that the determination of whether a State measure amounts to an indirect expropriation requires a 'case-by-case, fact-based inquiry'.[149] The different factors that ought to be taken into account in this inquiry according to the relevant annexes are typical elements of a proportionality analysis: the impact of the government action on the individual right, the extent of the government interference, and the character and objectives of the government action.[150] In such normative settings, the potentially negative consequences of proportionality do not materialize. Chapter 3, section II above has identified the rule of law, the risk of judicial lawmaking, and the arbitrariness of the balancing process as the main arguments against the application of proportionality.[151] Regarding the rule of law, the following statement by Waldron is of particular relevance to this subsection.

> According to most conceptions of the rule of law, individual citizens are entitled to laws that are neither murky nor uncertain but are instead publicly and clearly stated in a text that is not buried in doctrine.[152]

Against the background of this characterization of the rule of law, the application of proportionality in the process of identifying an indirect expropriation under a standard BIT provision raises serious concerns. After all, such a provision merely specifies that foreign investors are not to be expropriated except for a public purpose; in a non-discriminatory manner; and upon payment of prompt, adequate, and effective compensation. From the perspective of a foreign investor, it is not clear that a claim for compensation would require a proportionality analysis, even if the foreign investor suffered from a substantial deprivation of its property. The contrary, however, is true if an IIA contains an annex that sets out the understanding by the parties to the treaty of the provision on expropriation. In such cases, the text of the annex makes it abundantly clear that a non-discriminatory State action in pursuit of a public welfare objective will normally not sustain a claim for expropriation.

One may wonder why the drafters of the IIAs discussed in this subsection decided to take the detour of listing the relevant criteria in an annex instead of directly placing them in the body of the respective provision on expropriation. Two possible reasons for this practice go beyond mere stylistic considerations. The first relates to the parties' understanding of customary international law. The US, for example, clarified in its Model BIT that the relevant provision on expropriation 'is intended to reflect customary international law concerning the obligation of States with respect to expropriation'.[153] The same stipulation found its way into the US–Uruguay BIT[154] and the Rwanda–US BIT.[155] As we will see below,

---

[149] *See supra* notes 71–7 and accompanying text.   [150] *See* id.
[151] Chapter 3, notes 199–218 and accompanying text.
[152] Waldron, 'The Rule of International Law', at 17.
[153] Annex B(1) to the US Model BIT, *supra note* 68.
[154] Annex B(1) to the US–Uruguay BIT, *supra note* 71.
[155] Annex B(1) to the US–Rwanda BIT, *supra note* 72.

clarifications that the relevant annexes purport to reflect customary international law may also have an influence on the interpretation of older treaties without explanatory annexes.[156] Abandoning the formulation from standard BIT provisions altogether would make this argument more complicated. The second possible reason for making use of traditional formulations of IIA provisions in modern IIAs relates to the role of prior decisions in arbitral proceedings.[157] By adding an annex, States exclude consideration of case law not in line with the annex without dismissing as irrelevant the rest of arbitral jurisprudence on standard expropriation provisions.

Apart from rule-of-law concerns, the arbitrariness of the balancing process and the threat of judicial lawmaking are the main arguments against the application of the principle of proportionality. Concerns about the arbitrariness of the balancing process comprise the following two points of criticism: first, it is unclear what factors enter the balancing process; second, it is uncertain what weight the relevant factors carry.[158] These concerns are unjustified with respect to the application of the principle of proportionality in identifying an indirect expropriation under the annexes discussed in this subsection. As outlined above, such annexes provide a clear (albeit non-exhaustive) list of the factors that ought to play a crucial role in the balancing process.[159] Moreover, these annexes clarify that the public purpose tends to carry a greater weight in the balancing process than the property rights of foreign investors ('except in rare circumstances, non-discriminatory regulatory actions...do not constitute indirect expropriations').[160]

These elements provide a value system that guides the balancing process (and thereby significantly mitigates its subjective and arbitrary character) and militates against the risk of judicial lawmaking or activism. By outlining the relevant factors in the balancing process and establishing a certain hierarchical relationship among them, the parties to the relevant IIAs exercise considerable control over the decision-making process. Some of the IIAs discussed in this subsection contain mechanisms that further enhance the role of the contracting States in investor–State arbitrations. The following provision, which is part of several IIAs, is an important example:

Article 31

1. Where a respondent asserts as a defense that the measure alleged to be a breach is within the scope of an entry set out in Annex I, II, or III, the tribunal shall, on request

---

[156] *See infra* pp. 171–7. Note that the Canadian Model BIT (*supra note* 70), which is largely identical to the US Model BIT, does not contain such a statement with respect to the rules of customary international law on expropriation. Consequently, the BIT between Canada and Latvia (*supra* note 75) and the BIT between Canada and the Czech Republic (*supra* note 77) also lack this statement. Furthermore, other IIAs that largely follow the wording of the US Model BIT's annex on expropriation such as the KORUS FTA (*supra* note 79) and the ASEAN–ANZ FTA (*supra* note 81) omit the sentence on the customary international law character of the rules on expropriation as well.

[157] For the role of prior decisions in the reasoning of arbitral tribunals, *see* Chapter 4, notes 69–76 and accompanying text.

[158] *See* Chapter 3, notes 216–8 and accompanying text.

[159] *See supra* notes 69–81 and accompanying text.

[160] *See supra* notes 69, 70, 79, & 81 and accompanying text.

of the respondent, request the interpretation of the Parties on the issue. The Parties shall submit in writing any joint decision declaring their interpretation to the tribunal within 60 days of delivery of the request.

2. A joint decision issued under paragraph 1 by the Parties, each acting through its representative designated for purposes of this Article, shall be binding on the tribunal, and any decision or award issued by the tribunal must be consistent with that joint decision. If the Parties fail to issue such a decision within 60 days, the tribunal shall decide the issue.[161]

Hence, this provision grants the respondent the right to request an interpretation on certain issues by the parties to the treaty. The parties' joint interpretation is binding for the tribunal. In other words, with this mechanism the contracting States have limited the scope for third-party adjudication. Annexes I, II, and III, to which this stipulation refers, do not deal with the identification of an indirect expropriation under the relevant BIT.[162] However, in addition to Article 31, the US–Rwanda BIT, the US–Uruguay BIT, and the US Model BIT contain a more general provision that grants the treaty parties a certain control over the interpretation process. Article 30(3) of these treaties stipulates:

A joint decision of the Parties, each acting through its representative designated for purposes of this Article, declaring their interpretation of a provision of this Treaty shall be binding on a tribunal, and any decision or award issued by a tribunal must be consistent with that joint decision.[163]

Article 27(2),(3) of the ASEAN-ANZ FTA,[164] Article X(6) of the BIT between Canada and the Czech Republic,[165] and Article 11.22(3) of the KORUS FTA[166] contain very similar provisions. These provisions illustrate that the contracting States made nuanced choices regarding the degree that they delegated the resolution of disputes to third-party adjudication. In the absence of a joint decision by the parties to the treaty, it is for the arbitral tribunal to conduct a case-specific inquiry and reach its own conclusions.

In sum, the application of the principle of proportionality to the process of identifying an indirect expropriation under IIAs that define this concept along the lines of the 'mitigated police powers' doctrine does not give rise to serious concerns. It is neither a threat to the rule of law, nor does it entail an arbitrary balancing process or unwarranted judicial lawmaking. Rather, the text and structure of annexes such as those to the ASEAN–ANZ FTA suggest that a proportionality

---

[161] This is the text of Article 31 of the US Model BIT (*supra* note 68), the Uruguay–US BIT (*supra* note 71) BIT, and the US–Rwanda BIT (*supra* note 72). Article 11.23 of the KORUS FTA (*supra* note 79) contains a virtually identical stipulation.

[162] Annexes I, II, and III mostly specify certain sectors that are not fully covered by the substantive protections of the relevant BIT, e.g. the provisions on national treatment and most-favoured-nation treatment (*see* the explanatory notes in the US–Rwanda BIT, *supra* note 72, at 42, 54, and 65).

[163] *Supra* notes 68, 71, and 72.   [164] *Supra* note 81.   [165] *Supra* note 77.

[166] *Supra* note 79.

analysis is appropriate. Moreover, the application of the principle of proportionality in such legal settings brings to bear its positive features. Proportionality provides for an argumentative framework that identifies the relevant factors in the decision-making process. In this vein, proportionality ensures a certain degree of transparency, which reduces the scope for the introduction of subjective (or improper) elements into the decision-making process.[167] Furthermore, the principle of proportionality seeks to ensure that none of the interests involved is compromised to a greater extent than necessary for the advancement of a conflicting interest.

It is important to bear in mind, however, that the arguments presented in this subsection apply only to IIAs that contain very specific annexes on indirect expropriation. For other IIAs, the findings from subsection 1 remain unaltered: the ordinary meaning and the context of standard IIA provisions on expropriation do not suggest that determining the existence of an indirect expropriation involves a proportionality analysis. The following subsections analyse how other means of interpretation might change this tentative assessment.

3. The object and purpose of the relevant investment treaty

According to Article 31(1) VCLT, the ordinary meaning of the terms of a treaty shall be determined 'in the light of its object and purpose'. To clarify the potential role of the object and purpose of a treaty in the interpretation of IIA provisions on expropriation, this subsection tackles three issues. First, what are the methods an arbitral tribunal can use to determine the object and purpose of an IIA? Second, what is the object and purpose of an IIA? Third, what can the properly established object and purpose of an IIA add to the interpretation of a provision on expropriation?[168] The first of the three questions is relatively simple, at least from a theoretical perspective. All means of interpretation listed in Articles 31 and 32 VCLT may be referred to in order to determine the object and purpose of an IIA.[169] But treaties only rarely comment explicitly on their object and purpose. The same is true for IIAs. In the context of multilateral treaties, treaty interpreters regularly refer to *travaux préparatoires* in order to determine the object and purpose of the treaty. Negotiations leading to a (bilateral) investment treaty, however, typically do not produce such publicly available documents.[170] Often, there will simply be no *travaux* as the relevant treaty was based on a Model BIT. Consequently, arbitral tribunals mainly refer to its preamble when determining the object and purpose of an IIA.[171] Regarding the second issue—the concrete object and purpose

---

[167] *See also* Bomhoff, 'Balancing, the Global and the Local', at 576.

[168] For a similar approach regarding the general role of the object and purpose of a treaty in the interpretation process, *see* Fauchald, 'The Legal Reasoning of ICSID Tribunals', at 322.

[169] Villiger, *Commentary on the 1969 Vienna Convention*, Article 31, para. 13.

[170] McLachlan, 'Investment Treaties and General International Law', at 371–2.

[171] *See* Fauchald, 'The Legal Reasoning of ICSID Tribunals', at 322–3. However, Fauchald also noted that in most cases international investment tribunals did not provide any 'source' for their finding on the object and purpose of a particular IIA (id., at 322).

of IIAs—there are two broad strains within the jurisprudence of international investment tribunals. The first strain focuses on the role of IIAs as instruments for the protection of private property rights. The second strain perceives investment protection as a means to a greater end and emphasizes the contribution of foreign investment to the development and well-being of host States. According to this second view, IIAs seek to establish an equilibrium between the protection of private property rights and the right of host States to regulate in the public interest.

The tribunal in *Siemens v. Argentina* (which decided on the basis of the Argentina–US BIT) is usually cited as authority for the first approach, which defines the object and purpose of a BIT rather narrowly.[172] The tribunal held that it

shall be guided by the purpose of the Treaty as expressed in its title and preamble. It is a treaty 'to protect' and 'to promote' investments. The preamble provides that the parties have agreed to the provisions of the Treaty for the purpose of creating favorable conditions for the investments of nationals or companies of one of the two States in the territory of the other State.... The intention of the parties is clear. It is to create favorable conditions for investments and to stimulate private initiative.[173]

This description of the object and purpose of a BIT could be juxtaposed with the approach of the tribunal in *Saluka v. The Czech Republic*. The *Saluka* tribunal had to interpret the BIT between the Netherlands and the Czech Republic and stressed the need for a 'balanced approach'.

The protection of foreign investments is not the sole aim of the Treaty, but rather a necessary element alongside the overall aim of encouraging foreign investment and extending and intensifying the parties' economic relations. That in turn calls for a balanced approach to the interpretation of the Treaty's substantive provisions for the protection of investments, since an interpretation which exaggerates the protection to be accorded to foreign investments may serve to dissuade host States from admitting foreign investments and so undermine the overall aim of extending and intensifying the parties' mutual economic relations.[174]

There are obviously certain differences between the characterizations of the object and purpose of the relevant BIT by the tribunals in *Siemens* and in *Saluka*. Still, it is submitted that the differences between the two approaches is a matter of degree rather than principle. After all, the *Siemens* tribunal recognized that the protection of foreign investment under the BIT between Germany and Argentina is not an end in itself. Rather, the tribunal found that '[b]oth parties recognize

---

[172] *See, e.g.,* Anne van Aaken, 'Fragmentation of International Law: the Case of International Investment Protection', *Finnish Yearbook of International Law* XVII (2008) 91–130, at 126 n.178.

[173] *Siemens AG v. Argentine Republic*, ICSID Case No. ARB/02/8, Decision on Jurisdiction, 3 August 2004, para. 81.

[174] *Saluka*, Partial Award, para. 300. The tribunal in *Suez–Vivendi* and *AWG Group* adopted a similar approach regarding Argentina's BITs with France, Spain, and the United Kingdom. It stated 'that they all have broader goals than merely granting specific levels of protection to individual investors', and added that the 'protection and promotion of foreign investment' is 'only a means to an end' (*Suez–Vivendi* and *AWG Group*, Decision on Liability, para. 218).

that the promotion and protection of these investments by a treaty may stimulate private economic initiative and increase the well-being of the peoples of both countries'.[175] Furthermore, the *Siemens* tribunal did not invoke the object and purpose of the BIT in order to defeat the regulatory freedom of the host State on a broad scale. Rather, the tribunal referred to the object and purpose of the BIT when it observed that the treaty drafters seemed to use the words 'investor' and 'investment' interchangeably. Consequently, the tribunal declined to draw a negative conclusion regarding the scope of a BIT provision merely because this provision used only one of the two terms.[176]

In this context, it is also important to bear in mind that the preamble of the BIT between Argentina and Germany does not mention any values or interests beyond those that were addressed by the *Siemens* tribunal.[177] The preambles of more recent IIAs—especially of non-European States—tend to be more elaborate in their identification of relevant values and interests other than the protection of private property rights. This is certainly so when these preambles are compared to the traditionally slim preambles of the German BITs.[178] The differences between the Argentina–US BIT (concluded in 1991) and more recent US BITs based on the 2004 US Model BIT also reflect this development. This is not to say that the 1991 Argentina–US BIT completely ignores the broader dimension of BITs. The preamble of this treaty reads as follows:

The United States of America and the Argentine Republic, hereinafter referred to as the Parties;

Desiring to *promote greater economic cooperation* between them, with respect to invest-ment by nationals and companies of one Party in the territory of the other Party;

Recognizing that agreement upon the treatment to be accorded such investment will stimulate the flow of private capital and the *economic development* of the Parties;

Agreeing that fair and equitable treatment of investment is desirable in order to main-tain a stable framework for investment and *maximum effective use of economic resources*;

---

[175] *Siemens AG v. Argentine Republic*, ICSID Case No. ARB/02/8, Decision on Jurisdiction, 3 August 2004, para. 81.

[176] Id., para. 92.

[177] The preamble of the BIT between Germany and Argentina (*available at* <http://investment-policyhub.unctad.org/Download/TreatyFile/92>) reflects the wording of the German Model BIT (*available at* <http://www.iilcc.uni-koeln.de/fileadmin/institute/iilcc/Dokumente/matrechtinvest/VIS_Mustervertrag.pdf>), which reads as follows:

The Federal Republic of Germany and _____—desiring to intensify economic coop-eration between the two States, intending to create favourable conditions for investments by investors of either State in the territory of the other State, recognizing that the encour-agement and contractual protection of such investments are apt to stimulate private busi-ness initiative and to increase the prosperity of both nations—have agreed as follows:

[178] Interestingly, the German Model BIT of 2009 (*supra* note 177) has not followed the US and Canadian Model BITs in their efforts to provide for a greater regulatory leeway, neither in its preamble nor in its substantive provisions. Consequently, the preamble of the (renegotiated) BIT between Germany and Pakistan (concluded on 1 December 2009, *available at* <http://investment-policyhub.unctad.org/Download/TreatyFile/1386>) contains (essentially) the same preamble as the Argentina–Germany BIT (*supra* note 177) concluded in 1991.

Recognizing that the development of economic and business ties can contribute to the *well-being of workers* in both Parties and promote *respect for internationally recognized worker rights*; and

having resolved to conclude a Treaty concerning the encouragement and reciprocal protection of investment;

Have agreed as follows:[179]

The otherwise similar preamble of the 2004 (and 2012) US Model BIT differs from the Argentina–US BIT in one important respect: the preamble to the Argentina–US BIT mentions the public interest in the course of describing the positive effects of foreign investment. The preamble to the US Model BIT, however, addresses the possibility of conflict between private property rights and the public interest by emphasizing '[the desire] to achieve these objectives in a manner consistent with the protection of health, safety, and the environment, and the promotion of internationally recognized labor rights'.[180] The preamble to the US–Rwanda BIT contains the same passage.[181] The preamble to the US–Uruguay BIT adds 'the promotion of consumer protection' to an otherwise identical list.[182] The parties to the ASEAN–ANZ FTA took a different approach. While the preamble to this agreement does not comment on the substantive content of possibly conflicting interests, it explicitly 'reaffirms' the obligations of the parties under other international agreements.[183] The preamble in the KORUS FTA states that the parties

[desire] to strengthen the development and enforcement of labor and environmental laws and policies, promote basic workers' rights and sustainable development, and implement this Agreement in a manner consistent with environmental protection and conservation[.][184]

In sum, there is no doubt that IIAs protect the private property rights of foreign investors. It is debatable, however, whether the protection of these rights is an end in itself. Some States have become more explicit about the public interest in the preambles to their IIAs. Future arbitral tribunals might, therefore, be inclined

---

[179] Argentina–US BIT, *available at* <http://investmentpolicyhub.unctad.org/Download/TreatyFile/127> (emphases indicating references to the public interest added). For a critical view on the significance of these references to the public interest in the Argentina–US BIT, *see* Alvarez & Khamsi, 'The Argentine Crisis', at 470–1. Choudhury, on the other hand, concludes from the preamble to the Argentina–US BIT that 'the beneficiaries of the US–Argentina BIT are investors, workers and all nationals of the United States and Argentina who benefit from their countries' economic development.' (Barnali Choudhury, 'Exception Provisions as a Gateway to Incorporating Human Rights Issues into International Investment Agreements', *Columbia Journal of Transnational Law* 49 (2011) 670–716, at 707).

[180] *Supra* note 68. The preamble to the 2012 Model BIT is identical to that of the 2004 version. But note that the Canadian Model BIT (*supra* note 70) which is otherwise rather similar to the US Model BIT contains a slim preamble similar to the German Model BIT (*supra* note 177). The preambles in the Canada–Latvia BIT (*supra* note 76) and the Canada–Czech Republic BIT (*supra* note 77) follow the example of the Canadian Model BIT.

[181] *Supra* note 72.   [182] *Supra* note 71.   [183] *Supra* note 81.

[184] *Supra* note 79.

to build on the characterization of the *Saluka* tribunal when they determine the object and purpose of an IIA.[185]

This brings us to the third question raised at the beginning of this subsection: what can the object and purpose of an IIA contribute to the interpretation of a standard IIA provision on expropriation? To recall, standard BIT provisions allow for expropriations if they are in the public interest and accompanied by the payment of compensation. This rule itself seems to be a compromise between public policy considerations and investor rights. Hence, it is difficult to see how the (disputed) notion according to which the object and purpose of an IIA is to provide a balance between investor rights and the public interest should be able to provide clarity on the term 'expropriation'.

The ILC commented on the function of the object and purpose in the interpretation process as follows:

When a treaty is open to two interpretations one of which does and the other does not enable the treaty to have appropriate effects, good faith and the objects and purposes of the treaty demand that the former interpretation should be adopted. Properly limited and applied, the maxim does not call for an 'extensive' or 'liberal' interpretation in the sense of an interpretation going beyond what is expressed or necessarily to be implied in the terms of the treaty.[186]

In other words, treaty interpreters should not use the object and purpose of a treaty to revise the treaty.[187] This means that for IIAs with detailed annexes on indirect expropriations (discussed in the last subsection), the potential objects and purposes of the relevant IIA are immaterial. This is particularly important if one adheres to the notion that the only object and purpose of an IIA is the protection of private property rights. According to this view, all other concerns mentioned in the preamble of an IIA are mere 'hopes' or 'outcomes' associated with the protection of property rights.[188] Still, such an understanding of the object and purpose of IIAs cannot overwrite an annex that obliges arbitrators to consider the public interest in identifying indirect expropriations.

For standard IIA provisions that are not accompanied by a clarifying annex, the wording and the context often speak against the relevance of proportionality in determining the existence of an indirect expropriation.[189] The object and purpose of a treaty alone will hardly be sufficient to establish a contrary result. This is also true if one accepts the idea that the object and purpose of the relevant IIA goes beyond the mere protection of foreign investments. The next two subsections analyse whether the means of treaty interpretation reflected in Article 31(3) VCLT justify a different result.

---

[185] *See supra* note 174.

[186] ILC, *Commentaries on the Law of Treaties*, Articles 27–8, para. 6.

[187] Gardiner, *Treaty Interpretation*, at 197–8.

[188] *See* Alvarez & Khamsi, 'The Argentine Crisis', at 470–1 with respect to the Argentina–US BIT and arguably also Reinisch, 'Necessity', at 205.

[189] *See supra* notes 133–43 and accompanying text.

4. Subsequent agreement and practice

To recall, all the means of interpretation listed in Article 31(3) VCLT share one common feature: they are extrinsic both to the text of the treaty to be interpreted and to its 'context' as defined in Article 31(2) VCLT.[190] Furthermore, they are a 'mandatory part of the interpretation process' and are not hierarchically inferior to the other means of interpretation listed in Article 31 VCLT.[191] Article 31(3)(a) and (b) VCLT[192] are usually considered to constitute forms of 'authentic interpretation'. Some authors submit that these means of interpretation have 'binding force' on adjudicatory bodies since the 'parties to the treaty are their own masters'.[193] Article 31(3)(a) and (b) VCLT have so far received only very limited scholarly attention. In fact, the need for further clarification is so significant that the ILC Study Group 'Treaties over time', instituted in 2009, decided to put a special emphasis on the issues of subsequent agreements and practice.[194] In 2012, the ILC even decided to change the title of the Study Group to 'Subsequent agreements and subsequent practice in relation to interpretation of treaties'.[195] Hence, any attempt to resolve the doctrinal uncertainty surrounding Article 31(3)(a) and (b) VCLT in this subsection would be presumptuous. I will, therefore, largely confine myself to outlining some of the possible ways in which States might seek to establish an element of proportionality balancing in deciding on the existence of an indirect expropriation. Moreover, I will point to some factors that challenge the assumption that subsequent agreements and practice are unconditionally binding on arbitral tribunals.

International investment tribunals only very rarely make use of subsequent agreements and practice in the sense of Article 31(3) VCLT. And even when they do so, they usually do not refer to the relevant VCLT provision.[196] Some commentators have identified the involvement of private actors in investor–State arbitration as the reason for the limited recourse of arbitral tribunals to Article 31(3)(a) and (b).[197] After all, subsequent agreements and practice involve both contracting States of the BIT that gave rise to the relevant investor–State arbitration. In the dispute itself, only one of the two States is involved, together with a private party that cannot itself influence the interpretation of a treaty with the tools set out in Article 31(3)(a) and (b).

---

[190] *Supra* note 47 and accompanying text.   [191] *Supra* note 45–6 and accompanying text.

[192] For the wording of these provisions, *see supra* p. 87.

[193] Villiger, *Commentary*, Article 31, para. 16.

[194] ILC, Report of the International Law Commission on the work of its sixty-first session, UN Doc A/64/10 (2009), Annex A.

[195] *See* Georg Nolte, 'Introduction', in *Treaties and Subsequent Practice* (Georg Nolte ed., Oxford: OUP, 2013) 1–10, at 9.

[196] Fauchald, for example, only identified one instance in which an ICSID tribunal referred to a subsequent agreement (Fauchald, 'The Legal Reasoning of ICSID Tribunals', at 332 n.166, quoting *Philippe Gruslin v. Malaysia*, ICSID Case No. ARB/99/3, Award, 28 November 2000; the tribunal did not mention Article 31(3) of the VCLT in this case).

[197] McLachlan, 'Investment Treaties', at 372.

Nevertheless, Anthea Roberts has identified subsequent agreements and prac-tice as one of the most promising means to enhance the legitimacy of international investment arbitration.[198] Instruments States can use to recalibrate the balance between the public interest and investor rights include Model BITs, pleadings in arbitrations and interventions as non-disputing parties, public statements about their understanding of certain IIA provisions, and joint interpretations with the other parties to an IIA.[199] This subsection analyses whether such tools may give rise to a proportionality analysis in determining the existence of an indirect expropriation. I will first focus on subsequent agreements (a) before turning to subsequent practice (b).

a) Subsequent agreements

One of the rare settings in which international investment tribunals explicitly refer to Article 31(3) VCLT is in certain NAFTA proceedings.[200] This jurispru-dence relates to the interpretative note of the NAFTA Free Trade Commission (NAFTA FTC) of 31 July 2001 on a number of NAFTA Chapter 11 provisions. Article 1131(2) of NAFTA stipulates that an interpretation of a NAFTA provision by the FTC 'shall be binding' on a tribunal in an investor–State arbitration. The most significant part of the 31 July 2001 NAFTA FTC note is that it sought to clarify the concept of FET in Article 1105 of NAFTA. In response to the develop-ment of what was perceived as overly investor-friendly jurisprudence, the NAFTA FTC stated that the FET standard does 'not require treatment in addition to or beyond that which is required by the customary international law minimum standard of treatment of aliens'.[201]

Confronted with this FTC note, the tribunal in *Pope & Talbot* stressed that the reference to 'international law' in Article 1105 of NAFTA is to be interpreted against the background of Article 38 ICJ Statute. The tribunal found that the term 'international law' is significantly broader than the notion of 'customary interna-tional law' used by the FTC to limit the scope of Article 1105.[202] Consequently, the tribunal suggested that the FTC note of 31 July 2001 constitutes an amend-ment to the treaty and not its interpretation.[203] Finally, the assessment of the *Pope & Talbot* tribunal did not change the outcome of the case. The tribunal found that Canada had breached Article 1105 of NAFTA even if this provision was to

---

[198] Anthea Roberts, 'Power and Persuasion in Investment Treaty Arbitration: the Dual Role of States', *American Journal of International Law* 105 (2010) 179–225, at 191–5.

[199] Id., at 194.

[200] *See, e.g., Methanex v. United States,* Final Award, 3 August 2005, 44 ILM (2005) 1345, Part II, Chapter B, para. 21 ('[T]he Tribunal has no difficulty in deciding that the FTC's Interpretation of 31st July 2001 is properly characterized as a 'subsequent agreement' on interpretation falling within the scope of Article 31(3)(a) of the Vienna Convention').

[201] NAFTA FTC note of 31 July 2001 (*see* Chapter 4, note 132), para. B.2.

[202] *Pope & Talbot v. Canada,* NAFTA Arbitration, Award in Respect of Damages, 31 May 2002, para. 20.

[203] Id., para. 47.

be interpreted according to the FTC note.[204] Other NAFTA tribunals were more deferential to the characterization of the 31 July 2001 FTC note as an 'interpretation' of Article 1105 of NAFTA. The tribunal in *ADF Group v. United States*, for example, reasoned that the mere fact that the FTC issued the note under Article 1131(2) of NAFTA was sufficient for it to be characterized as a binding interpretation of Article 1105.[205]

The following example illustrates the potential relevance of this controversy for the interpretation of a BIT provision on expropriation. Let us assume that the parties to a BIT that does not include a provision similar to Article 1131(2) of NAFTA issue a joint declaration. According to this declaration, the provision on expropriation in the BIT is to be interpreted along the lines of the 'mitigated police powers' doctrine. Let us further assume that this BIT does not include an annex on the interpretation of the expropriation provision similar to the one in the US and the Canadian Model BITs. Would such a joint declaration be binding on an international investment tribunal and automatically subject the question of whether a certain State measure constitutes an indirect expropriation to a proportionality analysis?

If we categorize the declaration by the two States as an amendment to the BIT, the reasoning of the *ADC* and *Pope & Talbot* tribunals suggests that an arbitral tribunal might be able to ignore this document unless and until it is ratified by the two States.[206] This consideration regarding internal ratification processes does not apply if we qualify such a joint declaration as an interpretation of the BIT provision on expropriation.[207] Does this mean that such an interpretation by the 'masters of the treaty' is automatically binding for an arbitral tribunal? Article 31(3)(a) VCLT merely states that subsequent agreements regarding the interpretation of a treaty 'shall be taken into account'. This formulation is in line with the notion that none of the interpretative means listed in Article 31 VCLT is hierarchically superior to the others.[208] The most serious concern regarding the binding character of such interpretations is the involvement of non-state actors in international investment disputes. States have ceased to be the sole holders of rights and bearers of obligations in international law.[209] Human rights treaties are the most obvious examples of international treaties that create substantive and

---

[204] Id., paras. 67–9.

[205] *ADF Group v. United States of America*, ICSID Case No. ARB(AF)/00/1, Award, 9 January 2003, para. 177.

[206] *Pope & Talbot v. Canada*, NAFTA Arbitration, Award in Respect of Damages, 31 May 2002, para. 19; *ADF Group v. United States of America*, ICSID Case No. ARB(AF)/00/1, Award, 9 January 2003, para. 177.

[207] Note that the *Methanex* tribunal found that it would fall under the discretion of the relevant States whether a certain measure constitutes an interpretation or an amendment. This would also be true outside of the context of Article 1131(2) NAFTA and for such measures that entail significant changes for the application of the treaty (*Methanex v. United States,* Final Award, 3 August 2005, 44 ILM (2005) 1345, Part IV, Chapter C, paras. 19–22).

[208] *See supra* notes 43–7 and accompanying text.

[209] *See, e.g.,* Theodor Meron, *The Humanization of International Law* (2006); Parlett, *The Individual in the International Legal System.*

sometimes procedural rights for non-State actors. The position of foreign investors under IIAs with investor–State dispute resolution mechanisms is more intricate.

Three strains of argument dominate this debate.[210] First, it is possible to characterize IIAs as treaties that contain substantive and procedural rights for the parties only. According to this notion, investor–State dispute mechanism clauses merely permit investors to enforce the rights of their home State 'for the sake of convenience'.[211] If one chooses to follow this approach, there is little reason for arbitral tribunals not to strictly adhere to the interpretation of an IIA provision by the parties to the treaty.[212] Different considerations might apply, however, with respect to the other two possibilities of allocating the rights enshrined in IIAs, both of which enjoy considerable support in the jurisprudence of arbitral tribunals and legal scholarship.[213] According to the second theory on the nature of investor rights, IIAs establish substantive rights for the parties to the treaty only; however, investors enjoy the *procedural* right to enforce those substantive rights. Under the third theory, IIAs give non-State actors both procedural *and* substantive rights. Hence, investors have the procedural right to bring a claim before an arbitral tribunal alleging a violation of their own substantive rights.

The third theory (the 'substantive rights theory') entails the greatest concerns regarding the binding character of a joint interpretative note that proves to be disadvantageous for foreign investors. Assuming for the sake of argument that this theory is valid, the decisive question is to what extent the conferral of rights on foreign investors influences the normative weight to be accorded to a subsequent agreement on the interpretation of the IIA. The position of third-party beneficiaries under domestic law offers a helpful starting point. Under most contract law regimes, the promisor and the promisee will initially be free to rescind or modify a contract unless they had agreed otherwise. This changes, however, once the right of the third-party beneficiary has vested. From this point onwards, the promisor and the promisee will need the consent of the third-party beneficiary in order to change the contract. The ways in which the rights of third-party beneficiaries can vest vary among the different domestic legal orders. One of the typical scenarios under which the rights of third-party beneficiaries vest is that the third party relies on the contract and takes some corresponding action.[214] In order to transfer

---

[210] For a discussion of these theories in the context of countermeasures and the necessity defence, *see* Chapter 8, notes 40–6 and accompanying text.

[211] Roberts, 'Power and Persuasion in Investment Treaty Arbitration', at 184.

[212] Note that while such a practice appears to be unproblematic from an international law perspective, there remain serious constitutional law issues, especially if an IIA does not contain a similar clause as Article 1131 NAFTA. Notes of interpretation will typically be issued by the executive without legislative consent. If such an interpretation amounts to a modification of the treaty ratified by the legislator, notes of interpretation may undermine the constitutional allocation of powers between the executive and the legislator.

[213] *See, e.g.,* Roberts, 'Power and Persuasion', at 184 n.23 (with further references); Anne Peters, *Jenseits der Menschenrechte—Die Rechtsstellung des Individuums im Völkerrecht* (2014), at 277–86 (supporting the view that IIAs confer substantive rights on investors).

[214] Article 5.2.5 of the UNIDROIT Principles (*available at* <http://www.unilex.info/dynasite.cfm?dssid=2377&dsmid=109294>) provides that '[t]he parties may modify or revoke the rights conferred by the contract on the beneficiary until the beneficiary has accepted them or reasonably

this notion to the realm of foreign investment law, it is important to recall that a significant shift in risk and bargaining power occurs during the course of an investment.[215] Once the investment is in place, it is usually difficult for the foreign investor to withdraw from its investment without making losses. Therefore, one could argue that the rights of foreign investors under IIAs 'vest' once they make their investment.

There are also arguments against this private law analogy. Most importantly, the VCLT specifically regulates certain issues concerning third-party beneficiaries. Article 37(2) VCLT stipulates that if a treaty creates a right for a third State, 'the right may not be revoked or modified by the parties if it is established that the right was intended not to be revocable or subject to modification without the consent of the third State'. In other words, the parties to the treaty may adversely affect the position of the third State unless there is proof of a contrary intention of the parties at the time when the right came into existence. Obviously, the scenario addressed in the VCLT differs from the setting in which investor–State arbitration takes place as the former involves States only. Furthermore, both the private law analogy above and Article 37 regulate the 'revocation and modification' of a third-party right, while we are concerned here with an interpretation of a treaty. Still, both Article 37 and the private law analogy offer some guidelines for the normative weight adjudicators should accord to subsequent agreements in investor–State arbitration. First, there is little reason for a tribunal not to adhere to a subsequent agreement on interpretation that had become public before the investor made the investment. In contract law terms, the date of the investment is arguably the earliest possible point in time in which the rights of the foreign investor might vest. Second, by including 'survival clauses' in IIAs, States extend treaty protections even beyond the lifetime of the relevant treaty. Article XIV(3) of the Argentina–US BIT, for example, stipulates that the BIT provisions remain effective with respect to investments made prior to the termination of the treaty for another ten years from the date of termination.[216] It is arguable that a foreign

---

acted in reliance on them.' While the US Restatement (Second) of Contracts § 311 (1981) states in paragraph 2 that 'the promisor and promisee retain power to discharge or modify the duty [to an intended beneficiary] by subsequent agreement', paragraph 3 clarifies that '[s]uch a power terminates when the beneficiary, before he receives notification of the discharge or modification, materially changes his position in justifiable reliance'. For the UK, Section 2(1) of the Contracts (Rights of Third Parties) Act 1999 (Chapter 31) provides that 'where a third party has a right under section 1 to enforce a term of the contract, the parties to the contract may not, by agreement, rescind the contract, or vary it in such a way as to extinguish or alter his entitlement under that right, without his consent if…the promisor can reasonably be expected to have foreseen that the third party would rely on the term and the third party has in fact relied on it.' (*available at* <http://www.legislation.gov.uk/ukpga/1999/31/section/2>). *See also* Roberts, 'Power and Persuasion', at 211.

[215] *See supra* notes 64–7 and accompanying text.
[216] Article XIV(2) and (3) of the Argentina–US BIT reads as follows:

   2. Either Party may, by giving one year's written notice to the other Party, terminate this Treaty at the end of the initial ten year period or at any time thereafter.
   3. With respect to investments made or acquired prior to the date of termination of this Treaty and to which this Treaty otherwise applies, the provisions of all of the other

investor cannot be shielded from the negative effects of a joint interpretative note for a longer time than he would be protected against an outright termination of the treaty.

Another important consideration relates to the reasoning of the *Methanex* tribunal as to the 'binding' character of the 31 July 2001 FTC note. The tribunal stressed that the clear wording of Article 1131(2) of NAFTA puts foreign investors on alert as to the effect of such an interpretation.[217] The Canadian and US Model BITs and some more recent IIAs contain clauses similar to Article 1131(2) of NAFTA.[218] Does this mean that joint interpretative notes issued by States that are party to an IIA without a clause similar to Article 1131(2) are automatically irrelevant in the context of investor–State arbitration? The answer is probably 'no', but one may wonder how the lack of such provisions influences the normative weight that ought to be accorded to subsequent agreements on interpretation. If one takes the reasoning of the *Methanex* tribunal seriously, then the extent to which a foreign investor can expect a subsequent agreement on interpretation plays a crucial role for its normative weight. In other words, tribunals should consider the degree to which the relevant interpretation interferes with the reliance of the investor on the terms of the treaty. Consequently, agreements on interpretation of IIA provisions that obviously lend themselves to more than one possible interpretation should be given relatively great weight in the interpretation process. Conversely, if the wording of a provision seems to be unambiguous and the interpretation adopted by the contracting States is surprising in light of the text of the treaty, then the agreement on interpretation should carry a lesser weight.[219]

These considerations have the following implications for the normative weight of a subsequent agreement stating that a standard BIT provision on expropriation ought to be interpreted and applied according to the 'mitigated police powers' doctrine. I have argued that the text of standard BIT provisions on expropriation does not suggest that the question of whether a certain State measure constitutes an indirect expropriation depends on a proportionality analysis.[220] This

---

Articles of this Treaty shall thereafter continue to be effective for a further period of ten years from such date of termination.

[217] *Methanex v. United States,* Final Award, 3 August 2005, 44 ILM (2005) 1345, Part IV, Chapter C, para. 20.

[218] *See supra* notes 163–6 and accompanying text.

[219] In a similar vein, Anthea Roberts attaches considerable importance to the 'reasonableness' of the interpretation (Roberts, 'Power and Persuasion', at 209–10; *see also* Anthea Roberts, 'Subsequent Agreements and Practice: the Battle over Interpretative Authority', *in Treaties and Subsequent Practice* (Nolte ed., 2013) 95–102, at 99–100). José Alvarez also doubts that subsequent practice is automatically binding for adjudicatory bodies when third-party beneficiaries are involved (José E Alvarez, 'Limits of Change by Way of Subsequent Agreements and Practice', in *Treaties and Subsequent Practice* (Nolte ed., 2013) 123–32, p 126–32). Georg Nolte seems to take a different view when he emphasizes 'the role of states as masters of the treaty and law-givers' in the context of 'the possibility to retroactively affect and diminish the rights of private investors.' (Nolte, 'Reports for the ILC Study Group On Treaties over Time: Report 2', in *Treaties and Subsequent Practice* (Nolte ed., 2013) 210–306, at 237).

[220] *See supra* notes 133–9 and accompanying text.

consideration speaks against a binding force of a subsequent agreement that seeks to codify the 'mitigated police powers' doctrine. However, the jurisprudence of arbitral tribunals on indirect expropriations has never been consistent.[221] Consequently, foreign investors and their legal counsel should be alert to the possibility that an arbitral tribunal might judge the expropriatory character of a State action not only on the basis of its effects on the investment.

Ultimately, each case requires its own fact-specific assessment. Anthea Roberts, for example, characterizes the normative weight of interpretations by the parties to the treaty as 'a function of their timing and reasonableness'.[222] I have argued that there is little reason for an arbitral tribunal not to follow an interpretation that the parties to the treaty adopted before the investment had occurred. A subsequent agreement reached after the request for arbitration was filed that is not easily reconciled with the text of the treaty will have less normative force, in particular in the absence of a provision such as Article 1131(2) of NAFTA.[223]

b) Subsequent practice

Subsequent agreements are the most explicit form of action that States can take to influence the interpretation of a treaty after its conclusion. Consequently, the limitations to the binding character of subsequent agreements also apply to other forms of subsequent State action, i.e. subsequent practice within the meaning of Article 31(3)(b) VCLT. Moreover, there are some additional factors that have to be taken into account in the context of Article 31(3)(b). It is necessary that the subsequent practice be 'in the application of the treaty', and that it 'establishes the agreement of the parties regarding its interpretation'.[224] This agreement does not have to be explicit. In the words of Mark E. Villiger, it is sufficient that one of the parties to the treaty adopts an 'active', 'consistent', and not only 'haphazard' practice to which the other party or parties at least 'acquiesce'.[225] Are these requirements met if one party to an IIA adopts the 'mitigated police powers' doctrine as a respondent in an investor–State arbitration and the other party or parties to the same IIA do not object?

There are considerable reasons not to equate the lack of objection to the reasoning of the respondent State in an investor–State arbitration with the 'acquiescence' by the other contracting State(s). Most importantly, the only party to the treaty involved in an investor–State arbitration is the respondent. Something different might only be true in the case of a third-party intervention, or a scenario like one of those addressed by Article 30(3) of the US–Rwanda and the

---

[221] *See supra* pp. 126–31.   [222] Roberts, 'Power and Persuasion', at 212.

[223] *See also* id., at 213. For the importance of an explicit provision such as Article 1131(2) NAFTA regarding the 'binding' character of subsequent practice when third-party beneficiaries are involved, *see also* José E. Alvarez, 'Limits of Change by Way of Subsequent Agreements and Practice', *in Treaties and Subsequent Practice* (Nolte ed., 2013) 123–32, at 131–2.

[224] *See* the wording of Article 31(3)(b) VCLT, *supra* p. 87.

[225] Villiger, *Vienna Convention on the Law of Treaties*, Article 31, para. 22.

US–Uruguay BITs.[226] Therefore, there is typically no reason for the other party or parties to the relevant IIA to adopt a certain opinion on the legal reasoning of the respondent. To a certain degree, the latter is evidence of one of the very basic ideas of investor–State arbitration. Prior to the current legal framework, the protection of foreign investment often depended on factors such as the military and economic strength of the home State and its willingness to grant diplomatic protection.[227] Political considerations unconnected to the case of the foreign investor often greatly influenced the decision of host States to grant or not to grant diplomatic protection. By introducing dispute resolution mechanisms involving the foreign investor and the host State only, the parties to IIAs sought to depoliticize foreign investment disputes. Obliging home States to object to the reasoning of host States in investor–State arbitrations in order to prevent the establishment of subsequent practice within the meaning of Article 31(3)(b) would run counter to this basic idea.

Another aspect of State practice that might be of significant importance for the purposes of Article 31(3)(b) VCLT is the drafting of Model BITs.[228] Three caveats are appropriate here. First, Model BITs constitute State practice only of the party that has actually adopted the particular Model BIT. In order to establish an agreement of the parties to a particular IIA regarding its interpretation, some relevant practice of the other party or parties to the IIA will be necessary.[229] Second, it is of crucial importance to ascertain the purpose of the relevant Model BIT. If the sole purpose of the Model BIT is—as their name suggests—to provide a model for *future* BITs, it is hard to see how this instrument should constitute subsequent practice in the application of a treaty that was concluded before the Model BIT was adopted. Sometimes, the adoption of a new Model BIT will reflect the intention of a State to depart from current IIA standards in future treaties.

Something different is true, however, if and to the extent that the relevant State adopted a Model BIT in order to clarify its understanding of its current BIT obligations. US and Canadian Model BITs, for example, contain a significant number of provisions that introduce new concepts and elements to the BIT programmes of the two States. With respect to these provisions, it will be difficult to argue that they form subsequent practice in the application of BITs that predate the relevant Model BIT. This is not necessarily the case for those parts of Model BITs that elaborate in detail on traditional BIT provisions. The provisions on indirect expropriation in the Model BITs of Canada and the US might constitute valid examples in this respect.

The third and last caveat regarding the interpretative role of Model BITs relates to BITs concluded after the adoption of the relevant Model BIT. We have seen that the US–Rwanda BIT and the US–Uruguay BIT closely follow the structure and wording of the 2004 US Model BIT. The same is true for the Canada–Latvia

---

[226] *See supra* note 163 and accompanying text.   [227] *See also* Chapter 2, sections I–II.
[228] *See especially* Roberts, 'Power and Persuasion in Investment Treaty Arbitration', at 222–3.
[229] *See also* id., at 222.

BIT and the Canada–Czech Republic BIT with respect to the Canadian Model BIT. The value of introducing the Model BIT in interpreting these treaties is rather limited, as the particular BIT provisions merely reflect the stipulations of the underlying Model BIT. A more interesting question is what role Model BIT provisions play in the interpretation of BITs that postdate the relevant Model BIT but do not contain some of its salient elements. A treaty interpreter might be inclined to fill gaps in the BIT by referring to the Model BIT of one of the parties to the treaty. One should not underestimate the possibility, however, that the differences between the relevant BIT and the Model BIT are deliberate outcomes of the negotiations between the parties.

c) Summary

In sum, subsequent agreements and subsequent practice within the meaning of Article 31(3) VCLT may play a significant role in recalibrating the balance between the public interest and investor rights under IIAs, if States really wish to do so. Of course, one could argue that if States have such an ambition, they should renegotiate or amend their IIAs. However, such an undertaking requires considerable efforts, especially in light of the great number of existing IIAs.[230] Subsequent agreements within the meaning of Article 31(3)(a) bear particularly great weight in the interpretation process when they were reached before the relevant investment was made. In such scenarios, there is little reason not to treat subsequent agreements as binding on an arbitral tribunal. If the parties reached the agreement after the claimant had made its investment, the analysis of the normative weight of such an agreement should address the following factors. First, does the text of the relevant treaty provision indicate that it is open to more than one possible interpretation? Second, when exactly did the parties to the IIA agree on the particular interpretation? Third, does the IIA in question mention the possibility that the parties to the IIA may agree on its interpretation even during pending investor–State arbitrations?

This suggested methodology also applies to subsequent practice within the meaning of Article 31(3)(b) VCLT. The analysis in this context, however, involves some additional factors. Arbitral tribunals need to ensure that subsequent practice involves both parties to a BIT (or all parties to a multilateral IIA). Even though this might not necessarily require an 'active' practice by all the parties, arbitral tribunals should be careful not to infer acquiescence in such practice from the mere lack of opposition in the course of prior investor–State arbitrations or the current proceedings. Finally, arbitral tribunals need to ensure that the relevant State practice refers to the application of the treaty being interpreted. In other words, arbitral tribunals should not blindly impose the wording and structure of a unilateral Model BIT on the (presumably) carefully negotiated terms of a bilateral or

---

[230] *See also* id., who argues that such an attempt might involve prohibitive transaction costs (at 192).

multilateral treaty. A contrary practice by arbitral tribunals might have an adverse impact on the long-term capability of States to legislate on the international level in a meaningful, nuanced manner.

5. Systemic integration

It remains to be analysed whether the concept of systemic integration as reflected in Article 31(3)(c) VCLT justifies the application of the principle of proportionality in determining the existence of an indirect expropriation. The rules of international law to be taken into account under Article 31(3)(c) may stem from treaties, customary international law, or general principles of law.[231] Section III demonstrated that the ECHR does not militate for a proportionality analysis in the process of identifying an indirect expropriation.[232] The following subsections analyse whether customary international law (subsection (a)) or general principles of law (subsection (b)) may inform the reading of IIA provisions on expropriation.

a) Defining indirect expropriation through custom and creating custom through treaties?

Article 31(3)(c) VCLT plays a particularly important role when a treaty adopts a term that has a well-established meaning in customary international law.[233] If State measures that advance a public welfare objective in a proportionate way are by definition non-expropriatory under customary international law, then there would be a strong case for interpreting the term 'expropriation' in IIAs to the same effect. Similarly, a finding that even *disproportionate* State measures do not qualify as expropriations under customary international law—as long as they pursue a public welfare objective—would favour the 'police powers' doctrine. Indeed, there is some support for these notions. The 1961 Harvard Draft Convention on the International Responsibility of States for Injuries to Aliens, for example, states in Article 10(5) that:

An uncompensated taking of an alien property or a deprivation of the use or enjoyment of property of an alien which results from the execution of tax laws; from a general change in the value of currency; from the action of the competent authorities of the State in the maintenance of public order, health or morality; or from the valid exercise of belligerent rights or otherwise incidental to the normal operation of the laws of the State shall not be considered wrongful[.][234]

The American Law Institute adopted a similar approach. A subsection in the Restatement of Foreign Relations Law of the United States explicitly addresses

---

[231] Chapter 4, notes 83–8 and accompanying text.
[232] *Supra* notes 90–132 and accompanying text.
[233] *See* Chapter 4, note 200 and accompanying text.
[234] Richard R. Baxter & Louis B. Sohn, 'Responsibility of States for Injuries to the Economic Interests of Aliens', *American Journal of International Law* 55 (1961) 545–84, at 554.

the difference between indirect expropriations and non-compensable regulatory acts. The relevant passage reads as follows:

A state is not responsible for loss of property or for other economic disadvantage result-ing from bona fide general taxation, regulation, forfeiture for crime, or other action of the kind that is commonly accepted as within the police power of states, if it is not discriminatory[.][235]

It is important to bear in mind that these formulations merely reflect what certain scholars and institutions considered to be the state of customary international law or how they thought international law should develop. The relevant statements do not constitute State practice giving rise to customary international law, and it is doubtful whether these statements accurately reflected customary international law at the time when they were drafted. Rudolf Dolzer, for example, noted in 1995 that there is remarkably little guidance in State practice with respect to the definition of an expropriation. Consequently, Dolzer found that there had been no universally accepted definition for expropriation if the relevant act did not constitute a 'formal taking'.[236] Since Rudolf Dolzer made this statement the total number of IIAs has increased at least fivefold.[237] There is significant controversy as to whether IIAs constitute State practice that might give rise to customary international law, or whether their very purpose is to establish bilateral or mul-tilateral rules that deviate from custom. Thus far, this debate has been largely irrelevant for the definition of indirect expropriation. After all, most IIAs do not contain a clarification of this concept but simply presume its existence. The fact that arbitral tribunals differ greatly in their approaches to indirect expropriation suggests that the dramatic increase in the total number of IIAs did not cause or promote a universal understanding of the concept of indirect expropriation.[238]

However, we have seen that a new trend might have emerged. A significant number of IIAs are no longer silent on the constitutive elements of an indirect expropriation.[239] Within the ambit of these treaties, the existence of an indirect expropriation ought to be established along the lines of the 'mitigated police pow-ers' doctrine.[240] What does this practice mean for investor–State arbitrations under IIAs that contain similar provisions on expropriation but lack interpreta-tive guidance on the concept of indirect expropriation? An attempt to answer this question opens a new front for the debate on the effects of IIAs on the rules of customary international law.

In broad terms, there are two schools of thought on this issue. The first is com-prised of authors who argue that a dense web of identical (or very similar) BITs has given rise to, or in some cases fostered, rules of customary international law on the

---

[235] American Law Institute, Restatement (Third) of the Foreign Relations Law of the United States (1987) § 712(g).

[236] Rudolf Dolzer, 'Expropriation and Nationalization', *in Encyclopedia of Public International Law*, Vol. II (Rudolf Bernhardt ed., 1995) 319–26, at 322.

[237] *See* Chapter 2, notes 62–3 and accompanying text.   [238] *See supra* pp. 126–31.

[239] *See supra* notes 68–81 and accompanying text.

[240] *See supra* notes 145–67 and accompanying text.

treatment of aliens.[241] In the other camp are those authors who stress that States concluding BITs seek to deviate from customary international law or circumvent its uncertainties. Furthermore, a closer look at BITs would reveal that they vary significantly and hence constitute nothing more but the outcome of very specific negotiation processes.[242] In a similar vein, some authors point out that some States (especially developing countries) sign BITs out of economic considerations alone. Hence, States would widely lack the *opinio juris* element when concluding BITs that is necessary for the creation of customary international law.[243] Consequently, the current system of foreign investment law could have no influence on customary international law.

This debate might be less heated in the context of the question of how definitions of indirect expropriations in IIAs influence the understanding of this concept under customary international law. After all, authors who deny the impact of IIAs on customary international law usually seek to ensure that the balance between the regulatory freedom of States and the rights of foreign investors does not tilt (further) in favour of the latter. The clarifications on the concept of indirect expropriation in IIAs, however, seek to ensure that States can regulate in the public interest without being liable to foreign investors. In any event, a clinical isolation of customary international law from the current system of international investment law is not sustainable. Whether or not typical IIA provisions have transformed into rules of customary international law requires a case-by-case analysis of the two constitutive elements of custom: State practice that is uniform and consistent (albeit not necessarily universal), accompanied by *opinio juris*. Campbell McLachlan has described the relationship between IIAs and general international law as follows:

> The relationship is symbiotic. Developments in custom may, indeed should, influence the content of the treaty rule.... By the same token, the developments in the treaty rule...may influence custom.[244]

This view finds ample support in the jurisprudence of arbitral tribunals. A particularly illustrative example is the jurisprudence of several NAFTA tribunals on the FTC note of interpretation of 31 July 2001, which tied the FET standard in Article 1105 of NAFTA to the customary international law minimum standard of treatment.[245] The *Pope & Talbot* tribunal, for example, held that the customary international minimum standard of treatment was not 'frozen in amber at the

---

[241] *See, e.g.*, José E. Alvarez, 'A BIT on Custom', *New York University Journal of International Law and Politics* 42 (2009) 17–80, at 61–8; Andreas F. Lowenfeld, 'Investment Agreements and International Law', *Columbia Journal of Transnational Law* 42 (2003) 123–30, at 128–9.

[242] M. Sornarajah, *The International Law on Foreign Investment* (2010), at 206.

[243] *See* Cai Congyan, 'International Investment Treaties and the Formation, Application and Transformation of Customary International Law Rules', *Chinese Journal of International Law* 7 (2008) 659–79, at 664 nn. 24 & 27.

[244] McLachlan, 'Investment Treaties and General International Law', at 401.

[245] *See supra* note 201 and accompanying text.

time of the *Neer* decision' in 1926.[246] Instead, the tribunal found that BITs constitute relevant State practice that influences the content of customary international law.[247] However, the tribunal did not find it necessary to inquire into the current state of the minimum standard of treatment since Canada would have been in breach of this standard even according to the *Neer* criteria.[248]

We have seen that the tribunals in *ADF*, *Glamis*, and *Merrill* were more deferential to the binding character of the FTC note of interpretation of 31 July 2001.[249] Still, even those tribunals agreed that the international minimum standard of treatment has evolved since the *Neer* decision in 1926.[250] Interestingly, the tribunals differed with respect to the direction in which this standard has developed. The *Glamis* tribunal found that the perception of the international community as to what constitutes 'outrageous' State conduct may vary over time.[251] However, the tribunal held that the high threshold articulated in the *Neer* case adequately reflects the customary international law minimum standard of treatment and that the level of scrutiny remains the same.[252]

The *Merrill* tribunal took a more progressive view. It found that the *Neer* standard was historically limited to 'situations of due process of law, denial of justice, and physical mistreatment'.[253] The growing concern of international law with the rights of individuals would have led to an evolution of these standards through human rights law. The tribunal referred to these developments as the 'first track of the evolution' of the minimum standard of treatment.[254] In addition, the tribunal identified a 'second track' of the evolution of this standard in the context of 'business, trade, and investment'.[255] In sum, the tribunal found that the current state of the customary international law minimum standard concerning the treatment of foreign investors goes beyond the *Neer* standard. More specifically, the tribunal held that this standard 'protects against all such acts or behavior that might infringe a sense of fairness, equity, and reasonableness'.[256]

---

[246] *Pope Talbot v. Canada*, NAFTA Arbitration, Award in Respect of Damages, 31 May 2002, para. 57. On the *Neer* decision, *see supra* note 19 and accompanying text.

[247] Id., para. 62.　　　[248] Id., paras. 65–66.　　　[249] *See supra* notes 205–7.

[250] *ADF Group v. United States of America*, ICSID Case No. ARB(AF)/00/1, Award, 9 January 2003, para. 179; *Glamis Gold, Ltd. v. United States of America*, UNCITRAL Arbitration (NAFTA), Award, 8 June 2009, paras. 612–13; *Merrill & Ring Forestry LP v. Canada*, UNCITRAL Arbitration, ICSID Administered Case (NAFTA), Award, 31 March 2010, para. 193.

[251] *Glamis Gold, Ltd. v. United States of America*, UNCITRAL Arbitration (NAFTA), Award, 8 June 2009, paras. 612–3.

[252] Id., paras. 614–6. But note that the tribunal found that even this narrow standard covers 'legitimate expectations' of foreign investors that host States create through 'specific assurance[s] or commitment[s]... in order to induce investment.' (id., paras. 620–1).

[253] *Merrill & Ring Forestry LP v. Canada*, UNCITRAL Arbitration, ICSID Administered Case (NAFTA), Award, 31 March 2010, para. 197.

[254] Id., paras. 201–2, 205.　　　[255] Id., para. 201, 205.

[256] Id., paras. 210, 213. But note that the tribunal found that even such a broad understanding of the international minimum standard would not create 'legitimate expectations' of foreign investors to be exempted from '[e]mergency measures or regulations addressed to social well-being' (id., para. 233).

Without taking a position regarding the split of opinion between the *Glamis* and *Merrill* tribunals, the jurisprudence of NAFTA tribunals on Article 1105 strongly suggests that IIAs may have an impact on the rules of customary international law. The crucial issue is what this means for the recent trend of codifying the 'mitigated police powers' doctrine in IIAs. Tribunals should not readily assume that States attaching such annexes to their IIAs intend to deviate from a current definition of indirect expropriation in customary international law. Rather, some States might seek to codify what they consider to reflect customary international law when including such annexes. Annex B(1) of the US–Rwanda BIT and the US–Uruguay BIT, for example, explicitly state that the provision on expropriation 'is intended to reflect customary international law concerning the obligation of States with respect to expropriation'.[257] Other treaties with similar annexes do not contain this clarification. This is, for example, true for the KORUS FTA, the Canada–Latvia BIT, the Canada–Czech Republic BIT, and the ASEAN–ANZ FTA.[258] Still, this omission alone can hardly sustain the proposition that these States aspire to deviate from a notion of indirect expropriation that they consider to constitute customary international law. Furthermore, Model BITs may play an important role in the identification of custom. After all, Model BITs do not form the result of specific negotiation processes between two (or several) States. Rather, these instruments reflect what individual States consider to be appropriate and acceptable obligations in international law.[259] In this context, it is worth recalling that the Model BITs of both the US and Canada codify the mitigated police powers doctrine.[260] Article 6(2) of the 2007 Colombian Model BIT follows the same approach.[261]

Nevertheless, it is debatable whether these annexes do reflect the current status of customary international law on indirect expropriation. The idea that regulatory measures of general applicability do not constitute indirect expropriations is hardly new. We have seen that some arbitral tribunals and legal texts offered this view well before certain States started to integrate a corresponding clarification in their IIAs.[262] This circumstance arguably facilitates the creation of custom since State practice is not starting from scratch, so to speak. We have also seen, however, that this practice has not been consistent. On the contrary, much of it has focused on the 'police powers doctrine in its strict sense', while the annexes on expropriation appear to be codifications of the 'mitigated police powers' doctrine.[263]

---

[257] *See supra* notes 153–55. But note that it is also possible to understand this statement in a different way. Since Annex B(1) only refers to the treaty provision on expropriation and not the content of the annex, one might argue that it merely constitutes a confirmation of the customary international law character of the obligation to pay prompt, adequate, and effective compensation equivalent to the fair market value of the investment at the date of expropriation.

[258] *See supra* note 156.

[259] *See also* McLachlan, 'Investment Treaties and General International Law', at 394.

[260] *See supra* notes 68 and 70.

[261] *Available at* <http://ita.law.uvic.ca/documents/inv_model_bit_colombia.pdf>.

[262] *See supra* notes 29–49 & 234–5 and accompanying text. Of course, arbitral awards do not constitute State practice. However, to the extent that they refer to the reasoning and positions of the parties to the underlying treaty, they may shed some light on relevant State practice.

[263] *See supra* notes 35–49 and accompanying text.

Moreover, many of the more recent IIAs do not contain annexes in which the parties to the treaty would endorse the 'mitigated police powers' doctrine. Of course, for a rule to constitute customary international law, it is not necessary that the practice be universal. Still, it is important to note that some of the States with the largest IIA programmes have not followed the examples of the US and Canada. This raises the question of why these States refuse to elaborate on the notion of indirect expropriation, despite the history of diverging approaches to it. As at mid June 2012, Germany had concluded a significantly larger number of BITs (136) than the US (47) and Canada (29) combined.[264] Still, the German Model BIT of 2009 does not comment on the characteristics of an indirect expropriation. Rather, it contains a standard BIT provision on expropriation without further explanation.[265]

One may speculate why Germany did not follow the examples of Canada and the US. Germany has traditionally sought robust protection for its nationals abroad. So far, Germany has apparently not considered it necessary to readjust the balance between the regulatory freedom of host States and foreign investors. Something similar seems to be true for France, whose 2006 Model BIT provides for compensation in the case of expropriation without defining this term.[266] The State with the largest number of BITs after Germany is China (128 as at mid-June 2012).[267] The China–Czech Republic BIT, for example, in force since 1 September 2006, contains a standard BIT provision on expropriation unaccompanied by any definition of indirect expropriation.[268] The same is true for the China–Germany BIT, which entered into force on 11 November 2005.[269]

A trilateral investment treaty concluded between China, South Korea, and Japan in 2012, however, contains an definition of indirect expropriation along the lines of the US and Canadian Model BITs.[270] The same is true for the Canada–China BIT, also concluded in 2012.[271] CETA as it stands after the end of negotiations between the European Commission and Canda contains a definition on indirect expropriation modelled after the US and Canadian Model BIT as

---

[264] UNCTAD, *World Investment Report 2012, Towards a New Generation of Investment Policies*, at 199–202.

[265] Article 4 of the German 2009 Model BIT (*available at* <http://www.iilcc.uni-koeln.de/fileadmin/institute/iilcc/Dokumente/matrechtinvest/VIS_Mustervertrag.pdf>). *See also* Rudolf Dolzer & Yun-I Kim, 'Commentary on Germany's Model BIT (2009)', *in Commentaries on Selected Model Investment Treaties* (Chester Brown ed., 2013) 289–319, at 309–11.

[266] Article 5(2) French Model BIT, *available at* <http://ita.law.uvic.ca/documents/ModelTreatyFrance2006.pdf>.

[267] UNCTAD, *World Investment Report 2012, Towards a New Generation of Investment Policies*, at 199.

[268] Article 4 China–Czech Republic BIT, *available at* <http://www.unctad.org/sections/dite/iia/docs/bits/China_czechrep.PDF>.

[269] Article 4 China–Germany BIT, *available at* <http://www.unctad.org/sections/dite/iia/docs/bits/china_germany.pdf>.

[270] Protocol, item 2(b) China–South Korea–Japan trilateral investment treaty *available at* <http://www.mofa.go.jp/announce/announce/2012/5/pdfs/0513_01_01.pdf>.

[271] Annex B-10 Canada–China BIT, *available at* <http://investmentpolicyhub.unctad.org/Download/TreatyFile/600>.

well.[272] It will be interesting to see whether the Trans-Pacific Partnership (TPP), a treaty currently negotiated between twelve nations covering roughly 38% of world GDP (Australia, Brunei Darussalam, Canada, Chile, Japan, Malaysia, Mexico, New Zealand, Peru, Singapore, the US, and Vietnam)[273] will contain a similar definition on indirect expropriation. While it is currently uncertain whether the 'mitigated police powers' doctrine reflects customary international law, these treaties might soon make it difficult to argue that it does not.

In the meantime, it is worth recalling that if States consider the 'mitigated police powers' doctrine to accurately describe the concept of indirect expropriation, then they have several tools at their disposal to give legal expression to this view. It is worth recalling some relevant instruments in this regard: subsequent agreements, public statements as to the understanding of certain IIA provisions, notes of interpretation, and Model BITs.[274] A Model BIT of the EU would bring further clarity to the notion of indirect expropriation in international law,[275] as will the entry into force of the first IIAs concluded by the EU.

b) Introducing proportionality balancing into the concept of indirect expropriation through general principles of law?

We have seen in Chapter 4 that general principles of law belong to the 'rules of international law' that are to be taken into account in interpreting the terms of a treaty by way of Article 31(3)(c) VCLT.[276] On this basis, there are at least two ways in which general principles might justify the application of the principle of proportionality in determining the existence of an indirect expropriation. First, a corresponding understanding of the term 'expropriation' in domestic legal systems; second, an interpretation of IIA provisions on expropriation in light of proportionality as a general principle within the meaning of Article 38(1)(c) ICJ Statute.

The first possibility relates to what is arguably the best-established function of general principles in international law. In *Barcelona Traction*, the ICJ resorted to general principles in order to fill a gap in international law with an accepted concept on the domestic level.[277] A broad consensus among domestic legal orders that expropriations are to be identified by way of a proportionality analysis (or similar concepts) would support a corresponding approach on the international level. In this regard, an in-depth comparative study of the meaning of the term 'expropriation' in domestic legal orders would be necessary. The chances that

---

[272] *See supra* note 87 and accompanying text.

[273] *See, e.g.,* UNCTAD, *World Investment Report 2014, Investing in the SDGs: an Action Plan,* at 119.

[274] *See supra* notes 199–230 and accompanying text.

[275] On the relevance of acts by international organizations for the formation and confirmation of customary international law, *see* ILA, Statement of Principles Applicable to the Formation of General Customary International Law, at 19.

[276] *See* Chapter 4, notes 83–8 and accompanying text.

[277] *See* Chapter 3, note 311 and accompanying text.

such a project, if undertaken, would reveal a consistent pattern of proportionality balancing appear to be slim. On the contrary, the approaches of domestic legal orders in relation to 'indirect expropriations' seem to be very diverse. In this vein, Rosalyn Higgins found that 'most municipal law systems have themselves developed doctrines on the taking of property that are at best "incoherent"'.[278] Even the German Constitutional Court, arguably the greatest advocate of the principle of proportionality on the domestic level, does not resort to this principle in identifying an expropriation. The Court instead analyses whether the legislative or administrative act in question was aimed at the deprivation of concrete, subjective property rights.[279]

There is another way to introduce an element of proportionality balancing into the process of identifying an indirect expropriation: the notion of proportionality as a 'general principle' within the meaning of Article 38(1)(c) ICJ Statute. I have argued that the applicability of this principle on the international level depends on the legal setting in which it ought to be applied.[280] The wording and the context of a standard BIT provision on expropriation do not mandate the application of the principle of proportionality.[281] Still, proportionality balancing in legal settings that do not contain supporting textual markers is not without precedent.

The jurisprudence of the German Constitutional Court on constitutional rights and freedoms without limitation clauses constitutes one of the clearest examples for this practice.[282] It is important to note, however, that the German Constitutional Court subjects the application of the principle of proportionality in such settings to a crucial condition: the executive or the legislature may not restrict unconditionally guaranteed rights and freedoms for *any* public purpose. Rather, the conflicting interests must be derived from 'the constitutional value order and the unity of this fundamental value system.'[283] Deciding on the applicability of the principle of proportionality to legal settings on the international level that lack textual or contextual markers for a proportionality analysis involves the following question: to what extent does the international legal order provide for an objective value system comparable to domestic legal systems? A number of 'constitutional elements' in the international legal order were identified in Chapter 4.[284] The fact that the 'constitutionalization' of the international legal system is still lagging significantly behind that of domestic legal orders weighs against the application of proportionality in deciding on the existence of an indirect expropriation.

Moreover, the application of the principle of proportionality in this legal setting raises significant concerns regarding the rule of law and judicial activism. I have argued that the scope of an individual right ought to be apparent from

---

[278] Rosalyn Higgins, 'The Taking of Property by the State: Recent Developments in International Law', *Recueil de Cours* 176 (1982) 259–392, at 268.

[279] *See supra* note 53 and accompanying text.

[280] *See* Chapter 3, section IV.

[281] *See supra* pp. 152–3.   [282] *See supra* pp. 38–40.   [283] *See* Chapter 3, note 51.

[284] *See* Chapter 4, notes 95–155 and accompanying text.

the text of a treaty: a narrowing of this scope through legal doctrine that finds no support in the treaty text runs counter to the rule of law.[285] Let us recall that a standard IIA provision on expropriation stipulates that foreign investors have to be compensated when they are expropriated for a public purpose, even if this happens in a non-discriminatory manner. Foreign investors can hardly foresee that such a claim would be subject to an additional proportionality analysis. I have argued that something different is true when the annex to an IIA explicitly provides for an element of proportionality balancing in identifying an indirect expropriation.[286] This clarification, however, is missing in those IIAs that do not adopt the approach of the 2004 Model BITs of the US and Canada.

Critics of the principle of proportionality regularly point to the risk of judicial lawmaking or judicial activism.[287] We have seen that IIAs defining indirect expropriations in their annexes contain a number of instruments that greatly reduce or even eliminate this risk. Most notably, the wording of the relevant annexes skews the balancing process in favour of the public interest.[288] Furthermore, provisions such as Article 30(3) of the BITs between the Rwanda and the US or Article 27(2) and (3) of the ASEAN–ANZ FTA arguably allow the contracting States to intervene in the balancing process even during an ongoing investor–State arbitration.[289] However, these instruments are absent from IIAs that do not follow the approach of the 2004 Model BITs of Canada and the US. In sum, the criticisms of the principle of proportionality enjoy fertile ground regarding its application in identifying indirect expropriations under standard IIA provisions on expropriation.

VI. Conclusion

The analysis in section V addressed a variety of different means to exclude proportionate regulatory measures in the public interest from the scope of IIA provisions on expropriation. Incorporating a corresponding definition of indirect expropriation in new or renegotiated IIAs is the most straightforward approach. However, States are not limited to outright renegotiations of IIAs if they wish to recalibrate the balance between the public interest and the rights of foreign investors. Joint notes of interpretation, the adoption of Model BITs, and public statements may—under certain circumstances—have an effect on the interpretation of existing IIAs. All these forms of subsequent State practice require the willingness of States to tie the notion of indirect expropriation to a proportionality analysis. Some States might decide to refrain from this practice in the interests of more robust protection of their nationals abroad, or for the sake of attracting potential

---

[285] *See supra* note 152 and accompanying text.   [286] *See supra* pp. 153–7.
[287] *See* Chapter 3, notes 201–5 and accompanying text.
[288] *See, e.g., supra* notes 69–79 and accompanying text.
[289] *See supra* notes 163–4 and accompanying text.

investors by providing a greater degree of protection. If they decide to do so, arbitrators should not too readily read an element of proportionality into standard IIA provisions on expropriation that is absent from their wording when such States appear as respondents in investor–State arbitrations.

The concept of systemic integration, general principles, and the jurisprudence of other adjudicatory bodies can play a meaningful role in investor–State arbitration. However, arbitral tribunals should be mindful of the legal settings in which other adjudicatory bodies have developed certain solutions before importing them to investor–State arbitration. This is particularly true with respect to the jurisprudence of the ECtHR on Article 1 of the First Additional Protocol. In a similar vein, general principles seem to be of little assistance in deciding on the existence of an indirect expropriation in the context of a standard expropriation provision. The understanding of the term 'expropriation' varies significantly among domestic legal orders, and at least some domestic legal systems (such as the German one) identify expropriations without a proportionality analysis. This means there is little hope in attempting to distill a general principle from domestic legal systems according to which proportionate measures in the public interest are by definition non-expropriatory.

One may still wonder whether proportionality as a general principle within the meaning of Article 38(1)(c) ICJ Statute should have a crucial influence on the interpretation of standard IIA provisions on expropriation by way of Article 31(3)(c) VCLT. Under the methodology set out in this book, several considerations speak against such an approach. Standard IIA provisions on expropriation contain a clear rule according to which expropriations be accompanied by compensation even if they are non-discriminatory and adopted for a public purpose. Introducing proportionality into this mechanism without textual marker in the treaty raises serious concerns regarding the rule of law, the threat of judicial lawmaking, and the uncertainty on what rights and interests enter the analysis.

But there is another avenue within the concept of systemic integration through which proportionality might find its way into standard IIA provisions on expropriation. This book does not aspire to decide whether the 'police powers' doctrine (in its strict or mitigated form) constitutes customary international law. If it does not, States can give rise to such an understanding of the concept of indirect expropriation through relevant State practice. The recent trend in IIAs to define indirect expropriations along the lines of the 'mitigated police powers' doctrine suggests that a corresponding rule of customary international law is at least in the making. This rule, in turn, can be relevant in the interpretation of (older) IIAs without a clear definition of the concept of indirect expropriation by way of Article 31(3)(c) VCLT.

Finally, it is important to bear in mind that the 'mitigated police powers' doctrine does not automatically provide for more regulatory freedom than the 'sole effects' doctrine. After all, most arbitral tribunals that adopt the 'sole effects' doctrine require a 'substantial deprivation' of the investment.[290] In other words, if

---

[290] *See supra* notes 20–6 and accompanying text.

a State measure does not pass this threshold, it cannot qualify as an indirect expropriation. In the course of a proportionality analysis, however, the effect on the investment of the claimant is but one of several factors. This means that a State measure might qualify as an indirect expropriation even if it does not constitute a 'substantial deprivation'. For example, arbitrators applying the 'mitigated police powers' doctrine might consider the relevant measure disproportionately burdensome in light of the particular public interest at stake, and hence determine that the measure was expropriatory.[291] If the necessary degree of deprivation under the 'sole effects' doctrine is set at an appropriate level, regulatory measures that are proportionate and non-discriminatory will hardly qualify as indirect expropriations. This is borne out by the decisions of the *CMS, Enron, National Grid, Continental, LG&E, Metalpar,* and *Glamis* tribunals, which all rejected the expropriation claims.[292]

---

[291] Note that such an outcome is not possible under the two-step approach of the *Glamis* tribunal (*see supra* notes 47–9 and accompanying text).

[292] *See supra* pp. 126–7, 130–1.

6

Proportionality and the FET Standard

Most IIAs provide for FET and it is difficult to overestimate the practical importance of this concept. The jurisprudence arising from the 2001–3 Argentine crisis is a case in point: while no claimant succeeded on an expropriation claim, all but one of the tribunals found that Argentina violated the FET standard. The often inconspicuous positioning of the FET standard and its brief formulation in most IIAs do not reflect its central importance. The Argentina–US BIT, for example, provides for FET in a provision that covers this standard jointly with the separate standard of full protection and security. Article II(2)(a) stipulates that:

[i]nvestment shall at all times be accorded fair and equitable treatment, shall enjoy full protection and security and shall in no case be accorded treatment less than that required by international law.[1]

The first sentence of Article 2(2) of the Argentina–UK BIT contains a similar provision. It states that:

[i]nvestments of investors of each Contracting Party shall at all times be accorded fair and equitable treatment and shall enjoy protection and constant security in the territory of the other Contracting Party.[2]

The wording of these provisions indicates that the FET standard is of a very general character. Commentators often submit that the high volume of jurisprudence on FET by arbitral tribunals has not added much precision, conceptual clarity, or normative understanding to this standard.[3] This chapter analyses whether the principle of proportionality can alleviate some of these perceived shortcomings and guide arbitral tribunals in interpreting and applying FET provisions. It is structured as follows. Section I provides a brief introduction on FET, focusing on the relationship between FET and the international minimum standard of treatment and on the notion of legitimate expectations. Section II addresses the jurisprudence of the tribunals adjudicating claims arising from the 2001–3

---

[1] Argentina–US BIT, *available at* <http://investmentpolicyhub.unctad.org/Download/Treaty File/127>.
[2] Argentina–UK BIT, *available at* <http://investmentpolicyhub.unctad.org/Download/Treaty File/126>.
[3] *See, e.g.,* Wythes, 'Investor–State Arbitrations: Can the 'Fair and Equitable Treatment' Clause Consider Human Rights Obligations?', at 245; Schill, 'Fair and Equitable Treatment', at 151–2.

Argentine crisis, with a particular view to the tribunals' reasoning on the investors' legitimate expectations and the public interest. Section III makes a case for the application of the principle of proportionality in the context of the FET standard, based on the methodology developed in Chapters 3 and 4. The relationship between legitimate expectations of foreign investors and proportionality will be discussed in section IV. In 2012, a tribunal ordered Ecuador to pay US$1.77 billion to the US company Occidental because of a contract termination that in the tribunal's eyes violated the principle of proportionality. Section V analyses whether this decision could and should be understood to trigger a proportionality analysis under the FET standard whenever a State exercises its contractual rights. Section VI concludes.

I. Some basic features of the FET standard

1. FET and the international minimum standard of treatment

The content and scope of the FET standard is one of the most controversial issues in investor–State arbitration. This is hardly surprising, considering that most treaty texts do not offer more guidance than that host States violate the FET standard if their conduct falls short of being fair and equitable.[4] In the NAFTA context, the vagueness of the FET standard gave rise to what was perceived by the treaty parties as overly investor-friendly jurisprudence. Hence, in 2001 the NAFTA FTC issued an interpretative note on FET, specifying that Article 1105 of NAFTA does

not require treatment in addition to or beyond that which is required by the customary international law minimum standard of treatment of aliens.[5]

Some of the more recent IIAs follow the example of the NAFTA FTC and equate FET with the international minimum standard of treatment. Article III(1)(b) of the 2009 Canada–Czech Republic BIT, for example, stipulates in terms identical to the FTC note that FET does not go beyond the international minimum standard. The BITs between Canada and Latvia,[6] the US and Uruguay,[7] and the US and Rwanda[8] contain similar provisions. The same is true for Article 6(2)(c) of the ASEAN–ANZ FTA.[9]

While there may be a certain trend in more recent IIAs to tie FET to the international minimum standard, this trend is by no means uniform. The BITs between China and the Czech Republic and China and Germany, for example,

---

[4] For typologies of different FET clauses, *see* Kläger, *'Fair and Equitable Treatment'* (2011), at 9–22; Ioana Tudor, *The Fair and Equitable Treatment Standard in the International Law of Foreign Investment* (2008), at 19–52.

[5] Chapter 5, note 201.   [6] Article II(2)(b) Canada–Latvia BIT, Chapter 5, note 74.

[7] Article 5(2) US–Uruguay BIT, Chapter 5, note 71.

[8] Article 5(2) US-Rwanda BIT, Chapter 5, note 72.   [9] Chapter 5, note 81.

contain standard IIA provisions on FET that say nothing about customary international law or the international minimum standard.[10] The same is true for the German Model BIT of 2009.[11] CETA, the Free Trade Agreement agreed between Canada and the EU in 2013/14, seems to strike a middle ground. While it does not limit FET to the international minimum standard, it seeks to avoid an overly broad interpretation of the FET standard, in particular by listing certain categories of State conduct that are in breach of FET. The relevant provision—Article X.9—reads as follows:

[1.] Each Party shall accord in its territory to covered investments of the other Party and to investors with respect to their covered investments fair and equitable treatment and full protection and security in accordance with paragraphs 2 to 6.
[2.] A Party breaches the obligation of fair and equitable treatment referenced in paragraph 1 where a measure or series of measures constitutes:
  [a] Denial of justice in criminal, civil or administrative proceedings;
  [b] Fundamental breach of due process, including a fundamental breach of transparency, in judicial and administrative proceedings;
  [c] Manifest arbitrariness;
  [d] targeted discrimination on manifestly wrongful grounds, such as gender, race or religious belief;
  [e] Abusive treatment of investors, such as coercion, duress and harassment; or
  [f] A breach of any further elements of the fair and equitable treatment obligation adopted by the Parties in accordance with paragraph 3 of this Article.
[3.] The Parties shall regularly, or upon request of a Party, review the content of the obligation to provide fair and equitable treatment. The Committee on Services and Investment may develop recommendations in this regard and submit them to the Trade Committee for decision.
[4.] When applying the above fair and equitable treatment obligation, a tribunal may take into account whether a Party made a specific representation to an investor to induce a covered investment, that created a legitimate expectation, and upon which the investor relied in deciding to make or maintain the covered investment, but that the Party subsequently frustrated.
[5.] For greater certainty, 'full protection and security' refers to the Party's obligations relating to physical security of investors and covered investments.
[6.] For greater certainty, a breach of another provision of this Agreement, or of a separate international Agreement, does not establish that there has been a breach of this Article.[12]

Seeking to give content to the FET without tying it to the international minimum standard might turn out to have been a prudent decision by the CETA parties. The NAFTA FTC note equating FET with the international minimum

---

[10] Article 3(2) of the China–Czech Republic BIT, Chapter 5, note 268; Article 3(1) of the China–Germany BIT, Chapter 5, note 269.

[11] Article 2(2) of the German Model BIT, Chapter 5, note 265.

[12] Article X.9 of CETA (as it stood at the end of the negotiations between the European Commission and Canada) *available at* <http://trade.ec.europa.eu/doclib/docs/2014/september/tradoc_152806.pdf>

standard did not add much clarity. Rather, it gave rise to new interpretative issues.[13] In particular, there is debate on whether and to what extent the international minimum standard has evolved since 1926, the year in which *Neer* set a high threshold for a violation of this standard:[14]

the treatment of an alien, in order to constitute an international delinquency, should amount to an outrage, to bad faith, to wilful neglect of duty, or to an insufficiency of governmental action so far short of international standards that every reasonable and impartial man would readily recognize its insufficiency.[15]

Two main reasons exist why States may owe a higher level of protection to aliens under the international minimum standard today than they did in 1926. First, it is arguable that progress in the domestic and international rule of law has refined custom, and that today State conduct may constitute an internationally wrongful act without amounting to 'outrage.' Second, State conduct that was not sufficiently severe to be regarded as outrageous in 1926 might well appear outrageous to a contemporary observer. These and similar considerations caused some authors and tribunals to conclude that FET and the international minimum standard are in the process of converging, have converged, or never differed (that much) in the first place.[16] The precise contours of the international minimum standard are beyond the scope of this book. Suffice it to say that tying FET to the international minimum standard does not provide arbitrators with much guidance in interpreting and applying FET provisions. Roland Kläger rightly observed that the 'minimum standard is as indeterminate as fair and equitable treatment and thus unable to fill fair and equitable treatment with meaning'.[17] This chapter seeks to assess whether proportionality has a role to play for FET provisions that are not limited to the international minimum standard—neither by their text nor through other means of treaty interpretation. Whether the two concepts are identical or not is a matter of analysing the relevant treaty and of little interest to the broader purpose of this book.[18] However, if it is true that the conclusion of

---

[13] *See* Chapter 5, notes 241–56 and accompanying text.

[14] *See* Chapter 5, notes 246–56 and Kläger, *'Fair and Equitable Treatment'*, at 74–6.

[15] *United States (Neer) v. Mexico*, General Claims Commission—United States and Mexico, Decision, 15 October 1926, 21 *American Journal of International Law* (1927) 555–7, at 556. For possible development of the international minimum standard, *see* Chapter 5, notes 247–56 and accompanying text and Kläger, *'Fair and Equitable Treatment'*, at 74–6.

[16] *See* Chapter 5, notes 250–6 and Schill, 'Fair and Equitable Treatment', at 153–4 (with further references). The *Merrill* tribunal, for example, borrowed from the wording of the FET standard when it held that the international minimum standard 'protects against all such acts or behavior that might infringe a sense of *fairness, equity*, and reasonableness' (Chapter 5, note 256, emphasis added). In a similar vein, Argentina argued in *Continental* that the international minimum standard 'is a standard which means reasonability, proportionality, and no discrimination' (*Continental*, Award, para. 56).

[17] Kläger, *'Fair and Equitable Treatment'*, at 58.

[18] For the relationship between FET and the international minimum standard under certain treaties, *see, e.g., Glamis Gold Ltd. v. United States of America*, UNCITRAL Arbitration (NAFTA), Award, 8 June 2009, paras. 606–7, paras. 586–92; *Saluka*, Partial Award, paras. 292–5, 309; *Azurix Corp v. Argentine Republic*, ICSID Case No. ARB/01/12, Award, 14 July 2006, para. 361.

independent FET provisions influences customary international law, then much of what is said here may already be or become relevant to the international minimum standard as well.[19]

2. FET and legitimate expectations

Both scholars and arbitral tribunals consider the protection of legitimate expectations to be one of the key elements of FET provisions.[20] The way arbitral tribunals interpret FET provisions to arrive at this result provides important insights for the potential role of proportionality in the context of such provisions. In the absence of more specific textual guidance, arbitral tribunals sometimes consult dictionary definitions, which typically equate 'fair' and 'equitable' with 'just', 'even-handed', 'unbiased', and 'legitimate'.[21] Obviously, such definitions do not add much precision to the FET standard. Still, the term 'even-handedness' indicates that FET involves the reconciliation of several—often conflicting—interests.

Sometimes, the context of FET provisions offers insights into the meaning of 'fair and equitable'. The preamble to the US–Ukraine BIT, for example, provides that 'fair and equitable treatment of investment is desirable in order to maintain a stable framework for investment'.[22] The *Lemire* tribunal concluded from this part of the preamble that the FET standard 'is closely tied to the notion of legitimate expectations'.[23] Another interpretative means to give meaning to the FET standard is the object and purpose of IIAs. As outlined in Chapter 5, subsection V.3, determining the object and purpose of IIAs is not always a straightforward task. It is safe to assume, however, that IIAs seek to protect property rights qualifying as foreign investments under the relevant treaty—even though not necessarily as an end in itself but rather as a means to foster economic development through investment inflow. To attract investment, IIAs provide certain protections to mitigate risks that come with the investor's exposure to—and dependence on—the State's regulatory regime once the investment is made.[24] Against this background, it is only logical that expectations investors legitimately had when executing their

---

[19] For the relationship between IIAs and custom, *see* Chapter 5, notes 241–75 and accompanying text.

[20] *See, e.g.*, Kläger, *'Fair and Equitable Treatment'*, at 164–87; Schill, 'Fair and Equitable Treatment', at 163–6; Dolzer & Schreuer, 'Investment Law', at 132–40; Dugan, et al., 'Investor–State Arbitration', at 510–519; McLachlan, et al., *International Investment Arbitration—Substantive Principles*, paras. 7.101–7.114 (all with further references). Other factors which may give rise to a breach of the fair and equitable treatment standard include arbitrary treatment, a lack of transparency, denial of justice, inconsistent behaviour, or coercive treatment (*See* Dugan, et al., 'Investor–State Arbitration', at 507–510, 519–531; McLachlan, et al., *International Investment Arbitration*, paras. 7.80–7.100, 7.115–7.128).

[21] *Tulip Real Estate and Development Netherlands BV v. Republic of Turkey*, ICSID Case No. ARB/11/28, Award, 10 March 2014, para. 401; *MTD Equity Sdn. Bhd. and MTD Chile SA v. Republic of Chile*, ARB/01/7, Award, 25 May 2004, para. 113; *Saluka*, Partial Award, para. 297.

[22] US–Ukraine BIT, Preamble, para. 4 *available at* http://investmentpolicyhub.unctad.org/Download/TreatyFile/2366.

[23] *Joseph Charles Lemire v. Ukraine*, ICSID Case No. ARB/06/18, Decision on Jurisdiction and Liability, 14 January 2010, para. 264.

[24] *See* Chapter 5, notes 64–7 and accompanying text.

investments matter when assessing whether the host State's subsequent conduct was fair and equitable. In this vein, the Saluka tribunal held that

[a]n investor's decision to make an investment is based on an assessment of the state of the law and the totality of the business environment at the time of the investment as well as on the investor's expectation that the conduct of the host State subsequent to the investment will be fair and equitable. ... The standard of 'fair and equitable treatment' is therefore closely tied to the notion of legitimate expectations which is the dominant element of that standard.[25]

Does this mean that State measures that are not in line with expectations foreign investors had when making the investment automatically give rise to liability under FET provisions? The answer is no. Arbitral tribunals have clarified that purely 'subjective motivations and considerations' of foreign investors are not to be taken into account. Rather, the objective circumstances of the particular case determine whether the expectations of foreign investors are legitimate and reasonable.[26] Unlike stabilization clauses in investment agreements between host States and foreign investors, the FET standard does not protect foreign investors against regulatory changes per se. Every investor knows that laws may change, and if an investor expects each and every change to turn out to be advantageous to his or her investment, such an expectation is neither legitimate nor protected by FET. But what if certain expectations investors had *were* legitimate: does the host State by definition act unfairly or inequitably if its legislative or administrative acts run counter to such expectations? This question will be answered in section IV, after an analysis of relevant jurisprudence from the Argentine cases (section II) and an assessment of the potential role of proportionality in the context of FET (section III).

II. The FET standard and the Argentine financial crisis

1. Overview of the relevant jurisprudence

With the sole exception of the *Metalpar* tribunal, all tribunals dealing with claims arising out of the Argentine financial crisis found that Argentina breached the FET standard of the underlying IIA. In short, most tribunals reasoned as follows: Argentina established a specific regulatory regime in the public utilities sector in the 1990s to induce foreign investment.[27] Argentina explicitly promoted this regulatory regime when it asked foreign investors to invest in its public utilities sector and, thereby, created certain expectations on the part of foreign investors. Through the measures taken during its 2001–3 financial crisis, Argentina

---

[25] *Saluka*, Partial Award, paras. 301–2 (internal reference omitted).
[26] Id., para. 304; *MTD Equity Sdn. Bhd. and MTD Chile SA v. Republic of Chile*, ARB/01/7, Decision on Annulment, 31 March 2007, para. 67.
[27] *See* Chapter 2, subsection IV.1 for a basic survey of this regime.

frustrated these expectations. *Metalpar*, the only decision in which the FET claim was entirely dismissed, bears out how central industry-specific expectations and commitments were to the tribunals' FET analyses. The claimant in *Metalpar* was an investor in the automotive industry, who did not suffer from the dismantling of the regulatory regime in the public utilities sector. Instead, the claimant was merely affected by the general measures taken by Argentina in response to the financial crisis.[28] The tribunal emphasized that there was no bidding process leading to any contractual relationship between the claimant and Argentina that could have created similar expectations as in the other cases.[29]

In *Enron*, the tribunal held that Argentina had guaranteed that gas tariffs would be calculated in US dollars, converted into pesos for billing purposes, and adjusted semi-annually along the lines of the US Producer Price Index. Furthermore, the Argentine government had guaranteed that tariffs would not be subject to price control without compensation.[30] The tribunal reasoned that all this was part of Argentina's international marketing strategy and was enshrined in the statutory framework for regulated tariffs. Consequently, the tribunal found that the claimant 'had reasonable grounds to rely on such conditions'. Argentina completely dismantled this regulatory regime, and thereby breached the FET standard.[31]

The *CMS* tribunal, dealing with the same regulatory changes in the gas sector, reasoned along similar lines. It stated that

[t]he Treaty Preamble makes it clear...that one principal protection envisaged is that fair and equitable treatment is desirable 'to maintain a stable framework for investments and maximum use of economic resources.' There can be no doubt, therefore, that a stable legal and business environment is an essential element of fair and equitable treatment. The measures that are complained of did in fact entirely transform and alter the legal and business environment under which the investment was decided and made...It has also been established that the guarantees given in this connection under the legal framework and its various components were crucial for the investment decision.[32]

The *BG Group* case also involved an investor in Argentina's gas sector. The tribunal found that Argentina's derogation from the adjustment mechanism and the billing rules of the tariffs system constituted a breach of the FET standard. In reaching its conclusion, the tribunal relied both on the stability of the regulatory framework and the specific commitments given by Argentina.[33] In particular, the tribunal stressed that Argentina's specific commitments concerning the regulatory framework sought to provide for stability in the case of currency devaluation and cost variations.[34] Similar to the reasoning in *BG Group*, the *National Grid* tribunal considered legitimate expectations 'based on representations, commitments or specific conditions offered by the State concerned' to be a key factor in

---

[28] For an overview of these measures, *see* Chapter 2, subsection IV.3.
[29] *Metalpar SA and Buen Aire SA v. Argentine Republic*, ICSID Case No. ARB/03/5, Award, 6 June 2008, paras. 185–6.
[30] *Enron*, Award, para. 264.   [31] Id., para. 265.   [32] *CMS*, Award, paras. 274–5.
[33] *BG Group*, Final Award, paras. 305–7.   [34] Id., para. 310.

determining FET.[35] The tribunal found that Argentina violated the FET standard of the Argentina–UK BIT because it completely changed the regulatory regime with which it had actively sought to attract investments in the power sector.[36]

The *Continental* case involved a claimant in an insurance company incorporated in Argentina. Consequently, the tribunal did not have to decide on the dismantling of the regulatory regime in the public utilities sector. Its analysis focused on the more general measures adopted by Argentina, which included the temporary bank freeze, the prohibition of transferring funds abroad, the termination of the pegging of the peso to the US dollar, reduced interest rates, and the 'pesification' of outstanding debts. Two factors were particularly important for the tribunal's decision. First, the government did not significantly alter the regulatory framework of the insurance sector during the crisis.[37] Second, the claimant received no 'specific undertakings' in 'legislative, administrative, or contractual' form.[38] Furthermore, the tribunal held that the claimant had not made its investment in reliance on the more general legal framework since the claimant had entered the market before the relevant rules were established.[39] In sum, the tribunal concluded that the change of the convertibility regime of 1991 was not contrary to any legitimate expectations of the claimant.

Still, the *Continental* tribunal held that Argentina breached the FET standard in one respect. This finding related to Argentina's default on its debt, and rescheduling of government bonds and other financial instruments.[40] The tribunal found that for most of these financial instruments, Argentina's measures satisfied the requirements of the emergency clause in Article XI of the Argentina–US BIT. This was sufficient reason for the tribunal not to decide on the breach of the FET standard. Concerning Argentina's treasury bills, however, the tribunal reached a different conclusion. In 2004, Argentina offered a swap of the treasury bills in default against newly issued securities. The claimant declined this offer since it would have received only 30 cents per dollar and would have had to waive its rights.[41] The tribunal considered these conditions of the unilateral restructuring 'unreasonable' and concluded that Argentina had breached its obligations under the FET standard of the Argentina–US BIT.[42]

In *Suez–Vivendi*, *AWG Group*, and *Suez–InterAgua*, the tribunal held that Argentina violated the FET standard in two respects. First, the tribunal found that Argentina would have been under an obligation to revise the tariffs as provided in the concession contract and the regulatory framework, especially 'after the crisis had abated and economic growth returned'.[43] Second, the tribunal stated that Argentina breached the FET standard by forcing the claimants to renegotiate the

---

[35] *National Grid plc v. Argentina*, UNCITRAL Arbitration, Award, 3 November 2008, para. 173.
[36] Id., para. 180.   [37] *Continental*, Award, para. 258.   [38] Id., para. 260.
[39] Id., para. 259.   [40] *See* Chapter 2, notes 116–17 and accompanying text.
[41] *Continental*, Award, para. 220.   [42] Id., paras. 264, 266.
[43] *Suez–Vivendi* and *AWG Group*, Decision on Liability, para. 238; *Suez–InterAgua*, Decision on Liability, para. 218.

original concession contract.[44] The tribunal could not find a breach of the FET standard in the unilateral termination of the concession contract in 2006. While the claimants argued that Argentina had terminated the contract under false pretences, the tribunal found that the termination was pursuant to the contract and that it had no jurisdiction to conduct a substantive review of the related contract law issues.[45] In *Impregilo*, the tribunal found that Argentina's failure to restore the contractual equilibrium in the concession contrary to the relevant contract provision violated the FET standard under the Italy–Argentina BIT.[46]

The analysis in this subsection illustrates that a finding as to the compatibility of State measures with the FET standard is a very case-specific exercise. State measures that ran counter to expectations of the relevant claimant derived from either direct dealings with the State or industry-specific legislative commitments were likely to sustain an FET claim. In contrast, tribunals were hesitant to find a violation of the FET standard for general regulatory measures not targeted at the industry sector in which the investment was made. It is not the purpose of this chapter to offer any view as to whether the arbitral tribunals were right or wrong in their conclusions. Indeed, such an inquiry would require a familiarity with the facts of each individual case that only those directly involved in the specific proceedings are likely to have. For the significant number of cases resulting from the Argentine financial crisis still pending before arbitral tribunals, and other future cases involving economic crises, a more fundamental question is of greater relevance: what does the arbitral jurisprudence on the Argentine financial crisis reveal about the relevance of the public interest in deciding on a breach of the FET standard? We turn to this question now.

2. Public interest considerations

None of the Argentina tribunals found that emergency measures automatically violate the FET standard on the sole basis that they interfere with the interests of foreign investors. On the contrary, all tribunals accepted that States have to be able to take certain emergency measures without being liable to foreign investors. The *CMS* tribunal, for example, described the scope of this regulatory freedom as follows:

It is not a question of whether the legal framework might need to be frozen as it can always evolve and be adapted to changing circumstances, but neither is it a question of whether the framework can be dispensed with altogether when specific commitments to the contrary have been made.[47]

---

[44] *Suez–Vivendi* and *AWG Group*, Decision on Liability, paras. 239–43; *Suez–InterAgua*, Decision on Liability, paras. 219–23.
[45] *Suez–Vivendi* and *AWG Group*, Decision on Liability, paras. 200, 248; *Suez–InterAgua*, Decision on Liability, paras. 188, 226.
[46] *Impregilo*, Award, paras. 324–31.
[47] *CMS*, Award, para. 277. *See also Enron*, Award, para. 261.

Other tribunals reasoned along similar lines. The *National Grid* tribunal found that the relevance of the expectations of foreign investors in the context of BIT provisions on FET is subject to two important limitations. First, the protection of legitimate expectations through IIAs does not shield foreign investors from the 'ordinary business risk of the investment'. Second, the expectations of the foreign investor must be 'reasonable and legitimate' in the particular circumstances of the case.[48] Both the *National Grid* and *BG Group* tribunals referred approvingly to the reasoning in *Saluka*.[49] The *Saluka* tribunal held that the identification of a breach of a BIT provision on FET

requires a weighing of the Claimant's legitimate and reasonable expectations on the one hand and the Respondent's legitimate regulatory interests on the other.[50]

The *BG Group* tribunal described its task of taking into consideration both the investor's interests and the public interest under the FET provision of the UK–Argentina BIT in a similar vein:

The duties of the host State must be examined in the light of the legal and business framework as represented to the investor at the time that it decides to invest. This does not imply a freezing of the legal system, as suggested by Argentina. Rather, in order to adapt to changing economic, political and legal circumstances the State's regulatory power still remains in place. As previously held by tribunals addressing similar considerations, '...the host State's legitimate right subsequently to regulate domestic matters in the public interest must be taken into consideration as well.'[51]

The *Continental* tribunal emphasized the fact-specific character of the FET standard. It held that 'the concept of fairness [is] inherently related to keeping justice in variable factual contexts'.[52] The tribunal then identified the different factors that it would consider in deciding on a breach of this standard. This list included

---

[48] *National Grid plc v. Argentina*, UNCITRAL Arbitration, Award, 3 November 2008, para. 175. The *Merrill* tribunal (in a case unrelated to the Argentine crisis) characterized legitimate expectations of foreign investors in the particular circumstances of an emergency situation as follows: 'Emergency measures or regulations addressed to social well-being are evidently within the normal functions of a government and it is not legitimate for an investor to expect to be exempt from them'. (*Merrill & Ring Forestry LP v. Canada*, UNCITRAL Arbitration, ICSID Administered Case (NAFTA), Award, 31 March 2010, para. 233). Contrary to the Argentine cases, the *Merrill* case did not involve and any specific 'representations' by the respondent (id.).

[49] *National Grid plc v. Argentina*, UNCITRAL Arbitration, Award, 3 November 2008, para. 175; *BG Group*, Final Award, para. 298.

[50] *Saluka*, Partial Award, para. 306. Note that it is also possible to consider the balancing process as part of the inquiry of whether or not the expectations of foreign investors are 'legitimate' in the first place. The analysis of the *Saluka* tribunal in paragraphs 304–5 seems to suggest such an approach. The quotation above (para. 306), however, explicitly outlines a weighing of the 'legitimate expectations' of the foreign investor against the regulatory interests of the host State. The tribunal in *Suez–Vivendi* and *AWG Group* similarly vacillated between these two approaches. It stated that it 'must balance the legitimate and reasonable expectations of the Claimants with Argentina's right to regulate' (*Suez–Vivendi* and *AWG Group*, Decision on Liability, para. 236). However, it noted in the same paragraph that 'the legitimate and reasonable expectations of the investors...must have included the expectation that the Argentine government would exercise its legitimate regulatory interests'.

[51] *BG Group*, Final Award, para. 298.   [52] *Continental*, Award, para. 255.

factors such as the specificity of the political or legislative statements on which the investor relied, whether there was a contractual relationship between the investor and the host State, the degree of risk involved in the investor's field of business, the importance and extent of the changes that the State measures entailed for the investment, the 'relevance of the public interest pursued by the State', and whether the State sought to mitigate the negative consequences for the investment.[53] The tribunal did not elaborate, however, on how these factors relate to each other.[54]

The tribunal in *Suez–Vivendi*, *AWG Group*, and *Suez–InterAgua* focused on three factors in determining a breach of the FET standard: the expectations of foreign investors,[55] whether foreign investors have in fact relied on the assurances and regulatory framework of the host State and 'changed their economic position as a result',[56] and whether the expectations were legitimate and reasonable under the particular circumstances.[57] When scrutinizing Argentina's changes to its regulatory regime in the water sector, the tribunal adopted a balancing approach. It stated that

in interpreting the meaning of fair and equitable treatment to be accorded to investors, the Tribunal must balance the legitimate and reasonable expectations of the Claimants with Argentina's right to regulate the provision of a vital public service.[58]

The tribunal resolved the conflict between the different interests at stake by reasoning that Argentina would have had to exercise its right to regulate within the existing legal framework. Since Argentina's 'actions were outside the scope of the legitimate right to regulate and in effect constituted an abuse of regulatory discretion', the tribunal concluded that there had been a breach of the FET standard.[59]

Regardless of the outcome of the individual cases, the reasoning of the tribunals in the Argentine cases illustrates that the public interest matters in deciding whether the treatment of a foreign investor is 'fair and equitable'. Most tribunals found that both the interests of the foreign investor and the public need to be taken into account when deciding on a breach of the FET standard. Against this background, one may wonder why none of the tribunals—with the possible exception of the *Continental* tribunal[60]—made explicit use of a proportionality analysis when assessing whether Argentina breached the FET standard.[61] The

---

[53] Id., para. 261.　　　[54] Id., para. 262.

[55] *Suez–Vivendi* and *AWG Group*, Decision on Liability, para. 220.

[56] Id., para. 226.　　　[57] Id., para. 229.　　　[58] Id., para. 236.

[59] Id., para. 237. *See also supra* notes 43–4 and accompanying text. Arbitrator Pedro Nikken found this part of the decision contradictory (*Suez, Sociedad General de Aguas de Barcelona SA, and Vivendi Universal SA v. Argentine Republic*, ICSID Case No. ARB/03/19 and *AWG Group v. Argentine Republic*, UNCITRAL Arbitration, Decision on Liability, 30 July 2010 (Separate Opinion of Arbitrator Pedro Nikken), para. 40). While the tribunal allegedly balanced the 'right to regulate' against the expectations of the claimants, it found that this 'right to regulate' may only be exercised within the existing regulatory framework.

[60] While the *Continental* tribunal referred to 'reasonableness' and 'proportionality' (*see Continental*, Award, para. 227), it did not systematically go through the different steps of a proportionality analysis.

[61] The *LG&E* tribunal referred to proportionality in its indirect expropriation analysis (*LG&E*, Decision on Liability, para. 195) but not in the context of FET.

next section examines whether there is good reason for this reluctance, or whether proportionality provides an appropriate analytical framework for FET, available under the rules of treaty interpretation.

III. The case for the application of the principle of proportionality in deciding on a breach of the FET standard

1. Status quo: some, but no broad endorsement of proportionality by tribunals

The tribunals adjudicating claims arising out of the 2001–3 Argentine crisis are not alone in their hesitance to explicitly endorse proportionality as an analytical tool in interpreting and applying FET provisions. While there are some notable exceptions, references to proportionality in arbitral jurisprudence on FET are still rather scarce. One of these exceptions is the 2012 decision in *Occidental v Ecuador*, discussed in greater depth in section V. Here, the tribunal held that 'fair and equitable treatment has on several occasions been interpreted to import an obligation of proportionality'.[62] Three out of the four decisions relied on by the tribunal in support of this proposition, however, referred to proportionality in the context of expropriation but not FET: this is true for *LG&E*, *Azurix*, and *Tecmed*.[63] In *MTD v Chile*, the fourth decision cited by the *Occidental* tribunal, both parties agreed with Judge Schwebel's statement that FET 'encompass[es] such fundamental standards as good faith, due process, nondiscrimination, and *proportionality*'.[64] Still, the *MTD* tribunal did not engage in a proportionality analysis. Rather, the tribunal stated that it would follow the *Tecmed* approach,[65] according to which the host State, in order to avoid liability under an FET provision, has

to act in a consistent manner, free from ambiguity and totally transparent in its relations with the foreign investor, so that it may know beforehand any and all rules and regulations that will govern its investments.[66]

---

[62] *Occidental Petroleum Corporation and Occidental Exploration and Production Company v. The Republic of Ecuador*, ICSID Case No. ARB/06/11, Award, 5 October 2012, para. 404.

[63] Id., para. 404. See *LG&E*, Decision on Liability, para. 195; *Tecmed*, Award, para. 122; *Azurix Corp. v. Argentine Republic*, ICSID Case No. ARB/01/12, Award, 14 July 2006, para. 311.

[64] *MTD Equity Sdn. Bhd. and MTD Chile SA v. Republic of Chile*, ARB/01/7, Award, 25 May 2004, para. 109 (emphasis added). For others references to proportionality in the context of FET, see *Compañiá de Aguas del Aconquija SA and Vivendi Universal SA v. Argentine Republic*, ICSID Case No. ARB/97/3, Award, 20 August 2007, para. 7.4.26 and *EDF (Services) Ltd v. Romania*, ICSID Case No. ARB/05/13, Award, 8 October 2009, paras. 286, 293.

[65] *MTD Equity Sdn. Bhd. and MTD Chile SA v. Republic of Chile*, ARB/01/7, Award, 25 May 2004, para. 115.

[66] Id., para. 114 (referring to *Tecmed*, Award, para. 154).

This formulation of the *Tecmed* tribunal is widely considered to put too much of a burden on host States and not accurately to reflect the content of FET.[67] It is a justified concern that—if taken literally—the *Tecmed* formulation leaves insufficient room for host States to adapt their legal regimes to changing circumstances. If States incur international liability for any changes in their legal framework that might have an adverse effect on foreign investment, regulating in the public interest would be virtually impossible. The principle of proportionality, in contrast, provides a flexible tool to balance the different interests involved in a fact-specific and coherent manner. This does not mean that applying proportionality in the context of the FET standard is compatible with the rules of treaty interpretation. I will turn to this issue now.

2. Incorporating proportionality analysis through Article 31(3)(c) VCLT

It is common ground among tribunals that Article 31 VCLT governs the interpretation of FET provisions. We have seen above that the ordinary meaning of FET provisions and their context, as well as the object and purpose of IIAs, offer some guidance on the interpretation of FET provisions.[68] While the extent of this guidance may differ from treaty to treaty, it tends to be limited. The terms 'fair' and 'equitable' may be equated with 'just', 'even-handed', 'unbiased', and 'legitimate', and the notion of 'even-handedness' in particular implies the need for compromise and a balance between several interests.[69] Context and object and purpose usually reveal that investors should be able to expect a stable environment for their investment, which does not mean that States have assumed an obligation to compensate foreign investors whenever regulatory action has had an adverse effect on them. Obviously, such findings established through the interpretative means listed in Article 31(1) and (2) VCLT shed only little light on the content of FET. Against this background, it is surprising that tribunals are reluctant to resort to the means of treaty interpretation listed in Article 31(3) VCLT in interpreting FET provisions. We have seen that the concept of systemic integration enshrined in Article 31(3)(c) may provide useful guidance when (1) the treaty rule is unclear, (2) the relevant terms are 'by their nature open-textured,' or (3) the interpretation relates to 'generic terms'.[70] Standard IIA provisions on FET fall within all three of these categories, and therefore provide fertile ground for systemic integration.

The potential role of Article 31(3)(c) VCLT in the context of FET is a dual one. First, Article 31(3)(c) may warrant resort to proportionality as a general principle of law within the meaning of Article 38(1)(c) ICJ Statute. Second, Article 31(3) (c) VCLT may help to identify values and interests relevant to the proportionality

---

[67] *See, e.g, Saluka*, Partial Award, para. 304, *MTD Equity Sdn. Bhd. and MTD Chile SA v. Republic of Chile*, ARB/01/7, Decision on Annulment, 31 March 2007, paras. 66–7.

[68] *See supra* notes 21–6 and accompanying text.

[69] *See supra* note 21 and accompanying text.

[70] *See* Chapter 4, notes 199–201 and accompanying text.

analysis. Regarding the first issue, we have seen in Chapter 4 that general principles are among 'the rules of international law' to be taken into account under
Article 31(3)(c) VCLT.[71] Chapter 3, section I showed that proportionality is sufficiently established on the domestic level to pass the comparative law analysis
involved in identifying a general principle. Its transposability to international law,
however, depends on the particular normative setting in which proportionality
ought to be applied as a general principle. According to the methodology set out
in Chapters 3 and 4, arbitrators should consider the following three factors before
engaging in a proportionality analysis: (1) the threat of judicial lawmaking; (2)
the rule of law; and (3) the availability of a value system that guides the proportionality analysis and works against arbitrary outcomes.

Measured against these criteria, determining the existence of an indirect expropriation with the help of proportionality as a general principle encounters difficulties under standard IIA provisions on expropriation. As explained in Chapter 5,
standard IIA provisions on expropriation contain a clear rule according to which
expropriations must be accompanied by compensation even if they are non-discriminatory and adopted for a public purpose. Reading a proportionality analysis
into this rule raises significant concerns regarding the rule of law, the threat of
judicial lawmaking, and the uncertainty on what rights and interests enter the
analysis.[72] These concerns do not—or at least do to a much lesser extent—apply
in the context of FET.

The risk of judicial lawmaking or judicial activism materializes when adjudicatory bodies revise decisions taken by the legislator (in investor–State arbitration,
the treaty parties) under the mantle of proportionality balancing.[73] In the context
of IIA provisions on FET, States have made the decision that foreign investors
need to be treated fairly and equitably—nothing more and nothing less. Some
treaties contain FET provisions but do not grant foreign investors the right to
bring an FET claim before an arbitral tribunal.[74] Most treaties guaranteeing FET,
however, provide neutral third-party adjudication to decide what constitutes FET
under the particular circumstances of a given case. Hence, the treaty parties have
explicitly delegated the task of deciding whether a certain treatment was 'fair
and equitable' to arbitral tribunals; and they have done so despite the open-textured and highly case-specific character of FET. The legal setting of FET provisions is, therefore, very different from that of unconditionally guaranteed rights

---

[71] Chapter 4, notes 83–8 and accompanying text.

[72] Chapter 5, notes 280–9 and accompanying text. Note that these concerns do not apply when
the relevant IIA defines the concept of indirect expropriation along the lines of the (mitigated) police
powers doctrine (*see* Chapter 5, subsection V.2). Such State practice could foster or give rise to a rule
of customary international law according to which the (mitigated) police powers doctrine accurately
defines an indirect expropriation under customary international law, which could in turn influence
the interpretation of standard IIA provisions on expropriation (*see* Chapter 5, subsection V. 5.a).

[73] *See especially* Chapter 3, notes 201–7 and accompanying text.

[74] This is, for example, true for old Soviet-style BITs: *see, e.g.* Ripinsky, 'Commentary on the
Russian Model BIT', in Chester Brown, ed., *Commentaries on Selected Model Investment Treaties*, at
606 n.64 & 614–15. *See also* Chapter 5, note 4.

such as freedom of speech under US constitutional law, in the context of which accusations of judicial lawmaking through proportionality analysis are particularly prevalent.[75] Similar concerns are unjustified in the context of FET.

Regarding the rule of law, a comparison to standard IIA provisions on expropriation is again illuminating. Such provisions guarantee foreign investors that they will receive compensation if they are expropriated even if the expropriation is for a public purpose, non-discriminatory, and in line with due process. Foreign investors cannot see from the text of the treaty that this rule shall not apply if the public purpose is advanced in a proportionate way. The rule of law, however, implies that legal provisions shall be—in the words of Jeremy Waldron—'clearly stated in a text that is not buried in doctrine'.[76] These considerations speak against applying proportionality as a general principle in determining the existence of an indirect expropriation under standard IIA provisions on expropriations; but similar rule-of-law concerns do not apply in the context of FET provisions. IIAs assure foreign investors that they will be treated fairly and equitably. As mentioned above, the natural meaning of these terms implies an element of 'even-handedness'.[77] Hence, foreign investors are aware that certain situations might require the accommodation and balancing of several (possibly competing) interests.

The third caveat against the application of the principle of proportionality is that balancing requires a certain normative background; otherwise it risks being arbitrary and overly subjective.[78] This does mean that the application of the principle of proportionality in the context of the FET standard presupposes a value system that displays all characteristics of a domestic constitution. But a certain value system that guides and structures the proportionality analysis is necessary. It is clear that the protection of private property rights of foreign investors is central to IIAs. References to other values and interests in the relevant IIA, for example in its preamble, may be relevant to decide what is fair and equitable as well. This is particularly true for more recent IIAs, which tend to stress the importance of values and interests such as human health and the environment.[79]

This brings us to the second function of Article 31(3)(c) VCLT in interpreting and applying FET provisions: Article 31(3)(c) may help to identify the values and interests that are relevant in the proportionality analysis. Chapter 4 described the relevant methodology, and outlined its potential and limits. All of these points are relevant here, and there is no need to repeat them in their entirety. But it is worth recalling that Article 31(3)(c) allows treaty interpreters to resort to external rules that reflect multilateral or bilateral agreement on certain values. Rules and principles to be taken into account under Article 31(3)(c) may stem from treaties, customary international law, and general principles. This is an advantage of

---

[75] *See* Chapter 3, notes 150–87 and accompanying texts.
[76] Waldron, *The Rule of International Law*, at 17. *See also* Chapter 3, notes 208–14 and accompanying text.
[77] *See supra* note 21 and accompanying text.
[78] *See* Chapter 3, notes 215–18 and accompanying text.
[79] *See* Chapter 5, notes 180–4 and accompanying text.

the proportionality analysis under Article 31(3)(c) advanced in this book to (at first glance) bolder approaches such as Andreas Kulick's 'Global Public Interest theory': Kulick suggests balancing the public interest with the interests of foreign investors in the quantum phase, but only to the extent that the relevant public interest considerations have found their way into customary international law or constitute general principles of law.[80] The methodology suggested here provides for balancing when determining liability under FET provisions, and it does not exclude values derived from bilateral or multilateral treaties from the analysis.

Apart from providing relevant values, the international legal order even offers some hierarchical structure to frame a proportionality analysis—the concept of *jus cogens* and Article 103 of the UN Charter.[81] However, as described in Chapter 4, hierarchical factors will in most cases not be decisive.[82] Rather, the analysis is likely to turn on the issue whether national decision-makers took account of the relevant conflicting values in an appropriate way under the given circumstances. This idea corresponds with Konrad Hesse's notion of *praktische Konkordanz* in the context of conflicting values in constitutional systems. It is worth reiterating the core tenet of this theory:

Both legal values need to be limited so that each can attain its optimal effect. In each concrete case, therefore, the limitations must satisfy the principle of proportionality; that is, they may not go any further than necessary to produce a concordance of both legal values.[83]

In sum, proportionality analysis is a valuable tool for determining whether the relevant State measures have complied with the FET standard. Article 31 VCLT offers sufficient means to establish the normative background of the balancing process in each individual case. Guidance can be found within and—to the extent permitted by Article 31(3)(c)—outside the relevant treaty. If this is done properly, proportionality analysis in the context of FET provisions does not constitute a threat to the rule of law, nor is it apt to give rise to judicial lawmaking or arbitrariness.

While not decisive for the purposes of treaty interpretation, it provides comfort that Robert Alexy's theory on rules and principles seems to support the approach suggested here. There are arguably two ways to understand provisions on FET under Alexy's theory. Conflicts between the regulatory freedoms of host States and the private property rights of foreign investors in the FET context can be characterized as the collision of two principles.[84] Alternatively, it seems possible to argue that an FET provision constitutes a rule, in which the formulation 'fair and equitable treatment' refers to principles.[85] The principle of proportionality is

---

[80] Kulick, *Global Public Interest in International Investment Law*, at 209 & 305.

[81] *See* Chapter 4, notes 127–55 and accompanying text.

[82] *See* Chapter 4, notes 137–55 and accompanying text.   [83] Chapter 3, note 52.

[84] *See* Chapter 3, note 61 and accompanying text.

[85] *See* Chapter 3, notes 64–5 and accompanying text. Similar to Alexy, Niels Petersen has identified three scenarios in which principles are of particular importance: (1) situations in which there is no applicable rule; (2) situations in which rules refer either explicitly or implicitly to principles; and (3) situations in which rules are open to several interpretations and, therefore, need to be further

applicable under both alternatives and it seeks to ensure that the detriment to one of the values involved is no greater than factually and legally necessary for the purposes of the other.[86]

3. Refining but not contradicting existing jurisprudence

While proportionality analysis is not as yet firmly established in arbitral jurisprudence related to FET, it does not go against any major tenets of this jurisprudence either. Quite the opposite, applying proportionality coupled with the concept of systemic integration to FET provisions is compatible with existing jurisprudence and furnishes some of its most important elements with an analytical framework. As illustrated in subsection II.2, public policy considerations play a significant role in arbitral jurisprudence on FET, and many tribunals have recognized that in applying FET provisions both private and public interests have to be taken into account. The *Continental* tribunal, for example, identified a variety of different factors that it would consider in deciding on a breach of the FET standard. This list included the expectations of the claimant and the public interest.[87] However, the *Continental* tribunal did not clarify how these factors relate to each other. Instead, the tribunal abruptly announced its conclusions right after it listed the factors that it would take into account in its decision.[88] Proportionality analysis as outlined in the previous subsection provides a transparent analytical framework to make sure none of the relevant values and interests is compromised to a greater extent than necessary for the advancement of a conflicting interest.

In *Suez–Vivendi/AWG Group* and *Suez–InterAgua*, the tribunal balanced the interests of foreign investors with the host State's 'right to regulate'.[89] The notion of a 'right to regulate' in international law is not new; both arbitral tribunals and scholars have referred to it in the past.[90] It is unclear, however, what this concept actually means and what it entails. An IIA as a whole reflects a certain 'balance' between the interests of foreign investors and a host State's regulatory freedom (or its so-called 'right to regulate'). What else but its 'right to regulate' does a State exercise when it expropriates individuals? The purpose of IIAs is to limit the exposure of foreign investors to the regulatory moods of host States. States are free to expropriate foreign investors. But if they decide to do so they must pay compensation (usually in the amount of the 'fair market value' of the investment).

---

specified by underlying principles (Petersen, 'Customary Law Without Custom?', at 291). Again, FET provisions seem to fall under the second and/or the third scenario.

[86] *See* Chapter 3, note 63 and accompanying text.
[87] *See supra* note 53 and accompanying text.
[88] *Continental*, Award, paras. 261–2.   [89] *Supra note* 58 and accompanying text.
[90] For a survey in this respect, *see* OECD, International Investment Law: a Changing Landscape (2005), 43–72 (Chapter 2: '"Indirect Expropriation" and the "Right to Regulate" in International Investment Law'). Alvarez and Brink argue that all substantive guarantees in BITs ought to be balanced against a 'state's right to regulate in the public interest' (Alvarez & Brink, 'Revisiting the Necessity Defence', at 357–8).

The international legal order offers more concrete guidelines for the determination of what is 'fair and equitable' in a given situation than the so-called 'right to regulate'. The values and interests mentioned in the particular IIA play an important role in this context, and there is a notable evolution in contemporary treaty practice: preambles of more recent IIAs are increasingly elaborate in listing interests and values that are relevant in the context of the particular IIA.[91] As outlined in Chapter 4, Article 31(3)(c) VCLT may lead treaty interpreters to other interests and values that have to be considered in a particular situation. Against the background, it is surprising that the arbitrators in *Suez–Vivendi/AWG Group* and *Suez–InterAgua* did not comment on potential human rights obligations of Argentina when they interpreted and applied the relevant FET provisions.[92] This is not to say that they decided the case wrongly. Indeed, the tribunal considered a variety of different factors that lie at the core of every proportionality analysis. The tribunal pointed to some alternative means that would have allowed Argentina to protect the interests of the claimants without forfeiting the alleged goals of its regulatory measures.[93] In a similar vein, the *National Grid* tribunal weighed the factor that 'no meaningful negotiations took place' against Argentina.[94] The lack of such negotiations can determine the outcome of a proportionality analysis—as illustrated by a 1907 regional court decision discussed in Chapter 3.[95]

IV. Legitimate expectations: absolute protection or subject to proportionality balancing?

Section I established that the protection of legitimate expectations is one of the core elements of FET. It concluded with the question of whether State action

---

[91] *See* Chapter 5, notes 180–4 and accompanying text.

[92] In its decision on liability, the tribunal addressed 'human rights' only in passing when commenting on the customary international law defence of necessity. In contrast to this brevity, the tribunal had stated in prior procedural decisions that the subject matter of the dispute involved the water supply to 'millions of people' and that the tribunal might have to decide on 'complex public and international law questions, including human rights considerations'. (*Suez, Sociedad General de Aguas de Barcelona SA, and Vivendi Universal SA v. Argentine Republic*, ICSID Case No. ARB/03/19, Order in Response to a Petition by Five Non-Governmental Organizations for Permission to make an Amicus Curiae Submission, 12 February 2007, para. 18; *Suez, Sociedad General de Aguas de Barcelona SA, and Vivendi Universal SA v. Argentine Republic*, ICSID Case No. ARB/03/19, Order in Response to a Petition for Transparency and Participation as *Amicus Curiae*, 19 May 2005, para. 19). The *amicus curiae* submission of the Center for International Environmental Law discussed the relationship between human rights and the FET standard, *see Suez, Sociedad General de Aguas de Barcelona SA, and Vivendi Universal SA v. Argentine Republic*, ICSID Case No. ARB/03/19, Amicus Curiae Submission by the Center for International Environmental Law (CIEL) et al., 4 April 2007, at 16–21.) For further remarks on human rights and international investment arbitration, *see* Chapter 4, pp. 103–6 & 110–1.

[93] *Suez–Vivendi* and *AWG Group*, Decision on Liability, para. 235.

[94] *National Grid plc v. Argentina*, UNCITRAL Arbitration, Award, 3 November 2008, para. 179.

[95] *See* Chapter 2, note 39 and accompanying text.

that goes against an investor's legitimate expectations will automatically lead to liability under an FET provision. Some tribunals seem to assume that this is the case. In the 2004 *Occidental v Ecuador* decision, the tribunal held that 'there is certainly an obligation not to alter the legal and business environment in which the investment has been made'. Similarly, in *Parkerings v Lithuania*, the tribunal stated that

the Fair and Equitable Treatment standard is violated when the investor is deprived of its legitimate expectation that the conditions existing at the time of the Agreement would remain unchanged.[96]

Other arbitral jurisprudence, however, appears to consider the protection of legitimate expectation not to be absolute. The observant reader may have noted that some of the arbitral jurisprudence cited in this chapter explicitly referred to the balancing of the legitimate expectations of foreign investors with other interests. This is, for example, true for the *Saluka* tribunal, which reasoned that applying the relevant FET provision requires a 'weighing of the Claimant's legitimate and reasonable expectations on the one hand and the Respondent's legitimate regulatory interests on the other'.[97] The *Continental* tribunal followed a similar approach when it found that it needed to take into account factors such as the specificity of the political or legislative statements on which the investor relied and the relevance of the public interest at stake.[98] The same is true for the *Suez–Vivendi* and *AWG Group* tribunal, which held that in applying the FET standard it 'must balance the legitimate and reasonable expectations of the Claimants with Argentina's right to regulate'. In the 2010 *Lemire v Ukraine* decision, the arbitral tribunal held that it had to 'balance' several 'relevant interests' and consider the following factors:

- the State's sovereign right to pass legislation and to adopt decisions for the protection of its *public interests*, especially if they do not provoke a disproportionate impact on foreign investors;
- the *legitimate expectations* of the investor, at the time he made his investment;
- the investor's duty to perform an investigation before effecting the investment;
- the investor's conduct in the host country.[99]

This approach has the advantage that it allows for a flexible, case-specific analysis, taking into account all of the relevant interests involved. It risks, however, unduly frustrating expectations that are *legitimate*. To ensure a fair outcome of the balancing process, arbitral tribunals ought to pay close attention to the basis of the investor's legitimate expectations. *Parkerings v Lithuania* offers an instructive overview of

---

[96] *Parkerings-Compagniet AS v Republic of Lithuania*, ICSID Case No ARB/05/8, Award, 11 September 2007, para. 330.

[97] *Supra* note 50.   [98] *Supra* note 53.

[99] *Joseph Charles Lemire v. Ukraine*, ICSID Case No. ARB/06/18, Decision on Jurisdiction and Liability, 14 January 2010, para. 285 (emphasis added).

possible sources from which investors may derive their expectations: (1) explicit promises by the host State; (2) implicit assurances and representations by the host State; and (3) the domestic law at the time the investment was made.[100] The *Parkerings* tribunal had to deal with changes in legislation that reduced the parking fees a consortium of investors in the parking system of Vilnius was able to collect. The tribunal found that no explicit or implicit promises or assurances were made, and that a State is free to change its law 'at its own discretion' as a result of its 'sovereign legislative power'.[101] Adding that the claimant knowingly invested in a country in transition in the 1990s, the tribunal found that the claimant took the 'business risk' of changing legislation.[102] The tribunal finally dismissed all claims in their entirety.

To the extent that *Parkerings* stands for the proposition that a State does not automatically incur liability under FET if legislative changes have an adverse effect on foreign investors, the tribunal was right. Freezing the regulatory framework or certain parts of it at the time the investment was made is the function of so-called stabilization clauses and not the FET standard. States and foreign investors can and often do agree on such clauses in investment agreements, and the *Parkerings* tribunal rightly emphasized this point in its FET analysis.[103] Nevertheless, *Parkerings* should not be understood to mean that expectations investors derive from the host State's legal framework that are not accompanied by implicit or explicit promises or representations are automatically meaningless. The *Parkerings* tribunal itself noted that even in such situations a State may not 'act unfairly, unreasonably or inequitably in the exercise of its legislative power'.[104] This does not say much more than that State action must be fair and equitable, which is a rather coarse way of describing the content of the FET standard. A more nuanced approach seems to be possible under the proportionality analysis suggested here: legitimate expectations derived only from the regulatory framework when the investment was made enter the proportionality analysis, but they do so with less weight than expectations that rest on specific promises or representations.

At the other end of the spectrum, one may wonder whether the frustration of legitimate expectations that were raised by explicit promises of the host State should automatically lead to liability under FET without a proportionality analysis. The strongest way of making a promise in an investment context is probably to put it down in a contract. Some IIAs with FET provisions contain separate (so-called) umbrella clauses that elevate the breach of a contract between investor and host State to the treaty level—but others do not. This consideration speaks against the view that the frustration of legitimate expectations raised by promises of the host State automatically constitutes a breach of the FET standard. But legitimate expectations raised by explicit promises should have great weight in a proportionality analysis, and a host State will often violate the FET standard if it frustrates such expectations without compensating the foreign investor.

---

[100] *Parkerings-Compagniet AS v Republic of Lithuania*, ICSID Case No ARB/05/8, Award, 11 September 2007, paras. 331–2.
[101] Id., paras. 332, 334.   [102] Id., paras. 335–6.   [103] Id., paras. 336.
[104] Id., para. 332.

Having addressed the two extreme poles of the spectrum introduced above, the last category to be addressed is category (2): implicit assurances and representations by the host State. This category arguably comprises a broad range of different scenarios, which might in some instances not only verge on but also overlap with category (1) or (3). If a host State, for example, organizes conferences or other events in which it actively promotes its regulatory framework to induce long-term investment in a certain industry sector, then this should play a significant role in the proportionality analysis. Something similar ought to be true for industry-specific representations included in general legislation. Let's say legislation provides for a certain minimum feed-in tariff for electricity generated by renewable energies until the year 2025. A State is not barred by international law from later reducing this period to, say, 2017. But the expectations of a foreign investor who made his investment in reliance on payment of the specified feed-in tariff until the year 2025 will have considerable weight in a proportionality analysis. In conclusion, legitimate expectations are neither absolutely protected if they rest on specific promises nor irrelevant if derived from general legislation. Rather, the weight of legitimate expectations depends on the circumstances of each individual case and is determined by factors such as the specificity of the source giving rise to the expectation and the degree to which the source individualizes its addressees.

V. *Occidental v Ecuador*: proportionality as a restraint for States in exercising their contractual rights?

With the decision in *Occidental v Ecuador*, the year 2012 saw the largest publicly known ICSID award in history: a tribunal awarded $1.77 billion to Occidental[105] for a breach of the FET provision in the US–Ecuador BIT—and it did so because it considered Ecuador's termination of a contract to be disproportionate. While one of the arbitrators issued a dissenting opinion on damages, the tribunal's findings on both the relevance of proportionality and its application to the facts of the case were unanimous.[106] Regarding its impact on future jurisprudence, one may wonder whether this decision stands for the proposition that in exercising contractual rights States need to comply not only with the terms of the contract but also with the principle of proportionality. To shed light on this issue, a closer look at the facts and reasoning of the *Occidental* award is necessary.

In 1999, the claimant concluded a contract with Ecuador ('through' Petroecuador, the national oil company) regarding the exploration and exploitation

---

[105] The case was brought by Occidental Petroleum Corporation and Occidental Exploration and Production Company, two US companies. For ease of rererence, I do not differentiate between the two companies and refer to them both individually and jointly as 'Occidental' or 'the claimant'.

[106] *Occidental Petroleum Corporation and Occidental Exploration and Production Company v. The Republic of Ecuador*, ICSID Case No. ARB/06/11, Dissenting Opinion Brigitte Stern, 20 September 2012, para. 1.

of hydrocarbons of a certain part ('Block 15') of the Ecuadorian Amazon ('participation contract').[107] The participation contract was governed by Ecuadorian law and obliged the claimant to explore, develop, and exploit Block 15 at its own cost. In return, the claimant received a share of the oil produced from Block 15, referred to as the claimant's 'participation' and determined by a complex equation.[108] The participation contract set out strict conditions under which the claimant could assign its rights and obligations under the contract to a third party. These conditions included prior approval and authorization by both Petroecuador and the relevant ministry.[109]

In 2000, the claimant concluded a so-called farmout agreement with another company operating in the hydrocarbons sector, AEC ('the farmout agreement'). Farmout agreements are standard practice in the oil industry; they allow the use of less own capital and a reduction in exposure to in-country risk by including another company in the operations.[110] The farmout agreement provided for two phases. In phase one, AEC acquired a 40% 'economic interest' in Block 15 in return for contributions to the claimant's expenditures, payable from 2001–4.[111] In phase two, AEC would acquire legal 'title' in 40% of the claimant's participation, subject to two conditions precedent: payment of the relevant contributions from 2001–4, and governmental approval.[112] While the ministry was informed of AEC's involvement in the operations in 2000, no authorization of the farmout agreement was sought at that time: the claimant considered authorization unnecessary as no title was to be transferred in phase one.[113] The tribunal disagreed with this analysis and found that by not seeking authorization in 2000, the claimant violated clause 16.1 of the participation contract, which provided that:

16.1 Transfer of this Participation Contract or assignment to third parties of the rights under the Participation Contract, must have the authorization of the Corresponding Ministry, in accordance with existing laws and regulations, especially the provisions contained in Art. 79 of the Hydrocarbons Law and Executive Decrees No. 809, 2713 and 1179.[114]

The tribunal emphasized, however, that the claimant made an honest mistake and did not act in bad faith when it considered governmental approval of phase

---

[107] *Occidental Petroleum Corporation and Occidental Exploration and Production Company v. The Republic of Ecuador*, ICSID Case No. ARB/06/11, Award, 5 October 2012, paras. 105, 115.

[108] In 2005, the claimant's participation amounted to 70% of the oil produced from Block 15. If measured in net profits, however, the claimant allegedly received only 30% of total net profits between 1999 and 2006 (id., para. 116).

[109] Id., para. 119.

[110] Julian Cardenas Garcia, 'The Era of Petroleum Arbitration Mega Cases', *Houston Journal of International Law* 35 (2012) 537–88, at 544, 566–8; *Occidental Petroleum Corporation and Occidental Exploration and Production Company v. The Republic of Ecuador*, ICSID Case No. ARB/06/11, Award, 5 October 2012, para. 129.

[111] *Occidental Petroleum Corporation and Occidental Exploration and Production Company v. The Republic of Ecuador*, ICSID Case No. ARB/06/11, Award, 5 October 2012, para. 130.

[112] Id., para. 131.   [113] Id., paras. 351–64; 372–3.   [114] Id., paras. 119, 381.

one unnecessary.[115] Moreover, the claimant did not try to hide the involvement of AEC, but rather publicly announced that it entered into the farmout agreement.[116] The ministry itself stated in a memorandum dated 8 November 2000 that AEC already operated other fields in Ecuador, and that it could not see any 'impediment' for the 'future' assignment of the claimant's rights to AEC.[117]

On 12 July 2004, almost four years after the conclusion of the farmout agreement, an arbitral tribunal ordered Ecuador to pay $75 million to Occidental because Ecuador had violated Occidental's right to tax reimbursements in breach of the FET standard.[118] Ecuador did not recognize the award, and a State representative, the attorney general, openly declared that he was 'studying the contract linking Occidental with the country…to check whether the contractual norms have been strictly complied with'.[119] In August 2004, an internal memorandum came to the conclusion that the phase one transfer of economic interest to AEC in 2000 had violated the participation contract.[120] Upon request by the attorney general, the minister of energy asked the president of Petroecuador on 8 September 2004 to initiate the termination procedure under the participation contract.[121] The claimant denied the charges of non-compliance with the participation contract in a detailed letter dated 29 September 2004, and no further action by Ecuador to terminate the contract was taken until 2005.[122] During March and April 2005, the claimant had meetings with State representatives to find an amicable solution.[123] But after strikes, riots, and the ousting of the then Ecuadorian president, some government officials including the new minister of energy signed resolutions in which they undertook to take all necessary steps for the departure 'from Ecuador of the companies Occidental and…AEC'.[124] Political pressure to terminate the participation contract increased further in the months that followed.[125] On 15 May 2006 the minister of energy finally terminated the contract by governmental decree, followed by the seizure of the claimant's property and the oilfields over the next two days. Cited as legal basis of the decree, Article 74 of Ecuador's Hydrocarbons Law ('HCL') reads in material part as follows:

The Ministry of Energy and Mines may declare the *caducidad* of contracts, if the contractor:

[…]

11. Transfers rights or enters into a private contract or agreement for the assignment of one or more of its rights, without the Ministry's authorization.[126]

As mentioned above, the tribunal held that the transfer of the 40% economic interest to AEC would have required governmental approval. In conclusion, it found that the requirements of Article 74.11 were fulfilled,[127] which triggered the

---

[115] Id., para. 380.   [116] Id., para. 380.   [117] Id., para. 438(b).

[118] Id., paras. 438; 568. *See also Occidental Exploration and Production Company v. The Republic of Ecuador*, LCIA Case No. UN3467, Award, 1 July 2004.

[119] *Occidental Petroleum Corporation*, Award, para. 174.   [120] Id., para. 176.

[121] Id., para. 179.   [122] Id., paras. 180–1.   [123] Id., para. 185.

[124] Id., paras. 186–7.   [125] Id., para. 188–98, 438.

[126] Id., para. 121 (emphasis added).

[127] Id., para 381. As the tribunal found that the elements of Article 74.11 were fulfilled, it did not consider it necessary to analyse Article 74.12 and 74.13.

consequences set out in Article 74 according to which the Ministry '*may* declare the caducidad of contracts' (emphasis added). The tribunal reasoned that *caducidad* was not automatic ('may'). Rather, the ministry was obliged to exercise discretion, which involved both as a matter of Ecuadorian law and the FET standard adhering to the principle of proportionality.[128] In deciding whether *caducidad* was proportionate, the tribunal analysed what alternative means Ecuador had at its disposal to sanction the claimant's unauthorized transfer of economic interest to AEC. The tribunal emphasized that Article 79 HCL entitled Ecuador to request a transfer fee and to negotiate a more favourable participation contract—options that Ecuador had used in other instances.[129] When balancing the different interests at stake, the tribunal noted that the 2004 award against Ecuador 'led to a good deal of ill-feeling' against the claimant.[130] Regarding the rationale of the approval requirement, the tribunal deemed it legitimate that Ecuador—to protect its 'natural resources, and the income it can generate from them'—wished to carefully vet parties having 'access' or certain 'control over' those resources.[131] With the benefit of hindsight, however, Ecuador did not suffer any economic harm from the involvement of AEC.[132] And even at the time, the minister of energy expected the involvement of AEC 'to be a good idea as it was beneficial to the country'.[133] The tribunal found it 'overwhelmingly likely' that, if requested, authorization for the transfer would have been granted, in particular because AEC had been vetted by the government before and continued to receive further approvals.[134] Nevertheless, the tribunal accepted that Ecuador had a right to sanction the claimant for not soliciting the necessary approval to 're-emphasize the importance of adherence to its regulatory regime' and to convey a 'deterrence message'.[135] Depriving the claimant of its entire investment worth 'many hundreds of millions of dollars', however, was a disproportionate sanction.[136]

Whether one agrees or disagrees with the reasoning of the tribunal, its implications for cases in which States seek to exercise their contractual rights are limited. The contract was terminated by a governmental decree based on Ecuador's

---

[128] Id., paras. 396–409. The tribunal was not very specific as to the basis of its proportionality analysis under the FET standard. It referred to the role of proportionality in GATT jurisprudence (para. 402), domestic legal systems (para. 403), and the ECHR (para. 403), and noted that '[t]he obligation for fair and equitable treatment has on several occasions been interpreted to import an obligation of proportionality' by arbitral tribunals (para. 404). The notion of general principles within the meaning of Article 38(1)(c) ICJ Statute and/or the concept of systemic integration enshrined in Article 31(3)(c) VCLT were not mentioned by the tribunal.

[129] Id., paras. 429–34. Article 79 reads as follows (see id. para. 121):

> The transfer of a contract or the assignment to third parties of rights derived from a contract shall be null and void and shall have no validity whatsoever if there is no prior authorization from the Ministry of Energy and Mines, without prejudice to the declaration of *caducidad* as provided for in this Law. The State shall receive a premium for the transfer and the beneficiary company shall enter into a new contract under more favourable economic conditions for the State and for PETROECUADOR than the ones contained in the original contract.

[130] Id., para. 442.   [131] Id., para. 446.   [132] Id., para. 447.
[133] Id., para. 444.   [134] Id., para. 445.   [135] Id., para. 450.

[136] Id., para. 450. The tribunal noted that Ecuador's actions, apart from violating the FET provision, constituted an expropriation under the US–Ecuador BIT (id., para. 450).

hydrocarbons law, i.e. Article 74 HCL. The tribunal emphasized that the government proceeded explicitly under Article 74 HCL and not pursuant to the termination provisions set out in the participation contract,[137] which specified in material part that:

[t]his Participation Contract shall terminate...

21.1.1 By a declaration of forfeiture [*caducidad*] issued by the Corresponding Ministry for the causes and following the procedure established in Articles seventy-four (74), seventy-five (75) and seventy-six (76) of the Hydrocarbons Law, insofar as applicable...

21.1.2 Due to a transfer of rights and obligations of the Participation Contract without prior authorization from the Corresponding Ministry...

21.3 For the purposes of forfeiture and penalties, the provisions of Chapter IX of the Hydrocarbons Law shall be applicable.[138]

The tribunal noted that there was good reason for Ecuador not to proceed under clause 21.1.2 as the claimant did not transfer any of its 'obligations' arising from the Participation Contract to AEC during phase one of the farmout agreement.[139] Regarding clause 21.1.2, the tribunal held that the reference to the *caducidad* provisions in the HCL could only mean that the claimant accepted termination when the *caducidad* decree was lawful—and not when it violated, as here, the requirement of proportionality under Ecuadorian law.[140] Some might argue that it is for the judicial body having jurisdiction over the participation contract to make this call under Ecuadorian law, but this is not our issue here.[141] What matters for our purposes is that the tribunal did not say that when exercising its contractual rights Ecuador would have had to comply not only with the contractual terms but also with the principle of proportionality to avoid liability under the FET standard. The tribunal did not have to deal with this issue, for two independent reasons. According to the tribunal, Ecuador did not even *exercise* its contractual rights as it proceeded under the HCL;[142] and if Ecuador had proceeded under the contract, the termination would not have *complied* with its terms.[143]

Having established that *Occidental* provides no guidance on the issue whether proportionality may restrain a State in exercising its contractual rights, one may wonder what the right answer to this question is. Each case turns on its own facts, and much depends on the relationship between the exercise, if any, of administrative or legislative power and the particular contractual relationship. Nevertheless, as a basic rule, arbitrators should not turn to a proportionality analysis in such situations too readily. One of the main caveats against the application of the principle of proportionality is the risk of unwarranted judicial lawmaking. In the domestic constitutional context, this risk concerns the relationship between the

---

[137] Id., paras. 420, 433   [138] Id., para. 120.   [139] Id., para. 420.
[140] Id., para. 421.
[141] Some formulations of the tribunal suggest that it made the remarks on the interpretation of the participation contract *obiter dicta*: For example, the tribunal emphasized that what the claimant agreed to in the participation contract is irrelevant to actions taken outside and not pursuant to the contract (*see, e.g.* id., para. 423).
[142] *See supra* note 137 and accompanying text.   [143] *See supra* notes 138–40.

judiciary on one hand and the administration or legislature on the other. In international law, adjudicators typically risk engaging in unwarranted judicial lawmaking when they balance certain rights and interests for which a balance has already been struck by the treaty parties.[144]

Similar considerations apply here. If a foreign investor and a host State set out the terms under which one of them may exercise certain contractual rights, then it is not for arbitrators to overwrite this decision by a proportionality analysis. The contract is usually concluded before the investor makes his investment, and there is a strong assumption that the contract terms reflect what the parties considered a fair balance of mutual rights and obligations. Arbitrators should be cautious not to undermine this bargain by a proportionality analysis. Furthermore, in many legal regimes, the abuse of rights doctrine will provide for appropriate limits to a party's discretion in exercising its contractual rights.[145] Sometimes, tribunals might review whether the termination of a contract was justified under the terms of the contract; and these terms might even trigger a weighing and balancing of different interests akin to a proportionality analysis. This is very different, however, from holding a State liable under FET for a disproportionate exercise of rights that have been found to exist under a contract.

Recent jurisprudence supports the points made here. In *Vannessa v Venezuela*, decided in 2013, the tribunal had to deal with a State agency's termination of its contract for the exploitation of copper and gold with (a company controlled by) a foreign investor.[146] The tribunal found the termination justified under the contract because the foreign investor had, contrary to its contractual obligations, sold its interest to Vannessa, the eventual claimant.[147] The tribunal reasoned that within contractual relationships, States should not be held to higher standards than private parties. Thus, the tribunal held that '[i]t is well established that, in order to amount to an expropriation under international law, it is necessary that the conduct of the State should go beyond that which an ordinary contracting party could adopt'.[148] In its FET analysis, the tribunal emphasized again that the termination of the contract and the subsequent taking control of the mine 'were contractual responses to what the Tribunal considers contractual breaches'.[149] The tribunal added that in light of the circumstances of the investment and the contractual framework agreed between the parties, Venezuela's actions did not fall short of FET, however one may define this standard.[150] It remains to be hoped that other tribunals follow the example of the *Vannessa* tribunal and do not read into *Occidental* that the exercise of contractual rights is by definition subject to a proportionality test under FET provisions—because it is not.

---

[144] *See* Chapter 3, notes 201–7 and accompanying text.

[145] For a survey of the absue of rights doctrine under both domestic legal orders and international law, *see* Michael Byers, 'Abuse of Rights: an Old Principle, A New Age', *McGill Law Journal* 47 (2002) 390–431, at 392–404.

[146] *Vannessa Ventures Ltd. v. Bolivarian Republic of Venezuela*, ICSID Case No. ARB(AF)04/6, Award, 16 January 2013, paras. 56–60.

[147] Id., para. 112, 196, 201–8.   [148] Id., para. 209.   [149] Id., para. 221.

[150] Id., para. 222.

VI. Conclusion

Judging on a breach of the FET standard is a highly fact-specific exercise, and it is a truism to state that each case turns on its own facts. Thus, the often cited 1981 statement by F. A. Mann on the difficulties in giving general and abstract meaning to FET still holds true in many respects today:

A Tribunal would not be concerned with a minimum, maximum or average standard. It will have to decide whether in all circumstances the conduct in issue is fair and equitable or unfair and inequitable. No standard defined by any other words is likely to be material. The terms are to be understood and implied independently and autonomously.[151]

Nevertheless, the rules of treaty interpretation offer guidance for the interpretation and application of FET provisions that goes beyond Mann's statement. While each treaty is to be interpreted separately, the protection of legitimate expectations by foreign investors will often be an important component of the FET standard. As illustrated in section II, this does not mean that arbitral tribunals exclude public interest considerations from their analyses. Rather, tribunals emphasize that States may adapt their legislation to changing circumstances without incurring liability under the FET standard—in particular but not only in times of crisis. Tribunals have repeatedly held that reconciling the different interests at stake involves a balancing test, but they have rarely been explicit about the mechanics and analytical framework of this balancing exercise.

As demonstrated in section III, proportionality provides a valuable tool in this regard. In terms of treaty interpretation, the concept of systemic integration enshrined in Article 31(3)(c) VCLT plays a dual role here. First, it offers a solid basis for the application of proportionality as a general principle of law. Second, it helps to decide what values and interests are relevant in the proportionality analysis. If done properly, proportionality analysis in the context of IIA provisions on FET does not constitute a threat to the rule of law, nor is it apt to give rise to judicial lawmaking or arbitrariness. Rather, the different steps of a proportionality analysis make the reasoning of tribunals more transparent and enhance the probability that all relevant factors will be taken into account. Section IV established that the legitimate expectations of foreign investors are an important part of this proportionality analysis, and that the weight with which they enter the analysis depends to a large extent on the source from which they are derived.

Section V analysed the 2012 decision in *Occidental v Ecuador* in some depth. The tribunal found the termination of a contractual relationship disproportionate

---

[151] F. A. Mann, 'British Treaties for the Promotion and Protection of Investments', *British Yearbook of International Law* 52 (1981) 241–54, at 244.

and in violation of FET. For the reasons outlined in section V, however, this decision does not support the proposition that in exercising contractual rights, States need to comply not only with the text and spirit of a contract but also with the principle of proportionality to avoid liability. While proportionality should not impose an additional burden on States when it comes to the exercise of contractual rights, it bears emphasis that acting disproportionately is not the only way for States to violate the FET standard. Arbitral tribunals have applied the FET standard in a large variety of different factual situations, involving issues of transparency, denial of justice, inconsistent behaviour, coercive treatment, harassment, and procedural propriety.[152] In many cases, proportionality will be of little or no relevance, and a breach of the FET standard may be established without a proportionality analysis.

A last point to mention here is that neither the principle of proportionality nor the concept of systemic integration intrinsically favour the interests of either party to an investor–State arbitration. To recall, under Judge Schwebel's definition of FET, State action must not only comply with standards such as good faith, due process, and nondiscrimination, but also be proportionate.[153] Hence, proportionality offers protections to foreign investors they would not have if the principle of proportionality were irrelevant under the FET standard. On the other hand, the proposition that expectations of foreign investors (even if legitimate) enjoy no absolute protection under FET illustrates that proportionality can also play out to the advantage of host States. The concept of systemic integration is similarly neutral. Let us imagine that a host State seeks to fulfil its human rights obligations with measures that turn out to be disadvantageous for foreign investors. Under such a scenario, the introduction of human rights considerations into the process of balancing under an FET provision might weigh in favour of the host State.[154] However, resort to external rules can also prove to be advantageous for foreign investors. In *Saipem v Bangladesh*, for example, an ICSID tribunal referred to a decision of the ECtHR when it found that an arbitral award could be subject to expropriation.[155] Furthermore, some scholars argue that human rights law could influence the content of the international minimum standard.[156] Another

---

[152] *See, e.g.,* Dugan, et al., 'Investor–State Arbitration', at 507–510, 519–531; McLachlan, et al., *International Investment Arbitration*, paras. 7.80–7.100, 7.115–7.128; Dolzer & Schreuer, *Investment Law*, at 133–49.

[153] *See supra* note 64 and accompanying text.

[154] For a link between human rights and IIA provisions on fair and equitable treatment through Article 31(3)(c) VCLT, *see also* Vinuales, 'Access to Water in Foreign Investment Disputes', at 752–7; Simma & Kill, 'Harmonizing Investment Protection and International Human Rights', at 704.

[155] *Saipem SpA v. The People's Republic of Bangladesh*, ICSID Case No. ARB/05/07, Decision on Jurisdiction and Recommendation on Provisional Measures, 21 March 2007, paras. 130–2.

[156] *See., e.g,* Helmut Philipp Aust & Georg Nolte, 'International Law and the Rule of Law at the National Level', *in Rule of Law Dynamics* (André Nollkaemper, et al. eds., 2012) 48–67, at 63–5; Kingsbury & Schill, 'Investor–State Arbitration as Governance', at 28; McLachlan, *Investment Treaties and General International Law*, at 396–7.

approach seeks to determine FET by a comparative analysis of domestic administrative law systems.[157] To the extent that this analysis yields general principles of law, it may inform the content of FET provisions and result in additional protections for foreign investors in the future—subject to the limits of the concept of systemic integration set out in Chapter 4.

---

[157] Kingsbury & Schill, 'Investor–State Arbitration as Governance', at 27–8; Schill, 'Fair and Equitable Treatment, the Rule of Law, and Comparative Public Law', at 170–4.

7

Proportionality and NPM Clauses:
Article XI of the Argentina–US BIT

An increasing number of IIAs contain exception or NPM clauses permitting measures in the public interest that would otherwise violate the treaty.[1] The values and interests that exception clauses seek to safeguard vary from treaty to treaty. Issues addressed in these clauses include security interests, international peace, public order, health, environmental concerns, labour standards, and the integrity and stability of financial systems and institutions.[2] One of these clauses is part of the most frequently invoked treaty to bring an investor–State arbitration after NAFTA and the ECT: the US–Argentina BIT.[3] Article XI of this treaty states that:

This Treaty shall not preclude the application by either Party of measures necessary for the maintenance of public order, the fulfillment of its obligations with respect to the maintenance or restoration of international peace or security, or the protection of its own essential security interests.

This provision took centre stage in the arbitral proceedings instigated by US investors against Argentina for its emergency measures during the 2001–3 financial crisis. Arbitral tribunals reached different conclusions as to the proper interpretation of this provision, and the resulting divergent decisions fuelled the debate on the legitimacy of the current system of investor–State arbitration.[4] This chapter seeks to shed light on some of the interpretative issues that arose in the context of Article XI. The results of this analysis are not transferrable lock, stock, and barrel to NPM clauses in other treaties, even if worded in a similar or identical way to Article XI. Every NPM clause must be interpreted individually and in line with the

---

[1] UNCTAD, Bilateral Investment Treaties 1995–2006: Trends in Investment Rulemaking (2007), at 81; UNCTAD, World Investment Report 2012, Towards a New Generation of Investment Policies, at 151.

[2] *See, e.g.,* UNCTAD, Bilateral Investment Treaties 1959–1991, at 80–99 and the values and interests listed in Articles 10 and 11 of the 2004 Canadian Model BIT (*available at* <http://ita.law.uvic.ca/documents/Canadian2004-FIPA-model-en.pdf>).

[3] UNCTAD, Recent Developments in Investor–State Dispute Settlement (ISDS), IIA Issues Note, No. 1, at 9.

[4] *See, e.g.,* Burke-White & von Staden, 'Private Litigation in a Public Law Sphere: the Standard of Review in Investor–State Arbitrations', at 299.

interpretative means set out in Article 31 VCLT. Still, many of the considerations in this section will be relevant in the interpretation of other NPM clauses as well.

Section I provides an overview of the jurisprudence of arbitral tribunals and annulment committees that have analysed Article XI. I will then turn, in section II, to the relationship between Article XI and Article 25 ASR,[5] which all tribunals considered to be an accurate reflection of the customary international law defence of necessity. Section III discusses who is to decide whether a particular State measure meets the requirements of Article XI: the State invoking the NPM clause or the arbitral tribunal? The most controversial issue in the context of Article XI is arguably the interpretation of the term 'necessary'. According to one view, this element is to be equated with the 'only way' requirement of Article 25 ASR. This means that Article XI is unavailable when a State has alternative means at its disposal to deal with the relevant situation. These measures may be more expensive and less effective, but as long as they are available a State cannot rely on Article XI. According to a more regulator-friendly view, a measure is 'necessary' as long as the State acts within its 'margin of appreciation'. Section IV analyses these propositions and examines whether the application of the principle of proportionality would be a more appropriate way to interpret and apply the term 'necessary'. Section V deals with the consequences of a successful invocation of Article XI. It analyses whether a State has to compensate foreign investors for measures that meet the requirements of Article XI and for how long a State can rely on Article XI.

I. Arbitral jurisprudence on Article XI of the Argentina–US BIT

The first tribunal to decide on Article XI of the Argentina–US BIT was the *CMS* tribunal. While Argentina argued that this provision was 'self-judging', the tribunal clarified that it was the task of the tribunal to examine whether the requirements of Article XI were fulfilled.[6] The tribunal relied on the *Gabčíkovo* case, in

---

[5] To recall, Article 25 of the ASR reads as follows:
1. Necessity may not be invoked by a State as a ground for precluding the wrongfulness of an act not in conformity with an international obligation of that State unless the act:
   (a) is the only way for the State to safeguard an essential interest against a grave and imminent peril; and
   (b) does not seriously impair an essential interest of the State or States towards which the obligation exists, or of the international community as a whole.
2. In any case, necessity may not be invoked by a State as a ground for precluding wrongfulness if:
   (a) the international obligation in question excludes the possibility of invoking necessity; or
   (b) the State has contributed to the situation of necessity.
[6] *CMS*, Award, paras. 365–74.

which the ICJ held with respect to the requirements of the customary international law defence of necessity that 'the State concerned is not the sole judge of whether those conditions have been met'.[7] The *CMS* tribunal concluded that it had to conduct a 'substantive review', as opposed to a mere 'good faith' review.[8] While the *CMS* tribunal formally distinguished the customary international law defence of necessity from Article XI of the Argentina–US BIT, it conflated the two concepts.[9]

The *CMS* annulment committee severely criticized the reasoning of the arbitral tribunal without annulling the award. The committee found that the tribunal made a 'manifest error of law' by assuming that Article XI of the treaty had the same requirements as Article 25 ASR without analysing the relationship between the two provisions.[10] The committee stressed that Article XI does not share all of the substantive requirements of Article 25. For example, Article XI does not contain a provision similar to Article 25(1)(b) according to which no other essential interest of the other State or the international community as a whole must be seriously impaired.[11] The committee outlined two ways to characterize the relationship between Article XI of the Argentina–US BIT and Article 25 ASR, both of which lead to the conclusion that Article 25 is subsidiary to Article XI. The first approach considers Article 25 to be a primary rule of international law that excludes a breach of the BIT. As Article XI and Article 25 cover the same ground, Article XI, as *lex specialis*, excludes the applicability of Article 25 under this approach.[12]

The second approach considers necessity to be a secondary rule of international law. Accordingly, an arbitral tribunal would first have to clarify whether there has been a violation of a BIT provision. In a second step, the tribunal would have to examine whether Article XI sets in and prevents the violation of an international obligation. If the requirements of Article XI have not been met, a tribunal would still have to consider Article 25 ASR.[13] While the annulment committee did not state which of these two interpretative alternatives it preferred, it found that the *CMS* tribunal might have reached a different result if it had embraced one of the two possible interpretations. Since the tribunal did not do so, it never came to examine the specific requirements of Article XI. The committee concluded that if it 'was acting as a court of appeal, it would have to reconsider the Award on this ground'.[14] However, it held that there was no ground for annulment under Article 52(1)(b) ICSID Convention since the tribunal *did* apply Article XI (even if 'cryptically and defectively').[15]

---

[7] Id., para. 372 referring to *Case concerning the Gabčíkovo–Nagymaros Project* (Hungary v. Slovakia), Judgment, 25 September 1997, ICJ Reports 1997, 7–84, para. 52.

[8] *CMS*, Award, para. 374.

[9] *See* the tribunal's analysis of the customary international law defence of necessity in paras. 315–31 and of Article XI of the Argentina–US BIT in paras. 353–78 (in particular paras. 353 and 357).

[10] *CMS*, Decision of the Annulment Committee, paras. 130–2.

[11] Id., paras. 129–30.   [12] Id., para. 133.   [13] Id., para. 134.

[14] Id., para. 135.   [15] Id., para. 136.

Contrary to the findings of the *CMS* tribunal, the *LG&E* tribunal held that Argentina was 'excused under Article XI from liability' for any breaches of the US–Argentina BIT between 1 December 2001 and 26 April 2003.[16] Without elaborating on the relationship between Article XI and the customary international law defence of necessity, the tribunal stated that Article 25 ASR 'supports the tribunal's conclusion'.[17] Consistent with the findings of the *CMS* tribunal, the *LG&E* tribunal considered Article XI not to be self-judging.[18] The tribunal further found that a severe economic crisis could constitute an 'essential security interest' within the meaning of Article XI. In this regard, it found that '[w]hen a State's economic foundation is under siege, the severity of the problem can equal that of any military invasion'.[19] In concluding that the Argentine financial crisis met this threshold, the tribunal adduced the accelerated deterioration of Argentina's GDP, capital outflows that negatively influenced the Central Bank's liquid reserves, and the unemployment rate.[20] Arguably even more important were the social and political implications of the economic crisis. The tribunal stressed that Argentina had suffered from violent demonstrations and riots to such an extent that 'the country approached anarchy'.[21]

The tribunal then addressed the claimant's argument that the emergency measures were not the 'only means available' to respond to the crisis. Without explicitly clarifying the meaning of the term 'necessary' in Article XI of the Argentina–US BIT, the tribunal alluded to several different standards in its factual analysis. It reasoned that Argentina 'had no choice but to act' and that the suspension of tariff calculation in US dollars and the tariff adjustment according to the producer price index constituted a 'legitimate' approach.[22] It further found that the relevant emergency law as a whole was 'necessary' and 'legitimate'.[23] At one point, the tribunal seemed to restrict its scrutiny to a 'reasonableness' test when it stated that the 'severe devaluation of the peso against the dollar renders the Government's decision to abandon the calculation of tariffs in dollars *reasonable*'.[24]

The next decision of an arbitral tribunal involving Article XI of the Argentina–US BIT was *Enron*. Regarding the relationship between Article XI and the customary international law defence of necessity, the tribunal considered the two provisions to be 'inseparable' since the BIT did not define the various elements of Article XI.[25] Consequently, the tribunal merely deemed it necessary to establish that Article XI of the Argentina–US BIT was not self-judging.[26] Regarding the different elements of Article XI, the tribunal simply pointed to its negative conclusion on Argentina's customary international law defence of necessity.[27] The *Sempra* tribunal reasoned along the same lines as the *Enron* tribunal: it also limited its analysis of Article XI to the lack of its self-judging character.[28] When analysing the relationship between Article XI and Article 25, the tribunal stated that it:

---

[16] *LG&E*, Decision on Liability, paras. 229.   [17] Id., paras. 245, 258.
[18] Id., para. 214.   [19] Id., para. 238.   [20] Id., paras. 232–4.
[21] Id., para. 235.   [22] Id., para. 239.   [23] Id., para. 240.
[24] Id., para. 242 (emphasis added).   [25] *Enron*, Award, para. 334.
[26] Id., paras. 331–9.   [27] Id., para. 339.   [28] *Sempra*, Award, paras. 373–88.

[does not] believe that because Article XI did not make an express reference to customary law, this source of rights and obligations becomes inapplicable. International law is *not a fragmented body of law* as far as basic principles are concerned and necessity is no doubt one such basic principle.[29]

In June and July 2010, ad hoc committees annulled both the *Enron* and the *Sempra* awards, for very different reasons. The *Enron* committee annulled the award on grounds that relate to the customary international law defence of necessity, without commenting on Article XI of the Argentina–US BIT.[30] The *Sempra* annulment committee, in contrast, held that the tribunal wrongly conflated Article XI of the BIT and the customary international law defence of necessity.[31] While this finding was consistent with the *CMS* annulment decision, the *Sempra* committee went one step further: it found that the tribunal's refusal to interpret and apply the different elements of Article XI of the Argentina–US BIT constituted a failure to apply the applicable law.[32] This was sufficient reason for the tribunal to hold that the *Sempra* tribunal 'manifestly exceeded its powers' within the meaning of Article 52(1)(b) ICSID Convention.[33]

The *Continental* tribunal decided on Article XI of the Argentina–US BIT after the *CMS* annulment committee had outlined its understanding of the relationship between this provision and the customary international law defence of necessity. Following this guidance, the *Continental* tribunal interpreted Article XI as a separate treaty provision with elements not identical to those of Article 25.[34] Like all other tribunals dealing with the Argentine financial crisis, the *Continental* tribunal found that the invocation of Article XI of the Argentina–US BIT was not 'self-judging'.[35] Regarding the question whether a particular situation involves issues of 'public order' and 'essential security interests', the tribunal stated that it had to grant a 'significant margin of appreciation' to Argentina.[36] Having found that a severe economic crisis may thus trigger Article XI, the tribunal turned to the interpretation of the term 'necessary' in Article XI.

The tribunal explicitly rejected the view that the term 'necessary' has the same meaning as the 'only way' requirement in Article 25 ASR. Instead, the tribunal reasoned that Article XI was modeled on similar provisions in US treaties on Friendship, Navigation, and Commerce, which in turn reflect the wording of Article XX GATT 1947. Because of this, the tribunal saw fit to base its interpretation of the term 'necessary' in Article XI on the jurisprudence of GATT and WTO adjudicatory bodies on Article XX GATT and Article XIV GATS.[37] As a

---

[29] Id., para. 378 (emphasis added).

[30] *Enron Creditors Recovery Corp. v. Argentine Republic*, ICSID Case No. ARB/01/3, Decision on the Application for Annulment of the Argentine Republic, 30 July 2010, para. 405.

[31] *Sempra Energy International v. Argentine Republic*, ICSID Case No. ARB/02/16, Decision on the Argentine Republic's Application for Annulment of the Award, 29 June 2010, paras. 186–204.

[32] Id., paras. 205–10.   [33] Id., paras. 211–19.

[34] *Continental*, Award, paras. 162–8, with explicit references to the *CMS* annulment decision in n.236 & 239.

[35] Id., paras. 182–8.   [36] Id., para. 181.

[37] Id., para. 192. For a survey of this jurisprudence, *see* Chapter 3, notes 232–58 and accompanying text.

result, the tribunal held that the necessity of measures that are not 'indispensable' is determined by 'a process of weighing and balancing', which takes into account less infringing, alternative measures that are 'reasonably available'.[38] In the application of this standard to the case at hand, the tribunal (at least implicitly) adopted a two-step approach. It first established that Argentina's emergency measures 'contributed materially to the realization of their legitimate aims under Article XI'.[39] In a second step, the tribunal examined whether Argentina would have had less infringing, equally effective alternatives at its disposal.[40] In this regard, the tribunal bifurcated its analysis. It first looked at alternative measures during the emergency situation and then scrutinized whether Argentina could have avoided the crisis at an earlier time. It is crucial to remember that the State measures at issue in *Continental* did not include the changes to the regulatory framework in the public utilities sector. The tribunal had to deal only with the *corralito*, the devaluation of the peso, the pesification of US dollar-denominated debts, and the default, suspension of payment, and rescheduling of financial instruments held by the claimant.[41]

The tribunal found that the *corralito* was necessary to prevent capital flight out of the country since 'consultations and negotiations' did not constitute an 'alternative measure to urgent legislation or administrative action'.[42] Regarding the termination of the pegging of the peso to the US dollar and its devaluation, the tribunal rejected the claimant's submission that a 'voluntary debt exchange' or the 'full dollarization of the economy' would have constituted equally effective and less infringing means reasonably available. The tribunal reasoned that a debt exchange had proved to be ineffective in the past, and that a complete dollarization would have required strong support by the US government.[43] Moreover, the pesification of the dollar-denominated debts would have been a logical consequence of the stark devaluation of the peso. Without this measure, a large number of debtors would have gone bankrupt, and the country would have had to cope with an unsustainable bank 'bail-out'.[44] Hence, the de-dollarization of debts would have ensured a 'balanced distribution of the burden of the devaluation...charged to the entire community'.[45] As mentioned above, the tribunal considered certain parts of the measures related to the financial instruments held by the claimant to be covered by Article XI.[46] Regarding the treasury bills, however, the tribunal found that there was no reason for the claimant to accept the terms of the proposed swap. The tribunal stressed that Argentina offered the swap only in 2004, that its offer would have left the claimant with 30% of the original value of the bills, and that the claimant would have been required to waive other rights.[47]

---

[38] Id., paras. 193–5. The tribunal referred in particular to the cases *Korea-Beef* and *US-Gambling*. For these cases, *see also* Chapter 3, notes 233–43 and accompanying text.

[39] Id., paras. 196–7.   [40] Id., paras. 198–230.

[41] *See* Chapter 6, notes 37–42 and accompanying text.

[42] *Continental*, Award, paras. 204–5.   [43] Id., paras. 208–9.   [44] Id., para. 212.

[45] Id., para. 214.   [46] *See* Chapter 6, notes 40–1 and accompanying text.

[47] *Continental*, Award, para. 221. The tribunal said that Argentina could not rely on Article XI with respect to the treasury bills 'in the light of [these] factors'. But it did not state how this relates

The tribunal also examined whether Argentina could have taken certain measures before the crisis unfolded, instead of adopting the emergency measures later. In this context, the tribunal mentioned that the IMF had asked Argentina to reform its labour market and cut its public spending. While Argentina had not sufficiently adopted the recommended policies, the tribunal acknowledged that Argentina made 'reasonable efforts' appreciated by the IMF.[48] Moreover, even with the benefit of hindsight, there is significant disagreement about which macroeconomic polices would have been the most effective at the time. For example, fiscal austerity can make it more difficult to stimulate the economy. Some claim that such stimulation would have been necessary when the depression started.[49] The tribunal further noted that an earlier default would not have been an equally effective, less infringing means since it would not have left the claimant in a better position.[50] In a later part of its analysis, the tribunal analysed whether 'Argentina [has] contributed to necessity'. In this regard, the tribunal emphasized again that the international financial community and the IMF had welcomed parts of Argentina's political agenda at the time.[51] As, with the benefit of hindsight, the most promising approach to avoid the crisis would have been to act contrary to international advice, the tribunal concluded that Argentina's own conduct did not bar recourse to Article XI.[52] The *Continental* award survived scrutiny by an annulment committee, which neither explicitly embraced nor rejected the reasoning of the tribunal regarding Article XI.[53]

II. The relationship between Article XI and the customary international law defence of necessity

Three possible approaches towards the relationship between Article XI of the US–Argentina BIT and the customary international law defence of necessity arise from the jurisprudence summarized in the previous section. The first approach considers Article XI to be *lex specialis*, which renders the customary international law defence of necessity inapplicable.[54] According to the second approach, Article XI is basically equivalent to the customary international law defence of necessity.[55]

---

to its methodology. Arguably, it considered these factors to be relevant in its process of 'weighing and balancing'.

[48] Id., paras. 223–7.   [49] Id., para. 227 n.342.   [50] Id., paras. 228–30.
[51] Id., para. 234–5.   [52] Id., para. 236.
[53] *Continental*, Decision of the Annulment Committee, paras. 110–43. *See* Chapter 2, note 139 and accompanying text.
[54] This is the first of the interpretative alternatives offered by the *CMS* annulment committee (*see supra* note 1119). Reinisch seems to suggest a similar approach (Reinisch, 'Necessity', at 204–5).
[55] This approach was explicitly adopted by the *Enron* and *Sempra* tribunals (*see supra* notes 25 and 28). The most ardent supporter of this approach is José E. Alvarez, who appeared as an expert witness for the claimants in some of the cases against Argentina (*Sempra Energy International v. Argentine Republic*, ICSID Case No. ARB/02/16, Opinion of José E. Alvarez, 12 August 2005 *available at* <http://ita.law.uvic.ca/documents/Camuzzi_SempraAlvarezOpinion.pdf>). *See also* José E. Alvarez, 'The Return of the State', *Minnesota Journal of International Law* 20 (2011) 223–64, at 242–50, Alvarez & Khamsi, 'The Argentine Crisis', at 427–40. (Arguably sympathetic to

The third approach assumes that Article XI and the customary international law defence of necessity exist and operate independently of each other; one as a primary and the other as a secondary rule of international law.[56]

As the first approach differs from the third only with respect to the question whether Article 25 ASR is available when Article XI fails, it will be discussed in Chapter 8.[57] Regarding the second and the third approach, there is so much divergence of opinion that scholars do not even agree which approach is the predominant one. While Jürgen Kurtz opined in 2010 that the second approach ('confluence') is the 'dominant method', Alec Stone Sweet opined in the same year that this approach has been 'destroyed' by the decisions of the *CMS* annulment committee and the *Continental* tribunal.[58] It seems possible to establish equivalence between Article XI of the US–Argentina BIT and Article 25 ASR in at least two different ways. The first is to consider the two concepts to be interchangeable *ab initio*. The second possibility is to consider Article 25 to be a rule of international law relevant to the interpretation of Article XI as a matter of Article 31(3)(c) VCLT. I will address this second possibility when dealing with the distinct elements of Article XI. Here, it suffices to comment on the first possibility, i.e. Article XI as a mere reference to the customary international law defence of necessity. One of the most basic rules of treaty interpretation is that the words of a treaty matter. In this vein, as early as 1964, Fitzmaurice inferred the following 'principle of effectiveness' from the jurisprudence of the ICJ:

Treaties are to be interpreted with reference to their declared or apparent objects and purposes; and particular provisions are to be interpreted so as to give them their fullest weight

this view: Andrea K. Bjorklund, 'Economic Security Defenses in International Investment Law', *in Yearbook on International Investment Law & Policy 2008–2009* (Karl P. Sauvant ed., 2009) 479–503, at 493–8.) Some scholars have labeled this line of reasoning the 'conflation approach' or the 'method of confluence' (Christina Binder, 'Changed Circumstances in Investment Law: Interfaces Between the Law of Treaties and the Law of State Responsibility with a Special Focus on the Argentine Crisis', *in International Investment Law for the 21st Century—Essays in Honour of Christoph Schreuer* (Christina Binder, et al. eds., 2009) 608–30, at 613; Kurtz, 'Adjudging the Exceptional at International Investment Law', at 343).

[56] This is the second alternative suggested by the *CMS* annulment committee (*see supra* note 13) and the approach adopted by the *Sempra* annulment committee (*see supra* note 32) and the *Continental* tribunal (*see supra* note 34). The following authors support this methodology: Choudhury, 'Exception Provisions as a Gateway to Incorporating Human Rights Issues', at 708; Andreas von Staden, 'Towards Greater Doctrinal Clarity in Investor–State Arbitration', Czech Yearbook of International Law 2 (2011) 207–29, at 225; William W. Burke-White & Andreas von Staden, 'Investment Protection in Extraordinary Times: the Interpretation and Application of Non-Precluded Measures Provisions in Bilateral Investment Treaties', *Virginia Journal of International Law* 48 (2008) 307–410, at 320–4; Binder, 'Changed Circumstances in Investment Law', at 624–8; Kurtz, 'Adjudging the Exceptional at International Investment Law', at 356–9.

[57] *See* Chapter 8, subsection I.2.

[58] Kurtz, 'Adjudging the Exceptional at International Investment Law', at 343; Alec Stone Sweet, 'Investor–State Arbitration: Proportionality's New Frontier', *Law & Ethics of Human Rights* 4 (2010) 47–76, at 75. In 2014, with knowledge of the annulment decisions in *Sempra* and *Enron*, Stone Sweet confirmed his 2010 assessment and stated that the confluence approach (or the 'Orrego Vicuña' approach, named after the arbitrator who chaired the *CMS, Enron*, and *Sempra* tribunals) was 'eviscerated' (Stone Sweet & della Cananea, 'Proportionality, General Principles of Law, and Investor–State Arbitration', at 930).

and effect consistent with the normal sense of the words and with other parts of the text, and in such a way that a reason and a meaning can be attributed to every part of the text.[59]

Scholars understand and employ the 'principle of effectiveness' in a variety of different ways.[60] Richard Gardiner describes one of the more uncontroversial parts of this concept as the 'well-established principle that an interpretation is to be preferred which accords a meaning to every element of a treaty text'.[61] Neither this principle nor Article 31 VCLT forecloses the possibility that Article XI of the Argentina–US BIT ought to be interpreted in light of the customary international law defence of necessity. On the contrary, Article 31 offers different avenues to interpret Article XI consistent with Article 25 ASR, and they will be discussed below. It is incompatible with the rules of treaty interpretation, however, to deprive Article XI of any independent meaning *ab initio*. Nothing in the wording of Article XI suggests that this provision ought to be equated with the customary international law defence of necessity. Indeed, there are considerable textual differences between Article XI of the Argentina–US BIT and Article 25 ASR.[62] First, where Article 25 ASR negatively stipulates that 'necessity may not be invoked' except in narrowly described circumstances, Article XI clarifies that the Argentina–US BIT 'does not preclude' measures necessary for the protection of certain enumerated interests. Second, whereas Article 25 ASR requires that the peril is 'grave and imminent', that the State measure does not 'impair an essential interest' of other States or the international community as a whole, and that the invoking State has not 'contributed to the situation of necessity', such prerequisites are absent from the wording of Article XI.

Moreover, some structural and functional differences speak against equating the two provisions as well. Article 25 ASR will be discussed in depth in Chapter 8 but some remarks on the genesis of this provision and its function within the law of state responsibility are in order here. The ILC worked on the ASR for more than four decades, with F. V. García-Amador as the first Special Rapporteur for this topic (1955–61). García-Amador's focus was primarily on the treatment of aliens and his report contained only a short passage on 'exonerating circumstances'.[63] After García-Amador had left in 1961, the ILC decided not to elaborate on the substantive rules for the treatment of aliens. The focus shifted to more general rules, in particular the consequences of a breach of an international obligation.[64] In 1980, Roberto Ago presented a detailed and comprehensive survey of State

---

[59] ILC, Third report on the law of treaties, by Sir Humphrey Waldock, Special Rapporteur, *Yearbook of the International Law Commission*, Vol. II, 5–65 (1964), at 55, para. 12.

[60] For an extensive analysis, *see* Orakhelashvili, The Interpretation of Acts and Rules in Public International Law, at 392–439.

[61] Gardiner, *Treaty Interpretation*, at 65.

[62] For the text of Article 25, *see* Chapter 1, note 5.

[63] F. V. García Amador, Report on State Responsibility at the 8th Session of the International Law Commission, A/CN.4/96, *Yearbook of the International Law Commission*, Vol. II, 173–231 (1956), Contents (at 173) and paras. 183–91.

[64] James Crawford, *The International Law Commission's Articles on State Responsibility—Introduction, Text and Commentaries* (2002), at 1–2.

practice and scholarly writings on necessity,[65] which resulted in a 1980 draft article on necessity (Article 33). This draft article was already remarkably close to the final version of Article 25,[66] which was adopted in 2001 under the leadership of James Crawford. Since then, the General Assembly has 'welcomed' the ASR and commended them several times 'to the attention of Governments, without prejudice to the question of their future adoption or other appropriate action'.[67] The ICJ (in *Gabčíkovo* and in its *Wall* opinion) and all arbitral tribunals dealing with the Argentine financial crisis considered Article 25 to be an accurate codification of customary international law.[68]

Article 25 is located in Part One, Chapter V of the ASR, entitled 'circumstances precluding wrongfulness'. The function of such 'circumstances precluding wrongfulness' becomes obvious only when put into context with other provisions of the ASR. Article 1 stipulates that an 'internationally wrongful act' of a State entails its 'international responsibility', which is, according to Article 28, the legal consequences set out in Part Two of the ASR (including the obligation to make full reparation (Article 31)). Article 2 defines (a) attribution to the State and (b) a 'breach of an international obligation' as the constituting elements of a 'wrongful act'. A 'breach of an international obligation' in turn is described by Article 12 as an act that is 'not in conformity' with the requirements of a particular obligation, regardless of the source of this obligation. Necessity and the other 'circumstances' mentioned in Part One, Chapter V preclude the 'wrongfulness' of the act. In other words, they exclude the consequences as set out in Part Two by stipulating that there is no 'wrongful act' that would entail the 'responsibility of that State'.

While Article 25 ASR justifies otherwise wrongful conduct, Article XI is an exception clause that caters for emergency situations. This means that there is not even a breach of an international obligation (in the sense of the law of State responsibility) when the requirements of a treaty stipulation such as Article XI are fulfilled. Without such breach, there is no 'internationally wrongful act' (Article 2(b) ASR), which is the basis for an inquiry into whether Article 25 'preclud[es]

---

[65] Roberto Ago, Addendum to Eighth Report on State Responsibility, UN Doc. A/CN.4/318/ ADD.5–7, *Yearbook of the International Law Commission*, Vol. II, 14–51 (1980).

[66] *See* ILC, Report of the International Law Commission on the work of its 32nd session, *Yearbook of the International Law Commission*, Vol. II, Part Two, 30–63 (1980) at p. 34. Apart from some minor stylistic modifications, Article 25 in its final version differs from Article 33 of the 1980 draft articles in two respects. First, Article 25 stipulates in subparagraph 1(b) that the defence of necessity is not only excluded when the act seriously impairs 'an essential interest of the State towards which the obligation existed', but also when the obligation existed towards the 'international community as a whole'. Second, since the Commission decided to include a general provision on peremptory norms (Article 26), the original subparagraph (2)(a), which stipulated that necessity may not be invoked 'if the international obligation with which the act of the State is not in conformity arises out of a peremptory norm of general international law', was deleted.

[67] *See, e.g.*, GA Res. 62/61 of 6 December 2007.

[68] 'Legal Consequences of the Construction of a Wall in the Occupied Palestinian Territory', Advisory Opinion, 9 July 2004, ICJ Reports 2004, 136, para. 140; *Case concerning the Gabčíkovo– Nagymaros Project* (Hungary v. Slovakia), Judgment, 25 September 1997, ICJ Reports 1997, 7–84, paras. 50–52. In *Gabčíkovo*, decided in 1997, the ICJ relied on 1980 version of the draft articles (*see supra* note 66). For the Argentine cases, *see* Chapter 8, note 1.

the wrongfulness' of the relevant State measure. These considerations mirror the clarification of the ILC that 'it is not the function of the articles [on State Responsibility] to specify the content of the obligations laid down by particular primary rules, or their interpretation'.[69] In light of the above, it is difficult to argue that Article XI and Article 25 are functionally and structurally equivalent, even if there might be certain similarities between the two provisions.

Nevertheless, Alvarez and Khamsi opine that the two concepts ought to be equated for historical reasons. They submit that the US had incorporated exception clauses such as Article XI into its BITs only as an 'excess of caution', due to the uncertain status of the customary international law defence of necessity in the 1980s and '90s.[70] In other words, Article XI sought to ensure that the Argentina–US BIT would take account of situations covered by the customary international law defence of necessity (as understood by the US). Alvarez and Khamsi are right when they argue that Article 25 ASR was only adopted in 2001, and therefore does not necessarily reflect the status of customary international law when the Argentina–US BIT was concluded in 1991.[71] However, the 1980 ILC draft articles contained a provision on necessity that was very similar to the final version of Article 25.[72] Alvarez and Khamsi do not explain why the drafters of the US BITs did not mirror or at least approximate the formulation in this provision if they merely intended to codify customary international law.

Alvarez and Khamsi are also right when they point out that the text of Article XI of the Argentina–US BIT was derived from post-WWII FCN clauses, such as Article XX(1) of the Treaty of Amity, Economic Relations, and Consular Rights between the United States and Iran of 15 August 1955.[73] This provision reads in material part as follows:

The present Treaty shall not preclude the application of measures ... (d) necessary to fulfill the obligations of a High Contracting Party for the maintenance or restoration of international peace and security, or necessary to protect its essential security interests.[74]

If the US considered this an accurate codification of the customary law defence of necessity, one would have expected the US to press for a similar wording in Article 33 of the 1980 draft articles (and later in Article 25 ASR).

Still, it is not impossible that Argentina and the US intended to codify the customary international law defence of necessity in Article XI of the Argentina–US BIT. Treaty interpreters might be absolved from analysing the distinct elements of Article XI of the Argentina–US BIT if the US and Argentina had agreed that this provision should follow the status of the customary international law defence

---

[69] ILC, 'Commentaries on State Responsibility', *General Commentary*, para. 4(a).
[70] Alvarez & Khamsi, 'The Argentine Crisis', at 429.
[71] Id., at 428.   [72] *See supra* note 66.
[73] Alvarez & Khamsi, 'The Argentine Crisis', at 428.
[74] *Case concerning Oil Platforms* (Iran v. United States of America), Judgment, 6 November 2003, ICJ Reports 2003, 161, para. 32.

of necessity (see Article 31(4) VCLT). Ascertaining whether such a mutual intent existed at the time requires a complex fact-specific inquiry into the intentions of both Argentina and the United States, which is of little interest for the systemic issues discussed in this book. This chapter analyses Article XI as an independent treaty provision, and determines the relevance of Article 25 according to the interpretative means set out in Article 31 VCLT.

III. Is Article XI of the Argentina–US BIT self-judging?

While the tribunals deciding on Article XI of the US–Argentina BIT assumed that it is not 'self-judging', Burke-White and von Staden argue that this provision is 'implicitly self-judging' and subject to only very limited judicial review.[75] Self-judging clauses allow parties to IIAs to derogate from certain obligations based on their subjective evaluation of the factual and legal situation.[76] This section analyses whether XI is such a self-judging clause, and it proceeds as follows. Subsection 1 deals with the interpretative means listed in Article 31(1) VCLT and ICJ jurisprudence on Article 25 ASR. In light of recent developments in State practice, subsection 2 asks whether there is an emerging rule of customary international law according to which States may—on a self-judging basis—derogate from IIA protections for the sake of certain conflicting interests. Subsection 3 concludes with some observations regarding the treaty practice of the US after *Nicaragua*, which may shed further light on the interpretation of Article XI.

1. Ordinary meaning, context, object, and purpose, and some systemic integration

The wording of Article XI of the US–Argentina BIT does not indicate that this provision is self-judging, but language indicating a self-judging character of certain IIA provision is not foreign to the realm of international investment law. The US–Rwanda BIT and the US–Uruguay BIT (both modeled after the 2004 US Model BIT) contain provisions with clear textual markers for their self-judging character. Article 18(2) of these treaties stipulates that:

Nothing in this Treaty shall be construed...to preclude a Party from applying measures *that it considers* necessary for the fulfillment of its obligations with respect to the

---

[75] Burke-White & von Staden, 'Investment Protection in Extraordinary Times', at 381–6.

[76] *See, e.g.,* Stephan W. Schill & Robyn Briese, '"If the State Considers": Self-Judging Clauses in International Dispute Settlement', *Max Planck Yearbook of United Nations Law* 13 (2009) 61–140, at 68. On good-faith review with respect to Article XI, *see* Burke-White & von Staden, 'Investment Protection in Extraordinary Times', at 377. For a survey on the jurisprudence of international adjudicatory bodies with respect to self-judging clauses, *see* Schill & Briese, '"If the State Considers"', at 96–118.

maintenance or restoration of international peace or security, or the protection of its own essential security interests.[77]

This provision differs from Article XI of the 1991 Argentina–US BIT in two crucial respects. First, Article 18(2) contains a clear textual marker ('that it considers') limiting the scope of judicial review. Second, Article 18(2) omits the 'public order' of the host State from the list of interests for which States may resort to the NPM clause. The 'public order' element is particularly controversial and open to extensive interpretation.[78] Coupled with a self-judging exception clause, the notion of 'public order' would significantly undermine the substantive protections enshrined in an IIA. It is, therefore, probably no coincidence that the US dropped 'public order' from its explicitly self-judging exception clause. While this weighs against a self-judging character of Article XI, *e contrario* arguments based on a different wording in a subsequent treaty should be handled with great care. Nevertheless, one can probably say that the mere wording of Article 18(2) of the US Model BIT, and the provisions modeled after it, do no offer much support for a self-judging character of Article XI. The best point one can make in favour of the self-judging character of Article XI on the sole basis of the 'ordinary meaning' of its terms seems to be that the provision is silent on the degree of judicial review.

The context of the treaty terms and the object and purpose of the Argentina BIT appear to speak against a self-judging quality being assigned to Article XI. Article VII of the same treaty provides for arbitration in the case of a dispute regarding 'any right conferred or created' by this treaty. It is hard to see why Article XI should be treated differently from the other provisions in this treaty and be exempt from neutral third-party adjudication. The controversy about the object and purpose of BITs, and in particular that of the Argentina–US BIT, has been addressed above.[79] Even the more 'regulator-friendly' notion (according to which the object and purpose of this treaty go beyond the mere protection of private property rights) does not militate for a self-judging character of Article XI. The notion that an IIA seeks to accommodate several (possibly diverging) interests enhances the importance of neutral third-party adjudication. A neutral third party is in a better position than the contracting States to avoid intrinsically favouring any of the interests involved.

While there are significant differences between Article 25 ASR and Article XI of the Argentina–US BIT, these provisions share some important

---

[77] Chapter 5, notes 68, 71, and 72 (emphasis added). The 2012 Model BIT (Chapter 5, note 68) contains the same provision.

[78] For the interpretation of the term 'public order' in the jurisprudence of tribunals in the Argentine financial crisis, *see, e.g., Continental*, Award, paras. 171–4. On the debate about the interpretation of this term in general, *see* Alvarez & Khamsi, 'The Argentine Crisis', at 449–55 (for a narrow interpretation) and Burke-White & von Staden, 'Investment Protection in Extraordinary Times', at 357–61 (for a wider interpretation associating the term 'public order' with the police powers doctrine).

[79] Chapter 5, subsection V.3 (especially Chapter 5, note 179 and accompanying text).

characteristics and features. First, both provisions recognize that the public interest may require action that runs counter to the obligations under certain treaty provisions. Second, both provisions prevent a State from suffering the legal consequences that run from an internationally wrongful act. Hence, it is arguable that Article 25 ASR constitutes a rule of international law that is 'relevant' for the interpretation of Article XI according to Article 31(3)(c) VCLT.[80] This alone, however, says little about the normative weight that ought to be accorded to Article 25 in the interpretation of Article XI. It is submitted that this weight depends on the degree of textual, structural, and functional similarity between the two provisions and on whether other interpretative means militate for an interpretation different from the one suggested by Article 25. The ICJ held in *Gabčíkovo–Nagymaros* with respect to customary international law that:

the state of necessity can only be invoked under certain strictly defined conditions which must be cumulatively satisfied; *and the State concerned is not the sole judge* of whether those conditions have been met.[81]

Regarding the scope of judicial review, it is therefore irrelevant what normative weight out to be given to Article 25 ASR in the interpretation of Article XI. Both ICJ jurisprudence on Article 25 and the interpretative means listed in Article 31(1) VCLT speak against a self-judging character of Article XI.

2. Self-judging exceptions to IIA protections: an emerging rule of customary international law?

IIAs increasingly include exception clauses, some of which are explicitly self-judging. If there were an (emerging) rule of customary international law according to which States could derogate from IIA obligations on a self-judging basis to protect certain interests, then this might be relevant to the interpretation of Article XI as a matter of Article 31(3)(c) VCLT.[82] As already mentioned, more recent IIAs and Model BITs tend to put greater emphasis on public policy considerations than older IIAs.[83] Article 18(2) of the US–Rwanda and US–Uruguay BITs, modeled after Article 18(2) of the 2004 US Model BIT, is an example of a self-judging clause regarding the maintenance or restoration of international peace or security and the protection of the essential security interests of the host State.[84] In a similar vein, Article IX(5) of the BIT between Canada and the Czech Republic stipulates that:

---

[80] For the general methodology in this respect, *see* Chapter 4, notes 190–201 and accompanying text.

[81] *Case concerning the Gabčíkovo–Nagymaros Project* (Hungary v. Slovakia), Judgment, 25 September 1997, ICJ Reports 1997, 7–84, para. 51 (emphasis added).

[82] For the intricate relationship between IIAs, Model BITs, and the rules of customary international law, *see* Chapter 5, notes 239–75 and accompanying text.

[83] *See* Chapter 5, subsections III.3, V.2, V.3, and V.5.a.

[84] On this provision, *see supra* notes 77–8 and accompanying text.

[n]othing in this Agreement shall be construed:

(a) to require any Contracting Party to furnish or allow access to any information the disclosure of which *it determines* to be contrary to its essential security interests;

(b) to prevent any Contracting Party from taking any actions that it *considers necessary* for the protection of its essential security interests:

   (i) relating to the traffic in arms, ammunition and implements of war and to such traffic and transactions in other goods, materials, services and technology undertaken directly or indirectly for the purpose of supplying a military or other security establishment,

   (ii) taken in time of war or other emergency in international relations, or

   (iii) relating to the implementation of national policies or international agreements respecting the non-proliferation of nuclear weapons or other nuclear explosive devices[.][85]

Article XVII(6)(a) and (b) of the Canada–Latvia BIT and Article 10(4)(a) and (b) of the 2004 Canadian Model BIT contain the same provisions with the explicitly self-judging language ('which it determines'; 'that it considers necessary').[86]

That said, Article IX of the Canada–Czech Republic BIT, Article XVII of the Canada–Latvia BIT, and Article 10 of the Canadian Model BIT posit a whole array of 'general exceptions'. To assume that all of these exceptions are equally self-judging would be contrary to the nuanced and careful drafting of these provisions. Article IX(1) of the Canada–Czech Republic BIT, for example, contains a clause that resorts to the term 'necessary' as nexus requirement but lacks the self-judging element of Article X(5)(a) and (b). This provision states that:

nothing in this Agreement shall be construed to prevent a Contracting Party from adopting or enforcing measures *necessary*:

(a) to protect human, animal or plant life or health;

(b) to ensure compliance with laws and regulations that are not inconsistent with the provisions of this Agreement; or

(c) for the conservation of living or non-living exhaustible natural resources.[87]

A different formulation with respect to the means–end relationship and the applicable standard of review can be found in Article IX(2) of the Canada–Czech Republic BIT. This provision explicitly allows for '*reasonable measures for prudential reasons*' such as the 'protection of investors, depositors, financial market participants', 'the maintenance of the safety . . . of financial institutions', or the 'stability of a Party's financial system'.[88] Furthermore, the treaties based on the 2004 Canadian Model BIT contain detailed descriptions of the means–end relationship and applicable standard of review for transfer restrictions to cope with 'serious balance of payment difficulties'. Article IX(3)

---

[85] Chapter 5, note 77 (emphases added).   [86] Chapter 5, notes 69 and 75.

[87] Article XVII(2) of the Canada–Latvia BIT and Article 10(1) of the Canadian Model BIT contain the same provisions (emphasis added).

[88] *See also* Article XVII(3) of the Canada–Latvia BIT, and Article 10(2) of the Canadian Model BIT (emphasis added).

(b) of the Canada–Czech Republic BIT, for example, provides that the relevant State measures:

shall be equitable, neither arbitrary nor unjustifiably discriminatory, in good faith, of limited duration and *may not go beyond what is necessary* to remedy the balance of payments situation.[89]

The ASEAN–ANZ FTA also contains a significant number of exception clauses.[90] Article 1(2) of Chapter 15, for example, declares Article XIV of GATS (which is not self-judging) to be part of the agreement for the purposes of its provisions on trade in services, movement of natural persons, *and* investment.[91] In contrast, Article 2 of Chapter 2 of the ASEAN–ANZ FTA contains self-judging security exceptions reminiscent of the stipulations in the Canadian Model BIT.[92] With respect to other measures in the public interest, however, the exceptions mentioned in this chapter lack such self-judging elements. Article 1(4), for example, allows for

[m]easures *necessary* to protect national treasures or specific sites of historical or archaeological value or measures *necessary* to support creative arts of national value.[93]

We have seen that more recent US BITs contain self-judging exception clauses for measures related to peace and security.[94] The same treaties include exception clauses for environmental and labour concerns that are explicitly self-judging. Article 12(2) of the 2004 US Model BIT, the US–Rwanda BIT, and the US–Uruguay BIT states that:

Nothing in this Treaty shall be construed to prevent a Party from adopting, maintaining, or enforcing any measure otherwise consistent with this Treaty that *it considers appropriate* to ensure that investment activity in its territory is undertaken in a manner sensitive to environmental concerns.[95]

Article 13(2) of these treaties contains the same stipulation for labour concerns.[96] This does not mean that BITs that follow the example of the 2004 US Model BIT contain only

---

[89]   *See also* Article XVII(4)(b) of the Canada–Latvia BIT (emphasis added).

[90]   Chapter 5, note 81.   [91]   Chapter 5, note 81.

[92]   The most relevant passages of this Article read as follows:

Nothing in this Agreement shall be construed:
(a) to require any Party to furnish any information the disclosure of which *it considers contrary* to its essential security interests;
(b) to prevent any Party from taking any action which *it considers necessary* for the protection of its essential security interests:
   (i)   relating to fissionable materials or the materials from which they are derived;...
   (iv) taken in time of national emergency or war or other emergency in international relations (emphases added).

[93]   Emphasis added. *See also* the detailed guidelines for judicial review in Article 4(2) for measures adopted 'in serious balance of payments and external financial difficulties' (Article 4(1)).

[94]   *See supra* note 77 and accompanying text.

[95]   Chapter 5, notes 68, 71, and 72. The 2012 US Model BIT (Chapter 5, note 68) contains the same clause in Article 12(5).

[96]   The wording of Article 13(2) of the 2004 US Model BIT, the US–Rwanda BIT, and the US–Czech Republic BIT is identical to the wording of Article 12(2), with the only exception that the term 'environmental' is replaced by the term 'labor'.

self-judging exception clauses. Article 8(3)(c) of the US–Rwanda (and the US–Uruguay) BIT, for example, provides for certain exceptions to the prohibition of so-called 'performance requirements' that are similar to the GATT exception clauses discussed in Chapter 3, subsection III.1.b. Article 8(3)(c) states that certain stipulations in this article 'shall not be construed to prevent a Party from adopting or maintaining measures, including environmental measures:

(i)   *necessary* to secure compliance with laws and regulations that are not inconsistent with this Treaty;
(ii) *necessary* to protect human, animal, or plant life or health; or
(iii) related to the conservation of living or non-living exhaustible natural resources'.[97]

All the of the above indicates that recent State practice is far from being consistent regarding exception clauses and the relevant level of judicial scrutiny. In addition, some of the more recent IIAs do not contain exception clauses at all. In conclusion, there does not seem to be a rule of customary international law according to which exception clauses in BITs are self-judging that could be relevant to the interpretation of Article XI of the US–Argentina BIT.

3. Lessons from *Nicaragua v United States*

While the analysis so far speaks against the conclusion that Article XI of the Argentina–US BIT is self-judging, an analysis along the lines of Article 31(4) VCLT might establish a different result. It is arguably in this context that the arguments put forward by Burke-White and von Staden matter most. The two authors allege that the US has always considered exception clauses in BITs (and similar treaties) to be self-judging, at least since 1986.[98] One of their key arguments is the position taken by the US government in the *Nicaragua* case before the ICJ. In that case, the US argued that Article XXI(1)(d) of the 1956 FCN Treaty between the United States and Nicaragua was self-judging. The provision reads as follows:

The present Treaty shall not preclude the application of measures... *necessary* to fulfill the obligations of a Party for the maintenance or restoration of international peace and security, or *necessary* to protect its essential security interests.[99]

This provision is obviously very similar to Article XI of the Argentina–US BIT and does not contain a textual marker regarding its allegedly self-judging character either. It does not automatically follow, however, that the US indeed expected Article XI to be self-judging when it signed the BIT with Argentina in 1991. In the *Nicaragua* case, decided in 1986, the ICJ explicitly rejected the argument of the US that the security exception clause of the 1956 treaty

---

[97] Emphases added. *See also* Article 8(3)(c) of the 2004 US Model BIT.
[98] Burke-White & von Staden, 'Investment Protection in Extraordinary Times', at 381.
[99] *Case concerning Military and Paramilitary Activities in and against Nicaragua* (Nicaragua v. United States of America), Judgment, Merits, 27 June 1986, ICJ Reports 1986, 4, para. 221 (emphases added).

was self-judging. Shortly after the *Nicaragua* judgment, there was apparently significant discussion within the US government regarding its future policy on security exceptions in bilateral treaties.[100] As a result, the protocol to the BIT with Russia signed in 1992 explicitly declared an exception clause that was very similar to Article XI of the Argentina–US BIT to be self-judging.[101] While this treaty never entered into force, the great number of BITs concluded by the US in the early 1990s lack such a clarification. Moreover, there appears to be no other evidence that the US communicated an understanding that NPM clauses would be self-judging to any of its other BIT partners.[102] Rather, the inactivity of the US after the *Nicaragua* judgment suggests that the US did not want to resolve the tension between robust protection of its own investors abroad and its efforts to avoid liability vis-à-vis foreign investors at home solely in favour of the latter. The US–Egypt BIT (which entered into force on 27 June 1992) illustrates that the US knew precisely how to draft self-judging clauses. Article X of this treaty stipulates that:

This Treaty shall not preclude the application by either Party or any political or adminis-trative subdivision thereof of any and all measures necessary for the maintenance of public order and morals, the fulfillment of its existing international obligations, the protection of its own security interests, or such measures *deemed appropriate* by the Parties to fulfill future international obligations.[103]

Moreover, it is not sufficient for the purposes of Article 31(4) VCLT that the US intended Article XI of the Argentina–US BIT to be self-judging. Rather, it would be necessary for Argentina to have agreed with this notion when the treaty was concluded. The mere fact that Argentina argues today that Article XI ought to be self-judging is irrelevant for the purposes of Article 31(4) VCLT. Argentina and the US are free, of course, to reach an agreement (within the meaning of Article 31(3)(a) VCLT) on the self-judging character of Article XI without renegotiating the BIT. To date, this has not happened (to the best of the author's knowledge).

In sum, Article XI of the Argentina–US BIT should not be considered to be self-judging as long as no additional facts or insights require a re-evaluation of this interpretation on the basis of Article 31(3) or (4) VCLT. The same is true for other NPM clauses that resemble Article XI of the Argentina–US BIT and lack the explicitly self-judging language of Article 18(2) of the US Model BIT.

---

[100] Kenneth J. Vandevelde, 'Of Politics and Markets: the Shifting Policy of the BITs', *International Tax and Business Lawyer* 11 (1993) 159–86, at 172–3.

[101] Protocol to the US–Russia BIT, 31 I.L.M. (1992) 809–12, at 811, para. 9.

[102] Vandevelde, 'Of Politics and Markets', at 173.

[103] US–Egypt BIT, *available at* <http://investmentpolicyhub.unctad.org/Download/Treaty File/1123>.

IV. The nexus requirement: 'only way', 'margin of appreciation', or proportionality analysis?

One of the most controversial aspects of the arbitral jurisprudence on the Argentine financial crisis is the interpretation of the nexus requirement in Article XI of the Argentina–US BIT. In other words, when exactly is a State measure 'necessary' for the maintenance or protection of one of the interests listed in Article XI? Does it have to be the *only means* to cope with the situation or is it sufficient if it is the *least restrictive means* available? Another possibility would be to consider all State measures 'necessary' that fall within the host State's *margin of appreciation*. Arbitral tribunals have employed some of these standards and all of them find support in legal scholarship.[104] In 2010, Stone Sweet proposed applying the principle of proportionality to determine whether a certain measure is 'necessary' within the meaning of Article XI.[105] Stone Sweet's analysis focused on the policy rationales for the application of this principle in the realm of NPM clauses.[106] This section examines which of the different approaches is the most appropriate as a matter of treaty interpretation.

According to Article 31(1) VCLT, the starting point of the analysis is the ordinary meaning of the term 'necessary'. In this regard, it is probably not possible to say much more than that the term lies on a 'continuum', ranging from 'making a contribution to' to 'indispensable', and that it is 'located significantly closer to the pole of indispensable'.[107] The context of the term 'necessary' and the object and purpose of the Argentina–US BIT do not add much further clarity. Some might argue that if BITs have the sole purpose of protecting private property rights, then any exception clause within them ought to be interpreted narrowly. As explained above, however, the object and purpose of BITs is controversial, and it is unclear whether the protection of private property rights is the sole purpose of the Argentina–US BIT.[108] Regarding the purpose of NPM clauses, US BIT negotiator Vandevelde observed that the relevant provision in the 1983 Model BIT (which was in material part identical to Article XI of the Argentina–US BIT) was meant to strike a 'delicate balance' between maintaining flexibility for the US and ensuring a certain level of protection for its nationals investing abroad.[109] This comment suggests that neither an overly narrow nor an overly wide interpretation of Article XI is appropriate.

---

[104] *See* Alvarez & Khamsi, 'The Argentine Crisis', at 427–49 ('only way'); Kurtz, 'Adjudging the Exceptional at International Investment Law', at 365–70 ('least restrictive means test'); Burke-White & von Staden, 'Private Litigation in a Public Law Sphere', at 334–9 ('margin of appreciation').

[105] Stone Sweet, 'Investor–State Arbitration', at 67–76.

[106] *See*, in particular, id., at 75–76. In 2014, Stone Sweet buttressed his argument with a reference to Article 31(3)(c) VCLT and proportionality as a general principle of law (Stone Sweet & della Cananea, 'Proportionality, General Principles of Law, and Investor–State Arbitration', at 938).

[107] *See* Chapter 3, note 235 and accompanying text.   [108] *See* Chapter 5, subsection V.3.

[109] Kenneth J. Vandevelde, *United States International Investment Agreements* (2009), at 220.

In light of the above, the interpretative means listed in Article 31(1) and (2) VCLT seem to provide only very limited guidance on the interpretation of the term 'necessary' in Article XI. Furthermore, there is no subsequent agreement between the US and Argentina on the interpretation of the nexus requirement in Article XI. As outlined above, subsequent treaty practice is too diverse to offer useful insights regarding the interpretation of Article XI.[110] The following three subsections will examine whether Article 25 ASR, the margin of appreciation doctrine as developed by the ECtHR, or the principle of proportionality may inform the reading of the term 'necessary' in Article XI pursuant to Article 31(3)(c) VCLT.

1. Equating 'necessary' in Article XI of the Argentina–US BIT with the 'only way' requirement of Article 25 ASR?

Alvarez and others argue that the term 'necessary' in Article XI should be equated with the 'only way' requirement in Article 25 ASR by operation of Article 31(3)(c) VCLT.[111] It is arguable that the customary international law defence of necessity is a rule of international law that is 'relevant' in the interpretation of Article XI.[112] Accepting that Article 25 is relevant, however, does not clarify the normative weight that ought to be accorded to this provision in the interpretation of the term 'necessary'. Factors that should be taken into account in determining this normative weight include the textual, structural, and functional similarities between the two provisions, and the compatibility of the 'only way' requirement with the solutions suggested by the other interpretative means listed in Article 31.

As demonstrated above, Article XI and Article 25 share some similarities. Both provisions cater for situations in which the public interest requires action that may contradict obligations under certain treaty provisions. Furthermore, if invoked successfully, both provisions allow a State to avoid the legal consequences of an internationally wrongful act as set out in Part Two of the ASR.[113] But there are also significant differences between the two provisions, discussed in section II above.[114] For example, Article 25 is only available if the relevant State measure does not seriously impair an essential interest of the State towards which the obligation exists, or of the international community as a whole. There are also structural and functional differences between the two provisions. While the customary international law defence of necessity justifies an otherwise wrongful conduct, Article XI excludes a treaty violation.

As noted above, Vandevelde, one of the veterans of the US BIT programme, states that the purpose of exception clauses such as Article XI of the Argentina–US BIT is to ensure a certain 'balance' between the public interest and the rights

---

[110] *See supra* subsection III.2.
[111] Alvarez & Khamsi, 'The Argentine Crisis', at 437; Alvarez & Brink, 'Revisiting the Necessity Defence', at 333–5.
[112] *See supra* notes 80–1 and accompanying text.   [113] *See* text preceding note 80.
[114] *Supra* notes 62–69 and accompanying text.

of foreign investors.[115] It is difficult to see how this purpose could be accomplished when the term 'necessary' is equated with the 'only way' requirement of Article 25. The 'only way' requirement negates the necessity defence when *any* other means are available to cope with a particular situation, even if these means are more costly and possibly less effective.[116] All tribunals dealing with disputes arising out of the Argentine crisis agreed that an economic crisis may—in principle—trigger Article XI and/or Article 25 (even though they disagreed whether the situation in Argentina was severe enough to meet this threshold). In most economic crises host States have more than one means at their disposal to react to the crisis. Hence, equating the term 'necessary' with the 'only way' requirement would render Article XI meaningless in an economic context.[117]

As seen in Chapter 3, a significant number of domestic and international bodies outside the realm of investor–State arbitration have interpreted provisions that allow for certain measures 'necessary' for the protection of the public interest. None of them found that the relevant provision is unavailable when the State had *any* other means at its disposal, regardless of the costs and effectiveness of this alternative measure. This does not mean that the interpretation of Article XI of the Argentina–US BIT cannot lead to a different result. Still, the proposition that the host State cannot rely on Article XI when there is *any* other (even if more costly and less effective) way to act should not be adopted too readily. It bears emphasis that this proposition relies on the particular wording of Article 25 ASR ('only way'). Alvarez and Khamsi criticize that the *CMS* annulment committee put too much emphasis on the 'black letter formulations' of Article 25 when finding that the customary international law defence of necessity differs from Article XI.[118] The 'only way' requirement is probably the most distinctive and rigid element among the 'black letter formulations' of Article 25.[119] It comes as a surprise that Alvarez and Khamsi seek to read precisely this formulation into Article XI—despite their criticism of the 'false authoritativeness' of the text of Article 25.[120]

In sum, the findings in this subsection speak against equating the term 'necessary' with the 'only way' requirement. These considerations might be irrelevant if Argentina and the US intended to give a 'special meaning' to the term 'necessary' to the effect that a State measure is not 'necessary' if it is not the 'only way' to act (see Article 31(4) VCLT). Ascertaining such an intent of both Argentina and the United States at the time of the conclusion of the treaty is a fact-intensive exercise. Only the State parties or arbitral tribunals in possession of the relevant material are in a position to decide whether a corresponding intent existed when the treaty was concluded.

---

[115] *See supra* note 109.   [116] *See* Chapter 8, note 109 and accompanying text.

[117] For the unavailability of the customary international law defence of necessity in economic crises as a result of the 'only way' requirement, *see* Chapter 8, subsection II.3.

[118] Alvarez & Khamsi, 'The Argentine Crisis', at 436.

[119] *See also* Chapter 8, subsection II.3.

[120] Alvarez & Khamsi, 'The Argentine Crisis', at 436.

2. Transferring the margin of appreciation doctrine of the ECtHR to Article XI of the Argentina–US BIT?

While Alvarez and Khamsi rely on Article 25 ASR, Burke-White and von Staden refer to another external concept for the interpretation of the term 'necessary' in Article XI of the Argentina–US BIT. They argue that arbitral tribunals should apply the 'margin of appreciation' doctrine as developed by the ECtHR.[121] Burke-White and von Staden describe the margin of appreciation as a 'tool of judicial deference and self-restraint' that acknowledges that there will often be several ways to meet the requirements stipulated in a particular provision. In such cases, it would be 'first and foremost' for the domestic authorities to decide which measure to adopt.[122] Investor–State tribunals, in contrast, are ill-positioned to review governmental decisions since they are 'physically, politically, culturally, and socially' too far away.[123]

As a prefacing remark, it should be noted that the precise contours of the margin of appreciation doctrine and its relationship to the principle of proportionality are unclear.[124] Burke-White and von Staden state that the margin of appreciation doctrine is a

deferential standard of review according to which a panel will abstain from engaging in strict scrutiny of the facts of the situation and of the appraisal of these facts by the competent state authorities, to the extent that the respondent state has considered such facts in a non-biased manner and has drawn conclusions from it that pass muster under a reasonableness test.[125]

This approach is attractive at first glance. However, several caveats are necessary. From a doctrinal viewpoint, it is unclear why a concept developed by the ECtHR (for the interpretation of the ECHR) should be relevant for the interpretation of a treaty between Argentina and the US. To the best of my knowledge, the ECtHR has never claimed that the margin of appreciation doctrine constitutes a rule of customary international law or a general principle of law (within the meaning of Article 38(1)(c) ICJ Statute). The tribunal in *Siemens v Argentina* explicitly held that the margin of appreciation doctrine does *not* form part of customary international law.[126]

Still, if there were convincing policy rationales for the application of the margin of appreciation doctrine, arbitral tribunals might feel inclined to refer to this doctrine as an inspirational source. Several considerations go against such an

---

[121]   Burke-White & von Staden, 'The Need for Public Law Standards of Review in Investor–State Arbitrations', at 715–19; Burke-White & von Staden, 'Private Litigation in a Public Law Sphere', at 334–44; Burke-White & von Staden, 'Investment Protection in Extraordinary Times', at 370–5.

[122]   Burke-White & von Staden, 'Investment Protection in Extraordinary Times', at 374.

[123]   Id., at 372–3.

[124]   *See, e.g.,* Burke-White & von Staden, 'The Need for Public Law Standards of Review', at 702–3.

[125]   Id., p 705.

[126]   *Siemens AG v. Argentine Republic*, ICSID Case No. ARB/02/8, Award, 6 February 2007, para. 354.

approach. First, even in the context of the ECHR, the margin of appreciation doctrine is controversial. Judge de Meyer, for example, harshly criticized this doctrine in his partial dissent in *Z v Finland*:

The empty phrases concerning the State's margin of appreciation—repeated in the Court's judgments for too long already—are unnecessary circumlocutions, serving only to indicate abstrusely that the States may do anything the Court does not consider incompatible with human rights. Such terminology, as wrong in principle as it is pointless in practice, should be abandoned without delay.[127]

In a similar vein, Jeffrey A. Brauch identified the margin of appreciation doctrine as a 'threat to the rule of law'.[128] One of the reasons why scholars advocate a transfer of this doctrine from the ECHR to the realm of general international law is the hope for 'compliance-pull'.[129] In the field of investor–State arbitration, however, compliance is not so much an issue as it is in other areas of international law, mainly because of the availability of effective enforcement mechanisms.[130] Furthermore, the rationale of the margin of appreciation doctrine is closely linked to the heterogeneity of the legal frameworks and policy preferences of the 47 member states of the ECHR. The ECtHR grants a wider margin of appreciation if there is little common ground between the member States on a particular issue.[131] As Burke-White and von Staden point out, there is, for instance, insufficient agreement among the 47 members of the ECHR on the substantive content of 'morality'. Consequently, the member States enjoy a rather wide margin of appreciation when they regulate the freedom of expression for the 'protection of morals' based on Article 10(2) ECHR.[132] In the context of investor–State arbitrations involving a *bilateral* investment treaty, this rationale for the application of the margin of appreciation doctrine applies to a much lesser extent.

Another argument in support of the margin of appreciation doctrine is the assumption that courts would consider an issue only in the context of a specific dispute. Governments, on the other hand, tend to constantly monitor a particular development and accommodate short-term and long-term interests in their policies to ensure the best overall result.[133] This consideration should certainly carry weight in the context of inward-looking norms, i.e. norms that regulate the relationship between States and their own constituencies. Most human rights treaties contain restrictions that reflect a careful balance between the rights of individuals

---

[127] *Z v. Finland*, ECtHR, Reports 1997-I, Judgment (Merits and Just Satisfaction), 25 February 1997, at 358.

[128] Brauch, 'The Margin of Appreciation and the Jurisprudence of the European Court of Human Rights: Threat to the Rule of Law'.

[129] Yuval Shany, 'Toward a General Margin of Appreciation Doctrine in International Law', *European Journal of International Law* 16 (2005) 907–40, at 919.

[130] *See* Chapter 2, section III.

[131] Burke-White & von Staden, 'The Need for Public Law Standards of Review', at 702; Stone Sweet & Mathews, 'Proportionality Balancing', at 152.

[132] Burke-White & von Staden, 'The Need for Public Law Standards of Review', at 702. For the text of Article 10(2) of the ECHR, *see* Chapter 3, note 200.

[133] Shany, 'Toward a General Margin of Appreciation Doctrine', at 918.

and the interests of the national community. As members of a national community, individuals are the beneficiaries of restrictions put on the human rights and freedoms of others in the interest of society a whole. This line of thought applies to the relationship between foreign investors and host States only to a limited extent. Often, the interests of foreign investors at stake in the context of clauses such as Article XI of the Argentina–US BIT are adverse to the host State's interests with little prospect of a future trade-off. The ECtHR expressed a similar idea in *James*, when it found that 'non-nationals are more vulnerable to domestic legislation' and that 'there may well be legitimate reason for requiring nationals to bear a greater burden in the public interest than non-nationals'.[134]

Burke-White and von Staden's main reason for transferring the margin of appreciation doctrine to NPM clauses is to promote the 'legitimacy' of investor–State arbitration 'by returning national authorities to the center of decisionmaking'.[135] They do not argue that domestic courts should decide international investment disputes and not arbitral tribunals. Still, the claim that tribunals should defer to the decisions of domestic actors raises the question of whether domestic actors are indeed in a more 'legitimate' position to resolve conflicts between the interests of foreign investors and host States. Burke-White and von Staden stress the greater 'democratic legitimization' of domestic government institutions.[136] One may wonder whether a decision necessarily becomes more democratic simply because it is taken at a lower level. Rather, what appears to matter for the democratic legitimacy of a decision is that all stakeholders have been involved in the decision-making process.[137] In other words, it is of little avail in terms of democratic legitimacy if a decision is taken by a democratic entity if some of the principal stakeholders affected by the decision have no influence on the decision-making process.[138] Foreign investors are major stakeholders in international investment disputes, and are typically not involved in the decision making. Moreover, other stakeholders might live outside the borders of the host State, and may, therefore, be excluded from its democratic processes. This is, for example, true of neighbouring

---

[134] *See supra* note 117.

[135] Burke-White & von Staden, 'Private Litigation in a Public Law Sphere', at 339.

[136] Burke-White & von Staden, 'The Need for Public Law Standards of Review', at 714–15.

[137] Andreas L. Paulus, 'Subsidiarity, Fragmentation and Democracy: Towards the Demise of General International Law?', *in The Shifting Allocation of Authority in International Law* (Tomer Broude & Yuval Shany eds., 2008) 193–213, at 204–6. Mattias Kumm argues in a similar vein. He states that international law enjoys a presumption of legitimacy because it is the law of the international community and therefore 'deserves the respect of citizens in liberal constitutional democracies' (Mattias Kumm, 'The Legitimacy of International Law: a Constitutionalist Framework of Analysis', *European Journal of International Law* 15 (2004) 907–31, at 918). This presumption can be rebutted by certain normative considerations. One of these is the principle of subsidiarity, which requires a justification why a particular issue is more appropriately addressed on the international than on the domestic level (id., at 921–3). Kumm emphasizes that a typical justification for the handling of a matter on the international level is the involvement of outsiders (id., at 923).

[138] For a rather drastic but illustrative example, *see* Paulus, 'Subsidiarity, Fragmentation and Democracy', at 204: Palestinians in the West Bank not represented in the Knesset will not perceive a decision of this body on their treatment as 'democratic' simply because the Knesset is democratically elected.

communities that are affected by a host State's environmental measures (be it in a positive or negative way).

There are further reasons to see the democratic legitimacy of investor–State arbitration in a more positive light. The legitimacy of international law is regularly questioned on the basis of a democratic deficit on the international level.[139] Mattias Kumm rightly notes that these concerns should carry less weight in a treaty context as ratification through national parliaments provides a certain amount of democratic legitimacy.[140] The situation becomes more complex if international treaties create new lawmaking international institutions whose decisions directly affect individuals. The treaties establishing the European Communities, and later the European Union, granted far-reaching lawmaking powers to the European Council and the European Commission. Despite a gradual increase in the powers of the democratically elected European Parliament, it is still not as powerful as national parliaments on the domestic level. This is one of the main reasons why the European Union is frequently criticized as suffering from a 'democratic deficit'.

Another illustrative example is actions of the UN Security Council directed against individuals, for example the freezing of bank accounts of suspected terrorists.[141] The member States of the United Nations have agreed in Article 25 of the UN Charter to accept resolutions of the UN Security Council as binding. Still, the lack of meaningful judicial, administrative, or parliamentary review for the affected individuals gives rise to concerns regarding the 'legitimacy' of the relevant actions by the UN Security Council. International investment tribunals differ in many respects from lawmaking institutions. They do not pass laws of general applicability but decide discrete disputes arising out of an alleged breach of a host State's treaty obligations—despite the fact that future tribunals might take these decisions into account when rendering their own.[142] Furthermore, there are typically several provisions in an investment treaty that ensure that arbitral tribunals become active only after consultations and negotiations have failed.[143]

Another factor to bear in mind is that delegation of interpretative authority to a neutral body constitutes one of the key factors in the legalization of international relations. If a State opts for such delegation, with a corresponding obligation of its treaty partner(s), this decision is the outcome of its (democratic) decision-making

---

[139] For a visionary approach concerning democracy on an international level, *see* Richard Falk & Andrew Strauss, 'Toward Global Parliament', *Foreign Affairs* 80 (2001) 212–20. For a critical view, *see* Robert A. Dahl, 'Can International Organizations be Democratic? A Skeptic's View', *in Democracy's Edges* (Ian Shapiro & Casiano Hacker-Cordon eds., 1999) 19–36.

[140] Kumm, 'The Legitimacy of International Law', at 924. *But see also* Samantha Besson, 'The Authority of International Law—Lifting the State Veil', *Sydney Law Review* 31 (2009) 343–80, who argues that '(democratic) state consent is neither a sufficient nor a necessary condition of legitimacy' (at 371).

[141] On this and other measures adopted by the UN Security Coucil, *see* Thomas Meerpohl, *Individualsanktionen des Sicherheitsrates der Vereinten Nationen. Das Sanktionsregime gegen die Taliban und Al-Qaida vor dem Hintergrund des Rechts der VN und der Menschenrechte* (2008).

[142] *See* Chapter 4, notes 70–5 and accompanying text.

[143] *See, e.g.,* Articles VI, VII(2), and VIII(3) of the Argentina–US BIT.

process. Granting a margin of appreciation to one of the treaty parties once a dispute has arisen would undermine the capability of States to 'harden' their international obligations by agreeing on neutral third-party adjudication.[144] If States want to grant each other a 'margin of appreciation' when it comes to treaty compliance, they have several means at their disposal to do so. Setting out the 'self-judging' character of a provision or a certain 'margin of appreciation' in the relevant treaty is the most straightforward way. Subsequent agreements between the parties within the meaning of Article 31(3)(a) VCLT may have the same effect.[145]

Furthermore, the transfer of the margin of appreciation doctrine as developed by the ECtHR to Article XI of the Argentina–US BIT would probably not so much affect the interpretation of the nexus requirement, but rather more the question of whether there was indeed a threat to the host State's 'essential security interest' or the 'public order'. In *Stankov*, for example, the ECtHR found that the 'Contracting States have a certain margin of appreciation in assessing *whether* such a need exists, but it goes hand in hand with European supervision embracing both the legislation and the decision applying it'.[146] In a similar vein, the ECtHR held in *James* that it 'will respect the legislature's judgment as to *what* is "in the public interest" unless that judgment be manifestly without reasonable foundation'.[147] The reasoning of the *Continental* tribunal comports with this assumption. The tribunal held that:

interests such as 'ensuring internal security in the face of a severe economic crisis with social, political and public order implications' may well raise for such a party . . . *issues of public order and essential security interest objectively capable* of being covered under Art. XI. An interpretation of a bilateral reciprocal treaty that accommodates the different interests and concerns of the parties in conformity with its terms accords with an effective interpretation of the treaty. Moreover, in the Tribunal's view, *this objective assessment* must contain a significant *margin of appreciation*[.][148]

Finally, the margin of appreciation doctrine does not seem to find much support in the jurisprudence of the ICJ. In *Oil Platforms*, the ICJ had to apply a provision very similar to Article XI of the Argentina–US BIT. As noted previously, Article XX(1)(d) of the 1955 US–Iran Treaty of Amity, Economic Relations and Consular Rights allows each treaty party to take measures 'necessary to protect its essential security interests'.[149] In her separate opinion, Judge Higgins criticized the Court for finding that the United States committed an

---

[144] Abbott and Snidal consider 'delegation' to be one of the three main indicators of 'hard law', the other two being the 'binding' character of a legal obligation and its 'precision' (Abbott & Snidal, 'Hard and Soft Law in International Governance', at 421).

[145] For subsequent agreements and subsequent practice in investor–State arbitration, *see also* Chapter 5, notes 191–230 and accompanying text.

[146] *See* Chapter 3, note 268 and accompanying text (emphasis added).

[147] Chapter 5, note 114 (emphasis added).

[148] *Continental*, Award, para. 181 (internal references omitted) (emphases added).

[149] *See supra* note 74 and accompanying text.

internationally wrongful act without paying sufficient attention to the wording of Article XX(1)(d). The Court examined the facts of the case against the requirements of the right of self-defence in Article 51 of the UN Charter, especially whether the US action was 'necessary' and 'proportional'.[150] Judge Higgins arrived at similar criteria when interpreting the different elements of Article XX(1)(d). When inferring the requirement of proportionality from the term 'necessary', Judge Higgins mentioned in passing that this does not mean that the State invoking Article XX(1)(d) enjoys a 'margin of appreciation':

> The Court should next have examined—*without any need to afford a 'margin of appreciation'*—the meaning of 'necessary'. In the context of the events of the time, it could certainly have noticed that, in general international law, 'necessary' is understood also as incorporating a need for 'proportionality'.[151]

Judge Kooijmans was arguably more sympathetic to a 'margin of discretion' in the context of Article XX(1)(d), but he clearly differentiated between the governmental goal and the means chosen to achieve this goal:

> The evaluation of what essential security interests are and whether they are in jeopardy is first and foremost a political question and can hardly be replaced by a judicial assessment. Only when the political evaluation is patently unreasonable (which might bring us close to an 'abuse of authority') is a judicial ban appropriate. And although the choice of means to be taken in order to protect those interests will also be politically motivated, that choice lends itself much more to judicial review and thus to a stricter test, since the means chosen directly affect the interests and rights of others.[152]

In sum, neither the margin of appreciation doctrine nor the 'only way' requirement of the customary international law defence of necessity seem to be a perfect fit for the interpretation of the term 'necessary' in Article XI of the Argentina–US BIT. The next subsection analyses whether the principle of proportionality is a more appropriate tool for the interpretation of the nexus requirement in this provision.

3. Proportionality in the context of Article XI of the Argentina–US BIT

As seen in section I, the WTO-inspired Article XI analysis of the *Continental* tribunal addressed many factors that would matter in a proportionality analysis.[153] The assessment of the relevant facts by the tribunal involved intricate economic questions, controversially discussed in expert reports not available to the public. It is not the purpose of this subsection to decide whether the *Continental* tribunal

---

[150] Id., para. 51.
[151] *Case concerning Oil Platforms* (Iran v. United States of America), Judgment, 6 November 2003, ICJ Reports 2003, 161 (Higgins, J, concurring), para 48 (emphasis added). The Court itself did not refer to the 'margin of appreciation' doctrine in its decision.
[152] *Case concerning Oil Platforms* (Iran v. United States of America), Judgment, 6 November 2003, ICJ Reports 2003, 161 (Kooijmans, J, concurring), para 44.
[153] *See supra* notes 37–51 and accompanying text.

was right or wrong in its analysis. Rather, this subsection analyses whether in interpreting and applying Article XI arbitral tribunals should employ a proportionality analysis as a matter of treaty interpretation. The *Continental* tribunal justified its approach with a rather brief reference to exception clauses in US FCN treaties and Article XX GATT.[154] Some authors point out that there are significant structural differences between the WTO system and investor–State arbitration.[155] I agree with these authors that mere reference to trade law provisions with a wording similar to Article XI is insufficient reason to transport a WTO-inspired balancing test into Article XI. The issue discussed here is whether proportionality as a general principle of law within the meaning of Article 38(3)(c) ICJ Statute should inform the meaning of the term 'necessary' in Article XI by virtue of Article 31(3)(c) VCLT.

We have seen above that the interpretative means listed in Article 31(1) and (2) VCLT offer only very limited guidance on the interpretation of the term 'necessary' in Article XI.[156] Chapters 3 and 4 outlined the methodology to assess whether proportionality as a general principle should inform the interpretation of a treaty provision. To recall, it is important to consider three caveats before applying a proportionality analysis. In certain legal settings, proportionality analysis might (1) constitute a threat to the rule of law, (2) give rise to unwarranted judicial lawmaking, and/or (3) risk being arbitrary as it is unclear what interests enter the balancing process due to the lack of a relevant value system.[157]

Regarding the rule of law, it is worth remembering Waldron's postulate, according to which individual actors 'are entitled to laws that are neither murky nor uncertain but are instead publicly and clearly stated in a text that is not buried in doctrine'.[158] I have argued that the application of the principle of proportionality in the context of standard BIT provisions on expropriation raises serious concerns with respect to the rule of law. After all, such provisions stipulate that foreign investors must not be expropriated except for a public purpose; in a non-discriminatory manner; and upon payment of prompt, adequate, and effective compensation. It is not apparent from the text of standard BIT provisions on expropriation that a foreign investor would lose its right to be compensated if the State measure in question was proportionate.[159] These concerns do not apply to NPM clauses such as Article XI of the Argentina–US BIT. The text of Article XI makes it abundantly clear that a State may take measures 'necessary' for the protection of certain enumerated public interests, i.e. 'public order', 'international peace or

---

[154] *See supra* note 37 and accompanying text.

[155] Alvarez & Brink, 'Revisiting the Necessity Defense', at 349–52; Alvarez, 'Beware Boundary Crossings', at 25–37.

[156] *See supra* notes 107–10 and accompanying text.

[157] *See* Chapter 3, notes 199–218 and accompanying text. For an assessments of these factors in the context of standard BIT provisions on expropriation and the FET standard *see* Chapter 5, subsection V.5.b and Chapter 6, subsection III.2 respectively.

[158] Waldron, 'The Rule of International Law', at 17 (*see also* Chapter 5, note 152).

[159] *See* Chapter 5, notes 285–6 and accompanying text.

security', and the State's 'essential security interests'. For the same reason, there is no risk of judicial lawmaking in the context of Article XI of the Argentina–US BIT that would not have been envisaged by the parties to the treaty. The parties to the Argentina–US BIT decided to include an NPM clause in the treaty—and to refer the question of whether a particular State measure satisfies its requirements to third-party adjudication.[160]

Moreover, Article XI enumerates the public interest considerations that are relevant in the proportionality analysis, which provides significant guidance for arbitral tribunals. In certain legal settings, it might be unclear what factors enter the balancing process. This is particularly true in the context of standard BIT provisions on expropriation that contain neither a textual marker for a proportionality analysis nor an enumeration of conflicting interests that may trump investor rights.[161] In this context, it is also worth recalling that the US Supreme Court is reluctant to apply proportionality to fundamental rights, guaranteed by the US Constitution without textual limitations.[162] In the absence of limitation clauses, it may indeed be unclear whether and for the sake of which interests interference with unconditionally guaranteed rights is permitted. This is not a concern in the context of Article XI. Here, Article XI itself identifies the policy goals for the sake of which the host State may interfere with the protections set out in the US–Argentina BIT.

Furthermore, applying proportionality in the context of Article XI finds support in ICJ jurisprudence. The NPM clause interpreted by the ICJ in *Oil Platforms* specified that 'the Treaty shall not preclude the application of measures...necessary...for the maintenance or restoration of international peace and security, or necessary to protect...essential security interests.'[163] Both the Court and Judge Higgins in her separate opinion found that the parties could rely on this provision only if and to the extent that the relevant measures were proportionate.[164] Judge Higgins considered the term 'necessary' to trigger a proportionality analysis as a matter of 'general international law'.[165] This reasoning sits well with the proposition that one of the purposes of general principles is to provide guidance on the interpretation of treaty provisions that might be textually open to being assigned more than one meaning.[166] Article 31(3)(c) VCLT is the vehicle that transports general principles to the interpretation of open-textured treaty terms such as 'necessary' in Article XI.

A fully fledged proportionality analysis in the context of Article XI would require arbitrators to examine (1) whether the relevant measure was a suitable means to achieve its goal, (2) whether a less restrictive but equally effective alternative measure would have been available, and (3) whether the detriment to the

---

[160] *See supra* notes 77–103 and accompanying text.
[161] *See supra* notes 281–9 and accompanying text.
[162] *See* Chapter 3, notes 127 and 150–98 and accompanying text.
[163] *See supra* note 74 and accompanying text.
[164] *See supra* notes 150–1 and accompanying text.
[165] *See supra* note 151 and accompanying text.
[166] *See* Chapter 3, note 312 and accompanying text.

investor was proportionate when weighted against the benefits of the State measure. Jürgen Kurtz suggests limiting judicial review of exception clauses such as Article XI to the first two steps of this analysis. More specifically, he advocates a WTO-inspired analysis that examines whether a less restrictive alternative would have been reasonably available. The reasonableness of the alternative measure is to be judged by its administration and enforcement costs as compared to those of the adopted measure.[167] Kurtz states that arbitrators are ill-positioned to engage in the balancing process inherent in the third stage of the proportionality test. He suggests leaving the weighing and balancing of competing interests to national authorities.[168] I have argued that international law does not necessarily become more legitimate or democratic by referring decisions to the domestic level if those decisions affect outsiders.[169] The same caveats apply here. Furthermore, limiting proportionality analysis to its first two steps can render grave infringements of property rights lawful even if the advantage to the public interest is only minimal.

Kurtz doubts that 'courts, in general, are better assessors of values and empirical questions than elected representatives'.[170] This argument seems to go against proportionality analysis in general, not just on the international level. Chapter 3 addressed a large number of cases on the domestic and international level in which adjudicators resorted to the principle of proportionality. Of course, these decisions are only of limited relevance to investor–State arbitration, and they certainly do not constitute binding precedent. Still, they illustrate the kind of considerations that play a role in a proportionality analysis. Moreover, they offer valuable insights for situations in which the application of the principle of proportionality encounters certain difficulties. Some of these decisions are worth recalling at this point because they nicely illustrate the importance of the third step of a proportionality analysis.

As outlined in Chapter 3, subsection I.1, in 1907, the Prussian Higher Administrative Court had to decide on the interpretation of a limitation clause that enabled the police to 'take the necessary measures for the maintenance of public peace, security, and order'.[171] The administration ordered a factory owner to empty his pond for the protection of human health, with only 20 hours' notice. As the pond was essential for the operation of the factory, the Prussian Higher Administrative Court decided that the administration would have had to take account of the economic interests of the factory owner to the greatest extent possible under the particular circumstances of the case. The Court criticized that the administration had not contacted the factory owner before it issued its order. Consequently, the Court considered the administrative measure unlawful.[172] There is no reason why an arbitral tribunal should not take account of a State's efforts—or the absence thereof—to find a mutually acceptable solution before adopting the infringing measure. This is also true if the relevant measure has

---

[167] Kurtz, 'Adjudging the Exceptional at International Investment Law', at 369.
[168] Id., at 367.   [169] *See supra* notes 137–45 and accompanying text.
[170] Kurtz, 'Adjudging the Exceptional at International Investment Law', at 367.
[171] Chapter 3, note 34.   [172] *See* Chapter 3, notes 37–9b and accompanying text.

become the least restrictive one to achieve the respective goal by the time the State decides to take action.

Modern examples of limitation clauses containing the term 'necessary' as a nexus requirement that adjudicatory bodies interpreted to give rise to a proportionality analysis include section 33 of the South African Interim Constitution of 1993 and Articles 8(2), 9(2), 10(2), and 11(2) ECHR.[173] Some domestic courts resort to proportionality even if limitation clauses contain no (or more ambiguous) textual markers for a proportionality analysis. As noted in Chapter 3, subsection I.2 above, the Israeli Supreme Court interpreted Section 8 of the Basic Law: Human Dignity and Freedom as giving rise to a proportionality analysis even though its wording suggests a mere least restrictive means test ('to an extent no greater than is required').[174]

The judgment of the Israeli Supreme Court in *Beit Sourik* is particularly illustrative of the significance of the third step of the proportionality analysis. This case also provides an instructive example for how to deal with factual uncertainties. As explained in Chapter 3, subsection I.2, the Court examined whether an alternative, less infringing route of the fence (or wall) would have protected Israel's security interests as effectively. The Court found that there was no clear evidence that the alternative route would have been as effective as the one adopted. After this analysis, the Court decided that the respondent enjoys the benefit of the doubt and that the adopted route passed the least restrictive means test.[175] For the reasons outlined in the previous subsection, such a 'benefit of the doubt' solution is more appropriate than granting the respondent State a wide margin of appreciation *ab initio*. In the final step of its analysis, however, the Court decided that the adopted measure was disproportionate because the potentially greater level of security provided by the chosen route was only marginal as compared to the alternative route.[176]

It is a well-established principle that the party invoking a treaty provision needs to prove that all of its requirements are fulfilled. This means that in the context of Article XI it is for the host State to show that the three prongs of the proportionality test are met. The jurisprudence of the US Supreme Court on the different standards of scrutiny under US constitutional law follows a similar approach. In the context of intermediate and strict scrutiny, it is for the government to prove that the measure was 'substantially related to an important governmental objective' and 'narrowly tailored to achieve a compelling government interest', respectively.[177] The claimant bears the burden of proof only in the context of the rational basis test. This is a more deferential standard of review having less in common with the principle of proportionality than intermediate and strict

---

[173] *See* Chapter 3, notes 91 and 200.   [174] *See* Chapter 3, note 101 and accompanying text.

[175] *See* Chapter 3, notes 113–17 and accompanying text.

[176] *See* Chapter 3, note 121 and accompanying text.

[177] *See* Chapter 3, notes 140–9 and accompanying text. The claimant bears the burden of proof only in the context of the rational basis test, which is a more deferential standard of review further removed from the proportionality test than intermediate and strict scrutiny.

scrutiny.[178] There is yet another aspect of US Supreme Court jurisprudence on intermediate and strict scrutiny that seems to be an appropriate consideration in the context of investor–State arbitration: the governmental objective relied on in the proceedings must have been the *actual* reason for the State measure at the time the relevant measure was adopted. Unlike in the context of the rational basis test, it is not enough that the invoked public interest is merely a *conceivable* basis on which the State could have based its measure, while, in fact, the State acted out of a different motivation.[179]

The application of the principle of proportionality to NPM clauses such as Article XI is also compatible with Alexy's theory on rules and principles. The obligation to compensate a foreign investor for direct and indirect expropriations constitutes a rule under Alexy's theory. The same is probably true for Article XI, which clarifies that the Argentina–US BIT does not preclude measures that are necessary for the protection or maintenance of the public order, international peace and security, or the host State's essential security interests. To be more precise, Article XI of the Argentina–US BIT is a rule that constitutes an exception to rules (i.e. the substantive BIT provisions), and at the same time refers to principles.[180] After all, Article XI enumerates certain goals in the public interest, and clarifies that measures 'necessary' to protect those goals do not violate the treaty. Proportionality is an appropriate judicial tool in such situations.[181]

Of course, interpreting the term 'necessary' in NPM clauses as giving rise to a proportionality analysis will not solve all of the interpretative issues in the context of such provisions. Foremost, it will be for arbitral tribunals to interpret the interests listed in NPM clauses for the sake of which the substantive rights under a BIT may be limited. Burke-White and von Staden provide an overview of the public policy goals most frequently listed in NPM clauses. This compilation contains terms such as 'security interests', 'international peace and security', 'public order', 'public health', and 'public morality'.[182] These terms do not necessarily mean the same in every treaty. After all, the particular 'context' of a BIT (Article 31(2) VCLT), the means of treaty interpretation listed in Article 31(3) VCLT, and the possibility that the parties intended a special meaning to be given to a certain term (Article 31(4) VCLT) all play an important role in the interpretative process.[183] This is especially so with respect to open-textured terms such as 'public order' and 'public morality'.[184]

---

[178] *See* Chapter 3, notes 139–41, 232, & 266.

[179] *See* Chapter 3, notes 141 and 144 and accompanying text.

[180] For a similar characterization of Article XX of the GATT, *see* Petersen, 'Customary Law Without Custom?', at 291.

[181] *See* Chapter 3, note 65 and accompanying text.

[182] Burke-White & von Staden, 'Investment Protection in Extraordinary Times', at 349–68.

[183] *See* Chapter 4, section II.

[184] For various interpretations of these terms, *see* Alvarez & Khamsi, 'The Argentine Crisis', 450–1 (public order); Burke-White & von Staden, 'Investment Protection', at 357–61 (public order), 364–6 (public morality); Kurtz, 'Adjudging the Exceptional', at 360–1 (public order).

In the context of the Argentina–US BIT, all tribunals agreed that a severe economic crisis could pose a threat to a host State's 'essential security interests'.[185] Answering the question of whether the situation in Argentina in 2001–3, and Argentina's measures to deal with the crisis, satisfied the requirements of Article XI of the Argentina–US BIT is a fact-intense exercise. Proportionality offers an appropriate analytical framework to steer the analysis. It provides for transparency by obliging arbitrators to identify the different factors that play a role in their decision and explain how they relate to each other under the particular circumstances of the relevant case. Proportionality ensures that none of the interests involved (i.e. the private property rights of the claimant and the public interest) suffers more than necessary for the benefit of the other. In light of all of the above, the most appropriate tool to determine whether a State action was 'necessary' to attain one or more of the governmental goals outlined in Article XI appears to be the principle of proportionality.

V. The consequences of Article XI

Establishing proportionality as the relevant nexus requirement in Article XI of the Argentina–US BIT is of very limited use without knowing what will actually happen if a State demonstrates that a certain State measure passes the proportionality test. The text of Article XI merely states that the treaty 'shall not preclude' measures adopted in compliance with this provision. The claimant in *CMS* argued that Argentina owed compensation even if the tribunal was to find that the State could rely on Article XI for its non-compliance with certain treaty provisions.[186] There was no reason for the *CMS* tribunal to decide on this issue, since it rejected Argentina's arguments with respect to both Article XI and Article 25. Still, the tribunal stated that Argentina would have had to compensate the claimant even if the requirements of Article XI of the Argentina–US BIT had been met.[187]

The *CMS* tribunal based its reasoning on Article 27 ASR.[188] The *Enron* and *Sempra* tribunals followed essentially the same approach.[189] Article 27 states that a successful plea of necessity is 'without prejudice to... the question of compensation for any material loss caused by the act in question'. The *CMS* annulment committee rightly noted that Article 27 is a '"without prejudice" clause, not a stipulation'.[190] This means that the ASR do not clarify whether a successful invocation of Article 25 triggers a duty to compensate. The analysis in Chapter 8 will reveal, however, that there are strong arguments in support of the proposition that such a duty does exist. But this result cannot simply be transferred to Article XI,

---

[185] *CMS*, Award, paras. 359–360; *LG&E*, Decision on Liability, para. 238; *Enron*, Award, paras. 332–4; *Sempra*, Award, para. 374; *Continental*, Award, para. 178.
[186] For the position of the claimant, *see CMS*, Award, para. 386.
[187] Id., paras. 388–90. [188] Id., paras. 390.
[189] *Enron*, Award, paras. 344–5; *Sempra*, Award, paras. 393–5.
[190] *CMS*, Decision of the Annulment Committee, para 147.

as this provision is—according to the findings in section II—unlikely to be a codification of the customary international law defence of necessity phrased in different terms. Therefore, the question of whether a State owes compensation even if the requirements of Article XI are fulfilled deserves further consideration.

Unlike the *CMS* tribunal, both the *LG&E* and the *Continental* tribunals found that Argentina's measures to cope with the crisis were covered by Article XI.[191] In addition, both tribunals held that Argentina owed no compensation for damage done during the period in which it was entitled to derogate from the treaty protections as a matter of Article XI.[192] The *LG&E* tribunal noted that 'Article XI establishes the state of necessity as a ground for *exclusion from wrongfulness* of an act of the State, and *therefore*, the State is exempted from liability.'[193] This reasoning alone is insufficient to establish that a State does not owe compensation if the requirements of Article XI are fulfilled. The formulation of the *LG&E* tribunal ('a ground for *exclusion from wrongfulness*') characterizes the legal consequences of Article 25 ASR as a circumstance *excluding wrongfulness*. What was just said regarding the reasoning of the *CMS* tribunal applies to *LG&E* as well. Simply inferring the consequences of Article XI from Article 27 ASR is inappropriate. In any event, States are unlikely to avoid a duty to compensate under Article 25, as Chapter 8 will reveal.

That said, an obligation to pay compensation if a State can successfully invoke Article XI is—at least prima facie—contrary to the rules of State responsibility. Under these rules, a State is under an obligation to make full reparation for an internationally wrongful act. According to Article 2(b) ASR, an internationally wrongful act requires the 'breach of an international obligation'. Whether such a breach exists is to be determined by the relevant set of primary rules. International adjudicators usually first examine whether one of the substantive rights of the relevant treaty has been infringed. If the answer to this first question is 'yes', it is then necessary to determine whether a limitation clause excludes the violation of the particular treaty. The *CMS* annulment committee was very clear about the consequences of Article XI:

The answer to that question is clear enough: Article XI, if and for so long as it applied, excluded the operation of the substantive provisions of the BIT. That being so, there could be no possibility of compensation being payable during that period.[194]

---

[191] *See supra* notes 16–52 and accompanying text. None of the tribunals that had dealt with the Argentine crisis up to this point held that Argentina's measures were justified under Article 25. Even the *LG&E* tribunal, which found that Article 25 'supports the Tribunal's analysis', conceded that Article 25 'alone does not establish Argentina's defence' (*LG&E*, Decision on Liability, para. 258). The *Continental* tribunal explicitly stated that it did not have to comment on Article 25 since it considered the measures taken by Argentina to be covered by Article XI (*Continental*, Award, para. 162).

[192] *See Continental*, Award, paras. 164, 233. The *LG&E* tribunal was less clear in its reasoning but eventually reached the same result (*LG&E*, Decision on Liability, paras. 260–1).

[193] *LG&E*, Decision on Liability, para. 261 (emphasis added).

[194] *CMS*, Decision of the Annulment Committee, para. 146.

Some scholars have criticized this finding of the *CMS* annulment committee. Alvarez and Khamsi and Desierto argue that the State invoking Article XI of the Argentina–US BIT needs to compensate foreign investors for measures covered by this provision. Interestingly, these authors reach the same conclusion through diametrically opposed approaches. As explained above, Alvarez and Khamsi equate Article XI of the Argentina–US BIT with the customary international law defence of necessity. Consequently, they state that the 'traditional rule, codified at Article 27(b) ASR, continues to apply'.[195] Desierto, in contrast, argues that Article 25 ASR is completely irrelevant for the interpretation of Article XI as Article 25 does not even constitute a 'relevant rule of international law' within the meaning of Article 31(3)(c) VCLT. Desierto concludes from the wording of Article 31(3) ('taken together with the context') that there needs to be a 'linkage or nexus' between Article 25 and the 'context' of the Argentina–US BIT in order for Article 25 to influence the interpretation of Article XI.[196] While Alvarez and Khamsi argue that the US merely intended to codify the customary international law defence in Article XI, Desierto does not even detect a 'linkage' between the two concepts in light of the treaty's drafting history.[197] That said, Desierto thinks that Article XI does not exempt the host State from compensating the claimant as this provision would prevent an internationally wrongful act from arising only among the parties to the BIT. The investor–State relationship, on the other hand, would be unaffected by Article XI.[198]

Alvarez and Khamsi, and Desierto resort to textual and structural comparisons between Article XI and other provisions in the Argentina–US BIT to advance their respective points. These authors distinguish the wording of Article XI ('This Treaty shall not preclude') from formulations in other provisions of the Argentina–US BIT that are allegedly more explicit with respect to the inapplicability of the substantive BIT provisions.[199] One provision cited by both Desierto and Alvarez/Khamsi is Article I(2) of the Argentina–US BIT, which reads as follows:

Each Party reserves the right to *deny* to any company of the other Party the advantages of this Treaty if (a) nationals of any third country, or nationals of such Party, control such company and the company has no substantial business activities in the territory of the other Party; or (b) the company is controlled by nationals of a third country with which the denying Party does not maintain normal economic relations. (Emphasis added.)

---

[195] Alvarez & Khamsi, 'The Argentine Crisis', at 460.

[196] Diane A. Desierto, 'Necessity and Supplementary Means of Interpretation of Non-Precluded Measures in Bilateral Investment Treaties', *University of Pennsylvania Journal of International Law* 31 (2010) 827–934, at 911.

[197] Alvarez & Khamsi, 'The Argentine Crisis', at 428–40; Desierto, 'Necessity and Supplementary Means of Interpretation', at 911.

[198] Desierto, 'Necessity and Supplementary Means of Interpretation', at 882 & 907–8.

[199] Id., at 877–881; Alvarez & Khamsi, 'The Argentine Crisis', at 456–7.

The authors argue that the formulation 'to deny' constitutes explicit language indicating that the substantive treaty provisions are inapplicable.[200] Similar arguments are advanced with respect to Article II(1) ('to make or maintain exceptions'),[201] Article II(9) ('provisions of this Article shall not apply to'),[202] and Article IX ('Article VII and VIII shall not apply').[203] It is true that certain exception clauses in international treaties contain clearer language than the 'shall not preclude' formulation in Article XI of the Argentina–US BIT. Nevertheless, it is debatable whether this justifies the far-reaching conclusions drawn by Alvarez and Khamsi and Desierto.

As explained above, US FCNs from the 1950s inspired the language of Article XI. Article XXI(1)(d) of the 1956 Nicaragua–US FCN, for example, is largely identical to Article XI of the Argentina–US BIT and contains the 'not precluded' language.[204] The judgment of the ICJ in *Nicaragua* offers some valuable insights into the relationship between this provision and the rest of the 1956 treaty. It is true that the ASR were released only in 2001, as Khamsi and Alvarez point out when they warn against applying the distinction between 'primary' and 'secondary' rules in the context of the Argentina–US BIT signed in 1991.[205] Regarding the function and consequences of exception clauses such as Article XXI, however,

---

[200] Desierto, 'Necessity and Supplementary Means of Interpretation', at 87; Alvarez & Khamsi, 'The Argentine Crisis', at 456.

[201] Article II(1):

Each Party shall permit and treat investment, and activities associated therewith, on a basis no less favorable than that accorded in like situations to investment or associated activities of its own nationals or companies, or of nationals or companies of any third country, whichever is the more favorable, subject to the right of each Party *to make or maintain exceptions* falling within one of the sectors or matters listed in the Protocol to this Treaty. Each Party agrees to notify the other Party before or on the date of entry into force of this Treaty of all such laws and regulations of which it is aware concerning the sectors or matters listed in the Protocol. Moreover, each Party agrees to notify the other of any future exception with respect to the sectors or matters listed in the Protocol, and to limit such exceptions to a minimum. Any future exception by either Party shall not apply to investment existing in that sector or matter at the time the exception becomes effective. The treatment accorded pursuant to any exceptions shall, unless specified otherwise in the Protocol, be not less favorable than that accorded in like situations to investments and associated activities of nationals or companies of any third country. (Emphasis added.)

[202] Article II(9):

The most favored nation provisions of this Article *shall not apply* to advantages accorded by either Party to nationals or companies of any third country by virtue of that Party's binding obligations that derive from full membership in a regional customs union or free trade area, whether such an arrangement is designated as a customs union, free trade area, common market or otherwise. (Emphasis added.)

[203] Article IX:

The provisions of Article VII and VIII *shall not apply* to a dispute arising (a) under the export credit, guarantee or insurance programs of the Export-Import Bank of the United States or (b) under other official credit, guarantee or insurance arrangements pursuant to which the Parties have agreed to other means of settling disputes. (Emphasis added.)

[204] For the wording of Article XXI(1)(d), *see supra* note 99 and accompanying text.

[205] Alvarez & Khamsi, 'The Argentine Crisis', at 432.

the 1986 ICJ judgment in *Nicaragua* followed the same methodology as the ASR and the *CMS* annulment committee. The ICJ stated that 'Article XXI defines the instances in which the Treaty itself provides for exceptions to the generality of its other provisions.'[206] The Court explained the relationship between Article XXI and the other treaty provisions as follows:

Since Article XXI of the 1956 Treaty contains a power for each of the parties to derogate from the other provisions of the Treaty, the possibility of invoking the clauses of that Article must be considered once it is apparent that certain forms of conduct by the United States would otherwise be in conflict with the relevant provisions of the Treaty.[207]

In its analysis, the ICJ established that the US had infringed the freedom of navigation and commerce guaranteed by Article XIX(1) of the treaty.[208] In the context of the Court's analysis of whether the US could derogate from Article XIX, the Court explicitly referred to the position of the US in its counter-memorial on jurisdiction and admissibility. The Court stated that 'the United States relied on [Article XXI(1)(c)] as showing the *inapplicability* of the 1956 FCN Treaty to Nicaragua's claims'.[209] Against this background, it would be surprising if the drafters of the Argentina–US BIT of 1991 intended Article XI of this treaty to lead to any result other than the inapplicability of the relevant BIT provisions. Moreover, the ICJ turned to the issue of compensation only after it had established that the US could not rely on Article XX(1)(c).[210] This order of consideration would have made no sense if the 'shall not preclude' language of Article XXI were irrelevant for the purposes of reparation.

In *Oil Platforms*, the ICJ reiterated and affirmed the interpretative approach it had taken in *Nicaragua*.[211] However, the ICJ followed a different order of consideration. It first examined whether the requirements of Article XX(1)(d) of the 1955 US–Iran Treaty of Amity, Economic Relations, and Consular Rights were fulfilled.[212] After the Court had established that these requirements had not been met, it turned to the question of whether the US had infringed the freedom of commerce guaranteed by Article X(1) of the 1955 treaty. The Court finally answered this question in the negative.[213] The Court employed this order of consideration for a particular reason: if it had started its analysis with Article X(1), there would have been little reason to turn to Article XXI(1)(d) after the Court had established that the freedom of commerce was not infringed. However, the Court found it important to comment on the unlawfulness of the actions of the US in light of the international law on the use of force. As explained in Chapter 4, the Court addressed this issue when interpreting Article XX(1) along the lines of Article 31(3)(c) VCLT.[214] Whether one agrees with the order of consideration employed

---

[206] *Case concerning Military and Paramilitary Activities in and against Nicaragua* (Nicaragua v. United States of America), Judgment, Merits, 27 June 1986, ICJ Reports 1986, 4, para. 222.
[207] Id., para. 225.   [208] Id., para. 278–9.   [209] Id., para. 280 (emphasis added).
[210] Id., paras. 282–3.
[211] *Case concerning Oil Platforms* (Iran v. United States of America), Judgment, 6 November 2003, ICJ Reports 2003, 161, paras. 34–5.
[212] Id., paras. 43–78.   [213] Id., paras. 79–99.
[214] *See* Chapter 4, notes 22–4 and accompanying text.

by the ICJ or not, it is immaterial to the relationship between Article X(1) and Article XXI(1)(d) of the 1955 treaty. The US argued during the proceedings that the Court would not even have to examine whether the US contravened the principle of freedom and navigation under Article X if it found that the requirements of the NPM clause in Article XX(1)(d) of the 1955 treaty were fulfilled.[215] This proposition is incompatible with the notion that an NPM clause does not absolve a State from liability for the infringement of other treaty provisions.

As mentioned above, Desierto and Alvarez and Khamsi identify certain textual differences between Article XI and other provisions of the Argentina–US BIT that more explicitly exclude the applicability of the treaty than the NPM clause in Article XI.[216] It should be noted that the same differences between the wording of NPM clauses and other more explicit treaty provisions exist in several post-WWII FCNs of the US. Article XI(3) of the 1955 US–Iran treaty, for example, grants certain benefits to private enterprises. The third sentence of this paragraph specifies that the 'foregoing rule shall *not apply*, however, to special advantages given in connection with…manufacturing goods for government use, or supplying goods and services to the Government for government use…'.[217] In a similar vein, Article XVI(1) of the 1955 treaty provides inter alia for certain tax exemptions for consular officers. Article XVI(2) specifies that the 'preceding paragraph shall *not apply* in respect of taxes and other similar charges upon: (a) the ownership or occupation of immovable property situated within the territories of the receiving state; (b) income derived from sources within such territories…; or (c) the passing of property at death'.[218] Moreover, Article XVII of the 1955 US–Iran treaty follows a similar methodology as Article IX of the Argentina–US BIT.[219] Article XVII reads as follows:

> The exemptions provided for in Articles XIV and XVI *shall not apply* to nationals of the sending state who are also nationals of the receiving state, or to any other person who is a national of the receiving state, nor to persons having immigrant status who have been lawfully admitted for permanent residence in the receiving state.[220] (Emphasis added)

Hence the US–Iran treaty, just as the Argentina–US BIT, contained provisions that were more explicit about the inapplicability of treaty provisions than the NPM clause in Article XXI. However, neither the US nor the ICJ reasoned that Article XXI does *not* exclude a violation of the Iran–US FCN.[221]

One may wonder whether the involvement of private actors in investor–State arbitration justifies a different reading of NPM clauses in BITs such as Article XI of the Argentina–US BIT. Alvarez and Khamsi and Desierto refer to the object

---

[215] *Case concerning Oil Platforms* (Iran v. United States of America), Judgment, 6 November 2003, ICJ Reports 2003, 161 (Higgins, J, concurring), para. 6.
[216] *See supra* notes 199–203 and accompanying text.
[217] Iran–US FCN, 284 UNTS 93, at 126 (emphasis added).
[218] Id., at 130 (emphasis added).
[219] For the text of Article IX of the Argentina–US BIT, *see supra* note 203.
[220] Iran–US FCN, 284 UNTS 93, at 130 (emphasis added).
[221] *See supra* note 215 and accompanying text.

and purpose of the Argentina–US BIT as another reason why Article XI would not exclude compensation.[222] I addressed the issue of whether the object and purpose of the Argentina–US BIT is limited to the protection of private property rights, or whether it extends to economic development and other public interests, in Chapter 5, subsection V.3.[223] Even if the only object and purpose of the BIT is to protect private property rights, this is of little relevance to the interpretation of a provision that explicitly addresses possible conflicts between certain treaty obligations and the public interest. To reiterate, Vandevelde, who was involved in the early US BIT programme, described Article X(1) of the 1983 US Model BIT and, hence, also Article XI of the Argentina–US BIT as a 'delicate balance' between the abilities of the US to act freely and its desire to ensure a certain level of investor protection.[224] A 'balance' between two positions implies that both yield—to a certain extent—to the benefit of the other. If investors receive the same compensation regardless of whether Article XI sets in or not, this provision would be unable to bring about the 'balance' it purports to strike.

BITs are deeply embedded in the fabric of general international law. They provide for special rules, but they do not constitute self-contained regimes.[225] Regarding the compensation of foreign investors, BITs typically specify nothing more than that investments may not be expropriated except upon payment of prompt, adequate, and effective compensation.[226] The duty to compensate for breaches of substantive treaty provisions, for example for violations of the FET standard, is part of customary international law.[227] It appears to be uncontroversial that State measures covered by Article XI of the Argentina–US BIT do not constitute internationally wrongful acts.[228] A State's duty to compensate in the absence of an internationally wrongful act should not be assumed lightly. If the parties to the treaty had meant to establish such a duty, they could have clarified that a State invoking Article XI owes 'adequate' compensation to foreign investors.

As illustrated above, NPM clauses are increasingly common in IIAs.[229] To the best of my knowledge, there are no indications that States (foremost the US and Canada) assume that measures covered by these clauses entail an obligation to compensate. Indeed, it is difficult to see why States would go to the trouble of incorporating NPM clauses into their BITs if they did not expect to be exempted from liability when the requirements of such clauses are fulfilled. That said, if the US and Argentina intended, at the time of the conclusion of the treaty, to compensate foreign investors for measures covered by Article XI, this intent should prevail (see Article 31(4) VCLT). To establish such intent, specific evidence is necessary, and the burden of proof is on the party that is invoking

---

[222] Alvarez & Khamsi, 'The Argentine Crisis', at 457; Desierto, 'Necessity', at 881.
[223] *See* Chapter 5, notes 177–85.
[224] Vandevelde, *United States International Investment Agreements*, at 220.
[225] *See* Chapter 4, subsection III.1.a.
[226] *See, e.g.,* Article IV(1) of the Argentina–US BIT.
[227] *See* Chapter 8, notes 257–62 and accompanying text.
[228] *See also,* Desierto, 'Necessity', at 908.
[229] *See supra* notes 82–97 and accompanying text.

this special meaning.[230] Whether there is sufficient evidence of such a shared intention or not can be decided only by an arbitral tribunal in possession of the relevant material.

The last question to be addressed in this section is the length of time during which a State is absolved from liability by virtue of an NPM clause such as Article XI of the Argentina–US BIT. The applicable legal test appears to be straightforward, even though it might entail a complex factual analysis: a State should be able to rely on an NPM clause only as long as all of its requirements are fulfilled. This means that Argentina could rely on Article XI only as long as there was a threat to its 'essential security interests' or 'public order'. Under the proportionality analysis suggested in this book, the following additional factors should be taken into account: a breach of the BIT is excluded only as long as the relevant measures remain proportionate. In other words, grave infringements of private property rights might be covered by NPM clauses for a shorter period than relatively minor infringements. Furthermore, the point at which less infringing alternative measures become available marks the beginning—or the recommencement—of the host State's treaty violation.

VI. Conclusion

Each NPM clause has to be interpreted individually in accordance with the rules of treaty interpretation set out in Article 31 VCLT. For NPM clauses with a wording similar to that of Article XI, the interpretation process is likely to establish proportionality as an appropriate tool to determine whether State action is covered by the NPM clause. Article 31(3)(c) VCLT provides a solid basis to apply proportionality as a general principle to assess whether the relevant measure was 'necessary'. As shown in section IV, concerns regarding the rule of law, judicial lawmaking, and the lack of a value system to guide the proportionality analysis are unjustified in the context of clauses like Article XI. The text of such clauses puts investors on notice that a State may take measures 'necessary' for the protection of certain enumerated public interests, which mitigates possible rule-of-law concerns.

In the absence of language indicating the self-judging character of NPM clauses, the treaty parties will usually have referred the question of whether a certain State measure is indeed 'necessary' to neutral third-party adjudication. A tribunal applying proportionality analysis in such a legal setting is not engaging in unwarranted judicial lawmaking. Quite to the contrary, it is embracing the task conferred on it with an analytical tool that enhances the probability that all relevant factors are taken into account in a transparent manner. While in some legal settings it might be unclear what values and interests enter a proportionality analysis, this is of no concern in the context of NPM clauses such as Article XI.

---

[230] ILC, *Commentaries on the Law of Treaties*, Article 27, para. 17 and Chapter 5, note 144.

The values and interests to which investor rights may have to yield under certain circumstances are spelled out in the NPM clause itself.

As illustrated in section III, States make increasing use of NPM clauses when drafting IIAs. Such clauses are an effective means to make sure States have sufficient regulatory leeway to protect the specific interests set out in the relevant NPM clause without incurring liability under IIAs. Proportionality analysis seeks to ensure that a fair balance is struck between the property rights of foreign investors and the public interest when States rely on NPM clauses. Something different is true if the relevant NPM clause indicates that it is for the State to decide whether its actions were 'necessary'. While some NPM clauses have such a self-judging character, State practice is far from being consistent. Therefore, there is no emerging rule of customary international law according to which State measures based on NPM clauses escape judicial scrutiny. In the absence of explicit treaty language indicating the self-judging character of NPM clauses, there is a strong presumption that it is for the tribunal to decide whether a particular measure was 'necessary'.

We have seen in section IV that the margin of appreciation doctrine created by the ECtHR is hardly an appropriate means to interpret and apply the nexus requirement in Article XI of the US–Argentina BIT. While this doctrine risks unduly undermining IIA protections, incorporating the 'only way' requirement from Article 25 ASR into Article XI has the opposite effect. If the availability of any other means—even if more costly and less effective—would bar resort to Article XI, then the treaty parties could virtually never rely on Article XI in an economic context. As a matter of treaty interpretation, section II identified strong arguments against equating Article XI with the customary international law defence. As outlined in section IV, there is also little reason to interpret the term 'necessary' in Article XI in line with the 'only way' requirement of Article 25 by virtue of the concept of systemic integration. But reading the 'only way' requirement into NPM clauses is not the sole method of rendering such clauses useless for host States. Holding States liable to foreign investors regardless of whether State measures meet the requirements of NPM clauses or not has similar effects—and section V identified several arguments that speak against such an approach.

When applying proportionality in the context of NPM provisions, arbitrators should consider all elements of the proportionality test—suitability, least restrictive means test, and proportionality *stricto sensu*. Contrary to a scholarly suggestion discussed in section IV, the weighing and balancing inherent in the third step (proportionality *stricto sensu*) should be part of the analysis. In light of the jurisprudence analysed in this book, relevant considerations when weighing and balancing the different interests at stake ought to include the following: the degree to which the State measure infringes the rights of the claimant; the duration of the infringement; the likelihood that the apprehended peril would have materialized had the State not adopted the relevant measure; the extent and probability of imminent harm resulting from the realization of the apprehended peril; the importance of the specific governmental goal; the extent to which the public interest would have suffered if the State had adopted a less infringing but possibly less effective measure; the extent to which the adopted measure did achieve (or was likely to achieve) the stated goal; and whether the State has accompanied the infringing measure with compensation, which might render an otherwise disproportionate measure proportionate.

8

Proportionality and the Customary International Law Defence of Necessity

One of Argentina's main defences in the arbitral proceedings resulting from the emergency measures during its 2001–3 crisis was that of experiencing a state of necessity under customary international law. While all tribunals recognized that such a defence exists and was accurately codified by the ILC in Article 25 ASR, none of the tribunals found that Argentina could rely on it to justify its emergency measures.[1] Notwithstanding its ineffectiveness in the Argentine cases, some authors think that the necessity defence could and should play an important role in investor–State arbitration. If modified, so the argument goes, necessity could help to readjust the 'balance' between investor rights and the public interest and provide more regulatory freedom to States.[2] Such efforts find encouragement in the *Enron* annulment decision, which set aside an award with a narrow reading of the necessity defence for the tribunal's (lack of) reasoning regarding Article 25 ASR.[3]

While some consider the customary international law defence of necessity a promising tool to advance public interest considerations, others doubt whether necessity is applicable in investor–State arbitration at all. Such doubts usually arise from the object and purpose of BITs to protect foreign investment, NPM clauses as *leges specialis*, and the involvement of non-State actors in investor–State arbitration. Section I of this chapter examines whether and under what circumstances these factors might bar a tribunal in investor–State arbitration from releasing a State from liability regardless of a possible state of necessity. Section II analyses

---

[1] *See CMS*, Award, para. 255; *Enron*, Award, para. 303; *LG&E*, Decision on Liability, para. 245; *BG Group*, Final Award, para. 255; *National Grid plc v. Argentina*, UNCITRAL Arbitration, Award, 3 November 2008, para. 256; *Continental*, Award, para. 168; *Impregilo*, Award, para. 344; *Suez–Vivendi* and *AWG Group*, Decision on Liability, para. 258. The tribunal that probably came closest to accepting Argentina's plea of necessity as a matter of customary international law was the *LG&E* tribunal. But even this tribunal ultimately relied on Article XI of the US–Argentina BIT and not on Article 25 of the ASR. While some parts of the reasoning of the *LG&E* tribunal suggest that the tribunal considered the requirements of Article 25 fulfilled (*LG&E*, Decision on Liability, paras. 250–7), the tribunal clarified that 'this analysis concerning Article 25 of the Draft Articles on State Responsibility alone does not establish Argentina's defence' (id., para 259).

[2] Kent & Harrington, 'The Plea of Necessity under Customary International Law: a Critical Review in Light of the Argentine Cases', at 270.

[3] *See* Chapter 2, notes 136–8 and accompanying text.

the different elements of Article 25 and relevant jurisprudence from the Argentine cases. The purpose of section II is to assess whether necessity as codified in the ASR could play a meaningful role in investor–State arbitration—or whether certain elements of Article 25 are likely to frustrate such an ambition even beyond the Argentine cases. Section III evaluates whether arbitrators should expand the scope of necessity by applying a proportionality analysis to assess whether regulatory measures in the public interest are justified by necessity. Section IV addresses what is probably the most important issue regarding necessity for States and foreign investors alike: the consequences of a successful plea of necessity; if certain State action meets the requirements of Article 25, will the State invoking necessity have to compensate those who suffered from the exercise of this defence, and if yes, to what degree?

It is also important to clarify what this chapter will *not* do, which is to provide a comprehensive historic survey of the doctrine of necessity. Traces of this doctrine can be found in Roman, Christian, and Islamic law, and they have been revisited by other authors.[4] Like with so much of modern international law, the seventeenth-century writings of Hugo Grotius have had a strong influence on the development of the necessity defence as we know it today.[5] Grotius discussed the notion of necessity in the context of specific settings, e.g. a subject's right to resist his superior in case of 'extreme and imminent peril',[6] the use or destruction of private property in emergency situations,[7] or the 'right of passage over land and rivers' when foreign citizens or a whole people are in need of such transit.[8] Three centuries later, Burleigh Rodick extracted a set of general rules from Grotius' writings to arrive at the 'Grotian view on necessity':

1. There must be an absence of *mens rea* on the part of one who exercises the alleged right.
2. There must be a real and vital danger, either to life, or to property.
3. The danger must be imminent in point of time.
4. In seizing the property of neutrals the amount seized should be no greater than is necessary for the particular object in view.
5. Considerations must be given to the equities involved. The plea of necessity, for example, cannot be admitted when the person against whom the action is directed is in an equal state of necessity himself.
6. The person who has exercised the right is bound whenever possible to make restitution or to give an equivalent to the owner.[9]

---

[4] *See, e.g.,* Diane A. Desierto, *Necessity and National Emergency Clauses—Sovereignty in Modern Treaty Interpretation* (2012), at 64–9 (with further references).

[5] For the role of Grotius in the transition from medieval law to international law dominated by sovereign States, *see, e.g.,* Stephan C Neff, 'A Short History of International Law', *in International Law* (Malcolm D. Evans ed., 2003) 31–58, at 37, and Arthur Nussbaum, *A Concise History of the Law of Nations* (1950), at 2.

[6] Hugo Grotius, *The Law of War and Peace* (1625, James Brown Scott (ed.), Carnegie Endowment for International Peace, 1995), Book I, Chapter IV, para. VII, 148–56.

[7] Id., Book II, Chapter II, paras. VI–XI, at 193–6; and Book III, Chapter XII, para. I, at 745.

[8] Id., Book II, Chapter II, para. XII, at 196–200.

[9] Burleigh Cushing Rodick, *The Doctrine of Necessity in International Law* (1928), at 6.

During the 40 years in which the ILC worked on the ASR, the Commission reviewed not only such scholarly writings on necessity but also an even greater amount of relevant State practice and judicial decisions.[10] From this material, the ILC deduced the different elements of Article 25 ASR, which are today widely considered to reflect customary international law.[11] This chapter does not address the State practice and jurisprudence underlying the text of Article 25 in the abstract. Rather, parts of this material will be analysed where helpful to shed light on the applicability, elements, and consequences of the necessity defence. Moreover, this material provides valuable insights into whether the wording of Article 25 should be modified to more accurately reflect customary international law.

I. The applicability of Article 25 ASR in investor–State arbitration

To date, arbitral tribunals have not analysed in great depth the applicability of the customary international law defence of necessity in investor–State arbitration. Instead, tribunals have applied the elements of Article 25 ASR to the relevant facts, without a theoretical inquiry into the applicability of this doctrine. As mentioned in the introduction to this chapter, there are still some concerns regarding the applicability of Article 25 in investor–State arbitration. First, some scholars argue that the customary international law defence is excluded by virtue of the object and purpose of BITs as instruments for the protection of foreign investment. Second, NPM clauses (such as Article XI of the Argentina–US BIT) might constitute *leges speciales* that render the necessity defence inapplicable. Finally, the involvement of non-State actors in investor–State arbitration might exclude the applicability of the necessity defence. I will take each of these issues in turn.

1. Inapplicability of the necessity defence according to Article 25(2)(a) ASR?

Article 25(2)(a) ASR states that necessity may not be invoked if 'the international obligation in question excludes the possibility of invoking necessity'. In the words of the ILC, certain treaties are 'intended to apply in abnormal situations of peril for

---

[10] For futher comments on the genesis of Article 25, *see* Chapter 7, notes 63–7 and accompanying text.

[11] *See* the references in *supra* note 1; Bjorklund, 'Emergency Exceptions: State of Necessity and Force Majeure', at 474–5; Cynthia C. Galvez, '"Necessity", Investor Rights, and State Sovereignty for NAFTA Investment Arbitration', *Cornell International Law Journal* 46 (2013) 143–63, at 146; Roman Boed, 'State of Necessity as a Justification for Internationally Wrongful Conduct', *Yale Human Rights and Development Law Journal* 3 (2000) 1–43, at 42–3 who criticized the ILC's prior draft article 33 for precisely the missing reference to the interests of the 'international community as a whole' which was later inserted into Article 25(1)(b); *Case concerning the Gabčíkovo–Nagymaros Project* (Hungary v. Slovakia), Judgment, 25 September 1997, ICJ Reports 1997, 7–84, paras. 50–7.

the responsible State and plainly engage its essential interests'.[12] August Reinisch argues that the object and purpose of BITs renders Article 25 ASR inapplicable.[13] The *CMS* and *BG Group* tribunals also raised this issue.[14] The *CMS* tribunal stated that the Argentina–US BIT was 'clearly designed to protect investments at a time of economic difficulties or other circumstances leading to the adoption of adverse measures by the Government'.[15] Similarly, the *BG Group* tribunal did not dismiss the possibility that the relevant BIT 'implies such an exclusion', and that Argentina 'would not be entitled to invoke necessity to unilaterally revoke vested rights…designed precisely to operate in situations where a run on the currency would lead to a situation of necessity'.[16] Neither the *CMS* nor the *BG Group* tribunal reached a conclusion on the applicability of Article 25. Instead, both tribunals held that the requirements of the necessity defence were not fulfilled.[17]

Some tribunals explicitly rejected the view that the applicability of the necessity defence was excluded as a matter of Article 25(2)(a) ASR. The *Impregilo* tribunal stated that no obligation contained within the BIT 'preclude[s] Argentina from invoking the necessity plea'.[18] In *Suez–Vivendi*, *AWG Group*, and *Suez–InterAgua*, the arbitrators analysed the applicability of Article 25 as part of the process by which they considered whether the human right to water is to be taken into account in investor–State arbitration. The arbitrators reached the following conclusion:

> Argentina is subject to both international obligations, *ie* human rights *and* treaty obligation, and must respect both of them equally. Under the circumstances of these cases, Argentina's human rights obligations and its investment treaty obligations are not inconsistent, contradictory, or mutually exclusive. Thus, as discussed above, Argentina could have respected both types of obligations. Viewing each treaty as a whole, the Tribunal does not find that any of them excluded the defense of necessity.[19]

The ILC commentaries provide only one example for the inapplicability of the necessity defence according to Article 25(2)(a): reliance on military necessity is expressly excluded in certain humanitarian conventions applicable in armed conflict.[20] In the absence of an explicit exclusion, the object and purpose of a particular 'rule' and that of the relevant treaty as a whole should guide the decision on the applicability of Article 25.[21] The objects and purposes of BITs might vary from treaty to treaty but it is safe to assume that one of these purposes will always be the protection of private property rights. Experience shows that States are particularly prone to interfere with private property rights when the economy

---

[12] ILC, *Commentaries on State Responsibility*, Article 25, para. 19.
[13] Reinisch, 'Necessity', at 205. Andrea Bjorklund seems to sympathize with this view (Bjorklund, 'Emergency Exceptions', at 490).
[14] *CMS*, Award, para. 353; *BG Group*, Final Award, para. 409.
[15] *CMS*, Award, para. 354.　　　　[16] *BG Group*, Final Award, para. 409.
[17] *CMS*, Award, para. 355; *BG Group*, Final Award, paras. 410–12.
[18] *Impregilo*, Award, para. 355.
[19] *Suez–Vivendi* and *AWG Group*, Decision on Liability, para. 262; *Suez–InterAgua*, Decision on Liability, para. 240.
[20] ILC, *Commentaries on State Responsibility*, Article 25, at 19.
[21] *See* id., Article 25, at 19.

is faltering. BITs aim to protect such rights not only in times of macroeconomic stability, but also in times of crisis. Analogous to the exclusion of the necessity defence in humanitarian conventions, one could hence argue that the object and purpose of BITs implicitly excludes the necessity defence.

If States could evade their obligations under a convention providing rules for military action in armed conflict through an external concept of military necessity, then the convention would lose much of its *raison d'être*. It is debatable whether a similar conclusion is justified for the availability of the necessity defence in the context of IIAs. Such treaties apply in all the different political, economic, or military situations host States may find themselves in over the lifetime of a treaty. It appears to be quite a stretch to assume that the parties to an IIA intended to mutually relinquish the necessity defence reserved for extraordinary circumstances when concluding the relevant treaty. Furthermore, the inapplicability of necessity according to Article 25(2)(a) ASR arguably presupposes that the protection of private property rights is the sole object and purpose of the relevant treaty. At least IIAs that are more recent often do not exclusively focus on the protection of private property rights.[22] In such settings, the object and purpose of the treaty will provide only very limited guidance for the resolution of conflicts between private property rights and the public interest. Rather, adjudicators should interpret and apply the relevant treaty stipulations and the rules of general international law to resolve possible conflicts.[23] Necessity as codified in Article 25 ASR is part of these rules.

2. Inapplicability of Article 25 due to NPM clauses as *leges speciales*?

The *CMS* annulment committee suggested that Article XI of the Argentina–US BIT might constitute *lex specialis* and exclude the applicability of Article 25 ASR. Interestingly, the committee considered Article XI to constitute *lex specialis* only under the assumption that Article 25 constituted a primary rule of international law.[24] While the committee did not reach a view with respect to the legal character of Article 25, the ILC clearly stated that the ASR are a codification of secondary rules of international law.[25] The categorization of necessity as a secondary rule, however, does not automatically negate the possibility of a *lex specialis* relationship between NPM clauses and Article 25. The relevant provision on *lex specialis* in the ASR is Article 55, which specifies that:

These articles do not apply where and to the extent that the conditions for the existence of an internationally wrongful act or the content or implementation of the international responsibility of a State are governed by special rules of international law.

---

[22] *See* Chapter 5, subsection V.3.
[23] For the relevance of general international law in investor–State arbitration, *see* Chapter 4, subsections III. 1, III.2.a.
[24] *See* Chapter 7, note 12 and accompanying text.
[25] ILC, *Commentaries on State Responsibility*, General commentary, para. 1.

The ILC commentaries on Article 55 state that 'States often make special provisions for the legal consequences of breaches of [primary] obligations, *and even for determining whether there has been such a breach*. The question is whether those provisions are exclusive.'[26] The first part of this comment illustrates that States can agree on special rules regarding the consequences of the breach of a primary rule. For example, a treaty could include special provisions on restitution that modify (or exclude) Article 35 ASR.[27] The second part of this comment, quoted in italics, strongly suggests that NPM clauses that determine whether there has been a breach of an international obligation may also fall within the scope of Article 55.[28] A treaty rule is *lex specialis* if it provides a deeper or more detailed regulation on the subject matter.[29] In this vein, Maria Agius argues that if States provide for derogation clauses (i.e. NPM clauses) in a particular treaty, the customary international law defence of necessity is inapplicable.[30]

There is no generic answer to the question of whether a particular NPM clause excludes the applicability of Article 25 ASR. Rather, the answer is likely to vary from treaty to treaty. Regarding the Argentina–US BIT, an inquiry into the applicability of Article 25 alongside the NPM clause in Article XI of the treaty is mainly an academic exercise. If Article XI sets in, there is no reason for the arbitral tribunal to address Article 25 as there is no breach of an international obligation that could be justified by Article 25. Conversely, if the requirements of Article XI are not fulfilled, it is almost impossible for the responding State to meet the high threshold of Article 25, especially because of the strict 'only way' requirement.[31] That said, the decision of the *Enron* annulment committee gives reason to rethink the interpretation of the requirements of the necessity defence, which will be done in section III. If more lenient approaches towards the interpretation of Article 25 hold sway, this provision might play a significant role in investor–State arbitrations in the future, regardless of whether the relevant treaty contains an NPM clause.

The main reason why the necessity defence may be relevant even in the context of treaties that contain NPM clauses is that Article 25 covers State action adopted for any 'essential interest' of the host State. Most NPM clauses allow interference with private property rights only for the furtherance of specific policy objectives. Article XI of the Argentina–US BIT, for example, lists 'the maintenance of public order', 'the maintenance or restoration of international peace or security', and the protection of 'essential security interests' as permissible public policy objectives. The relevant provision of the (2004 and 2012) US Model BIT contains an even

---

[26] Id., Article 55, para. 1 (emphasis added).   [27] Id., Article 55, para. 5.

[28] Roberto Ago also recognized the possibility of a *lex specialis* relationship between the customary international law defence of necessity and special treaty provisions (Ago, *Report on State Responsibility*, para. 67).

[29] Mark E. Villiger, *Customary International Law and Treaties* (1985), para. 87.

[30] *See, e.g.,* Maria Agius, 'The Invocation of Necessity in International Law', *Netherlands International Law Review* 56 (2009) 95–135, at 119.

[31] *See infra* section II.

more limited list than Article XI of the Argentina–US BIT: the 'public order' clause is not part of Article 18(2).[32] Hence, certain regulatory measures that do not serve one of the public policy objectives listed in an NPM clause might still fall under the scope of Article 25.

In deciding on the applicability of Article 25 in the context of IIAs that contain NPM clauses, the following question ought to guide the analysis: is the relevant NPM clause meant to expand or limit the regulatory freedom of the host State compared to the situation that would exist if the clause were not part of the treaty? If an interpretation according to Article 31 VCLT leads to the conclusion that the relevant clause seeks to *expand* regulatory freedom, then Article 25 should be applicable if the NPM clause does not set in. If the relevant clause intends to *limit* the regulatory freedom of the host State, as compared to the situation under customary international law, then recourse to Article 25 should be denied. Again, the answer to this question might vary from clause to clause as well as from treaty to treaty. Most of the more recent IIAs that contain NPM clauses take account of the public interest to a greater extent than BITs from the twentieth century.[33] In those cases, there is little reason to assume that Article 25 is not applicable if the requirements of the relevant NPM clause are not fulfilled.

3. Inapplicability of Article 25 due to the involvement of non-State actors?

The last issue to be addressed in this section is whether the involvement of non-State actors in investor–State arbitration has an effect on the applicability of Article 25. The *BG Group* tribunal briefly mentioned the possibility that Article 25 might cover the relations between States only, without commenting any further on this issue.[34] This notion does not appear to be in line with the view of the ILC, which describes the scope of the ASR as follows:

[T]he present articles are concerned with the whole field of State responsibility. Thus they are not limited to breaches of obligations of a bilateral character, e.g. under a bilateral treaty with another State. They apply to the whole field of international obligations of States, whether the obligation is owed to one or several States, to an *individual or group*, or to the international community as a whole.[35]

The ILC was not as clear about the applicability of Part Two of the ASR (Articles 28–39) to disputes involving non-State actors as this general statement might suggest. Article 33(2) stipulates that Part Two 'is without prejudice to any right, arising from the international responsibility of a State, which may accrue directly to any person'. According to the ILC, this 'without prejudice' clause clarifies that

---

[32] *See* Chapter 7, note 78.
[33] *See*, e.g., Chapter 5, subsection III.3 and Chapter 7, subsection III.2.
[34] *BG Group*, Final Award, para. 408.
[35] ILC, *Commentaries on State Responsibility*, General commentary, para. 5 (emphasis added).

it is for the applicable primary rules to determine whether non-State actors can invoke the responsibility of the relevant State directly.[36] Part One (which includes Article 25), in contrast, applies to all international obligations, whether they are owed to other States, non-State actors, or both. The ILC described this principle as follows:

State responsibility extends, for example, to human rights violations and other breaches of international law where the primary beneficiary of the obligation breached is not a State. However, while Part One applies to all the cases in which an internationally wrongful act may be committed by a State, Part Two has a more limited scope.[37]

That said, there is some controversy surrounding the question of whether all of the circumstances precluding wrongfulness in Part One of the ASR are applicable in investor–State arbitration. This is particularly true with respect to countermeasures. The relevant provision (Article 22 ASR) reads as follows:

The wrongfulness of an act of a State not in conformity with an international obligation towards another State is precluded if and to the extent that the act constitutes a countermeasure taken against the latter State in accordance with Chapter II of Part III.

The crucial issue here is whether lawful countermeasures justify breaches of international obligations only with respect to the State that committed the prior wrongful act or also vis-à-vis foreign investors from that State. This question became relevant when US investors instigated NAFTA arbitrations against Mexico because of a 20% tax on any drink containing a sweetener not made from cane sugar. Mexico argued that the tax was a countermeasure taken in response to a prior violation of NAFTA by the US.

Before turning to the positions taken by the different tribunals, a few words on the ILC codification of countermeasures as a circumstance precluding wrongfulness are in order. The ILC clarified that the relevant act a State seeks to justify under the ASR must be directed against the State that committed the prior wrongful act, and that countermeasures only preclude wrongfulness in relation to that State. The phrases 'if and to the extent' and 'countermeasures taken against' in Article 22 make this clear.[38] The ILC recognized that countermeasures might have negative effects on the position of other States or non-State actors. Third parties must tolerate these effects as long as they do not amount to a violation of an international obligation owed to them.[39] Consequently, NAFTA tribunals dealing with the Mexican soft drink tax analysed whether Mexico owed its NAFTA Chapter XI obligations directly to foreign investors or merely to the other parties to NAFTA.

---

[36] Id., Article 33, para. 4. The ILC identified IIAs as an example where primary obligations are owed to non-State actors, and where those actors can invoke the responsibility of the relevant State directly (id.)

[37] Id., Article 28, para. 3.   [38] Id., Article 22, paras. 4–5.

[39] Id., Article 49, paras 4–5.

There are three main theories on the rights and positions of foreign investors under IIAs,[40] and the relevant NAFTA tribunals have referred to all three of them. According to the 'derivative rights theory', all obligations in an IIA are merely owed on an inter-State level. Hence, when investors instigate arbitral proceedings they are, as the *ADM* tribunal put it, 'stepping into the shoes and asserting the rights of their home State'.[41] The second theory says that investors have a procedural right to bring a claim, while the substantive obligations under the relevant IIA remain on the inter-State level. This is the theory favoured by the *ADM* tribunal, which found that the countermeasures in question did not infringe the investor's procedural right to bring a claim.[42] According to a third theory, the substantive BIT provisions are directly owed to the foreign investor.[43] Under this theory, countermeasures, even if lawful, cannot justify the breach of an IIA provision vis-à-vis foreign investors. The *CPI* and *Cargill* tribunals favoured this theory.[44]

While the nature of investor rights is therefore of crucial importance in the context of countermeasures, it is submitted that this issue is immaterial when it comes to the customary international law defence of necessity. This is true even where one assumes that foreign investors enjoy substantive rights under BITs. Contrary to countermeasures, the necessity defence operates independently of any prior conduct of another actor.[45] The act justified by necessity does not require an internationally wrongful act by another State nor does it need to be directed against a certain State. Rather, necessity justifies the breach of any international obligation under the strict requirements of Article 25. There is no limitation as to the number of potential obligors: the act will be justified concerning any State against whom the relevant obligation is owed. The same holds true for non-State actors. This does not mean that the necessity defence is indifferent to the effects of the act on others. Article 25(1)(b) stipulates that the necessity defence is excluded if the relevant act 'seriously impair[s] an essential interest of the State or States toward which the obligation exists, or of the international community as a whole'. Moreover, as we will see below, resort to necessity entails a duty to compensate.[46] These considerations, however, relate to the elements of the necessity defence and its consequences—and not to its very applicability.

---

[40] For an overview of these theories, *see* Parlett, *The Individual in the International Legal System*, at 106–19. *See also* Chapter 5, notes 209–14 and accompanying text.

[41] *Archer Daniels Midland Company and Tate & Lyle Ingredients Americas, Inc v. United Mexican States*, ICSID Case No. ARB (AF)/04/5 (NAFTA), Award, 21 November 2007, para. 162. On this theory in general, *see* Parlett, *The Individual in the International Legal System*, at 109.

[42] *ADM*, Award, para. 179. The tribunal found that the countermeasures were disproportionate and could, therefore, not justify the breach of NAFTA obligations (id., paras. 160 and 180).

[43] Parlett, *The Individual in the International Legal System*, at 111.

[44] *Corn Products International, Inc v. United Mexican States*, ICSID Case No. ARB (AF)/04/1 (NAFTA), Decision on Responsibility, 15 January 2008, para. 167; *Cargill, Incorporated v. United Mexican States*, ICSID Case No. ARB(AF)/05/2 (NAFTA), Award, 18 September 2009, para 553.

[45] *See* ILC, *Commentaries on State Responsibility*, Article 25, para. 2.

[46] *See* subsection IV.1.

That said, a 2007 decision of the German Constitutional Court triggered some discussion on whether the necessity defence is available in investor–State arbitration.[47] During its financial crisis, in December 2001, Argentina defaulted on its external debt (that is it failed to meet due principal and interest payments). This default has resulted not only in several investor–State arbitrations but also in domestic court proceedings brought by private individuals against Argentina. In 2007, the German Constitutional Court rendered a decision on the question whether Argentina could invoke necessity as a defence in German court proceedings against private bondholders. The Court recognized that Article 25 ASR constitutes an accurate codification of customary international law.[48] However, the Court found that Article 25 applies only to relationships governed by international law, and not to those governed by private law. Hence, the German Constitutional Court held that there is no rule of general international law that entitles a State to suspend the performance of its *private* law obligations vis-à-vis individuals in situations of necessity.[49]

A closer look at the reasoning of the German Constitutional Court reveals that its decision, even if considered correct, is of minor importance for claims based on the violation of BIT obligations. Notably, the Court did not contradict the reasoning of the *CMS* and *LG&E* tribunals, which applied Article 25. Rather, the Court explicitly referred to these decisions and clarified that the *CMS* and *LG&E* tribunals decided on BIT obligations governed by *international* law.[50] Contrary to its position regarding *private* law claims brought before domestic courts, the Court did not doubt that Article 25 is applicable to disputes governed by international law, whether they involve private individuals or not.[51]

Hence, the decision of the German Constitutional Court does not cast doubt on the notion that the breach of substantive investment treaty obligations may be justified by Article 25. The decision on jurisdiction and admissibility in *Abaclat*—a case brought by private bondholders against Argentina—confirms this point. In analysing whether the relevant governmental acts might prima facie have breached a BIT provision, the tribunal distinguished the mere failure to fulfil payment obligations from sovereign acts, which included in particular legislative measures Argentina took to modify its payment obligations.[52] As a result,

---

[47] Stephan W. Schill & Yun-I Kim, 'Sovereign Bonds in Economic Crisis: Is the Necessity Defense under International Law Applicable to Investor–State Relations? A Critical Analysis of the Decision by the German Constitutional Court in the Argentine Bondholder Cases', *in Yearbook on International Investment Law & Policy* 2010/2011 (Karl P. Sauvant ed., 2011) 485–512, at 487.

[48] BVerfG, 2 BvM 1/03, Decision of 7 May 2007, para. 36. (Paragraph numbers refer to the German language version of the decision.)

[49] Id., para. 49.   [50] Id., para. 53.

[51] Id., para. 48. August Reinisch made the same point in his expert opinion requested by the German Constitutional Court (August Reinisch, 'Sachverständigengutachten zur Frage des Bestehens und der Wirkung des völkerrechtlichen Rechtfertigungsgrundes "Staatsnotstand"', *Zeitschrift für Ausländisches Öffentliches Recht und Völkerrecht* 68 (2008) 3–43, at 22 (para. 69) and 23 (para. 75)).

[52] *Abaclat and others v. Argentine Republic*, ICSID Case No. ARB/07/5, Decision on Jurisdiction and Admissibility, 4 August 2011, paras. 313–4 and 321–4.

the tribunal found that Argentina might have violated the relevant BIT provisions on FET, expropriation, and non-discrimination by its sovereign acts.[53] And as explained above, the German Constitutional Court did not doubt that Article 25 is available as justification against breaches of such BIT provisions.

Under one scenario, however, the reasoning of the German Constitutional Court might become relevant for tribunals dealing with the violation of substantive BIT obligations. Many BITs contain so-called 'umbrella clauses', which oblige the parties to the treaty to fulfill any obligation arising from contractual relationships or specific undertakings made by the host State. In *Abaclat*, the claimants made an alternative contention in the event that the tribunal considered the relevant claims to be contractual. The claimants argued that the dispute would fall within the jurisdiction of the tribunal by operation of the umbrella clause in the Chile–Argentina BIT. According to the claimants, this umbrella clause would have been applicable through the most favoured nation clause in Article 3(1) of the Italy–Argentina BIT.[54] As the tribunal found that the claims at stake were treaty claims, it did not have to reach a view on this argument. There is some debate on the question as to whether an umbrella clause turns a contract claim into a treaty claim.[55] This debate is beyond the scope of this book. Suffice it to say here that the reasoning of the German Constitutional Court could only become relevant for tribunals dealing with the violation of BIT obligations when an umbrella clause does *not* elevate contract claims to the treaty level.

In this context, it is important to recall that the German Constitutional Court referred with approval to a number of decisions by international courts and tribunals that applied the doctrine of necessity.[56] In three cases cited by the Court—*Serbian Loans, French Company of Venezuela Railroads*, and *Russian Indemnity*—the relevant disputes involved contract claims.[57] States exercising diplomatic protection brought the relevant claims before the respective courts and tribunals. As explained in Chapter 2, the exercise of diplomatic protection is a right of the State and not of the individual.[58] Hence, to the German Constitutional Court, the invocation of the necessity defence in these cases concerned exclusively the inter-State level.[59] The German Constitutional Court concluded that there was no State practice accompanied by *opinio juris* to support the existence of a rule of customary international law entitling States to invoke necessity against contract claims by private individuals.[60]

Justice Lübbe-Wolff issued a dissenting opinion severely criticizing the reasoning of the majority. Lübbe-Wolff found that it would be contradictory to grant defaulting States the necessity defence against creditor States but not against

---

[53] Id., paras. 314, 326. A more definitive statement was not necessary at this stage of the proceedings.

[54] Id., para. 310.

[55] *See, e.g.,* McLachlan, et al., *International Investment Arbitration—Substantive Principles, paras.* 4.94–4.116.

[56] BVerfG, 2 BvM 1/03, Decision of 7 May 2007, paras. 45–60.

[57] Id., paras. 54–60.   [58] *See* Chapter 2, notes 43–9 and accompanying text.

[59] BVerfG, 2 BvM 1/03, Decision of 7 May 2007, paras 57, 59, 60.   [60] Id., para 33.

private individuals. According to the 'object and meaning' of the necessity defence, its invocation could not be restricted to the inter-State level.[61] Lübbe-Wolff's reasoning received significant scholarly support. Stephan Schill and Yun-I Kim, for example, argue that the strict dualistic approach of the majority opinion, with its categorical distinction between the inter-State level and the relations between States and individuals, constitutes a legal anachronism.[62] The strongest argument against the limitation of the necessity defence to the inter-State level relates to standing.[63] Prior to the current systems of investor–State arbitration and human rights adjudication, individuals very rarely had standing before international courts and tribunals.[64] Decisions by international courts and tribunals concerning the plea of necessity, therefore, almost by definition focused on the inter-State level. This does not mean, however, that States intended the necessity defence to be inapplicable if a private law claim is brought directly before an international court or tribunal—or the courts of a foreign State. In sum, the involvement of private actors in investor–State arbitration is unlikely to lead to the inapplicability of Article 25.

II. The status quo: practical unavailability of necessity in investor–State arbitration

As mentioned above, the tribunals in the Argentine cases all considered Article 25 ASR to be an accurate codification of the customary international law defence of necessity, but none of them found that Argentina's emergency measures were justified by it.[65] This unanimous holding—and the particular reasoning adopted by some tribunals—provokes the question whether necessity as codified in Article 25 may play a meaningful role in investor–State arbitration at all. Focusing on the Argentine cases, this section examines which elements of Article 25 make it so difficult for States to successfully invoke necessity—and whether States can realistically expect to pass the relevant hurdles in future crises. Answers to these questions are necessary to determine whether and how proportionality analysis could render the necessity defence more useful to States in investor–State arbitration.

This section is structured around the different elements of Article 25, which can be easily inferred from the provision's wording:

1. Necessity may not be invoked by a State as a ground for precluding the wrongfulness of an act not in conformity with an international obligation of that State unless the act:

---

[61] Id., para. 86.
[62] Schill & Kim, 'Sovereign Bonds in Economic Crisis', at 496, 501; Stephan W. Schill, 'Der völkerrechtliche Staatsnotstand in der Entscheidung des BVerfG zu Argentinischen Staatsanleihen—Anachronismus oder Avantgarde? ', *Zeitschrift für ausländisches und öffentliches Recht und Völkerrecht* 68 (2008) 45–67, at 52–6.
[63] *See also* Schill & Kim, 'Sovereign Bonds in Economic Crisis', at 498.
[64] *See* Chapter 2, notes 29–38 and accompanying text.
[65] *See supra* note 1 and accompanying text.

(a) is the only way for the State to safeguard an essential interest against a grave and imminent peril; and

(b) does not seriously impair an essential interest of the State or States towards which the obligation exists, or of the international community as a whole.

2. In any case, necessity may not be invoked by a State as a ground for precluding wrongfulness if:

(a) the international obligation in question excludes the possibility of invoking necessity; or

(b) the State has contributed to the situation of necessity.

The stipulation in Article 25(2)(a) according to which necessity may not be invoked if '[t]he international obligation in question excludes the possibility of invoking necessity' concerns the applicability of Article 25 and was dealt with in subsection I.1. Before addressing the individual elements of Article 25, a few general remarks on this provision relevant to all of its components are in order. The very first sentence of Article 25 makes it abundantly clear that necessity can only be invoked in exceptional circumstances. The provision starts with the formulation 'necessity may not be invoked'—and then qualifies this basic rule in the course of the elaborate Article 25. The elements of the necessity defence are phrased as a list of cumulative elements that need to be met if an exception to the basic rule should apply.[66] The ILC clarified in its commentaries that the purpose of this negative wording was to stress the exceptional character of the doctrine.[67] There is also no doubt that the different elements of Article 25 are subject to judicial scrutiny. In this vein, the ICJ held in *Gabčíkovo* with respect to the elements of the necessity defence that 'the State concerned is not the sole judge of whether those conditions have been met'.[68] With these observations in mind, we now turn to the various elements of Article 25.

1. Grave and imminent peril for an essential interest

Article 25(1)(a) ASR provides that necessity may only be invoked 'to safeguard an essential interest against a grave and imminent peril'. For some tribunals deciding the Argentine cases, Argentina's measures to combat the economic and financial crisis did not serve such an 'essential interest'. The *CMS* tribunal did not categorically deny that an economic crisis may give rise to the necessity defence when it held that 'the need to prevent a major breakdown, with all its social and political implications, might have entailed an essential interest of the State'.[69] But while the tribunal conceded that the crisis was 'indeed severe', it held that 'the relative

---

[66] The ICJ has confirmed that the different elements of the necessity defence have to be fulfilled cumulatively, as indicated by the clear wording of Article 25 and its predecessor in the 1980 draft articles (*Case concerning the Gabčíkovo–Nagymaros Project* (Hungary v. Slovakia), Judgment, 25 September 1997, ICJ Reports 1997, 7–84, at 51).

[67] ILC, *Commentaries on State Responsibility*, Article 25, para. 14.

[68] *Case concerning the Gabčíkovo–Nagymaros Project* (Hungary v. Slovakia), Judgment, 25 September 1997, ICJ Reports 1997, 7–84, para. 57.

[69] *CMS*, Award, para. 319.

effect that can be reasonably attributed to the crisis does not allow for a finding on preclusion of wrongfulness'.[70] The *Enron* and *Sempra* tribunals reached the same result but were more explicit in their reasoning. They found that the relevant peril must go against the very existence of the State for the State measure to serve an 'essential interest':

The Tribunal has no doubt that there was a severe crisis and that in such context it was unlikely that business could have continued as usual. Yet, the argument that such a situation compromised the *very existence of the State and its independence* so as to qualify as involving an essential interest of the State is not convincing. Questions of public order and social unrest could be handled as in fact they were, just as questions of political stabilization were handled under the constitutional arrangements in force.[71]

The notion that the necessity defence is related to the preservation of the very existence of the State is rooted in natural law approaches such as the eighteenth-century writings of Emmerich de Vattel. In *The Law of Nations*, Vattel established a direct link between a so-called 'right of self-preservation' and the doctrine of necessity:

[t]he right of self-preservation carries with it the right to whatever is necessary for that purpose, for the natural law gives us the right to all those things without which we can not satisfy our obligations.[72]

Vattel further specified that:

[a] Nation or State has the right to whatever can assist it in warding off a threatening danger, or in keeping at a distance things that might bring about its ruin. The same reasons hold good here as for the right to whatever is necessary for self-preservation.[73]

Inspired by Vattel, some scholars would assume that there exist certain supreme rights and duties of States apart from the positive rules of international law. These rights were mostly considered to be hierarchically superior to treaty law or custom.[74] Among these 'natural rights', the right of self-preservation prevailed over all other rights or duties. Amos S. Hershey, for example, found that a State has the 'right... to take such measures *as it may deem necessary* for its own safety and defence'.[75] Such an omnipotent, self-judging right of self-preservation obviously lends itself to abuse and undermines the very idea of an international legal order

---

[70] Id., paras. 320–1.

[71] *Enron*, Award, para. 306 (emphasis added). The *Sempra* award contains virtually the same wording, except for some minor editorial differences (*Sempra*, Award, para. 348).

[72] Emmerich de Vattel, *The Law of Nations or the Principles of Natural Law Applied to the Conduct and to the Affairs of Nations and of Sovereigns* (1758, James Brown Scott (ed), Carnegie Institution of Washington, 1916), Book I, Chapter II, § 18, at 14.

[73] Id., § 20, at 14.

[74] Amos S. Hershey, for example, found that 'these rights have, in fact, a broader and deeper significance than the ordinary positive rules of the Law of Nations of which they are in large measure the ultimate basis or source, and have even greater obligatory force' (Amos S. Hershey, *The Essentials of International Public Law* (1912), at 143).

[75] Id., at 144.

that seeks to put certain restraints on the exercise of power. Georg Schwarzenberger aptly summarized the consequences of such a right of self-preservation:

If self-preservation were an absolute and overriding right, the rest of international law would become optional, and its observance would depend on a self-denying ordinance, revocable at will by each State, not to invoke this formidable super-right.[76]

While Schwarzenberger's rejection of an overriding right of self-preservation reflects the current status of international law, this does not necessarily mean that States can rely on the necessity defence without a threat to their very existence. But the argument that such an existential threat is necesary to trigger the necessity defence has lost much of its historical underpinning. State practice and judicial decisions confirm this account, and illustrate how the doctrine of necessity has decoupled from the right of self-preservation over time.

References to the right of self-preservation were still quite common in the late nineteenth and at the beginning of the twentieth century. In 1903, Venezuela and France set up a mixed claims commission to resolve disputes arising out of the 1898–9 Venezuelan revolution.[77] The commission consisted of one commissioner from each party and one umpire (appointed by the Queen of the Netherlands) who would render an opinion only when the two commissioners disagreed.[78] In *French Company of Venezuela Railroads*, the umpire held that Venezuela was not responsible for its failure to repay its debts to a French company. While the umpire found that Venezuela's 'own preservation was paramount', the decision does not say that necessity is available only if the existence of the State is at stake:

The umpire finds no purpose or intent on the part of the respondent Government to harm or injure the claimant company in any way or in any degree. Its acts and its neglects were caused and incited by entirely different reasons and motives. Its first duty was to itself. Its *own preservation* was paramount. Its revenues were properly devoted to that end. The appeal of the company for funds came to an empty treasury, or to one only adequate to the demands of the war budget.[79]

---

[76] Georg Schwarzenberger, 'The Fundamental Principles of International Law', *Recueil de Cours* 87 (1955) 195–383, at 344.

[77] 'Mixed Claims Commission France–Venezuela Constituted Under the Protocol signed at Washington on 27 February 1903', *reprinted in* United Nations Reports of International Arbitral Awards X, at 3–4.

[78] *See* Article I and II of the Protocol dated 27 February 1903, 'Mixed Claims Commission France–Venezuela Constituted Under the Protocol signed at Washington on 27 February 1903', *reprinted in* United Nations Reports of International Arbitral Awards X, at 3–4.

[79] *French Company of Venezuelan Railroads Case*, Mixed Claims Commission France–Venezuela, Opinion of the Umpire, 31 July 1905, United Nations Reports of International Arbitral Awards X, 335–55, at 353 (emphasis added). The umpire used the term '*force majeure*' and not 'necessity'. At the time of the decision, tribunals used these two terms fairly interchangeably. According to contemporary doctrine, necessity contains an element of 'free choice', which is absent from *force majeure* (ILC, Report of the International Law Commission on the work of its fifty-third session, Yearbook of the International Law Commission, Vol. I (2001), Article 23, para. 1). A State resorting to the necessity defence might act in an emergency situation, but it is still willfully committing the particular act. In a situation of *force majeure,* in contrast, it is materially impossible for the State to comply with an international obligation (id., Article 23, para. 1). In most cases, budgetary constraints will force States to prioritize their expenses. The very act of prioritization involves an element

In 1912, an arbitral tribunal set up by Russia and Turkey followed a similar line of reasoning, albeit with a different outcome. In the 'preliminaries of peace' of 1878, Turkey had agreed to compensate Russian subjects and institutions located in Turkish territory for losses suffered during the war between the two States.[80] The issue submitted to arbitration (and decided in what became known as the *Russian Indemnity* case) was whether Turkey owed 20 million francs interest on its initial debt of 6 million.[81] Turkey adduced its financial problems between 1881 and 1902 as defence for its late payment. The tribunal acknowledged that Turkey was forced to 'make special application of parts of its revenues' because of 'financial difficulties of the utmost seriousness, increased by domestic and foreign events'.[82] But the tribunal also pointed out that Turkey was able to obtain loans at decent rates, pay back some of those loans, and reduce its public debt by approximately 350 million francs.[83] In light of the comparatively small initial debt of 6 million francs, the tribunal rejected Turkey's defence since the repayment would not have 'imperil[led] the existence of the Ottoman Empire *or seriously compromise[d] its internal or external situation*'.[84] This indicates that a threat to the very existence was one alternative under which the tribunal would have accepted Turkey's defence, but serious consequences for Turkey's 'internal or external situation' might have sufficed as well.

While *French Company of Venezuela Railroads* and *Russian Indemnity* contain at least references to self-preservation, other decisions and instances of State practice are devoid of any connection between 'necessity' and existential threats. One of these examples is the 1893 *Russian Fur Seals* controversy. When British and US hunting near Russian territorial waters threatened to exterminate seals, the Russian government prohibited hunting of fur seals by a decree that extended beyond Russian territory. In a letter to the British ambassador, the Russian foreign minister identified an 'absolute necessity of immediate precautionary measures' and underlined 'the essentially precautionary character of the above-mentioned measures, which were taken under the pressure of exceptional circumstances'.[85]

The *Torrey Canyon* incident is another case in point. In 1967, the Liberian oil tanker *Torrey Canyon* had an accident close to British territorial waters, and the leaking oil was a threat for the English coast and its environment. After several attempts to contain the oil on board had failed, the British government decided to bomb the abandoned ship in order to burn the remaining oil. Interestingly,

---

of 'free choice'. Consequently, it is difficult to imagine a situation in which a financial crisis could lead to a situation of *force majeure*.

[80] *Russian Indemnity* (Russia v. Turkey), Award, 11 November 1912, *reprinted in American Journal of International Law* 7 (1913) 178–201, at 182.

[81] Id., at 187.   [82] Id., at 195.   [83] Id., at 196.

[84] Id. (emphasis added). Like the umpire in *French Company of Venezuela Railroads*, the tribunal used the term '*force majeure*' instead of 'necessity'. For the difference between these two concepts, *see supra* note 79.

[85] ILC, 'Force majeure' and 'fortuitous event' as circumstances precluding wrongfulness: survey of State practice, international judicial decisions and doctrine—Study prepared by the Secretariat, Yearbook of the International Law Commission, Vol. II, Part One, 61–227 (1978), para. 155.

no protest of any government against the British plan to destroy the vessel was reported, and the silence of the international community arbugaly indicated a consensus on the lawfulness of the British measures.[86]

Another example to be mentioned here is the ICJ decision in *Gabčíkovo–Nagymaros*. In 1989, Hungary suspended works on a joint dam project with Slovakia (then Czechoslovakia) on the river Danube because of environmental concerns. While this suspension was contrary to Hungary obligations under a 1977 treaty, the ICJ 'ha[d] no difficulty in acknowledging that the concerns expressed by Hungary for its natural environment...related to an "essential interest."'[87] Ultimately, the ICJ rejected Hungary's necessity defence since the environmental ramifications of the project were dependent on the final rules of operation, which had not even been agreed when Hungary stopped its works.[88] Hence, the court did not consider the relevant peril to be 'imminent' as required by the ILC codification.[89]

All of the above strongly indicates that a threat to the very existence of a State is only one way for its 'essential interests' to be at stake. In his 1980 report to the ILC, Roberto Ago described the circumstances that could give rise to the necessity defence as

a grave danger to the existence of the State itself, its political or economic survival, the continued functioning of its essential services, the maintenance of internal peace, the survival of a sector of its population, the preservation of the environment of its territory or a part thereof, etc.[90]

In line with Ago's report, the 2001 ILC commentaries relied on a number of cases in which the relevant 'essential interest' had nothing to do with the very survival of the State.[91] Without providing a specific list of interests, the ILC suggested a case-to-case analysis to determine whether a particular interest qualifies as 'essential':

The extent to which a given interest is essential depends on all the circumstances and cannot be prejudged. It extends to particular interests of the State and its people, as well as of the international community as a whole.[92]

Unlike the *Sempra* and *Enron* tribunals, most of the Argentina tribunals commenting on the 'essential interest' prong followed the guidance provided by the

---

[86] *See* ILC, *Commentaries on State Responsibility*, Article 25, para. 9.

[87] *Case concerning the Gabčíkovo–Nagymaros Project* (Hungary v. Slovakia), Judgment, 25 September 1997, ICJ Reports 1997, 7–84, para. 53.

[88] Id., para. 55.

[89] Id., para. 55. For a general criticism of the 'imminence' prong and a proposal to exclude this element from the analysis, *see* Julio Barboza, 'Necessity (Revisited) in International Law', *in Essays in International Law in Honour of Judge Manfred Lachs* (Jerzy Makarczyk ed., 1984) 27–43, at 40–1.

[90] Ago, *Report on State Responsibility*, para. 2.

[91] ILC, *Commentaries on State Responsibility*, Article 25, paras. 4–12.

[92] Id., Article 25, para. 15.

ILC. The *LG&E* tribunal, for example, held that peril to an 'essential interest' does not necessarily require that there be a threat to the very existence of the State:

What qualifies as an 'essential' interest is not limited to those interests referring to the State's existence. As evidence demonstrates, economic, financial or those interests related to the protection of the State against any danger seriously compromising its internal or external situation, are also considered essential interests. Roberto Ago has stated that essential interests include those related to 'different matters such as the economy, ecology or other.'[93]

The arbitrators in *Suez–Vivendi*, *AWG Group*, and *Suez–InterAgua* also had little difficulty in finding that Argentina sought to safeguard an 'essential interest' by adopting the relevant measures. They stated that '[t]he provision of water and sewage services to the metropolitan area of Buenos Aires certainly was vital to the health and well-being of nearly ten million people and was, therefore, an essential interest of the Argentine State'.[94] The *Impregilo* tribunal reasoned along similar lines, and explicitly held that a peril to an 'essential interest' does not necessarily involve a threat to the very existence of the State:

In the Arbitral Tribunal's view, the term 'essential interest' can encompass not only the existence and independence of a State itself, but also other subsidiary but nonetheless 'essential' interests, such as the preservation of the State's broader social, economic and environmental stability, and its ability to provide for the fundamental needs of its population. It follows that, in addition to Argentina's overall stability, the need to provide the population with water and sewage facilities represented an 'essential interest' [...][95]

In sum, the jurisprudence, State practice, and ILC material reviewed in this subsection strongly suggests that the customary international law defence of necessity is not limited to situations in which States face existential threats. The approaches taken by the *LG&E, Suez–Vivendi, AWG Group, Suez–InterAgua*, and *Impregilo* tribunals on this issue seem to accurately reflect the current state of customary international law. Contrary to what the reasoning of the *Sempra* and *Enron* tribunals might suggest, the 'essential interest' requirement in Article 25 is no reason why the necessity defence would be unavailable to States in a severe economic crisis.

2. No serious impairment of another essential interest

Article 25(1)(b) ASR provides that the necessity defence is excluded if the relevant State measure 'seriously impair[s] an essential interest of the State or States towards which the obligation exists, or of the international community as a whole'. Generally, the tribunals dealing with the Argentine financial crisis did not analyse

---

[93] *LG&E*, Decision on Liability, para. 251 (internal reference omitted).
[94] *Suez–Vivendi* and *AWG Group*, Decision on Liability, para. 260; *Suez–InterAgua*, Decision on Liability, para. 238.
[95] *Impregilo*, Award, para. 346.

this requirement in great depth. The *LG&E* tribunal, for example, simply stated that '[i]t cannot be said that any other State's rights were seriously impaired by the measures taken by Argentina during the crisis'.[96] The *CMS* tribunal recognized that the Argentina–US BIT is 'also of interest to investors as they are specific beneficiaries and for investors the matter is indeed essential'.[97] Nevertheless, the tribunal concluded that 'it does not appear that an essential interest of the State to which the obligation exists has been impaired, nor have those of the international community as a whole. Accordingly, the plea of necessity would not be precluded on this count.'[98] Similarly, the arbitrators in *Suez–Vivendi* and *AWG Group* stated that 'Argentina may have injured the Claimants' interests, but it is difficult to see how Argentina's actions impaired an essential interest of France, Spain, the United Kingdom, or the international community'.[99] The *Impregilo* tribunal also refused to take the claimant's interests into account under Article 25(1)(b). The tribunal held that:

The interests of a small number of a Contracting State's nationals or legal entities are not consistent with or qualify as an 'essential interest' of that State. It follows that any impairment of those interests is irrelevant for purposes of the paragraph.[100]

Some authors wonder whether such jurisprudence gives too little weight to the interests of foreign investors. August Reinisch, for example, finds that the interests of individuals may have to be 'balanced' against the interests of the State invoking the necessity defence.[101] Andrea Bjorklund argues that the State-centric approach of the tribunals in the Argentine cases puts foreign investors at a disadvantage as they will usually not be able to convincingly argue the interests of their home States in arbitral proceedings.[102] The drafting process of Article 25 contains some support for such concerns. As mentioned above, Article 33 of the 1980 ILC draft articles was almost identical to Article 25. But one significant difference between the two provisions is that Article 33 limited the interests that may outweigh the interests of the State invoking necessity to the bilateral level. Article 33 mentioned only the interests of the 'State towards which the obligation exists'; the reference to the 'international community as a whole' was missing in the 1980 draft.[103] It is safe to assume that today the 'international community' does not only include States but also other entities and individuals.[104]

While it is therefore difficult to argue that foreign investors are not part of the international community, Article 25(1)(b) does not refer to the interests of individual members of this community but rather to those of 'the international community as a whole'. The term 'international community as a whole' goes back

---

[96] *LG&E*, Decision on Liability, para. 257.   [97] *CMS*, Award, para. 358.

[98] Id., para. 358.

[99] *Suez–Vivendi* and *AWG Group*, Decision on Liability, para. 261.

[100] *Impregilo*, Award, para. 354.   [101] Reinisch, 'Necessity', at 201.

[102] Bjorklund, 'Emergency Exceptions: State of Necessity and Force Majeure', at 487.

[103] *See* Chapter 7, note 66.

[104] *See, e.g.,* Crawford, *State Responsibility*, Introduction, at 40–1.

to *Barcelona Traction*, where the ICJ distinguished a State's obligations in the field of the treatment of aliens and their property from obligations *erga omnes*:

When a State admits into its territory foreign investments or foreign nationals, whether natural or juristic persons, it is bound to extend to them the protection of the law and assumes obligations concerning the treatment to be afforded them. These obligations, however, are neither absolute nor unqualified. In particular, an essential distinction should be drawn between the obligations of a State towards the international community as a whole, and those arising vis-à-vis another State in the field of diplomatic protection. By their very nature the former are the concern of all States. In view of the importance of the rights involved, all States can be held to have a legal interest in their protection; they are obligations *erga omnes*.[105]

There are not many rules of international law that give rise to obligations *erga omnes*, i.e. obligations owed to the international community as a whole. In *Barcelona Traction* and in the advisory opinion on the *Wall in the Occupied Palestinian Territory*, the ICJ saw obligations *erga omnes* in the prohibitions of aggression, genocide, slavery, and racial discrimination, in the duty to respect the right to self-determination, and in certain obligations under international humanitarian law.[106] Breaches of *erga omnes* obligations may have far-reaching consequences under the law of State responsibility: States other than the injured State have the right to invoke the responsibility of the State violating the relevant obligation.[107]

It is important to bear in mind that Article 25(1)(b) excludes the necessity defence when an 'essential interest' of the international community as a whole is 'impaired', and not only when the State invoking necessity *violates* an *erga omnes* obligation. But it is also clear that not every detrimental effect on the interests of single actors will qualify as an impairment of the interests of the international community *as a whole*.[108] Against this background, Article 25(1)(b) does not seem to constitute an insurmountable hurdle for States to invoke the necessity defence in investor–State arbitration—and the Argentine cases bear this out.

---

[105] *Case concerning the Barcelona Traction Light and Power Company Limited* (Belgium v. Spain), Judgment, 5 February 1970, ICJ Reports (1970) 3, para. 33 (emphasis in the original).

[106] Id., para. 34; *Legal Consequences of the Construction of a Wall in the Occupied Palestinian Territory*, Advisory Opinion, 9 July 2004, ICJ Reports 2004, 136, para. 155. The ILC declined to provide a list of *erga omnes* norms, which would be of very 'limited value' since the concept of obligations *erga omnes* is not static but 'evolve[s] over time' (ILC, *Commentaries on State Responsibility*, Article 48, para. 9). The most likely candidates for the category of *erga omnes* obligations (beyond the examples mentioned by the ICJ) are international norms that involve so-called 'community interests', such as the ban on the use of force, the protection of the environment, and respect for international human rights (Bruno Simma, 'From Bilateralism to Community Interest in International Law', *Recueil de Cours* 250 (1994) 221–384, at 237–43).

[107] *See* Article 48(1)(b) and (2) of the ASR. Article 42 ASR sets out under what circumstances a State qualifies as an 'injured State'.

[108] Andrea Bjorklund notes that even taking into account the interests of foreign investors might not greatly influence the outcome of an Article 25(1)(b) analysis. In her view, the 'primarily financial' interests of foreign investors will regularly seem 'trivial' compared to the 'interests of a State in protecting its financial and political security and well-being' (Bjorklund, 'Emergency Exceptions', at 487).

3. The 'only way' requirement

Article 25(1)(a) ASR requires that the adopted measure be 'the only way' for the State invoking the necessity defence to protect its essential interest. The ILC clarified that the mere availability of other means negates the necessity defence, even 'if they may be more costly or less convenient'.[109] The ICJ endorsed this approach in *Gabčíkovo*, where the Court outlined concrete measures that Hungary could have adopted in lieu of abandoning the project to protect its environmental interests.[110] Significantly, the ICJ did not inquire into the effectiveness or cost of these alternative measures, which included construction works to regulate river flows and the processing of river water to supply Budapest with clean water.[111] The ICJ confirmed this approach in its *Wall* opinion, where it found that '[i]n the light of the material before it, the Court is not convinced that the construction of the wall along the route chosen was the only means to safeguard the interests of Israel'.[112]

Against this background, it is not surprising that the *CMS, Sempra, Enron, Suez–Vivendi, AWG Group*, and *Suez–InterAgua* tribunals found that Argentina's measures did not meet the high threshold of the 'only way' requirement.[113] The *CMS* tribunal observed that economists have identified alternatives to the measures adopted by Argentina, 'including dollarization of the economy, granting of direct subsidies to the affected population or industries and many others'.[114] Without commenting on the potential effectiveness of these alternatives, the tribunal concluded that 'the measures adopted were not the only steps available', and hence rejected the necessity defence.[115] The notion that the mere existence of a variety of approaches to address an economic crisis excludes the necessity defence was also expressed by the *Sempra* and *Enron* tribunals:

A rather sad global comparison of experiences in the handling of economic crises shows that there are always many approaches to addressing and resolving such critical events. It is therefore difficult to justify the position that only one of them was available in the Argentine case. While one or the other party would like the Tribunal to point out which alternative was recommendable, it is not the task of the Tribunal to substitute its view of the Government's choice between economic options. It is instead the Tribunal's duty only to determine whether the choice made was the only one available, and this does not appear to have been the case.[116]

---

[109] ILC, *Commentaries on State Responsibility* Article 25, para. 15.
[110] *Case concerning the Gabčíkovo–Nagymaros Project* (Hungary v. Slovakia), Judgment, 25 September 1997, ICJ Reports 1997, 7–84, paras. 55–7
[111] Id., paras. 55–6.
[112] *Legal Consequences of the Construction of a Wall in the Occupied Palestinian Territory*, Advisory Opinion, 9 July 2004, ICJ Reports 2004, 136, para. 140.
[113] *CMS*, Award, para. 324; *Enron*, Award, para. 308; *Sempra*, Award, paras. 350–1; *Suez–Vivendi* and *AWG Group*, Decision on Liability, para. 260; *Suez–InterAgua*, Decision on Liability, para. 238.
[114] *CMS*, Award, para. 323. [115] Id., para. 324.
[116] *Sempra*, Award, paras. 350–1. The same passage, bar minor editorial differences, is part of the *Enron* award (*Enron*, Award, paras. 309–10).

The arbitrators in *Suez–Vivendi and AWG Group* adopted a similar approach. They noted that 'Argentina could have attempted to apply more flexible means to assure the continuation of the water and sewage services to the people of Buenos Aires and at the same time respected its obligations of fair and equitable treatment'.[117]

The only tribunal that found that Argentina's measures were the 'only way' to deal with the crisis was the *LG&E* tribunal. To be noted at the outset, the *LG&E* tribunal did not rely on Article 25 but made this finding in passing.[118] While the reasoning of the *LG&E* tribunal regarding the 'only way' requirement was as brief as that of the other tribunals, it reached the opposite result:

In this circumstances, an economic recovery package was the only means to respond to the crisis. Although there may have been a number of ways to draft the economic recovery plan, the evidence before the Tribunal demonstrates that an across-the-board response was necessary, and the tariffs on public utilities had to be addressed.[119]

The *LG&E* tribunal adopted a very general approach to the 'only way' requirement. Instead of identifying distinct measures and then explaining why there were no other means available to attain the respective governmental goal, the tribunal simply relied on the necessity of *a* recovery package. This line of reasoning does not differ significantly from arguing that *some* action was necessary, and justifying the breach of international law on that ground.[120] The strict approach taken by the other tribunals with respect to the 'only way' requirement might be similarly dissatisfying. In an economic crisis, States will always have a variety of options at their disposal. The ILC's comment that 'the plea is excluded if there are other (otherwise lawful) means available, even if they may be more costly or less convenient' leads, in practice, to the result that the necessity defence will hardly, if ever, be available in an economic crisis.[121]

In this context, it should be noted that parts of the *Enron* award were annulled on the ground that the tribunal failed to address certain issues concerning the 'only way' requirement. The annulment committee held that taking the term 'only way' literally was just one of at least two ways Article 25(1)(a) could be interpreted. Under this interpretation, the necessity defence would be excluded 'if there were genuinely no other measures that Argentina could possibly have adopted in order to address the economic crisis'.[122] The annulment committee, in

---

[117] *Suez–Vivendi* and *AWG Group*, Decision on Liability, para. 260. The *Suez–InterAgua* tribunal reached the same conclusion regarding the water and sewage services in Santa Fe (*Suez–InterAgua*, Decision on Liability, para. 238).

[118] The tribunal found that 'the protections afforded by Article XI have been triggered in this case, and are sufficient to excuse Argentina's liability' (*LG&E*, Decision on Liability, para 245). It added that the 'necessity standard as it exists in international law (reflected in Article 25 of the ILC's Draft Articles on State Responsibility) supports the Tribunal's conclusion' (para 245). Elsewhere in its award, the tribunal clarified that Article 25 'alone does not establish Argentina's defense' (para. 258).

[119] Id., para. 257.

[120] For further criticism of the generality of the approach by the *LG&E* tribunal, see Bjorklund, 'Emergency Exceptions', at 486–7 and Reinisch, 'Necessity', at 200–1.

[121] See also Reinisch, 'Necessity', at 200.

[122] *Enron Creditors Recovery Corp. v. Argentine Republic*, ICSID Case No. ARB/01/3, Decision on the Application for Annulment of the Argentine Republic, 30 July 2010, para. 369.

essence, suggested the least restrictive means test as another possible interpretation of the 'only way' requirement. Article 25(1)(a) would then require that 'there must be no alternative measures that the State might have taken for safeguarding the essential interest in question that did not involve a similar or graver breach of international law'. Furthermore, the annulment committee criticized that the tribunal did not address the question of whether the 'relative effectiveness of alternative measures' matters.[123]

The comments of the annulment committee on Article 25(1)(a) resemble the interpretation of a treaty provision according to Article 31 VCLT. It is debatable whether such an approach is appropriate. The ASR purport to codify customary international law. As such, they ought to facilitate the identification and application of a particular source of international law. It is, of course, always possible to argue that a certain provision of the ASR does not accurately reflect customary international law. However, this is different to suggesting, as the *Enron* annulment committee did, that the 'only way' requirement might not have to be understood according to its 'literal meaning'. The ILC specified that the 'only way' requirement excludes the plea of necessity if there are 'other...means available, even if they are more costly or less convenient'.[124] The least restrictive means test suggested by the annulment committee is difficult to reconcile with this statement.

The *Enron* annulment committee rightly noted that, according to the literal meaning of Article 25(1)(a), 'the principle of necessity under customary international law could rarely if ever be invoked in relation to measures taken by a Government to deal with an economic crisis'.[125] It is submitted that the proper conclusion to be drawn from this concern would have been to question whether the text of Article 25(1)(a) accurately decscribes contemporary customary international law or whether the 'only way' requirement should be abandoned in favour of a more lenient standard. Before addressing this issue in section III, I will turn to another element of the necessity defence as codified in Article 25: the non-contribution requirement.

4. The non-contribution requirement

Article 25(2)(b) ASR states that a State may not invoke necessity if it 'has contributed to the situation of necessity'. While not apparent from this wording, the ILC clarified in its commentaries that the contribution must be 'sufficiently substantial and not merely incidental or peripheral' in order to exclude the necessity defence.[126] The only tribunal in the Argentine cases which held that the necessity

[123] Id., para. 370–1.   [124] *See supra* notes 109–12 and accompanying text.
[125] *Enron Creditors Recovery Corp. v. Argentine Republic*, ICSID Case No. ARB/01/3, Decision on the Application for Annulment of the Argentine Republic, 30 July 2010, para. 369. For a case study of whether the 2008 bank crisis in Iceland could give rise to the necessity defence in its current form (with a negative conclusion), *see* Kent & Harrington, 'The Plea of Necessity under Customary International Law', at 264–8.
[126] ILC, *Commentaries on State Responsibility*, Article 25, para. 20.

defence was not excluded by Article 25(2)(b) was the *LG&E* tribunal. The tribunal stated that '[t]here is no serious evidence in the record that Argentina contributed to the crisis resulting in the state of necessity'.[127] The absence of more extensive reasoning by the tribunal can partly be explained by the fact that it did not rely on Article 25 but instead on Article XI of the Argentina–US BIT, which does not contain a provision similar to Article 25(2)(b).[128] The other main reason for the tribunal's finding was that it placed the burden of proof in the context of Article 25(2)(b) on the claimant.[129] This approach appears to be in opposition to what the ILC had in mind when drafting Article 25. James Crawford clarified in his second report that the 'onus of proof' for all circumstances excluding wrongfulness lies with the State invoking the relevant defence.[130]

All other tribunals analysing the requirements of Article 25 ASR found that Argentina's own actions and omissions had substantially contributed to the economic crisis.[131] The *National Grid* tribunal, for example, acknowledged that external factors played a role in the emergence of the crisis.[132] Nevertheless, it rejected the necessity defence on the following grounds:

> Internal factors such as external indebtedness, fiscal policies or labor market rigidity were under the control of the Respondent and created a fertile ground for the crisis to develop when in the late nineties the external factors adduced by the Respondent came to play.[133]

The arbitrators in *Suez–Vivendi*, *AWG Group*, and *Suez–InterAgua* also found that a confluence of developments abroad and domestic shortcomings had given rise to the situation of necessity. The arbitrators found that Argentina's 'excessive public spending, inefficient tax collection, delays in corresponding to the early signs of the crisis, insufficient efforts at developing an export market, and internal political dissension and problems inhibiting effective policy making' had substantially contributed to the crisis.[134] The arbitrators noted that if global factors alone had been responsible for the crisis, it is difficult to see why other countries did not find themselves in the same situation as Argentina.[135]

---

[127] *LG&E*, Decision on Liability, para. 257.

[128] As mentioned before, the *LG&E* tribunal stated that its analysis of Article 25 'alone does not establish Argentina's defence' (*see supra* note 118).

[129] *LG&E*, Decision on Liability, para 256 ('Claimants have not proved that Argentina has contributed to cause the severe crisis faced by the country').

[130] James Crawford, *Addendum to Second Report on State Responsibility*, UN Doc. A/CN.4/498/Add.2 (1999), para. 349.

[131] *CMS*, Award, para. 329; *Enron*, Award, para. 312; *Sempra*, Award, para. 354; *National Grid plc v. Argentina*, UNCITRAL Arbitration, Award, 3 November 2008, paras. 259–60; *Suez–Vivendi* and *AWG Group*, Decision on Liability, para 263; *Impregilo*, Award, paras. 356–9.

[132] *National Grid plc v. Argentina*, UNCITRAL Arbitration, Award, 3 November 2008, para. 259.

[133] Id., para. 260.

[134] *Suez–Vivendi* and *AWG Group*, Decision on Liability, para. 264; *Suez–InterAgua*, Decision on Liability, para. 242.

[135] *Suez–Vivendi* and *AWG Group*, Decision on Liability, para. 264; *Suez–InterAgua*, Decision on Liability, para. 242.

The *Enron* tribunal was less specific with respect to the factors constituting Argentina's contribution to the crisis. Instead, it opined that 'although each party claims that the factors precipitating the crisis were either endogenous or exogenous, the truth seems to be somewhere in between with both kind of factors having intervened'.[136] In a similarly general manner, the tribunal found that the crisis 'has not been the making of a particular administration as it is a problem that had been compounding its effects for a decade, but still the State must answer as a whole'.[137]

The *Enron* annulment committee decided that the cursory reasoning of the tribunal amounted to a failure to apply the applicable law within the meaning of Article 52(1)(b) ICSID Convention. The committee noted that there were several ways to understand Article 25(2)(b). According to the literal meaning of the provision, 'any causal link' between the behaviour of the State and the situation of necessity would be sufficient to exclude the necessity defence. The questions whether the State was blameworthy for its conduct, and whether the effects of its shortcoming were foreseeable, would be irrelevant under this interpretation.[138] In light of the tribunal's comment that Article 25(2)(b) is 'the expression of a general principle of law devised to prevent a party taking legal advantage of its own fault', the annulment committee found that the tribunal did not adopt a literal interpretation.[139] The annulment committee held that, in this case, the tribunal would have had to specify what behaviour amounts to 'fault', which it failed to do. The annulment committee listed deliberate conduct, recklessness, and negligence as possible standards.[140] The annulment committee concluded that the tribunal simply applied an expert opinion of an economist (Professor Edwards), instead of providing a legal definition for the expression 'contributed to the situation of necessity'.[141]

The *Impregilo* tribunal rendered its decision after the *Enron* award was annulled. Possibly with this decision in mind, the *Impregilo* tribunal addressed the question of whether the relevant conduct must have been 'deliberate (i.e. intended to bring about the state of necessity) or reckless or negligent, or even caused by a lesser degree of fault'. The tribunal found that there is no need for a State's contribution

---

[136] *Enron*, Award, para. 311.   [137] Id., para. 312.

[138] *Enron Creditors Recovery Corp. v. Argentine Republic*, ICSID Case No. ARB/01/3, Decision on the Application for Annulment of the Argentine Republic, 30 July 2010, para. 387.

[139] Id., para. 388 (referring to *Enron*, Award, para. 311).

[140] *Enron Creditors Recovery Corp. v. Argentine Republic*, ICSID Case No. ARB/01/3, Decision on the Application for Annulment of the Argentine Republic, 30 July 2010, para. 389. Alvarez-Jiménez suggests a two-step approach: If the State acted with 'reasonable diligence', no further analysis is required and the necessity defence cannot be excluded by way of Article 25(2)(b). If the State's conduct does not meet this standard, tribunals need to examine in a second step whether the State's contribution to the necessity defence was 'substantial' (Alberto Alvarez-Jiménez, 'Foreign Investment Protection and Regulatory Failures as States' Contribution to the State of Necessity under Customary International Law—a New Approach Based on the Complexity of Argentina's 2001 Crisis', *Journal of International Arbitration* 27 (2010) 141–77, at 149).

[141] *Enron Creditors Recovery Corp. v. Argentine Republic*, ICSID Case No. ARB/01/3, Decision on the Application for Annulment of the Argentine Republic, 30 July 2010, paras. 391–3.

to be 'specifically intended or planned' to exclude the necessity defence. Instead, it could also be '*inter alia*, well-intended but ill-conceived', and still keep a State from successfully invoking necessity.[142] In this context, the tribunal referred to the finding of the ICJ in *Gabčíkovo–Nagymaros*, according to which Hungary was precluded from relying on the state of necessity because 'it had helped by act or omission to bring it about'.[143] In *Gabčíkovo*, the ICJ stressed that Hungary itself concluded the very treaty whose implementation it later complained would entail harsh environmental consequences. The Court further reasoned that the parties were aware of most of the project's environmental risks when they concluded the treaty in 1977. Moreover, Hungary had pressed for an acceleration of the works only a few months before its decision to abandon the project in 1989.[144]

Concerning the required level of the contribution, the *Impregilo* tribunal relied on the formulation of the ILC, according to which it must be 'sufficiently substantial and not merely incidental or peripheral'.[145] The application of these principles to the facts of the particular case led to the same conclusion as that reached by the other tribunals. While recognizing that market developments abroad played an important role, the tribunal found that:

Argentina's own economic policies over several years prior to the crisis rendered the economy of the country vulnerable to exogenous shocks and pressures, and impacted adversely the sustainability of its economic model on the national and local levels. The Arbitral Tribunal, notes by way of example, Argentina's long-term failure to exercise fiscal discipline, including control of provincial spending and of the subsidization of the Provinces by the central government; and its inability to adopt labor and trade policies consistent with the country's currency board. The resulting high indebtedness and inflexibility in Argentina's markets hampered substantially the country's ability to cope with external shocks, leading to the 2001 crisis.[146]

Indeed, it is difficult to argue that a State's own policy choices do not have a significant impact on its economy. It is, therefore, hard to see how a State coping with an economic crisis could ever rely on the necessity defence. This is certainly true if one strictly follows the formulation in Article 25(2)(b) according to which the necessity defence is unavailable if the State 'has contributed to the situation'. Like most of the other elements of Article 25, the non-contribution requirement seeks to minimize the risk that States abuse the necessity defence. As Roberto Ago explained:

---

[142] *Impregilo*, Award, para. 356.

[143] Id., para. 356, note 94 (referring to *Case concerning the Gabčíkovo–Nagymaros Project* (Hungary v. Slovakia), Judgment, 25 September 1997, ICJ Reports 1997, 7–84, para. 57).

[144] *Case concerning the Gabčíkovo–Nagymaros Project* (Hungary v. Slovakia), Judgment, 25 September 1997, ICJ Reports 1997, 7–84, para. 57.

[145] *Impregilo*, Award, para. 357 (referring to ILC, *Commentaries on State Responsibility*, Article 25, para. 20, *see also* supra note 126).

[146] *Impregilo*, Award, para. 358.

It would obviously be out of the question for a State intentionally to create a situation of danger to one of its major interests solely for the purpose of evading its obligation to respect a subjective right of another State.[147]

This rationale of the non-contribution requirement is further borne out by a comparison between Article 25(2)(b) and a similar stipulation in the context of the *force majeure* provision of the ASR. Article 23(2)(a) provides that *force majeure* does not preclude the wrongfulness of an act if

the situation of *force majeure* is due, either alone or in combination with other factors, to the conduct of the State invoking it.[148]

Under this provision, it is less likely that a State's contribution excludes the State's defence than under Article 25. For Article 23(2)(a) to preclude *force majeure*, it is not enough that the State has 'unwittingly contributed' to the relevant situation 'by something which, in hindsight, might have been done differently but which was done in good faith'.[149] The ILC explains the more rigid approach in Article 25(2)(b) with the need to impose narrower limitations on the 'necessity' defence than on *force majeure*.[150] *Force majeure* differs from necessity insofar as the former leaves the State no choice on whether and how to react in a particular situation—and consequently does not lend itself as readily to abuse as necessity.[151]

Concerns regarding the abuse of the necessity defence permeate the entire text of Article 25. While the ICJ and the Argentina tribunals did not hesitate to consider Article 25 an accurate codification of customary international law, the status of necessity as a rule of international law was much less clear just a few decades ago.[152] Some considered a customary international law defence of necessity neither existent nor desirable—often because of its potential of abuse in a wide range of settings.[153] When Roberto Ago prepared his 1980 report, he was aware of these concerns. Ago reached the conclusion that it was better to include necessity as a 'safety valve' in the ASR and to stress its exceptional character than to ignore it.[154] In this vein, Roberto Ago acknowledged that

the concept of 'state of necessity' is far too deeply rooted in the consciousness of the members of the international community and of individuals within States. If driven out of the door it would return through the window.[155]

---

[147] Ago, *Report on State Responsibility*, para. 13.

[148] Article 24(2)(a) contains the same subparagraph with respect to 'distress'.

[149] ILC, *Commentaries on State Responsibility*, Article 23, para. 9.

[150] Id., Article 25, para. 20.   [151] *See supra* note 79.

[152] As late as 1990, an arbitral tribunal questioned the existence of the customary international law defence of necessity (*Rainbow Warrior* Case (New Zealand v. France), Decision, 30 April 1990, R.I.A.A., Vol. XX (1994) 217–84, at 254).

[153] *See, e.g.,* Eduardo Jiménez de Aréchaga, 'International Responsibility', *in Manual of Public International Law* (Max Sorensen ed., 1968) 531–603, at 542–3.

[154] *See in particular,* Ago, *Report on State Responsibility*, paras. 12–13, 75–6, 79–80.

[155] Id., para. 80.

Some might find that—with the benefit of hindsight—the text of Article 25 strikes a poor balance between avoiding abuse and the tempering of unbearable consequences of 'adhering at all costs to the letter of the law'.[156] In its desire to avoid the abuse of the necessity defence in certain settings, so the argument could go, the ILC rendered the necessity defence unavailable in an economic context. In this regard, it bears emphasis that none of the cases or State practice with an economic background collected by the ILC seem to explicitly state that the necessity defence is unavailable if the State contributed to the emergency situation.

As seen in this section, the 'only way' and 'non-contribution' requirements in Article 25 make it virtually impossible for States to successfully invoke necessity in an economic crisis. One way to facilitate recourse to the necessity defence would be to abandon the 'only way' requirement and instead ask whether the State measure was a 'proportionate means' to protect its 'essential interests'[157]—and include the State's 'contribution' as one factor in this analysis. If a State intentionally, or by gross negligence, contributed greatly to the situation of necessity, it would be very difficult (if not impossible) to justify grave violations of BIT provisions. If, however, the State did not act negligently, the contribution of the State is of little magnitude, and the infringement of private property rights is small in scale, then a different assessment might be appropriate. Such a flexible approach to the State's contribution would bring Article 25 more in line with similar concepts on the domestic level. Binder and Reinisch point out that domestic law provisions do not automatically exclude the possibility of adopting emergency measures only because the State's prior actions or omissions have contributed to the emergency situation.[158] While modifying Article 25 in that way seems to be attractive at first glance and would certainly increase the relevance of necessity in economic crises, section III analyses whether such an approach would indeed be appropriate.

III. The principle of proportionality: the only way forward?

We have seen in the previous section that the wording of Article 25 renders the necessity defence virtually unavailable in economic crises. Abandoning the 'only way' and 'non-contribution' requirements in favour of a proportionality analysis that includes the State's contribution to the emergency as one relevant factor would provide for more flexibility.[159] The existence of alternative measures to deal

---

[156] Id.

[157] *See also* Reinisch, 'Necessity', at 201; Bjorklund, 'Emergency Exceptions', at 485; Michael Wilson, 'The Enron v. Argentina Annulment Decision: Moving a Bishop Vertically in the Precarious ICSID System', *University of Miami Inter-American Law Review* 43 (2012) 347–76, at 369; Kent and Harrington support the application of a reasonableness test in the context of Article 25 (*see* Kent & Harrington, 'The Plea of Necessity under Customary International Law', at 255).

[158] Christina Binder & August Reinisch, 'Economic Emergency Powers: a Comparative Law Perspective', *in International Investment Law and Comparative Law* (Stephan W. Schill ed., 2010) 503–40, at 539.

[159] *See supra* notes 157–8 and accompanying text.

with an economic crisis would not automatically exclude the necessity defence. Rather, the inquiry would focus on whether the alternative measures would have been less infringing and equally effective, and whether the adopted measure was (on balance and taking the State's contribution to the situation of necessity into account) appropriate. This section discusses and assesses doctrinal pathways for such an approach, together with their respective risks and benefits. Subsection 1 analyses whether the current status of the customary international law defence of necessity warrants the abandonment of the strict 'only way' requirement in favour of a more flexible proportionality analysis. Subsection 2 addresses possible inter-actions between necessity in customary international law and general principles within the meaning of Article 38(1)(c) ICJ Statute.

1. Modifying the ILC codification: replacing the 'only way' requirement with the principle of proportionality?

Contrary to some other codification projects of the ILC, the ASR have not resulted in a multilateral treaty. As is well known, the purpose of the ILC is not only the codification of international law but also its progressive development.[160] While the ICJ and all Argentina tribunals took a contrary position, some scholars consider Article 25 to be an instance of progressive development as opposed to an accurate codification of custom.[161] The fact that none of the cases or instances of State practice relied on by the ILC to arrive at the wording of Article 25 dealt with *all* of the elements of this provision lends some support to this scholarly view.[162] Furthermore, as noted in section II, the 'non-contribution' requirement in Article 25(2)(b) seems to enjoy relatively little support from the material analysed by the ILC but rather be the result of the ILC's efforts to avoid the abuse of the neces-sity defence.[163] As a first step in assessing whether the 'only way' requirement should be replaced with a proportionality analysis, I will analyse to what degree the material adduced by the ILC supports the inclusion of the 'only way' language in Article 25.

---

[160] The ILC was established by the General Assembly in 1947 to give effect to Article 13(1)(a) of the UN Charter (GA Res. 174(II) of 21 November 1947). This provision empowers the General Assembly to 'initiate studies and make recommendations for the purpose of...encouraging the progressive development of international law and its codification.' Article 1 of the Statute of the ILC stipulates that the object of the Commission is the 'progressive development of international law and its codification'. (GA Res. 174(II) contains the Statute of the Commission. Even though the statute has been amended by several resolutions, Article 1 has remained unchanged. For an institu-tional study of the ILC in general, *see* Herbert W. Briggs, *The International Law Commission* (1965)).

[161] *See, e.g.*, Robert D. Sloane, 'The Use and Abuse of Necessity in the Law of State Responsibility', American Journal of International Law 106 (2012) 447–508, at 453, 471; Desierto, *Necessity and National Emergency Clauses*, at 114. For the relevant jurisprudence, *see supra* note 1.

[162] While the ICJ adressed (more or less) all elements of Article 25 in *Gabčíkovo* (which the ILC included in its 2001 commentaries) it is important to bear in mind that the ICJ relied on the 1980 ILC draft article on necessity (*Case concerning the Gabčíkovo–Nagymaros Project* (Hungary v. Slovakia), Judgment, 25 September 1997, ICJ Reports 1997, 7–84, paras. 49–56), which was almost identical to Article 25.

[163] *See supra* notes 147–56 and accompanying text.

One of the earliest decisions involving necessity is *Neptune*, rendered by a commission constituted under the Jay Treaty referred to in Chapter 2.[164] After Great Britain had entered into war with France in 1793, the British government issued an instruction to stop and detain all foreign vessels carrying food to France.[165] Acting under this order, a British warship seized the *Neptune*—an American vessel carrying food to Bordeaux—and brought it to Portsmouth in Great Britain. The vessel was released but the cargo was ordered to be sold to the British government at a low price.[166] One of the main defences of the British government in the proceedings was necessity. It argued that it was threatened with extreme food shortage when the order to seize foreign vessels was issued.[167] The argument did not go through and the commission awarded the difference between the price paid by the British government and the one the owners could have achieved had they sold their cargo in France.[168] The opinion of commissioner Pinkney dealt with the appropriate means–end relationship:

We are told by Grotius that the necessity must not be imaginary, that it must be real and pressing, and that even then it does not give a right of appropriating the goods of others *until all other means of relief* consistent with the necessity have been tried and found inadequate.[169]

In a similar vein, commissioner Trumbull found that

[t]he necessity which can be admitted to supersede all laws and to dissolve the distinctions of property and right must be absolute and irresistible, and . . . *all other means* of self-preservation shall have been exhausted.[170]

In *Neptune*, the commissioners therefore indeed seemed to consider the necessity defence to be available only if the chosen measure was the only means to protect the relevant interests at stake. A communication between Great Britain and Portugal in the first half of the nineteenth century offers similarly strong support for the 'only way' requirement. A treaty between Great Britain and Portugal required Portugal to grant certain privileges and immunities to British citizens, inter alia to respect their property.[171] Some of this property was seized to sustain the Portuguese armed forces. Jenner, a British law officer, acknowledged the existence of the necessity defence, but stated that it may be exercised only under strict conditions. Jenner wrote that he

do[es] not apprehend, that the Treaties between this Country and Portugal are of so stubborn and unbending a nature, as to be incapable of modification under any circumstances whatever, or that their stipulations ought to be so strictly adhered to, as to deprive the Government of Portugal of the right of using those means, which may be *absolutely and*

---

[164] For the dispute resolution mechanism of the Jay Treaty, *see* Chapter 2, notes 33–7 and accompanying text.

[165] '*The Neptune*', *Jefferies, Master: Provision Case*, Award, 20 June 1797, *reprinted in* John Bassett Moore, *International Adjudications*, Vol. IV (1931) 372–443, at 373.

[166] Id., at 374, 440.   [167] Id., at 398.   [168] Id., at 441.

[169] Id., at 398, 399 (emphasis added).   [170] Id., at 433 (emphasis added).

[171] Lord McNair, *International Law Opinions*, Vol. II (1956) 231–2.

indispensably necessary to the safety, and even to the very existence of the State. The extent of the necessity... must be imminent and urgent.[172]

The *Caroline* incident and its consequences lend strong support to the 'only way' requirement as well.[173] On 29 December 1837, the Caroline, a ship owned by American citizens, was carrying cargo in support of Canadians rebelling against Great Britain. After the US government had unsuccessfully tried to prevent this activity, British forces set the steamer on fire in US territory. While *Caroline* is today usually adduced in the context of anticipatory self-defence, in a time unfamiliar with the prohibition of the use of force, the incident was considered to be a case of necessity.[174] In the aftermath of the incident, Great Britain and the US largely agreed on the prerequisites of the plea of necessity, even though the two countries differed on the question of whether these requirements had been met in the case at hand. The correspondence between the two governments culminated in a statement by Secretary of State Webster, according to which a State resorting to necessity must prove

a necessity of self-defense, instant, overwhelming, *leaving no choice of means*, and no moment for deliberation.[175]

An important case that involves the conflict between business interests and regulatory powers is *Oscar Chinn*. In 1931, the global depression had severe consequences for trade in the Congo, then a Belgian colony.[176] In order to alleviate the situation, the Belgian government decided to decrease the costs of river transportation. To this end, it advised Unatra, a Belgian transportation company operating in the Congo, to cut its tariffs. In return, the Belgian government promised to reimburse the company for its losses.[177] Oscar Chinn, a British subject operating a river transport service in the Congo, claimed that these measures created a 'de facto monopoly' in favour of Unatra that forced him out of business.[178] The UK argued before the PCIJ that such a 'de facto monopoly' was not in line with the 'freedom of trade' and 'freedom of navigation' Belgium undertook to respect in the Congo. Since the PCIJ found that Belgium had not breached any treaty obligations or general international law,[179] it did not have to comment on the doctrine of necessity. The separate opinion of Judge Anzilotti, however, contains some seminal statements on necessity, which lend further support to the 'only way' requirement:

No one can, or does, dispute that it rested with the Belgian Government to say what were the measures best adapted to overcome the crisis: provided always that the measures

---

[172] Id., at 231–2.   [173] *See, e.g.,* Randelzhofer, 'Article 51', para. 39.

[174] For a detailed account of the *Caroline* incident and the subsequent exchange of diplomatic notes, *see* John Bassett Moore, *A Digest of International Law*, Vol. II (1906) 409–14.

[175] *See* id., at 412 (emphasis added).

[176] *The Oscar Chinn Case* (United Kingdom v. Belgium), Judgment, 12 December 1934, PCIJ Series A/B 63 (1934) 65–152, at 71.

[177] Id., at 71–4.   [178] Id., at 75, 85.

[179] Id., at 83–8. For the text of the relevant treaty provisions, *see* Convention Revising the General Act of Berlin, February 26, 1885, and of the Declaration of Brussels, July 2, 1890, signed at Saint-Germaine-on-Laye September 10, 1919, 8 LNTS 25–38, at 31–5.

selected were not inconsistent with its international obligations, for the Government's freedom of choice was indisputably limited by the duty of observing those obligations. On the other hand, the existence of that freedom is incompatible with the plea of necessity which, by definition, *implies the impossibility of proceeding by any other method* than the one contrary to law.[180]

While by no means do all cases and instances of State practice adduced by the ILC in the drafting process of Article 25 address the required means–end relationship, the 'only way' requirement finds significant support in the material discussed in this subsection. One may still wonder whether a refinement of the necessity defence is appropriate. The *Torrey Canyon* incident described above[181] and its consequences provide a good example for such a refinement in a subsystem of international law. In the aftermath of this incident, States established a new legal regime to regulate the powers of coastal States to protect their territories from pollution: the International Convention Relating to Intervention on the High Seas in Cases of Oil Pollution Casualties of 29 November 1969.[182] Parts of the wording of Article I are reminiscent of Article 25 ASR. It states that:

[p]arties to the present Convention may take such measures on the high seas as may be necessary to prevent, mitigate or eliminate *grave and imminent danger* to their coastline or related interests from pollution of the sea by oil...which may reasonably be expected to result in major harmful consequences.[183]

Article V of this Convention outlines a proportionality analysis to determine whether the State measures were indeed 'necessary' under the particular circumstances of the case:

Measures taken by the coastal State in accordance with Article I shall be *proportionate* to the damage actual or threatened to it.

Such measures shall not go beyond what is reasonably necessary to achieve the end mentioned in Article I and shall cease as soon as that end has been achieved; they shall not unnecessarily interfere with the rights and interests of the flag State, third States and of any persons, physical or corporate, concerned.

In considering whether the measures are *proportionate* to the damage, account shall be taken of
(a) the extent and probability of imminent damage if those measures are not taken; and
(b) the likelihood of those measures being effective; and
(c) the extent of the damage which may be caused by such measures.[184]

The United Nations Convention on the Law of the Sea (UNCLOS) contains a similar provision in its Article 221, which allows States to take 'proportionate' measures to protect their coastlines or related interests against pollution through a maritime 'casualty'.[185] The two conventions constitute fine examples for the

---

[180] Id., at 114 (emphasis added).   [181] *Supra* note 86 and accompanying text.
[182] United Nations Treaty Series, Vol. 970 (1975) No. 14049, at 212–6. The Convention came into force on 6 May 1975 after the fifteenth ratification (at 213).
[183] Id., at 212 (emphasis added).   [184] Id., at 214 (emphasis added).
[185] The full text of Article 221 of UNCLOS reads as follows:

emergence of proportionality analysis in legal settings traditionally governed by the customary international law defence of necessity. So why not harness this doctrinal refinement for customary international law, which might be the very root of primary rules on emergency situations anyway?

We have seen in Chapter 5 that treaty making can influence customary international law.[186] This applies both to the Law of the Sea conventions just mentioned and the dense web of roughly 3000 BITs and IIAs. Against this background, it is at least arguable that a consistent pattern of NPM clauses that allow for emergency measures in times of economic crisis might have an effect on the customary international law defence of necessity. States increasingly include NPM clauses in their Model BITs and BITs, and the analysis in Chapter 7 has revealed that proportionality is likely to be an appropriate means to interpret and apply some or even many of these clauses. The interests protected by NPM clauses, however, are far from consistent. States include NPM clauses in their treaties for reasons as diverse as the protection of 'essential security interests', the protection of 'human, animal or plant life or health', the 'conservation of living or non-living exhaustible natural resources', the 'maintenance of the safety of financial institutions', the 'stability of a party's financial system', the protection of 'historical or archaeological value', and the support of 'creative arts of national value'.[187] This means that States make nuanced choices in their IIAs as to when and how investment protection may have to yield to other interests. It is important to bear in mind that the customary international law defence of necessity may justify treaty breaches for the sake of any 'interest' ('as long as this interest is essential'). Coupled with a proportionality analysis, this would render Article 25 de facto a 'super-NPM clause', and undermine the choices made by States in their IIAs.

Some States do not include NPM clauses in their BITs at all. As explained by US BIT negotiator Kenneth J. Vandevelde, NPM clauses in US BITs (such as Article XI of the Argentina–US BIT) sought to strike a 'delicate balance' between the regulatory freedom of the US and the protection of its nationals investing abroad.[188] States that do not include such clauses in their BITs presumably do so for the following reasons: either they seek a very robust protection of their investors abroad, or they intend to attract foreign investors by offering them a particularly stable legal framework, or both. Reducing the threshold for a successful invocation of the necessity defence by abandoning the 'only way' requirement

---

Nothing in this Part shall prejudice the right of States, pursuant to international law, both customary and conventional, to take and enforce measures beyond the territorial sea *proportionate* to the actual or threatened damage to protect their coastline or related interests, including fishing, from pollution or threat of pollution following upon a maritime casualty or acts relating to such a casualty, which may reasonably be expected to result in major harmful consequences. (Emphasis added.)

[186] Chapter 5, notes 241–5 and accompanying text.
[187] *See* Chapter 7, notes 1–2 & 82–97 and accompanying text.
[188] Vandevelde, *United States International Investment Agreements*, at 220.

would make it more difficult for States to legislate effectively on the international level through their treaties.

Another factor to be borne in mind is that enhancing the relevance of Article 25 in investor–State arbitration by replacing the 'only way' requirement with a proportionality analysis might have repercussions in other areas of international law. The drafting process of Article 25 shows that States have invoked the necessity defence in a variety of different circumstances, some of which involved military means.[189] In investor–State arbitration, the exercise of the necessity defence is subject to judicial scrutiny. Many other areas of international law lack such neutral third-party adjudication—and the risk of abuse of the necessity defence is particularly present in these areas.[190] One should not forget that if States consider a more lenient standard for necessity as that codified in Article 25 to be appropriate, they can change the status quo through relevant State practice. With the increase of international fora in which States can articulate their views, changes in custom may arguably occur through a relatively short duration of State practice, as illustrated in Chapter 4.[191] In any event, clarifying that the strict wording of Article 25(1)(a) does not accurately reflect customary international law would not be a difficult first step for States to take. In the absence of such State action, the better arguments speak currently against replacing the 'only way' requirement in Article 25 with a proportionality analysis as a matter of customary international law.

2. Necessity and the principle of proportionality: custom versus general principles?

So far, the discussion on necessity in this section has focused on necessity as a rule of customary international law. There is some support for the notion that necessity constitutes a general principle of law as well.[192] Justice Lübbe-Wolff took this view in the Argentine bonds case before the German Constitutional Court discussed in subsection I.3.[193] Lübbe-Wolff did not examine the doctrine of necessity under various domestic legal systems. Rather, she adopted a more general approach and reasoned that domestic legal systems contain mechanisms to ensure that States facing private law claims can still fulfill their most essential tasks in times of crisis.[194] In Italy, this result would be achieved through the rules of sovereign immunity.[195] In the US, the possibility of suspending domestic court proceedings and State immunity on the enforcement stage would provide sufficient protection for States that need to restructure their debt.[196]

---

[189] *See, e.g., supra* notes 164–82 and accompanying text.

[190] For the ILC's efforts to minimize the risk of abuse inherent in the necessity defence, *see supra* notes 153–6 and accompanying text.

[191] *See* Chapter 4, notes 108–26 and accompanying text.

[192] Schill & Kim, 'Sovereign Bonds in Economic Crisis', at 505–8.

[193] BVerfG, 2 BvM 1/03, Decision of 7 May 2007, paras. 81, 91.   [194] Id., para. 94.

[195] Id., paras. 92.   [196] Id., paras. 93.

August Reinisch and Christina Binder took a more specific approach. These authors analysed the legal regimes governing emergency measures in the UK, France, Germany, and the US. In contrast to Justice Lübbe-Wolff, Binder and Reinisch examined the distinct elements of the various domestic rules (for example the threshold requirements and limitations of the necessity defence) in detail.[197] They found that the respective domestic legal orders are too diverse to give rise to general principles of law within the meaning of Article 38(1)(c) ICJ Statute.[198] In any event, it is important to bear in mind that even those who consider necessity to constitute a general principle of law do not suggest that the requirements of this principle are any different from those set out in Article 25 ASR.[199] Therefore, the characterization of necessity as a general principle might be relevant to the question of whether the necessity defence is *applicable* in private law proceedings before domestic courts. It seems to be irrelevant, however, for the analysis of the *requirements* of the necessity defence in international law.

An issue that deserves closer attention is whether general principles of law can inform the content of Article 25. In particular, one may wonder whether the principle of proportionality could constitute the proper nexus requirement for Article 25, and replace the strict 'only way' requirement. General principles of law may provide guidance on issues not resolved by treaties or customary international law.[200] Furthermore, there is no reason to assume that rules of customary international law (or treaty norms) are hierarchically superior to general principles of law. Still, there is a certain *lex specialis* relationship between the sources of international law reflected in Article 38(1)(c) ICJ Statute.[201] This means that if States resolve a legal issue on the international level in a particular way—be it through treaties or State practice leading to customary international law—there is little reason to overwrite this decision by resort to general principles of law. The 'only way' requirement in Article 25 ASR is a threshold that is more difficult to meet than the proportionality test. The ILC, the ICJ, States, and arbitral tribunals have expressed the view that Article 25 constitutes an accurate codification of customary international law. The main rationale for the strict wording of Article 25 is that States should not be able to evade their international obligations too readily. If States consider a more lenient standard to be appropriate, they can change the status quo through relevant State practice—and some of the relevant means in this regard were discussed in the previous subsection.[202]

Moreover, the application of the principle of proportionality in the context of the necessity defence raises serious concerns regarding the rule of law, judicial lawmaking, and arbitrary outcomes. These three factors are to be considered applying

---

[197] Binder & Reinisch, 'Economic Emergency Powers', at 513–38.

[198] Id., at 538–40. In a similar vein, Sloane, 'The Use and Abuse of Necessity in the Law of State Responsibility', at 469–70. Sloane opines that if necessity constitutes a general principle at all, this principle would be limited to the right of self-preservation (at 470).

[199] *See* Schill & Kim, Sovereign Bonds in Economic Crisis, at 508–10.

[200] *See* Chapter 3, notes 310–11 and accompanying text.

[201] *See* Chapter 3, note 310 and accompanying text.

[202] *Supra* notes 186–91 and accompanying text.

proportionality as a general principle in international law.[203] To recall, the rule of law requires that the scope of guaranteed rights under a treaty be apparent from its text. Reducing the scope of a guaranteed right by legal doctrine without textual support is problematic from a rule-of-law perspective. I have argued that proportionality analysis in the context of the FET standard and Article XI of the Argentina–US BIT does not contradict this understanding of the rule of law.[204] A more careful analysis is appropriate with respect to BIT provisions on expropriation.[205] Some States address rule-of-law concerns by including in their BITs definitions of the term 'expropriation' that incorporate a proportionality analysis.[206] In contrast, the notion that a breach of BIT obligations can be justified as long as the relevant emergency measures are proportionate is apparent from neither the relevant BIT, nor the wording of Article 25, nor relevant State practice. Replacing the only way requirement in Article 25 with a proportionality test therefore raises serious concerns regarding the rule of law.

According to Robert Alexy's theory on proportionality balancing, unconditionally guaranteed rights cannot be restricted for *any* public purpose.[207] Rather, the conflicting interest must be derived from the (in the words of the German Constitutional Court) 'constitutional value order and the unity of this fundamental value system'.[208] As explained in Chapter 4, the international legal order has some hierarchical elements.[209] Furthermore, Article 31(3)(c) VCLT provides for a certain value system on the bilateral or multilateral level in the interpretation of treaties. In addition, Article 25 contains some elements that provide certain guidance for a proportionality analysis. One of the factors that matter in a proportionality analysis is the extent of the threat and the urgency of the adopted measures. Article 25(1)(a) clarifies that nothing short of a 'grave and imminent peril' suffices for the purposes of the necessity defence. Furthermore, Article 25(2)(a) specifies that the necessity defence is excluded as soon as a conflicting 'essential interest' is 'seriously impaired'.

Still, Article 25 grants States the necessity defence for the protection of *any* 'essential interest'. Replacing the 'only way' requirement with the principle of proportionality would risk subjecting international obligations to the general condition that their fulfillment does not disproportionately burden the State's policy preferences. This amounts to a freestanding balancing test. To the extent that domestic law embraces such freestanding balancing tests, this happens against a very strong constitutional background, which international law still lacks despite some constitutional features.[210] Even if international law had such a strong constitutional background, conditioning treaty commitments to a freestanding balancing test would undermine the ability of States to make nuanced choices in their

---

[203] *See* Chapter 3, section II.
[204] *See* Chapter 6, subsection III.2 and Chapter 7, subsection IV.3.
[205] *See* Chapter 5, subsection V.5.a.   [206] *See* Chapter 5, subsection V.2.
[207] *See* Chapter 3, note 199.   [208] Chapter 2, note 51 and accompanying text.
[209] *See* Chapter 4, notes 127–55 and accompanying text.
[210] *See* Chapter 4, notes 1–17 & 95–155 accompanying text.

treaties. If States could (temporarily) dispense of their treaty obligations as long as it served one of their 'essential interests' in a proportionate way, it would be very difficult for them to make credible commitments in treaties regarding issues they deem important. The effects would be felt not only by individual States but by the international community as a whole: releasing States from their international obligations whenever indicated by a proportionality test would bring considerable uncertainty and instability to international relations. On balance, the better arguments speak against a replacement of the 'only way' requirement in Article 25 with a proportionality analysis. There are much better ways for States to readjust the balance between the public interest and the rights of foreign investors if they wish to do so, in particular through the incorporation of NPM clauses in IIAs.

IV. Consequences of a successful plea of necessity

While we have seen in section II that the strict requirements of Article 25 make it very difficult for States to rely on the necessity defence in investor–State arbitration, section III has identified certain doctrinal pathways that show how this might change at some point in the future. Therefore, some comments on the consequences of a successful invocation of the necessity defence appear to be in order. The text of the ASR provides only very limited guidance on this issue. Article 27 stipulates that:

The invocation of a circumstance precluding wrongfulness in accordance with this chapter is without prejudice to:
(a) compliance with the obligation in question, if and to the extent that the circumstance precluding wrongfulness no longer exists;
(b) the question of compensation for any material loss caused by the act in question.

Paragraph (a) addresses compliance, and the cautious 'without prejudice' wording indicates that necessity does not necessarily relieve the invoking State permanently of its duty to adhere to its international obligations. In its commentaries, the ILC was more explicit. The Commission clarified that the 'obligation regains full force and effect' as soon as the circumstances precluding wrongfulness cease to exist.[211] Similarly, the ICJ held in the *Gabčíkovo–Nagymaros Project* case that

the Treaty may be ineffective as long as the condition of necessity continues to exist; it may in fact be dormant, but... as soon as the state of necessity ceases to exist, the duty to comply with treaty obligations revives.[212]

When it comes to compensation, the case is not so straightforward. Analogous to Article 27(a), the text of Article 27(b) indicates that a State's reliance on necessity does not automatically negate a duty to compensate. But the ILC gave little

---

[211] ILC, *Commentaries on State Responsibility*, Article 27, para. 1.
[212] *Case concerning the Gabčíkovo–Nagymaros Project* (Hungary v. Slovakia), Judgment, 25 September 1997, ICJ Reports 1997, 7–84, para. 101.

guidance on whether a successful plea of necessity indeed entails a duty to compensate, and merely stated that:

Without the possibility of such recourse the State whose conduct would otherwise be unlawful might seek to shift the burden of the defence of its own interests or concerns on to an innocent third State.[213]

While there is ample jurisprudence on the question of compensation for internationally wrongful acts, so far no arbitral tribunal or international court has awarded compensation following recourse to Article 25. This is not very surprising since all courts and tribunals analysing Article 25 concluded that its requirements had not been fulfilled in the relevant case. The next subsection seeks to shed light on the issue of whether a State invoking the necessity defence incurs a duty to compensate.

1. A duty to compensate?

Jurisprudence from the time before the adoption of the ASR yields significant support for a duty to compensate even if the wrongfulness of State measure is precluded by necessity. In the *Neptune* case introduced in section III, for example, commissioner Pinkney found that, even if justified by necessity, the British seizure of goods from an American vessel bound to France would have required compensation:

Great Britain might be able to say to neutrals 'You shall sell to us,' but it does not follow that she could also say 'You shall sell to us upon worse terms than you would have procured elsewhere in the lawful prosecution of your commerce.'[214]

The *Company General of the Orinoco* case contains similar considerations.[215] In the 1880s, Venezuela granted various concessions to a French company for the exploitation of the Upper Orinoco and Amazonas as well as for certain infrastructure projects.[216] To avoid military conflict with Columbia, who claimed sovereignty over parts of this area, Venezuela rescinded the relevant contract.[217] The umpire considered the rescission to be a 'sovereign right' of Venezuela. While the umpire did not directly refer to necessity, his reasoning was very reminiscent of this concept,[218] and he held that Venezuela owed compensation for the exercise of its 'sovereign right':

---

[213] ILC, *Commentaries on State Responsibility*, Article 27, para. 5.

[214] 'The Neptune', Jefferies, Master: Provision Case, Award, 20 June 1797, *reprinted in* John Bassett Moore, *International Adjudications*, Vol. IV (1931) 372–443, at p. 400. For further comments on *Neptune, see supra* notes 164–70 and accompanying text.

[215] *Company General of the Orinoco Case*, Mixed Claims Commission France–Venezuela, Opinion of the Umpire, 31 July 1905, United Nations Reports of International Arbitral Awards X, 250–85.

[216] Id., at 250.

[217] For relevant diplomatic correspondence and other documents, *see* id., at 257–67. The boundary issue was finally settled in favour of Columbia (id., at 269).

[218] *See,* id., at 280–1.

[Venezuela] considered the peril superior to the obligation and substituted therefor the duty of compensation. ...A careful study of the event connected with this Governmental act, and of those which followed, reveals nothing which in any degree lightens the responsibility or in any part changes the relation which the respondent Government assumed toward the Company General of the Orinoco and its creditors when it exercised this sovereign right.[219]

In 1926, the Council of the League of Nations established a commission to investigate certain military activities at the Bulgarian-Greek border.[220] A treaty stipulation entitled members of the Bulgarian minority in Greece to choose Bulgarian nationality. Those who made use of this option had to leave Greece but retained both their immovable property and a right to return.[221] After large parts of the Bulgarian minority had left Greece, the government decided to settle Greek refugees from Turkey on the abandoned property. At some point, parts of the Bulgarian minority who had first left Greece decided to return. Without directly invoking the doctrine of necessity or its consequences, the commission acknowledged that returning the real estate was no option but found that the Bulgarian minority should be compensated:

[T]he number of these persons at the present in Bulgaria is considerable. Most of them left property in Greece for which they have received no compensation. Under the pressure of circumstances, the Greek Government employed this land to settle refugees from Turkey. To oust these refugees now in order to permit of the return of the former owners would be impossible...Nevertheless, if these Bulgarians are to be asked to give up a right, it is only just that they should be compensated for the value of the property they left behind them.[222]

In *Gabčíkovo–Nagymaros*, the ICJ briefly but unequivocally commented on the duty of compensation as a consequence of a successful plea of necessity. Rejecting Hungary's necessity defence, the Court 'point[ed] out that Hungary expressly acknowledged that, in any event, such a state of necessity would not exempt it from its duty to compensate its partner'.[223] Apart from relevant jurisprudence, legal doctrine also appears to support a duty to compensate following an invocation of the necessity defence. Some scholars suggest that the categorization of necessity as an excuse would entail a duty to compensate, while its characterization as a justification would negate such a duty.[224] There seem to be good reasons,

---

[219] Id., at 280, 282.

[220] Report of the Commission of Enquiry into the Incidents on the Frontier Between Bulgaria and Greece, League of Nations—Official Journal 7 (1926) 2, at 196–210.

[221] Id., 209. (The relevant treaty was the 'Treaty between the Principal Allied and Associated Powers, and Greece, concerning the Protection of Minorities in Greece' concluded on 10 August 1920, *available at* <http://www.pollitecon.com/html/treaties/Treaty_Concerning_The_Protection_Of_Minorities_In_Greece.htm>).

[222] Id., 209.

[223] *Case concerning the Gabčíkovo–Nagymaros Project* (Hungary v. Slovakia), Judgment, 25 September 1997, ICJ Reports 1997, 7–84, para. 48.

[224] *See, e.g.*, Kent & Harrington, 'The Plea of Necessity', at 262–3; Bjorklund, 'Emergency Exceptions', at 510–11; Vaughan Lowe, 'Precluding Wrongfulness or Responsibility: a Plea of Excuses', *European Journal of International Law* 10 (1999) 405–11, at 410.

however, to consider necessity to be justification, and nevertheless uphold a duty to compensate. This is, for example, what the ICJ did in *Gabčíkovo*, when it repeatedly stated that a successful plea of necessity would 'justify' Hungary's conduct but nevertheless found that reliance on necessity entails a duty to compensate.[225]

Unlike the ICJ, most scholars refer to the customary international law defence of necessity as an 'excuse', often to stress its exceptional character.[226] The differences between the two concepts are rarely clarified; Bin Cheng's remark that necessity 'justifies *and* excuses an otherwise wrongful act' is a particularly clear case in point.[227] One argument against categorizing Article 25 an excuse is to avoid its intermingling with concepts that are invoked when scholars struggle with tensions between the law and moral or political considerations. These concepts include 'mitigating circumstances',[228] 'humanitarian necessity',[229] 'extreme necessity',[230] 'moral necessity',[231] and the 'illegal but justified' approach.[232] Through them, scholars seek to take account of moral dilemmas posed by situations like that in Kosovo around 1999 without creating precedents for the unwarranted use of force under the disguise of humanitarian motives. Unlike Article 25, these considerations do not lead to the preclusion of wrongfulness under the law of state responsibility.[233] Some authors nevertheless put such political and moral considerations and the notion of excuses on the same footing.[234] Therefore, it seems advisable not to use the term 'excuse' in the context of Article 25.

[225] *Case concerning the Gabčíkovo–Nagymaros Project* (Hungary v. Slovakia), Judgment, 25 September 1997, ICJ Reports 1997, 7–84, paras. 48, 57. In *Neptune,* necessity was also referred to as a justification ('*The Neptune', Jefferies, Master: Provision Case,* Award, 20 June 1797, *reprinted in* John Bassett Moore, *International Adjudications,* Vol. IV (1931) 372–443, at 398, 433).

[226] Andrea K. Bjorklund, 'Economic Security Defenses in International Investment Law', *in Yearbook on International Investment Law & Policy 2008–2009* (Karl P. Sauvant ed., 2009) 479–503, at 502; Bjorklund, 'Emergency Exceptions', at 511; Georg Schwarzenberger, *International Law—International Courts* Vol. II (1968), at 30; Desierto, *Necessity and National Emergency Clauses,* at 49; Agius, 'The Invocation of Necessity in International Law', at 115–16; Burke-White & von Staden, 'Investment Protection in Extraordinary Times', at 321; James Crawford, 'Revisiting the Draft Articles on State Responsibility', *European Journal of International Law* 10 (1999) 435–60, at 444. Lowe seems to favour the 'excuse' approach for all circumstances precluding wrongfulness except for self-defence (*see* Lowe, 'Precluding Wrongfulness', at 410). Simma and Verdross, in contrast, classify necessity as a justification (or *Rechtfertigungsgrund*) (Simma & Verdross, *Universelles Völkerrecht,* para. 1290).

[227] Bin Cheng, *General Principles of Law as Applied by International Courts and Tribunals* (1953) 74 (emphasis added).

[228] Thomas M. Franck, *Recourse to Force: State Action Against Threats and Armed Attack* (2002), at 184.

[229] Bruno Simma, 'NATO, the UN and the Use of Force: Legal Aspects', *European Journal of International Law* 10 (1999) 1–22, at 12, 22.

[230] Thomas M. Franck, 'The Use of Force in International Law', *Tulane Journal of International and Comparative Law* 7 (2003) 7–19, at 13.

[231] Franck, *Recourse to Force,* at 186.

[232] *See* Anthea Roberts, 'Legality vs. Legitimacy: Can Uses of Force be Illegal but Justified?', *in Human Rights, Intervention, and the Use of Force* (Philip Alston & Euan Macdonald eds., 2008) 179–213, at 179, describing the view of Thomas Frank who refers to 'illegal and yet legitimate' (Franck, *Recourse to Force,* at 182) and 'illegal but morally justified' actions (id., at 184).

[233] Bruno Simma, for example, drew a clear line between legality and the moral consideration of 'humanitarian necessity' (Simma, 'NATO, the UN and the Use of Force', at 22).

[234] *See, e.g.,* the following remarks by Ian Johnston:

While not controlling for the proper categorization of Article 25, it is illuminating how domestic legal systems draw the line between justifications and excuses. Most scholars seem to assume that justifications render a certain conduct lawful, while excuses simply exclude the 'blameworthiness' of the actor.[235] In the words of George Fletcher, justifications intend to 'channel... behavior in the future', and excuses are merely 'an expression of compassion for one of our kind caught in the maelstrom of circumstance'.[236] This means that justifications in domestic law tend to acknowledge that a certain act served a 'superior interest'.[237] Excuses, on the other hand, cater for unlawful actions that occurred in exceptional situations under difficult psychological circumstances.

To recall, Article 25(1)(b) ASR provides that the necessity defence is excluded if the relevant State measure 'seriously impair[s] an essential interest of the State or States towards which the obligation exists, or of the international community as a whole'. The ILC clarified that for a certain State measure to meet this requirement '[t]he interests relied on *must outweigh* all other considerations'.[238] Such a value judgment established through the weighing of conflicting interests is typical for justifications and not for excuses. Section 3.02 of the US Model Penal Code, for example, contains a justification, which accepts that the chosen course of action was the 'lesser evil':[239]

Conduct that the actor believes to be necessary to avoid a harm or evil to himself or to another is *justifiable*, provided that... the harm or evil sought to be avoided by such conduct is greater than that sought to be prevented by the law defining the offense charged.[240] (Emphasis added.)

> Excuses function as individualized expressions of understanding about the pressure of circumstances, not as general guides to action. As Bruno Simma put it in characterizing NATO's intervention in Kosovo, the event was 'ad hoc and distinctive'; it was a 'singular case' from which no general conclusions could be drawn. It is precisely because the international community has not been able to devise a set of guidelines for determining when the use of force for humanitarian purposes or against terrorists would be justified that the *necessity excuse* is invoked.

Ian Johnstone, 'The Plea of 'Necessity' in International Legal Discourse: Humanitarian Intervention and Counter-terrorism', *Columbia Journal of Transnational Law* 43 (2005) 337–88, at 356 (emphasis added) (internal references to Simma, 'NATO, the UN and the Use of Force').

[235] Albin Eser, 'Justification and Excuse: a Key Issue in the Concept of Crime', *in Justification and Excuse—Comparative Perspectives*, Vol. I (Albin Eser & George P. Fletcher eds., 1987) 17–65, at 20–1; Johnstone, 'The Plea of 'Necessity' in International Legal Discourse', at 351.

[236] George P. Fletcher, 'The Individualization of Excusing Conditions', *Southern California Law Review* 47 (1974) 1269–310, at 1308.

[237] Eser, 'Justification and Excuse', at 54.

[238] ILC, *Commentaries on State Responsibility*, Article 25, para. 17 (emphasis added).

[239] Fletcher criticizes that the Model Penal Code does not take account of situations in which the objective standard of 'lesser evil' is not met by the defendant. Therefore, Fletcher sees room for an additional notion of necessity as an excuse; for example, if someone (under certain circumstanes) kills two men in order to save the life of one (*see* Fletcher, 'The Individualization of Excusing Conditions', at 1284–5).

[240] The full text of § 3.02 is as follows:

§ 3.02. Justification Generally: Choice of Evils.

In German law, necessity is well established both as a justification and an excuse. 'Justifying necessity' is codified in section 34 of the German Criminal Code and contains an element of 'superior interest' similar to that in section 3.02 of the US Model Penal Code:[241]

A person who, faced with an imminent danger to life, limb, freedom, honour, property or another legal interest which cannot otherwise be averted, commits an act to avert the danger from himself or another, does not act unlawfully, *if, upon weighing the conflicting interests, in particular the affected legal interests and the degree of the danger facing them, the protected interest substantially outweighs the one interfered with.* This shall apply only if and to the extent that the act committed is an adequate means to avert the danger.[242] (Emphasis added.)

'Excusing necessity' (sometimes referred to as duress) is codified in section 35 of the German Criminal Code, and does not require that the protected interest outweigh the impaired interest.[243] Rather, section 35 takes account of the special subjective motivation of the defendant and his desperate psychological situation.[244]

The French Penal Code codifies necessity in Article 122-7, which is usually considered to be a justification (*fait justicatif*):[245]

A person is not criminally liable if confronted with a present or imminent danger to himself, another person or property, he performs an act necessary to ensure the safety of the

> (1) Conduct that the actor believes to be necessary to avoid a harm or evil to himself or to another is justifiable, provided that:
>   (a) the harm or evil sought to be avoided by such conduct is greater than that sought to be prevented by the law defining the offense charged; and
>   (b) neither the Code nor other law defining the offense provides exceptions or defenses dealing with the specific situation involved; and
>   (c) a legislative purpose to exclude the justification claimed does not otherwise plainly appear.
> (2) When the actor was reckless or negligent in bringing about the situation requiring a choice of harms or evils or in appraising the necessity for his conduct, the justification afforded by this Section is unavailable in a prosecution for any offense for which recklessness or negligence, as the case may be, suffices to establish culpability.

[241] Eser, 'Justification and Excuse', at 54.

[242] The English translations of § 34 and § 35 are provided by the German Ministry of Justice, *available* at <http://www.gesetze-im-internet.de/englisch_stgb/englisch_stgb.html#StGB_000P34>. For slightly different translations, *see* id., at 54 n.91 and id., at 58 n.115.

[243] The text of section 35 is as follows:

> A person who, faced with an imminent danger to life, limb or freedom which cannot otherwise be averted, commits an unlawful act to avert the danger from himself, a relative or person close to him, acts without guilt. This shall not apply if and to the extent that the offender could be expected under the circumstances to accept the danger, in particular, because he himself had caused the danger, or was under a special legal obligation to do so; the sentence may be mitigated pursuant to section 49 (1) unless the offender was required to accept the danger because of a special legal obligation to do so.

(*See* the references provided in *supra* note 242.)

[244] Kristian Kühl, '§ 35 Entschuldigender Notstand', *in Strafgesetzbuch—Kommentar* (Karl Lackner & Kristian Kühl eds., 2011)268–73, para. 1.

[245] Bernard Bouloc, *Droit Pénal Général* (2009), para 403; Hervé Pelletier & Jean Perfetti, *Code Pénal* (2012), Article 122-7, para 1.

person or property, except where the means used are disproportionate to the seriousness of the threat.[246]

Notably, the last part of Article 122-7 introduces an element of weighing and balancing ('except where the means used are disproportionate'). As mentioned above, this objective exercise is a characteristic feature of justifications and not of excuses.

Private law concepts of necessity on the domestic level often constitute justifications as well—and nevertheless trigger a duty to compensate. Tort law in the US generally recognizes the doctrine of necessity, and the victim will usually have a claim for compensation although necessity is considered to be a justification and not an excuse.[247] The German Civil Code contains two codifications of the doctrine of necessity, both of which are justifications that trigger a claim for compensation. Section 228 is often referred to as 'defensive necessity' since the peril arises precisely from the object that is destroyed or damaged by the relevant (defensive) action.[248] The provision reads as follows:

A person who damages or destroys a thing belonging to another in order to ward off from himself or from another a danger threatened by the thing does not act *unlawfully* if the damage or destruction is necessary to ward off the danger and the damage is not out of proportion to the danger. If the person acting in this manner caused the danger, he is obliged to *pay damages*.[249]

Section 904 of the German Civil Code sets out 'offensive necessity' as a general justification for infringements of someone else's property, and it provides that the owner may claim compensation for the act justified by necessity.[250]

The owner of a thing is not entitled to prohibit the influence of another person on the thing if the influence is necessary to ward off a present danger and the imminent damage is disproportionately great in relation to the damage suffered by the owner as a result of the influence. The owner may require compensation for the damage incurred by him.[251]

In sum, international jurisprudence, a concern for a clear differentiation between Article 25 and mere moral or political considerations, and domestic notions of necessity support both the categorization of Article 25 as a justification and the

---

[246] Translation provided by the French government, *available at* <http://www.legifrance.gouv.fr/Traductions/Liste-des-traductions-Legifrance>.

[247] *See, e.g.,* Claire Finkelstein, 'Tort Law as a Comparative Institution', *Harvard Journal of Law & Public Policy* 15 (1992) 939–63, at 942–3 and 947.

[248] Tilman Repgen, '§ 228 Notstand', *in* J. von Staudingers *Kommentar zum Bürgerlichen Gesetzbuch mit Einführungsgesetzen und Nebengesetzen, §§ 164–240* (Nobert Haberman & et al. eds., 2004) 804–18, para. 1.

[249] Translation provided by the Ministry of Justice, *available* at <http://www.gesetze-im-internet.de/englisch_bgb/index.html> (emphasis added). The phrase 'does not act unlawfully' in this provision indicates that § 228 constitutes a justification and not an excuse.

[250] Hans Hermann Seiler, '§ 904 Notstand', *in* J. von Staudingers *Kommentar zum Bürgerlichen Gesetzbuch mit Einführungsgesetz und Nebengesetzen, §§ 903–924* (Karl-Heinz Gursky & et. al eds., 2002), para. 2; id., para. 28; Hartwig Sprau, '§ 823', *in Palandt—Bürgerliches Gesetzbuch,* 2009) 1239–87, paras. 30, 41; id., para. 30.

[251] Translation provided by the Ministry of Justice, *available at* <http://www.gesetze-im-internet.de/englisch_bgb/index.html>.

notion that a successful plea of necessity triggers a duty to compensate. All of this tells us little, however, about the relevant standard of compensation, to which we turn now.

2. The relevant standard of compensation

No investor–State tribunal has so far awarded compensation for acts justified by Article 25, and there is therefore no jurisprudence on the relevant standard of compensation following a successful plea of necesssity in investor–State arbitration. Scholarly comments tend to turn on considerations of equity. Ripinski and Williams, for example, argue that such compensation must 'distribute equitably between the parties the burden of losses incurred during emergency situations'.[252] These authors further state that 'arbitrators will inevitably base their decisions on what they see as equitable and reasonable in the circumstances of a particular case'.[253] While it is indeed difficult to be more specific, some additional insights follow from a juxtaposition of the necessity defence with other legal settings involving issues of compensation in investor–State arbitration: (1) State measures covered by NPM clauses; (2) expropriations complying with standard IIA provisions; and (3) unjustified breaches of IIA provisions, i.e. internationally wrongful acts.

While NPM clauses in IIAs tend to prevent a breach of an international obligation from arising, the customary international law defence of necessity merely excludes the wrongfulness of this breach. It is, therefore, safe to assume that a successful plea of necessity will entail a larger amount of compensation than reliance on NPM clauses, which may relieve States from paying any damages.[254] There are certain similarities between acts justified by necessity and expropriations complying with standard BIT provisions. Both require that the relevant act be based on a public purpose. A successful plea of necessity, however, implies that the State acted in order to protect an 'essential' and superior interest, rather than just *any* 'public purpose'. Furthermore, standard BIT provisions on expropriation do not require that the public interest in question be threatened by a 'grave and imminent peril'. Rather, it is for the State to decide under which circumstances it will expropriate foreign-owned assets, provided the expropriation serves a public purpose and is non-discriminatory. Hence, there is no reason to assume that an amount of compensation that would have been sufficient to render an expropriation lawful is inadequate for the purposes of the necessity defence. In other words, a successful plea of necessity should not entail a higher amount of compensation than that which the host State would have had to pay to expropriate the foreign investor. Under most IIAs, expropriations are only lawful if accompanied by compensation

---

[252] Ripinsky & Williams, *Damages in International Investment Law*, at 352.
[253] Id., at 353.   [254] *See* Chapter 7, section V.

based on the 'fair market value' of the asset as at the time of the expropriation (or as at the time at which the decision to expropriate became public).[255]

At the other end of the spectrum, the necessity defence differs from the third category mentioned above—internationally wrongful acts—insofar as the State measure justified by necessity is not considered to be 'wrongful'. It seems fair to say that a State act justified by necessity involves a lower degree of 'illegality' than a 'wrongful act' and should, therefore, must not entail a larger amount of compensation. The consequences of violations of IIA protections are governed by customary international law. As far as pecuniary remedies are concerned, there is little doubt that the principles formulated by the PCIJ in the *Factory at Chorzów* case are applicable in investor–State arbitration.[256] The PCIJ held that:

The essential principle contained in the actual notion of an illegal act—a principle which seems to be established by international practice and in particular by the decisions of arbitral tribunals—is that reparation must, as far as possible, wipe out all the consequences of the illegal act and re-establish the situation which would, in all probability, have existed if that act had not been committed. Restitution in kind, or, if this is not possible, payment of a sum corresponding to the value which a restitution in kind would bear; the award, if need be, of damages for loss sustained which would not be covered by restitution in kind or payment in place of it—such are the principles which should serve to determine the amount of compensation due for an act contrary to international law.[257]

By stating that 'reparation must...re-establish the situation which would, in all probability, have existed if that act had not been committed', the PCIJ identified the key element for measuring the compensation due for an internationally wrongful act: a comparison between the real situation at the time of the judgment and the situation that would exist if the 'wrongful act' had not been committed. A large number of investor–State tribunals relied on the *Chorzów* principles in

---

[255] Many IIA provisions on expropriation follow in substance the World Bank Guidelines on the Treatment of Foreign Direct Investment, ILM 31 (1992) 1379–84. The first three sections of Article VI of these guidelines read as follows (at 1382):

1. A State may not expropriate or otherwise take in whole or in part a foreign private investment in its territory, or take measures which have similar effects, except where this is done in accordance with applicable legal procedures, in pursuance in good faith of a public purpose, without discrimination on the basis of nationality and against the payment of appropriate compensation.
2. Compensation for a specific investment taken by the State will, according to the details provided below, be deemed 'appropriate' if it is adequate, effective and prompt.
3. Compensation will be deemed 'adequate' if it is based on the fair market value of the taken asset as such value is determined immediately before the time at which the taking occurred or the decision to take the asset became publicly known.

[256] Ripinsky & Williams, *Damages in International Investment Law*, at p. 31 (with further references); Marboe, *Calculation of Compensation and Damages in International Investment Law*, paras. 7.04–7.06. Reisman and Sloane observe that '*Chorzów* Factory remains, notwithstanding the passage of more than 70 years, the seminal international decision about compensation under international law' (Reisman & Sloane, 'Indirect Expropriation and its Valuation in the BIT Generation', at 135).

[257] *Factory at Chorzów*, Merits, at 47.

determining compensation for unlawful expropriations and violations of the FET standard. Particularly illustrative for our purposes is the *CMS* case, which contains a number of interesting considerations regarding the assessment of a hypothetical situation—the key element in the application of the *Chorzów* principles.[258]

While the *CMS* tribunal rejected Argentina's argument that the economic crisis justified its recourse to the necessity defence, the crisis constituted a compensation-reducing element under the *Chorzów* principles in several ways, including the following: first, the tribunal held that if the tariffs had been calculated in US dollars in compliance with the FET standard, domestic demand for gas would have decreased because of the economic crisis. This decrease would have diminished the claimant's revenues.[259] Second, the tribunal found that without pesification the claimant would have been able to greatly increase its revenue, at least once the crisis was over. Under such circumstances, however, Argentina would have been allowed to significantly decrease the tariffs on the basis of the tariff review system of the original legal framework.[260] Finally, the tribunal further decreased the amount of compensation because of 'operation and maintenance expenditures' that the claimant would have incurred but for Argentina's measures in violation of the BIT.[261]

It is important to bear in mind that the application of the *Chorzów* principles may, under certain circumstances, lead to the result that the amount of compensation for a wrongful act is lower than the sum payable for a lawful expropriation at the time of the State's action. This is simply the consequence of the fact that the amount of compensation due for lawful expropriations is usually to be determined at the time of the expropriatory act. Determining compensation for a wrongful act, on the other hand, demands an inquiry into a hypothetical development until the date of the award. These considerations bring us to the following conclusion: the necessity defence should not entail compensation that exceeds the amount of compensation payable for a lawful expropriation. In any event, the amount of compensation is limited to the sum that the claimant would have been able to recover under the rules of customary international law on compensation for wrongful acts. Of course, this 'double ceiling' does not resolve all issues that might arise regarding the appropriate amount of compensation. Still, it provides at least some guidance for tribunals, which so far have not analysed the standard of compensation in the context of acts justified by Article 25.

V. Conclusion

The analysis in section I of this chapter showed that the customary international law defence of necessity is, in principle, applicable in investor–State

---

[258] Even the *CMS* annulment committee—which in other respects opined that the award 'contained manifest errors of law' and that it 'suffered from lacunae and elisions' (*CMS*, Decision of the Annulment Committee, para. 158)—acknowledged that 'the Award is one of the most detailed decisions on damages in ICSID case-law.' (Id., para. 154)

[259] *CMS*, Award, para. 444.   [260] Id., para. 456.   [261] Id., para. 458–62.

arbitration—despite a ruling of the German Constitutional Court that cast doubt on this proposition. In practice, however, it is very difficult for States to rely on the necessity defence (as codified by the ILC and applied by the ICJ and investor–State tribunals) in times of economic crises. As seen in section II, the reasons for this practical unavailability of the necessity defence are the strict 'only way' and 'non-contribution' requirements of Article 25. One way to enhance the relevance of the necessity defence in investor–State arbitration would be to replace the 'only way' requirement with a proportionality analysis. This analysis could include the extent of the State's 'contribution' as one relevant factor without excluding the necessity defence by definition if the State's policies contributed to the emergence of the crisis.

Section III analysed two doctrinal pathways to incorporate such a proportionality analysis into Article 25. The first pathway focused on developments within the customary international law defence of necessity. We have seen that the 'only way' requirement enjoys reasonable support in the State practice and jurisprudence that underlies the wording of Article 25. Still, States can influence the content of the customary international law defence of necessity in several ways, for example by clarifying their understanding of the 'only way' requirement in Article 25 or other relevant legal expressions in international fora. As long as States are unwilling to take these steps, there is little reason to think States want to facilitate recourse to the necessity defence. In light of the variety of contexts in which States have invoked necessity in recent centuries, it is important to bear in mind that reducing the threshold for this defence may have ramifications beyond investor–State arbitration.

The second doctrinal pathway for establishing a proportionality analysis in the context of Article 25 is the interaction between customary international law and general principles of law. General principles may inform the content of (unclear) customary international law, and it is therefore at least arguable that proportionality as a general principle of law may have a bearing on the means–end relationship in Article 25. However, such an approach raises several concerns. The notion that a breach of BIT obligations can be justified as long as the relevant emergency measures are proportionate is apparent from neither the relevant BIT nor Article 25 and therefore runs counter to the rule of law from the perspective of foreign investors. Moreover, letting respondent States avoid their treaty obligations as long as the relevant measures serve one of their 'essential interests' in a proportionate way would overwrite the nuanced bargains they made with their treaty partners. This would bring instability to international relations and uncertainty for foreign investors.

Section IV commented on the consequences of a successful plea of necessity—which might become particularly important if States take the steps to refine the customary international law defence of necessity outlined in section III. While the ASR provide little guidance on this issue, the better view is that the invocation of the necessity defence entails a duty to compensate. Contrary to what is probably the predominant view in legal scholarship, Article 25 is better characterized as justification than as excuse, which does not mean that the relevant State escapes payment of damages. Regarding the relevant standard of compensation, section IV has augmented notions of equity with insights from a comparative analysis of other legal settings in investor–State arbitration that involve issues of compensation. A review of the *Chorzów* principles and their application illustrated that investors are not sheltered from macroeconomic developments in times of crisis. Rather, these factors, as well as developments subsequent to the treaty violation, matter when it comes to the consequences of internationally wrongful acts. The same principles should cap the amount of compensation payable for the exercise of the necessity defence, and so should the value of the investment as at the time when the acts justified by necessity occurred.

9

Summary and Concluding Remarks

Through a combination of substantive treaty protections, procedural tools, and robust enforcement mechanisms, the current system of investor–State arbitration constitutes one of the most effective means for the protection of non-State actors in international law. States conclude IIAs to protect their nationals abroad and/or to attract foreign investors in the hope that they will contribute to their own prosperity and development. The protection of foreign investment will therefore often not only be compatible with the public interest but be a matter of the public interest itself. Nevertheless, investor–State disputes typically deal with alleged treaty infringements that respondents argue occurred in the public interest. Conflicts between different rights and interests arise in almost every legal order, and are often resolved through a proportionality analysis. Chapter 3 illustrated that this is particularly true for a significant number of domestic constitutional orders and some international law regimes such as the WTO and the ECHR. The comparative study in Chapter 3 concluded that proportionality constitutes a general principle of law within the meaning of Article 38(1)(c) ICJ Statute that may be relevant to the interpretation of IIAs.

This book does not suggest that arbitrators should apply a free-floating proportionality analysis whenever investor rights conflict with other interests. Rather, arbitrators should be mindful of the relevant legal setting before engaging in proportionality analysis. Chapter 3 identified three factors arbitrators should take into account before applying the principle of proportionality in investor–State arbitration: (1) the risk of unwarranted judicial lawmaking; (2) rule-of-law concerns; and (3) the risk of arbitrary outcomes due to uncertainty as to what interests matter in a proportionality analysis and what weight they carry. Value orders provided by constitutions mitigate the third concern on the domestic level. International law might not have a unitary value system comparable to that of domestic constitutions; but IIAs do not operate in isolation from the rest of international law. Chapter 4 discussed whether and to what extent the principle of systemic integration enshrined in Article 31(3)(c) VCLT may compensate for the lack of a comprehensive constitutional value order. We have seen that Article 31(3)(c) allows arbitrators to resort to external rules under certain circumstances. It is important to bear in mind, however, that Article 31(3)(c) is only one of the several means of treaty interpretation. Arbitrators should first carefully consider the ordinary meaning of the treaty terms, their context, and the object and purpose of the treaty, before considering external rules. Where States have made certain choices in IIAs, arbitrators should not overwrite them.

Through this analytical prism, this book examined the current and potential role of proportionality in IIA provisions on expropriation, the FET standard, Article XI of the US–Argentina BIT, and the customary international law defence of necessity. Chapter 5 established that States have a variety of different means at their disposal to exclude proportionate regulatory measures in the public interest from the scope of IIA provisions on expropriation. The most explicit form of doing so is to include corresponding definitions of the concept of indirect expropriation in IIAs—a practice that States are increasingly adopting. States can also bring about such an understanding of indirect expropriation for existing IIAs that contain no definition of this concept, for example through subsequent agreement in the form of joint notes of interpretation—subject to the limitations set out in Chapter 5.

In the absence of clear guidance from the parties to an IIA, however, tribunals should not too readily read a proportionality analysis into IIA provisions on expropriation. To recall, standard IIA provisions on expropriation merely specify that expropriations are permissible as long as they serve a public purpose, comply with due process, are non-discriminatory, and are accompanied by compensation. The wording and context of such provisions does not suggest that foreign investors receive no compensation only because the relevant State measure was proportionate in light of a conflicting value or interest. Chapter 5 showed that reference to ECtHR jurisprudence cannot justify such a result either. However, there is a trend in treaty making to include a definition of indirect expropriation that excludes proportionate regulatory measures in the public interest from the scope of IIA provisions. If this trend persists—in particular in regional IIAs such as CETA, TTIP, or TTP—there is a strong argument that the mitigated police powers doctrine reflects customary international law. Such a rule of customary international law would be relevant to the interpretation of other IIA provisions on expropriation by virtue of Article 31(3)(c) VCLT, and militate for a proportionality analysis in identifying an indirect expropriation even if not indicated by the text of the relevant treaty.

Chapter 6 identified the FET standard as particularly fertile ground for the application of the principle of proportionality and the concept of systemic integration. Tribunals recognize that the FET standard often requires the accommodation of competing interests. Proportionality offers an argumentative framework for a transparent and stringent case-specific analysis and does not constitute a threat to the rule of law, nor is it likely to give rise to judicial lawmaking or arbitrariness. It bears repeating that both the inclusion of a proportionality analysis in adjudicating FET claims and the consideration of external rules may play out to the advantage of either investors or States. Proportionality analysis is neutral: it provides for a 'fair balance' of the competing interests at stake and ensures that none of them is impaired more than necessary for the benefit of the other.

As demonstrated in Chapter 7, NPM clauses with a wording and structure similar to that of Article XI of the Argentina–US BIT are also likely to give rise to a proportionality analysis. Such provisions list values and interests that may conflict with investor rights and, therefore, provide for a value system that frames the proportionality analysis. As a result, concerns about judicial lawmaking, the rule of law, or arbitrary outcomes of the proportionality analysis are even less justified here than they are for the FET standard. Article 31(3)(c) VCLT constitutes a solid basis to apply proportionality as a general principle in such settings. Proportionality analysis is a transparent and efficient tool for resolving conflicts between the competing interests at stake—a task States have referred to neutral third-party adjudication for non-self-judging NPM clauses. Hence, incorporating NPM clauses in IIAs constitutes an effective means for States to ensure they are not liable to foreign investors for proportionate measures in the public interest without unduly undermining investor protections in IIAs.

Something different is true for the customary international law defence of necessity discussed in Chapter 8. While this defence is, in principle, applicable in investor–State arbitration, it is almost impossible for States to successfully invoke necessity in times of economic crisis. The replacement of the strict 'only way' requirement with the principle of proportionality would facilitate recourse to the necessity defence. However, the better arguments seem to speak against such an approach. Proportionality analysis in the context of the necessity defence would allow States to evade their international obligations as long as the resulting harm was proportionate compared to a benefit to the national community. Such an approach runs counter to the international rule of law. Moreover, this far-reaching use of the principle of proportionality would undermine the ability of States to make meaningful choices regarding the balance between investor rights and other interests in IIAs. Nevertheless, States may bring about such an understanding of the necessity defence in several ways. If they wish to do so, an important first step would be to clarify—outside arbitral proceedings—that they do not consider the strict 'only way' requirement to reflect customary international law. Even if modified, however, the necessity defence can bring only limited relief to host States as they are under an obligation to pay damages for acts justified by necessity, albeit not necessarily to the same degree as for internationally wrongful acts. Therefore, focusing on the necessity defence distracts from more important tasks faced by States and the international community, one of which is to find suitable rules for the insolvency of States.[1]

If States wish to recalibrate the balance between investor rights and the public interest in international investment law, they have more sophisticated and nuanced means at their disposal. States can, for example, include NPM clauses in

---

[1] For various efforts in this regard, *see* Christoph G. Paulus, 'Should Politics be Replaced by a Legal Proceeding?', *in A Debt Restructuring Mechanism for Sovereigns* (Christoph G. Paulus ed., 2014) 191–212, at 197–211; Ugo Panizza, 'Do We Need a Mechanism for Solving Sovereign Debt Crises? A Rule-Based Discussion', *in A Debt Restructuring Mechanism for Sovereigns* (Christoph G. Paulus ed., 2014) 223–39, at 234–7; Anna Gelpern, 'A Skeptic's Case for Sovereign Bankruptcy', *in A Debt Restructuring Mechanism for Sovereigns* (Christoph G. Paulus ed., 2014) 261–78, at 276–8; Christoph Paulus, 'Rechtliche Handhaben zur Bewältigung der Überschuldung von Staaten', *Recht der Internationalen Wirtschaft* 55 (2009) 11–7.

their IIAs and/or clarify in annexes to IIAs that proportionate regulatory measures to protect public welfare objectives do not constitute indirect expropriations.
Subject to the caveats outlined in Chapter 5, States can influence the interpretation of IIAs even after their conclusion through subsequent agreements and practice. Furthermore, States should realize that their contributions to a value order
on the international level might influence the interpretation of IIAs. Within the
limits set out in Chapter 4, Article 31(3)(c) VCLT provides for a mechanism to
take account of rules of international law outside the four corners of IIAs. Hence,
treaty making in other fields such as environmental and human rights law can
make a difference. Such cooperation on the international level is preferable to
retreating to the domestic level, be it by abandoning the system of investor–State
arbitration or more subtle means such as self-judging NPM clauses. States should
take an active role in shaping the values of the international community, ideally
on a global or multilateral level, but also through their bilateral relationships.

For arbitrators, it is important to bear in mind that every IIA in itself reflects a
certain balance between the protection of foreign investment and other interests.
States conclude IIAs to protect their nationals abroad, attract foreign investment,
or both. In the past, the protection of nationals and their investments might have
been the sole or dominant reason for traditionally capital-exporting States to conclude IIAs. Today, the picture is more complex. To mention just two factors,
developing States increasingly conclude IIAs between themselves, and traditionally capital-exporting States find themselves at the receiving end of investor–State
arbitrations more often than they used to. The bargain struck between investment protection and other interests in a particular IIA indicates to what extent
the treaty partners consider foreign investment and its protection to be in the
national interest. Foreign investment can create jobs, make significant contributions to GDP, increase exports, lead to beneficial intellectual property transfer in
such crucial areas as food production and clean energy, improve training of local
staff, enhance productivity, generate additional tax income, lead to efficient use
of underutilized resources, and import best practices for addressing social and
environmental issues.[2]

The 2012 UN Conference on Sustainable Development held in Rio de Janeiro
established a working group that would provide a proposal to the UN General
Assembly for sustainable development goals (SDGs).[3] In July 2014, the working
group submitted its proposal, comprising seventeen goals to be attained by 2030,
to the General Assembly. The relevant list included the eradication of hunger, the
availability and sustainable management of water and sanitation for all, access

---

[2] UNCTAD, World Investment Report 2014, Investing in the SDGs: an Action Plan, p. iii;
UNCTAD, World Investment Report 2011, Non-Equity Modes of International Production and
Development, pp. 147–8; UNCTAD, World Investment Report 2010, Investing in a Low-Carbon
Economy (2010); p. 121; UNCTAD, World Investment Report 2009, Transnational Corporations,
Agricultural Production and Development (2009), p. 133.
[3] General Assembly, UN DOC A/67/634, para. 1.

to affordable and reliable energy, and the building of resilient infrastructure.[4] Reaching these goals requires a stark increase in investment, particularly in transportation, water and sanitation, telecommunications, energy, and agriculture. According to UNCTAD estimates, total investment needs are approximately $5 to $7 trillion per year. Measured against current investment, UNCTAD identified an investment gap of between $1.9 and $3.1 trillion annually in key areas such as power, transport, and water in developing countries alone, and stated that much of the needed investment will have to come from the private secctor.[5] While sufficient funds appear to be available on a global scale, there is reluctance to invest them abroad because of regulatory uncertainty.[6] IIAs are an important means to work against this uncertainty. When concluding IIAs, States have to weigh and balance the advantages of foreign investment and the protection of nationals abroad on one hand with possible disadvantages of foreign investment and its protection on the other. It is not for arbitrators to undermine the balance struck in a particular IIA through a proportionality analysis. But proportionality is a valuable tool to elucidate the bargain inherent in every IIA to reconcile conflicting interests.

---

[4] Outcome Document of the Open Working Group for Sustainable Development Goals, 17 July 2014, p. 5 (*available at* <http://sustainabledevelopment.un.org/content/documents/4518SDGs_FINAL_Proposal%20of%20OWG_19%20July%20at%201320hrsver3.pdf>).

[5] UNCTAD, World Investment Report 2014, Investing in the SDGs: an Action Plan, at 140.

[6] Id., at 136; UNCTAD, World Investment Report 2011, Non-Equity Modes of International Production and Development, at iii.

Bibliography

Abbott, Kenneth W. & Snidal, Duncan, 'Hard and Soft Law in International Governance', *International Organizations* 54 (2000) 421–56

Agius, Maria, 'The Invocation of Necessity in International Law', *Netherlands International Law Review* 56 (2009) 95–135

Ago, Roberto, 'Addendum to Eighth Report on State Responsibility', UN Doc. A/CN.4/318/ADD.5–7, *Yearbook of the International Law Commission*, Vol. II, 14–70 (1980)

Alexy, Robert, *Theorie der Grundrechte* (Frankfurt am Main, Suhrkamp 1986)

Alexy, Robert, 'Constitutional Rights, Balancing, and Rationality', *Ratio Juris* 16 (2003) 131–40

Allott, Philip, 'State Responsibility and the Unmaking of International Law', *Harvard International Law Journal* 29 (1988) 1–26

Alvarez, José E., 'Beware Boundary Crossings', New York University Public Law & Legal Theory Research Paper Series, Working Paper No. 14-51 (September 2014) *available at* <http://papers.ssrn.com/sol3/papers.cfm?abstract_id=2498182>

Alvarez, José E. & Khamsi, Kathryn, 'The Argentine Crisis and Foreign Investors: a Glimpse into the Heart of the Investment Regime', in *Yearbook on International Investment Law & Policy 2008–2009* (Karl P. Sauvant ed., Oxford: OUP, 2009) 379–478

Alvarez, José E., 'A BIT on Custom', *New York University Journal of International Law and Politics* 42 (2009) 17–80

Alvarez, José E., 'The Return of the State', *Minnesota Journal of International Law* 20 (2011) 223–64

Alvarez, José E. & Brink, Tegan, 'Revisiting the Necessity Defense: Continental Casualty v. Argentina', in *Yearbook on International Investment Law & Policy 2010–2011* (Karl P. Sauvant ed., New York: OUP, 2011) 319–74

Alvarez, José E., 'Limits of Change by Way of Subsequent Agreements and Practice', in *Treaties and Subsequent Practice* (Georg Nolte ed., Oxford: OUP, 2013) 123–32

Alvarez-Jiménez, Alberto, 'Foreign Investment Protection and Regulatory Failures as States' Contribution to the State of Necessity under Customary International Law—a New Approach Based on the Complexity of Argentina's 2001 Crisis', *Journal of International Arbitration* 27 (2010) 141–77

Amador, F.V. Garcia, 'Report on State Responsibility at the 8th Session of the International Law Commission', A/CN.4/96, *Yearbook of the International Law Commission*, Vol. II (1956) 173–231

Andenas, Mads & Zleptnig, Stefan, 'Proportionality: WTO Law in Comparative Perspective', *Texas International Law Journal* 42 (2007) 372–427

Aust, Helmut Philipp & Nolte, Georg, 'International Law and the Rule of Law at the National Level', in *Rule of Law Dynamics* (André Nollkaemper, et al. eds., Cambridge: CUP, 2012) 48–67

Barak, Aharon, *Proportionality* (Cambridge: CUP, 2012)

Barboza, Julio, 'Necessity (Revisited) in International Law', in *Essays in International Law in Honour of Judge Manfred Lachs* (Jerzy Makarczyk ed., The Hague: Martinus Nijhoff Publishers, 1984) 27–43

Baxter, Richard R. & Sohn, Louis B., 'Responsibility of States for Injuries to the Economic Interests of Aliens', *American Journal of International Law* 55 (1961) 545–84

Beatty, David M., *The Ultimate Rule of Law* (Oxford: OUP, 2004)

Behrens, Peter, 'Towards the Constitutionalization of International Investment Protection', *Archiv des Völkerrechts* 45 (2007) 153–97

Bernhardt, Rudolf, 'Article 103', in *The Charter of the United Nations—a Commentary* (Bruno Simma, et al. eds., Oxford: OUP, 2002) 1292–302

Besson, Samantha, 'The Authority of International Law—Lifting the State Veil', *Sydney Law Review* 31 (2009) 343–80

Binder, Christina, 'Changed Circumstances in Investment Law: Interfaces Between the Law of Treaties and the Law of State Responsibility with a Special Focus on the Argentine Crisis', in *International Investment Law for the 21st Century—Essays in Honour of Christoph Schreuer* (Christina Binder, et al. eds., Oxford: OUP, 2009) 608–30

Binder, Christina & Reinisch, August, 'Economic Emergency Powers: a Comparative Law Perspective', in *International Investment Law and Comparative Law* (Stephan W. Schill ed., Oxford: OUP, 2010) 503–40

Bjorklund, Andrea K., 'Emergency Exceptions: State of Necessity and Force Majeure', in *The Oxford Handbook of International Investment Law* (Peter Muchlinski, et al. eds., Oxford: OUP, 2008) 459–522

Bjorklund, Andrea K., 'Investment Treaty Arbitral Decisions as Jurisprudence Constante', in *International Economic Law—the State and Future of the Discipline* (Colin B. Picker, et al. eds., Portland, OR: Hart, 2008) 265–80

Bjorklund, Andrea K., 'Economic Security Defenses in International Investment Law', in *Yearbook on International Investment Law & Policy 2008–2009* (Karl P. Sauvant ed., Oxford: OUP, 2009) 479–503

Boed, Roman, 'State of Necessity as a Justification for Internationally Wrongful Conduct', *Yale Human Rights and Development Law Journal* 3 (2000) 1–43

Bogdan, Michael, 'General Principles of Law and the Lacunae in the Law of Nations', *Nordic Journal of International Law* 46 (1977) 37–53

Bomhoff, Jacco, 'Balancing, the Global and the Local: Judicial Balancing as a Problematic Topic in Comparative (Constitutional) Law', *Hastings International and Comparative Law Review* 31 (2008) 555–86

Bouloc, Bernard, *Droit pénal général* (Paris: Dalloz, 2009)

Bowett, William, 'State Contracts with Aliens: Contemporary Developments on Compensation for Termination or Breach', *British Yearbook of International Law* 59 (1988) 49–74

Brauch, Jeffrey A., 'The Margin of Appreciation and the Jurisprudence of the European Court of Human Rights: Threat to the Rule of Law', *Columbia Journal of European Law* 11 (2005) 113–50

Braun, Tillmann R., 'Investitionsschutz durch internationale Schiedsgerichte', *TranState Working Papers* 89 (2009) 1–23

Briggs, Herbert W., *The International Law Commission* (Ithaca: Cornell University Press, 1965)

Brower, Charles N. & Schill, Stephan W., 'Is Arbitration a Threat or a Boon to the Legitimacy of International Investment Law?', *Chicago Journal of International Law* 9 (2009) 471–98

Brower, Charles N. & Blanchard, Sadie, 'What's in a Meme? The Truth about Investor–State Arbitration: Why It Need Not, and Must Not, Be Repossessed by States', *Columbia Journal of Transnational Law* 52 (2014) 689–779

Brownlie, Ian, *Principles of Public International Law* (Oxford: OUP, 2008)

Burke-White, William W. & von Staden, Andreas, 'Investment Protection in Extraordinary Times: the Interpretation and Application of Non-Precluded Measures Provisions in Bilateral Investment Treaties', *Virginia Journal of International Law* 48 (2008) 307–410

Burke-White, William W. & von Staden, Andreas, 'Private Litigation in a Public Law Sphere: the Standard of Review in Investor–State Arbitrations', *Yale Journal of International Law* 35 (2010) 283–346

Burke-White, William W. & von Staden, Andreas, 'The Need for Public Law Standards of Review in Investor–State Arbitrations', in *International Investment Law and Comparative Law* (Stephan W. Schill ed., Oxford: OUP, 2010) 689–720

Byers, Michael, 'Abuse of Rights: an Old Principle, A New Age', *McGill Law Journal* 47 (2002) 390–431

Chalamish, Efraim, 'The Future of Bilateral Investment Treaties: a De Facto Multilateral Agreement?', *Brooklyn Journal of International Law* 34 (2009) 303–54

Cheng, Bin, *General Principles of Law as Applied by International Courts and Tribunals* (London: Stevens & Sons, 1953)

Choudhury, Barnali, 'Exception Provisions as a Gateway to Incorporating Human Rights Issues into International Investment Agreements', *Columbia Journal of Transnational Law* 49 (2011) 670–716

Christoffersen, Jonas, *Fair Balance: Proportionality, Subsidiarity and Primarity in the European Convention on Human Rights* (Leiden: Martinus Nijhoff Publishers, 2009)

Clapham, Andrew, *Human Rights Obligations of Non-State Actors* (Oxford: OUP, 2006)

Clayton, Richard & Tomlinson, Hugh, *The Law of Human Rights—Vol. I* (Oxford: OUP, 2008)

Cohen-Eliya, Moshe & Porat, Iddo, 'The Hidden Foreign Law Debate in Heller: the Proportionality Approach in American Constitutional Law', *San Diego Law Review* 46 (2009) 367–413

Congyan, Cai, 'International Investment Treaties and the Formation, Application and Transformation of Customary International Law Rules', *Chinese Journal of International Law* 7 (2008) 659–79

Corporate Europe Observatory & Transnational Institute, *Profiting from Injustice* (2012)

Crawford, James, 'Revising the Draft Articles on State Responsibility', *European Journal of International Law* 10 (1999) 435–60

Crawford, James, 'Addendum to Second Report on State Responsibility', UN Doc. A/CN.4/498/Add.2 (1999)

Crawford, James, *The International Law Commission's Articles on State Responsibility—Introduction, Text and Commentaries* (Cambridge: CUP, 2002)

Cremer, Hans-Joachim, 'Eigentumsschutz', in *EMRK/GG—Konkordanzkommentar* (Rainer Grote & Thilo Marauhn eds., Tübingen: Mohr Siebeck, 2006) 1222–345

Dahl, Robert A., 'Can International Organizations be Democratic? A Skeptic's View', in *Democracy's Edges* (Ian Shapiro & Casiano Hacker-Cordon eds., New York: CUP, 1999) 19–36

de Aréchaga, Eduardo Jiménez, 'International Responsibility', in *Manual of Public International Law* (Max Sorensen ed., London: Macmillan, 1968) 531–603

de Vattel, Emmerich, *The Law of Nations or the Principles of Natural Law Applied to the Conduct and to the Affairs of Nations and of Sovereigns* (1758, James Brown Scott ed, Carnegie Institution of Washington, 1916)

de Wet, Erika, 'The Emergence of International and Regional Value Systems as a Manifestation of the Emerging International Constitutional Order', *Leiden Journal of International Law* 19 (2006) 611–32

de Wet, Erika, 'The International Constitutional Order', *International and Comparative Law Quarterly* 55 (2006) 51–76

Delbrück, Jost, 'Proportionality', in *Encyclopedia of Public International Law*, Vol. III (Rudolf Bernhardt ed., Amsterdam: North-Holland, 1997) 1140–44

Desierto, Diane A., 'Necessity and Supplementary Means of Interpretation of Non-Precluded Measures in Bilateral Investment Treaties', *University of Pennsylvania Journal of International Law* 31 (2010) 827–934

Desierto, Diane A., *Necessity and National Emergency Clauses—Sovereignty in Modern Treaty Interpretation* (Leiden: Martinus Nijhoff Publishers, 2012)

Di Pietro, Domenico, 'The Use of Precedents in ICSID Arbitration: Regularity or Certainty?', *International Arbitration Law Review* 10 (2007) 92–103

Dolzer, Rudolf, 'Expropriation and Nationalization', in *Encyclopedia of Public International Law*, Vol. II (Rudolf Bernhardt ed., Amsterdam: North-Holland, 1995) 319–26

Dolzer, Rudolf & Schreuer, Christoph, *Principles of International Investment Law* (Oxford: OUP, 2008)

Dolzer, R. & Kim, Yun-I, 'Commentary on Germany's Model BIT (2009)', in *Commentaries on Selected Model Investment Treaties* (Chester Brown ed., Oxford: OUP, 2013) 289–319

Dorsen, Norman et al., *Comparative Constitutionalism: Cases and Materials* (St Paul, Minn: West, 2003)

Douglas, Zachary, 'Other Specific Regimes of Responsibility: Investment Treaty Arbitration and ICSID', in *The Law of International Responsibility* (James Crawford, et al. eds., Oxford: OUP, 2010) 815–42

Doyle, Michael W., 'The UN-Charter—a Global Constitution?', in *Ruling the World? Constitutionalism, International Law, and Global Governance* (Jeffrey L. Dunoff & Joel P. Trachtman eds., Cambridge: CUP, 2009) 113–32

Dugan, Christopher F., et al., *Investor–State Arbitration* (New York: OUP, 2008)

Dugard, John R., 'First Report on Diplomatic Protection at the 52nd Session of the International Law Commission', A/CN.4/506 (2000)

Dunoff, Jeffrey L. & Trachtman, Joel P., 'A Functional Approach to Global Constitutionalism', in *Ruling the World? Constitutionalism, International Law, and Global Governance* (Jeffrey L. Dunoff & Joel P. Trachtman eds., Cambridge: CUP, 2009) 3–35

Dworkin, Ronald, *Taking Rights Seriously* (Cambridge, Massachusetts: Harvard University Press 1977)

Ehlers, Dirk, 'Die Europäische Menschenrechtskonvention: Allgemeine Lehren der EMRK', in *Europäische Grundrechte und Grundfreiheiten* (Dirk Ehlers ed., Berlin: De Gruyter, 2009) 25–80

Ehlers, Dirk, 'Die Grundfreiheiten der Europäischen Gemeinschaft: Allgemeine Lehren', in *Europäische Grundrechte und Grundfreiheiten* (Dirk Ehlers ed., Berlin: De Gruyter, 2009) 209–69

Elias, Olufemi & Lim, Chin, '"General Principles of Law", "Soft" Law and the Identification of International Law', *Netherlands Yearbook of International Law* 28 (1997) 3–49

Engle, Eric, 'The General Principle of Proportionality and Aristotle', *Ius Gentium* 23 (2013) 265–75

Eser, Albin, 'Justification and Excuse: a Key Issue in the Concept of Crime', in *Justification and Excuse—Comparative Perspectives*, Vol. I (Albin Eser & George P. Fletcher eds., Freiburg: Max-Planck-Institut, 1987) 17–65

European Commission, 'Investment Provisions in the EU–Canada Free Trade Agreement' (CETA) (3 December 2013)

Falk, Richard A., 'The Pathways of Global Constitutionalism', in *The Constitutional Foundations of World Peace* (Richard A. Falk, et al. eds., Albany: State University of New York Press, 1993) 13–38

Falk, Richard A. & Strauss, Andrew, 'Toward Global Parliament', *Foreign Affairs* 80 (2001) 212–20

Fassbender, Bardo, 'Rediscovering a Forgotten Constitution—Notes on the Place of the UN Charter in the International Legal Order', in *Ruling the World? Constitutionalism, International Law, and Global Governance* (Jeffrey L. Dunoff & Joel P. Trachtman eds., Cambridge: CUP, 2009) 133–47

Fassbender, Bardo, *The United Nations Charter as the Constitution of the International Community* (Leiden: Martinus Nijhoff Publishers, 2009)

Fauchald, Ole Kristian, 'The Legal Reasoning of ICSID Tribunals—an Empirical Analysis', *European Journal of International Law* 19 (2008) 301–64

Finke, Jasper, *Die Parallelität internationaler Streitbeilegungsmechanismen: Untersuch ung der aus der Stärkung der internationalen Gerichtsbarkeit resultierenden Konflikte* (Berlin: Duncker & Humblot, 2003)

Finkelstein, Claire, 'Tort Law as a Comparative Institution', *Harvard Journal of Law & Public Policy* 15 (1992) 939–63

Fischer, Peter, 'Transnational Enterprises', in *Encyclopedia of Public International Law*; Vol. IV (Rudolf Bernhardt ed., Amsterdam: North-Holland, 1985) 921–6

Fletcher, George P., 'The Individualization of Excusing Conditions', *Southern California Law Review* 47 (1974) 1269–310

Fletcher, George P., *Rethinking Criminal Law* (New York: OUP, 1978)

Franck, Thomas M., *Recourse to Force: State Action Against Threats and Armed Attack* (New York: CUP, 2002)

Franck, Thomas M., 'The Use of Force in International Law', *Tulane Journal of International and Comparative Law* 7 (2003) 7–19

Freeman, Alwyn V., 'Recent Aspects of the Calvo Doctrine and the Challenge to International Law', *American Journal of International Law* 40 (1946) 121–47

Friedmann, Wolfgang, 'The Use of "General Principles" in the Development of International Law', *American Journal of International Law* 57 (1963) 279–299

Cynthia C. Galvez, '"Necessity," Investor Rights, and State Sovereignty for NAFTA Investment Arbitration', *Cornell International Law Journal* 46 (2013) 143–63

Giorgio Gaja, 'General Principles of Law', in *The Max Planck Encyclopedia of Public International Law—Volume IV* (Rüdiger Wolfrum ed., Oxford: OUP, 2012) 370–8

Gardam, Judith G., *Necessity, Proportionality and the Use of Force by States* (Cambridge: CUP, 2004)

Gardbaum, Stephen, 'The Myth and the Reality of American Constitutional Exceptionalism', *Michigan Law Review* 107 (2008) 391–466

Gardbaum, Stephen, 'Human Rights and International Constitutionalism', in *Ruling the World? Constitutionalism, International Law, and Global Governance* (Jeffrey L. Dunoff & Joel P. Trachtman eds., Cambridge: CUP, 2009) 233–57

Gardiner, Richard K., *Treaty Interpretation* (New York: OUP, 2008)

Garner, Bryan A., *Black's Law Dictionary*, (pocket edition, New York: West Publishing Co, 2006)

Gattini, Andrea, 'Case Law: Joined Cases C-402 & 415/05 P', *Common Market Law Review* 46 (2009) 213–39

Gazzini, Tarcisio, 'General Principles of Law in the Field of Foreign Investment', *Journal of World Investment & Trade* 10 (2009) 103–19

Geck, Wilhelm K., 'Diplomatic Protection', in *Encyclopedia of Public International Law*, Vol. I (Rudolf Bernhardt ed., Amsterdam: North-Holland, 1992) 1045–67

Gelpern, Anna, 'A Skeptic's Case for Sovereign Bankruptcy', *in A Debt Restructuring Mechanism for Sovereigns* (Christoph G. Paulus ed., Oxford: Hart, 2014) 261–78

Giglio, Gabriel Goméz, 'Emergency Law and Financial Entities in Argentina', *Journal of International Banking Law and Regulation* 10 (2003) 397–405

Gomez-Lobo, Andres & Foster, Vivien, 'The 1996–97 Gas Price Review in Argentina', in *Natural Gas: Private Sector Participation and Market Development* (Suzanne Smith ed., Washington: The World Bank, 1999) 78–87

Grabenwarter, Christoph & Marauhn, Thilo, 'Grundrechtseingriff und -schranken', in *EMRK/GG—Konkordanzkommentar* (Rainer Grote & Thilo Marauhn eds., Tübingen Mohr Siebeck, 2006) 332–77

Grimm, Dieter, 'Proportionality in Canadian and German Constitutional Jurisprudence', *University of Toronto Law Journal* 57 (2007) 383–97

Grotius, Hugo, *The Law of War and Peace* (1625, James Brown Scott (ed.), Carnegie Endowment for International Peace, 1995)

Gutteridge, H.C., 'Comparative Law and the Law of Nations', *British Yearbook of International Law* 21 (1944) 1–10

Hackworth, Green Haywood, *Digest of International Law*, Vol. III (Washington, DC: US Govt Printing Office, 1942)

Henkin, Louis, 'Infallibility under Law: Constitutional Balancing', *Columbia Law Review* 78 (1978) 1022–49

Henkin, Louis, *International Law: Politics and Values* (Dordrecht: Martinus Nijhoff Publishers, 1995)

Hershey, Amos S., *The Essentials of International Public Law* (New York: Macmillan, 1912)

Hesse, Konrad, *Grundzüge des Verfassungsrechts der Bundesrepublik Deutschland* (Heidelberg: C.F. Müller, 1999)

Higgins, Rosalyn, 'The Taking of Property by the State: Recent Developments in International Law', *Recueil de Cours* 176 (1982) 259–392

Higgins, Rosalyn, *Problems & Process: International Law and How We Use It* (Oxford: Clarendon, 1995)

Hill, Sarah F., 'The "Necessity Defense" and the Emerging Arbitral Conflict in its Application to the US–Argentina Bilateral Investment Treaty', *Law and Business Review of the Americas* 13 (2007) 547–67

Hobe, Stefan & Griebel, Jörn, 'New Protectionism—How Binding are International Economic Legal Obligations During a Global Economic Crisis?', *Goettingen Journal of International Law* 2 (2010) 423–35

ICSID, *History of the Convention*, Volume I (Washington 1970)

ICSID, *History of the Convention*, Volume II, Part 2 (Washington 1968)

ICSID, *Report of the Executive Directors* (Washington 1965)

ILA, 'Statement of Principles Applicable to the Formation of General Customary International Law' (2000)

ILC, 'Third Report on the Law of Treaties, by Sir Humphrey Waldock, Special Rapporteur', *Yearbook of the International Law Commission*, Vol. II, 5–65 (1964)

ILC, 'Draft Articles on the Law of Treaties with Commentaries', *Yearbook of the International Law Commission*, Vol. II, 187–274 (1966)

ILC, '"Force majeure" and "fortuitous event" as Circumstances Precluding Wrongfulness: Survey of State Practice, International Judicial Decisions and Doctrine—Study prepared by the Secretariat', *Yearbook of the International Law Commission*, Vol. II, Part 1, 61–227 (1978)

ILC, 'Report of the International Law Commission on the Work of its Thirty-second Session', *Yearbook of the International Law Commission*, Vol. II, Part 2 (1980)

ILC, 'Report of the International Law Commission on the Work of its Fifty-first Session', *Yearbook of the International Law Commission*, Vol. I (1999)

ILC, 'Articles on Responsibility of States for Internationally Wrongful Acts with Commentaries', *Yearbook of the International Law Commission*, Vol. II, 20–143 (2001)

ILC, 'Report of the International Law Commission on the Work of its Fifty-third Session', *Yearbook of the International Law Commission*, Vol. I (2001)

ILC, 'State Responsibility, First Statement of the Chairman of the Drafting Committee' made at the 2681st to 2683rd meetings, held from 29 to 31 May 2001, *available at* <http://untreaty.un.org/ilc/sessions/53/english/dc_resp1.pdf> (2001)

ILC, *Articles on Diplomatic Protection with Commentaries* (2006)

ILC, *Fragmentation of International Law: Difficulties Arising from the Diversification and Expansion of International Law* (2006)

ILC, 'Report of the International Law Commission on the Work of its Sixty-first Session', UN Doc. A/64/10 (2009)

IMF, 'Evaluation Report, The IMF and Argentina 1991–2001' (Washington 2004) *available at* <http://www.imf.org/EXTERNAL/NP/IEO/2004/ARG/ENG/pdf/report.pdf>

IMF, 'Lessons from the Crisis in Argentina' (Washington 2003) *available at* <http://imf.org/external/np/pdr/lessons/100803.pdf>

Jenks, C. Wilfried, *The Proper Law of International Organisations* (London: Stevens & Sons, 1962)

Johnson, D.H.N., 'Prize Law', *in Encyclopedia of Public International Law*, Vol. III (Rudolf Bernhardt ed., Amsterdam: North-Holland, 1997) 1122–8

Johnstone, Ian, 'The Plea of "Necessity" in International Legal Discourse: Humanitarian Intervention and Counter-terrorism', *Columbia Journal of Transnational Law* 43 (2005) 337–88

Kadelbach, Stefan & Kleinlein, Thomas, 'International Law—a Constitution for Mankind? An Attempt at a Re-appraisal with an Analysis of Constitutional Principles', *German Yearbook of International Law* 50 (2007) 303–47

Kadelbach, Stefan, 'Ethik des Völkerrechts unter Bedingungen der Globalisierung', *Heidelberg Journal of International Law* 64 (2004) 1–20

Kadelbach, Stefan & Kleinlein, Thomas, 'Überstaatliches Verfassungsrecht. Zur Konstitutionalisierung im Völkerrecht', *Archiv des Völkerrechts* 44 (2006) 235–66

Kaiser, Karen, 'Art. 1 ZP I', in *EMRK—Konvention zum Schutz der Menschenrechte und Grundfreiheiten—Kommentar* (Ulrich Karpenstein & Franz Mayer eds., München: C.H. Beck, 2012) 359–76

Kaufman, Eileen, 'Deference or Abdiction: a Comparison of the Supreme Courts of Israel and the United States in Cases Involving Real or Perceived Threats to National Security', *Washington University Global Studies Law Review* 12 (2013) 95–159

Kent, Avidan & Harrington, Alexandra R., 'The Plea of Necessity Under Customary International Law: a Critical Review in Light of the Argentine Cases', in *Evolution in Investment Treaty Law and Arbitration* (Chester Brown & Kate Miles eds., New York: CUP, 2011) 246–70

Kingsbury, Benedict & Schill, Stephan W., 'Investor–State Arbitration as Governance: Fair and Equitable Treatment, Proportionality and the Emerging Global Administrative Law', in *50 Years of the New York Convention—ICCA International Arbitration Conference* (Albert Jan van den Berg ed., Alphen aan den Rijn: Kluwer Law International, 2009) 5–68

Kingsbury, Benedict & Schill, Stephan W., 'Public Law Concepts to Balance Investors' Rights with State Regulatory Actions in the Public Interest—the Concept of Proportionality', in *International Investment Law and Comparative Public Law* (Stephan W. Schill ed., Oxford: OUP, 2010) 75–104

Kläger, Roland, *'Fair and Equitable Treatment' in International Investment Law* (Cambridge: CUP, 2011)

Kleinlein, Thomas, 'Judicial Lawmaking by Judicial Restraint? The Potential of Balancing in International Economic Law', *German Law Journal* 12 (2011) 1141–74

Knahr, Christina, 'The New Rules on Participation of Non-Disputing Parties in ICSID Arbitration: Blessing or Curse?', in *Evolution in Investment Treaty Law and Arbitration* (Chester Brown & Kate Miles eds., New York: CUP, 2011) 319–38

Kolb, Robert, 'Principles as Sources of International Law (With Special Reference to Good Faith)', *Netherlands International Law Review* 53 (2006) 1–36

Kommers, Donald P., *The Constitutional Jurisprudence of the Federal Republic of Germany* (Duke University Press, 1997)

Koskenniemi, Martti, 'The Politics of International Law', *European Journal of International Law* 1 (1990) 4–32

Kriebaum, Ursula, *Eigentumsschutz im Völkerrecht* (Berlin: Duncker & Humblot, 2008)

Krommendijk, Jasper & Morijn, John, '"Proportional" by What Measure(s)? Balancing Investor Interests and Human Rights by Way of Applying the Proportionality Principle in Investor–State Arbitration', in *Human Rights in International Investment Law and Arbitration* (Pierre-Marie Dupuy, et al. eds., Oxford: OUP, 2009) 422–51

Krugmann, Michael, *Der Grundsatz der Verhältnismäßigkeit im Völkerrecht* (Berlin: Duncker & Humblot, 2004)

Kühl, Kristian, '§ 35 Entschuldigender Notstand', in *Strafgesetzbuch—Kommentar* (Karl Lackner & Kristian Kühl eds., München: C.H. Beck, 2011) 268–73

Kulick, Andreas, *Global Public Interest in International Investment Law* (Cambridge: CUP, 2012)

Kumm, Mattias, 'The Legitimacy of International Law: a Constitutionalist Framework of Analysis', *European Journal of International Law* 15 (2004) 907–31

Kumm, Mattias, 'The Cosmopolitan Turn in Constitutionalism', in *Ruling the World? Constitutionalism, International Law, and Global Governance* (Jeffrey L. Dunoff & Joel P. Trachtman eds., Cambridge: CUP, 2009) 258–324

Kurtz, Jürgen, 'Adjudging the Exceptional at International Investment Law: Security, Public Order and Financial Crisis', *International and Comparative Law Quarterly* 59 (2010) 325–71

Lauterpacht, Hersch, *Private Law Sources and Analogies of International Law* (London: Longmans, Green, 1927)

Leckner, Theodor & Perron, Walter, '§ 34 Rechtfertigender Notstand', in *Strafgesetzbuch—Kommentar* (Adolf Schönke & Horst Schröder eds., München: C.H. Beck, 2006) 673–700

Legum, Barton, 'Investment Disputes and NAFTA Chapter 11, Remarks', *ASIL Proceedings* 95 (2001) 202–5

Lerche, Peter, *Übermaß und Verfassungrecht* (München: Heymann, 1961)

Lipstein, Kurt, 'The Place of the Calvo Clause in International Law', *British Yearbook of International Law* 22 (1945) 130–45

Lord McNair, *International Law Opinions,* Vol. II (Cambridge: CUP, 1956)

Lowe, Vaughan, 'Precluding Wrongfulness or Responsibility: a Plea for Excuses', *European Journal of International Law* 10 (1999) 405–11

Lowenfeld, Andreas F., 'Investment Agreements and International Law', *Columbia Journal of Transnational Law* 42 (2003) 123–30

Marboe, Irmgard, *Calculation of Compensation and Damages in International Investment Law* (Oxford: OUP, 2009)

Mann, F. A., 'British Treaties for the Promotion and Protection of Investments', *British Yearbook of International Law* 52 (1981) 241–54

McLachlan, Campbell, 'The Principle of Systemic Integration and Article 31(3)(c) of the Vienna Convention', *International and Comparative Law Quarterly* 54 (2005) 279–320

McLachlan, Campbell et al., *International Investment Arbitration—Substantive Principles* (Oxford: OUP, 2007)

McLachlan, Campbell, 'Investment Treaties and General International Law', *International and Comparative Law Quarterly* 57 (2008) 361–401

Mclachlan, Campbell, 'The Evolution of Treaty Obligation in International Law', in *Treaties and Subsequent Practice* (Georg Nolte ed., Oxford: OUP, 2013) 69–81

Meerpohl, Thomas, *Individualsanktionen des Sicherheitsrates der Vereinten Nationen—das Sanktionsregime gegen die Taliban und Al-Qaida vor dem Hintergrund des Rechts der VN und der Menschenrechte* (München: Utz, 2008)

Miles, Kate, *The Origins of International Investment Law—Empire, Environment and the Safeguarding of Capital* (Cambridge: CUP, 2013)

Meron, Theodor, *Human Rights and Humanitarian Norms as Customary Law* (Oxford: Clarendon, 1989)

Meron, Theodor, *The Humanization of International Law* (Leiden: Martinus Nijhoff Publishers, 2006)

Moore, John Bassett, *A Digest of International Law*, Vol. II (New York: The Macmillan Company, 1906)

Moore, John Bassett, *International Adjudications* (New York: OUP, 1931)

Mosler, Hermann, 'General Principles of Law', in *Encyclopedia of Public International Law*, Vol. II (Rudolf Bernhardt ed., Amsterdam: North-Holland, 1995) 511–27

Neff, Stephan C., 'A Short History of International Law', in *International Law* (Malcolm D. Evans ed., Oxford: OUP, 2003) 31–58

Nußberger, Angelika, 'Das Verhältnismäßigkeitsprinzip als Strukturprinzip richterlichen Entscheidens in Europa', Neue *Zeitschrift für Verwaltungsrecht (NVwZ)*—Beilage 32 (2013) 36–44

Nolte, Georg, 'Thin or Thick? The Principle of Proportionality and International Humanitarian Law', *Law & Ethics of Human Rights* 4 (2010) 244–55

Nolte, Georg, 'Introduction', in, *Treaties and Subsequent Practice* (Georg Nolte ed., Oxford: OUP, 2013) 1–10

Nolte, Georg, 'Reports for the ILC Study Group On Treaties over Time: Report 1— Jurisprudence of the International Court of Justice and Arbitral Tribunals of Ad Hoc Jurisdiction Relating to Subsequent Agreements and Subsequent Practice', in *Treaties and Subsequent Practice* (Georg Nolte ed., Oxford: OUP, 2013) 169–209

Nolte, Georg, 'Reports for the ILC Study Group On Treaties over Time: Report 2—Jurisprudence Under Special Regimes Relating to Subsequent Agreements and Subsequent Practice', in *Treaties and Subsequent Practice* (Georg Nolte ed., Oxford: OUP, 2013) 210–306

Nussbaum, Arthur, *A Concise History of the Law of Nations* (New York: Macmillan, 1950)

OECD, *International Investment Law: a Changing Landscape* (2005)

Orakhelashvili, Alexander, *Peremptory Norms in International Law* (Oxford: OUP, 2006)

Orakhelashvili, Alexander, *The Interpretation of Acts and Rules in Public International Law* (Oxford: OUP, 2008)

Panizza, Ugo, 'Do We Need a Mechanism for Solving Sovereign Debt Crises? A Rule-Based Discussion', *in A Debt Restructuring Mechanism for Sovereigns* (Christoph G. Paulus ed., Oxford: Hart, 2014) 223–239

Parlett, Kate, *The Individual in the International Legal System—Continuity and Change in International Law* (Cambridge: CUP, 2011)

Paulus, Andreas L., 'Commentary to Andreas Fischer-Lescano & Gunther Teubner: the Legitimacy of International Law and the Role of the State', *Michigan Journal of International Law* 25 (2004) 1047–58

Paulus, Andreas L., 'Jus Cogens in a Time of Hegemony and Fragmentation—an Attempt at a Re-appraisal', *Nordic Journal of International Law* 74 (2005) 297–334

Paulus, Andreas L., 'Subsidiarity, Fragmentation and Democracy: Towards the Demise of General International Law?', in *The Shifting Allocation of Authority in International Law* (Tomer Broude & Yuval Shany eds., Oxford: Hart, 2008) 193–213

Paulus, Andreas L., 'The International Legal System as a Constitution', in *Ruling the World? Constitutionalism, International Law, and Global Governance* (Jeffrey L. Dunoff & Joel P. Trachtman eds., Cambridge: CUP, 2009) 69–109

Paulus, Andreas L. & Leiß, Johann Ruben, 'Article 103', in *The Charter of the United Nations—a Commentary* (Bruno Simma, et al. eds., Oxford: OUP, 2012) 2110–37

Paulus, Christoph G., 'Rechtliche Handhaben zur Bewältigung der Überschuldung von Staaten', in *Recht der Internationalen Wirtschaft* 55 (2009) 11–17

Paulus, Christoph G., 'Should Politics be Replaced by a Legal Proceeding?', *in A Debt Restructuring Mechanism for Sovereigns* (Christoph G. Paulus ed., Oxford: Hart, 2014) 191–212

Pellet, Allain, 'Article 38', in *The Statute of the International Court of Justice* (Andreas Zimmermann, et al. eds., 2nd edition, Oxford: OUP, 2012) 731–870

Pelletier, Hervé & Perfetti, Jean, *Code Pénal* (Paris: Litec, 2012)

Perkams, Markus, 'The Concept of Indirect Expropriation in Comparative Public Law—Searching for Light in the Dark', in *International Investment Law and Comparative Public Law* (Stephan W. Schill ed., Oxford: OUP, 2010) 107–50

Peters, Anne, 'Humanity as the A and Ω of Sovereignty', *European Journal of International Law* 20 (2009) 513–44

Peters, Anne, 'Membership in the Global Constitutional Community', in *The Constitutionalization of International Law* (Jan Klabbers, et al. eds., Oxford: OUP, 2009) 153–262

Peters, Anne, *Jenseits der Menschenrechte—die Rechtsstellung des Individuums im Völkerrecht* (Tübingen: Mohr Siebeck, 2014)

Petersen, Niels, 'Customary Law Without Custom? Rules, Principles, and the Role of State Practice in International Norm Creation', *American University International Law Review* 23 (2008) 275–310

Petersmann, Ernst-Ulrich, 'Human Rights, Constitutionalism and the World Trade Organization: Challenges for World Trade Organization Jurisprudence and Civil Society', *Leiden Journal of International Law* 19 (2006) 633–67

Petersmann, Ernst-Ulrich, 'Human Rights, International Economic Law and "Constitutional Justice"', *European Journal of International Law* 19 (2008) 769–98

Petersmann, Ernst-Ulrich, 'International Rule of Law and Constitutional Justice in International Investment Law and Arbitration', *Indiana Journal of Global Legal Studies* 16 (2009) 513–33

Peterson, Luke E., *Human Rights and Bilateral Investment Treaties: Mapping the Role of Human Rights Law within Investor State Arbitration* (The International Center for Human Rights and Democratic Development, 2009)

Peterson, Luke E., 'NGOs Permitted to Intervene in South Africa Mining Case and—for the Second Time at ICSID—Tribunal Offers Would-be Petitioners to be Given Access to Case Documents', *International Arbitration Reporter* 2 No. 16 (2009)

Posner, Richard A., 'Pragmatism versus Purposivism in First Amendment Analysis', *Stanford Law Review* 54 (2002) 737–52

Proukaki, Elena Katselli, *The Problem of Enforcement in International Law— Countermeasures, the Non-Injured State and the Idea of International Community* (London: Routledge, 2010)

Randelzhofer, Albrecht & Nolte, Georg, 'Article 51', in *The Charter of the United Nations—a Commentary* (Bruno Simma, et al. eds., 3rd edition, Oxford: OUP, 2012) 1397–428

Randelzhofer, Albrecht & Dörr, Albrecht, 'Article 2(4)', in *The Charter of the United Nations—a Commentary* (Bruno Simma, et al. eds., 3rd edition, Oxford: OUP, 2012) 200–34

Randelzhofer, Albrecht, 'Article 51', in *The Charter of the United Nations—a Commentary* (Bruno Simma, et al. eds., 2nd edition, Oxford: OUP 2002) 788–806

Ratner, Steven R., 'Regulatory Takings in Institutional Context: Beyond the Fear of Fragmented International Law', *American Journal of International Law* 102 (2008) 475–528

Regan, Donald H., 'The Meaning of "Necessary" in GATT Article XX and GATS Article XIV: the Myth of Cost–Benefit Balancing', *World Trade Review* 6 (2007) 347–69

Reinisch, August, 'Necessity in International Investment Arbitration—an Unnecessary Split of Opinions in Recent ICSID Cases? Comments on *CMS v. Argentina* and *LG&E v. Argentina*', *Journal of World Investment & Trade* 8 (2007) 191–214

Reinisch, August, 'Sachverständigengutachten zur Frage des Bestehens und der Wirkung des völkerrechtlichen Rechtfertigungsgrundes "Staatsnotstand"', *Zeitschrift für Ausländisches Öffentliches Recht und Völkerrecht* 68 (2008) 3–43

Reisman, W. Michael & Sloane, Robert D., 'Indirect Expropriation and its Valuation in the BIT Generation', *British Yearbook of International Law* 74 (2003) 115–50

Rensmann, Thilo, *Wertordnung und Verfassung* (Tübingen: Mohr Siebeck, 2007)

Rensmann, Thilo, 'Völkerrechtlicher Enteignungsschutz', in *Rechtsfragen internationaler Investitionen: Tagungsband zum 13. Münsteraner Außenwirtschaftsrechtstag 2008* (Dirk Ehlers, et al. eds., Frankfurt am Main: Verlag Recht und Wirtschaft, 2009) 25–54

Repgen, Tilman, '§ 226 Notstand', in *J. von Staudingers Kommentar zum Bürgerlichen Gesetzbuch mit Einführungsgesetzen und Nebengesetzen, §§ 164–240* (Nobert Haberman et al. eds., Berlin: Sellier, 2004) 804–18

'Report of the Commission of Enquiry into the Incidents on the Frontier Between Bulgaria and Greece', *League of Nations—Official Journal* 7 (1926) 2, at 196–210

Riedel, Eibe & Arend, Jan-Michael, 'Article 55(c)', in *The Charter of the United Nations—a Commentary* (Bruno Simma, et al. eds., 3rd edition, Oxford: OUP, 2012) 1566–602

Ripinsky, Sergey & Williams, Kevin, *Damages in International Investment Law* (London: BIICL, 2008)

Ripinsky, Sergey, 'Commentary on the Russian Model BIT', in *Commentaries on Selected Model Investment Treaties* (Chester Brown ed., Oxford: OUP, 2013) 593–621

Roberts, Anthea, 'Legality vs. Legitimacy: Can Uses of Force be Illegal but Justified?', in *Human Rights, Intervention, and the Use of Force* (Philip Alston & Euan Macdonald eds., Oxford: OUP, 2008) 179–213

Roberts, Anthea, 'Power and Persuasion in Investment Treaty Arbitration: the Dual Role of States', *American Journal of International Law* 105 (2010) 179–225

Roberts, Anthea, 'Subsequent Agreements and Practice: the Battle over Interpretative Authority', in *Treaties and Subsequent Practice* (Georg Nolte ed., Oxford: OUP, 2013) 95–102

Rodick, Burleigh Cushing, *The Doctrine of Necessity in International Law* (New York: Columbia University Press, 1928)

Root, Elihu, 'The Basis of Protection to Citizens Residing Abroad', *American Journal of International Law* 4 (1910) 517–528

Rubenfeld, Jed, 'A Reply to Posner', *Stanford Law Journal* 54 (2002) 753–67

Sachs, Michael, 'Artikel 20', in *Grundgesetz* (Michael Sachs ed., München: C.H. Beck, 2011)

Sarkar, Rumu, 'A "Re-Visioned" Foreign Direct Investment Approach From an Emerging Country Perspective: Moving From a Vicious Circle to a Virtuous Circle', *ILSA Journal of International and Comparative Law* 17 (2010–11) 379–92

Sadurski, Wojciech, *Rights Before Courts: a Study of Constitutional Courts in Postcommunist States of Central and Eastern Europe* (Heidelberg: Springer, 2005)

Schill, Stephan W., 'Der völkerrechtliche Staatsnotstand in der Entscheidung des BVerfG zu Argentinischen Staatsanleihen—Anachronismus oder Avantgarde? ', *Zeitschrift für ausländisches und öffentliches Recht und Völkerrecht* 68 (2008) 45–67

Schill, Stephan W., *The Multilateralization of International Investment Law* (Cambridge: CUP, 2009)

Schill, Stephan W. & Briese, Robyn, '"If the State Considers": Self-Judging Clauses in International Dispute Settlement', *Max Planck Yearbook of United Nations Law* 13 (2009) 61–140

Schill, Stephan W., 'Fair and Equitable Treatment, the Rule of Law, and Comparative Public Law', in *International Investment Law and Comparative Public Law* (Stephan W. Schill ed., Oxford: OUP, 2010) 151–82

Schill, Stephan W., 'International Investment Law and Comparative Public Law—an Introduction', in *International Investment Law and Comparative Public Law* (Stephan W. Schill ed., Oxford: OUP, 2010) 3–35

Schill, Stephan W., 'The Multilateralization of International Investment Law: Emergence of a Multilateral System of Investment Protection on Bilateral Grounds', *Trade, Law and Development* 2 (2010) 59–86

Schill, Stephan W. & Kim, Yun-I, 'Sovereign Bonds in Economic Crisis: Is the Necessity Defense under International Law Applicable to Investor–State Relations? A Critical Analysis of the Decision by the German Constitutional Court in the Argentine Bondholder Cases', in *Yearbook on International Investment Law & Policy 2010/2011* (Karl P. Sauvant ed., Oxford: OUP, 2011) 485–512

Schill, Stephan W., 'Deference in Investment Treaty Arbitration: Re-conceptualizing the Standard of Review', *Journal of International Dispute Settlement* 3 (2012) 577–607

Schlesinger, Rudolf B., 'Research on the General Principles of Law Recognized by Civilized Nations', *American Journal of International Law* 51 (1957) 734–53

Schlink, Bernhard, 'Proportionality in Constitutional Law: Why Everywhere but here?', *Duke Journal of Comparative and International Law* 22 (2012) 291–302

Schlochauer, Hans-Jürgen, 'Jay Treaty' in *Encyclopedia of Public International Law*, Vol. III (Rudolf Bernhardt ed., Amsterdam: North-Holland, 1997) 4–7

Schreuer, Christoph H., *The ICSID Convention: a Commentary* (Cambridge: CUP, 2001)

Schreuer, Christoph H., 'Non-Pecuniary Remedies in ICSID Arbitration', *Arbitration International* 20 (2004) 325–32

Schreuer, Christoph H. et al., *The ICSID Convention—a Commentary* (2nd edition, Cambridge: CUP, 2009)

Schwarzenberger, Georg, 'The Fundamental Principles of International Law', *Recueil de Cours* 87 (1955) 195–383

Schwarzenberger, Georg, *A Manual of International Law* (London: Stevens, 1967)

Schwarzenberger, Georg, *International Law—International Courts* Vol. II (London: Stevens, 1968)

Seiler, Hans Hermann, '§ 904 Notstand', in J. von Staudingers Kommentar zum Bürgerlichen Gesetzbuch mit Einführungsgesetz und Nebengesetzen, §§ 903–924 (Karl-Heinz Gursky, et. al eds., Berlin: Sellier, 2002)

Shany, Yuval, 'Toward a General Margin of Appreciation Doctrine in International Law', *European Journal of International Law* 16 (2005) 907–40

Simma, Bruno & Alston, Philip, 'The Sources of Human Rights Law: Custom, Jus Cogens, and General Principles', *Australian Year Book of International Law* 12 (1988-89) 82–107

Simma, Bruno, 'From Bilateralism to Community Interest in International Law', *Recueil de Cours* 250 (1994) 221–384

Simma, Bruno, 'NATO, the UN and the Use of Force: Legal Aspects', *European Journal of International Law* 10 (1999) 1–22

Simma, Bruno, 'The Work of the International Law Commission at Its Fifty-First Session (1999)', *Nordic Journal of International Law* 68 (1999) 293–361

Simma, Bruno & Killl, Theodore, 'Harmonizing Investment Protection and International Human Rights: First Steps Towards a Methodology', in *International Investment Law for the 21st Century—Essays in Honour of Christoph Schreuer* (Christina Binder, et al. eds., Oxford: OUP, 2009) 678–707

Simma, Bruno, 'Miscellaneous Thoughts on Subsequent Agreements and Practice', in *Treaties and Subsequent Practice* (Georg Nolte ed., Oxford: OUP, 2013) 46–49

Sionaidh Douglas-Scott, *Constitutional Law of the European Union* (Essex: Pearson, 2002)

Sloane, Robert D., 'The Use and Abuse of Necessity in the Law of State Responsibility', *American Journal of International Law* 106 (2012) 447–508

Sornarajah, M., *The International Law on Foreign Investment* (2nd edition, Cambridge: CUP, 2010)

Spiermann, Ole, 'Humanitarian Intervention as a Necessity and the Threat or Use of Jus Cogens', *Nordic Journal of International Law* 71 (2002) 523–43

Sprau, Hartwig, '§ 823', in *Palandt—Bürgerliches Gesetzbuch* (Peter Bassenge, et al. eds., München: C.H. Beck, 2009) 1239–87

Stein, Torsten & von Buttlar, Christian, *Völkerrecht* (München: Vahlen, 2012)

Steingruber, Andrea Marco, *Consent in International Arbitration* (Oxford: OUP, 2012)

Stern, Klaus, 'Zur Entstehung und Ableitung des Übermaßverbots', in *Wege und Verfahren des Verfassungslebens: Festschrift für Peter Lerche zum 65. Geburtstag* (Peter Badura & Rupert Scholz eds., München: C.H. Beck, 1993) 165–175

Stern, Klaus, *Das Staatsrecht der Bundesrepublik Deutschland—Band III/2—Allgemeine Lehren der Grundrechte* (München: C.H. Beck, 1994)

Stone Sweet, Alec & Giacinto Della Cananea, Proportionality, General Principles of Law, and Investor–State Arbitration: a Response to José Alvarez', *NYU Journal of International Law and Politics* 46 (2014) 911–54

Stone Sweet, Alec, 'Investor–State Arbitration: Proportionality's New Frontier', *Law & Ethics of Human Rights* 4 (2010) 47–76

Stone Sweet, Alec & Grisel, Florian, 'Transnational Investment Arbitration: From Delegation to Constitutionalization?', in *Human Rights in International Investment Law and Arbitration* (Pierre-Marie Dupuy, et al. eds., Oxford: OUP, 2009) 118–136

Stone Sweet, Alec & Mathews, Jude, 'Proportionality Balancing and Global Constitutionalism', *Columbia Journal of Transnational Law* 47 (2008) 73–165

Strupp, Karl, *Das völkerrechtliche Delikt* (Stuttgart: Kohlhammer, 1920)

Tamanaha, Brian Z., 'A Concise Guide to the Rule of Law', in *Relocating the Rule of Law* (Gianluigi Palombella & Neil Walker eds., Oxford: Hart, 2009) 3–15

Tams, Christian J. & Zoellner, Carl-Sebastian, 'Amici Curiae im internationalen Investitionsschutzrecht', *Archiv des Völkerrechts* 45 (2007) 217–43

Teubner, Gunther & Fischer-Lescano, Andreas, 'Regime-Collisions: the Vain Search for Unity in the Fragmentation of Global Law', *Michigan Journal of International Law* 25 (2004) 999–1046

Trachtman, Joel, P. 'Trade and...Problems, Cost-Benefit Analysis and Subsidiarity', *European Journal of International Law* 9 (1998) 32–85

Tribe, Laurence H., *American Constitutional Law* (2nd edition, New York: Foundation Press, 1988)

Tribe, Laurence H., *American Constitutional Law—Volume One* (3rd edn, New York: Foundation Press, 2000)

Tsakyrakis, Stavros, 'Proportionality: an Assault on Human Rights?', *International Journal of Constitutional Law* 7 (2008) 468–93

Tudor, Ioana, *The Fair and Equitable Treatment Standard in the International Law of Foreign Investment* (Oxford: OUP, 2008)

UN Econ. & Soc. Council [ECOSOC], Committee on Economic, Social and Cultural Rights, *General Comment No. 15*, U.N. Doc. E/C.12/2002/11 (20 January 2003)

Uibopuu, Henn-Jüri, 'Interpretation of Treaties in the Light of International Law: Art. 31, para. 3(c) of the Vienna Convention on the Law of Treaties', *Yearbook of the Association of Attenders and Alumni of The Hague Academy of International Law* 40 (1970) 1–42

UN, Conference on the Law of Treaties, First Session, 26 March–24 May 1968, A/CONF.39/11 (1968)

UN, 'Responsibility of States for Internationally Wrongful Acts: Compilation of Decisions of International Courts, Tribunals and Other Bodies', Report of the Secretary General of 1 February 2007, A/62/62 (2007)

UNCTAD, *Bilateral Investment Treaties 1959–1991* (1992)

UNCTAD, *Bilateral Investment Treaties 1995-2006: Trends in Investment Rulemaking* (2007)

UNCTAD, *Investor–State Dispute Settlement and Impact on Foreign Investment Rulemaking* (2007)

UNCTAD, *International Investment Rule-Making: Stocktaking, Challenges and the Way Forward, UNCTAD Series on International Investment Polices for Development* (2008)

UNCTAD, *Latest Developments in Investor–State Dispute Settlement, IIA Monitor No. 1* (2008)

UNCTAD, *World Investment Report 2008, Transnational Challenge and the Infrastructure Challenge* (2008)

UNCTAD, *World Investment Report 2010, Investing in a Low-Carbon Economy* (2010)

UNCTAD, *World Investment Report 2011, Non-Equity Modes of International Production and Development* (2011)

UNCTAD, *Latest Developments in Investor–State Dispute Settlement, IIA Issue Note No. 1* (2011)

UNCTAD, *World Investment Report 2012, Towards a New Generation of Investment Policies* (2012)

UNCTAD, *Recent Developments in Investor–State Dispute Settlement (ISDS), IIA Issues Note, No. 1* (2014)

UNCTAD, *World Investment Report 2014, Investing in the SDGs: an Action Plan* (2014)

van Aaken, Anne, 'Fragmentation of International Law: the Case of International Investment Protection', *Finnish Yearbook of International Law* XVII (2008) 91–130

van Aaken, Anne, 'Defragmentation of Public International Law Through Interpretation: a Methodological Proposal', *Indiana Journal of Global Legal Studies* 16 (2009) 483–512

Van Harten, Gus & Loughlin, Martin, 'Investment Treaty Arbitration as a Species of Global Administrative Law', *European Journal of International Law* 17 (2006) 121–50

Van Harten, Gus, *Investment Treaty Arbitration and Public Law* (Oxford: OUP, 2007)

Van Harten, Gus, et al., *Public Statement on the International Investment Regime* (31 August 2010) *available at* <http://www.osgoode.yorku.ca/public-statement-international-investment-regime-31-august-2010/>

van Rijn, Arjen, 'Right to the Peaceful Enjoyment of One's Possessions (Article 1 of Protocol No. 1)', in *Theory and Practice of the European Convention on Human Rights* (Pieter van Dijk, et al. eds., Antwerpen: Intersentia, 2006) 863–93

Vandevelde, Kenneth J., 'A Brief History of International Investment Agreements', *U.C. Davis Journal of International Law & Policy* 12 (2005) 157–94

Vandevelde, Kenneth J., 'Of Politics and Markets: the Shifting Policy of the BITs', *International Tax and Business Lawyer* 11 (1993) 159–86

Vandevelde, Kenneth J., *United States International Investment Agreements* (Oxford: OUP, 2009)

Verdross, Alfred, *Die Quellen des universellen Völkerrechts* (Freiburg: Rombach, 1973)

Verdross, Alfred and Simma, Bruno, *Universelles Völkerrecht* (Berlin: Duncker & Humblot, 1984)

Vile, John R. A, *Companion to the United States Constitution and its Amendments* (Westport: Praeger, 2006)

Villiger, Mark E., *Commentary on the 1969 Vienna Convention on the Law of Treaties* (Leiden: Brill, 2009)

Villiger, Mark E., *Customary International Law and Treaties* (Dordrecht: Nijhoff, 1985)

Vinuales, Jorge E., 'Access to Water in Foreign Investment Disputes', *Georgetown International Environmental Law Review* 21 (2009) 733–58

von Krauss, Rupprecht, *Der Grundsatz der Verhältnismäßigkeit in seiner Bedeutung für die Notwendigkeit des Mittels im Verwaltungsrecht* (Hamburg: Appel in Komm., 1955)

von Staden, Andreas, 'Towards Greater Doctrinal Clarity in Investor–State Arbitration: the CMS, Enron, and Sempra Annulment Decisions', *Czech Yearbook of International Law* 2 (2011) 207–29

Vranes, Erich, 'Der Verhältnismäßigkeitsgrundsatz', *Archiv des Völkerrechts* 47 (2009) 1–35

Waibel, Michael et al., 'The Backlash against Investment Arbitration: Perceptions and Reality', *in The Backlash against Investment Arbitration*, (Michael Waibel, et al., eds, Texas: Wolters Kluwer Law & Business, 2010) xxxvii–li

Wälde, Thomas W. & Sabahi, Borzu, 'Compensation, Damages, and Valuation', in *The Oxford Handbook of International Investment Law* (Peter Muchlinski, et al. eds., Oxford: OUP, 2008) 1049–124

Waldron, Jeremy, 'The Rule of International Law', *Harvard Journal of Law & Public Policy* 30 (2006) 15–30

Walter, Christian, 'Constitutionalizing (Inter)national Governance—Possibilities for and Limits to the Development of an International Constitutional Law', *German Yearbook of International Law* 44 (2001) 170–201

Williamson, John, 'From Reform Agenda to Damaged Brand Name—a Short History of the Washington Consensus and Suggestions for What to do Next', *Finance & Development* 40 (2003) 10–13

Wilson, Michael, The Enron v. Argentina Annulment Decision: Moving a Bishop Vertically in the Precarious ICSID System', *University of Miami Inter-American Law Review* 43 (2012) 347–76

Wythes, Annika, 'Investor–State Arbitrations: Can the "Fair and Equitable Treatment" Clause Consider Human Rights Obligations?', *Leiden Journal of International Law* 23 (2010) 241–56

Index